Ray Parkin's
Wartime Trilogy

Ray Parkin's Wartime Trilogy

Out of the Smoke
Into the Smother
The Sword and the Blossom

MELBOURNE UNIVERSITY PRESS

ERRATA

The author has noted the following typographical errors in the text as it was originally published:

Out of the Smoke

page 255, line 13 for Warsprite *read* Warspite
page 266, line 9 for J.U. 8JB's *read* J.U. 87B's
page 275, line 8 for torpodoes *read* torpedoes

The Sword and the Blossom

page 865, line 26 for beautifying *read* beatifying

I would like this volume to be a memorial to those in war
who, sent on suicide or hopeless missions,
did not count the cost, but paid the ultimate price.

MELBOURNE UNIVERSITY PRESS
(an imprint of Melbourne University Publishing)
PO Box 1167, Carlton, Victoria 3053, Australia
mup-info@unimelb.edu.au
www.mup.com.au

Out of the Smoke first published by The Hogarth Press, London, 1960.
Into the Smother first published by The Hogarth Press, London, 1963.
The Sword and the Blossom first published by The Hogarth Press, London, 1968.

This edition first published 1999
Paperback edition 2003

Printed in Australia by Tecprint

National Library of Australia Cataloguing-in-Publication entry

Parkin, Ray, 1910- .
    Ray Parkin's wartime trilogy: Out of the smoke, Into the
    smother, The sword and the blossom.
    ISBN 0 522 85067 7.
    1. Parkin, Ray, 1910- . 2. Perth (Cruiser). 3. Burma-Siam
    Railroad – History. 4. World War, 1939–1945 – Personal
    narratives, Australian. 5. World War, 1939–1945 – Prisoners and
    prisons, Japanese. 6. World War, 1939–1945 – Naval operations,
    Australian. 7. Prisoners of war – Japan – Biography. 8. Prisoners
    of war – Australia – Biography. I. Parkin, Ray, 1910–Out of the
    smoke. II. Parkin, Ray, 1910–Into the smother. III. Parkin, Ray,
    1910–The sword and the blossom. IV. Title. V. Title: Wartime
    trilogy.
    940.547252

CONTENTS

CONTENTS

The Sword and the Blossom

Foreword

Ray Parkin did not cause the events in this book. He happened
to be there and his instinct was always to try to understand
things by describing them accurately.

When he was thirty-one, Ray was captured by the Japanese.
He had been in the Australian Navy for nearly half his life,
entering the service in 1928, joining HMAS *Perth* when she was
commissioned and serving on her every day until she was sunk.
He was at the wheel during the Battle of Matapan, the battles
of Greece and Crete in the Mediterranean in 1941 and the
battles of the Java Sea and the Sunda Strait in 1942. In this last
action, HMAS *Perth* was sunk and two-thirds of the ship's
company of 683 were killed.

Ray was captured at Tjilatjap on the south coast of Java and
went into prison at Bandoeng. The prisoners who met here
became known as Weary Dunlop's 'Thousand'. They were taken
north by ship to Changi, in Singapore, and then up through
Malaya to work on the Burma–Siam railway. When the war
finished, Ray was working in a coal-mine under the Inland Sea
in Japan. One morning he noticed a cloud rising in an unusual
way. It was the Nagasaki atom bomb, forty miles away.

During his three and a half years of captivity, Ray kept a
record of events and made drawings and paintings. This was a
summary offence. If his captors had known he was doing it, he
would have been executed. His materials were scrounged,
adapted and invented. In Bandong he wrote in tiny writing on
individual sheets of toilet paper. He met another prisoner who
had been a bookbinder and got him to sew them together. Any
scrap of paper he could find was useful. He had a small pencil
he could put under his tongue when being moved about. When
Ray was taken by ship to Japan, Weary recognised that the
work couldn't be smuggled and he volunteered to look after it
in Thailand. He carefully packed it inside a false bottom in his
office table, where he was also hiding the drawings of Jack

Chalker and others. After the war, Weary brought it all back to Australia in mint condition.

Some years later, Ray's war memoirs became three books. The first, *Out of the Smoke,* tells the story of the ship, her sinking and her surviving crew as they become accustomed to captivity. *Into the Smother* describes the experience of the Burma–Siam railway. When the Australian Prime Minister spoke at a commemoration ceremony at Hellfire Pass on Anzac Day 1998, he quoted from this book. The third book, *The Sword and the Blossom,* reflects on the period of captivity in ways which acknowledge the lessons of survival and which explore the philosophical strength and subtlety of one who could view his captivity as 'a kind of freedom'.

The books were published, initially at the instigation of Laurens van der Post, by The Hogarth Press in London in 1960, 1963 and 1968. They hum with action and documentary description and are written plainly by an observer keen to record actual events. They are wise, tolerant books and reveal a man not thrown from his purpose by hatred and not blinded to beauty and good sense by great catastrophe.

In June 1999 Ray won both the Non-fiction Award and the Book of the Year Award in the NSW Premier's Literary Awards for his superb work *H.M. Bark* Endeavour. In his speech at the awards dinner Ray described himself as 'a blow-in'. This is not humility. Ray is a confident man who knows what he sees. The value he places on his work, however, is a practical one. It needs to be worth doing and it needs to be done well.

As to what Ray finds worth doing, we find a clue in a letter he wrote many years ago to Alan Marshall:

> I do not consider myself as a writer per se, nor as such am I an artist. I cannot write or draw as an exposition of facility because I am painfully aware of my limitations of both facility and aesthetics and on every hand feel outclassed. But I feel I can still work in a way within these limitations so as to use my writing and drawing as part of an exploration of life

itself in an attempt to encapsulate what small discoveries or experiences one might make or have, to help expand one's awareness and inner space of natural relationships for an unharassed personal equilibrium.

There is a balance in things which appeals to Ray. During the 1960s his knowledge was instrumental in pinpointing the exact location of HMAS *Perth* on the seabed in Sunda Strait and assisting in the analysis and assessment of material brought to the surface.

When he was at sea, his bosun's 'call' (the whistle used to pipe orders) was kept in a little metal container called a save-all, which was fixed to the bulkhead near the wheel. When David Burchell dived on to HMAS *Perth* he found a save-all and brought it back. It happened to be the one from the wheelhouse bulkhead and, after twenty-five years at the bottom of the sea, it hangs today on the wall above Ray's desk.

Just as his intention in telling the story of H.M. Bark *Endeavour* was to put the reader on the ship, so in describing his wartime experiences Ray wants his readers to understand things, to know how it was and perhaps to sense how they themselves might have dealt with the experience. I am delighted that this remarkable trilogy is once again available. I know of no other books about the experience of Japanese captivity which so impress and inform the reader of today.

John Clarke
Melbourne
July 1999

What Reviewers Have Said

Out of the Smoke

'This noble book ... he is a writer of exceptional talent. All through the narrative the reader is aware of a man with a spirit capable of being enlarged by experiences that might well have diminished others.' *Country Life*

'Here, recollected in tranquillity, is the very stuff of which heroic poetry is composed ... Mr. Parkin tells this magnificent story with love, humility, great understanding and compassion, and a laconic, unsparing veracity ... In my judgment this is one of the noblest personal stories to emerge out of the welter of books written about World War II.' *Books to Read*, BBC Radio

'The sincerity and vivid recollection of the landing of some hundred or so men on a coral reef off the mainland are not likely to be forgotten.' *Bookman*

'This is a most moving and unusual book of great quality—a chronicle of one of the most heroic sea battles ever fought ... marvellously clear-sighted ... the book opens in such a trance of shock that the story of *Perth*'s final battle is not told until two-thirds of the way through the lifeboat journey, where it stands in dazzling relief of action and energy against the exhausted shipwreck sequences of dazed, oil-soaked men crawling out of the sea over live coral on the island.' *Queen*

'... as exciting a story of human endurance in the face of difficulty as [the reader] has ever come across ... Anyone who has been at sea will lap up this story from the first page to the last.' *Illustrated London News*

'... ranks among the most stunning descriptions of any naval action of the war.' *Sunday Dispatch*

'The sea battle ranks with those of Grenville and Nelson, and the quality of this experience permeates the book which is written with the most moving and exacting honesty.' *Sunday Times*

'... a deeply moving tale of self-imposed discipline and unyielding resolution in the face of the most daunting difficulties ... If Mr Parkin never writes another word he will have given the world something truly memorable in this humbly told tale about the ship that he loved and the ordeal that he and his comrades underwent after she was lost.' *Economist*

'... the great nobility of those Australian sailors shines through all its pages ... Even as a "hostilities only" sailor I understood something of the mystique which binds a sailor to his ship. But I have never had it revealed to me so movingly than from the pen of this ex-chief petty officer.' *Reynolds News*

'Aglow with truth, it is undoubtedly one of the few great books to come out of the war ... written from notes painfully compiled and concealed during captivity—on toilet paper and other scraps, at one time with a forbidden pencil stump concealed under the author's tongue ... Action, thought and emotion are real, stark, inspiring ... Oddly, the pronoun "I" appears only once, and then seemingly by accident.' *Sydney Sun*

'In all my reading experience, it is—to use a dangerous word—unique ... it has a special dimension rarely found in stories of action; *Seven Pillars of Wisdom* and *Venture to the Interior* also have this dimension, which gives spiritual meaning to physical experience ... Although there is much casual, understated heroism in *Out of the Smoke*, there are no heroics; nor is there a scintilla of humbug.' *Age*

'Parkin has an eye for detail that is both touching and disturbing. He is not a romantic concerned with painting an Anzac Day-pub-talk picture of Australian servicemen. He shows both the strengths and weaknesses of the men.' *Sun News-Pictorial*

'It is much more than just another war book: for Mr. Parkin writes with penetrating insight into the minds of his shipmates; and in his understanding of the affection with which seamen regard their ship he reminds one very strongly of Joseph Conrad ... high praise indeed. Mr. Parkin does not look back on any of his sufferings in anger or bitterness. Rather does he remember with unquenchable pride the ship he fought in and the men who manned her. His book deserves to take a place alongside the greatest tales of the sea.' *Naval Review*

'Mr Parkin tells the story so simply, so unemotionally, that the reader becomes only slowly aware of its immensity ... Always a graphic artist, Mr Parkin brings to this story a brave and poetic quality, a sincere and human quality that cannot be overpraised.' *Australasian Post*

'Quite the most haunting World War II book of the year ... almost unclassifiable ... Although superficially a story of personal experience, it is the product of a poetic mind, and it has a timeless and luminous beauty.' *Age Literary Supplement*

'It is a tale of courage hardly ever surpassed in the annals of the sea, and one of the few great books so far written about World War II.' *Bulletin*

'*Out of the Smoke* should be compulsory reading in every Australian high school, lest we forget.' *West Australian*

Into the Smother
'... probably the finest POW writing in English'. Max Harris, *Australian*

'This is an awful, stirring, and essential journal, not touched up, of events as they occurred, by a writer on whom the presence of death conferred a piercing vision of life; how it survived is a saga in itself.' *Observer*

'From his experiences Mr. Parkin distilled spiritual enrichment and a philosophy based on a new respect for the enduring strength of the human body and on a conviction of the fundamental need to maintain integrity under the severest adversity. To those who have not suffered as he has, this is a humbling and disturbing book.' *Times Literary Supplement*

'*Into the Smother* tells much about the horror camps which no merely accurate statement of the facts could possibly convey. The reason of this is that Parkin sees as a poet and writes as a poet. A host of other men might each see an incident and describe it faithfully, yet produce nothing more than a true report; Parkin, describing the self-same incident, would endow it with a quality of revelation.' John Hetherington, *Age*

'*Into the Smother* has claims to a permanent place in war literature. It is so sensitively and delicately written that the reader feels something of the agony of the overworked captives, and in particular of the author who has succeeded in writing about the enduring qualities of the human spirit.' *Geelong Advertiser*

'. . . a factual book whose primary aim is not reportage . . . but a delicately-structured examination of men's spirits and souls under unimaginable stress . . . This book, one of the most distinguished in any genre which Australians have written in recent years, has crept up on us. There is a wonderful quality in this book of a vision compassionate and quiet, of a wisdom that only comes when some kinds of men and women have been passed ten times through the flames that temper the soul.' Stephen Murray-Smith, *Australian Book Review*

'Ray Parkin gives a personal view of what it was like in hideous, toiling heat and disease-ridden jungles; an intensely moving picture that sums up what it was like for so many others who were taken prisoners-of-war and put to work by the Japanese.' *Australian Traveller*

'. . . a documented account, stripped naked of everything but stark facts.' *Ballarat Courier*

'It is impossible not to be moved to deep pity and compassion . . . a notable addition to prisoner-of-war literature.' *Canberra Times*

'. . . the great virtue of this account, although compiled day by day, is its objectivity: there is no moaning, no self-pity, no trace of morbidity . . . the book is not a mere chronicle of human cruelty and misery, but holds implicitly a commentary on human nature that is relevant outside the camp still.' *Sunday Times*

'*Into the Smother* is built up out of diary extracts smuggled away from the Japanese; the technique, in building up a whole picture piece by piece, is extremely effective; and this book has a permanent quality about it which we rarely see. It is a book for all men to reflect on, and has an aspect of greatness about it.' *Today's Writing*, ABC Radio

' . . . a book which may live and be read beyond our time . . . In its revelation of the moral and spiritual strivings of man reduced by captivity and cruelty to sheer animality, I thought of *Amiel's Journal*; and in its interweaving of reflections upon man and nature my mind went back to Thoreau living by Walden Pond . . . I am sure that for Australians it will be the most vivid, the most balanced and most authentic record of those terrible 15 months in Thailand that they have yet been given.' *West Australian*

'Mr. Parkin is indeed a most unusual man. Not only does he possess a remarkable gift for vivid description of scenes and persons, but he illustrates his work himself, and his character is such that, for all the modesty with which he tells his story, it is obvious that he became an outstanding leader throughout the terrible ordeal . . . ' *Naval Review*

'A great memorial to these men's appetite for life and life's sweetness in even the most savage adversity.' *Oxford Mail*

The Sword and the Blossom
'. . . his gift of finding a telling and evocative phrase, the skill of his drawings which illustrate the narrative and, above all, his capacity to enter into the feelings of men enduring great privation, put it into a class of its own . . . The two earlier volumes were lifted far above the normal level of such stories by the author's sensitivity to his physical surroundings and his striving to find some underlying meaning behind the suffering and degradation of his experiences. These elements still feature in this continuation of the story, with particular stress on an attempt to understand the complexity of the Japanese character.' *Times Literary Supplement*

'The narrative is quietly written, with poetic feeling, but with a shattering frankness . . . Ray Parkin sees beyond the surface. He looks into the hearts of his men and women, Japanese as well as Australians, and he shows them as they really are.' *The Age Literary Supplement*

'Mr. Parkin gives the reader a remarkable insight into the Japanese way of thinking, and lights his ghastly experiences with magnificent prose.' *Western Daily Press*

'This is a remarkably evocative book—illustrated by Parkin himself—and ought to be required reading for all those who . . . aspire to insight on men caught up in the macabre unreality of modern warfare.' *Australian*

'Parkin refuses to either vengeful or splenetic. He doesn't take his chance to pay off old scores, and this is noble, moving and admirable. Instead, he forgives his one-time tormentors, and his argument is classic. As he sadly points out, war does *not* ennoble and many of his own comrades behaved despicably . . . [he] obliquely infers that the act of self-preservation is neither gentlemanly nor nice and that there is a touch of bestiality in the best of us anyway.' *Age*

OUT OF THE SMOKE

RAY PARKIN

with an Introduction by Laurens van der Post

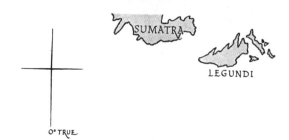

SUMATRA

LEGUNDI

SUNDA
STRAIT

Boat's track ....

Survivors' average course to Sangieng - - - -

Road party –Anjer to Labuhan ————

MAGNETIC

NEARLY STATIONARY   YARN 0°5'E (1927)

0° TRUE

VERLATEN IS
623'
ACTIVE VO

𝒢REAT CHANNEL

Sail found in sand

614   LEGON DAMERGARING ....

525   Winkle Beach

PRINCES IS   Water Beach –Anzac named
RASKA
1050

SECOND POINT

PRINCES CHANNEL   MEW BAY
MEW IS

FIRST POINT
FRIAR ROCKS ☆ FL.EV 30 SEC. 165 FT. 18 M. Lighthouse
JAVA HEAD ☆Lighthouse
0930/9TH

Indian Ocean

LONGITUDE EAST GREENWICH   5'   10'   15'   20'   25'

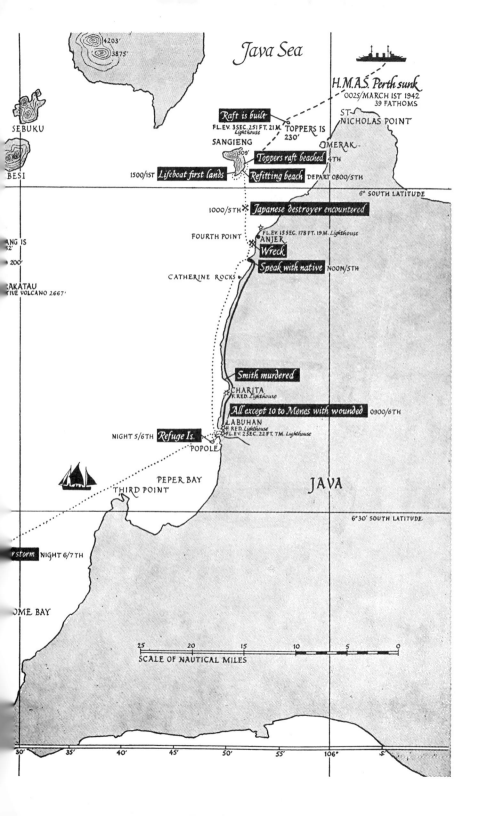

Java Sea

4203'
3875'

SEBUKU

BESI

Raft is built
FL.EV. 3 SEC. 251 FT. 21 M.
Lighthouse
SANGIENG
509'

TOPPERS IS
230'

H.M.A.S. Perth sunk
0025/MARCH 1ST 1942
39 FATHOMS
ST.
NICHOLAS POINT

OMERAK
4TH

Toppers raft beached

1500/1ST *Lifeboat first lands*   *Refitting beach* DEPART 0800/5TH

6° SOUTH LATITUDE

1000/5TH *Japanese destroyer encountered*

ANG IS
32'

200'

FOURTH POINT
FL.EV. 15 SEC. 178 FT. 19 M. Lighthouse
ANJER
Wreck

KAKATAU
IVE VOLCANO 2667'

CATHERINE ROCKS

Speak with native NOON/5TH

Smith murdered

CHARITA
F. RED. Lighthouse

All except 10 to Menes with wounded 0900/6TH

LABUHAN
F. RED. Lighthouse
FL.EV. 2 SEC. 22 FT. 7 M. Lighthouse

NIGHT 5/6TH *Refuge Is.*
POPOLE

PEPER BAY
THIRD POINT

JAVA

6°30' SOUTH LATITUDE

rstorm NIGHT 6/7TH

OME BAY

25   20   15   10   5   0
SCALE OF NAUTICAL MILES

30'   35'   40'   45'   50'   55'   106°   5'

"This finely spun fabric" (see p. 242)

OUT OF
THE SMOKE

The Story of a Sail

RAY PARKIN

With an Introduction by
Laurens van der Post

1960
THE HOGARTH PRESS
LONDON

This story is for

THELMA, MY WIFE

INTRODUCTION

By LAURENS VAN DER POST, o.b.e.

I HEARD this story first from the writer himself in a Japanese camp for prisoners of war. Since then seventeen eventful years have gone by, and still I find on meeting it again in these pages that it has lived with me as if I had heard it only yesterday. Part of the reason is in the nature of the story itself; it is one of the great stories of war at sea. Although my years of service in the British army and my warm affection for it prejudice me in these matters, I am aware that the sailor invests his conduct in battle with a quality those of us who are compelled to fight with our feet on the ground cannot wholly match. Precisely why this should be invites an essay into the mystery of imagination and its effect on the texture of human behaviour for which there is no room here. I can only say I believe it to be something born out of the special relation that the sailor has with his ship, and the profound emotion which both sea and ship sustain in his spirit. Conrad is the obvious example of the artist with an almost extra-sensory perception of this subtle fact, but ironically no people have been more conscious of it than the enemy against whom the battle described here was fought. The Japanese even have a special word for it: they call it "Maru" and they used to join this ancient suffix to the names of their ships. Their knights, too, before the concept of chivalry degenerated into a psychological aid to totalitarian warfare, added "Maru" to the names they gave their swords. Priests also applied it in numerous ceremonies of their own. But, one and all, they did this to denote that the swords or ships thus named differed from ordinary inert matter, not merely obeying the will but becoming instruments of the spirit, and thus making an intangible contribution of their own to the quality of human performance. So imponderable is this "Maru" aspect of things that it is almost impossible to define in purely intellectual terms. One has to experience it to know what it is. But I can safely say that no one could read "Out of the Smoke" without achieving a clear comprehension of its reality which my inexpert attempt at description cannot possibly convey. In these pages it is everywhere swelling the tide of action and resolution just as the moon, even when invisible, draws the sea to its fullness. The result is that this story naturally takes place high in the company of ships like Grenville's *Revenge*, trapped off the Azores; Nelson's men of war, outnumbered on several oceans; Cradock's *Monmouth* and *Good Hope* caught against the fatal sunset at Coronel; the tiny *Glow-Worm* having "its light quenched" in the stormy North Sea, as Sir Winston Churchill put it at the time, and many another vessel whose example made heroism a routine of the British sailor in battle.

The other thing that makes this book so remarkable is both the writer, and the way he tells his story. No great event is properly accounted for until it has been described by the person who, because of what he is in himself, stands in a special relation to it, and who despite the din and confusion of the battle and his own immediate duties continues to hold a watching brief for the future. The writer of this book is such a man. A professional sailor in the Royal Australian Navy, he was a chief petty officer and quartermaster in the cruiser *Perth* with which this story is concerned. He steered the ship in her final battle in the Sunda Strait, was one of the last to leave her and the last but one to speak to her heroic captain. Among the survivors he was one of the few with an experience round enough to tell the story of the ship both from within the ship and right up to her end. Moreover, he had the capacity to do so.

I remember the first time I met him. A newcomer, I was walking around the crowded Japanese prison when I saw a bearded young man with a battered coolie's straw-hat on his head, sitting as far apart as possible from the crowd and impervious to the clamour. He was engaged in painting. I went and stood behind him and watched a corner of the prison swiftly taking shape on his board. In the centre of the picture like a symbol of triumph over defeat and confinement, a flaming Spathodia (or, as the Malays have it more feelingly, a Slippers-of-God Tree) soared above the high barbed wire fence. There and then we became friends, and though I knew him for only a few weeks, for he was soon taken away to work on the Siam-Burma railway, what we experienced was so real that we have continued to correspond to this day. Not once in those rather terrible weeks did I notice any sign of decline in his urge constantly to make, shape and create things. It has also survived the peace-time test, perhaps more exacting because less obvious, of having to make a living and support a family with grace. The illustrations he has made for this book, as well as the book itself, speak eloquently for themselves in this regard.

But why did so creative a person wait 17 years to tell the story? The answer is both between and in the lines he has written. I know from my own experience that there are things in war which cannot immediately be told. When Wordsworth spoke of art as "Emotion recollected in tranquillity" he may have given the world merely a subjective explanation of how he fashioned his own poetry, but his definition, in a sense, is valid for the writer whose immediate subject is war. There are emotions in war that can be recollected only when one is certain of one's tranquillity. The emotion which compelled this story is one of them. It is one of the writer's many qualities that he recognized this and had the confidence and patience to wait for the tranquillity in which the emotion could emerge in its entirety and integrity. Yet even at this distance some of the effect of shock and violence remains, and rightly so because without it the tale would be incomplete. The trance of disaster is so profound that only when the writer is sailing a salvaged life-boat back to Australia (as he hopes), can his imagination deal with the fate of his beloved ship and her crew. Then the full story of *Perth* unfolds like a flower that opens only at night.

The writer, I am convinced, was born an artist before life turned him into a quartermaster. The book is full of detail whose importance only the instinct of an artist could have selected, and the portraits of the survivors are not only drawn by an acute observer but interpreted by a generous, live and compassionate mind. There are unforgettable sketches of individuals, each in his unique way a microcosm of the macrocosm of the horror and pity of war. There is, for instance, the portrait of the little English girl with yellow hair and her young injured brother who appear with the flotsam and jetsam of the shattered European empires in the East on the coral island to which the writer swam from his sinking ship. There is a portrait of the captain of *Perth*, tough in its tenderness, and numerous others, from seamen and stokers right up to one of my favourite characters, met afterwards in prison—a 19-year-old Australian Naval Officer who, one day, when I asked why he was so deep in thought, replied: "I was just thinking how I love the smell of gun powder. You do too, don't you sir?"

But to end where I began, with the "Maru" aspect. A writer who has also had considerable experience of war at sea not long ago wrote a book called "The Ship That Died of Shame". That was fiction. "Out of the Smoke" is the true story of a ship which died so free of shame that she has come alive again in a greater way. As long as men who were destined to be brothers need to be reminded of how they murder one another, this story will remain as the memorial of *Perth* and the men who sailed in her.

CONTENTS

ILLUSTRATIONS AND MAPS

ILLUSTRATIONS

Portraits of Mr Carr, Mr Wyatt, Ken, and Darky made in Java during captivity, were lost. The drawing here of Mr Carr is from memory only

ACKNOWLEDGEMENTS

I wish to acknowledge my debt to the following authors and publications: Commander W. K. Karig, USNR, and Lieutenant W. Kelly, USNR, *Battle Report*; Samuel Elliot Morrison, *The Rising Sun in the Pacific*; C. Hermon Gill, *Royal Australian Navy* 1939-42; and to the Department of Navy for permission to use, as source material, certain official reports.

I have used these works as reference for the skeleton on which to hang the survivors' tales which I was fortunate enough to be able to bring out of Japanese prison camp at the end of the war. By that time many of the tellers of the tales were dead. If any account is at variance with history, I hope the historians will understand. They are not to be held responsible for anything in this book—for this story is told largely from the point of view of the men at the time.

I want to thank also Messrs Hutchinson & Co (Publishers) Ltd and Admiral of the Fleet, Viscount Cunningham of Hyndhope, especially, for his personal permission to quote certain passages from his *A Sailor's Odyssey*. In reply to me, he wrote: "Waller was a grand man, outstanding among the many fine men who did so well in those hard Mediterranean days, and a great loss to all the Navies of the Commonwealth. Had he lived he would have gone far."

This would be incomplete without mention of Laurens van der Post who, having read the opening chapters of this book in a prison camp, in 1942, latterly encouraged me to finish the story. To C. Day Lewis for his kind and understanding editing, and my publishers for every kindness and encouragement they have offered me, I would like to express my gratitude.

Foreword

TIME: February-March, 1942

PLACE: Java

THIS record contains more than the men in the lifeboat could possibly have known; but, I believe, not more than materially affected them or contributed to the climate in which they were then living. It is not meant to be a detailed or exhaustive history; however, truth, so far as it can reasonably be ascertained, has not been transgressed.

I think it has been made clear what are simply impressions of the time, as opposed to firm fact; both of which are inextricably woven into the truth of the men's experience. Thus it differs from a categorical history of events only.

Superlatives used in quotations can be evaluated according to their source. Superlatives in my own narrative I believe to be a simple statement of fact under the compulsion of that fact: subjective or objective.

It is an attempt to reconstruct the atmosphere of the time—a tragic and disheartening time for the West. In the naval actions, the focus is necessarily on H.M.A.S. *Perth*; for the rest the focus is on a few men.

It is, therefore, meant to be representative of men and ships who have faced their Saint Crispin's Day together.

It tries to avoid sensationalism out of respect for, and in memory of, all those who have died in the cause of— we know not what: except it was a duty laid upon them.

R. PARKIN

But if the cause be not good, the King himself hath a heavy reckoning to make when all those legs and arms and heads, chopped off in a battle, shall join together at the latter day and cry all, "We died at such a place"; some swearing; some crying for a surgeon; some upon their wives left poor behind them; some upon the debts they owe; some upon their children rawly left. I am afeard there are few die well that die in a battle; for how can they charitably dispose of any thing, when blood is their argument? Now, if these men do not die well, it will be a black matter for the king that led them to it; who to disobey were against all proportion of subjection.

Henry V, IV, i

DRAMATIS PERSONAE

List of main characters in this story (except the first three, in order of appearance).

H.M.A.S. Perth (ex *H.M.S. Amphion*). Six-inch cruiser. Commissioned for Royal Navy June 1936; re-named *Perth* and commissioned Royal Australian Navy June 1939. Modified *Leander* class, 6980 tons, 72,000 horse power, speed 32.5 knots. 1939, West Indies, Central Atlantic, Caribbean Sea. 1940-41, Eastern Mediterranean, action at Malta, Greece, Crete, Matapan and Syrian campaign. 1941-42. Western Pacific. Battles of Java Sea and Sunda Strait.

	Action Station
Captain H. M. L. Waller, D.S.O., R.A.N.	Commanding officer of *Perth*
Lieutenant-Commander J. A. Harper, R.N.	Navigating Officer
John (Dirk), Seaman Petty Officer.	Action Chief Quartermaster
Ben, Leading Seaman.	4-inch H.A. Director
Dick, Able Seaman.	Port Pom Pom gun's crew
Fatty (Hilton Arrat), Petty Officer.	In charge 4-inch H.A. Director
Jim (Dresden), Leading Seaman.	"Y" Shell Handling Room
George (Yew), Able Seaman.	Captain's Enemy Bearing Indicator
Ken (Day), Chief Telegraphist.	In charge Main Wireless Office
Mr Cross, Lieutenant, R.A.N.R.(S).	Bridge: Assistant Navigator
Jacky (Bunting), Yeoman of Signals.	Flag Deck
Cookie, Stoker Petty Officer.	After Fire and Repair Party
Ginger, Acting Petty Officer.	After Electrical Repair Party
Mr Stewart, Lieutenant-Commander (S).	After .5 Machine Guns
Darky (Gregory Oliver), Able Seaman.	4-inch Gun's crew
Blackie (Wolfe), Petty Officer.	Captain of "Y" Turret
Mr Carr, Lieutenant, R.A.N.R.(S).	After Bridge
McMurtee, Stoker.	After Engine Room
Smithy, Engine Room Artificer.	After Engine Room.

Part 1

SANGIENG—INERTIA

I

To the swimmer, the island at first appeared as a line of rocks. Then it grew bushes and trees along a low shore. That was as he encountered a strong, south-sweeping current, the choppy surface of which threw oil-fuel in his face and made him afraid lest it should get into his lungs.

He saw two trees on the hill behind the shore, and grimly took a bearing to work out the direction he must swim to prevent being swept past the island. If he missed this island, it would be (in his own language) "up all bags and hammocks!"

He swam squinting and blinking, through the dollops of oil-fuel flung in his face. It was oil-fuel from last night's seventeen or eighteen sunken ships. Several times he thought how easy it would be to stop swimming. How comfortable it would be! He had been swimming since midnight, and it was now around nine or ten in the morning.

He knew something of the power of the sea because he had spent years on it, and he did not delude himself: there was the shore; here was he. Between them lay water—absolutely impersonal water—which did not care whether he lived or died; which was kinder and gentler to a lowly mollusc than to him.

He had seen so many die.

He kept on swimming and blinking up at those two trees as best he could. He knew he was losing ground and being swept down to leeward. But there was a point of land jutting out. . . . The current tore at him, and stubbornly he swam against it. His legs and his arms seemed to slip through the water without doing any good.

He was tired—dangerously tired. When a man is so tired, he does not care: except for rest.

The water became calmer. He blinked at the trees again. *The bearing had changed! It was opening!* He shuddered to think how close he had been to giving up. The thought of safety, after nine or ten hours drifting in the dark, was more unreal than dying. He felt a spinning giddiness as if he were between two worlds.

Ahead, about twenty yards out from the beach, was a man. He was a dark man, almost black. He seemed to be stalking fish in the shallows: bent with his chest close to the surface of the sea, and making a cautious, halting, jerky progress toward the shore.

He kept swimming.

He touched ground; then swam a little further and stood up. It took a few moments for his numbed feet to feel; he got them off the bottom quickly, for he had been standing on live coral, growing with its spiky, upstretched branches. These had collapsed and plunged him ankle deep among the sharp jelly-oozing stumps which took flesh from his legs and feet like peel from a potato. He cursed as he re-floated himself. He knew too well the evil poison of live coral which could rival the tropical ulcer.

He watched the man catching fish close to shore. He saw him get closer and closer, and then fall on his face with the wavelets softly hissing in the coral sand about him. The swimmer then knew the man had not been fishing.

As carefully as he could, he dragged himself over the coral, which was only a few inches under the surface. He let his body trail and hauled himself ahead for all the world like a crayfish. Eventually he had to walk. With curses, cuts and cringing gait he arrived beside the other man, who rolled over and looked up.

"Who's that?" he asked, as if it were pitch dark instead of bright morning.

"Me," said the swimmer informatively.

The other peered closer. "Bloody oil-fuel," he said. "Can't tell who you are."

"Dirk," the swimmer insisted. "How are you, Ben?"

"Oh," said the other with recognition, "*you*, John. I didn't think your mob would get out below there."

"Well, we did," said John; "the Auxiliary W/T people too. We left just after the second torpedo got her."

"They told us to scram after the first. They could see it was hopeless and we couldn't do no good up there."

"See many in the water?"

"Oh yes, lots. Hell of a lot got away. Don't know where they are now. This current split 'em up a bit."

"Nearly split *me* up too. Left a raft out there to swim in. Johnno, the capt'n's cox'n, and an ord. No sign of 'em out there now. Looks like the current got 'em."

"Yes," said Ben, with full knowledge of the subject, "it's a bastard!" And they both looked out over the sea which, last night, had swallowed up so many of their mutual friends. The dark streak which was running down past the island had drowned more after the sun came up. Some perhaps, were still drowning in it. Oil-fuel.

Somewhere out in the ruffled water rose a long, wailing cry for help—repeated and repeated. There was something desperate and frightened in it. As if the man were not calling because he needed help but because he was scared stiff. It was like someone overawed by a terrible loneliness and trying, with his own voice, to shatter its finality. He went on calling.

Ben and John looked out in the general direction and saw a head and an upraised arm. And again the desperate cry came. They gave one unanimous shout.

"Swim!"

"He's through the current and in a backwater. Why don't he swim?"

"Digger, if you can yell like that you're strong enough to swim a little more. I'm not!"

They looked at the blood oozing through the oil-fuel on their legs. "No sir," said Ben, "I've had enough of that coral for today."

They sat, and watched, and listened. The newcomer kept on making little cries even after he was ashore. "Oh! Oh! Oh!" he kept on repeating hoarsely, consumed with horror.

"We couldn't help you, mate," Ben explained. "We had to come through that there ourselves."

"Oh! Oh! Dead Yank out there kept follerin' me around. Drifting. Pushed him away with my foot. Kept follerin'. I was drifting on a piece o' wood. Took his lifebelt off and pushed him away. Heard you yell—and swum. My bloody eyes! Can't hardly see a thing. Who are you? Oh, my eyes! Couldn't get rid of that Yank. Kept follerin'!"

The man was unstrung. When he opened those eyes in his oil-blackened face they were bloodshot and tears no longer came to flood them.

"We're going to look for water and see what we can see."

"I'm buggered. I'll stay!"

They left him there, face down on the coarse coral, still groaning hoarsely: "Oh! Oh! my eyes!" But there was nothing they could do.

The narrow beach was some ten or fifteen feet wide with trees overgrowing it and pushing branches out over the shallows. Odd bits of wreckage: an old boat's cover; a mast with broken halyards attached; a few oddments of first field-dressing kits half buried in the bigger lumps of coral above high water; and a couple of lifebelts hung on branches—oil-stained. Someone else had landed here not long since. There was a kapok lifebelt, too, of American pattern, bone dry.

"Shipwreck seems to be the fashion hereabouts lately," remarked Ben.

Ben and John wondered if there were any survivors of previous sinkings here. They felt that there were some of their own crowd. Groups of them had been bobbing about close by at dawn. Even now, as they looked out over the rising sepia-coloured reef, they could see more survivors. But it looked as if they were being swept past the island. Such rafts as the survivors had were not manœuverable, and the swimmers were miles too far down to beat that current.

There was a boat out there with a sail hoisted. There was no wind and the sun was getting hot. Heads were bobbing around. A Japanese destroyer steamed close, stopped engines, and the sail was lowered. The two on the beach were not sure at the time whether this boat had been sent from the destroyer to pick up last night's survivors or not. But they knew of no other boat. However, the ship steamed away again to maintain its ceaseless submarine patrol in the Strait of Sunda. A few aircraft were heard overhead, but the two men found them difficult to identify. Anyway, what the hell, now? The complete satisfaction of having both feet on solid land so possessed them that they had not begun to think past it.

They stood in the shallow water where the sand was finer and set about getting the cursed oil-fuel off each other. Their inflatable lifebelts, with the oil-soaked jersey covers, were hung in the trees beside the others. They stood black, naked and streaked in tones from deepest sepia to raw sienna. They scrubbed each other with sand. Their clothes (a pair of blue jean shorts and a torn overall between them) they treated similarly. The whole business was not very successful, but it at least scraped some of the stuff off. They proceeded naked, carrying their rags, and gingerly picked their way around the shallow water along the beach where the trees made it impossible to go by land.

As they went, they examined odds and ends—empty pemmican tins and bits of wood and cases. Fifty yards off-shore a clinker-built ship's lifeboat bumped restlessly on the reef. "She looks to have a bad hole in her," John remarked.

Not far from here they struck inland and became conscious again of their tender feet, which had been soaked in the sea since the previous midnight. They broke through the trees which bordered the beach, and were confronted with a narrow plain some two hundred yards wide. This was covered with a broad-leafed sword-grass. Young banana palms sprouted here and there. The coming heat of the day glared already on the matt surface of the grass. Rising beyond this flat was a steep hill. Away to the left John saw the two trees he had used for his bearings. On the ridge of the hill was a cultivation of maize, some paw-paw and pumpkin. On the plain itself, showing dry and parched, was the sloping nepa-thatch of two or three small huts pressed in on all sides by the prolific grass.

Here was water. Here was habitation. This meant putting on their wet, oily clothes again.

"Got to be decent, I suppose," Ben said.

"Oh, indubitably," John acquiesced with mock dignity.

They went forward along the narrow path of grass which was trodden down like a mattress beneath their feet, and it led them to the first house. The path became smooth, brown earth and quite hard. Beyond was another hut over the top of a patch of yams whose leaves seemed so neat and formal. In this hut pumpkins lay in a yellow and green heap with some native sails and a few tools. There was nobody there. They passed on to the next hut.

They went with natural caution. They did not know what the temper of the people here would be. And they were tired of animosity.

When they arrived at the hut they found some black men mooching around. Some were lying down on the ground or on bamboo slats; a couple were just wandering without much purpose. Then they were suddenly recognized for more oil-stained survivors. It was difficult to identify one another.

"There's water in the well over there; it's pretty good."

"Seen anyone here who owns these huts? The people who live here?"

"Don't know. When *we* landed and came here, old boy gave us a cup o' tea each and shoved off. Don't know where he's gone. Seems to have cleared out."

The day remained still, with rising heat, and the leaves seemed to ring with the hot glare. There was little to do except to wait and see how many of the others turned up.

For four days since they had arrived in Java they had

been kept at it. Air-raids, surface actions (by day and night), sinkings by submarines and, finally, sunk themselves at midnight by four torpedoes after an hour's fierce action. They had all spent upwards of eight hours in the water, the first part of which was made more uncomfortable for them by falling projectiles and exploding torpedoes. They had had no sleep for the past two nights. The last meal had been supper on the previous night. They were bemused. They were so weary. The only thing was sleep. The heat was taking their remaining strength. So they slept—five or six of them there, Micawber-like, waiting for something more to turn up.

Thus passed the forenoon for some on March 1st, 1942.

2

Six men were drifting together on or around the same raft. A wounded man lay uncomplaining. They were to the northward of Toppers Island, a small beehive lump of stone supporting a few trees and two Javanese light-keepers. The south-bound current of Sunda Strait split here and swept past, set over toward Sangieng Island, and went on past Krakatau and Java Head to the Indian Ocean.

At varying distances from this group others were bobbing about. The cruiser's people had been broadly scattered by dawn. Some distance from the raft men sighted a lifeboat drifting empty. Three of them left to swim for her. Eventually they reached her and found her half-full of water. She was a cumbersome steel lifeboat. They laboured heavily with her without much success. By this time the raft had come to within a few hundred yards of the boat and another man came over. Between them they then managed to get the rest of their people off the raft and into the boat. Most of them were practically naked and black with the oil-fuel which lay thick on the water in the current. The wounded man was suffering from shrapnel wounds in the arms, thighs and testicles. He did not complain. Indeed, he apologized.

By this time the sun was fairly well up and hot. The calm sea made a reflecting mirror for the heat, and was ruffled, dark-blue only along the line of the current. They were being swept past Sangieng Island. The boat was bailed and they began picking up others.

All forenoon it went on. Struggling with heavy oil-soaked oars which slipped around in their hands, and caused blisters—mental and physical. The boat was heavy and slow, high-sided, stiff; and it lay on the men's hands like a thing dead.

The survivors were so thick with oil that it was imposs-ible to handle them. Greasy hands slid from other greasy hands and arms, and the man they were trying to recover slopped back into the sea with a breathless curse. They could only get men out of the water by passing a bight of rope under their armpits and heaving them over the gun-wales, where they slid into the bottom of the boat in a sloppy heap like gaffed marlin. In agitated moments they cursed the boat. Dragging oil-covered, exhausted men over her black gunwales was back-breaking. At last there were about thirty men in the boat.

Three, four and five miles down the Strait were other heads, some just visible on the smooth surface. A Japanese destroyer moved among the nearer ones. The current had kept them in the centre of the Strait, sweeping them inwards towards the great Krakatau. It looked as if they would be swept on to that pitiless stretch of open water: the Indian Ocean.

Those in the lifeboat managed to get a sail on her and

pull up against the current, trying to make Sangieng. There was no wind and the sail only annoyed the rowers. Frayed nerves and brittle tempers began to show: there was bickering born of discomfort, suffering and fatigue, accentuated by the knowledge of their poor progress. It was only bullying and driving on the part of some of the older men that kept them going. But they *had* to keep going or get swept out to open ocean. It took them hours to make good the two miles back to the northwards. With some difficulty they found a break in the rock-bound shore and landed on a beach not fifty feet wide at the end of a rockless channel as short and as square as a graving dock. They landed amid the guttering and gloating of sea along the rocksides—it was miraculous that they had got safely over the last fifty yards.

With the boat pulled up high and dry, the men tumbled ashore and lay down, dead-beat. It was about three o'clock in the afternoon.

3

It was about this time that John awoke. He had dozed restlessly, with conflicting thoughts of past and future. Thoughts of his wife and two children. When they heard the news of the loss of the ship they would not know whether he was alive or dead. Thinking of the shock to them filled him with a haunting hopelessness—helplessness. He could do nothing about it. He must try to thrust it from him. He did not yet know about the boat.

Taking a blunt, long-bladed knife which he found in the hut, he made his way back to the beach. Insects rose and hovered over the curved and arching sword-grass which seemed to hiss and ring with the heat as he passed it. The sun beat down on his back like a fire. He came out on the

Survivors, 1942

beach to a small cleared patch where grass had recently grown over the charcoal remnants of a burnt bamboo hut at the foot of a straight-trunked canary tree. A few bamboo frames still stood. John wondered if this were the work of previous survivors or the natives. Two or three stakes stood out in the pale sandy-green of the little cove: perhaps they were used to guide native craft.

He pushed on to the water's edge and went to the left. The worm-eaten, slimy logs which rolled and bumped beneath overhanging trees told of the grim inevitable victory of the sea. Under its surface all its little citizens seemed to gloat, cuddled safe. He did not like wading in bare feet. The sharp coral and sticks were a menace—they could be so poisonous. He came to where they had seen the old boat's cover that morning and set about getting himself a wardrobe. Protection from the sun was necessary and from the chill of nights. So he cut a square big enough to wrap around him with an overlap of about eight inches. It reached from his neck to just above his knees. In the appropriate places he coaxed (for the knife was blunt and would only cut by beating it against the canvas on a bit of coral) two slits in it. Thrusting his arms through them, he had a rudimentary coat. He then proceeded to introduce two "buttons" in the front. From the cover he cut a couple of short lengths of codline lacing. To the ends of these he spliced two pieces of coral about the size of his little finger, as toggles.

As he did it he wondered how old the "toggle" was, for though he had seen it pretty widely used at sea, he felt that it was one of the really primitive ideas still surviving in its original form. The earliest of mariners had used it, before their euphroes and dead-eyes, which were now gone, but the toggle still endured, perhaps because of its very simplicity. Maybe it had first appeared in kampongs of people who had never seen the sea. Perhaps hunters of the aurochs and the sabre-toothed tiger had known it. His mind was not on the present but the vibrant past. He spliced two eyes on the other side of the coat and put it on, fastened the two white toggles and let the square neck fall in a broad lapel.

Now! The next step—what did he need? A covering for nights. He cut himself a square of canvas. He did not want to go too heavily on the cover—some instinct of con-servation held him back. So the result was that the piece he cut himself was just too small for an effective blanket, which he often rued in the dark, still hours when an annoying chill played about his back and mosquitoes attacked his ankles and feet. Sitting in the dappled shadows on the loose coral of the narrow beach, he was naked with his new clothes beside him. The boat's cover conformed to the plan of the boat and around the edge at intervals were deep triangular flaps, fitted with lanyards of inch stuff. He sawed one of the lanyards through to make a belt for the coat. Several flaps had been cut off by him in trimming his coat and blanket. Now he sat with one on his knees reflecting what he could do with them.

As he looked out from under the dark, low-hanging foliage he saw a panorama of sea and mountains. To him, then, it was only of mild interest. In another world out there was activity. A destroyer moved endlessly up and down, north and south, vigilant and aggressive, on patrol. A landing on Merak was being covered by naval forces, and the occasional boom of gunfire reached him across the water. Merchant ships, carrying troops, with only super-structure, masts and funnels visible above the intervening sea-horizon, made a long, slow, quaint procession. There

The dying boat

were almost forty of them. A float-plane reconnaissance or two droned back and forth overhead, seen occasionally through the leaves above, or beneath them out to eastward over the Java coast. That morning, as Ben and he had stood watching, bombing aircraft had come over and fighters had roared about. But it was vague. Some bombs were dropped over the Japanese troopers; hull down it was hard to tell. A single ship a little to the southward, abreast Anjer light, was near-missed with a stick of bombs. John had seen that—the great explosion of enfoamed seawater shooting skywards, almost obscuring the ship. Good to be on the outside looking on, he thought. And the ships moved steadily up and down close to Java with a slow deliberation that spelled success. So, in that other world, an invasion went on with all the completeness of modern invention, while the naked man turned to his piece of canvas and was more concerned with making a hat out of it.

He pondered on that thought a little and looked intently at the dark, blue line of the lively, chopping sea tearing down just outside the brown reef. It seemed as if, when he had swum through that current, he had indeed swum to a different world. His forehead wrinkled. "Like the bloody Styx," he thought. He was in a place unaffected by the world of yesterday. He made the hat by fashioning it into a cone and fastening the edges with a knotted rope yarn. It made him think of the first time he had been treated to "turkey lolly" and the swarthy vendor had so cunningly twisted the bag out of a square of paper; and how the taste of that pink and white stuff was really the taste of the clever bag made so neatly, and of the exotic colours.

He looked out at the grey lifeboat on the reef. As it bumped, the loose tanks within gave a mournful echo.

A jagged tooth of coral held her and she half floated on it. He felt drawn to her—but the thought of having to tread over that live coral shelf! Taking the bits of canvas ready cut, he fitted them with rope yarn laces. Cutting coconut leaves and folding them to fit beneath his soles, he wrapped a piece of canvas about each foot.

It was slow and difficult progress: the coral collapsed as he brought his weight down; the water pressure swilling inside soon exposed his soles and marooned him in the middle. It was half-expected, but it disgusted him. He would wait another day and seek a brighter idea in footwear before going out to the boat. He was garbed in the newly fashioned coat and the tall Crusoe-like headpiece which made him look as if wildness were his normal state.

He came back to the shore on all fours, feeling for footholds that were not so sharp or not so weak that they would break and jamb his foot. As he reached the sandy bottom closer in, he straightened up.

Fifty yards up the beach he saw a skiff, painted grey, clinker-built, and with her mast stepped. The stem was ashore and a bowline ran across the coral strip to a tree. The lowered sail was draped on the yard, and a bight or so of the sheets stuck out over the stern. The boat rocked gently, the water slapping with a quiet flatness under the counter. In the sea, a few feet out from the transom, stood a man, half naked, with trousers rolled above his knees.

"How y' goin', mate?" he called in an everyday voice.

John was curious, but not surprised. Not any more. He made his way along to the man. This was where he had come ashore that morning. His eyes took it in as he approached. The boat had the look of having been brought there deliberately as part of a voyage. Her gear wore a weathered look so that, among the apparent disorder, there was the pattern of things falling naturally into place. About six feet above the water's edge a man squatted over a smoother piece of coral, intent upon sharpening his knife—a naval clasp-knife. He did not look up until John was stepping from the water in front of him. His face was serious and quiet; but with dark, imperious eyes which gave a relentless firmness to his mouth.

"How'r' yuh?" he said simply, feeling the edge of the blade. John said, "Not bad." The man went on sharpening.

Just by him, a little in front, sat a Malay woman in the conventional tight breast-compressing bodice and a black skirt of some light stuff. She was young and had a good face and a warm brown skin. Smooth, black hair was drawn to a bun at the back of her head. Before she looked up at the newcomer she had been watching two very lovely children in front of her. The youngest, a boy of five with white hair, was playing with the intriguing shapes of the coral fragments between his legs. The elder, a girl of eight, nearly as fair, was his sister, and she plaited strips of coconut leaf. Both of the children looked up at John, and the look went right through him in a thrill of pain. He had a boy and girl, both fair, of three and six. The children remained quite silent.

Lying askew to the water's edge, and almost in it now the tide was making, was an oil-covered form, face down. The oil was on him like half-dried treacle and there was no difference between the appearance of his skin and the overall suit he wore. The woman looked at him compassionately and up at John with deep, sincere eyes, "He's been like that all day. We gave him water when we came. He is sleeping. It is his eyes. They hurt and he rubs them He can't see." Just then the man groaned, shifted restlessly and was still again.

The man sharpening the knife looked up. "Missus can't do nothin' for it." He shook his head. "Got nothing."

The other man had followed John in from the stern of the boat and stood dripping and shiny-black from the knees down. More oil-fuel was coming in with the tide. He was whiter and more slender than the man with the knife. Younger too. Over the gunwale of the skiff, near the bow, hung a very soiled, once-white drill naval singlet with the characteristic square blue-jean neck band.

John did not attempt to explain the group. He simply accepted it. His mind was tired and his sensitivities dulled. But he looked at the singlet and the younger man. "Navy?" he asked.

"I am," the youngster replied, and appeared more ready to talk than the other. "Tug's not. Nor the other one."

"Other one?"

"Yes, gone foraging," said Tug, "to see what he can get."

"How many of you?"

"Six. Other one and us."

"What ship?" This was addressed to the younger man.

"*Vendetta.*"

"*Vendetta?* But she didn't . . ."

"No, she got away all right. I was in hospital—Singapore. Got a job driving wounded down from Johore Baru. Got away in the skiff. Made our way down the coast. Tug was in Singapore. They were bombed out of their ship—an old Chinese coaster. This is his fifth shipwreck this war."

John looked toward Tug, who stopped sharpening a moment and glanced up to nod. "We'd only a grenade-thrower and a Lewis. They were high levellers," he added significantly. His knife was still not sharp enough.

"I think I saw you out in the tide this morning."

Bombed-out!

"Yes, destroyer came over and we had to lower our sail."

"Where'd you come from?"

"Sumatra. Left last night."

"Then you'd be crossing about the time we were there?"

"Yes, we saw you."

"Pretty hot for you, eh?" And John looked from the man with the knife to the woman and the children playing silently with coral and grass, and back to the slender young speaker who only said, "Yes, we saw you."

He thought of it later. What the young man had seen was some twenty destroyers and a few cruisers protecting a total of about fifty ships from two cruisers. After a fierce fight in the close waters of the Strait lasting just over an hour, the two cruisers had run out of ammunition and been torpedoed. All that was left of them was a few survivors. Between eight and fifteen enemy, including warships, had gone with them. It was a bad night to have spent in the Strait in a sixteen-foot skiff.

John looked at the children and spoke to them. "What are your names?" he smiled.

"Mary," said the girl. "And Robin's my brother." And both of them fixed him with frank, wide eyes which had a sort of dumb appeal in them.

"Mummy and we left Daddy in Singapore and came away in a boat." Robin was quite silent. "Mummy said we were to wait. . . . I don't know where my Mummy is." Her voice went faster, and choked toward the end. Her lips quivered and her eyes filled quickly. She sobbed. Robin simply looked at her as if he were half-puzzled but quite sympathetic, and then he went on playing with his pebbles.

"Stow it! Stow it, Mary," growled Tug, still sharpening.

"Don't, Mary," the Malay woman said, "Mummy is all right."

"Where—how did you pick them up?"

"Bombed out in Banka Strait. We picked up Missus and them coming through." This was Tug speaking.

"They told us to go to the saloon because there was an air-raid on. The aeroplanes came over and there were some big explosions, and the ship started to sink. They told us to go to the boats; but I could not find any and I jumped into the water. I found something—a thing—"

"A raft," supplied the *Vendetta* rating.

"—and dragged myself on to it. And when I looked up the ship was coming down on top of me. It was falling over. I prayed and it missed me."

"And the children?"

"I found them in the water near me and pulled them on with me."

"That's how we found them. We were in by the shore when this happened."

"Did you get any others?"

"We had thirteen in the boat, but it was too many. We left some to take a chance in Sumatra. We've been fourteen days from Singapore. Pulling most of the way. No wind. Some days we pulled for thirteen hours. Got stuck on the mud near Banka for a whole tide." He paused and then continued, "We had a vote and made Tug skipper, and we do whatever he says."

This made John look again at Tug. Tough, weather-bitten, taciturn, a man about thirty looking stern enough to be cruel. But he was not. It was a deep sense of unswerving responsibility. And he spoke: "We're trying to

make Timor, or mebbe Australia. Travel by night mostly
and stick to the coast. Put in and rest up and fossick.
Mebbe two months."

"Got a chart?"

"No, an atlas. Got it handy, Missus?"

She got the book. John sat down carefully, conscious
that beneath his coat were no pants.

"Page ten and eleven."

"Yes, I've got it."

And John, for the first time, had an idea just where he
was. Tug leaned forward and traced his proposed course
roughly with his forefinger.

"That's ocean coast to the south."

"I know," Tug replied.

"Well, I hope you have luck."

"We'll do it all right."

The water lapping at the feet of the sleeping man transferred their attention to him. He was waking now and
rolling over to sit up.

"How you doing now?" John asked.

"Ah, that's better after that sleep. But my bloody
eyes—"

"Don't touch 'em," warned John, "blink 'em hard.
But don't touch 'em. You'll only get more in."

"Got any water anywhere?"

"Yes, here's some water," said the young chap, whose
name was Bill Jenkins. And he gave him a mug with
water.

The man drinking, a short young man of twenty-two
or so, paused and looked up at John with his near-blind
eyes. "How many of our mob here?"

"About eight or ten so far. Maybe some more further
up the beach. There looked to be a crowd ahead of me

who would make it there! Seen anyone else?" he asked of
the others.

"Nobody 'cept you."

John was looking at Robin and suddenly noticed a
great round sore on his knee. Mary had brushed the flies
away and told him not to let them get on it.

"What happened to his leg?"

"It was sun-burn and we burnt it with lysol—and he
don't keep it covered from the sun."

"Lysol neat?"

"M-m-"

"Whew!"

Mary said, "He won't keep the flies away from it, and
now he can't put his leg properly straight." John thought
it was pleasant to hear her high, well-articulated speech.
But Robin only looked at her with a faint grin on his face
as if his sister's concern were amusing. He still remained
silent.

"Tropics are crook for a sore like that."

"Robin never complains. Do you Robin?" Missus put
in. Robin simply shook his head, but did not raise it. He
looked slightly embarrassed.

John gazed out at the destroyer now steaming slowly to
the south. After a short silence he said, "When are you
shoving off from here?"

Tug answered, "Might spend a couple of days here.
Depends what we find. Want water and some food."

"There's plenty of water here."

"Yes. We'll cross to the mainland by night."

"Do they take any notice of you?" He nodded toward
the destroyer.

"Only told us to lower our sail this morning. But you
c'n never tell."

John shook his head.

"Listen, Frank," he said to his oily shipmate, "when you feel ready to move you can find us easy enough. Follow the beach around there. To the right. There's a bit of a sandy cove and it's clearer. You'll see an old bamboo shed—just a couple of bits standing. Rest's burnt. And a big tree. Turn in and right behind the burnt shed there's a path through the grass. Keep bearing left till you see some huts. We're there. I'll go back now to see what's doing. Most of 'em should have had a sleep by now—and it's getting a bit cooler."

Then he turned to the others and said, "Well, so long! I'll see you some more before you sail. Good-bye, Missus," he smiled an oil-caked smile for her. "Good-bye, Mary! Good-bye, Robin! So long!"

And he waded back along the shore, treading tenderly. On the way near the huts he ate a few tomatoes the size of marbles. When some of them saw him in his new suit, they hailed, "Hi Robinson Crusoe!"

4

A fire had been kept going since the natives had vanished. It was a poor sort of a blackfellow's fire, but when they wanted it they coaxed life back into the miserable grey ashes between the fire stones. A couple of kerosene tins were filled from the shallow well cut down in the coral deposit. With hot water and odd bits of rag and the coral sand used as an abrasive, several of the men stood dirty and naked in the meagre shade of a paw-paw and rubbed each other raw. It was painful work, but the oil-fuel was hateful enough to warrant it.

One of the crowd was standing lanky and nude alongside a cold fire, and another was rubbing the white ash on him.

Then they changed about. Each, with his eyes tightly closed, was doing his own head. They rubbed ash into their hair, to absorb some of the oil. Their skins burned fiercely in the sun.

The kampong was a poor one. John looked around and took it in. There were three huts set at fifty-yard intervals along its length. There were two small wells between the three huts: the water in them was sweet enough, though hard. They appeared to be tidal, so the water must be seawater filtered through the lime of the coral strata. This intrigued John and, as he gazed, squatting on the edge, he saw a great, gleaming, brown toad sitting jewelled with armchair comfort on a cool, sandy ledge over the shallow, clear pool at the bottom.

The cultivation was of cassava over the whole area close to the huts, thrusting its hand-like leaves, on long thin stems, under the eaves where there were no walls. At the north end grew a few tomato bushes with a lot of the small, marble-like sweet fruit on them. A patch on the hill, for a couple of hundred feet up, had been tilled, and there grew some maize (now 1ipe) and green paw-paw. Above that grew the wild Java Bush.

The kampong, off the hard beaten path, was dusty and full of coral fragments. Some scrawny chickens with long legs and hard thighs scratched and pecked about. A roué rooster pecked and prowled, and caused a squawking scatter now and again among the hens.

The afternoon wore on. Men looked about for themselves, attended to themselves, and thought to themselves. There was no leader, and there was no party—only a number of men whom chance had assembled under one thatched roof, after they had come in from the beach to find water.

Two of the huts were only sloping roofs with two or
two-and-a-half walls. The low side was the open side. In
the first one, at the northern end, was a small fireplace and
a beaten earth floor and a bamboo bench which occupied
the full length of the high side. On it were rags which might
have been bedclothes; beneath it were a few pumpkins,
a native sail, a mast and a rudder. There were also some
rusty old tools. A few yards from the entrance there was
a well. Here were six very sure, very self-contained young
fellows who would far rather continue their adventures
alone, without outside opinion or advice. They were
energetic and already they had ideas about leaving this
boatless island. Undaunted, but in some respects unthinking, they formed a tight little group of healthy men who
hated a burden. Geographically, too, they were a little
separated from the rest. The path curved between their
hut and the next, and the tall yam-tops cut them off.
They lived a separate civic life, attending subsequent meet-
ings of the community only with a sort of tolerance of a
scheme-of-things into which they refused to be dragged.

The second and centre hut was the poorest of the lot.
So far about eight men had come down there. It, too, was
a simple sloping-roofed affair, whose low side was only five
feet high. The raised platform for sleeping was two feet
high, and a bare six feet wide. The whole hut was fifteen
by ten feet. The bare earthen floor held a couple of rude
fireplaces. Three or four pumpkins lay under the communal bunk, and cluttered at one end of the hut were
maize on the cob in the husk, a tin of claggy, sour rice and
some dirty little mugs. There was only a back wall of
plaited bamboo and two half-end walls. Here the yam
leaves intruded.

The third and main hut was palatial compared with the

others. At one end was a cooking-room running from front to back. In it were cooking-utensils, the shallow iron pan bowls for frying, etc., and tin cups, plates, a spoon or two and a knife. This smoke-blackened room had a separate door to the outside. The rest of the house was made up of two bedrooms, each with its own door which opened on to a common verandah, and elevated on floors a foot or so above ground. In the bedroom were some mattresses, bedclothes and other odds and ends later discovered. Men lay on the verandah now, not thinking what to do.

Men were still personal, within themselves: still getting themselves straight, which is the responsibility of any man so that his personal affairs do not become a community problem. This life was not yet twelve hours old. It took some thinking over.

John joined the bathers.

5

Another swimmer swept to the south past Sangieng and looked at the island intently. "It's this or nothing," he thought. A freak of the current set him around the south-eastern promontory of the land upon which he looked so wishfully. He began to swim with very definite purpose, and the faint, undulating swell from the Indian Ocean helped to bear him northwards to safety. Eventually he landed through the surf, which rolled him over on the rocks until he crawled ashore. In the sun, on the edge of the wild grasses, he lay resting. The severe rocky hills looked down timelessly and unmoved. Insect life continued around him with all the self-absorption of childhood. When some energy returned to him, he wandered about the rock-bound shore to the eastward. There he found the boatload of sleeping and exhausted men sprawled near their beached boat.

He sat down with them.

6

Ben wandered around the island, exploring with irrepressible hope. He had cut across to the beach from the camp and then picked his way along the loose, steep and narrow coral beach there. He went southward. Back towards the centre of the island, above a short plain, were steep hills. Rising steeply on his left from the plain, and then dropping quite abruptly into the sea, was a promontory a hundred feet high and nearly half a mile long—for all the world like a young Gibraltar extending diagonally.

Ben decided to cut behind this hazard. After breaking his way through some wooded tangle he was among grass growing in low clumps. It rustled in the occasional puffs of wind which came like a hot breath across the sand and shell-strewn plain. Over the pale, hazy-green of the plain he saw the south coast of the island rise in sheer rock-cliffs, the feet of which were strewn with islets looking like bits of the island torn out by a giant hand and flung in anger from the summit. Some of them still carried the shaggy polls of topsoil; vegetation and trees with grotesque, searching, vine-like trunks writhed down over the rocky crags. Distance blued the deep shadows; here and there a patch of brilliant emerald glowed. Ben viewed the extent of the island thus for the first time. "She's bigger than I thought," he reflected.

His gaze had been captured by these more salient features of the landscape, but as he swept it to the left, he saw something which affected him more than scenery. It was the mast of a boat. He pushed forward eagerly and there found the sprawled figures of many of his shipmates. "Ho there! Wakey! Wakey!" he called. They looked up, and questions flew. Ben told them of the others.

Almost all went back with Ben to the kampong. More of what had happened last night was pieced together. The newcomers drank avidly at the wells. Indecision and tiredness still left them without a plan for the future. None could tell if any attempt would be made to rescue them. The situation in Java was unknown.

The fact of having survived last night, and now being able to sleep without drowning, was sufficient. The heat of the afternoon overtook them again.

There was some talk of going back for the remaining wounded man. One had already made his way around with the others, having only a couple of shrapnel wounds which, though painful, did not prevent him from walking.

7

Five men were left in the little cove with four-foot walls of jagged volcanic rock. One was wounded; his companions had rigged the mainsail on a couple of oars to shelter him. Only one of them was over thirty years of age. The youngest were the swimmer and another able seaman and a short, dark-headed stoker who, like the rest, was a black treacly mess, but whose eyes were giving him much more trouble, for his eyelids were glued together. Only occasionally did he glimpse the glare of the sun. Dick, the injured man, was young also. Looking out from where they sat, they could see Krakatau thrusting its cone up, jagged and blue.

Some hours passed. The wounded man was given some water from the lifeboat's barricoes. At last the older man stood up and turned to look across the shimmering grasses towards the low belt of tangled trees and bush into which the others had vanished.

"Look here," he said in a voice which held something of exasperation and disgust. "It doesn't look as if the others are coming back. I think we'll see if we can get Dick back ourselves."

The others made gestures of assent and shifted uneasily with a sort of hopeless lassitude. Their wills were as tired as their bodies. The blind stoker was too miserable.

The man who made the decision was of middle height and thick-set. They called him Fatty. He reached into the boat and pulled out the triangular staysail. "Look," he said. "What if we carry him in this in a sitting position? One of us can take the head and the others can take the clew and the tack. The one with the head will have to hold it up." He was not counting the stoker in, for he did not appear to be capable of helping. "What do you think, Dick?"

"All right with me," Dick said quietly.

"We'll give it a try," said the swimmer, whose name was Jim. "Come on, George, my old tarpot!" he added to the other able seaman and gave him a shove with his foot.

They gathered up the wounded man and sat him in the foresail. The blood drained from his face and a spasm of pain crossed it. He was naked and they thought it was better to leave him so. There was nothing to cover him with that was not oil-soaked. Everything shone black with it, including the patient. His wounds were open and un-dressed—filled with the oil-fuel and oozing the blackest of red when he was moved. They found him abnormally heavy to carry although he was only a slight man. They had not staggered clear of the beach when he fainted. They could not work a co-ordination between the three of them, and he was twisted first this way and then that. They had to give it up out of sympathy for the man, who said, between fainting spells, "I don't think it's very good."

They put him down and got two oars and the mainsail with which they improvised a stretcher. They were forced to get the stoker to take one corner: he stumbled along with them like a blind man with a lead dog. They had to rest every fifty yards; then it was hard work to get the blind man to his feet again. With painful short marches, they literally drove themselves on. When they started to break their way through the bush to pick a path, they did not fully realize what it meant. Without boots, feet were cut by thorns and broken branches. They had to take detours, often without making a foot of progress. They rested the man in the stretcher while they tore at the jungle with their hands to make an opening. The stoker at each stop would sink down and fall asleep. When they were ready to go on, he had to be shaken roughly and kicked to his feet. With one hand on the shoulder of one of the bearers, he stumbled behind. Each man had his own troubles and discomforts. Each man seemed to develop a hard shell of self inside of which his misery seethed. It was the wounded man's never complaining which kept things under control.

They became bushed. A sense of futility settled on them and they were deciding to bed down there and then, come what may: snakes, ants, mosquitoes or any thing else. Then they heard a distant "Coo-ee": a call which Australia has sent around the world. They answered, realizing that it was the other party. It was an hour before dark, and it took the newcomers about half an hour to find them by constant coo-eeing and reply. The new party were all footsore. With their help, the wounded man was taken back to the boat, where, it was decided, Fatty, Jim, George and the wounded man, Dick, should spend the night and be collected in the morning.

The others returned to the kampong.

The wounded man was made as comfortable as possible with the sails. The stoker had gone back with the others. The remaining three slept on the beach. The night became cold and they shivered. About one o'clock a storm broke with a deluge of rain. Mosquitoes whined viciously; so they buried themselves in the sand for refuge and slept. It was not until the next morning they discovered Dick's wounds being tormented by streams of ants. But he had not complained.

8

In the kampong men had collected in groups in the huts. They talked in a scrappy sort of way. There was a little food which they shared, but it was hardly worth while. A tin of pemmican was put into a kerosene tin with water so that when it boiled there was only a suspicion of taste in it. It was hot and the men told each other it was all right— and tried to believe it themselves. They were too disinclined to *disbelieve* it, for they did not want to accentuate their state of need and ill-luck by complaints. It was typical of the conversation too. They dwelt upon their good fortunes. And in the grimmest of things they discussed there was kept alive that spark of humour imperative to a sense of balance. Such as a short laugh over a man who had cried, help, he could not swim; yet who beat the good swimmers to floating wreckage. Or the grimmer one of a man who called desperately to God to save him—the first time in years he had used the name without blasphemy. The general feeling was one of sufficient-unto-the-day-is-the-evil-thereof. They needed rest. That shaped the picture as the light of day was overlaid with the swift downfall of dark. The fires glowed and smoked beneath the thatch; men coughed and hoped the fires would keep the mosquitoes away.

They slept in close, uncomfortable rows on the raised bamboo slats. They stank with oil: a smell they endured but hated. Odd rags covered them. If the rags were on top, they did not keep out the cold or mosquitoes from below. If they were placed under them, they were no protection on top. Restless, cold, stiff and mosquito-bitten, but they slept. It rained and became colder. They grunted and squirmed uncomfortably, vowing to do something about it next day. It would be good to feel the warmth of the sun again. Forgotten was the sun that had scorched and sapped them yesterday. Only the warm enlivening beams of a morning sun and long cool shadows were remembered. They slept on fitfully.

The black velvet foliage of night paled to green and became real. Gone were the immovable impressions, grotesque and towering, born of the baffling vagueness of the heavy, clouded night. The men saw trees now, leaves, other men, and the posts which supported the roof beneath which they had slept.

The ragged fringe of leafy thatch, dead and dark, straggled and touched the fresh, stiff, green hands of the yam trees stretched on thin, smooth arms multitudinously from the man-high single stalk of their being. They were pale, clean hands, washed in the night by rain, and now held forth as if for inspection. Throughout the whole plantation the yam trees stood up straight and held their hands out—all clean and they knew it; so they stood still, with the self-assurance of regulars on parade. A trifle bored. Here and there in the ranks an early morning rumour of that inveterate gossip, the wind, caused a stir. But they became still again and stood as before. And thus they stood while the colours of day were hoisted over the tree-tops: red and the paling colours of light. Around them, the rabble of the undisciplined grasses. Only the yams stood erect and disciplined, and on them shone glistening buttons that were drops of rain, shot through with light—each one a microcosm of crystal. On the hillside stood the maize: ripe in tattered clothes, pitifully attempting to imitate the soldierly yam. Among them towered a few paw-paws—straight and neat with a broad topee of leaves on top. These stood like exasperated old colonels despairing over volunteers.

Amid this soldiery of nature the men in the huts were like horses in a stable. They attended no parades. Their world was another one. They did not see the soldiers, the volunteers and the exasperated colonels. They saw only the shape of things that appeared in their minds.

In the rising sun they saw dark blood and thick oil-fuel and the flash of explosion. The clouds were tipped with flashes and soaked in oil-fuel and blood. Within John was born a silent, sullen animosity against the sunrise.

It was the depression of men awakening; of men who had slept chilled and uncomfortably through the night, waiting for morning. Now it had come, they had to break the shackles of lethargy. It was as if they were unwilling to stretch out their legs and surrender that little patch of warmth they had cuddled to their bellies with inthrust hands and up-drawn knees.

One by one they stirred and moved about. They spoke sentences to each other, but these were outside each man, like his arms and his legs. Each was still a locked vault filled with private thoughts; with ideas he would not let out. Which somehow he *could not* let out. Each was thus excommunicate from the other. They spoke outside themselves, yet with habitual feeling.

"What a bonza night," one said, like a prayer of thanksgiving for perils safely past.

"It was a bastard," came a doleful chant like an orthodox response.

"O-o-o-h, A-h-h-h," yawned a man on the bamboo slats. "Ten million mosquitoes, and five thousand bamboo trees, and every one of 'em left a mark. Good-morning!" and, after stretching on his neck and heels, he flopped on to his back. "Feathers 'a' got bones in 'em," he murmured less audibly.

A brightly-jewelled, green snake slithered down the thatch and landed with a light soft plop at the bare feet of a man looking without emotion over the yam tops. He killed it with a piece of firewood before it could slide away. Some others came over to look at it curiously. "Tree snake," one opined. "Drop outa the trees on to you." The man who had killed it, still with the piece of wood in his hand, stood unmoving. He eyed the snake with all the distaste of men since Adam for the traditional, sinister reptile.

"Kick it out of the way, there." And it was kicked into the bare, tilled earth of the yam patch for the ants to clean out.

"Is the fire still going?"

"Dunno. I got up a coupla times last night and put some wood on, but chucked it in eventually."

"Ken and I sat over it talking till pretty late. We put a big bit on before we turned in."

"Better blow the ashes up. Might be a spark."

A man with a bit of mouldy canvas about his middle got down on all fours and raked among the ashes. Another one got the dried husks of maize and shredded them fine. Then a few sticks and twigs.

"Still warm," mused the man, searching; and he blew fine, white clouds of ash in little cumulus eddies, looking for a spark.

"Here's a go," he said hopefully, when he saw a wink as faint as the first star at twilight. He reached for the dry tinder and gently piled it on; nurtured it stick by stick, sliver by sliver. Watching them blacken as if ink was soaking in. Breathing on the whitening edge which melted like ice-cream until it glowed. Smoke began to rise, white-blue, and fill the low-roofed structure and filter vapourlike from the top. Inside, it swirled slowly round. Soon the firemaker had the building to himself.

"Let him have it, he's happy."

"Hah!" The flames started to flicker, and then of course the others came back and all wanted to put wood on it.

"*I'll* look after this," the producer said quite emphatically.

"Better get something to eat, I suppose," suggested Ken. "What've we got?"

"Sweet Fanny Adams," said a tall, dirty man with blond hair concealed by black oil and the fire ash he had rubbed in it. He was an officer. It was Lieutenant Cross.

"Cook up some paw-paw and pumpkin. Chuck in a couple of tomatoes."

"Worse than the chief cook's idea of soup."

"What happened to old Bob?"

"Don't think he got out. She stopped a couple there near the galley. Nobody saw him in the water. Sammy Burton was in the water, though. He's near Bob in action. He died in the water—back shot away."

"M-m-m, I never struck anyone who'd seen him either."

"Well, what about this? We cook it?"

"Might as well. Keep us going till we get organized."

"Get organized! That's what we kept saying since the day we commissioned in Pompey in '39. 'When we get settled down!' Old Flip started it. And we were still saying it a week ago!"

"But we *were*," insisted John. "She was as good a fighting ship as any. She took all that shellfire *and* four torpodoes *and* she never caught fire. *And* she did not stop firing until she had no ammunition left. It's a pity she's gone." He shook his head. "It's more than just the loss of a cruiser or a crew. It's her *experience*; and she was one of those good gunnery ships."

"You've got to hand it to the Engineer Commander. He had the Fire Parties and Damage Control like no other ship. Yes, sir!"

"She was a great little ship. See her when she went?" Just after the fourth fish hit her. Down she went by the bow, lifted her screws clear—*and they were still turning.* Strike me! There was *no* stopping her!"

A couple of men came along from the larger hut. Everyone was glad of the morning sunshine. The well was visited and they drank deeply. Nobody seemed fussy about food at the moment. The whole prospect of the future came up. Was it to be marooning with the meagre fare of a nomad? Would it be rescue? Or would it be escape?

The meal was a couple of mouthfuls of half-cooked

paw-paw or pumpkin. They told themselves it would keep them going. Yet after a most arduous four or five days, a sinking, a night in the water and a foodless day and an uncomfortable night, they were not so fussy about food this morning. They were living upon suspense.

"Wonder what'll happen? What'll they do about us?"

"Might send a Catalina up to search. Ought to make a ground sign."

"Yeh, so the Nips can see it. Look, they got a recco up already! Fat chance!"

The group looked up and, droning high across the Strait and rising up above the trees from the east, appeared a float plane. As it passed over the island they drew discreetly into cover.

"Still, they must know we went. We were making enemy reports, weren't we, Ken?"

Ken was a Sparker. He nodded.

"Well they won't *leave* us here surely."

"Hard to say. Depends how things are going in Java. Might be a chance if we kept air supremacy for awhile."

"They kept us here fighting anyway. Why do that?"

"Perhaps they're going to make a stand."

"Oh, I think so, surely!"

"Well, they're banging away in the hills over there."

"What about the boat?"

"She's all right."

"Got a sail?"

"Yes, water barricoes and some biscuits and milk."

"Sounds all right. She's a chance, anyway."

"There's about fifty of us."

"Yes, I know. Board of Trade allocate her for forty. And you know what *they* are. More on the outside, hanging on, than inside."

"Ah well, we'll all have to see about that later."

"Yes, there's a lot of things to be considered. Better all get ourselves in as best shape as we can first."

The conversation shuttle-cocked thus from one to another, skimming the surface. They were not aware of the situation in Java. There was much they did not know which has since become history.

"What about the wounded chap and those other jokers with him?" Ben broke in.

"Yes, they'll have to be brought around today sometime. But they've got milk, biscuits and water. More than we've got here."

"Have to fetch 'em at low tide to get him round the beach."

"It'll be hot then."

"Have to do it, that's all."

"Well, about eleven o'clock, fellers, we'll go around." Two waterproof watches had survived, so they still were the slaves of marked hours.

"O.K., O.K.," came a few cries of assent trailing off.

9

Oil-fuel was still a problem. It never ceased to be.

"How are your eyes, Neil?"

"Pretty sore. Can't see much."

"Bathed 'em?"

"Yes. Yes, can't get rid of it, though. Stuff sticks in my eyelashes and eyebrows."

"Let's try some fire ash. See if that will do any good." The pair walked over to an old fire where there was some fine white ash. Neil was told to lean forward while the other lightly scooped the finest of the ash off the tip. "Close your eyes tightly." And he flung it up in little jerks into the eyes of the other. "Now dust it in with your fingers and see if it absorbs any of the stuff. Maybe it'll wash out later."

Jacky, Neil's cobber, came over. "What's this—ash? What d'y' do? Rub it in? Think I'll try some. What's it like, Neil?"

"Don't know yet. But the idea sounds all right."

"I'll try it." And he proceeded to rub the ash over his face and in his hair. "My eyes are not as bad as Neil's, but I got the bloody stuff thick all over me. Makes you stink and feel terrible. Clogs up your skin and you can't sweat."

"Yes. Likely to be poisonous, too, on sores."

"Don't talk about sores; wait till that coral gets to work!" This was Ben. "That's something the crowd in the boat dodged. Not many of us with sores so far."

"Have to watch it getting around the beach in the shallow water. Stone fish too. Get one of those and you're a goner."

"Nice places these tropical islands. Romantic."

"Well, I'd rather have a bar of soap than a hula girl any day."

"Romance! Look at us!"

Oil! Oil! The rotten, treacle-black, sticky, stinking muck, which had spread over the water in the night in a heavy, slimy foam, polluting everything. Drowning men had coughed and choked and sputtered in it, their eyes had filled with it. Men had died under a black, shapeless, gleaming headstone which deserted them and clung to the living like a persistent indefatigable enemy.

Here were so many men made alike by the black skin of oil encasing them. Many had found themselves naked in the water not knowing how they got there—victims of

JIM

JOHN

FATTY

JACKY

some explosion which had denuded them; and fighting their way clear to the water, they had no memory of it. Others more fully clad had cast off boots and shirts or trousers in the water. A few had swum in shorts or overalls. But all of this clothing was soaked just as fully as if it had been put in a bucket of fuel-oil and held submerged.

In the sun their black was changed to a sepia brown. Those whose eyes were bad could not bear to open them to the light—the light of morning growing stronger and hotter. They sat rather helplessly with their eyes closed. They hoped the flowing tears, which would run dry sometimes, might heal the burning. It seemed that nothing else would.

Ben was stalking the rooster with a stone in his hand. "Ho, you can count your days, my boy. You'll be in the pot soon." He let drive with the stone and there was a thump on the boney little carcass which made a noise like a drum. There was a spurt of dust under the spurs of the bird's long legs and a squawk as it dashed off. The hens scattered and the cock pulled up somewhere in the maize patch beyond them: from thence it crowed defiantly, to regain ascendency over his personal domain.

"All right," said Ben. "You can cackle. It might be your last. That was only practice."

Shortly after there was a commotion among the hens.

"He's taken you serious," Ken laughed.

"Watch where those hens go—there'll be eggs. Gawd, they're skinny, though. Only like an egg with legs themselves."

"There's not much to eat on this island. I mean there's enough *now*. But not once we started on it, it wouldn't last more'n a week."

"I reckon it'd be a good idea if we got all the provisions

under one roof and organized a central galley with an equal ration each."

"That'd be a fairer way, all right, and we'd know where we stood."

"Have we got anyone can cook?"

A black, unrecognizable face said it could if some one would give it a hand.

"I'll give you a hand, Stokes," volunteered one.

"What about them up in the far hut? Ginger and Co.?"

"They'll have to go with the mob, that's all. Majority rules!"

"How many of us here?"

"Wait a minute. One—two—seven'n five—twelve—four at the well—sixteen—"

"Some more inside, Ben!"

"Oh yes. How many?"

"Eight."

"Well, they know what they can do. They can't run the island."

"They reckon they will find their own way to the mainland. They say there's a canoe big enough for them they've discovered in a river along the beach. But the river has no outlet. They'd have to carry it."

"We could soon give 'em a hand with it."

"Well then, it's settled about the cooks and the meals?"

"Yes."

"What about meals. Two a day? After all, more people suffer from over-eating than over-drinking."

"We can try it, anyway."

"All right: morning and night—we've had the morning one."

"Have we?" asked an innocent.

"You have," said someone with finality. "Fill up on water at the well."

"I wish I'd eaten that last supper the night we left Batavia. Zepps in the clouds! Boy, oh boy! Snags and mash!"

"They were tinned sausages, and I *thought* I didn't like them."

"Getting near time to go for the wounded bloke, fellers. Who's going?"

"Look, it's no good us all going down to get Dick. Who's got the best footwear?"

"I'll go." And one after another a number of them volunteered to make the trip.

"O.K. boys! What about moving off! Got to catch the tide!" And off they moved through the bush track which led to the beach. Ben led this party because he had made the journey the day before. When they broke through the bush on to the beach they saw two figures to the south. They hailed them and got a wave in return.

The two men were walking painfully through the shallows. The water flashed as they pushed their legs forward or stumbled, and their hands smote the surface. Their knees bent and their haunches dropped. It all came from a warning spasm in their tender feet, which winced involuntary at almost any contact. Sharp broken branches, half buried, stabbed them and lumps of sharp coral seemed to lure their feet like magnets. Even the coarse sand was like a compact pressure of needle points which the implacable hand of the sea-bed pushed up. It magnified the feeling of personal misery, enlarging the World-within-a-man which makes for pain, so that the world outside is diminished and, because it appears not to suffer too, takes on the unreality of deadness.

The little party watching them approach could feel their every step.

"Crook feet! This *bloody* coral!"

"The dead stuff's not so bad. It cuts yer, but it's not poisonous."

"That live stuff's the daddy, though. It cuts you under the feet. It breaks and cuts your ankles as you crash. And that stinkin' jelly-muck in it poisons you." This was Ken.

"Who are these blokes?"

"Come over from the boat p'raps."

"Fancy trying to recognize anybody over twenty yards. All look like black fellas."

"P'r'aps it's just as well. Nips won't pay us so much attention. Wonder if they'll worry over us?"

"I thought they would have put a landing party ashore for us yesterday."

"It looked like it when they came so close in. I was ready to make for the scrub."

"Yes, that was when they told the skiff to lower her sail. I don't suppose they'll pick us up until the landing over there is finished."

"They're still moving transports over there. She's a mansize landing. Seem to be steaming a bit further in. There's the destroyer patrol. Up and down—never stops."

"Hullo, look! ack-ack! See the bursts up over the leading ships! Destroyers or a cruiser sending it up. Can't see any aircraft."

"Here, Nobby," Ken broke in, "you were in the water near me when that destroyer came and steamed amongst us. Did you hear that Jap yell out when one of our fellows asked for a line?"

"Eh? Oh yeh! That bloke that yelled out: 'We good boys now, Aussie?'"

"Weren't they clean, though. Every one in a white suit. They had their lights on."

"Looked as if they had manned ship to cheer or something."

"No, I think that was just their upper deck mob lining the guard-rails to have a screw. Did they pick any of our blokes up? Anyone notice?"

"Yes, one bloke. Don't know who he was. They got him aboard and fixed his hands behind his back and marched him forrard."

"Got him for information I suppose."

"I suppose so."

"They were careful enough getting under way, though."

"Yes, he just kicked his screws ahead and drifted clear."

"Bloody smart-looking ship, too."

"Yes, by God. It made me feel all the dirtier in the water watching them inboard all dry and clean, with engines under them."

"Look at 'em now out there. Steaming up and down. Got all the soap and food they need."

"It's Fatty and a stoker, I think," someone said, as the two men drew near.

"Watcher there, Fatty, my boy! What sort of a night you have?"

"My feet," said Fatty, with a comic face of pain which was no exaggeration, "are ready to chuck their hands in."

"Yeah, we saw you coming up."

"I met Stokes here wandering on a tour of exploration," Fatty explained. "I got tired of waiting for you mob. We came right around the beach. Right around that whacking great headland. You come to fetch Dick, did you? I left

George and Jim around there with him. If you make a stretcher of the sail and a couple of oars, it'll be best, I think. Where's this camp of yours?"

"In there by that tree. You'll see the track. Can't miss it," Ken informed him. "S'long. See you later."

With their improvised footwear they had to proceed carefully. The heavy, loose coral was steep, and to walk easily along the shore a man needed one leg shorter than the other. It was amazing how immense a man's mind could become, and how little the world outside him: that tiny childish destroyer out there slipping diminutively along on the little bit of shining glass with the tiny hills behind, cut out of pale blue little bits of paper.

At last they reached the turn-off.

"That's the way Fatty and Stokes came around. Must be a coupla mile that way."

"Yes, that's the patch o' scrub we found them in last night."

They had got to the stage where the effort was telling. But, each of them was deep within his own remote inner-world. The men, automaton-like, went on over the grass-tufted coral flat to where the boat lay high and dry and a few round-headed stones pressed dangerously under her bilges.

"Wonder if she'll be too far gone by the time we get to her?" Ken said.

"Hope not," said George. "Jim and me tried to get her off those bricks. She's too heavy. Need more hands."

"How's Dick?"

"Pretty crook, I think," confided Jim; "and the ants got at him last night. But he don't complain."

"Will we start back with him now? What do you say? Or do you want to rest?"

"No, we can make it. Sooner we can get Dick on a mattress, the better."

They got together the sail on its yard and folded it as much as they could, for it was pretty rotten and weathered. With two oars they completed the job. Gently they put the patient on it. Not a murmur. Instead, a tired boyish smile with teeth strangely white against the oil-caked face and body. He was quite naked. Each of them saw the jagged holes in his thigh and groin, and the one in his wrist. They felt a moving admiration for him which was sentimental, with a film of vague hate smeared at the back.

One steadied his head while the others moved and lifted. It seemed almost as if he were being pressed down, he was so heavy. Being careful strained them. They grew tired and cut their feet, but they only rested Dick when it looked as if he were going to faint. Walking tortured them more now, but it hurt them less; for they no longer slipped away into the sea of self-feeling.

The sun was getting hotter. When they rested in the sun, they held up the foresail, which covered him, to shade him. As they reached the sea on the other side of the neck, they found the tide flooding.

"Won't have to waste any time."

"How you feeling, Dick? This'll be the worst part!"

"I'm all right. Sorry to be such a nuisance."

"Don't be a —" He was called an unmentionable name, which carried an utter affection with it.

So they pushed on through the water with the wounded man shoulder high, each of them dreadfully afraid of falling, so that the muscles of their stomachs strained into hard stiffening lumps which they could feel like tight belts. Before, their feet had winced so quickly at a touch; now, they trod down firmly without drawing back, and it did not trouble them if they were cut or not. It was different now, somehow. A man did not feel that isolation in immensity. Things went on around him. A man trod on a stone and it hurt. But that wasn't *all*. It was only a man treading on a stone.

"There's the tree," Ken said with a cheerfulness of relief.

"There she blows!"

"You beaut!"

"How y' feeling, Dick?"

For a moment there was no reply.

"All right."

But it had been an effort.

Presently someone said, showing how their thoughts were circling, "See the old *Houston* at the finish?" "On fire fore and aft. No ammunition, but still firing with a bloomin' *pom-pom*. You could see the tracer not going half the distance to the Jap cruiser belting her."

"Gosh, she was a sight in the searchlights, with those eight-inch salvos all around her. The fall of shot stuck up like the war-memorial at Albury—just how you see it when you come through in the Sydney Express—floodlit."

"If they all fight like she did, no matter. No ship could do more."

They were now off the beach and striking in to the camp.

10

When the party had gone for the wounded seaman, the rest had spread out, each about his own business. The couple at the well rubbed and scrubbed themselves sore until the rags they had were black and worn useless.

"Did you rub ash in first?"

"Around my face and neck and arms. Helps take the burn out, doesn't it?"

"Yes, but you got to be careful of the bits of charcoal or coral from the fireplace. She drags a bit when you're scrubbing off."

"Well, anyway, we're *here*. What about them poor cows carried past here? They've got my sympathy. She was hot out there yesterday and none of 'em could have any water. She's hot again now."

They were in strips of sun and shade beneath the banana palm's broad, tattered leaves which arched overhead to the brink of the well. On the edge of the well was a small bucket with a long rope of coconut fibre attached, the other end of which had a short thick stick tied by its middle. The well was about two feet across and roughly circular. It looked cool, and the white bones of coral showed clean and washed against the dull yellow of the sand. At the bottom, over the sandy floor, the pool lay still and clear about eighteen inches deep. When a man leaned over to drop the bucket in, it mimicked him, turned him upside down, doubled the distance and, without a sound, set him looking at his black visage in the sky-blue background. On a small ledge, eighteen inches up, a large brown toad with gold flecked eyes looked inscrutably and unmoving at the wall opposite. He was there yesterday. He was there for ever.

"Think they'll make the mainland? Any of 'em?"

"Hard to say. If they didn't, a lot would give up and fall asleep. Then the sharks. Wouldn't be too many left by today. Maybe some on rafts."

"Don't envy them. Look like going right out into the Indian. There were a lot yesterday towards the middle of the Strait. No water—gosh!"

Men kept on like this in their conversation. They wondered and speculated whenever they talked with each other. When they were silent, they were usually thinking of private things such as relations and people distant.

There in the sun by the large hut a few still talked and pottered about with footwear, a loin-cloth, or a hat. Some lay around in the shade of the building without the will or energy to move. "Cookie" was on the job, organizing his utensils and supplies. Some rice was found, but it would only be enough to last a day or so. However, Cookie's job was to use whatever came to his hand for the moment.

The heat and the glare; and the effort of thought. They felt tired, more tired and without energy than ever before in their lives. They had been left nerveless by the uprooting of all that was usual in the past. War had been thrust upon them. But that was different. It had been put *on* them. Now they had had so much torn *out* of them: their memories had become unreal and mocking. This new life, these new things—they had not the will or energy to absorb now. They washed till they were sore, and they were still as filthy as ever. They slept or lay around until their bones ached, and still they were tired. They were hungry, but they did not want to eat. The thought of effort, of doing anything, crushed them; but they had to face it.

II

"What d'y' say we go along 'n' see this canoe they spoke about, John?" This was Ben, sitting on the edge of the verandah.

"Where is it, do you know?"

"Oh, somewhere round the beach t' the north. Isn't that so, Suh?" Here he turned to an officer, a gunnery man in overalls without a belt. They were unbuttoned down the front and hung like a clown's suit as he bent bewildered over the strange shoe he was making.

"What's that, Ben? Oh, cripes! I dunno. Ginger said somewhere round the beach. In a river or creek or some dam' place."

"Well, we can go along that track we came in yesterday ... You know where we came to the left—it looked as if it went a good way to the right too."

"Well, who's coming?" John called. "We're going to look at this canoe or have a bit of an explore anyway. Might find some more blokes up that way."

Two others, throwing off the oppression of inertia, said "all right," and the four started out. They picked their way past the well to the first hut. As they passed the little grass shed Ben ducked his black freckled face under the eave and said:

"Going to do a bit of exploration. Anyone coming?"

There was no reply.

On they went snaking in a shallow "S" on the smooth, hard, brown path left, then right, which brought them by the remaining hut in which Ginger and his tight little group of adventurers sat.

"Good-day, boys!"

There was a civil reply. But Ben and John felt the stiffening of resistance. There was something different here from the attitude of the others. John looked harder at them. He had been a petty officer. Not that that mattered in these circumstances, but he had had to size up situations like this before. The thing had to be done without an open breach. But it had to be done just the same.

"The mob's decided to eat all together, boys. They reckon this separate eating is too wasteful. Some will get fat while others go hungry. And we don't know how long we'll be here yet."

John stood at the entrance just beyond the eave and the sun beat down on him. Just behind him on the path waited the others. The tight little group sat up in a row looking very well cared for. On the earthen floor in front of them Ginger was boiling up some tomatoes and pumpkin which gave off wisps of white vapour stirred out from the shallow iron pan by the cook's trailing stick as he stood and listened. There they were: comfortable and unwanting, silently refusing to give it up. But John spoke as if he took for granted that their reason or a generous instinct would lead them to accept so simple and just a suggestion.

There was a grumble of "Why disturb us?" They could get along on their own without troubling anyone. They had plans all worked out. They were entitled to make a break for it if they could.

John conceded them all this. But he was nearly openly angry, for he usually saw red when people started talking about what they were "entitled" to.

Ben said, very directly, "What about the others? What about the wounded? Do you expect us to do *all* the dirty work?"

It was getting near an open breach. That would get them nowhere. "Well," John said, "the majority want it. Mr Cross and Mr Stewart and the other two officers are for it. It's the only sensible thing to do."

"Yes, but what about us? Do you expect us to stay here forever if we reckon we've got a chance?"

"No, you don't have to do that. If you want to go, you can always take your share of provisions with you."

"As a matter of fact, if we can get any parties away," said Ben, "we'll only be too willing to give them a hand."

This brought them round a bit. Let them think it over.

"Well, that's the idea. There'll be a general meal at the end hut about sunset. That's the first meal all together. There's a stoker P.O. cooking. It's up to us all to help each other. Be seein' yuh."

And the four moved on.

"Y' know, some blokes want everything," reflected Ben.

"We'll have to watch those guys."

"Best thing's to get them on their way."

"Let's hope this canoe will suit them. There's six of them."

"May take more. There's others want to get away too, and take a chance on the mainland."

"That might be our best chance, you know: to disperse and get through the country in small groups."

"Tjilatjap's a naval base. If you could get through to there before the Japs."

"I wonder what the position on the island is? They seem to be still resisting over the way in Merak. There's still gunfire in the hills."

"Hard to tell. Well, we can get organized and see what we can do. Have to talk it over with the whole crowd of us together."

The track was just wide enough for one man, so they walked in single file. It ran like a dark channel, and it was a little damp where the sun had not yet penetrated. The down-trodden blades were brown and made a thick mat. They were very glad of this. Their feet were tender. Trees began to grow nearer the path and at more frequent intervals, as if the hill were forcing them out. The whole gradually converged into a wall of growth through which the path still wound successfully.

"Seems to be a well-used path. Looks as if something's been dragged along here lately. See that grass beside the track—it's been pushed over."

"Well, we're going in the jungle country now, boys. Watch the mossies."

They had a fair passage to the edge of what looked to be a dark lagoon. It was muddy with black, viscous mud which rose in little grey clouds, almost whitish, when it was disturbed. To get to the water one had to climb over the thin, twisted trunks of trees with fine, rough bark. The trees seemed to swoop towards the water. Their branches twined like arms with arthritic joints, some of them dipping their thin hands of leaves and twigs on to the slimy depths: dark green and black over the green-black water which reflected the trees above with a clear and silent perfection—but it was lies. That was not the water at all. The water was dark and thick with slimy mud at the bottom. The calm beauty, the smooth and enticing serenity of the pool curving away until it vanished, still unended, around the bend between the thick, green, round-topped walls of leafy trees whose skirts touched the water, was a mask. In the sun, the trees were a rich ochre-green, almost golden; in the shade, rich with the dark greens of a Constable. They rose as if it were not their skirts but their bosoms breasting the water whose surface shone pale and beautiful—not with a metallic shine, but the smooth shine, almost a bloom, of healthy skin—of a loved skin.

"By Gee," said Ben, "she's a beautiful spot all right. Looks cool, doesn't it?"

"Yes, look at the mossies! Hind legs of 'em like Kanga-bloomin'-roos!"

"Big black ones. It's not the bite that hurts, but the kick when they take off, I reckon."

The mosquitoes swarmed in on them: black flecks raising itchy lumps.

"Wonder if they are malaria ones? Malaria ones don't bite in the sun. There's a *bit* filtering through. Let's hope anyway."

As soon as they had arrived, they had all seen what looked like a black log in the water. A line ran from it to the tree on which a couple of them now stood over the water.

"Capsized!"

"Give a haul on the painter there!"

Those on the tree hove it up together. The trunk swayed up and down with the tugging, and the quietness of the pool was broken. The maw of the pool broke forth from its beautiful mask and spewed swirling black saliva as the sucking teeth, which had held the hull of the capsized canoe, were drawn away. An eel swam out of it like a great worm from a gullet, and escaped. As the men let go their grasp, the craft sank back and slowly capsized again.

It was a heavy dug-out canoe with sockets and places for the outrigger carved out of the solid sides. There was a place for a plug which was missing. There was also a stern-fast running across to the other side of the pool so that she would not come quite close enough to them for a man to embark. None of them felt inclined at that stage to wade into such sinister-looking waters.

They broke off a branch, and by balancing precariously over on the outboard end of a tree Ben succeeded in several times righting the canoe. Each time they watched her go back with the same slow roll, for all the world as if the bottom of the pool had sucked the life out of her. Well, they were too few to get her out of the water. It was no good putting in a plug and bailing her if she were going to capsize again. Leave her. Send a party round tomorrow or sometime.

"Let's get out of these mosquitoes before they eat us alive!"

None of them was properly dressed for protection. Ben had on his greasy blue jean overalls which flopped around unbuttoned, without sleeves and rolled up to the knees. John wore his canvas coat which had no sleeves, and beneath he had contrived a pubic band made out of a worn bodice-cum-brassiere affair he found about the hut. It was a small thing indeed—Javanese women are doll-like. The other two merely had rags wrapped this way or that about their middles in a rough attempt at propriety. They were pleased to be back on the open grass track.

"They can get half a dozen in that, easy. She's got plenty of freeboard. They could make the island in that and run down the coast if necessary. Inside the Strait, anyway."

"Yes, they shouldn't have any trouble in getting their outrigger shipped. They only need a bit of lashing."

"They'll be right."

"Let's hope so."

They trudged on.

After a while they came to the place where the path branched. Just showing over a couple of low bushes to the left was a boat's masthead.

"Hullo," exclaimed John, "the skiff party are there! Come and have a word with them."

"Those are the people you spoke with yesterday?"

"Yes, chap off the *Vendetta*'s with them."

"Wonder do I know him?" said Ben.

"You may—he's from Melbourne."

And they broke through to find a party with a fire

going at the base of a big tree. The skiff, with a bow-fast to a root and a stern anchor laid out, washed in the shallows of a low tide. Some clumps of slime-grown coral showed above the calm, hot surface of the cove. The sea was undulating imperceptibly so that dark shapes beneath just rippled the top of the water, and they looked like the backs of cruising sting-ray. It was more coral. The flat, almost regular beat of the sea on the oil-ringed tide mark of the shore betrayed its pulse.

Missus was there, and the two children. The *Vendetta* sailor was smashing up firewood. "Goo'day," he greeted and they replied. Missus was combing her shiny black hair. She smiled up at them. The children looked up at the first sound. Mary's eyes were large and sad, Robin's were large and curious.

"Hullo, kiddies!" said Ben. "What's your names?"

Mary said, "He's Robin," and Robin's eyes drooped shyly and he grinned bashfully as little boys do. "And I'm Mary."

"How do you do. I'm Ben," he said solemnly. "What have you got there?"

"We're plaiting these leaves together. We're not very good, really."

"Oh, but you are," encouraged Ben. "They are *all right*. They'd make bosker mats for a teapot and things."

Mary was quite puzzled by the Australian "bosker" as Ben rendered it. But she liked this friendly man and she smiled a little shyly at the praise.

A hot, clear day with insects buzzing in the grass. The hills, close, warm and still: tenanted by sunny trees with deep shadows on their white, burly trunks. The lazy, drooping banana palms: lazy like an old mare at a manger. Children quietly playing beside a Malay woman combing her hair—she was quite handsome, and they were childishly beautiful. They sat beneath the green and dappled shadows of the tree. The sea with its quiet monotonous slap-splash and faint hiss afterwards. The cloudless sky and pale-blue, distant mountains of Java. The boat gently rocking. A man piling firewood, and a smoking fire curling upwards lazily. And Ben talking with the children.

But around the beach was a thick, black oil-ring; the water's edge was mottled with its froth. The Malay woman had a soldier husband somewhere in Malaya, dead or alive. The children were without parents. They were playing with a man who was filthy with oil, and whose lips and eyes gleamed in his face like a nigger minstrel's; whose fair hair was the colour of tarred hemp, whose clothes stank with oil, and whose three companions looked just like him. And up and down the Strait patrolled the destroyer, as if it were set on preventing these people getting back into the world. It seemed to say, "You're dead, whatever you might think."

Yet they were alive. Warm and sensually alive, feeling the warmth of the sun and standing amid beauty. True, the beauty mocked them; but they saw it and recognized it.

"Where're the others?" John asked.

"Gone scrounging. We're shoving off on the tide tonight. Going to fill up with a good feed before we sail."

"There's some chickens round the kampong."

"Yes, Tug's gone."

"Tonight, eh! High water about six, or a bit later. The current will be making then. It'll help you down."

"Yes, we've got to dodge that destroyer."

"Pretty dangerous at night," Ben put in. "I mean if he sees a black shadow, he's just as likely to open fire, thinking you're a sub."

"Well, we've just got to take that chance. I think we'll slip well down below the patrol before we cross."

"Yes, they only go about six or seven miles to the south."

"What's this sore on the young fellow's knee?" Ben asked.

He was told.

"Haven't you got anything to put on it?"

"No, we ran out of our stuff."

"I think we've got something. Came up from the boat. Would it be all right if we took him back to the camp and stuck on a bit of a dressing?"

"How about it, Missus?"

"It would be very good," she said.

"Will you come with us, Robin, to get your leg fixed up?" The boy nodded, but kept his head shyly down. Mary gave Ben a look of gratitude. She hated that sore on her brother's knee. The flies would not let it be. Strange indeed must have been her thoughts as she watched her brother carried over the brink of the beach into the island she never really saw. How different it all was from her home—her father's home. He was a judge in Singapore. Everybody there spoke precisely. It was clean, with people in white clothes. There were motor cars. Servants moving obsequiously. Cool drinks and plenty of food. There was a school and other children. Now, only she and Robin. No mummy or daddy. She wanted to find her mummy. Tears flooded her eyes; she held her head low.

"Don't, Mary," softly whispered Missus, and put an uﾞ .erstanding hand on her shoulders. "Mummy's all right. We'll find her." And she thought hopelessly of her own husband. She wanted him too. She had seen her world destroyed. Even as she came south it was still being destroyed. All these men blown up in their ships and trying to get back to their own world. Her world was behind, still in flames. Even about her. They had thought to find safety in Java. But destruction was travelling faster than they. Looking down with her hand on Mary's shoulder, she was filled with compassion for the children. They, too, had seen all this. They had seen it in their own strange, half-seeing, childish way. She thought it unspeakably brutal that such things should happen to them. At the same time she felt her impotence—one woman whose husband they had taken. Women and children were unconsidered, if they got in the way. Yet they could not get out of the way.

"Have a good feed when Tug gets back, Missus?"

"Yes," she said in a friendly tone; "won't we, Mary?" Mary nodded and her tears were drying. She picked up her coconut leaves again

12

Robin arrived in the kampong on Ben's shoulders, and he saw more men. It must have given him some cause for childish wonder, if he had not had it all knocked out of him. It was hard to tell with the child, for he never laughed, nor did he sulk. Unconsciously he was stoical. The men liked him and were far more demonstrative than he. They talked to him far more than he cared to answer, so he resorted to gestures which were often no more than looks from his large grey eyes. Their enthusiasm bewildered him a bit, but he still liked them. They made things seem a bit more usual somehow. He caught at the childish impression that life was a bit of a game still. Men seemed a lot like others he had known. These men were very dirty, but that did not worry him because everybody was—it was like the game of the moment. He liked watching them. While he was getting his leg dressed he almost laughed at Ben making an elaborate pantomime of stalking the rooster, finishing up with a tremendous leap which was utterly futile.

John found that Robin had no hat, so he set about making him one which would be an exact replica of his own. "Tailor made," he said as he fitted it on the boy's fair head. The lad was shyly amused and proud, and had to be prompted to a "Thank you" by the other man from the skiff. Tug and he were there. They were ready to go back—a fowl had died and they had some other things also. Now they were going to wait for Robin and take him back. Dick lay on his mattress in the corner of the verandah and watched the child with great interest. As John looked at them both, he caught an impression of there being no difference in their ages—only in size.

Soon Robin was taken back to the beach: a couple of fellows went with Tug and his companion to help them.

"There'll be some scran when you come back."

"You beaut!"

It was Ben who had called out. He turned to the man who had become cook, "What have you got for us, Cookie?"

"It's a sort of a stew. I don't know how it will go. There's a chicken in it."

"A chook! Cookie, your blood's worth bottling!"

13

The stew contained rice, tomatoes, pumpkin, paw-paw, some yams and yam-leaves and the hen. It had caught on the bottom when cooking and there were little carbon flakes in it. But Cookie got only praise. They all insisted that it was good.

Gradually the crowd collected. Someone suggested: "What about having a meeting? Getting organized?"

"Yes, we ought to see how many's here."

"When?"

"Now. Got to do it sometime."

"All right," said Mr Cross, an ex-Merchant Service officer. "Let's get a pencil and paper. Ken—will you write the names down?"

"Yes. I've already written down the people who used this hut last night."

"Well, we'll muster them and get the rest and see where we are."

"Someone had better go along and get Ginger and his gang of braves."

They began writing down the names. Presently a messenger who had been dispatched came back with two of the people generally spoken of now as "Ginger's Mob".

"Ginger and the others have gone exploring. They didn't know this meeting would be on."

"What do they reckon on finding?" asked Mr Cross.

"They say when they were coming in yesterday, they saw a two-masted schooner. They think she's sheltering anchored at the other end of the island."

"What do they think they can do with her if they get her?"

"They reckon they can take her—swim out."

"They'll find it pretty tough going round that end of the island."

"Hope they do get her—solve the problem for all of us."

"How long are they going to be away?"

"Said they might be gone a couple of days. They only took a bottle of water each. Said they could live on what they could get."

"What'd they think this is—Robinson Crusoe's Island or the Swiss Family Robinson or something?" Ben muttered in a tone of sceptical disgust.

"They got big ideas all right!" said another.

"Let's hope they have some luck, lads, anyway," said Mr Stewart pacifically.

"Well, let's get their names anyway; then the first part of this business will be over."

They were taken. All the names were called over and accounted for. "That gives us, let me see—" Ken was computing—"Forty-nine, all told."

"Forty-nine."

There was a short silence, like an involuntary service to the rest of the seven hundred ship's company. The yam leaves shone rigid in the glare. The hillside looked dry. There was the scrape of a solitary spoon on a plate. An audible sipping of a man standing near-naked just beyond the shadow of the hut. His own shadow was etched black around his feet in the dust.

"Well, what are we going to do?"

"First, I think we have to decide: What's the situation over there."

"They are still having a go over the channel, so they haven't got past there yet."

"I think our best chance is to get ashore over there, split up into small parties and make a break, east."

"There's a railhead at Anjer. Might be a chance if we got to that."

"Depends where the Japs are. How strong they are."

"Well, we might beat them if we can get to Tjilatjap in time."

"That means travel by road. Boat's too slow."

"Ship's lifeboats are no good to sail. All right running

with the wind. But you can't point 'em. They make as much leeway as headway," Mr Cross put in. "What's this one?"

"She's steel, about twenty-three feet and for forty persons."

"She'd get us all over to the mainland, anyway."

"That's the best chance, I reckon. Small parties on foot. Natives will help. Pick up a car or a bike."

"Tjilatjap's between two hundred and fifty to three hundred miles."

Others, who thought they should stick to the boat, began discussing what was the best course to take. Some were for going north and along the top of Java.

"Might pick up a better boat, or a ketch or something. Then we could make the whole voyage to Australia."

"What about wind? This time of the year's no good for wind. We are round the doldrums now. More chance with the open sea to the south."

"That's all ocean coast. There's only two ports in six hundred miles of coast. Not a good place to beach a boat if you wanted to; it's lousy with coral and you'd get a big surf all the time."

"We might make Tjilatjap, and we might be in time."

Ken, John, Fatty and a few others were saying nothing. To them two ideas were obvious. There were too many to make any sort of a trip by boat further than the mainland. Let those who wished go by land. If they split up, there would be a fairer chance of someone getting through; and one of the things sticking in these men's minds now was the wish to establish communication with their old world and let people know they were alive. The other problems were secondary.

The more who travelled by land, the better for the boat.
Everybody soon saw the issue.

Mr Cross put the proposition up. "Well, let's get the
parties sorted out. Ken will put a cross alongside all those
who want to make a break by land. Right-o, fellas, we'll
get your names."

When the count was finally made, there were some
twenty-nine for the land party, and the remainder for the
boat. Ben was one of the land party. He and four others
were going together. They had talked it over before. The
real problem was the transport to the mainland for them.
So far the boat was the only means they had. The canoe
was a probable one also. True, a rescue party might even
now be sent for them. Yet, though they had no means of
telling, they all assumed that nothing could stop Java
from falling. The strange stillness, which had overawed
Batavia on the night they left, had created an ominousness
which they still felt and could not throw off. They decided
that time was the important factor. Therefore it was
important to get the boat ready for action.

"Too late to bring her around now. Never shift her till
high water, and that's not till just on dark."

"We'll send a party around in the morning. Has she
been holed?"

"Not unless she's done it since we left. There were a
couple of rocks under her I didn't like. We'd better get
her as soon as possible, anyway."

Ben was stalking a hen. He was bent like a slinking
Indian, and the hen step by step was keeping the same
distance in front.

"I'll get you yet—or one of your cobbers."

"Ben!" called Mr Cross.

"Sir!" said Ben, springing hatless to an exaggerated

attention in the scorching sun and facing the officer who was in the shade with most of the others.

"What're you blokes going to do—I mean about gear?"

"Something to carry water in and a bit o' maize or something. That's all we want. Should be plenty of food and water over there."

"I was wondering about provisions from the boat."

"Oh, cripes, no! Keep 'em! You'll need 'em in the boat. We'll be able to get along. Look at that dog! If we're here long enough we'll have you, my boy. Not much more meat on him than a big rat, tho' "

"Well, if you fellers are all fixed, it's just a matter of getting the boat rigged and ready for sea. How long will that take?"

"Depends on the gear," said John.

"It's not *too* bad," Fatty put in. "Mind *you*, it's not A 1 at Lloyd's or anything like that."

"I'm wondering if it's any good anyway—ship's life-boats *won't* sail. We'd need a fair wind. Even from the sou'east it's no good. It'd mean beating all the way."

"Well, you won't be wanting any of the land party, will you? We won't be doing anything more this afternoon, eh? If you want a hand, let us know. I'm going to do a bit of exploring—never know what you might find."

And the land party melted about the kampong, leaving the twenty boat party. The four officers had elected to stay with the boat. There was one young Engineer, a Sub-lieutenant, a Paymaster Lieutenant-Commander and a seagoing Reserve Lieutenant. The remainder of the party were mixed: sparkers, seamen, stokers and signalmen. They were chief petty officers, petty officers, leading rates and ratings.

The general idea was agreed upon—to sail for Tjilatjap,

and perhaps Australia. Although the day was still hot, the men were gradually coming to life. Each according to his own imagination was stirred. Some had a blind hope that came of confidence in the older ones' "knowing all about it". Something to *do* at last! To hell with blasted inertia! They had been made generous and eager by this sudden spirit, which refreshed them like a thunder shower. Self had shrunk to its normal size, ready for action in the world without.

Part 2

SANGIENG—ACTIVITY

I

THUS activity was born.

Mr Stewart was spokesman, being the senior person present. But discussion was informal, for the officers had willingly given up the privileges of their rank, and they lost no respect thereby.

"Well," said Mr Stewart, "what we've got to have is a skipper for the boat. I think you'll all see that it is necessary."

"What about you, sir?" Fatty suggested.

As a leader he was qualified; but he said, "It doesn't have to be an officer."

"I suggest John," Ken said.

There was some more murmuring discussion. Mr Stewart asked for a show of hands. Then he said: "Petty Officer Dirk!"

"Sir!" answered John, embarrassed.

"Well, Dirk—You're skipper!"

John was so surprised that he found it hard to speak. He felt an unreality about it. Why pick him? He wished he could feel that their faith were justified.

For the officers, Mr Stewart and Mr Cross, he had the deepest admiration. The way in which they had put the decision into the hands of the men had taken some courage, and perhaps some natural feeling of wounded pride. Yet they had resolutely done it.

John wondered if he had not merely presented a possibility for the men to express a freedom from normal discipline. The distinction between "Officer" and "Rating" is one which holds the rating a bit like a coiled spring in tension.

2

It was decided to get the boat round to the other beach tomorrow and start to refit her. Half a dozen seamen would do for that. The rest would work on provisions. Mr Stewart would take charge of that party with Mr Robey and Mr Black.

"Mr Cross, Fatty, Ken, Jim, George, Darky! All right for the boat party—refitting?" John suggested.

"O.K."

"She's right."

"Anybody feel like taking a walk along to the wrecked lifeboat and salvaging some of the gear tonight?" John asked.

Mr Stewart and Mr Cross said they would. On the way through the kampong they had to pass by the hut of the rugged individualists. They were all there except one. Mr Cross told them briefly what had been decided upon, pointing out with apparent innocence how it left them free to their own devices although, in certain respects, responsible to the whole party until the expedition was begun.

"How did you get on with your exploration, Ginger? See the schooner?"

"We got around so far and couldn't get any further. It's too wild. Impossible." He was a bit embarrassed from chagrin, and it went against his grain to have to discuss a failure. He had set off with such outspoken confidence about swimming around headlands and the like. Nature had set a limit on Ginger, and he did not care for it. He was chastened. He felt that they, like Nature, were eager to bowl him out.

"What do you reckon on doing now?"

"Oh, we'll take the canoe. *We'll* get along all right."

"We're getting together all the gear we can that's likely to be of use: tools and things. So if you've got any stuff, we'll collect it tomorrow and take it down to the beach where we are going to refit the boat. Be the best place to get the canoe in shape too. We're going to the beach to look over the lifeboat."

As they arrived on the beach they came upon the skiff's party eating a meal. The children each had a drumstick and were thoroughly preoccupied. Missus had a plate on her knees, and two of the men were standing up. They greeted one another casually, although Mr Stewart and Mr Cross had seen only Robin before.

"Going to have a look at the boat out on the reef there," said John, being more familiar with them.

"Good stuff there," said the *Vendetta* chap. "We got some."

"When're you shoving off?"

"On the tide, about dusk."

"See you before you go. We'll be back," John called over his shoulder and moved on to catch up. "Good crowd, those," he said as he overtook them. "Had a pretty tough spin. Thought they would make Batavia and be safe. Now they are still as far away from freedom as ever."

"Are they going on with the kiddies?" asked Mr Cross.

"Think so. They are talking about holding the coast to Timor."

"To the south?"

"That's what they said."

"Tck," went Mr Cross's sceptical tongue, "don't think they'll make it in *that*. It's all ocean coast." He shook his head. As a matter of fact, he had no confidence in the lifeboat's ability either. Only the wildest luck, in his opinion, would make a passage possible. John and the rest had the greatest respect for his opinion, too. He was a merchant service officer and knew these boats for what they were. Also he had made an ocean trip in a yacht and knew that there were definite limits to what even a boat with good sailing qualities could do. His knowledge and opinion were respected, but for the time the men were playing with the idea of luck, of miracles. It kept the future brighter, and helped to combat morbid contemplation. Mr Cross had felt himself bound to say the things he honestly believed. But action, even though fruitless, in the end could never be a wholly barren thing.

Eventually they came opposite to where the boat bumped dolefully. They found the mast, a boom, the boat's cover, and the three or four lifebelts hanging in the branches of the trees which overhung the water.

"It's pretty sharp all the way out. Want something on our feet to get out there."

They bound their feet with bits of canvas and, naked, made their way out to the boat. They had to cross the field of living coral, branching upwards in a spiky stubble. Here and there clumps were exposed, olive and brown with calm little pools between them.

The tide was flooding, but not yet too deep for them to reach the wreck.

The boat, bumping, made a hollow noise beneath the broad, sweeping sky now edged whitely with tails of

celestial mares. Not all the space of the flowing sea—
flowing swift and darkly blue against the island now—
could set free this imprisoned sepulchral voice moaning
shackled within the restless, wooden hull. The edge of
the fast-flowing current slid past the boat.

John and Mr Cross climbed aboard. She was half full as
the tide rose within her. John felt a deep, poignant emotion
stir within him for this boat, so lonely—dying. And, even
while she died, so many attendant mourners, the unknown
living-dead of her past, were present. The man who had
nailed the red and white diagonally-stripped bunting flag
to the six-foot staff; the man who had planed its hexagonal
surface; the man who had coiled the line so neatly on the
canvas sea anchor and stopped it tight with rope yarns.
The biscuit tank with its cover removed and contents
gone—who had done that?

"Don't see any marks on her. I wonder what ship?" Mr
Cross said.

"Search me," said John. "I wonder if she came from that
bombed-out ship we saw derelict on Saturday morning?
Just before we got to Batavia after the Java Sea action. She
was burnt out and listed well to port. Remember? Her port
lifeboats' falls were overhauled right down to the water."

"What'll we take of this stuff?"

"Take all the movable stuff—never know what might
come in handy. The tanks for a start. Don't lose the
butterfly nuts or the rubber washer for the door."

So they got the gear out of her. The oars they passed
over the side first, and the two in the water held them
together. Then came the rudder, the flag on the staff, the
sea anchor and the boat's anchor. Together with the
movable bottom boards and locker doors they were
lashed to form a raft. Then they unbolted the biscuit locker

from beneath one of the midship thwarts and passed it out also. The boat's crutches were broken from their galvanized chain lanyards, and the ten put carefully in the tank. The last thing was the painter, which John unshackled after some difficulty with the salt-encrusted shackle pin. The bow ring where it was fixed was in an awkward position.

"A man's gotta curse," he explained from his constricted position, "or he'll bust." At last it was free. Mr Cross had already gone over the side, and others stood waiting, waist deep, in the water which was beginning to swirl threateningly. For a moment, as he stood on the thwarts facing aft, he looked across at the eternal destroyer and at the distant mountains of Java which had taken on a roseate glow from the low-hung sun at his back to the westward. It was peaceful. It was distant.

Then he cast his critical glance over the boat. "What about this canopy-frame? Probably just the thing to rig a bow-dodger in the other boat."

"Better bring it," Mr Cross said. "Don't wan't to walk over this bloody coral any more."

The journey back to the shore was awkward. The raft had to be piloted. They got to the edge of the lapping water and hove all the salvaged gear well above the high-tide mark. Then they sat and rested. It surprised them how they had to rest after so short a labour. They had not been much more than half an hour out at the boat.

John could still hear her bumping and the imprisoned voice sounding plaintive, like an earth-bound spirit.

3

"Shall we go back now?" suggested Mr Stewart. "Have a yarn with the skiff's people and wish them good luck?"

So, they stepped into the warm sea and started to wade back along the beach. As they rounded the point they could see the skiff being loaded by three men. She was bows-in to the beach: before her short mast, things were being piled high so that at the stern, where the deadwood of her keel was cut away just below the lower pintle, there showed a little space.

"Arse-up like a swan," Mr Cross said poetically.

"Gosh, they're game," Mr Stewart said admiringly.

They splashed their way out of the water, cursing the oil-fuel they could not dodge. The tide had brought in another instalment which ringed the beach with a black ribband six feet wide.

Mr Cross bade "good-evening" to Missus in a self-conscious sort of way, and then applied his conversation to the children. This was the first time he had seen them together or had opportunity for direct conversation with them. He asked their ages, and Mary answered him. He told them he had a boy and girl at home just like them, and they were waiting for him with their mummy. He had said this without thinking. Mary, who had been listening intently, started to talk at the mention of a "mummy". It was a quick flood of talk, which got faster and faster, and less and less intelligible, until, with brimming eyes, she started to whimper. Robin looked up round-eyed and silent. Mr Cross glanced over at Missus with an awful look of self-condemnation, wishing he could have bitten his tongue out. And just when they had been getting so interested in his story.

"Can it, Mary!" growled Tug as he went past with a bundle on his shoulder. The child looked up and took a great sniff of a sob in an endeavour to obey.

Robin wore the tall, Robinson-Crusoe-like hat that

John had made for him. Mary's fair straight hair was bare. "Haven't you got one, Mary?" John asked. She shook her head bashfully. "Oh, then we'll soon fix that up!" They had brought some of the boat's cover with them for sleeping that night. So, with a borrowed knife he soon had one of the flaps off. "Now," he said laughing, "lean forward and we'll fit you with the latest from Paris." The two children in the same sort of hats, looked at each other and grinned.

The *Vendetta* sailor said, "What do you think of *them*? Your face and necks won't get burnt now!"

Mary, with the instinct of her sex, said, "We'll have to see that Robin keeps his on, shan't we?" And Robin's look was a mixed one of guilt and bravado. Little boys with fussy sisters *should* shock them from time to time, he thought. Missus smiled affectionately at these men who made such a fuss over children and laughed so much over little things like Robin's look at his nagging sister.

Two of the men stood by the boat, their thighs rich black and gleaming brown as the undulating oily water rose and fell. The stern anchor had been laid in and the boat squared to the beach. Tug came up to those around the big canary tree and announced, "Well, we're all ready to shove off. Ready, Missus?"

"Yes," she said. "All ready!"

Nobody shook hands. In their atlas the skiff's party were taking a list of the then known of *Perth*'s survivors. The *Perth*'s people also had their names. Missus walked down the beach with the hem of her skirt slightly lifted. When she reached the water's edge, Tug lifted her in his wiry arms and swirled his way to the stern of the boat, while the other two picked up the children from the beach and placed them alongside her. As they were deposited, Tug saw that each was clutching a bundle of leaves.

"Put them out," he ordered.

Robin said that he wanted them.

"Put them *down*!"—and he smacked the backs of their hands so that the leaves were scattered and spread flat, drifting on the calm evening sea. Both children wept loudly.

"Shut up, shut up!" he said harshly. But they howled on. The men got into the boat and ran out a pair of oars. She was deeply laden and preserved very little freeboard, so there was something duck-like about her. Slowly they pulled away in the mother-of-pearl atmosphere of the evening. The light seemed brighter on the hills beyond the Strait. Here they were in a gossamer of shade from the hills behind them. The children cried on the quiet evening air as the boat picked its way out of the little cove and vanished around the tree-fringed point.

They were gone.

4

The party on the shore—about eight or nine—with a kind of unanimous and inaudible sigh, went away, leaving the beach deserted as the shadows deepened and the oil, like a black and slimy serpent, writhed long and sinuously around the narrow sand, black and gleaming through the night.

When they arrived back at the big hut they found Cookie with a plate of boiled rice. They had some salt with it and found it good.

There was a little more deliberation about getting a sleep that night. With the blunt long knives they found in the huts, they made a small party to slash some of the

The skiff departs

tufty grass for mattresses. They cut and reaped beneath a great guinea-gold moon in the stillness of the kampong.

"She doesn't look bad in the moonlight—the old kampong, does she?" Ken said to John.

"No, *she's* all right," he replied. "It's the genus homo that's gone wet. There's nothing wrong with the world."

"It makes you mad, doesn't it? Look at us blokes here: our people don't know where we are; a good ship gone to the bottom, a lot o' blokes lost, and—and—well, what the hell!"

"It's the hard way, always the hard way. That's the only way people will wake up. You've got to hammer 'em silly to knock any sense into 'em. They never believe you when you *tell* them, and then they make a hell of a song when it happens. And *who's* going to change it?"

"You tell me. But it's tough though, when you *know* it's bound to happen, and then *you'll* be the first one for the chopper."

"Just a nice good old-fashioned nightmare, only it's dinkum."

"Which reminds me," Ken yawned, "I think I'll trap some myself. Big day, probably, tomorrow."

The golden moon climbed higher, changed her standard and turned to silver, pale and bright, while little cloud wisps drifted across her expressionless face, putting an evanescent frown on blankness. The trees were dark and still with a silver leaf here and there. The men slept, and the fires were dopey, blinking eyes of red.

5

The men began to stir with Nature and the dawn as the last planet hung like a solitary electric lamp in the east. A little longer while the blood began to flow and the energy of thought to kindle. A few strained " 'Mornin's" or " 'Day's" as each stretched himself, arching on shoulders and heels in what looked like an attempt to tickle his navel on a piece of down-hanging attap from the roof. They swilled themselves at the well and shivered. They said, "I feel one hundred per cent now"; beat their chests with no great energy, then stumbled back to the hut, sat on the bed boards of bamboo, scratched their heads which rolled in uproarious yawns: then they relapsed into a still, unthinking contemplation of their dirty feet in the dust. They were awake.

Eventually they all forgathered down at the big hut. Cookie was hard at it making tea. Tea was all they could have for breakfast. About noon they hoped for something solid. Groups of them stood around and discussed what they and others had to do that day. Mr Stewart talked over with John his ideas for getting provisions together. John need not concern himself there.

Most of his thoughts, however, were with the boat. In the past he had never missed a chance to rig and sail a boat. A shipmate had once told him that his ribs overlapped— he was clinker built. And whether it was Java, Sydney Harbour or the West Indies, the job was essentially the same. He looked about for the others. They had a tide to catch. Eight of them went. The tide was just beginning to make, and they did not know how long they would have to wait for the boat to refloat.

"You won't get her off till full water, I don't reckon," Fatty said.

"Anyway," Mr Cross said, "it's a spring tide—the moon is full. If that don't float her off, nothing will."

"You know, we've been lucky. I don't know about you, but I didn't give it a thought: the moon's been waxing and must've been real full last night. If she'd been waning while we've been doing nothing this last couple of days—"

"We'd have had to wait a fortnight at least to get enough water again," finished Mr Cross.

"We've been lucky all right!"

"Wonder if the tide's at the same state on the south side of the island?"

"Probably, but you never can tell."

Here they broke off from the beach and took the track which led them across the neck to where the boat lay. When they arrived, they sat down to take a rest and consider the next step.

There lay the boat on the smooth, moist sand, slewed on her side. She had a look of absolute immobility. They would have to get at her soon, but as yet the short skimming water from the surf was not reaching her. They looked at the beach apprehensively—had the tide already passed full water?

"You—" George began, searching for invective.

"Hold it," Ken put in, "she's still making."

The gear inside was higgledy-piggledy as they had left her. Barricoes, oars, stretchers, mast, anchor and other odds and ends were strewn about above high water on a low bank.

"Marvellous how such a little gear can look so untidy," Fatty said.

"Like a midshipman's chest—everything on top and nothing handy," George added. They got up and went over to the boat to make a survey of her. There was about a foot of water in her and, inert as she was, she looked more like a tank than a boat to them.

"She's made water," Fatty said. "Might be the plug, might be a hole."

"Some spray and some rain—I hope."

"Let's see if we can move her. Might be a chance," John said.

They hove and they struggled, all to no purpose. They strained until it seemed that their heads would burst.

"Not—a—bloody—chance," panted Mr Cross.

"Look! a rock! Under her starb'd side. The way she's dented, it's doing her the world of no good."

"We'll have t' try to dig her out."

Down on their hands and knees two of them went, to grovel and scoop away the coarse sand that cut their fingers. But it was soon apparent that this was no loose rock but part of the mother reef. It was useless to dig.

The next wave came a little higher, splashed against the boat and back into the faces of the diggers.

"There's a chance," panted John, who was one of the diggers. "Undermine her and let the sea drag the stuff out. She might slew then."

The tide was still making and the turbulence around them became greater. She *did* move. Just a fraction. So each time a sea came in they struggled frantically.

"Like a bloomin' loose tooth," George said disgustedly.

"That rock's the trouble. It's foul of the keel now."

The keel protruded four inches below the garboard of the boat. They dragged down the heavy wooden stretchers, burrowed under the keel and shoved them in. The undermining of the sea had now become a handicap, for it tore the sand out and left her more heavily on the rock.

"I don't like it," George said sourly. "Much more of this and it will be through the bloody bottom."

They got pieces of wood; heaved and strained this way and that; flopped on their hands and knees to dig a handspike in. The water rushed in and over them, but they worked on submerged. As they came up for a gasp of air, they spat out salt water, sand and vitriolic opinions of the situation. They called and hove together.

The water went down and left them streaming with their hair plastered, salt and flat, over their faces. But she was still there.

"*She'll* go. Just wait for the next big one. We'll get her."

The water surged about them like a pack of hungry beasts. There was the bottomless sensation of the sand swirling away from under their feet. They lifted, pushed and panted. The sand bit into their feet like glass and slid away like quicksand. They groped desperately around the keel under the water with their handspikes. Then, what they had been striving for so fiercely—a lurch and a bump. In a little while they had her afloat.

Now came the scarcely less arduous task, of keeping her square to the surf, and to stop her being swept sideways into the jagged rock walls of the cove, which was no wider than the length of the boat. The boat now seemed enormous, buoyant and high-sided. She became bigger than the Trojan Horse: they dangled from its bridle, wrenched this way and that. But always they managed to scramble to their feet in time to save her from those rock walls. They got rope and passed the ends over the side. A couple crawled on to the rocks at either side and they soon had her moored off the bow and quarter. Then she was able to surge there to her heart's content, though the boat-keepers could not trust the lines too far and had to play her like a great fish. All the gear was piled into her haphazardly, crutches were shipped and oars made ready. One hand stood by in the bow with a boat hook ready to fend off. They warped her out into deep water. There were four in the boat already. The two on the quarter lines boarded alternately by drawing the boat to them, while a hand in the boat fended off with the loom of an oar. Watching the send of the sea, the man on shore took his chance and jumped. The men on the bow lines were last. They threw their lines aboard and jumped into the water, swimming a couple of strokes, and then being hauled over the gunwales.

The cove was too narrow to permit the oars being worked. Each man stood on a thwart and paddled, poled or fended off as best he could. The boat rolled and pitched violently in the constriction of the rocky cleft, threatening to send them over the side at any moment. The unused oars slithered and rattled across the thwarts and over the toes of the crew.

So, slowly progressing and abruptly tossing, they made their way to open water. They had to get their oars out smartly, for the ground swell was making itself felt over fifty yards to seaward and the ground was sown with clumps of coral reef and rock. The cox'n watched those above the surface. The bowman with his boat-hook either fended off when he could, or called orders to the rowers.

"Hold water starb'd, up hard port." And over the port bow he would make a jab at the submerged shape with all the weight of his body behind the boat-hook, until the bow sheered sharply away. They hugged the shore as much as they dared, each having in mind sharp memories of the current. They did not know just how it swept past the south-east corner of the island, but they did know that they had to round that point to get to the other beach. Off the point they could see scattered rocks and an islet with growth on its poll.

The morning was sunny, and old enough to be hot. The

sky had a dry look and was thinly lime-washed with high cirrus clouds. This, the southern side of the island, was in cool dark-green shadow, standing darkly above the pale green shallows with the choppy blue outskirts in which the boat rode. Blue and hazy were the steep cliffs along the west coast—almost ultramarine. To the south, the cobalt silhouettes of Krakatau and its satellites sat flat on the straight sea-horizon. And the metal of the boat grew hot.

They pulled uncomfortably at the oars. There is always animosity between a sailor and his oar. He masters it, or it masters him. It is a feeling inseparable from rowing with heavy ash oars from fourteen to seventeen feet long. And this boat had heavy, oil-soaked ones with all the devil in their warped blades. At first they viciously attacked the rower's wrists, then the forearms and shoulders: when he lay right back, the base of the spine had the skin rubbed through. Thus they rowed, with this inner animosity burning slowly.

Until they reached the corner, they were almost within the shadow of the high bluff. They piloted between the shoals and through the devious channels which lay inside the islet off-shore. Just beyond, they marked the dark stream of the current they hated so much.

"Well! Look in there, will you?" cried the bowman astoundedly as they rounded the last point. "It's another life-boat! A wooden one, and she looks in fair nick, too."

They all turned and became full of speculation. Where had *she* come from? Were there more survivors on the island? Their crowd? Or Japs?

The thought of another boat at their disposal was too good to be true. Each felt a shadow of suspicion, which was the natural child of disbelief. Yet there she was, lying square to the beach, grey-painted and clinker-built, with touches of spar brown around the gunwale capping and over her inside. She really looked better than the boat they were in. The bights of her lifelines hung regular and unbroken; there was the minimum of oil-fuel about her water line. As they could see her, she looked sound and well found.

This added haste to the way in which they beached their own boat. A couple of hands bent a length of line to the painter and made it fast to some gnarled roots above the tide. Others laid out a stern anchor, burying the fluke and weighting it with loose rocks. This finished, they went across to the new discovery and looked her over with inevitable hope; for she seemed to them, then, as a good omen of sure deliverance. She had oars, boat-hooks, rudder, tiller, water barricoes, but no mast or sails. She was the normal double-ended lifeboat, about twenty-three feet long and almost identical with the one wrecked out on the reef. They found a tin canister in her, about six inches in diameter, containing only a pair of parallel rulers of the walking type. In the sternsheets there was a weathered copy of a *National Geographic Magazine*.

"Well, what do you make of her?"

"Someone's been lucky. Probably found her washed up on the beach somewhere."

"She looks as if she's been used all right. The chart's gone, f'r instance. Then she's abandoned."

"She may have been washed clear of the mainland after they left her."

"By golly! There's been some shipping sunk round these parts lately. Shouldn't be surprised if we finish up with a boat each."

It seemed as if everything to make their successful escape possible were being thrown into their laps. Good luck, they unconsciously felt, was a working of the gods in their favour. And they were ready to see it at the drop of the hat. Now that the manifold works of Man had been taken from them, they had created for themselves the need of divine intervention. Seeing Man projected in true proportion upon the screen of infinite and eternal Nature, their own insignificance dawned upon them, so that there rose within them the cry for importance—to be noticed, to be indulged and to be cared for. When the greater God pulls men up short, leaves them vulnerable and helpless, then the lesser gods are called back.

"Well, it's what I call *good luck*! *Someone's* on our side!" Fatty said, looking almost as if he could see the silent and invisible procession of the old jungle gods and the sea gods coming to form a circle of beneficence about them.

"The crowd from her must have gone up to the camp. We'll go up and get some food, if any, and come back and work in the boat afterwards," John suggested. "I'd like to get the strong of this boat business."

It was the land party who had found her, stranded on a sandy beach two miles northward. This was the crowd who had decided that their best chance lay in splitting into small groups and making their way by land. They had thought to get over to somewhere near Anjer light. They did not think that Anjer had fallen yet. Their precise knowledge of the lie of the land over there was small— only a vague mental picture augmented by a brief perusal of the skiff's atlas, and a rough tracing taken with the idea of reaching Tjilatjap. They had noted the railheads on the west coast, but lost interest in Merak. They must get away quickly. And now, here was a boat: the twenty-nine of them could leave as soon as they liked.

Since they only wanted to make the short passage across

the Strait, they all agreed that they would leave as much gear behind as they could for the other boat. They cut clubs and made other such preparations, as each thought fit. A glass bottle here and there, for water. They cobbed some maize and made it up in small rag bundles. Thus equipped, half-naked, with "boots" good for a couple of miles at the most, they were now ready to walk the entire six hundred miles of Java and evade hostile forces *en route*.

They were impatient that whole afternoon and slept only fitfully that night. Ben, with an organized hunting party, slew the rooster. After that, he sat back like a man whose time has come. Now he had nothing to do but wait for the morrow.

Someone said, "Why not make a break in the night?"

"Yeah," Ben replied by way of discouragement, "and have some bomb-happy gun's crew banging away at us for a sub."

"Not bloody likely."

Impatience spread to the boat party too. It was hard to convince some of them that there was work to do on the boat before she was fit to take to sea.

"Listen," John said to them, "this is not a bloody book. It hasn't been written, so the script writer won't pull you out of the drink and lug you ashore like we used to pull out the Saturday Afternooners on Sydney Harbour. We'll do what we can: so take it easy!" Some were steadied by this, but some were disappointed. However, there was no more argument.

6

John did not want to get to sea and find that he had forgotten something vital that should have been done.

There was plenty that they would have to do without, goodness knows. But he had to make the best of what they had. So he and his party got what scraps of food Cookie had raked up and made their way back to the beach.

As they passed Ginger's hut, they found a conference.

"Going in the morning, eh Ginge?" John asked.

"Well, as a matter of fact—we're thinking of going in the canoe after we rig her. With a sail we reckon we can get a good way down the coast. We're willing to have a go at Australia—working down the islands, of course."

As they passed on, John remarked disgustedly, "They *would* do that—just to put things in the blue. They know we want that sail for the lifeboat."

"They talk as if all they had to do was to hop in a boat and go where they liked. Think every boat's a ferry service."

"I know you don't think a lifeboat will sail to windward, Mr Cross," remarked John; but with a bit of extra sail she may do a little better. We'd need luck with wind, too."

"Well, they haven't gone yet," Fatty said calmly.

They were carrying the mainsail and foresail upon which the wounded man had been brought to the camp. This, with some other gear, they deposited at the foot of the big tree where there was a small, flat, grassy patch about ten feet across.

Next, they set to work, to empty the boat. Oars rattled out first and were passed chain fashion up the beach. Bottom boards, stretchers, buoyancy tank covers and so on, until there was nothing movable left in her. She was foul with oil-fuel, which they attacked like an enemy. Drenching her down, they went to work with sand and canvas to scour her as best they could.

Three men in the boat, two more on the beach; and all the woodwork being painfully scrubbed—how on earth could that have any bearing upon the saving of their lives or the preservation of their freedom? But this was an activity of emotion, not of reason. They scorched in the sun, their knuckles became raw and bleeding, and they burnt themselves on the sun-heated metal of the boat. Energy was drained from them, their oil-clogged pores brought them close to heat-stroke; but they had raised within themselves an implacable antagonism for this stinking stuff which men had sucked out of the earth, started a war over, torn open good ships and covered the face of the sea with.

John and Mr Cross made a pile of the boat's gear, checking and sorting against their further needs. Tools, such as they were, and all the useful gear were put to hand. Apart from the cleaning of the boat, nothing else was done to her that day; but they pored over some suggestions for the re-rigging of her sails.

A little later Mr Cross said slowly, "You know, I can't see us getting fair winds. And even if we should pick up the Trades, Australia would be right in the wind's eye."

John knew that Mr Cross was talking sense. "Still," he said, "there's not much else we can do but give it a burl."

"No," Mr Cross said: "but it might be a good idea not to get too far out into the Indian Ocean. You might get left out there with no chance to recover the land."

"And if we stick to the coast there are reefs and lee shores."

John let himself be deluded into thinking that an extra mast, if it could be fitted, would work wonders. But this would not solve the problem of leeway, he knew, and he put it out of his mind again. He was wholly humble before

Nature; knowing that he could not reasonably expect her to show him special favours. To himself he summed it up thus: "Act as if the whole project is possible, do what we can, and if the powers that be decree otherwise, then so be it. But don't let's throw our bloody ego in the face of an eternal wisdom."

They had quite an array of gear; it almost embarrassed him, for it would make failure look like incompetence. But with all this great stock, there was one thing they needed more. That was *wind*. And not just any wind, but wind in the right direction.

They had plenty of spars, it seemed: three masts and a gaff with metal gooseneck, besides the yard to which the mainsail was laced. The sails were in poor condition and looked as if they would have to be constantly repaired: there was the rub—repaired with what?

It was a long afternoon to this little band of men so intent on scraping off from their little iron tank the traces of oil which loomed larger than time for them just then. The sun was sinking lower and the heavy shadows were creeping bluely across the coral to the boat, where a patch of shade splurged on the bow at the waterline, like blue-black ink, on the absorbent ground of oil-soaked paint. The depth of shadow made the sea surface a warm, smooth opalescence, and the boat a splash of gold ochre in the sun.

"How you going, Ken?" John called. "Think we'll get her cleaned up tonight?"

"I don't know: all except the oars, I s'pose. They take some doing."

"Oh, well, it doesn't matter about those so much. You can get on with those while we are working on the boat."

"How's the boat coming along, Fatty?" John called.

"She's just about okey-doke, master. There's a bit of sand in the bottom yet. Still, I don't think it matters much. *Per*-sonally *I* think she's all right."

John leaned on the gunwale unthinkingly and burnt his arm. He scooped up a double handful of water and cooled himself a leaning place. "Jolly good show!" he said mocking the very British type known to both of them.

"Thankee kindly, Guv'nor. The oil has been successfully evacuated—another naval triumph. But am I *weak*?"

"What do you reckon? Can we make a start on the rigging in the morning?"

"Yes, I reckon so."

"Well, we've got the gear sorted. There's a hell of a lot to do on the sails though; they're rotten."

"What sailmaking gear we got?"

"Fanny Adams! A bit of wire and some ropeyarn."

"They found some cotton and a couple of needles, you know."

"Not thread?"

"No, just that housewife's stuff."

"M-m-m-m. Not much use. Probably make some sort of needle of wire and use ropeyarn." John turned up towards the beach to the men working on the oars: "Who feels like a nice long sewing job that'll be no picnic?"

"What about it?" Ken asked Jacky. "That job'll about do us."

"All right by me," Jacky, who was a Signal Yeoman, replied.

"Right," said John, "those rags are all yours. Down the luff the mains'l's rotten; the head's weak and she'll want at least one patch—you'll be worth your weight in fishhooks if you can made 'em anyway serviceable."

"Tomorrow's the day," Ken said.

The sun was low: the shadows had crawled right over the boat now, and lay flat and extended on the water beyond. Mr Cross called, "What do you fellers say, call it a day?"

"Call it a day!"

"Reckon a couple ought to sleep here tonight. Better sure than sorry. Who'll make up a number with me?" John said.

"I'll be in it," both Fatty and Ken volunteered at once. "That'll be enough to handle either of them if they start to break adrift."

They marched back to the kampong, looking more like a bunch of shady characters bent on pillage than a band of tired men going home for a meagre dollop of boiled rice. They seemed to personify all the beggary of the East. They bobbed along in an irregular string, head and shoulders above the grass bordering the track. Around them the trees on the hills embroidered thick dark lace on the crimson field of departing day. The bush was held in breathless suspense, with an impatient croak or chirp waiting for night to begin.

Their rice was soon eaten and they talked with some of the others on the day's doings. They had carried all spare gear to the foot of the big tree, so that the cove was taking on the look of a buccaneer's lair. Then Ben had suggested that, while there were plenty of hands, they could get the water barricoes filled. It was heavy work, but after they had filled the first two they discovered, in the tall grass, just back from the beach, another well, which held good water. Then the land party dispersed, each man to his own devices.

7

Ken, Fatty and John made their way back to the boats.

"Tide's on its last legs," Fatty decided.

"Yes," Ken agreed, "just about full."

"A good chance to get a stern line on 'em and moor them taut fore and aft, then they'll ride the falling tide all right," John said.

In turn they hauled each boat off-shore as far as the painter would allow, weighed the stern anchors and searched for fresh holding ground on a clump of coral.

"O.K.," John called at last. "All fast! Haul in!" Then they waded ashore, satisfied that the boats would be all right for the night.

They lay on the boat's cover, gazing into the illimitable and comforting space between the stars. The bright stars were companionable—it was like looking on the lights of one's home town, after years of absence, and finding them full of promise and memory.

"Wonder if our folks know the ship's sunk?"

At midnight it would be three days.

"I s'pose so. We made enemy reports when it started."

"But they wouldn't know whether we were safe."

"I wish they did."

"That's what keeps worrying me—Mum and Dad are getting on, and Mum's health is not too good."

"This sort of thing's no good for them."

"The wife'll worry like mad, I suppose, bound to. It's tough on them, worrying."

"It's a rotten suspense."

"They won't know how many survivors, and probably think the worst. After all, there's not many of us left."

"Maybe if they let them know we were sunk close to shore it wouldn't be so bad," Fatty said hopefully.

"Well, mums and wives seem to take a hell of a lot of convincing that their men are dead," Ken added.

And they fell asleep without noticing the stars being blotted out or hearing the distant thunder. Two hours later there was a great clap of thunder right overhead, whose echoes went rolling away along the invisible valleys of the air. They were awake, but lay without speaking, as if a word spoken would bring the wrathful skies down upon them.

"It won't be long now," John ventured at last.

"Beautiful Java," Fatty intoned.

"It couldn't just rain—it's got to hold you in suspense."

"Don't worry, it'll come."

And it did. Sheets of water swept over them, and they ducked beneath the porous cover. It flowed in rivulets under them as well. A hundred thousand hurtling hooves drummed on the cover in deafening commotion. After an hour the stars came back and winked at them over the great joke that had been played on them. The degenerate cover was not entirely useless, for it now kept the wind off their wet bodies, though little devils of draughts chilled them, so they lay in death-like stillness to preserve little pockets of warmth.

The high-pitched whine of tiny and beautiful engines, moving small transparent wings at incredible speed, grew in volume. Abruptly it stopped. The sudden cessation seemed louder than the noise. It was ominous.

"Where did that one lob?"

"You'll know in a minute, if you've copped him!"

Then the air was filled again with the tiny screaming of engines.

"This is as bad as bloody Malta," Fatty said; "and what can you do about it?"

"Pull your head in, same as we did in Malta," Ken replied.

So they pulled the canvas over their heads and withdrew into the fetid atmosphere of dank flax, oil-fuel and warm, wet bodies. Even here they were invaded, and the imprisoned motors seemed a thousand times more shrill, dinning inside their very brains. Then at last, tired of it all, they slept.

Daylight found them sitting up, tousled, and inspecting the direct hits of last night's raid. They stood up and stretched themselves, while they looked down at the two boats riding on the full breast of the tide. The wooden clinker one had made a bit of water, but she rode well enough. They went naked down to the water and, carefully avoiding the oil, waded out to their waists and laved themselves. Then they picked up their rags and oddments of canvas, and started back to the camp. But before they cleared the beach, down trooped the land party.

They gathered into a few groups for a final talk—men who had known each other over the years in peace and war in the navy, who had been shipmates many times before, and had said good-byes when going on draft to other ships. But this time it was do or die, and in the peculiar quietness of their "Good lucks" and Good-byes" a hint of it showed.

The land party were taking with them several copies of the names of the survivors. Some had made rough maps of Java which, on such a small scale, could be no more useful than lucky charms. Still, it was thought then that they had a very good chance of getting through to the allied lines, despite the unopposed landing at Merak just across the way. They hoped to get through with the help of friendly inhabitants. Jan, the gunner's mate, and a small group, were having a final word with Ken and others while Ben was squaring off the boat in preparation and getting her bailed. Some stood on the water's edge and stared across the Strait, wondering what awaited them there. They looked, too, at the grey silhouette of the patrolling destroyer: would she get them?

"Well, Jan," Fatty said, "good luck!"

"Thanks, same to you blokes!"

"We'll be all right."

"Come on, boys," Ben yelled across the coral. "She's rearin' to go! On the oars, slaves!"

"Good-bye Ken, John, Fatty. See you in Aussie!"

Down the beach they trooped and climbed aboard. Ben was at the tiller, and the oars were being run out and waving in the clear morning air like the legs of a drunken spider. They were black against the pale, calm surface of the sea.

A man stood in the bow conning the boat, prodding the bottom with a boat-hook, sounding their way.

"Paddle ahead. Plenty of water. Whoa! hold her! coral ahead! Go to port! Steady! Righto, me hearties, heave away again."

Eventually they were out over the tide-covered shelf, and the oars began to pick up a stroke. The boat grew smaller to those on the beach.

"Wonder what the destroyer will do?"

"It won't be long before we know, anyway."

But the destroyer, on a southern beat of her patrol, went well down below them and gave the boat a chance to get past.

"Might 'a' thought they were niggers," John said, with a sense of relief.

"Well, they look as if they should make it now," Ken decided.

"Wonder if the Nips will have a committee for them over there," Fatty mused.

After gazing out at the vanishing boat for a long while they turned, by mutual consent, and made their way back to the camp.

"I didn't see Ginger and his mob there with the others in the boat," Fatty remarked with a puzzled expression.

"No," John said, "they're set on rigging that canoe. Reckon they can sail to Australia or America, or somewhere adventurous."

"Well, where's the canoe? Still in the bloody creek! What do they want us to do? Pack up and give them a hand, I suppose." Ken demanded with some heat.

"If we had to stay together on this island for long, we'd have to screw down on those blokes," Fatty said. When he was roused, he ceased to be the jovial, tubby funny-man and became a man of simple, direct action.

Back at the camp they found a cup of wishy-washy tea. It was hot, though, and good to them. There was a strange quality about the meals they ate on that island. Later, in the boat, they could hardly remember what they *had* eaten ashore.

8

Twenty-three had just departed. Twenty-six remained: six rugged individualists, and the twenty for the boat. Now some of the boat party were getting impatient and wanting to know when they were going to get under way. John and Mr Cross put their case: it was not like catching a train; the boat had to be overhauled and re-rigged; they would have to try and repair the original rig and add an extra mast to carry extra sails; there was no provision in the boat's design for this mast, so it would take time to work out. They also tried to point out, without discouraging the men, that ships' lifeboats were poor sailers, not to be compared with service boats.

This sobered most of the men; but there were still those who expected a story-book ending to the affair, which would come without particular effort on their part.

"What is tomorrow?"

"March the fifth."

"Thursday."

"Is that right?"

"Yep, it's four days since we were sunk."

"Well, we'll try and have the boat ready by tomorrow. No guarantee, but we'll give it a fly."

"Well, if we can make our departure tomorrow, I think we should have a good feed before we go—on full tummies we'll stand a better chance." This was Mr Stewart speaking.

"Hear, hear!"

"Bloody fine idea!"

"There's a couple of sheep here, down by a hut towards the beach where we got the boat. They're at the hut at night."

"Better snaffle one at least."

"They're pretty skinny. Knock 'em both off."

"We could eat 'em all right, but better not rob the old boy too much: he doesn't look too prosperous."

"I'll dress it when you want it," George said.

So the crowd split up to appointed duties. Ginger's party were a bit dismayed. "Leave tomorrow? We haven't

got our canoe round yet. We can't manage it on our own."
So six of the provision party gave them a hand, and in the
middle of the forenoon they broke through on to the beach,
staggering with the controversial canoe. As soon as it was
slewed into position on the beach, Ginger's eye lighted on
the tempting array of boat's gear by the tree. He thought
they were selfish when they deliberated before handing
anything over to him. Fatty silenced him with, "I didn't
see you cutting your bloody feet out there on the reef
trying to salvage any of this stuff."

"You only want the canoe to get you over to Java."

"But we might be able to make it all the way."

Mr Cross looked sceptical. John did nothing to disguise
his look of utter disbelief. "There are *twenty* of us. You
don't *need* the sail. You had decided to go by land,
remember? You can't expect to have the pick of the gear
just to leave it to rot on the beach. We need that native
sail."

This was the first stand taken. But John had made up
his mind, and was prepared to back himself to any length;
and the whole of John's party felt the same. Ginger, who
could see a hole through a ladder, accepted the situation
wisely. At no time was the question of naval seniority or
rank invoked. It was settled on a much older order than
even His Majesty's Service.

With the air thus cleared, work was resumed on the
beach. The sail proved a long job. The roping from the
peak to the tack was broken away and the cloth was
rotten. "Use ropeyarn to fix the roping," Ken suggested.
"It won't tear the cloth so much."

"Yes, prick the sail with a pusser's dirk, double a piece
of wire for a needle and haul your ropeyarn through with
that," Jacky agreed.

Jim and Darky carried on scouring the woodwork. It was a hard, monotonous and thankless job, for the boat would have sailed just as well with unscoured woodwork. But it did matter so far as the comfort of the men who sailed the boat was concerned.

Mr Cross sat himself in the shade of the canary tree and went to work on the compass. "She's pretty right I think; needs a bit of a clean up, that's all," he said to John.

"She seems all right to me," John agreed. "No bubble, anyway. How's the lamp?"

"I've got to have a look at that yet. It's a bit corroded."

"Well I'll get down to the boat and make a start."

"What are you going to do?" Mr Cross asked.

"Try to work out how to step another mast in her, aft, to carry that native sail. Then there's the question of a weather dodger forrard, and an awning too, if possible."

John limped across the beach to the boat, where Fatty was waiting by the bow.

"What's to do, old boy." Fatty greeted him.

"Look at the gear on the main, will you? We'll get that set up. But before we step it, reeve an extra set of halyards: there's an extra sheave in the cap of one of the masts by the tree."

Together they stepped the mast, the only one for which the boat was fitted. The mast-clamp on the thwart was bent, but with a tomahawk and some determined bush-carpentry they got it closed and the pin driven well home, and secured the shrouds lazily to the chain plates.

"Both the lanyards need renewing," John remarked.

"Yes," Fatty said, "but that won't take long."

"Right," John said with satisfaction and decision; "the mizzen! Let's select the best of those three masts up there—

"Refitting Beach", Sangieng, 1942

one with a square heel and a decent sheave. Give me a hand, Hilton, old boy."

"To prove my great love for you, John, my tulip, I'll even walk across that bloody beach for you—and get a drink of water."

"Good idea."

When they were back, John took the decrepit hand-saw and cut a recess in the teak strongback which ran across the boat about three feet from the stern-post. Then he fitted the masthead with four shrouds. These he made fast to the rings to which the outside lifelines were fastened. He fitted the mast with rope parcelling to avoid chafe against the strongback, and lashed it back to the lifting hook. The heel he secured with stout chocks hammered down wedge-like against solid parts of the hull. The most difficult part was to devise lashings to hold these in place, for although they were beautifully taut now, the working of a boat in a seaway would "work a hundred quid out of a miser," as Fatty put it.

John at length stood up and luxuriously stretched his cramped back and neck. "She works!" he exclaimed, "I think. Now I want to try and fit that canopy frame forrard for the dodger."

"Good idea too: it might stop a big greenie gobbling us up one dark night."

They succeeded in fixing this by jamming one hoop against the mast so that the hinge wedged firmly beneath the gunwale between the converging bows. By lashing it to the mast, they got it stayed fast.

"That's a drop of all right. Better than I thought."

"Yes, now all we have to do is to cut the bow-end of the boat's cover and secure it on. She's tailor-made. You beaut!"

"Going to do it now?"

"No, just cut the canvas and stow it in the fore-peak here: we can rig it under way."

"Now the awning—lash a spare mast between these two, eh? That'll make the ridge."

"And the rest's a soda."

"Yes, we've even got the cleats for the cover-lacing."

It did not take them long to lay hold of the next best mast and lash it fore and aft so that it just cleared the foot of the mainsail when hoisted two blocks. This brought it to just about the height of a man's shoulder as he sat on the thwarts. Then they hoisted the main and foresail, setting them and planning the best lead for the sheets and the best position to belay the halyards, having in mind that they would all be needed in dark, wild conditions.

"Don't want the bloody things fouling and jamming when the panic's on." Fatty remarked.

Ken and Jacky had not finished with the mainsail, but by setting it as they had now done they were all able to get a better idea of what was still needed.

"A good blow 'ud knock the guts out of it," Ken said.

"Well, you've done it a hell of a lot of good, already," John said: "the head-lacing and the throat-lashing want a bit of toil still—the rest we'll have to hold together with prayer, that's all."

They lowered the sails and carried the main back across the beach to the patch of grass on which they had been working. Each of the sail-makers felt some glow of satisfaction. What had seemed so hopeless and thankless, when they were working on it—the frustration of inadequate tools and material aggravated by the heat and the nagging discomfort of their oil-caked bodies—these were swept away by the sight of the sail hoisted and spread in the light breeze. Their work had seemed to come to life.

"We'll take the cover down and cut the dodger and the awning."

"You know, I think we will make it by tonight," Fatty said.

"Not far short, anyway," John replied.

"I've been thinking about that native sail for the mizzen. If it fits, it should work the same as the mizzen of a whaler. It's got a nice belly in it for light winds."

The sail they spoke of was a white triangular one of cotton with a picturesque red patch running up a couple of cloths from the bottom. John hauled on the sheet until the boom was fore and aft. Even the vague hot air that was stealing through the stillness over the placid water filled the sail in a smooth curve without the vestige of a wrinkle.

"Not so dusty. Just the sort of sail you need in this part of the world," Ken called to them across the beach. And John was so pleased with the lucky fitting that, like a boy with a new toy, he hauled the sheet and let it go alternately, just to watch the sail fill and spill the wind so gracefully with slow languorous motion.

"Luck's a fortune," he remarked:" the mast's only just high enough to take it."

The forenoon was being brazed into noon—a cloudless and glaring noon. Their skins and the boat grew hot; every surface in the sun grew too hot to touch. Though it beat down impartially, each man, when he let himself dwell on it, felt that it was seeking to torment only him, while nature remained calm and unaffected. In the boat John and Fatty constantly threw water over the parts they were working on. George and Darky worked at the water's edge and kept themselves wet. Ken, Jacky and Mr Cross kept to the shade of the tree.

"How you going, Darky?" Fatty called. "Any of it ready to go back in the boat?"

"Yes, mate, all except a few oars. Those bludgers take some cleaning up."

The tide was low: they dragged the woodwork back to the boat and hove it aboard after carefully swilling all the sand from it. First of all they fitted the bottom boards into place: then came the covers for the buoyancy tank lockers.

"That's that," Fatty said thankfully, straightening himself up and showing a strangely suffused face under the nigger brown of the oil-fuel. "Bloody awkward under some of these thwarts there. Raise a blood pressure."

"She begins to look like a boat now." John said. "But I'd like to see some decking forrard."

"For the wounded?"

"Yes, and for some of the provisions. They want to be kept as dry as possible and out of the sun."

"We've got to keep the thwarts clear for pulling."

"I know, but if we deck in from the mainmast forrard, we won't lose anything: it will give us a good fore-peak."

"We could try it."

So, with spare boards from the other boats they easily rigged this deck.

They climbed from the boat and picked their way tenderly across the beach. "So we can think a bit," John explained. The seven of them sat in the shade. Mr Cross was near the barricoes and held a tin while Jacky dipped out water for them.

"What provisions have we got?"

"There's the pemmican and biscuits and tinned milk we found with the boat."

"Maize, some paw-paw, a few sticks of green bananas."

"They found some sugar cane," George said.

"If we could get some coconuts it would help."

"They tried to find some of those, but had no luck. No trees on the island except those young ones just through the bush there."

"What else?"

"There's still a bit of rice, I think."

"Well, we could cook the lot of that and eat it first."

"We'll have to get busy about the stowing of all this," John said. "Give 'em a good stow; we don't want loose gear about. Especially barricoes. If they get shaken, we lose all our water."

Presently they returned to work, making up and stowing spare gear. They stranded rope down into yarns for stops, halyards were overhauled and stopped out to the shrouds on rotten yarn to be both clear and handy. The water casks were stowed tightly: there were four of them, and they fitted nicely athwartships between the stroke and next thwart forward. Word was sent to the provision party to send down what they had ready. Oars were selected and stowed. They put in four spare ones and two boat-hooks, and some light spars which would be just the thing for bearing out the sails in light winds.

"Too bloody smooth," Fatty said. "We're getting on too well."

John had felt an air of expectancy and excitement creeping over him, and with it, of course, that inevitable doubt.

Just then Fatty looked along the beach and saw a crowd of human figures coming around the point at the north end of the cove. His heart sank. "Get on this mob, willya! Who the hell could they be? Someone just in time to spoil our fun!"

It was too far to tell who they were, except they looked dark.

"Japs or natives?"

The invaders were, in fact, regarding them suspiciously too. The others looked up at Fatty's cry.

"I thought something like this would happen."

"Who are they, anyway?"

"Don't know. Grab something heavy, that's all."

"Might be Jap survivors."

"We'll soon find out."

"Don't do anything," Mr Cross warned, "just wait and see if they start."

Part 3

TOPPERS

I

VOICES in the dark.

"Who's that?"

"*Perth*'s here! Who're you?"

"Capt'n o' the Quarterdeck, Petty Officer Wolfe!"

"Come alongside, small party here."

"That you, Mr Carr?"

"Yes, it's me."

Petty Officer Wolfe swam over to the voices.

"What you got—a raft?"

"No, just a ring buoy and our blimps."

"Which way are you making? For the land?"

"We have been. Seems to be a current setting us down."

"That's what I thought."

"Those lights flashing down there—what are they?"

"One's on an island; the other's on the mainland of Java, I think," Mr Carr supplied.

"I feel a bit done, sir," one of the swimmers said.

"Keep it going, lad," Mr Carr encouraged; then he spoke to the man resting in the circular buoy: "do you think you could swim a while now, son?"

"I think so, sir."

"Good! That's the stuff! Here you are, lad, take a rest."

The tired swimmer thankfully got inside the cork circle and spread his elbows and hung there. He wondered how long more. They had been swimming towards that dim land for hours and it got no nearer; and in the darkness the loom of the land, against the faint glimmer of the sky, looked so close. He had not realized, until they had spoken of it now, that they were being swept down in a current. They *must* be getting nearer. The more experienced had watched those two flashing beacons and had seen the inexorable change of bearing. The young fellow in the lifebelt suddenly felt hope and energy flow from him, but he still retained a faith in the older men to outwit the sea, as a child sees in its father the power to circumvent any calamity.

"Looks like we'll have to have a go at that island," Wolfe said.

"I'm afraid it does," Mr Carr replied. "It's a pretty small lump of rock, and I don't know whether it's a watched light or not."

"Anyway, it's solid and won't sink under us."

They swam down in the current toward the island which, to them, was simply the left-hand light winking in the dark. They took turns of being towed in the lifebuoy. Action was a boon, cushioning the swift events of the past few days, which had culminated in the sudden urgent necessity for each man to leap into the black midnight sea to save his life. The fact that the sea was being torn in livid rags by shell fire from many ships, and criss-crossed by the wakes of shark-like torpedoes, made the sea no less welcome: a sea that proved for so many of them an end by violent explosion, by smashing from underwater detonation, by horrible treacly strangling in the thick oil-fuel from ships bleeding to death.

All they could carry was a thought so light, yet so much the man himself, that it added absolutely nothing: it was in fact the man stripped of everything civilization had ever offered him. He became the essential being as supplied by God; he threw off the humanly sacrosanct bonds of Reason and Intellect and became the incredibly efficient child of Instinct.

But now that single winking light was witholding their minds from agonizing contemplation of a horrible void. One light, two hundred and fifty-one feet higher than their gleaming, oil-soaked faces: a brief flash every three seconds, over and over, to save them from horrific reflections. Down this flickering beam they swam, carried by the strong south-bound current of Sunda Strait. They swam with an endurance which surprised them. They felt that they could not go on, yet found it equally impossible to give up. They were discomfited by thoughts of sharks.

"Nobody was taken by sharks in the *Prince of Wales* and *Repulse* affair, I heard," Wolfe said to steady them; but he was not so sure himself. "Oil-fuel keeps 'em away."

"It must be four o'clock by now," one of them said.

"Easy, I reckon. It's one of the longest middle watches I've ever put in."

"What time's dawn?" another asked longingly.

"Somewhere between six and seven, I suppose."

The water was not cold, but they all felt the chill of numbness creeping through them.

"I'd like to see that sun poke up."

"I wonder what it will reveal?" Mr Carr reflected. And there followed a long silence during which the hump of rock they were making for loomed higher. The light winked on disinterestedly, high above them now, over the black water. The rock, it was no more than that, was scarce two hundred yards long on the waterline and its apex rose well towards the southern end. The way they

"Toppers Island"

were being set would take them along the eastern side, so they were edging in as close as they could.

"Do you feel like making the effort?"

White water creamed around the rocks on the shore.

"Bit of a swell somewhere."

Otherwise the sea was calm enough. Not long ago the moon had set behind the thick, broken cloud banks. Edging them with silver, it made the ragged edges decorative and mockingly romantic above the low, undulating world on which they lay pressed down by night.

2

As they approached within striking distance, their efforts increased and each man was swimming strongly with a single-minded determination to reach the solid land. All night they had thought of this moment and wondered if it would ever be. Each man lost consciousness of those around him and fought stubbornly for that first touch of land. Petty Officer Wolfe held the island in a sullen, almost malevolent, stare as if demanding that the island should not swim one stroke away from him as he swam towards it. Following his threatening gaze, he swam with grim concentration. But the rocks seemed no nearer.

In the faint suggestion of dawn the world seemed cold and uninterested indeed. The rocks were changing from black to a rich sepia and umber; the close foliage hung motionless. Growing so securely on the sides of the razor-backed island, so green, so heavily verdant, trees shed a cold impersonality over the foolish creatures whose roots were not fixed.

Thus the island appeared to the swimmer. Swim as he might, Petty Officer Wolfe saw the island move slowly by. He turned more into the stream to slow the passing and to edge closer to the shore. Some freak was preventing him, but his stubborn spirit was not broken. Such indeed was his single-mindedness that, had the island sunk beneath the sea, he would have continued to the place it had lately occupied. He could be as inimical as the rock itself. Slowly he was taken along the southern side of the island. He was still wearing an overall suit and an athletic singlet. On his feet were a pair of sandals: they were good sandals, he thought—too good for swimming in. Around his chest was his jersey-covered blimp. He was all too conscious of their weight. Too late to get them off now! If he did, the island would be gone from him for ever.

He could get no closer. Just past the western end he suspected that the current, which had split to pass, rejoined with greater force. He was struggling now to hold the lee. He found he was losing ground. "Now or not at all!" he gasped inwardly. He strove with all that remained of his strength and fought it out with the current. His mind filled with invectives that burned inside him like a fuel and drove him on above his strength. He would consume himself completely to beat that satanic current. Without sense of time he strove to gain, inch upon inch, until he could no longer be sure whether he was gaining or losing.

His numbed hand struck hard rock and the skin of his knuckles came off. It was not painful, and he only felt the dull impact of it. He grabbed at the rock like a greedy man. It was volcanic and, below the water, short sea grass grew on it; as he clung, he lay there just like the grass. The impulse to sink gently under the surface, to rest forever on its beautiful smoothness, was overpowering and almost caught him off guard.

Slowly, floating himself in, he hauled toward the shelf of rock clear of the sea. The guttering water surged whitely about him. A little rest and then, with a tremendous sigh, he crawled from the sea and lay beaten, in a coma, above the tide.

He lay there a long while: he will never know how long. Distant detached thoughts hovered in the pre-dawn about him. How many were still struggling? Where were they? Who was he talking about? He couldn't seem to remember. There were seven hundred of us. But destruction had been complete, violent and swift. Must have been over a week ago. His hands gripped the loose rocks under him, and he felt a surge of exultant gladness sweep over him as he lay there. Whether he slept or not, he did not know; but it was full daylight when he sat up and began to look around him.

In the crevices of the rocks was wreckage—fresh wreckage. "Last night's?" he wondered. "Might be! Must'a' got a few of the convoy as well as the others. Didn't take long to get washed up. This *floated* here, and I bloody well had to kill myself to make it!" Suddenly he felt thirsty. He pulled off his shirt and tore it into strips to make a head-covering. The sun was up, and hot searching rays stabbed out between the fracto-cumulus in the east, which glittered like a glass window in a church. He looked up at the vertical wall of rock and trees above him, feeling very small and very tired.

"Looks a couple of hundred feet," he thought, and began to drag himself up to the summit. It was an hour or more before, pushing through some lime trees near the top, he saw the cap of the lighthouse. The thick, ribbed lense glinted in the sun and was hooded like the head of a rocket. It stood upon a high frame tower. In a few more minutes he was in the open, out of the trees. There were more of his shipmates there: they greeted one another

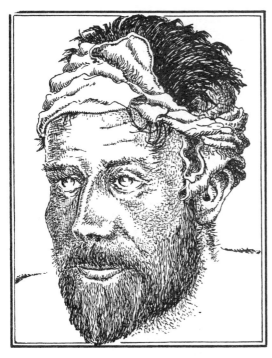

BLACKIE

GEORGE

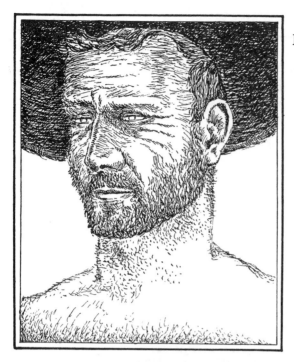

MR CARR

CAPTAIN
H. M. L.
WALLER,
D.S.O., R.A.N.

eagerly. There were the six he had been in the water with, and seven others. They had landed at various places and converged on the lighthouse.

Two Javanese in European dress (shorts, shirts and shoes) were the light-keepers: they had given the men a smoke of native tobacco in bark papers—"like the clippings of a blackfella's beard," said one. It was dark and strong and made their heads reel. But it was, nevertheless, a smoke they all long remembered. A little boiled rice and small, dried fish was set before them with black tea. There were not enough plates and cups, so they had to take turn about. Some drank out of coconut shells.

Some of the men addressed Wolfe as "Blackie", but the younger ones used a deferential "Petty Officer" or "Chief". As a formidable Captain of the Quarterdeck he had commanded this respect from young A.B.s and Ords.

Besides Mr Carr there were four other officers. All spoke, of course, of the past eventful night and tried to remember whom they had seen in the water, whom they knew as dead, and whom wounded. They found it surprisingly hard to remember: impressions had been vivid but confused. Presently someone suggested that they should go down to the beach again to see if there were more survivors. About seven went to the eastern end, the most likely point of approach. Blackie and an A.B. went to the other end. The light-keepers had let them have some kerosene to swab off the hated oil-fuel.

Blackie and his Quarterdeckman climbed along the rocky shore and noted wreckage jammed in crevices.

"Jap stuff, I should think."

"Must'a' been some ships sunk last night."

"Well," Blackie said with a faint grin, "I can vouch for one—ours."

"Do you think we sunk many?"

"Oh, I think so. Mind you, there were so many of 'em you didn't have time to notice much. In 'Y' turret we would fire a few rounds at one target and then shift to another. We was going like that all the time. But we got some of the convoy, I think—couldn't miss 'em at that range. And perhaps some destroyers were hit too."

"It was pretty fierce while it lasted, wasn't it?"

"You're telling me it was! And the old turret never missed a round right up to the time we were hit. As a matter of fact, she never missed a round since the ship commissioned."

The youngster looked at him in complete belief. There had always been some sacred bond between the Captain of the Quarterdeck and his turret. His power of invective against anyone who criticized or interfered with his beloved six-inch gun turret had caused the younger members of his part of ship to refer to him as the "Black Wolf".

They continued around the island, noting wreckage and seeing no one. It was after ten o'clock when the parties had left the house to search, and after one o'clock when they got back. On their return, Blackie and the A.B. found eleven new arrivals. Curiously enough all the newcomers were Americans: survivors of U.S.S. *Houston*. They had been rescued from the sea by the *Perth*'s people. A young Australian Pay Sub-lieutenant had swum out with a light line to their assistance and they had been dragged back by men on shore. Four of them, on a raft, had been thus saved as they swept close by. A further three were clinging to another float. The rest were saved at different points along the southern side. All of them were pretty well exhausted and had to be passed over to the care of the light-keepers.

The final count of survivors there was twenty-five. There were fourteen *Perth*'s and eleven *Houston*'s. The Americans were: one Medical Commander (who had a scalp wound), three seamen, one Photographer, one private, three Yeomen of Signals and two Quartermasters. They came from diverse parts of the U.S.A.: two from Iowa, one each from Colorado, Michigan, Indiana, Texas, Oregon, California, Florida, Kentucky and Mississippi. The Australians included five officers of various branches, two sick-berth ratings, four seamen, one engine-room, and one telegraphist, one cook rating. They came from the east and west of the continent—Queensland, New South Wales, Victoria and Western Australia. It was almost as if night had reached down into the sleeping sea and, scooping half-way across the world, had left them sitting high and dry upon this small rock in the sea looking at each other for the first time.

The Americans did not talk much. There was another meal of rice, fish and tea, after which (according to one of them) they lay down and died. This they did in the two rooms of the house.

The island was Toppers Island. On most maps and charts it has no shape or outline. Not much more than a rock, it is marked on the chart with a red blot to indicate a lighthouse. It is in the Strait of Sunda, away to the north-east and nearer to Java than Sumatra. It lies north-east of Sangieng Island some eight miles. A leg-of-mutton shape obstruction, with the low knuckle to the east and the high bluff to the west, it supports enough soil for some thick vegetation, but has a bald stone apex upon which stands the lighthouse's steel-frame tower, twenty-five feet high. From the top, a steel ladder runs down to earth, whence the bare lime-washed stone extends away until, after thirty yards, it runs slap into the house.

The building, some forty feet by twenty-five, had a narrow verandah encompassing three sides, which on the fourth and south side widened to six feet. The building was divided in two by a wall across the centre, making two rooms about sixteen feet square, each entered by an independent door. The western one was the normal bed-room and contained one double bed, an iron four-poster, painted black, with a high frame from which hung a mosquito net; otherwise the room was bare. There was a window in the northern wall of each room. The other room contained, besides the soundly sleeping inmates, a flat-topped table-desk in the corner. A chair was shoved close up to it, and the drawers showed on either side of its wooden back. On the table was an old brass telescope covered with black leather and verdigris. Some books were heaped behind the speckled blotter. They were atlases, tide tables and shipping registers. An electric torch lay askew. Suspended from the board ceiling on brass chains hooked in tripod was an oil lamp with a large glass chimney and a round enamel parasol shade.

It was a white house. The square pyramid of corrugated roof shone in the hot sun: this was the watershed for the water tanks ranged below. Between the house and the light tower, just off the eastern end, was the wash place— a shed eight feet square, with a trough and concrete floor beneath a corrugated lean-to roof. Water for this came from three iron tanks fixed up the hill a bit. Off the north-eastern corner was the kitchen, about six feet from the main building. It contained a copper and a hemispherical cooking-pan. Along the eastern side on the ground were five more square tanks, just above the kitchen. They were cross-connected and the water was drawn from a tap in the lower one. Above the south-west corner were four more tanks, while just below the north-west one was a small store shed.

Here lived the light-keepers of Toppers Island, tending the lamp and keeping records for the Dutch Navigation Authorities. But now, all at once, they found that they did not know the nationality of their employer nor, indeed, from which hemisphere he came—East or West. But the survivors could not divine their feelings. The light-keepers were hospitable. They gave meals which were of necessity simple but not niggardly: they gave tobacco. These men were of a different stamp from those natives on Sangieng, who were Bantam people.

Late in the afternoon the men began to awaken and bestir themselves, though very lethargically. The reaction of the survivors was of two distinct kinds. The Americans were perfectly satisfied to sit and wait to be taken off. They were quite sure that this would happen. The Australians were not so sure: they had not the Americans' unlimited confidence in America.

"Our tin-cans will come up here and blow all their goddam tin-cans clean to hell."

"Do you think so, Yank?"

"I surely do, guy. Our fellows won't let these yellow basstids get away with this."

"Where are you going to get all these ships?" a sceptical Australian asked.

"Oh, we got plenty of tin-cans."

"What do you call 'tin-cans'?"

"Dam' destroyers. Tin-cans, that's what we call 'em."

"Pity they didn't give us a few more for this last job of ours."

"It doesn't sound as if they had so many to spare. Surely they did not expect us to *win* against that force last night?"

"We were almost out of goddam ammo before we started."

"Well, I think we must have been a suicide force just to slow them down," Blackie remarked, "and that's why I don't think we'll see your tin-cans, Yank."

"They'll surely come, don't worry."

"Time will tell."

So the Americans were content to wait. But the Australians found themselves wondering. Someone said, "Policy put us here and I'm afraid Policy will bloody-well leave us here." Blackie had seen enough in the morning to convince him of that. Merak looked only three or four miles away. They could make out the suggestion of a small pier and a group of buildings. This small feature on the map had obviously become important to the Japanese. The convoy had moved in close and anchored. It was silhouetted against the blue of the shoreward hills and the sun glittered on the busy water around them. Barge-loads of troops were moving in and landing. Destroyers patrolled around and in amongst them. To the northward, between Java and Sumatra, and to the southward, past Anjer, two destroyers went ceaselessly back and forth. In the basin below Merak lay a small aircraft carrier. Several float-planes were in the air. A single aircraft had zoomed up from the south and let go a stick of bombs with more alacrity then accuracy. It tore the water to white rags about fifty yards off the carrier's bow. The sky suddenly flowered with the wild barrage festooning the air. That was the one act of Allied resistance that Blackie witnessed.

That was all he was to see. "Tin-cans," he said to himself, "some hopes!"

There were no cruisers in sight.

"Don't see any of those cruisers we fought last night."

"Where do you suppose they are?"

"I don't know, but it shows you how sure they must have been about taking this bloody island."

"Look how deserted Batavia was last night!"

"Seems to me they ran away before they were touched. Probably the joint's lousy with fifth column." Blackie's disgust was patent. He had lost a lot of friends last night— men with whom he had grown up, since he was a lad of fourteen in the old *Tingira*, training ship. On the one hand he saw people of authority fleeing in motor cars and comandeering large aircraft; on the other was a meagre force sent out to sell themselves as dearly as they could; but they were expendable, and had to be expended. "Well, *I'm* glad we stayed," he said bitterly to the young able-seaman alongside him, "at least the Navy won't stink because of us." The young able-seaman found, now that he thought about it, that he was very glad too; but he hoped that his mother would not worry too much. He had only been at sea seven months.

Soon after this, fighters appeared and patrolled at a bare two thousand feet above them. Float-planes kept up an anti-submarine patrol over the Strait. As the ships finished disembarking, they got under way and moved unescorted and independently to the north-west as if, Blackie thought, making up towards Palembang. "Look! No escort, wouldn't it make you mad?" Blackie fumed. "They *know* we've got nothing against them." He blasphemed. "Greece and Crete, we were beaten, but we bloody-well fought it out. We raised the cost and saved some of our swattie cobbers. We should have had Andy here!"

"Who's Andy?"

"Andrew Cunningham, our C-in-C. in the Med. They *might* have still got us, but we would have had a bit more to say."

"Why, what was wrong with the Dutch Admiral?"

"What was *right* with him? He only made the best target in the world with his ships. We were all in *close column* with only two of his ships able to engage. He lost his destroyers, without even using them."

"Well he got *himself* sunk on the night of the Java Sea action."

"That was another thing," Blackie growled. "Moonlight night, enemy in the vicinity, reccos overhead dropping flares, under twenty-knots and no *zig-zag in close formation.* And we steamed down that line of flares— four cruisers looking like four cathedrals. What I want to know is why they didn't get the bloody lot of us instead of just the two Dutchmen? *That* was a freak."

This was quite a revelation to the youngster, for the swift and confused actions they had fought over the past four days would probably never be fully sorted out in his mind. But to Petty Officer Wolfe all this was held in comparison against the clock-like and Nelsonic efficiency of the Eastern Mediterranean Fleet in which they had served under Andrew Cunningham, their own personal Nelson. "Last night was better," Blackie said: "our own Skipper ran the show. We got stuck into them and did something. I'd go anywhere under Hec. Waller. Andy wouldn't be ashamed of us over last night."

Around seven in the evening they were supplied with another meal of rice, fish and tea.

"Wonder how long the food'll hold out?"

"Perhaps the keepers expect the Service Boat soon."

"What? With that going on over there?"

"H'm, s'pose not."

For a while the conversation drifted to those they had seen in the water. They were surprised to find that things which had seemed so vivid at the time could grow so vague just when they tried to recall them. "When did you blokes abandon ship?" Blackie asked the *Houston's* survivors.

"Waal," one answered slowly, "Ah was just closing the dam' breach-plug in my eight-inch gunbox when there was a hell of an explosion. The next thing I know *I'm* swimming in the sea."

"There sure was one hell of an explosion. She seemed to be afire all over."

"I don't think we had any bricks left except some small stuff—some guy was firin' *them* off too."

None of them seemed too clear how they got in the water except for this "hell of an explosion".

During the day they had talked over the possibility of building a raft with which to make their way off the island. "There seems to be plenty of wreckage about the rocks," Blackie had said.

"Oh yes, we saw some too—*hatch-planks*, in fact."

"We saw more stuff further on. A couple o' jumping-ladders with plenty of cordage on them."

"Yes, well, maybe we could. We would have to see about it in the morning."

"Where would we go then?"

"I don't know; but we wouldn't go *there*!" Blackie said, pointing over to Merak.

"No, that's true enough. What about an atlas—I saw

one on the table inside. Simmonds," he turned to the lad on his right, "would you see if you could get hold of it, lad?"

Simmonds was back in a few moments. It was a Dutch school atlas intended, apparently, for use in the Netherland East Indies. On a double page of Western Java they found what they wanted. It showed them some of Sumatra, and Sunda Strait. Midway between Java and Sumatra was an island marked "Sangieng" also "Dwars-in-den-weg". That was the land they could see to the south. It was about eight miles away. In a short conversation with the Javanese they found out that there were some people living there who cultivated food.

"That seems a good first step, anyway."

3

At 5 a.m. next day they began to stir. The Americans said, "Think you guys are crazy: you'll get blown to hell out to sea and never be heard of again."

"What are *you* going to do? Sit here till Kingdom Come?"

"Guess I can sit on my fanny until our fleet comes up these here straits."

"O.K., Sam," one of the Australians said, "but us Wallabies don't trust anybody as much as you do."

So the Australians made their way down the steps to the sea. The great drops of dew on the broad tapioca leaves were just catching the first upflung rays of the sun. Down on the tide mark they set about salvage. It was taken to a small beach in the centre of the southern side. The rope-ladders were brought here, then the hatch planks—they were good oregon timbers a foot wide and three inches thick, and over six feet long. At 8 a.m. they called a halt and went back to have breakfast.

The sun was now fairly risen, the cloud broken up and the heat evident. With the food they had begun to sweat. From the steps they could see the Japanese destroyer approaching from the north. It reached the southern limit of its beat only five-hundred yards off-shore. All at once there was a great explosion and a broad area of the surface shuddered, went white, then leapt into the air.

"Depth charge!" one of them remarked.

"Musta got a ping!"

The ship clapped on a few revolutions and moved snakily about the sea. Nothing more happened and she settled down again.

"I'd like to see one of our tin-cans and watch 'em blow those goddam sons o' bitches sky high."

"D'y'reckon?" laconically queried an Australian.

"Guy, they surely would. You watch 'm!"

"Like the other night?"

"Aw," the American said seriously, "that was damned unfair. We never had a chance."

"No school ties in war-time, mate!"

The raft party were away again. All day they worked. Two spars, fifteen feet long, were found. They were eight inches at the heels. "Sisters!" Blackie gloated to Mr Carr. Two rafts were found, upon which seven of the Americans had arrived. "Not unlike the ones we took aboard just before we left Batavia," they said.

"Nice of Batavia to give us rafts to crawl ashore on after they'd sold us out!"

The next find was a tin which floated high in the water. It contained small biscuits, the size of the top joint of a man's finger. They were packed in cheap cotton bags with a string at the neck. Some Japanese characters were poorly printed on the bags—some thirty of them, each no more than a quarter of a pound. Yet Morgan's treasure could scarcely have fired such excitement. They also gathered a quantity of deal planks.

Later that afternoon a couple of youngsters came up the beach bearing two boxes which looked, to the rest of them, like ·303 ammunition cases. They put them down and pulled off the wooden covers, then bent back the metal lining they had already torn along the soldering. Each tin was chock-full of banknotes.

A couple of them bent down and carefully picked up a few notes with a peculiar air of dread. One box contained guilder notes, and the other cent notes. All bore the significant lettering: DE JAPANSCHE REGEERING.

"Japanese occupation money," Mr Carr said.

"They're certainly confident. These must have been printed months ago."

"Singapore! Stronghold of the East! What bloody Bovril!"

"Take it up and give it to the light-keepers."

They went on building the raft. The two spars formed the port and starboard frames, and they lashed the hatch-planks across with cordage from the jumping-ladders.

"What about water?"

"That's right. You can never tell where the next will come from."

"Well, young Simmonds and I saw some casks around the rocks yesterday—they were filled with cherries."

"Eatable?"

"I don't know. We broached one and it stunk."

"What's this they are bringing up now?"

"That's them!"

The casks were bucket-shaped and bound with plaited

cane hoops. A lid was jammed on the top, fitted with a two-inch bung.

"Good casks, but what about the taste?"

They decided to turn out the contents and try to scour the containers with saltwater and sand. Mr Carr looked contentedly over all the gear they had collected.

"Considering the size of the place," he said, "we've collected a wonderful store."

They took the money and the biscuits, and climbed the two-hundred steps to their evening meal. The day was now gold under a westering sun and they, too, felt something of the rich mellowness of the evening, because they were satisfied with the day's progress.

After supper, they talked again about the recent action. "Why, you guys were firing before we had closed up at general quarters!" an American remarked.

"Yes," said another. "That show the night the *Java* and *De Ruyter* were blown up—you had a couple of salvoes off; and when we were ready, it was over."

"Yes. We opened fire at 9,700 yards," said Blackie. "Our second and fifth broadsides were observed to hit. Torps gave us that over the broadcast system."

"Then what happened?"

"Just broke off, that's all. Enemy retired in smoke."

"But you guys always got the first rounds off."

"Brought up in a tough school," Blackie smirked. "*Ajax* and *Perth* spent a lot of time on the Aegean Patrol. They called us the 'hair-trigger twins'."

"See much action?"

"Enough to smarten up our drill," Blackie said with exaggerated nonchalance. "We were bombed with the *Illustrious* in Malta; then there was the Battle of Matapan, the battles and evacuations of Greece and Crete; and bombardments all the way round from Damour to Tripoli. I think there were about two hundred and fifty air-raids too." Blackie laid it on thick.

"No wonder you guys got itchy trigger fingers!"

"You blokes fought bloody well yourselves."

4

After breakfast the next morning they organized into various parties. Cask scourers; raft builders; paddle makers. Among the wreckage they had found two oars, and somehow they finished up with just thirteen paddles. But their superstition was not strong enough to make them discard any. It was a simple matter, with the spars and planks they had, to complete the raft: the only difficult task was to secure the lashing so that they had enough for the whole job. Two men came down just as they were finishing, with half the paddles already made.

"'Bout ready for her trials," Blackie called.

Eight of them gathered around and, with a few hearty heaves, launched the raft into shallow water. Mr Carr was a big young man, largely muscled and of a slightly swarthy complexion. He now stood above the others looking rather like a pirate chief satisfactorily launching a nefarious scheme. "I think we ought to be proud of her," he said.

The men boarded her; paddled her into deep water; turned her round; brought her back. "She'll do!" By the time they had secured her, the shadows had appreciably lengthened. They made her fast head and stern between the tides, and there she lay for the night. They filled the casks with water and took them down to the beach. Someone looked into the biscuit tin.

"Strike me! The tin's half empty! Who's been digging out on the bloody biscuits?"

Mr Carr made a brief inspection. "About a dozen bags gone. Any of you lads been eating them?" Nobody had.

"Well, they're gone. No good making a fuss about it—we'll be off tomorrow."

They all settled down to their last night on Toppers Island. In the morning they breakfasted on rice, fish and tea. Impatiently they trooped down to the beach. Most of the Americans came too. They repeatedly told them they were crazy. The voyagers were given a small bag of rice as well as their biscuits and water. It did not take them many minutes to get the stuff aboard. First the two oars, a ring lifebuoy, the paddles, the water and the biscuits and then the men followed. The raft was still not quite awash. They hauled aboard their stern lines and the paddles began to thrash the water as they drew away.

5

Each man had a paddle, and Mr Carr had an oar over the stern to keep her on course. Slowly, as they drew away, the Americans merged into the rocks and were dwarfed beneath the rising hump of the island. All had to stand to paddle, and their motley rigs mingled in a confused dark mass, making strange parallelepiped with flailing limbs splashing wildly about its perimeter. Rags were wound about their heads to protect them from the sun. There were once-white drill naval singlets, sad-looking serge sailors' trousers and even sadder oil-soaked blue jean overalls, some of the sleeves of which had gone to make "stocking" caps.

The day was clear and, on a low smoky shore to the south-east, the dark phallus of the Anjer light rose against the blue hills beyond. There was a light chop on the sea pinpointed with spangles from the low sun. Beneath them the sea was dark blue. Anjer lay over their port bow—

Sumatra was to starboard, and ahead was Sangieng—a mere low craggy outcrop above their close horizon.

Their progress was slow. No wake was visible astern and, after they had put Toppers a certain distance behind, it seemed to tow along with them. But they had found the current and gradually they were convinced that they were making progress. The destroyer to the south slowly continued its way. She was parallel and to the eastward of them. As she came north each time, they watched her approach anxiously over their port side. This happened four times as they made the crossing.

They had been under way now for about two hours. Toppers looked small indeed. The horizon behind them was slicing up leaving the lighthouse till last. Sangieng had grown taller and wider. They could see vegetation now.

"I'm dry!"

"Me too!"

"What about a drink?"

"What do you say, Mr Carr?"

"Yes," said Mr Carr, "I think we might have a small one."

A coconut shell was got out of the biscuit tin. It took two or three of them to pour a drink. Two held the cask waist-high on their fore-arms and controlled the tilt with their two free hands. It was tricky, for the raft lurched in the slight sea.

Sangieng was rising before them now. They could see the fringe of trees above the beach. There were hills, steep and tree-covered. To the north-west the ruggedness increased. They observed two grass huts near the shore, which did not seem many hundreds of yards away from them now. They had been over three hours on the water. They were growing tired from continued paddling.

"Right-o, boys! Give it the works! This is the last lap."
The nearness aggravated them.
"We're being swept down!"
"The bloody current's got us!"
"Come on lads, put your backs into it!"
They sweated and fumed and paddled harder in their anxiety.
"The current must split and race down both sides of the island," one of them gasped.
"*Paddle*! Don't natter!"
"Save—your—breath—and—*paddle*!"
They all laboured desperately. The current had taken them by surprise. "Bloody tropics!" one of them gasped.
"Keep stroke. *Stroke*! *Stroke*! *Stroke*!" Blackie called in an effort to steady them.
Gradually they edged closer into shore several hundred yards below the huts.
"A body!" one of the paddlers on the port side exclaimed.
"A Jap!"
The body floated idly, face downwards. It was that of a man dressed in blue overalls torn at the waist. With a paddle they turned him over, revealing the short-cropped oriental head of a Japanese sailor. Crabs and sea lice were crawling voraciously over the vulnerable parts. A push with the paddle and the body bobbed away with the gentleness of a swan.
The raft touched the beach and was quickly dragged high and dry. The beach was not wide, but it ran away unbrokenly for almost a mile. They gazed curiously about their new environment, then made for the huts they had seen as they approached.
"There's footprints here!"

"Where? Give us a look!"

"Going towards the hut, it looks like."

"Well, there's somebody here, anyway."

"Natives—we know that."

A few yards further and they found a box. "What's that?"

"Grenades—hand grenades," Blackie said. "Dutch; don't muck about with them. Never know what they will do."

When they arrived at the huts they found them deserted, except for centipedes and scorpions. They had passed some newly split coconut husks on the beach, but there was no sign of humanity. A few odd utensils, all useless, were scattered about. The walls were pasted over with Dutch and American newspapers. They filed out again into the sun. In the undergrowth they discovered a small well. It was sweet and cool, and they drank liberally.

"Well, what do we do?" Mr Carr said, wiping his mouth with the back of his hand.

"One party east; one party west!"

"Then all come back here and sort ourselves out again."

"Each party stick together—you don't know what you'll strike!" Blackie cautioned.

"Yes," added Mr Carr, "and don't go inland—stick to the beach."

Blackie went with one party to the north and west; Mr Carr took the others south and east. Soon they came to a river connecting with the sea. There was no current. On the opposite side they saw two white square rafts painted with red patches.

"They look like a couple of ours!"

"Could be, too. That would mean some of our blokes probably."

"Look! Another body!"

"You're right. Another Jap."

The body was floating, just touching the shore on which they stood. It was incredibly bloated, the clothing on it stretched to bursting point. Around the waist was a heavy leather belt into which there were still thrust brass cartridge tubes. The belt seemed in danger of cutting the distended body in two.

"Matelot all right," Blackie said. "He must have been number two—the breachworker—of an open gun. Destroyer, I suppose."

"Well, his troubles are over, anyway."

"And his wife or mother will always be left to wonder how it happened."

"I wonder if what we hear about their dying is right? They say they don't mind."

"I wonder how they are with their womenfolk—do they care?"

"They are like us, I suppose—some do, some don't."

Across the river there grew a difficult tangle of undergrowth, the beach stopped dead and hills rose abruptly. "Not much to push on for there," they decided, and they made their way back to the huts. Presently one of the others came running back excitedly.

"There's some of our fellows around there!"

"How many?"

"Oh, about thirty."

"Know any?"

"Yes, there's the Chief Tel., the Chief Q.M., some officers and the P.O. in charge of the A.A. Director."

"John, eh!" Blackie mused. "Thought he musta copped it, down there. Glad he made it. Been with that bloke since 1935. We've gone from ship to ship together—seven years without a break." He explained to the others, "We were made P.O.s together on the same day at the same table by the same Captain."

They wasted no time getting around to their newly-discovered shipmates. After the first greetings, they went over the last night's action.

"We got the order to abandon ship," Blackie was saying, "and cleared out of the turret after the word had been passed to the blokes below. I got on the upper deck—there were still shells bursting about. The ·5's had been hit and nearly all the carley floats smashed up. I made my way forrard to my abandon ship station—the second whaler. When I got on "X" deck, all I could see was flame and bursting shell all over the joint. I was sure that I was not going through *that* to get to a boat that wouldn't be there."

"Hitting us up there too, eh?"

"Yes, "X" turret had been hit—both guns were off the trunions and pointing *outwards*. Then I went aft on to the quarterdeck to see about getting the floats free. I was trying to clear the big one just abaft the depth charge rails, when the third fish hit her just under "X" turret. It blew me clean over the side. I went down and down. I was spinning like a top. Then I started to come up. Was I glad! I sucked in air like mother's milk."

"That was the mob I saw on the quarterdeck as I floated past. Looked like millions of 'em."

"Yes, there was a hell of a lot blown up then," Fatty said.

"It was after this that I found Fatty in the cutter," Blackie went on. "I climbed in."

"And you were no sooner in than *she* sank. And we had to abandon ship for the second time in an hour. I was jack of it, I can tell you," Fatty recalled lugubriously.

"Well, what did you expect? Her bottom was shot away with shrapnel."

"Yes, but I could not see *that* in the bloody dark, and I was getting tired of this abandon-ship business. It was getting monotonous. Then I had to go around blowing up bloke's blimps. Why *they* could not do it I *don't* know. A man's as wet as a scrubber!"

Meanwhile, as Mr Carr came around the point, he sighted the boat with the masts stepped and looking ready for sea. He strode forward eagerly. Fatty had been working hard, and was glad the job was nearly over—soon they would be under way.

Mr Carr strode to the boat with a pleased and possessive light in his eyes. He clapped his hands wide apart on the gunwale, saying, "Well, how many'll she take?"

Fatty was knocked speechless with the coolness of it.

Part 4

DECISION

I

THE recognition between the two parties—Topper's and Sangieng's—had been without guile or ambiguity. The Topper's hailed: "Who are you? Yanks?"

"Yanks be buggered, we're Aussies!"

There were questions about the boat, which the newcomers contrasted with their raft. They imagined that they were delivered already. But Fatty said to John, "What do we do now? There's fourteen of 'em. It was bad enough with our twenty-two."

"I don't think we'd make it—couldn't carry enough provisions."

"It's not that we aren't glad to see them, but somehow you can't help feeling like you do."

"It's a kick in the guts all right—just when we thought we had things set!"

"You'd think a man 'ud feel different at a time like this when it's sort of life or death. Still, there it is: he's not much different from other times."

"Self-preservation, I'd reckon. It's a duty, too, if you've got any responsibilities."

Mr Carr was talking the boat question over with Mr Cross. Mr Cross was still sceptical about the boat's sailing qualities. Mr Carr agreed with his logic; but he felt an inner confidence that something would happen to get them by. He was eager to try, and so were the boat party.

But they knew that the more there were, the less their chances. Curiously, they were not thinking of personal deliverance when they spoke of the boat's chances. For some of them the boat had taken on some of the personality of their late ship. The last voyage in their ship had been abruptly and violently terminated at the northern end of these straits; now, half-consciously within them, the idea persisted that *her* voyage should be continued. They were thinking as seamen, with that strange monk-like devotion of seamen to the Sea and the Ship.

Fatty was sitting on a thwart, watching John cool his feet in some water in the bottom of the boat. John was looking away across the Strait through the hot air at the destroyer just making her turn north again. At the southern end of the cove, blackened, oil-stained rocks were revealed above the half-tide. Suddenly he saw the dark shape of a native canoe impelled by four intent-looking Malays. "Hullo," he muttered, "what's going to happen *now*?"

"Strike me pink! Huh, it never rains but it pours. What do *they* want?"

"I don't know—but here's another boatload and—just look!—another half a dozen walking round the point."

John picked up a heavy tiller. Those on the beach had also seen the newcomers and were standing in expectant attitudes.

What struck them as curious was that the natives were all quite well dressed, in sarongs, shirts and coats. On their heads were velvet flower-pot hats. There were womenfolk with them. The whole party could have been returning from a visit. Yet the men felt a strange ominous intensity in their approach.

Slowly the canoes came on, the walkers on the beach carefully keeping abreast of them. The paddlers drove their paddles through the water, trailing thin black eel-like wakes, diminishing as the canoes lost way. Then they would drive them in again, plunging the bows in a faint gurgle as radiating ripples ran from the sides. They passed ten yards ahead and clear of the boat, then turned towards the two stakes driven into the shallows—one near the water's edge, and one to seaward.

"That must be a channel," John remarked.

The coral scrunched as the walking natives passed the boat. They cast it a covetous look to their right, and another to their left at the gear piled under the canary tree. They walked on to the canoes without a word. The women had already disembarked and straightway crossed the beach up to the bush-fringe, where they remained half-concealed. The outriggers were dragged up high and dry.

"They've come to stay," Mr Cross said.

The natives approached the white men with seeming resolution. They knew what they wanted; but how could they get it? With oriental diplomacy they avoided an immediate clash, because they were not sure of their relative strength. It was not hard for them to see some of their own possessions among the sailors' store. They pointed to them, and the white men brazenly shook their heads, so they gathered their women and departed in the direction of the kampong.

"Reminds me of householders returning after a flood—they don't know what they'll find," John said.

"You can't blame them for being hostile on us."

"You can't blame *us*, either."

"And that's how wars start: *nobody* is to blame."

It was not long after this when the provision party and the Topper's came trooping back to the beach. They came in a ragged column, head and shoulders over the

grass, carrying odd things and looking like native porters.

Mr Cross called, "What's up?"

"Niggers kicked us out."

"Kicked you out?"

"They said we had to leave; they had brought their families back."

At that moment Mr Stewart and Mr Wyatt arrived.

"We had to move away to avoid trouble. They wanted us to leave everything. But we've managed to rescue just about the lot," Mr Stewart told them.

"What about the stew with the sheep?" Jacky asked anxiously.

"We got that—Cookie went through with it as soon as he saw them coming. Here it comes now!"

Gradually the whole crowd assembled. The natives arrived, too, and started to poke about after their possessions. They were allowed to take some, as a matter of policy. The sailors equalled those orientals in oriental cunning. In good enough part, feeling almost philanthropic, they gave the natives back the things they managed to discover—but what they wished to keep vanished from native ken for ever. Sensing this, the temper of the Malays became edgy. They were mollified a little when they were given to understand that they could have the spare oars and other gear the sailors did not require.

The survivors possessed two watches between them, which the Malays coveted. They haggled in a tongue incomprehensible to the Australians, but their actions were not so obscure. The leader of the natives was a man in a dark red sarong and a white shirt, over which he wore a well-tailored European coat. On his head was a black velvet Javanese cap. He kept his hand in his right-hand pocket, closed over the butt of an automatic pistol. He was evidently ready for trouble, but had no wish to pre-cipitate it. Both sides were watching each other closely. Some of the Malays looked into the stew tin. They saw a couple of bones and, pointing to them, cried, "B-a-a-a-a!" and one of them histrionically pointed to himself, evidently as the erstwhile owner.

But George, who had slaughtered the animal, replied with equal pantomime, "No!" Shaking his head he pointed into the fire-blackened tin and crowed in a high-pitched voice, "Cock-a-doodle-doo-oo!" This quickly became a bedlamite battle of B-a-a-a-a-a's and Cock-a-doodle-doo-oo's. The Malays tried to extract payment from the survivor's stores by way of reparations. The Australians became adamant.

A small detachment of natives took Ginger's canoe into the bush. When Ginger saw the canoe vanish, he watched with a fascinated, fainting incredulity. He fell to haggling with one of the natives for a passage to the mainland. The native agreed, and Ginger smirked around at the others with self-satisfaction. But the price proved to be the snag. Ginger had a watch which would not go and an Australian £1 note. The unreasonable native wanted a watch that would go and money he could spend. Ginger was disturbed at this astounding attitude. He then offered six guilders. The native acquiesced, and indicated he would take them off at sundown. At last the natives drew off; but at sunset the one who was going to take Ginger and five others over the Strait did not return.

John and Fatty had had a tense time down at the boat. A couple of Malays had poked about, at first with a touch of arrogance. Both the sailors watched them quietly but intently, realizing that at any moment they might have to take direct action. They did not want to do this; but it was clear that they would not have the slightest hesitation. This was the same with every man on the beach. It was perhaps the undercurrent of their resolution which put restraint on the natives. John had quickly pulled their own sail over the light cotton one which had belonged to the natives. They were quite willing to fight for this, but the issue was avoided.

After the natives withdrew, it was unanimously decided that nothing was to be served by staying further on the island. The boat was ready but not stored. Blackie, Mr Carr, John and Fatty stood by the boat while the others carried the gear down. Between the second and third thwarts they stowed the cherry casks and the square tank they had taken out of the old lifeboat. Right forward under the deck built in the bow-sheets, they stowed a few small stalks of bananas, some paw-paws and melons. Some cobbed maize was wrapped in an old piece of sail-cloth and put on top of the rest to keep it clear of the bilges. After she was loaded, the more responsible watched her critically as she scraped and bumped at her moorings. This led them to discuss the relative merits of steel and wooden boats.

"It only needs one good bump and she's done for. Repairs are a dockyard job."

And they still talked over the crowd there would be in the boat. "Do you think they'll all stick to the boat when we get over to the mainland?"

"How many of your blokes would take to the road, do you think, Mr Carr?"

"I don't know, Mr Carr replied with deliberate hesitation. "I'd have to ask them. For myself, I should like to stick to the boat."

Meanwhile there was a hubbub under the tree. Cookie

was standing over the blackened tin of stew. Men were waiting impatiently and pressing forward as the strong aroma assailed their nostrils. Each felt a primeval urge to get near that food. Hunger is more fundamental than sex, someone said. "I've had it all frightened out of me—and I don't mean hunger," another confirmed.

There they stood, heads forward, noisily sucking food from their hands, with the whites of their eyes gleaming animal-like in their mahogany oil-stained faces, shifting aside mechanically as they felt the press of another body against them. For platters, they had taken leaves as big as their hands, which they now thrust forward to the cook with a curious mixture of brutal demand and humble supplication.

This was the first real meal the Sangiengers had had. Topper's had eaten regularly; yet, if anything, they had been given the preference. Stranger still, the man who had killed and dressed the meat got none at all.

After they had finished sucking their teeth and licking their grimy stubble, some went up to the well and had a long drink. Then most of them settled around on the beach, talking over whatever took their fancy.

As night drew on they secured the boat for the hours of darkness. They passed the oars out to make more room for those sleeping in the boat. John and Blackie, naked, waded well out with the stern anchor and secured it in a great cabbage-clump of coral. The wounded men were put on the foredeck and made as comfortable as possible with the sails. In all, twenty men managed to cram themselves into the boat. The movement that night in the boat was for all the world like the primitive concatenate nerve-system of the common earthworm: no brain, but one cell nudged the next until the whole was aware of a general desire to turn this way or that, in a semi-hypnotic state, obeying this instinctive urge.

Night came gently. The blue was pale and softly invaded with the pink bridal-blush anticipating the night. It was sweet and calm and cool, with the invisible charm of velvet caressing the senses. The blue grew deeper, the shadow-drenched foliage turned more richly green and black. The blush of the sky soared high and faint in infinity, and was seen only through a gossamer-fine cirrus veil, like a woman's skin. The warm yellow tongue of the camp fire, red-rooted beneath the square black tin of boiling rice, danced whimsically, turning men's faces into tragi-comic masks as mobile as melted wax. They sat about and fed the mocking flames well into the night. In twos and threes they bedded down, rising at times to stretch stiff and chilled limbs impressed with coral rubble, and to throw a stick or two on to the fire.

2

In the early hours of the morning a breeze came up and, on the shallow bosom of the falling tide, the boat jarred her keel. A couple in the stern sheets lifted their heads and shoulders clear of the awning they had rigged and cocked an eye over the side to watch her antics. They decided that they were harmless and sank back to sleep or stupor. Those on the beach slept more fitfully: occasionally, after they had risen to stretch, they remained sitting and staring into the embers, muttering disjointed phrases. Tomorrow was a closed door which only tomorrow could open—it was not for them to try.

At last the door of the morrow did swing slowly ajar. It was opened on leaden hinges on a leaden-lined day whose dome was flattened by heavy clouds. Objects loomed and became concise in the even leaden light. The cloud-mantle was rent in the east for a moment; a few shafts of sun fell in fleeting pools of fire on the grey sea. There was no wind. The water lapped the beach with a dull leaden slap. The boat rode quietly on a rising tide. The men saw the growing light, but were reluctant to relinquish the thoughts of night. They were to make a voyage. They thought of other voyages—famous ones. They dreamed that this would be famous too.

Part 5

DISILLUSIONMENT

I

THOSE on the beach were first to be roused. They sat up, speculated about the day, sought a drink, stretched and yawned. Naked, they waded waist-deep into the sea, plunged forward swimming a few easy strokes, and stood up again. As they walked back to the shore they shook the water from their heads and wiped it from their eyes with a gesture of both hands which might have been huge histrionic grief. One by one the occupants of the boat now crawled forth to join the others. The last few unrigged the awning and stowed it on the watercasks.

The fire was beginning to make smoke as it was stoked with slightly damp wood. It seemed a miserable thing by daylight after its mockery of the men in the dark. The men gathered around, each receiving a dollop of boiled rice—some warm, some cold, and some burnt. It was a thick agglomerate mess they held in their fingers and ate. Saltless and tasteless, it stuck to the points of their whiskery stubble: when they wiped the backs of their hands across their mouths, the stubble congealed in one starchy streak.

Three or four natives came down to the beach. As soon as they were spotted, Mr Cross issued a warning to watch everything—nothing else was to be given up. A general call was given for each man to look to his own personal arrangements and stand by to move off. The sick-berth attendants were doing all they could for the wounded. All men drank deeply at the well. Then they clambered aboard.

"Stow thick and leave the way clear for pulling," John called.

"Shake it up! Shake it up!" Blackie yelled. "Can't be all day. Some one take a boat-hook and con us out."

The boat was now floating ten yards from the beach, just inside the reef. "Settle down there! Make it snappy! Get the oars out! There's a bit of a current setting down there—stroke port! Keep her square—give the stroke oars room there—you'll have to crowd in the stern-sheets a bit till we settle down."

Heavily laden as they were, they only just cleared the reef, after touching, backing and creeping ahead again cautiously. But at last they were into deep water and settled to a steady stroke. They looked back on the island which had been their home for four days. Already it was a stranger to them. The green of the trees quickly turned to grey and lay low on the leaden sea. It was only half an hour since they had started, yet already they seemed far from the land on all sides, the sea looming large all around them. Toppers Island was only a dot ahead of the patrolling destroyer now making a short leg to the north-west before its southern turn. The horizon ruled itself darkly across in front. Sangieng was distant, showing the ruggedness of its western side, for the current had swept them down a little. Further to the south and west were the high islands towards Sumatra: Sebesi could only be seen at times; but Krakatau with its two satellites, Verlaten and Lang Islands, rose darker and hermit-like. Krakatau, that father of disturbance, stuck his head into the clouds and brooded on the indigo sea, withdrawn from mortal things. A curtain of rain swept from the west as if he had drawn it over for further privacy. The rain-curtain was livid against the twilight grey of the world down there, and it followed a sharp leading edge in a narrow strip compressed between sky and sea. It moved like a silent and distant train. There were several of these trains moving in various directions and passing at a distance around the boat. One swept from the north behind Anjer, Java's Fourth Point, making the lighthouse there stand black-etched above a chiselled shore. It was towards Anjer they were steering.

"Transport to Tjilatjap," was the thought in many heads. Unconsciously they were still thinking to complete that last mission of the ship. *Perth* had been dispatched to Tjilatjap for orders. Before they had begun that last fight, the Captain over the broadcast system had said, "The ship is bound for Tjilatjap. With a bit of luck we should be there tomorrow." Well, they still needed that bit of luck to make Tjilatjap, and they wanted some facts to work on. The sailor mind, despite its simple romantic nature, is always happier with facts than fancies. Even some of the most fantastic sailor yarns are based upon fact.

"Anjer may have fallen."

"Better steer a bit to the south'rd and find a quiet spot to have a look around. A lighthouse or any landmark's not the place to go."

Ginger's party of six were going to take their own chances as soon as they could land. Many others were uncertain, each man being free to choose for himself. The close-packed sky was smooth and cold and dark, a few tatters of nimbus draped here and there in rags. The boat moved forward with the short sullen stroke of a duty-boat. Pulling the oars double-banked is difficult work, calling for more concentration than when one has an oar to oneself. More spines are jarred by the looms of the oars behind, and more knuckles are skinned. The forearms of the man on the outboard end of each oar cramp more quickly because of curtailed movement. Hands on the oars amidships are pinched between the opposing looms.

The boat was overflowing with a swarm of dirty humanity: black stubble-grown faces in which showed ridiculously pink mouths and red-rimmed, bloodshot eyes; hair dull as stringy-bark. The rowers had been changed again, for they had been under way just over two hours now. Most of the world about them was blotted out. Only the dark line of Anjer remained, like a strip of blue serge. The Japanese destroyer, going dead slow as if she were drifting, came down through the rain from Merak. On this course she would pass them very close.

"*If* she passes!"

"Pull a bit harder, boys! Might take us a bit clearer."

"Well, she's coming down—she hasn't altered course."

"With a bit of luck she will pass astern."

"Don't say that 'bit of luck' business—you know what happened last time."

Slowly the destroyer came down and passed them without a sign of recognition. Could it be as easy as that?

"Don't take any notice—they think we're wogs. Break up the stroke—make it ragged."

The destroyer was not one of the Jap's latest: she was canoe-bowed, two-funnelled, mounting probably a 12-cm. gun on the foredeck, and a pair or more of torpedo tubes in the well-deck before the bridge. Abaft the bridge she was much like a British ship. The gun's crew were standing about in white duck-suits near the fo'c's'le gun. Heads on the compass platform were clearly visible. It was a strange feeling to be thus far ignored.

"I don't like it."

Enemy destroyer

Then the destroyer began to alter course. She came around to port a mile below them. Tension mounted.

"That brings them across our bows."

"Looks as if they are going to see what makes us go."

"Well, it was fun trying, boys."

"What'll they do? Open fire?"

"Pick us up—I *hope!*"

"What about stopping? Do you reckon they'd risk stopping on patrol?"

"They might ram us!"

Slowly the ship turned across their bows, passing from port to starboard. She had not altered her speed one revolution. They could feel themselves being watched.

"The wolf goes around the sick sheep."

"Break the stroke and pull."

The ragged men pulled on, trying hard to keep their eyes in the boat. In their mind's eye they could see vividly the prowling grey ship on the backdrop of the great, grey eternity about them. But they could not keep quiet. "What's she doing now?" a voice asked. Those in the stern-sheets could see.

"Same course, slightly opening."

"Tell 'em to keep on it."

The sky had turned dark. Daylight was excluded and they lay in a vast cold twilight of unreality. Rain marched about on the plain of the sea in walls, like companies manœuvering in line over a battlefield. In this strange labyrinth of marching rain-squalls the boat and the prowling ship were alone. Two countries were at war. The world was at war. Navies, armies, air armadas in titanic struggle; while here, in a world apart, wrapped thickly in an element of Nature, two small opposing units floated silently near each other.

"She's altering course again—don't look!" came a quick warning. "We'll give you the drum what's happening."

"To *starboard*! That's away from us. Maybe they're going to shove off."

"It looks like . . . *Ah*! . . . She's still swinging. She's going right through one hundred and eighty degrees. Perhaps she's going back north."

"I'd give a million quid to know if she's taking any notice of us."

"She's gone past one-eight-o. Coming up now from our port bow!"

"How far distant?"

"Not far. I can see blokes on the fo'c's'le standing round."

"Gun's crew, that's what they are. Are they closed up to the gun?"

"Don't bloody-well like it."

The destroyer was closing them now. She had steadied on a course which would bring her near. There was a sudden flurry amongst the Japanese sailors on the fo'c's'le: they scurried aft, as if to ammunition lockers, and then dashed forward under the gunshield.

"This is it! Stick your hands over your ears—there's going to be a bang."

All heads spun with anxiety to the enemy ship. Around the gunshield they could see the frantic movement of the sailors. "What the bloody hell? They're all flapping like bats—what the . . ."

"Ha! Putting on their bloody oil-skins—look at this whacking great squall coming up!"

The relief of the men was so great that there was not one of them who was not shaking a little.

The ship no longer stood between them and their

course. Her speed increased slightly as she drew away. Then the rain squall, black as night, came down over them all.

2

The escape, and the deluge of rain which enveloped them, gave them new life. They pulled with fresh energy into the black squall, as if it were a sanctuary. Exuberance burst out like a spring on a mountainside.

"One thing, when we get ashore the natives'll be able to tell us where the Jap is."

"If *they* can't trick the Japs, nobody can."

"I can just imagine how they'd gloat to see the Nips off."

"We'll all be black enough with this oil-fuel—all we need is a sarong and we'll be right."

"They'd feed you too. It should be easy."

"What we want is to get there quick—no mucking about."

"Can't tell how far the Jap is—it looked pretty rotten in Batavia."

"Yes, but perhaps they just let the west part of the island go to draw him on. When they get him ashore, they'll get stuck into him."

"The Yanks must have a good base at Tjilatjap. They do things in a big way."

"Yeah, you watch 'em get aircraft up. The Nips can't last."

"Well, but look at the ships he used in the invasion—all second-hand junk he'd been buying up for years. Wonder how many Wallaby ships were in that last lot?"

The rain swept north. The horizon was an indigo line, above which the long panel of rain ran like an extended curtain dropped from the frieze of cloud above—a grey drape twenty miles long. Behind this the Japanese destroyer and all the Japanese activity was shut. They made no curtain calls. The boat was now about a mile off Anjer.

"Better go a bit further south, there," Fatty suggested. "Drop below Anjer Point—put it between us and the Japs. That rain won't stay there for ever."

"Hey! What's that over there?" John called suddenly. "I see it! It looks like a ship!"

John moved the tiller over. "Let's have a look at it."

Hope rose unreasonably again. But, as they drew closer, Jacky said, "Just a hulk. Been there bloody years."

They turned south and, feeling their way inshore, they were lucky enough to be conned in by some natives. They could not beach the boat, but had to lie outside a rock ledge which was steep-to. They lay to a stern anchor and bowline. Some of them landed over the bows. It was now about 11.30 a.m. The brief sun was again behind the overcast. The sea was grey and indigo. Ashore the fine groves of coconuts grew out of a luscious sward. Parallel to the shore, a hundred yards back, ran a road: they could not see it, but it was obvious from the occasional passage of bicycles and, now and then, small carts drawn by Timor ponies on rapid, diminutive hoofbeats. The groves of palms, stretching far north and south, stood as quiet as cathedral cloisters in the still grey tropic noon. Hope seemed rational again. After the wildness of Sangieng, this calm orderliness of things impressed them: a macadamized road, a grassy path alongside, bicycles, horses, and probably cars.

Mr Cross and a group were talking to a Javanese wearing a white shirt and a rich wine-red sarong. A couple more natives hung about, while others passed without much curiosity. John got the impression that the Javanese was some sort of an official, for he seemed to be speaking with authority. Mr Cross had a little Malay and the native had a little English. The Japs were about, but had not yet reached Labuhan. "Labuhan's about twenty miles south," Mr Carr informed them.

"If we can get there before them, we might pick up a small vessel and make a real break."

"Then we don't want to waste time."

"We can't all go by road—there's the wounded."

"I'm with the boat, for better or worse," John said.

"Me too," said Fatty.

"Yes, well," Mr Cross called above the din, "we want to get sorted out. All those for the road—ashore! All for the boat—in the boat!"

Mr Stewart addressed the land party. "Right, chaps— Labuhan is about twenty miles south, down the road. They say there's a port there: probably some small ships left. The sooner you get there, the more chance you have. That's all."

"What about the rice, sir? Think we should dish it out? It will be sour soon, else."

"Yes, right. Pass it out!"

The black tin was hauled out. They passed it round the boat first, and each man scooped four fingers of glutinous rice. Ashore it was given the same treatment. By sheer luck it was distributed evenly.

"Any complaints?" shouted Fatty, imitating the Duty Officer of the Day at Dinner Rounds. There were plenty of jeering replies. They were saying the things they would have loved to have said in the past, if it had not been for stern naval discipline and King's Rules and Admiralty Instructions. Officers and men equally enjoyed this release.

Blackie sat there with his oil-soaked singlet wrapped turban-wise about his oily head. A pair of oily combination overalls were tied around his waist by the knotted arms. His torso was bare except for hair and oil. His beard was oil-caked and his scraggly mustache half hid his lips.

"You used to be flash going ashore all right—real tiddley," Jacky said to him. "But—Oh, brother!—when you came back aboard! I can remember you coming back in, Alex. You were *only* two days late—you looked just like you do now."

Blackie grinned sheepishly. "You ——," he pronounced. "I've been trying to forget my past indiscretions. Just because a man goes ashore for a bit of relaxation and good company after a month or more of that monastic life a bloke's got to lead in a 6-inch turret."

"Huh!" Snorted Fatty, "hark at the High Priest of 'Y' Turret."

"Who're *you*?" Blackie came back. "Saint Bloody Stylites of the High Angle Director—stuck up on that long bloody tower—you worshipped that silly useless thing!"

"Is *nothing* sacred to you? You Black Prophet!"

One of the road party cast off the bowfast, and with a few shouts and waves they parted.

"You'll be sorry," was Jacky's last word.

3

The boat was hauled over the stern anchor, which was quickly weighed. Oars were run out with a rattle and, with her head turned south, the boat began to crawl like a great ten-legged beetle towards Labuhan.

"There's a few less in the boat."

"Hope they make it all right. They should—travel faster than us, and the natives are friendly."

"How's the wind?"

"No good—up and down."

"Keep pulling. We'll get a puff sometime."

"This Labuhan sounds good," Mr Carr said. "Big possibility of picking up a small trader. We could sneak down by Java Head and get through by night. Then right out into the Indian." There was a gleam in his eye as he contemplated this exciting possibility.

"Be there by dusk, I think."

"Not without a wind."

"She's not an easy boat to pull."

"That sail lashed amidships is awkward." John showed the back of his right hand: the knuckles were grazed red and smooth, with pin spots of blood on them. Others were the same. The boat moved so slowly that it hardly seemed worth the effort. On the rowers' right, Java stretched interminable and never-moving. Would Anjer, astern, never drop below the horizon?

"Are we bloomin' well towin' it?" Jim asked disgustedly.

"Pretty country, though," George said.

"Yeah, but this oar is spoiling my view just now, mate."

"And so we say farewell—" one of them began.

"All right, all right, you blokes, fair go!" George pleaded. "This beautiful island of Java with its waving palms and friendly people and noble blue mountains (if you don't believe me, take a pike over your shoulder at that lot) and its lovely climate."

The same-seeming palms stood along the beach; behind these, huge and blue, rose five or six mountain peaks, the highest of which was just on six thousand feet: a difficult contrast against which to measure the boat's progress, slow as a beetle in treacle.

"There's a bit less of Anjer now."

"I believe you're right."

It seemed a long time before they passed Catherine Rocks, off a point just four miles below their starting point.

"How long Australia at this rate?"

"Never make it."

But they lost Anjer light behind Catherine Rocks with great relief. "It was like having a bucket dragging over the stern," Jacky said.

John looked at the sea intently. "Puff!"

"Catspaws—fitful," Mr Cross answered.

"What there is is astern, I think. Might help us."

"Set the mizzen and help us find the wind—it won't get in the way."

"Oars!"

The oars stopped clear of the water: John came aft from the thwart on which he had been pulling, and bent on and hoisted the native cotton sail.

"Stand by! 'Way together!"

The rowers went on with their mechanical stroke and watched the idly flapping sail. When that sail filled they could stop pulling at the oars. Fatty, who was on the stroke thwart, gazed up with wide blue eyes at the loosely hanging sail, which half-filled like a red-patched balloon and then collapsed again.

"Like a West Indian banana boat," he remarked vacantly, and then with a sudden animation called to John at the tiller, "and *you* look like the proprietor. You remember me, mistair? Harbour Street, Shanghai Lil's, Dirty Dick's—me veree good customaire!" Then, breaking off this line completely, he turned to the startled youngster on the thwart beside him. "How are you, Wings? Happy in the Service? Are you studying for promotion?"

Ken, from the next thwart forward, said, "Don't take

any notice of him, Snow—he's as wet as a scrubber: been in the Navy too long. Deaf as a beetle—says it's gunfire. Know what it is?"

"No."

"Pusser's Custard! If you eat too much it sends you deaf. Don't stay till you eat as much as him!"

Half an hour later the light native sail was drawing, steadily. They hoisted and set the main and laid in their oars. The breeze came from the starboard quarter out of the north-west. "A soldier's wind," John said.

"Now you can admire the scenery, Jim," Ken said.

"It *is* nice, you know. Not too hot, and a nice breeze," Jim admitted.

It was the first time they had had the boat under sail. It was good to feel her work for herself at last. "Must be doing five knots," an ordinary seaman said.

"Only one and an onion," Fatty corrected.

"Two at the most," Mr Cross said.

"It'll probably freshen later—see that rain sweeping about those mountains—there's something driving that," Blackie observed.

John had fallen silent: a comfortable mood of contemplation had settled on him—a mood in which he could feel genuine humility without inferiority or defeat. He was gazing over the four mountain peaks. The lowest was three thousand and the highest was six thousand feet. They came rolling out of the south-east like stupendous Southern Ocean combers upon a running ship. They were blued, indigoed and purpled with the spindrift swirl of low nimbus cloud masses which were here jagged, there soft: black like ink under their bellies and weeping rivers of water in extended sheets. High above, the clouds rose in white cumulus columns glaring in sunshine against the ragged cerulean patches of space beyond. Because of the swirling cloud and the changing nature of the storm moving across the face of the island, the mountains themselves seemed to undulate with the great primeval force of cosmic change, as if they were being moulded before his eyes. Great mountains subservient! Then what was he? This handful of oil-stained men in the boat—what a speck, what an invisible moment in Time they were!

This thinking had given John a power, a sense of untouchability, as if he were beyond the reach of tragedy. He had felt thus before, when it seemed that Hitler was sending his air-force day after day, month after month, only to destroy *him*. With nerves nearly at breaking point, he had been forced to think to some purpose. "Think, to save your soul," he said to himself. So he came to forswear the egocentric point of view. It was hard, for he loved his ego dearly: but he perceived that, with death constantly imminent, to consider one's own death as the central tragedy of Time was to get so out of touch with reality as to suffer a thousand worse horrors.

John trimmed the sheets and jiggled the tiller automatically, steering for a point just above Labuhan. As he took in the sheet an inch or two and moved the tiller a fraction, he compared those niggardly movements with the colossal forces of air, water and electrics over on those mountains.

"We'll get that rain eventually," Mr Carr's voice broke across his reverie. "It's playing all around the mountains—it'll come out of the foothills soon."

"The breeze is freshening—hauling a bit to the west, too."

"Aft sheets! We'll stand off that point a bit. Looks like a shoal there. We'll get to windward."

They were now approaching the point behind which they hoped to find Labuhan. Beyond the rocks on that point was a small, low island, not half a mile long. The sea was broken and confused there and, contrary to Mr Carr's prediction, a white squall was sweeping up from the southwest under a low, fast ceiling. A small native boat with a square white spritsail was flying before it. As it was passing out of sight behind the palms on the end of the land, the sail fluttered wildly for a moment, to be doused by one of the black, ant-like figures. Then both ants paddled the dark little splinter of wood swiftly inshore.

"Suppose there's quite a bay behind there."

"Not much by the atlas," Mr Carr said. "Should have thought we'd have seen something at anchor by now."

"Look, sir! There's *got* to be something—they can't leave us like this," said Jacky.

Along the shore of this northern part of Labuhan, palms grew right out to the end of the point, and it was possible to see the sea on the other side through a frieze of trunks.

"I'll give the point plenty of clearance and go between those half-tide reefs: they'd be a quarter-mile apart."

The wind and sea freshened about them. "Pity we didn't get this before—we could have beaten the land party easy."

"Wonder how they're going?"

"Be there now, I suppose. Might have got bikes or anything."

In another quarter of an hour they were round the point and staring at the bay of hope itself.

4

"There's yer ships, boys!" Jim jeered. "One each!"

"Not a bloody raft even!"

"Who said it was a *port*? You couldn't get a dico in here!"

"Well, the atlas shows a railhead."

"We'd better go in and show them the atlas," said Blackie.

They dropped the sails and started pulling.

"But there's been something," one of them said in a puzzled tone. "Look! A concrete wall, and see those steel-framed towers—they look like beacons. They don't do that for nothing."

"That looks like the mouth of a river."

"It's marked on the atlas."

"Allah be praised!" Blackie said, devoutly raising his eyes to heaven. "Something's right at last."

The river formed a narrow estuary about fifty yards wide. Square across the mouth were half a dozen lines of breaking waves.

"Sand-bar—slap across her!"

"Looks like only a foot of water."

"Give her a go, anyway."

"Give way together—pull easy!"

"Keep her square!"

They rode the insweeping waves and were dropped in the trough a couple of times before there was a dull grinding and the boat surged to a standstill. "Fit men over the side! Keep her square! Unship the rudder!" Gradually they worked her over the bar.

Mr Cross said, "A small party only, to go ashore and see what's doing. The remainder stand by the boat—and be ready to clear out. Turn her now."

About eight of them waded ashore. As they were bringing in the boat, they had noticed a continuous stream of natives crossing the river from the town to the palms, beneath which they vanished in a meandering line north-ward.

"Look at 'em!" Jacky cried, "Get a cork-eye at this bloke! He's got a chest o' drawers on his head—they've all got something—wardrobes, po-cupboards, the whole works!"

"They're bailing out—that's what they are doing."

"Before the Japs come."

The rubble and concrete wall on the other side extended away in a curve from the mouth of the river; it ceased where a graded earth bank took its place. Above the earthen section rose two galvanized iron sheds. A little further left, an elevated petrol tank stood on a steel frame marked *Shell*. Beneath it was a rude service station.

"Road there!" John remarked. They pushed across the ford, with Jacky and John last, moving against the stream of the black exodus. On the far bank among the stragglers was one of darker mien than the rest. As he passed he made a sudden grab at John's wrist. John swung and evaded him.

"What's the score, mate?" and he saw that the man was armed with a two-foot parang which he started to swing menacingly.

"Don't like the look in that coon's eye." Jacky said.

The Malay was half crouched, his knees slightly bent, his left arm stretched toward John and his right drawn back with the sharp parang gripped in a slightly shaking hand. He was talking short guttural phrases and pointing to John's left wrist.

"Y'disc—your identity disc! That's what he's after."

John glanced down at his wrist and there, against the oil-stained skin, the pale gold disc gleamed temptingly.

"He's not going to get it," John told Jacky flatly.

Labuhan, 1942

The disc held strong sentimental ties for him. His wife had sent it to him when they were in the Mediterranean. Many times he had soberly thought that this was all that would have been left recognizable of him. He still had hopes of getting back to his wife with it around his wrist. This was dampening that hope. A couple more natives, attracted by the row, had come close.

John and Jacky were bare-footed, and naked except for their oil-stained shorts. They were equipped only for flight. But if anything started, John would have to dodge that swinging parang and they would have to close pretty smartly. But what would the rest be doing? Probably they would be submerged beneath a black avalanche and beaten to death. A vivid picture of Captain James Cook's murder presented itself unbidden to John's mind: the chill it sent through him helped him to decide. It seemed to John that the truculent Malay was making more of a show now he had an audience. Could he be bluffing? John took a deep breath: there was only one way to find out. "Jacky," he called. "You just walk on as if you're not interested— follow the others."

"And what are *you* going to do?" Jacky demanded. "That's a murderous great knife he's got there."

"Can't keep my eyes off the bloody thing. Right-oh, get walking."

John had only a vague idea of what he was going to do; it was the right moment that counted, he thought. The native was still talking loudly, now at John, now at his countrymen.

"Don't worry about it, mate, it's not worth a cracker." John knew his words meant nothing to the black, but he hoped the off-hand tone would calm the bandit down. He even affected a laugh—the hollowest laugh on record, he later admitted. Yet that laugh probably saved his life. It had to be very circumspect, for to deride a man in the Malay's condition was likely to precipitate murder. One of the other natives spoke and laughed as well. The man with the knife turned indignantly on him. John knew that, if he did not act now, there would not be another chance. So he turned his back squarely on his attacker and walked away, keeping a firm rein on himself. Jacky had reached the end of the sheds: he was looking back as John started his walk.

"How'm I going, Jacky? I can feel that bloody knife between my shoulders every step I take."

"Just keep walking. He's arguing with the other bloke—he don't know what to make of it. He hasn't moved. He's got the knife up in the air and he looks as if he's goin' to bust out bawlin'.—You've beaten him!"

They turned the corner into Main Street. It had been built by man to give Labuhan life: a place for man to mark on the map; a place for a couple of beacons to flash in the dark at the mouth of a muddy little river; a place served by a fussy fire-fed little locomotive running on tracks from the great mills of Herr von Krupp, and equipped with police, post office, regulations. Methodically the Dutch had done it, and the place was neatly tabbed in the file of their colonization. But men of another civilization, bent on unashamed depredation, swept down from the north; and they had hardly set their feet upon Java before the Dutch had fled. No sooner had the blond rulers turned their backs than the black Malays (the Bantaams) did what they had wanted to do for years. With the repressive shackles broken, they swarmed into Main Street and up-rooted it. The shops on either side stared out of hollow, eyeless sockets, their insides ripped out; windows, shutters and doors were pulled down and smashed where they lay. Some were gutted with fire; all were looted. The blood of the looters had risen with the drumming pulse of easy victory. The nameboards of the Chinese proprietors were scattered about like headstones in a desecrated cemetery. The street was morbid with desolation—papers, shattered books of carefully kept accounts, photograph albums, bits of printed rags, broken glass, pencils, beads broadcast, postcards, tins, bottles lay where they had been stamped on insensately by a mob excited to fanatical frenzy in their new-found freedom and power.

"Coo!" Jacky breathed, "we were luckier than we guessed, back there."

They both glanced apprehensively over their shoulders. But the street was deserted.

"Better catch up with the others and stick together," John said, looking about him with a fascinated horror. The whole street seemed to say, "Do you see? *I'm dead*! I no longer *am*. Civilization doesn't amount to much, does it? In a few minutes the niggers come in, tear it to pieces and march back to the bush."

What he had seen, he later reflected, was the murder of an idea. Tragedy is the death-struggle of an idea in the face of a changed reality: as, when a friend dies, we suffer until our acceptance of his death is complete. As long as our minds are unready for the new conception, there is tragedy.

They passed out of the town and across the bridge over the river. Skirting a road block, they turned left along the main road and, about five hundred yards further on, they came up with the others, who were talking to someone through an iron palisade fence. It was a Chinaman, armed with a rifle. He had been barricaded in the house for three days with two of his friends, who were also armed. The looters had gone mad in the town, burning and pillaging. They had made several attempts on his house, but he had been able to beat them off each time. Numbers of people had been murdered—Chinese mostly. Perhaps the Malays were growing quieter now, but it would take little to start them again. This Chinaman had a radio. Batavia had fallen two days ago, he told them. The Nipponese were broadcasting, telling the people to cease resistance and help build a Greater Asia Co-prosperity Sphere.

"Some of your fellows came through here the day before yesterday—a Commander and a Padre. I advised them to give themselves up to the Japanese. I hear that they have not been bad to prisoners. They could not be worse than the very bad Malays."

"We have some wounded. Have you any bandages?"

The man with the rifle went into the house to see what he could get. As he was going through the door, Jim called, "Y' haven't got any soap, have you?"

They stood outside the fence and waited. They saw no one. "Doesn't look so hot, does it?" Blackie commented.

"The Japs seem to be pretty well in control now."

"I wonder, if we did get to Tjilatjap, what we should find?"

The Chinaman returned with a handful of clean rags and two small pieces of soap. This was all he could give them. They talked a little more with him, and again he urged them to go up the railway to Menes. "It's much safer," he said. "You cannot last long against the black men—they are treacherous and there are many thousands."

They thanked him and returned along the road to the boat, after arming themselves with heavy branches for clubs.

"I wonder how those blokes are getting on, walking?"

"Funny we haven't seen them yet," Mr Cross said, echoing the common anxiety which suddenly came to them all. "There should be some sign of them by this!"

They became tense as they approached the river, fully prepared now if the need arose. They met a couple from the boat about to enter the town. "All back, boys," Blackie called. "This place ain't healthy any more. We'll see if we can find a spot further down the coast for the night."

"I don't like the way that little crowd over there is watching us. I wouldn't be surprised if they were thinking of eating us."

They had just cleared the bar when they heard a loud hail from the town-side of the river. About a dozen running figures were shouting for them to come back. They ran out on the southern arm of the river mouth.

"Our blokes! They're our blokes!"

"Thank Christ!" Blackie said devoutly. "Let's hope they all turn up now."

They dared not go back inside the bar, but picked the men up to seaward, just outside the river entrance—twelve of them.

"Where are the others?"

"Don't know! We came down in separate parties."

"Have any trouble with the niggers?"

Mr Stewart, who was one of this party, told a depressing tale of hostility and treachery from the natives along the road. They had been forced to run for it several times. And now here were only twelve out of the twenty who had set out so hopefully a few hours ago.

5

The sea was leaden grey, with an undulating swell running in to the shore and spending itself with seething whiteness about the rocky ledges. The sky was leaden; the cloud was heavy, smooth and low. The men's hearts were leaden too. They had so unthinkingly counted on the friendliness of the natives to help them past the Japs. This sudden-seeming treachery left them numb. With this inadequate boat, their lack of clothes and protection, their bodies spent by a hectic week or more of fighting and sleeplessness in the ship before the long hours in the midnight sea—after all this they were tottering and bewildered. Even this fertile island was now denied them.

They explored a little way to the south, where there was a flat muddy beach, but the water was still very shallow a long way off-shore. The officers were silent and serious. Ken, Fatty, Jacky and John looked at each other in the stern-sheets with unspoken thoughts.

"Well," said John at last, "we've got to find a bit of beach comfortable and deep enough for a pierhead jump."

"We'll need to set good watches too. Now the niggers know we're about, they're bound to have a go at us," Mr Cross ruefully remarked.

"Look," cried George. "What about that small island off there?"

They had been so intent on searching the coast that they had not thought to look off-shore.

John put the tiller over and gave the order to give-way. This island was a godsend—it eliminated the chances of a surprise attack. As the boat's head swung away towards the island, Jacky who was on the stroke oar cried, "Look!" With the quick eye of a signalman he had sighted someone running through the palms. They heard a piercing shout and saw the flying figure wave an arm wildly above its head. "A nigger!"

"He's no blackfella," Blackie said with decision, "he's got overalls on." And again came the piercing shout.

"He's in a panic," Jim said. "Wonder if those black bastards are after him."

"Hold water, port; up hard, starboard," called John. With the tiller hard over, the boat was turning in her own length.

"Give way, together! Macaronies, boys! It's only a burst! Give it to her!" The lumbering boat gathered way and gave a faint chuckle of bow-water. The man was still shouting, but they could see no one in pursuit. It seemed as if he dared not take his eyes off the boat: one hand, they noticed, was pressed to his chest as if to stop his heart from bursting.

John was confronted with a problem. He was taking the boat straight in, but the shore was an unbroken rock-shelf. How was he going to get close enough to pick the man up and, at the same time, keep the boat from being lifted bodily by the swell and dumped on the rocks? That would be the finish of the lot of them. He turned the boat and approached stern-first, using the oars to counteract the send of the incoming sea. The fleeing man had stopped shouting and was recklessly clambering over the needle-sharp rocks towards them.

"It's Stoker McMurtee," one of them cried. "Him and E. R. A. Smith were in the road party together."

They could hear the man now; great strangled sobs came from his tortured lungs. The wild whites showed in his eyes, startling in his almost black, oil-stained face. The hand on his chest was clamped over a broad bloodstain, and the blood had run down his arm and dripped from his elbow.

John had to ignore the man's pitiful state. "We can only

take the boat in so far—then he'll have to jump into the drink and we'll pull him inboard. Now, you fellas on the oars, don't take your eyes off me! Do what I say when I say it! Nothing else! Right?"

Fatty said, "I'll go over the side and grab him when he hits the water. Ken, Blackie and Jacky—stand by to haul him in."

"Right!" called John decisively. "Now—back together —easy." He had shipped an oar over the stern instead of the rudder. He said he was not going to risk the boat, but the very coldness of the decision gave him more confidence. Fatty would take care of the man; he would take care of the boat. He brought her in until the blade of his sweep touched the rocks. This would give them the minimum safety. Fatty slipped into the water, and a couple of strong, swift strokes brought him to the edge below the suffering man. Blackie and Jacky bellowed, "Jump, mate, we can't come any closer."

But the poor fellow seemed suddenly to lose his nerve: he baulked, as if some unnamed horror stared up at him from the dark swirling water. He had come across those sharp rocks without a thought of their cruelty. A man in his normal senses could never have done it. But now, that dark water with the boat beyond—his salvation so near— he did not have the courage left to grasp it.

Fatty was in danger of being lifted up by the sea and dropped on the rocks, which would cut his naked skin to shreds. "Jump," he cried in impatient anxiety, "for Christ's sake jump!" But the man was as petrified as the rocks on which he stood—gripped in a terrible indecision. John had to watch over the stern for the rocks, and over the bows for the incoming swell—watch for that big one which comes every now and again. This shelf was volcanic, and the sea had worn it into a million hard needle-points: it could puncture the taut skin of their boat as easily as a pin would a balloon.

"Way together!" he called urgently, and the rowers drove their blades into the water and rose off the thwarts, heaving with rigid arms and straining backs against the sluggishness of the boat. The broken white water swirled around McMurtee's knees.

"Jump, Mac! *Jump!*" Fatty urged again, swimming right in and risking bad laceration. He held up an imploring extended arm. McMurtee fell rather than jumped. Fatty grabbed him and with a few strokes had him alongside the boat, which John had allowed to drop back again. Blackie, Ken and Jacky reached over and with one concerted heave dragged the injured man in and sat him on the stroke thwart. Fatty followed.

"Give way, together!"

When the boat was well clear, John called, "Oars!" and all the blades came clear of the water and stopped. Then he turned his attention to Stoker McMurtee. Unstrung and still giving those awful shivering sobs, he sat with Mr Carr and Mr Cross kneeling before him. Mr Carr gently took the hand from the great bloodstain on his chest. There was no wound under it. The blood had run down the man's right elbow, and Mr Carr turned the palm up: the fingers were half clenched. Prising them slowly open, he saw a long gash across the palm from the base of the little finger to the space between the index finger and thumb. So deep and jagged was it that it seemed a miracle that the top of the hand had not fallen away. Mr Carr muttered, "What do we do with that?" John, leaning over his shoulder and without any special knowledge, said, "Clean pad of kero in the palm, close the fingers,

bandage it—and hope." They did this and improvised a
sling.

John got the boat under way again and was making for
the little island off-shore. "Refuge Island," some one
said grimly; and thereafter, that is what they called it.
"The bastards!" came another voice. McMurtee gradually became quieter: occasionally, with a shudder, he
muttered, "Smithy!"

The group in the stern-sheets looked at one another,
half-guessing the trouble. "What happened, there, Mac?"
Fatty asked quietly, in a matter-of-fact voice. McMurtee
looked up. He realized it was Fatty who had pulled him
through the water to the boat in those last horrible
moments. Gradually he began to talk.

McMurtee and Smithy had left the boat with the others
and made south down the broad road flanked with palms.
Both were fit men. Smithy was a young fair fellow of
medium height, wiry and athletic; McMurtee was solid
and tough and taller. They had pushed on and were soon
well ahead of the others. They had passed several small
groups of attap huts, and then a village. On the further
side of this a group of five or six natives were gathered. As
the pair came up with them they asked, "Labuhan?" and
pointed ahead. There was a short useless exchange of conversation which nobody understood. Then came a word
both sides knew: "tobacco."

McMurtee said, "He's asking us for smokes, Smithy."

One of the natives stepped forward and thrust a hand
into Smithy's overall. Smithy pushed him away without
ceremony. In a moment the others all crowded in and drew
long parangs. McMurtee saw a great blade flashing down
on to his head and his right hand instinctively shot up
to ward it off. The savage edge bit deeply. He turned to

Smithy. Smithy was on the ground, already dead, with his boyish head cloven and two frenzied natives hacking away at his body with their parangs. What the shock had been to McMurtee could only be vaguely appreciated by those others in the boat, but perhaps it had saved his life. For, in that paroxysm of grief and shock, he had run without heed. No wonder he was so far gone when they got him.

"He would have come at least five miles," Jacky marvelled.

"He's tough," Blackie replied.

Now McMurtee sat, emptied right out. No one pressed him further. He was allowed to sit quietly and listen to the casual conversation about him, or gaze over the grey sea, full of his own strange thoughts. As they rowed over to Refuge Island, the men felt pretty sure that the natives would make an attempt on them that night. They thought they saw a few skirting through the palms, and said they were keeping track of them.

The landing was easy, the beach being steep and pebbly, and the water quite clear all round. They pulled the boat well up and lifted Dick, the wounded man, ashore and made him as comfortable as possible on the sails by the bushes at the top of the beach. McMurtee and the other walking-wounded were helped up there also. Several made short sorties about the islet, but the light was beginning to go and they did not discover much. They gathered wood and lit a fire with one of the friction flares. The fire was concealed in the bush against the spying eyes of the natives, and its warmth and life comforted them.

6

They held a general council of war. The officers acquainted the men with the situation ashore as it had been made known to them, and there followed a general discussion. Already the boat was losing its attraction for many of them. They were used to steam turbines and regular schedules. Somehow they could not get their minds out of steam-turbine gearing. They had seen and realized for the first time the great limitations of a boat dependent on the wind—a boat, more-over, built to save life only by floating, or, at most, running before a wind, not made to lay close to the wind and beat like a yacht.

Now, with the darkness around them, by the light of a flickering fire on a remote foreign beach, having only had four fingers of sticky, near-sour rice and one drink of water in one long, laborious tropic day, they felt discouraged. They were half-ready for any change of plan, since the present one seemed to be leading into a dead end.

The Chinaman appeared to have told them nothing more than the truth. The natives were not to be taken lightly: there were thousands of them, all of the same wicked temper, and treacherous. The Japanese were taking over the island almost unopposed—probably faster than any of them could travel without transport. They were faced with two possibilities: direct attack from the natives, or betrayal by them to the Japanese. The natives would seek to gain favour, no doubt, with the conquerors from the north. In a densely populated place like Java, with its labyrinthine village-life, it would be impossible to move ashore undetected. In the same way the boat could hardly land anywhere along the coast without someone seeing them and spreading the news. They would not be able to move.

These were the things which confronted them squarely now. The implications were sinking right in. Short of sailing right out into the Indian Ocean and heading for

Australia, they could only live on borrowed time. But the Indian Ocean was vast and the winds unfavourable, apart from the shortcomings of the boat. They were getting back to the only decision it seemed feasible to make; yet it was a decision none of them really wanted to make.

There is a stigma about surrender, no matter how inevitable. It is criticized, usually, by smug, comfortable people, after the enemy has been defeated. One politician has gone so far as to say that to pay prisoners of war in enemy hands three shillings a day subsistence would only be to encourage defection in the fighting forces of the future. Unreasonable views like this colour public opinion, because we are all a bit self-righteous and smug at heart: in spite of ourselves, we get just a little secret lift from the downfall of another.

Yet great men have surrendered. There is a point of no-surrender when a rabid ego, to preserve itself, will destroy all else. There is a point of no-surrender which is honourable and valuable—when surrender would cause a dangerous precedent and damage the cause for which we fight—these men had willingly fought their ship to her death for just that reason. And there is a point of no-surrender which is just plain stupid, caused by a fixed idea of what people will think: this is the greatest force yet devised for the moral destruction of the weak.

Nelson, whose great moments of transcendental joy were those of action against any odds in the face of the King's enemies, was more than once moved to compassion for an enemy being uselessly sacrificed by commanders who should have concluded an honourable surrender—commanders probably driven to this criminal extremity by what people, safe by their firesides, would think.

And now these men on the beach were being tried by

the invisible, merciless court whose judge and jury listened, not to the defendants, but to their own self-righteous clamour—a court assembled, not to try and judge impartially, but to establish itself as sinless. This kind of judgment was revealed, for example, when a certain man came home at last after three and a half years of Japanese incarceration. He had helped to build the "death railway". He had laboured in tropic jungle and oriental snow, above the ground, and in coal mines beneath the sea. He had buried many of his friends and suffered dehumanizing sicknesses. And now he came home with a mild gratitude that it had been no worse; that he had, by the grace of God, survived. Among the friends there to welcome him was a Pharisee who took him by the lapel and said, "You have no idea what it has been like here in Australia, while you have been away. Tea was rationed, and clothes—it was awful!" The ex-prisoner felt guilty in spite of himself, and muttered that he had indeed been lucky to have escaped all this.

The men's decision had to be made in the face of the Pharisees. To the Pharisee, there could be only one possible decision: take the boat, with her limited provisions and lack of sailing qualities—take her straight out into the Indian Ocean and sail her, to the glory of sensational literature (which is the sacred gospel of the Pharisee) to Australia or Hell. What magnificent passages might be written, about gaunt scarecrow figures with mad-staring eyes leaping to death in the frenzy of an intolerable thirst or practising cannibalism in the bows on a corpse hidden under a mouldering piece of canvas.

The thought of Pharisaic verdicts on their action made the men uneasy and unsure. They gathered on the beach by the boat in the short twilight. Some of them gazed across at Labuhan, half-expecting the natives to come out in a fleet of war canoes. A group of the older ones were by the fire, trying to formulate some action.

"I think the men should have some food," Mr Stewart said.

"Biscuit?"

"What about a bit of pemmican, too? It's been a long day."

"The youngsters are a bit disheartened—it'd cheer 'em up," Ken said.

Two tins of pemmican were opened. Mr Cross got out the biscuits and handed them to Mr Carr, who spread the paste on with a jack knife. The men stepped up in turn.

"Pemmican? What's that?" an ordinary seaman asked.

"Don't take it serious, lad, it's all bull!" Blackie said drily.

Thirty-two biscuits had been handed out and, as each man received his ration, he gave his name and rating to Mr Wyatt. At this rate they had eleven meals left. That was eleven days at one biscuit a day, supplemented by the other stuff occasionally. But would one biscuit a day be enough?

Two measures of water had been served to each man— one-third of a pint. Watches were set from volunteers, each trick being only half an hour. The boat was secured and they slept on a split-yarn ready for emergency. But the night passed without incident.

7

With the first streaks of daylight the men began to stir. They refreshed themselves in the sea, and several small parties went out on short exploratory trips. All seemed heartened by the fact that the natives had not attacked.

They had really expected it. So much of yesterday was faded now like a bad dream. To their pleasant surprise, one of them stumbled across a shallow well in the bush, which meant that everyone could drink his fill. But, strangest of all, was the discovery of two small packets of Capstan cigarettes on a sandy spit at the other end of the islet. Some of the cigarettes were beyond salvage; but then it was a miracle that any had survived, because it appeared that they had come there water-borne.

Soon there was a loud hail for all men to muster. They gathered on a flat sandy strip fringed with low green bushes. They formed in a fairly regular circle facing Mr Stewart, as senior member, at the head.

"Well, chaps," he began, "you all know what happened yesterday. You know what things are like with the Japs and the natives. With our limited water and provisions, and our present numbers, the boat only offers a slim chance."

"And the wounded," someone added.

"Yes, the wounded—they need proper attention as soon as possible."

Mr Cross cleared his throat. "Now you don't want to get any fancy ideas about this boat performing miracles. It won't. I know it won't. These boats are only made to keep afloat and save life."

"What about the sails?"

"Those sails aren't much good except for running with the wind behind you. We want to go the other way. All long boat-voyages have been made to the westward in this hemisphere. The *Trevessa's* boats went west, and so did Bligh."

"Couldn't we go west?"

"We could, but God knows where we would end up. Out of sight of land, we could steer west till kingdom come and still be making easting in a current, without knowing. We don't know enough about the locality."

"West is right into Jap territory, dearies," Jacky reminded them.

"If you get to sea," Mr Carr advised them, "and you can't fix your position, you've got no hope of setting a course."

"That's right," Mr Cross added. "You could only go on dead reckoning; and believe me, the way these things can behave, that's exactly what it would be—*dead* reckoning. Without instruments it would be foolhardy."

"It's all right for Saturday-afternooners on Sydney Harbour: they can take a chance with patrols to pick 'em up. We are supposed to know better."

"I know it would be nice to make a miracle voyage and have headlines in the papers about it, and all be heroes. But you don't need to be told about that."

"And there's still the wounded, sir," Jacky reminded them.

Blackie clinched it. "Listen," he said, "when we were sent to Java, you know what Admiral Helfrich said: we were there to a finish. All right. We fought to a finish. We fought till our ammo was gone and they came in and fished us. No attempt has been made to rescue us. And it won't be, don't worry. As a fighting force we're written off. If we got a signal through to Navy Office now, we'd get the reply 'Look after yourselves—we can't.' "

"We've done what we can, lads. Now I think we owe a little thought to parents and wives."

"And I wonder what *they* know about us at the moment?"

Ken, who had been Chief Telegraphist in the ship, said, "We made an enemy report, and then amended it. They knew we were engaging an enemy force of superior but unknown strength. That is all they know. Nothing else was sent."

"They'll guess the rest. But they won't know the casualties."

"We'll just be 'missing after enemy action.' "

"If someone could get through and let them know, it would be a help."

"Well, the boat could give it a go."

"It would have to be a minimum crew."

"Enough to man her, and as few as possible to eat the provisions."

"I think ten men would be a minimum," John said. "You couldn't manage her in a surf with less on the oars."

They talked this over for a while, before deciding that an attempt should be made. It meant that the rest would have to stay behind, and the decision was not reached entirely without qualms: that invisible court was still nagging each man. It was a ticklish business, again, to select men for the boat. Quite a number wanted to go. John had been elected to take charge of the boat at Sangieng. Mr Carr was the leader of the Toppers Islanders. Neither had relinquished his command. Now it was spontaneously suggested that Mr Carr and John should pick a boat's crew: a total of ten fit men.

Mr Carr chose first: Alfred Wolfe, Petty Officer.

John picked: Hilton Arrat, Petty Officer.

Then in turn came: Enoch Wyatt, Sub-lieutenant; Ken Day, Chief Telegraphist; Jack Bunting, Yeoman of Signals; Jim Dresden, Leading Seaman; George Yew, Able Seaman; Gregory (Darky) Oliver, Able Seaman. It was not easy to pass good men by, but ten was the limit. So the matter was settled.

Gear was stowed in the boat, water barricoes topped up from the well and the wounded made as comfortable as possible in the fore part. Then all hands embarked and shoved off. The boat was pulled over to the bar at the river mouth. A canvas stretcher was made for Dick. The landing party hopped out in the green, sandy shallows and stood a little irresolutely about the boat's gunwale. They all wished one another good luck and gave lingering handshakes.

"Well, see you in Sydney."

"I'll buy you a pot."

"I'll drink it."

"We'll celebrate with biscuits and pemmican."

The majority of the party had soon waded off, and the wounded were safe in the shade of the palms waiting for Mr Stewart and Mr Cross, the senior officers. Now they too followed; and the boat's crew stood by the boat watching them depart.

Part 6

PRINCES ISLAND

I

THE party ashore vanished in a compact group, with a wave. The boat's crew silently shoved their boat to seaward and climbed aboard.

It was 9.30 a.m. The sea was of pale, shining blue glass. There was no breath of wind, and Refuge Island stood deserted on its own translucent reflection: green, dripping into the azure sea. With only four oars manned, they passed it on their port hand. They had decided to pull in two watches, four oars being enough to give the boat steerage-way over the still surface. They were in a kind of mental vacuum created by the departure of the others, the decisions that had been made, and the uncertain future which lay before them.

Once Refuge Island lay well astern, they seemed to be in a dream world where images stood about them at distances which no amount of toil at the enslaving oars would alter. Princes Island lay high, blue and remote ahead; Java lay green and closer to port; Old Man Krakatau with his two satellites stood on the line of the horizon—three overlapping blue cones broad on the starboard bow; Sumatra, a faint distant silhouette, was away over to starboard; astern, Refuge Island had sunk for ever from their gaze.

"If we've got to pull to Australia, we've had it." Jim said, expressing the general feeling of futility.

"Well, we needed to get clear of the land," Blackie said.

"Yes, we couldn't just sit there like a lot of bollards and wait," Fatty agreed.

"I think there's a breeze coming up, I see a few cats-paws," John said hopefully. "What about setting the sails?"

For a while the sails flapped uselessly as the boat rolled. The fitful puffs, which died at birth, exasperated the men. At last enough wind, faint though it was, filled the sails and allowed them to lay in their oars.

"Pulling's got whiskers on. Doesn't get you anywhere," Fatty said.

"It wouldn't take long to exhaust a man."

"Well," John said, "I think the oars should only be used to get us somewhere definite—within sight."

"I think we should set watches, lads," Mr Carr announced. A couple of them looked askance at each other. Bit pretentious, they thought, trying to run a lifeboat like a bloody battleship.

"Think it's worth it?" said Fatty deprecatingly.

"I do," said Sub-lieutenant Wyatt, "got to have a routine: keeps up the morale."

"Some routines I've worked," Jacky grumbled, "have only kept up my blood pressure."

"I think it's a good idea," John said. "It means order and no arguments when something has to be done. We'll have to get rest, so why not organize it?"

"Right."

"There's ten of us. How do you split that up?"

"Three watches and one spare man."

It did not take them long to select the watches. John took the Red Watch with Jim and Darky; Mr Carr took the White Watch with Fatty and Ken; Blackie took the

Blue Watch with Mr Wyatt and George. Jacky was made Dayman, and was to look after the worn gear.

"How about setting the watches?" Mr Carr said.

"Shall we start with Red?"

"Fair enough, I'm there now," John said from the tiller. "Jim, you take over the mainsheets; and Darky, you take the foresheet. Watch closed up, Mr Carr."

"Very good. White Watch will have the Afternoon, and Blue the First Dog."

It was then 11 a.m. by Jacky's watch. From now on, the wristwatch was handed over to the man at the helm at the change of each watch. The breeze had increased a little, but it was still impossible to hold the boat very close to the wind. They would not clear the jutting point of Welcome Bay on this tack. In the Afternoon Watch the wind increased and all watched with interest as the boat was pinched into the wind with each puff to try and weather the point. It was a lesson on the capabilities of the boat, and it was not encouraging. However, the wind shifted a point, and in the First Dog Watch the promontory was abaft the beam, well to leeward. And now they were in the middle of the southern end of Sunda Strait: about equidistant from Krakatau, Princes Island and the shores of Welcome Bay on Java.

In the Last Dog Watch the wind died and left them there. And it was as a primeval amphitheatre that John afterwards thought of that place in which, he always insisted, he had seen the greatest show on earth.

With the stillness, great soaring cumulus clouds rose in the west, cutting off the sunset and its colour, bringing a cold gloom down on them prematurely. The colossal cumulus anvils rose in great atomic pillars, dwarfing the mountains. "Anvils" the meteorologist calls them; and on each anvil in this vast celestial forge can be hammered out, in a couple of minutes, enough electric energy to supply a large city for fifty years.

From the feet of these great atomic piles, legions of black nimbus clouds rolled across Sunda Strait from the westward like endless Atlantic winter-combers. The light became darker than dusk and lighter than night, as if neither would own it: it was like a dread threat of complete anarchy. The sea was pressed flat into a leaden sheet with the weight of the oppressive atmosphere. The boat lay dead-still, microscopic in the great brooding scene; but to the men it was not microscopic—it was the centre of the cosmos.

John ordered Jim to brail up the main and take a couple of turns of the brails to secure the sail to the mast. He himself stood on the strongback and hove the boom of the mizzen up to the mast, then with a few deft turns secured that sail to its mast with the overhauled sheets. Now only the small triangular foresail was set: it hung limp.

"Look at those clouds hanging like big black bags of water about to burst," Blackie remarked.

"Like walking under the udders of a thousand giant cows, kinda," Jim said impressed by their shapes—so hard, distended and smooth.

The undersides of these clouds were black, but between the spherical forms they gleamed with a peculiar, steely, blue-grey light. The sky was now completely covered and the mountains to the east, beyond Pepper Bay, were swirling their heads in its massive turbulence. Searching lances of lightning stabbed outwards and downward, spitting and hissing on the sullen sea. The thunder rolled about voluminously with the deep sonorousness of an organ in a cathedral. Out of the gloom came a roaring hiss

Rain, Sunda Strait

which swept over them. They felt as if they were being beaten to the bottom of the boat with an avalanche of pebbles. It was not hail, but enormous drops of water smacking down everywhere.

John gasped. His oil-soaked hair was plastered over his face, and a thick layer of water streamed over him as if he were standing under a waterfall. With both hands he gripped the gunwale and stood bowed, muscles tensed, resisting the great weight of water falling upon him, and gazing with a fascinated rapture at the sea.

Each huge raindrop was striking the water like a bullet— thousands upon thousands of them until, by a trick of optics, a continuous after-image was registered on his visual screen. An order had come out of chaos and there, dancing on the surface of the sea, were the coronets of splashes from the bomb-like rain drops, whose ever-widening rings radiated and intersected to make the flat sea a mosaic floor.

"Roll on, my Twelve," said Jacky.

"Roll up that bloody awning and help me catch some water," Fatty said.

The blackened tin in which they had cooked the rice was washed out, and the boat's cover was spread across the boat and funnelled into it. Meanwhile each man had been licking his chops, savouring the sweet water running down his face. They caught more than half a tinful. The rain abated, and the night became a vast, empty and draughty room in which they shivered. Vagrant winds blew this way and that, chilling them without sailing the boat. It was not worth spreading the sails. It was now after 8 p.m. and White Watch were on deck. John had handed the timepiece over to Mr Carr.

"When did we last eat?" enquired Fatty.

"This morning on Refuge Island," Blackie replied dolefully.

"No wonder my backbone's trying to unscrew my navel."

Blackie, who was stand-by watch, got ten biscuits out of the tank and handed them around. "All right, you herring-gutted lot, take plenty—*one* each, and cut the big ones in half."

Each man nibbled his biscuit with care and precision. They were learning to make a full meal out of one square dry biscuit.   ___

2

John was off watch now until 4 a.m., when Blackie would call him for the Morning Watch. He wanted to sleep, but was unsettled. It was not anxiety, he told himself, but a vague kind of excitement. It was as if he had been partly initiated into a great secret and was now waiting for the final and complete revelation of the principle of life. He was on the verge of something—but how to capture it and make it a permanent idea? He knew now that, if it took him all his life, he would pursue it to the end. Perhaps the search was the thing itself: the constancy of thought one brought to it; the faith that it was there; the patience and humility before it; the realization that it was miracle in itself; the knowledge that, no matter how impersonal it may seem, it is scrupulously just and infinitely wise.

But why should he think of this now? Why should he not be thinking of his hard wet bench, or a dozen other discomforts?—the wet plaited native grass mat he had pulled around him, that was growing warm and steamy with a pungent stench? or the stiffness in his knees, shoulders, arms and legs? Yet he found he was annoyed if these discomforts intruded on his thoughts. He brushed them aside, feeling that there was some revelation imminent here in this primeval cradle of storm. The continual gunfire of thunder about them, the continual lightning-sheets of it, jagged lances and claws of it—John felt something akin to all this stirring within himself. Was it that tremendous gamut of cosmic force he had seen, from the great cumulus anvils to the coronetted splashes of the rain-drops? The cloud and the raindrop: both equally important and intrinsically the same. The idea sprang to John's mind: "Here, if anywhere, is a self-portrait of God!"

All through the First Watch this great amphitheatre echoed with the gigantic crashes of thunder, cracking like two worlds in collision and rolling away to Eternity. And, through it all, the boat and the crew were allowed to lie unmolested.

"Listen to that, will you!" Blackie was saying. "If that's not the dead spit of 'Y' Turret in anger!"

"Gives me the creeps," George said. "It's the battle of Sunda Strait all over again. Like a battle of ghost ships! Brings it all back, don't it?"

"Can't get it out of my head. I expect to see the ship steam in sight at any minute. Listen! Six-inch salvos!"

Each new flash and crack of lightning and thunder reminded them of that last night. All the brilliance, swift-ness and violence of the action, and the finale with the ship going under them and the Captain's order, "Every man for himself!"

3

John felt a shake and heard a whisper in his ear, "Right-o, me hearty, rise and shine—it's all yours." He sat up with a jerk. One of the first things he was conscious of was the dank stink of the sodden straw mat he had pulled around him. The thunder had stopped. The only noises in the world were those of the sleeping crew—deep measured breathing, and a staccato snore from the bows. Cloud had broken up, so that some clean rain-washed stars showed brightly. A light breeze was blowing and the boat was just making way, close-hauled on the starboard tack. Silently he moved aft to the tiller and took over from Mr Wyatt. Blackie handed him the watch, which he strapped on his wrist. Darky took the foresheets from George; Jim took the mainsheets from Blackie. The few clothes they wore were still wet and the light breeze made them shiver. Jim and Darky could crouch below the gunwale; but John, steering, had to sit above it.

The breeze increasing, the boat moved steadily through the water on an easy reach for Princes Island. At daybreak they were coming up with the land nicely. The first shafts of sunlight through the broken cloud were a voluptuous pleasure to them after cringing from the wind through the hours of darkness. Princes Island was a large rugged place, but they had no intention of exploring it: all they wanted was a good beach for the boat. With the morning so calm, clear and peaceful, John felt something like a Columbus who had sailed into a new world. Well, he had too, for he knew the world would never be the same to him again. He had been reborn last night in Sunda Strait.

Approaching as close to shore as possible, they found a flat sandy beach after piloting the boat over reefs and shoals. The tide was full and they were able to put her up on a good piece of sand. Spreading the sails to dry, they carried all the provisions ashore to the shelter of the over-hanging trees on the low, grassy ledge above the beach. They then sat down to review the situation.

"That mains'l's going to take some keeping in one piece," Blackie said. "Lucky if she stands a good blow."

"She's all we've got, mate." Jacky said.

They drew a rough map on the sand above the receding tide: Java and Princes Island; then, away down in the bottom right-hand corner was the west coast of Australia. When it was finished it told them nothing more than that Australia was to the south-east, which they already knew. They knew, too, that they would have to sail right into the wind's eye to get there.

"No instruments except a compass."

"Can't see that at night," Fatty reminded them.

"That means we would be blind half the time," John said.

"We couldn't get a fix," Mr Carr said.

"If we did get a fix, we would have nowhere to put it."

"We'd never know what drift we were making either, lads," Mr Carr said.

"By Guess and by God," said Jacky.

They left it at that. This was the sort of thing they had talked out before and never seemed to get any further. They all knew the answers, but none of them was ready to admit it—that the ocean passage was a long slim chance against all sailor common sense.

4

They decided to skirmish along the beach. John went north. There, strewn along the shore, were half-buried canned-fruit cases with their bottoms out. As John bent over them he felt a twinge of homesickness, for the contents had been grown and canned in the Goulburn Valley of Victoria, close to home. Each time he came across them he felt a flush of exasperation. Apart from an occasional bit

of other wreckage, there was nothing of significance. But
at the north end of the beach, on some rocks among the
mangroves, were some sizable green and white striped
winkles. John marked them down for a meal and returned
to the boat.

He found Mr Wyatt making a pair of bamboo dividers.
They were very neat and quite efficient. John admired
them. But, he thought ruefully, we have no chart to walk
them across. Mr Wyatt had felt the urge to do something
useful—even if it were only a pretence to save him from
the mental doldrums. John knew that he too had done
much the same in rigging the boat: those little extras
could have little effect on their ultimate fate, but they
were born of a sailor's pride in his vessel.

Further down the beach he found Mr Carr, Jacky, Ken
and Fatty. They were looking at some cases—four or five
of them, metal lined. They had been broken open with
the old hand axe from the boat.

"Phew! What a pong!" Jackie sniffed.

"Ammonia," Ken said.

"That will be real useful," Blackie said, coming up with
them. "We can eat it."

"Well," Fatty said hopefully, "how about, there, using
the metal part for water containers?"

"We'll try it, anyway," Mr Carr said.

"Hey!"

They turned to see Jim and George coming up from the
south.

"Take a pike at this!" Jim shouted. They were carrying
a long package between them. It was in a canvas cover.

"Well I'll be——"

"You beaut! You bloody beaut!"

"At last we've got something useful!"

217

"Where'd you get them?"

"We were just about to turn back," Jim said, "when I saw something sticking out of the sand. It was half-buried."

"Took two of us to pull it out," George added.

"Undo that lanyard and give us a look—don't crow yet!" said the sceptical Blackie. The lanyard at the end of the canvas cover was undone. George dived his hand in to grasp the end of the contents, while Jacky grabbed the cover at the other end and walked away with it. Out came a neatly made-up boat's sail already laced to its yard.

"Well I'll be ——! I don't believe it!"

"It's an omen, boys," Jim said.

John and Fatty were busy laying the sail out on the wet, tide-deserted sand to examine its condition.

"Here you are, Blackie," Fatty said elatedly, "feast your beer-sodden eyes on this lot! There's a *fores'l* as well!"

"Four-stranded rope sheets," John remarked. "They would be American, I'd reckon—ours are three-stranded."

"Well, they're brand new—I bet they have never been hoisted."

"It can blow now, boys, *this'll* do us for a storms'l— she's stronger than that rotten rag we have now."

"Don't be too hard on that rag," Jacky said loyally, "Ken and me gave our youth to get the bloody thing in one piece."

"Don't worry," John soothed him, "it's still a better fair-weather sail than this—it's much bigger."

"We can set an extra jib now to balance that native sail aft."

This, they thought, was the first bit of real luck so far. Coming so soon after the sinister experience in Labuhan, it was hard for them not to exaggerate its importance. They worked away on the boat with a new confidence until about noon, then called a halt. Under the trees they each had one dipper of water from the barrico. The dipper contained just one-sixth of a pint. They rested, surprised to find how quickly they tired now. Later they collected half a bucket of winkles, lit a fire with one of the signal flares, and boiled the shell fish in salt water. About an hour before sunset they sat down together and ate their meal.

"Ate their meal" is perhaps a euphemism: these shell fish, even in death, offered no little resistance. They would not come out of their shells as the men expected they would. To pick them out with sharpened slivers of wood was difficult.

"Who'd be a Robinson Crusoe?" snarled the disgusted Blackie.

"I know," John suggested, "crack 'em between two bits of rock like walnuts."

Thereupon arose a swinelike noise of sucking, spitting and cursing.

"Look here," Fatty said, "by the time we have eaten this lot, we'll all be in line to lay eggs."

"You're not kidding, I've eaten more shell than fish so far."

They sucked away doggedly to the end; but, though they had saved some of their precious biscuit, they could only feel they had eaten a meal of salt-water and shell.

For reference they called that place Winkle Beach; and thereafter, whenever the name was mentioned, there always came a resounding "*Bloody winkles!*"

5

They slept aboard that night, each man doing his trick of lookout from the shore, by the stores. John's trick was from 2 to 3.15 a.m. Shortly after he had taken over, he saw a great lantern hung in the sky. Its sudden appearance sent a chill through him. He was sure it had not been there a moment ago. It was undulating slightly, he thought. A ship? Can't see any sidelights. No red or green. Must be an anchor light. On the fore-stay. How the hell did it get so close without him noticing it? The Japs! They've come to get us. But a ship as close as that would be aground, surely? Cautiously he moved down the beach, so that he could see the light without the intervening branches. As he stepped into the clear he took two deep, thankful breaths. The lantern was a planet hung low in the east. It was clearly spherical and of great brilliance. Even so, looking through the branches again, he found it was still difficult to shake off the illusion—the ghost of a ship seemed to hover just off-shore for the rest of his trick.

6

Next morning they had a biscuit and a measure of water each. All the gear was put back in the boat, and they left at 9 a.m. Moving down the island to the south in the hope of finding a watering place, they came to a narrow wedge-shaped bay which looked like the mouth of a stream. They rowed in until the mangroves closed across the head of the opening. There they spent a lot of time looking for the stream, but, if there was one, they did not find it. Jim and Jacky got a couple of nasty gashes from broken mangrove stumps under the water. They gave up, and pulling out proceeded down the coast. Soon they sighted a couple of coconut palms just back from the beach. A few hundred yards further on they came upon the relics of a stick-pile jetty with a derelict hut on its end.

"Signs at last," Jim said.

"Must be water," George said, "else they wouldn't build that here."

"Reckon we ought to give it a go, there, anyway." Fatty said.

"We'll get those coconuts back there, too."

They put the boat ashore on a good shelving sandy strip. Bending the grapnel to the end of the painter, they ran it to the butt of a small tree. Then they laid out the stern anchor and the boat rode handsomely. Wading ashore, they began to walk up the beach.

"I'm bombo! I'm ding-bats!" Jacky suddenly wailed. "Can anybody see what I can see?"

Thousands of shells on the beach had arisen as one and moved to the right and slightly away from them. Then, suddenly, they sank again to immobility. As the men advanced a few paces more, all the shells got up again and marched to the left and away from them.

"Hermit crabs!" John exclaimed, recognizing these peculiar little denizens of other fishes' deserted homes. As they outgrow each shell, they leave it to find a larger one in which to insert their vulnerable, chili-shaped bodies. One claw is much bigger than the other as if, at some stage of evolution, the whole species had become victims of poliomyelitis. The arrangement, however, is practical: it allows the crab to withdraw into the host shell so that the small claw is retracted and covered by the larger, which does the job of the 'cat's eye' of the ordinary shell fish. And thus they can sit in smug security until danger is past.

"The beach is lousy with them," Darky said.

"They *real*?" Jacky pleaded, "They *dinkum*? Oh! I thought it was me sinful past."

"It's a feed, anyway, lads," Mr Carr called.

"A *feed*? Y'can't eat pink elephants! What d'y'think a pink elephant'd taste like?"

"Put him in the shade, boys," Ken said, grinning. "Buntin' tossers are crackers to start with. Don't expect him to get any better."

"We'll have a feed tonight, anyway—get big ones only, there's plenty here," John said. They were sitting resting and the beach remained stationary.

"What's to do?" Fatty asked presently.

"Those coconuts," said George.

"Water," said Ken.

"Pink elephants," murmured Jacky.

7

Jim, George, Mr Carr and Blackie took the broken-handled hatchet and went after the coconuts.

"If we get water here," Ken said, "we'll use those cherry casks—if we can scour them good enough. The bottles too."

"I'll give the casks a good go with sand," Jacky volunteered.

"We'll go into the water-getting when the others get back."

"Yep," John agreed; "meanwhile let's give the boat a final louse over and see that everything's ready for sea."

They set about providing sea-lashings for everything. It had always been a principle with John that a boat under sail, no matter how lively, should move as one piece. He loved the feel of a boat under sail, everything snug and secure, with no other sound but that of wind and water against hull and sails. So they checked everything—shrouds and lanyards and halyards, looking to the lead and run, and providing spares where possible. "This is more important than any Admiral's Inspection, Fatty, old boy," John said.

They were just wading back to the beach from the boat when the coconut party reappeared.

"Twenty-two," Mr Carr called.

"You beaut! Who climbed after them?" Jacky wanted to know.

Jim looked at him in disgust. "Have *you* tried to climb a tree, lately? You'll find this diet we been on kinda takes the monkey outa yuh. We chopped 'em down."

George gave a broken guffaw. "Fair go, Jim, don't 'xaggerate! We didn't *chop* 'em down—we *gnawed* 'em down. Look," he chuckled, "a little baby squirrel could'a' done it quicker."

"I hope no one hears about this," Blackie growled, "I'm ashamed. Bloody heroes!"

"You murdered two trees for twenty-two coco-lousy-nuts?" Jacky cried.

"Naw," George croaked, "*they* murdered *us*! Look at our hands!" And he held out his upturned palms to show them the broken blisters he had received from the rough, broken-handled axe.

"Men," Fatty said impressively, "I'm proud of you! Errol Flynn couldn't have done better."

It was obvious that the "coco-bloody-nut heroes", as Blackie called them, had had to work hard for the nuts. Since the drink in the storm on the previous night, they had each had only one-sixth of a pint of water, and they had spent several hours pulling the ungainly boat in the hot sun on those soul-blistering ash oars. It was now after 1 p.m.

"How about we splice the mainbrace?"

Each slowly sipped his sixth of a pint in turn from the pannikin. Then they set about looking for water. Back from the sea a hundred yards was an evil-smelling swamp.

"Nice drop of fever water," Jim observed.

Ken said, "It smells like it's dead."

"Let's fill the casks with that," Blackie said, "and all commit Harry Carey or something."

"There's no stream running into the swamp?" Mr Carr asked.

"No," Ken said, "not as far as we could see. We poked about a bit, but you can't get far."

"Well," John suggested, "what about we dig for some between the sea and the swamp and see what we get?"

"It won't take all of us—how about those hermit crabs? We want a good feed of them tonight."

Jim, George and Blackie said that they would get them. "Better take Jacky, too," Ken said, "then maybe he'll find out they are real and come out of the horrors."

So they collected the biggest of the shell fish and, not wanting a repetition of the Winkle Episode, they cracked the shells and extricated the odd-bodied inhabitants until the tin was almost half full. Jacky held up a specimen to the others. They looked at the chili-shaped abdomen now so vulnerable, so soft, so pallid and corpse-like. This was surmounted by a twisted, one-sided thorax with one pincer claw three or four times the size of the other.

"Ain't it 'orrible?" Blackie insisted.

"I dunno," George said in slow, measured tones. "With you in the background—with your dirty, scabby, oil-fuelled face, with yer clogged-up bugwhiskery ziff, with yer walrus mo droopin' in rags over yer snarlin' teeth—well—I dunno! Another look at you and they don't look so bad, y'know."

"Besides," Jim said, "y'c'n eat the crabs—but a cannibal'd knock up on Blackie."

They put some sea-water in the tin and placed it over a fire lit with a signal flare. "These flares are not so hot," Blackie remarked after struggling with one. "They've just about had their time."

George tended the fire while the others walked over to the water diggers. The two digging were breathless, having nothing more to dig with than boards: the coral deposit was stubborn. The rest were looking intently at the bottom of the hole, giving the impression of dirty, rapacious ruthlessness. Were they burying a victim or exhuming a treasure?

"Here," John panted and threw his board out of the hole, "someone else have a go."

"Same again," Ken grunted and climbed out.

Mr Carr and Fatty took their places. After a while water started to seep in. "A little deeper yet," Mr Carr panted. Then the sides started to cave in and the sand became sloppy. "Taste it!" Fatty put some of the wet sand to his lips and sucked it. "Hard to tell," he said, "not *real* salt, anyway. Can't tell whether it's this or the pong of the swamp." Carefully scooping the sand at the bottom, they were able to make a shallow pool from which they could bail. They found it was brackish, but thought it fit enough to drink.

"What if we put some charcoal in it?" John suggested. "It might absorb some of the impurities."

"Give her a go there, anyway," Fatty agreed. "They use it in gas masks."

"It couldn't make it more horrible," Blackie said sourly.

"We'll use this stuff before the Sangieng water," Mr Carr said.

"If it starts to send us mad, we can switch," said Jacky.
"How'll we tell?" George chuckled.

They stowed the water in the cherry casks and in the bottles for which Mr Wyatt and Blackie had cut wooden bungs. Then they gathered at the top of the beach near the fire and yarned. They had done all that they could think of for the boat. John was conscious that they had done a little more: each man had indulged himself in his own small way—and it had given comfort to the mind. "Like whistling in the dark," John thought; "well, it works too, sometimes."

8

They speculated over the contents of the tin on the fire.
"Hope they taste better than they looked."
"They're nice and pink anyway."
"This is Sunday," Jacky suddenly reminded them.
"So what?"
"Well, how about we celebrate?"
"On what?" Blackie asked.
"Hermit crabs, Jap biscuits—and little lollies," Jacky said.

So they made it a feast, more by the way they went at it than by what they ate. They consumed the crabs, eating only the soft bodies and discarding the deformed claws and the tiny legs upon which they had dragged their continually changing homes. Then Mr Carr took the Japanese kit-bag Blackie handed him. It was a double-ended sausage bag tied at each end to sling across the shoulder. From this they took a small calico bag of biscuits. "They're about the same size as the small bone of a pig's trotter," Jacky said. "What's the issue? How many's she run?"

"One bag enough?"

"Pretty lousy. Don't be shonkey with 'em!"

"Come on, another bag! Hang the expense! Put it on my slop-chit," Fatty said.

From the two bags they each got five biscuits and three little lollies.

"Now for a drink of water!"

This was bailed out of the waterhole. After they had drunk, they fell to talking. They all felt optimistic. They dreamed wild dreams aloud to each other: it was like having taken a ticket in a big-prize lottery, and dream-spending the prize money right away. At the same time, at the back of their minds, they realized that this might be just another ticket to tear up after the draw.

This afternoon, as Mr Carr and the rest of them stood in the water by the bows of the boat, Fatty had said, "She ought to have a name. There's no honour and glory in a ship without a name!"

"Got no Princess Marina here, this time," said Blackie, nostalgically.

"What did she say, again?" Fatty asked.

"She said, 'I rename this ship *Perth*, and may God bless all who sail in her.' And she said it very nicely, too."

"What'll we call this one, then?"

"I don't know what she *has* been—some time British— but Jap just before we got her," Fatty said.

"She's Wallaby now, anyway," said George, "so we'll give her a Wallaby name."

"How about *Anzac*?"

"Good idea! The old Zacca's gone—that name's not on the list now. We'll grab it."

"All right," Mr Carr said, "I rename this ship *Anzac*—"

"And God help all who sail in her!" George chuckled.

227

John took a piece of charcoal and inscribed the letters A-N-Z-A-C on either bow, cutting deeply into the thick, coagulated oil there.

"Daa-da-da—ta-da-da-da-daaaaaaa!" sang Jacky to the tune of the 'Still', used to call ships to attention for saluting in passing. They all gave very admiral-like salutes of extreme carelessness and brevity. Such was the christening ceremony of ship's lifeboat *Anzac*, on Sunday, March 8th, 1942.

Peace settled over the Strait of Sunda, which became a broad mirror in the dusk: Old Man Krakatau was smoking a last pipe before night fell, and as they looked out, the derelict bamboo jetty wove lazy snakes on the barely audible sea. The boat rode quiet and serene like a resting swan contemplating its own reflection. The breath of Nature was warm. The men, having done everything they could, settled to an untroubled sleep. There were questions which could not be answered until they had passed beneath the velvet vault of this lovely starry night. As did their Elizabethan forebears, they reposed their souls in the hands of God.

Part 7

JAVA HEAD

I

As they looked astern at the bamboo jetty it merged with the tangle of growth ashore, and the highest peak, called Raska, towered a thousand feet above, less than a mile away. The day was moderately overcast, the wind was light. The oars had been boated and the sails set. They were close-hauled with the wind SSE., hoping to clear Java's First Point and Java Head in one reach.

"She'll do her deep-water trials, now."

"Now we'll find out if Mr Cross was right or not."

"I don't reckon he'd be far wrong," said Blackie, at the tiller.

"Don't *cruel* it before we get under way," Jacky snapped.

"She's carrying a bit too much weather helm," John told them. "Rig the bowsprit and the Yankee fores'l—that should help to balance the mizzen."

This was done and, as the wind increased and the ruffled sea turned a sparkling blue, the sails drew into firm curves without flutter or wrinkle. Shrouds were set up, sheets trimmed and the halyards made up, coiled and stopped, clear for instant running. Oars were lashed out to their own sides of the boat. Boat-hooks and bearing-out spars were hung in beckets so that they would not roll about but could be drawn forth as easily as cutlasses. John sat on the strongback on the lee side and looked the boat over critically.

"Well, it's up to the old girl herself, now," Ken said.

Over the port bow and gradually falling abeam was Mew Island. Friar Rocks were beginning to appear at the foot of the Point like a row of jagged teeth upthrust from a lower jaw. As they raised them further and brought them fairly abeam, white foam could be seen about them. On the point above stood an ideal conception of a lighthouse: a straight, white column above seething treachery. A brilliant shaft of sunlight streamed through a break in the clouds; and only this pure column, in all the three hundred and sixty degree circle in which they lay, was dramatically lit.

"I wonder what those light-keeper jokers are doing over there? Wonder if they'll report us?" Jacky queried.

"What *us*?" Darky said scornfully.

"Well, we're only a mile or so out, and they'd have a good glass."

"Look," Blackie said, pointing high in the air to the northward, over their quarter. They could see, below the cloud, a small familiar shape. It was a single-engined float plane with its two long floats splayed beneath like the webbed feet of an alighting albatross.

"Just a coincidence."

"They all make me nervous."

"He could come down and have a look at us—and if he felt like it, he could have a bit of target practice."

"Nice thought!" Mr Wyatt said.

They watched the plane in silence. Overhead, he seemed to hesitate: he flew a little to the left, and then to the right, as if puzzled. To their immense relief, he then took a wide circle and went south and east. "Keep going, mate," Jim encouraged, "we won't sink any of your bleedin' Navy."

But each was more relieved than he cared to admit then. This enemy plane was an unwelcome intrusion: they had slipped through into another world, which had nothing to do with the Japs. It was a simple world, as old as the sea. War had put them out of the war—all right, let it leave them out now! They had enough to do. So, for the time being, war did leave them alone.

Mr Carr and John sat watching the wake. Occasionally they glanced at one another, but said nothing. Blackie looked at Jacky's watch on his wrist. It was exactly 9.30 a.m. and the lighthouse was dead abeam. They all remarked it. "Remember the log," John said. This was taken by them as their actual point of departure, the beginning of the voyage. The breeze was now sufficient to heel the boat and give her steady headway. It was a good opportunity to find out how she sailed. That is why Mr Carr and John were watching the wake. The others were watching the bow-wave.

"Like a destroyer," Darky said: "must be doing six knots."

Mr Carr, looking in the wake said, "Two, perhaps."

"What?"

"That's about all."

"Gawd struth," Jim said disgustedly, "are we goin' to Australia?"

"Never mind the speed," John told them, "look at the wake."

"What do you mean?"

"I mean that the way we are headed, our wake is trailing up to windward nearly forty-five degrees."

"Yeah?"

"That means all that is *leeway*."

"Struth! Can't we point any closer?"

"That wouldn't do us any good—besides, she's as close as she'll go. It's just within three points."

"Where does that get us?"

"Back where we started—or further, if we have to beat dead into the wind," Blackie explained. "To get to windward you have to make port and starb'd tacks—each time you're about forty-five degrees off the wind, zig-zagging towards it. Right?"

"Yes."

"Well, you're dropping off forty-five degrees by your wake, which means you are practically only going *sideways* to your course each time."

"Oh!"

"It will be no South-east Trade for Australia—even if we found it. Eastwards we have the land with us to give us some idea. Westwards we have only ocean or Japs, and no instruments. God knows where we would be."

After clearing Java Head, they held their course for some time to gain sea-room. Java Head! This was the first time John had seen it, for he had been watch below and turned in when they had passed to the northward. Now, in spite of their problems, he looked at that point of land with reverence. This was a salient point not only in geography, but in history too. The history of a sea phase: of romance and unbelievably hard facts of argosies of spice and tea. Down this Strait and by this headland Anson and Drake had passed. Over this narrow strip of water, difficult water, sailing ships had for centuries come and gone. Helpless vessels in the landlocked strait, becalmed, had been attacked by the Malay pirates—the same breed as had, this very week, murdered some of *Perth*'s ships-company. The urgent necessity of making money from tea had sent beautiful ships racing past this point. They sailed under legendary names, adding further legend to them. *Sir Lancelot, Ariel, Taeping, Hallowe'en, Cutty Sark, Caliph, Belted Will, Fiery Cross, Thermopylae, Titania, Lahloo*—these names sprang unbidden to John's mind in stately procession, filling him with a deep, silent reverence for the past. The past which was so much a part of that world in which they were now sailing—how he wished he were closer to that past, for then he would not be so ignorant in this present!

But to this extent at least he was a realist. He was conscious of the limits of his knowledge—he had only so much experience—so much opportunity, and so much wasted opportunity: therefore, just *so* much knowledge. You can't get more out of the pot than you put into it, he reasoned. Luck could help him; but his reverence for the eternal order of things was too deep for him to expect the Universe to change step just to make a pretty story out of his life. When, back on Sangieng, they had elected him to skipper the boat, he was privately appalled, though immediately flattered. He was known to have been, in the past, mad on boat-sailing, venturing forth when others would not face the rough weather. They knew he had enjoyed this, and so it won him the kind of reverence which the ancients had for the eccentric or insane. John found himself resenting this, though for reasons of morale he could not deny it. That he was frailly human and pitifully limited he was only too well aware. But why must everyone want nothing less than complete success? Was that always more important than the being or the doing? He was prepared to go from day to day as long as necessary; but he knew he was not going to immolate himself for the sake of a myth or to make a sensational story; nor would he spend his life, if he retained it, hating his failures or inventing stories to justify them. If he failed, it would be a measure of himself and he would know himself just that much better.

The wind veered south and they went about on to the starboard tack, heading a bit better than east-south-east. The land was now under their lee. "All right in daylight," John said, "but we wouldn't want it at night."

"No fear," Mr Wyatt said.

All afternoon they held this course, until they raised Kelapa Island fine on the port bow. They all looked at the atlas. On that scale it looked quite an impressive day's run. They reviewed the provision situation.

"At one biscuit a day, we've got thirty-six days left."

"How about the water?"

"On minimum rations—one-third of a pint a day: I'd reckon about fifty days."

"That counting that 'orrible stuff?"

"Yep!"

On the starboard bow, grey rain-squalls were seen sweeping up towards Kelapa. They had just been able to distinguish Trowers Island beyond Kelapa, but now it was obscured. Kelapa was insubstantial and cold, mist-grey; white horses galloped before the increasing wind; and John, now at the helm with the Red Watch, laid the boat closer to it.

"Looks like we might weather Kalapa yet," John said. With the increasing wind, the boat appeared to sail much better.

"You beaut," Fatty said, delighted.

But darkness came down before they made the island. Mr Carr relieved John. A biscuit spread with pemmican and a measure of water were issued. Slowly they chewed and relished the biscuit: but with the water it was different; they had only one pannikin and, while drinking, each man could feel the impatience of the others. Therefore only the last man could take his full time over it, so this was a privilege given to each in strict turn.

2

Just before dark they had gone about on to the port tack and, as the wind backed a few points, they were headed almost due south. The lighthouse could still be seen winking over their starboard quarter. Mr Carr counted carefully. "Flashing white, every thirty seconds," he pronounced. At 8 p.m., with Java Light still winking confidentially, John relieved Blackie for the First Watch. He was to find out what the hours of darkness could mean.

There was no "star to steer her by". The stars were asleep in a thick blanket of overcast. There was no light for the compass. John was steering by the wind and the repeated flashes of Java Head became their Pole Star. South was safe: it put the reef-bound coast further to leeward and took them south for their next easting. As yet the weather had set no pattern, nor had the watches recurred often enough to take on a rhythm. By about 9 p.m. the watches below had gone to some sort of rest. The side-benches held three each side, and the midship thwarts each took one. But the positions were varied throughout the voyage by fad, fancy, invention, exasperation and boredom. It was surprising that, with only ten men in the boat, it seemed impossible for at least two men not to be touching each other. As the men became enervated and short-tempered, the touching of them was like two sticks in the hands of an Australian aboriginal— it soon produced smoke and heat as readily as flint on steel. This was mostly in the dark hours, when each man had drawn about him a comforting caul of isolation—

those silent hours when we revel in expansive dreams or cringe in apprehension.

John sat at the tiller. It was dark, but he could see the livid gleam of the bow-wave; he could sense, and almost see, the set of the sails. He could feel the movement of the boat which told him the shape of the sea. He could see, astern, the flash of the light—a spark of life in the dark womb in which they now swam.

The boat was quiet, the breeze was dying, and a warm breath of air enveloped them. John looked into the darkness uneasily. Away astern, skeleton-white forks of lightning fingered out bonily as if clawing at the hills of Java. Thunder was muffled and distant. Soon the warm air was moving in gusts and increasing steadily. John laid the boat on a course by the wind, keeping the light over his port quarter. Then the light blurred and vanished. The boat held good way and steered firmly. He was confident that he had the feel of her: close-hauled, with the wind and sea on the port bow—just a touch of weather helm.

The wind increased. Wave-crests were now breaking. The boat lay well over, held firmly by the wind. Her speed increased, and now and again she would drop into the trough with a great splash, shouldering the seas aside with assurance. John felt the joyous thrill which can only come from a boat under sail flying through the wind and water. "This is what we want," he exulted, "this will push us on." Still the wind increased. The seas became higher and steeper. "Too much weather helm," John decided. "Here, Jim!" he called, "snatch a turn with your sheets. Hold the tiller a tick; I'm going to furl the mizzen." Quickly he hauled away the topping lift of the boom, belayed it around the strongback, overhauled the sheets and passed them around the mast and sail as a gasket.

Then he took the tiller again. "That should ease her," he said to Jim, invisible to him in the darkness. All he could see now was the faint phosphorescence of the broken water outside the boat. It was by the feel of the sea on the port bow that he was now sailing.

"Seas're getting up a bit," Jim remarked.

Now the boat was pitching violently and crashing into the troughs of the waves with a booming from her metal skin. It unsettled the watches below.

"Better see the shire council about this bloody road. What do we pay our rates for?" growled Jacky.

All of them were now sitting up to brace themselves. Lightning slithered out and crackled on the sea. It lit up a heavy inferno-like sky. Thunder enveloped them; the wind increased, adding to the pandemonium. Sheets of water beat down on them from the clouds, and the shattered wave-crests swept across them like broken window-glass. The lightning continually flared, to vanish before a picture was formed on the retina. It gave John a sensation of near-blindness. All that was left to him was the feel of the sea. Desperately he felt for it holding the boat true to it—the sea *must* give the direction of the wind.

The movement was so wild now that all hands were clinging on to avoid being thrown out of the boat. It was rearing up, crashing down, heeling far over. Men were gasping from the violence of it. John knew he had to keep the boat sailing at all costs. As long as she moved, she lived. Stop her, and the sea would pounce on her from all sides. Those livid flashes of lightning, which lit up everything in a magnesium glare, revealed nothing. Nevertheless, John endeavoured to watch close aboard over the weather side for the racing crests, thinking only, "Which way do they run? Keep them on my port bow!"

In the littoral of the Styx

Water Beach, Princes Island, 1942 (see p. 222)

Close hauled

Suddenly there was a great thunderous clap, which seemed to come from inside the boat. She was wrenched violently sideways as if she had been kicked like a football.

"Good God!" he heard Mr Carr's voice out of the dark.

"What's up with you? Can't you hold a bloody course?" came Blackie's shout of anger.

"What the hell are you talking about? I've got the sea over the port bow. What bloody more can I do?" John shouted back, no less angry.

"*Port* bow?" screamed Blackie. "We've jibed!"

Suddenly the boat, the whole sea and the world itself seemed to drop from under John. If the sea was on the port bow, then the wind must be on the *other* side to have jibed them! The mainsail had come across the boat with one mighty explosion from starboard (where it was sheeted in) to port. They were lucky to have mast or sail left. It was just as well he had taken such care with the shrouds and fitted preventers, which had seemed superfluous then. But he was still spinning in the abyss. Spray and rain were contradicting one another: the pitching of the boat told him nothing, either.

"Where *is* the bloody wind?" he yelled.

Mr Carr came to his rescue. He was standing in the stern-sheets, not an arm's length from John but completely invisible to him, and inaudible too, unless he shouted. Mr Carr's hand had found the clew of the mainsail, and he could feel its pull to port.

"On the starb'd quarter! Put your helm *down*!" he bawled. "Jim," he snapped to another invisible figure, "snatch the sheet out of that fairlead and pass it over to port."

"Ease your helm! Hold her there!"

They were now close-hauled on the starboard tack—

but not too close, lest they should come up into the wind unexpectedly and lie helpless in irons. They tried to keep the wind broad on the bow. A sheet of lightning of longer duration than the rest revealed a sea that was crazy—a sea that was crossing itself dangerously.

For over an hour the storm raged at its worst, and during that whole time Mr Carr gave John helm orders. He was acting as John's "seeing-eye". But Mr Carr, too, was blind; he was reading the mainsail as a blind man would read braille, with his hand on the smooth, taut curve at the foot of the sail.

Within two hours the sea had gone down and was running true with a fine steady breeze. Clouds drew back to reveal star-spangled patches of velvet sky. Java Head was winking indefatigably—but now it was on the *port* bow!

"We've been turned right round!" John exclaimed. "We're heading straight back for the coast."

"Just shows you, there, how easy it would be to pile up if the weather stayed bad," Fatty said.

They went about on the port tack, and the rest of the night was uneventful.

3

When John came off watch at midnight and lay down on the hard wooden side-bench, he did not go to sleep at once. Lying on his back, he watched the stars show momentarily through the clouds. He reflected on what he thought was a miserable exhibition on his part. In ordinary times you don't just bluff others—you bluff yourself too, and don't know it. When your bluff is called, you find out. He was glad he had found himself out. I shall be a bit more of a wake-up now, he thought: we *do* kid ourselves, and forget the next fella's just as good.

What about those sailors a hundred years ago? the men who sailed the Tea Clippers and the Wool Clippers or any of the sailing ships then? We think we are a bit superior to them: we are educated. Educated for what? And what do we really know about these men? They were poor: they had hardly any clothes: they had less food and only token pay. When they completed a voyage, they got drunk, whored, went broke and were shanghaied, or meekly sought another berth. Always back to the sea, because they knew nothing else. They were ignorant, dumb brutes to pull, haul, furl and stow; to chip, paint, scrub, rig and blacken-down. That's what we usually think.

But, lying here at sea off Java Head, where so many of these simple men had passed, John felt that he had entered a great sanctuary inhabited by the gentle souls of these mortally profane and bawdy sailors. They had sailed their ships on nights like this, and in the dark confusion there had been no confusion at all—the myriad blocks, halyards, gaskets, pins, cleats, ringbolts and braces were all woven into a purposeful design. This finely spun fabric of the sailing ship was like the warp and woof of Time and Space itself. Time and again they would come back to it. No! They were not just drunk out-of-works looking for a job. When they joined their ships each time, they were homing on a deep instinct—deeper than consciousness could ever explain to them.

Take the Figure-head as a symbol of the ship's soul. Every spoke of the wheel has moved it; every halyard, every brace has given it the activity of life; every man, too, who has trodden her decks or climbed aloft in her, has left something of himself in that figure-head. Thrashing her way to windward, shouldering a path through wild seas with her weather bow, dripping and shaking. Running

242

before a gale with her kicking helm in the hands of the best men, under lower tops'ls only, the men aloft desperately trying to keep the rest of the sails in the gaskets to prevent them from being blown to ribbons. A greybeard with a boiling top comes up swiftly from astern, swooping beneath the counter, lifting the ship roughly on its hoary shoulders and pushing the figure-head down in the boiling of the bow. The mountain of water rushes forward, filling the waists and leaving the deck-houses and fo'c's'le like lonely little islands. There is a dreadful pause: she drags like lead—awash like a rotten log. Then the bows rise again on the sweeping wave, belching foam and loose water, and she slips back into the windless valley between moving ranges of water. There she wallows, emptying her washports.

So for years the ship goes on, pounding and pounding. And just as a bar of iron, being beaten, will have magnetism induced into it because it lies between the north and south magnetic poles; so does the ship, lying between the Celestial and Terrestial Poles, through which flow the lines of psychic force, have induced into her the magnetism of a soul.

4

John began to awaken about seven o'clock. The night had been somewhat uncomfortable: the iron knees running across at intervals from the side of the boat kept probing at him, and the pungent stench of his sodden grass mat almost suffocated him. He growled when Darky, sleeping in the next billet forward, kicked his head with restless feet. Only the noises of the boat were comforting during those dark, chill hours. Nevertheless, at no time had he regained full consciousness until he heard Mr Carr call, "Heave-ho, lads! Rise and shine!"

The whole crew sat up and looked at one another: dull lustreless hair, black oil-soaked skins whitish in salt-caked patches, and each face framed in the horror of a ten-day beard.

"Gawd!" shuddered Jacky, "This is the real crook part of ship wreck—having to look at you bastards."

They sluiced themselves with sea water from over the side, flicked off the surplus with their hands and sat on the gunwales facing the sun like sea gulls to dry. Blackie had the boat on an easterly course with a light wind.

"At least we're goin' the right way," Jim praised the coxswain.

The sea was pale with a faint, long swell. The sky was clear, and the new sun was pleasant on their encrusted skins.

"What about breakfast?" Fatty suggested.

One biscuit and one measure of water were issued. At eight o'clock, Red Watch closed up. They washed the boat down with salt water and bailed her out. They discovered that the cherry casks of fresh water were ruined by the sea. Many of the bottles were also empty—they had capsized and the wooden corks had leaked.

They talked over the water shortage, deciding that they would continue with the present ration and, if that became intolerable, they would put in somewhere. They all accepted this. There were no real problems of conduct or discipline in the boat: they had all come from a hard discipline and been conditioned to take things as they found them. In the past they had had to submit to many harsh and outrageous decisions—things about which they belly-ached at the time, making a great noise on the mess-decks, but accepting them just the same, for the Navy and the ship are paramount. The fact that they were now serving in their H.M.A.S. *Anzac* laid upon them the same obligation of simple duty.

By 9 o'clock there was not a breath of wind. The boat rolled slightly on the oily swell. The sea surface became polished, smoky glass. The sky took on a coppery tinge around the horizon, and the sun was a molten ball climbing slowly to the meridian. Pale and powder-blue, faint and distant like smoke, a diminutive silhouette of a couple of Java's mighty peaks lay on the horizon. Except for a slight rolling, the boat was immobile.

"Seems a good opportunity to list the survivors in the log," Mr Carr said.

The log was a book John had picked up in Main Street, Labuhan. It was an album-like book almost as big as a family bible. It had thick, brown leaves which were permeated with the pleasing spicy smell of cinnamon. In it, at Water Beach, John had made a sketch of the boat, showing the bamboo jetty and Krakatau. He had been detailed to keep the log. Already they had listed the skiff's party with the Malay woman and the two children; the Americans of Topper's Island; and the twenty-two *Perth*'s who had left Sangieng in the wooden boat with the split plank, as well as the party they had left at Labuhan. John, under the appropriate dates, had jotted down a skeleton log of their doings.

And now was the first real opportunity to set about piecing together the events of those days before the sinking. They began with their arrival in Sourabaia and worked through, fitting the pieces as best they could. They had a fair cross-section to work from.

Mr Carr had been in the after conning position, the secondary navigation bridge. Mr Wyatt had been in the transmitting station down in the bottom of the ship and the heart of the 6-inch control. George was on the bridge, on the captain's port enemy bearing indicator. Jim was in charge of "Y" shell handling room. Blackie was Captain of "Y" turret, from the gunhouse to the magazine. Ken was the Chief Telegraphist stationed in the main wireless office. Jacky was a Yeoman of Signals on the flag deck at the foot of the foremast, abaft the bridge structure. Almost vertically above him sat Fatty in the 4-inch high-angle director which, except for the masthead, was the highest manned position in the ship. Darky was on the 4-inch gun deck, an ammunition number. John was Action Chief Quartermaster down in the lower steering position. So, from their various points of view and experience, they each contributed to a mosaic of their recent past.

"Seemed fishy, right from the jump," Jim said.

Part 8

JAVA SEA

I

THEY had arrived in Sourabaia to join the ABDA Force—American, British, Dutch and Australian—and to become part of the Eastern Striking Force. They were new in the area. They thought they were going to stop the rot which had started in Singapore. It was February 26th, 1942.

What they did not know was that on the 23rd General Wavell had received orders to leave Java and set up headquarters elsewhere. The General was convinced that further defence of Java was futile. Since the 24th, Admiral Doorman had been at sea with his ships. On the 27th, Admiral Helfrich reluctantly gave permission for the British cruisers *Dragon, Danae* and *Hobart,* with destroyers *Tenedos* and *Scout,* to withdraw from the area; but he later complained that one-third of available sea-power had not been there at the show-down.

Thus Admiral Doorman was left with his own flagship, *De Ruyter* (5·9-inch cruiser), supported by cruisers *Java* (5·9-inch Dutch), *Houston* (8-inch American), *Exeter* (8-inch British), and *Perth* (6-inch Australian). His destroyers were *J. D. Edwards, Alden, Ford* and *Paul Jones* (American); *Kortenaer* and *Witt De With* (Dutch); *Encounter; Jupiter* and *Electra* (British). This was the force which *Perth* had joined at about 2 o'clock in the afternoon of the 26th.

It was a low grey day: smoke was rising thickly from two

bombed-out ships, as well as from several warehouses ashore. Japanese raiding planes had just departed. *Perth* had entered harbour under an Air Raid Red, and had not let go her anchor until the Green was passed. There were no Allied fighters to be seen: it made a dismal and gloomy picture. Older members of the ship's company read the signs and remembered the fall of Greece and Crete. They knew then, without any official information, what sort of a job they had on hand. They had lived through this sort of thing at least twice before. They knew that those past escapes had been sheer luck. What they did not anticipate was the type of leadership they would have to endure, or the unfair handicaps placed on that leadership. Those handicaps, inherent in such a hastily formed and mixed group, were to be faced with whatever ready philosophy one could muster; but the lack of intelligence and liaison from shore headquarters was heartbreaking.

The British Prime Minister had already sent a message to O.C. British Air Forces in Java: "Every day gained is precious, and I know that you will do everything humanly possible to prolong the battle." The sailors knew nothing of this, but their intuition left them in no doubt as to the desperate state of affairs.

On arrival, Captain Waller went over to the flagship, while the ship's company anxiously awaited his return to confirm or scotch wild rumours. As soon as the Captain had returned, it was announced that they would proceed to sea at 8 p.m. Reconnaissance had reported a large, heavily escorted convoy headed south towards Sourabaia. The striking force was to intercept it and destroy it. The Captain said, "We hope to meet the Nips tonight and give them hell." It looked easy on paper. The report was: Course SW., near Arenos Island—30 transports, two cruisers and four destroyers. Admiral Helfrich ordered, "You must continue attacks until enemy is destroyed."

It seemed bad from the beginning. As the fleet was getting underway, *De Ruyter* collided with a tug and water-barge, sinking them both. This caused some delay and affected the spirits of the men. It was dark when the Force finally cleared the channel and the mine-fields off Sourabaia Strait. American bombers had attacked a convoy near Barwean Island, but Doorman received no inkling of this until four hours later. At 1 a.m. the Squadron altered course to intercept. *Perth* remained closed up at Action Stations all night.

By morning, nothing had been sighted, and nothing had happened except that the men's nerves had become brittle from disappointment and lack of sleep. *Perth's* radar revealed aircraft prowling above the cloud-layer. At 9 a.m. a single aircraft, high and fast, dropped a stick of bombs between the cruisers and destroyers, near *Jupiter*. They were shadowed continually. Sometimes there was a feint and the A.A. crews went into action. This cat-and-mouse game went on all day. The enemy could obviously avoid all contact with the utmost ease. The situation was passed back to headquarters. The reply came: "Despite air-attacks you will proceed eastwards. Search for and attack enemy." Doorman replied significantly: "Was on eastward heading after search from Sapoedi to Rambang. Success of which depends on getting good reconnaissance information, which last night *failed me*. Destroyers will have to refuel." At 12.40 p.m. he made a further signal: "This day the personnel reached the limit of endurance: tomorrow the limit will be exceeded." Shortly after this they began to retire towards Sourabaia, to lie behind the minefields and refuel the destroyers.

Throughout *Perth* there was general frustration and weariness, accentuated by the enemy's power to sit over them with aircraft and make fools of them on the surface. They were denied all air support—the only four Brewster Buffaloes were escorting the four remaining dive-bombers. The depressing atmosphere of the fall of Greece had returned.

"Left out on our own again, like a shag on a rock!" Fatty said bitterly.

2

"The force was returning from an abortive sweep carried out the night before," wrote Captain Waller in his action narrative.

As the squadron sailed through the swept channel, a sudden rain-squall came down, catching the Bridge personel before they could get their oilskins. The Captain, with the rest of them, was drenched. He sent his steward to get him dry shorts, a shirt and a towel. Then, standing just abaft the chart table amidships, he stripped himself naked and vigorously rubbed himself down, unconcerned and unselfconscious amid his officers and men.

George said, "The only thing I thought a bit funny was that he didn't have his pipe."

At 2.27 p.m. a reconnaissance report was received of an escorted convoy with a strong covering force, west of Barwean Island. All ships altered course one-eight-o degrees and steamed back up the swept channel to the sea. "We are altering course to intercept the enemy."

"I bloody-well hope so," grumbled the sceptics.

Admiral Nishimura was perfectly well informed of all this. He had deployed his forces to his own satisfaction and was steaming ahead for contact, holding all the trump cards. He knew the forces and the disposition with which he had to deal.

The Allies were expectant but guessing. The ships at sea were blind, and headquarters ashore seemed reticent in passing on intelligence; and from this derives the whole pattern of the action, as *Perth* saw it.

The Allies had turned to make contact with the enemy. The order was now: destroyers—*Electra* ahead, with *Encounter* to port and *Jupiter* to starboard, forming the screen. The cruisers followed in column: *De Ruyter* (Flag), leading *Exeter*, *Houston*, *Perth* and *Java*. The destroyers had been leading on entering the channel but now, with the exception of the British, they were unable to take station ahead. *Kortenaer* had boiler trouble and could not make more than 24 knots; she was now 4,000 yards to port of *Edwards*. The Americans had been ordered to the disengaged bow, but because of bad machinery they could not pass ahead of the Dutchman.

Fatty said, "What we really needed there was Andy Cunningham and the Eastern Med. Fleet. I coulda cried when I saw what was happening!"

"Imagine how old Hec must have felt," Ken said, "after he'd been a Flotilla Skipper with a fleet like Andy's. Of course, the crook engines were not the Dutchy's fault."

"No, but what happened later on was," George put in. "Hec was nearly crying at some of the things that were done."

"After all," Mr Wyatt said, "the force had been so hastily formed—and the Dutch hadn't fought a naval engagement for a couple of hundred years. How could he do better?"

At 4 p.m., *Electra* made an enemy report back to the

racing ships steering north-west. She reported two battle-ships, one four-funnelled cruiser and destroyers.

"That gave me a nasty taste in my mouth—the battlers bein' there," George said.

"Yes, but they amended it to two modern eight-inch cruisers," Ken reminded him.

The squadron increased to 26 knots and, at 5.14 p.m. the enemy was sighted by the cruisers. *Perth* broke out her battle ensigns at the fore and main mastheads. Curiously, this simple routine act had a stimulating effect on some of the veterans of *Houston*. "That meteor flag of England sure looked good," they said.

Two 8-inch cruisers, *Hagura* and *Natchi* and destroyers; and, nearer, a *Jintsu* cruiser with a destroyer flotilla, moved from left to right on approximately a parallel course. At 4.16 p.m., the Japanese heavy cruisers opened fire at 28,000 yards, directing it towards *Exeter* and *Houston*, who opened fire in turn at 4.17 and 4.18 p.m. respectively. *Jintsu* opened fire about this time on *Electra*, in the van.

The Japanese fire was accurate, pitching pretty close, short or over. The men fighting the ships from below could hear the abrupt, slapping crash of the projectiles exploding in the water. Those on deck heard the cracketing as they passed low overhead. John, on the wheel, could hear this vicious sound come echoing down sixty feet of voice-pipe from the bridge. This increased the tension for those below, who could see nothing of what went on in the brilliant sunshine above. They longed for the reassurance of their own main armament making reply. The accuracy of the enemy fire was assisted by aircraft spotting, which reported back the fall of shot and every alteration of course ABDA made. It made them sitting ducks. The range was now between 26,000 and 28,000 yards.

Although *Exeter* and *Houston* appeared to be the main targets, the light cruisers were being surrounded by splashes too. The whole of the Allied Force was left in close formation: thus the 6-inch ships were in the unenviable position of being out of range, but forming a vulnerable target for the enemy. Captain Waller wrote in his narrative: "*Perth* was still out of range of the enemy cruisers, and I found this long period of being Aunt Sally very trying without being able to return the fire." But George and Fatty recalled that at the time he had said much more—and with Anglo-Saxon simplicity. He was appalled at the tactics. He wanted a Nelsonian order: Engage the enemy more closely.

"What possible bloody good can we do here?" he fumed. "We should be in there having a whack at them—not sitting here waiting to be sunk."

3

It must be remembered that this man talking was no novice. He had fought from the beginning of the war, two years and nine months ago, against all sorts of odds. To him the odds were only incidental to the job in hand. He had led the 10th Destroyer Flotilla, better known as the "Scrap Iron Flotilla". I think it was the Germans who christened it. Captain Waller was not trigger-happy. Cool, detesting show and pretension, he wanted only unadorned efficiency. He was quick to scold, but quicker to let a man up again. On one occasion, the Quartermaster had fallen foul of the Officer of the Watch over the misinterpretation of an order. It began to look as if the O.O.W. would take the matter through the official red-tape and the Captain would find himself obliged to disrate the leading seaman. Hec sensed this quickly and, going straight to the voice-pipe, called sharply, "Quartermaster!" "Sir!" came the reply. "Don't be so bloody wet!" and the incident was closed.

At the Battle of Matapan, acting independently during the night of dog-fights in which the destroyers were involved, he had torpedoed a cruiser, damaged another and badly damaged a destroyer. This was the man who now, naturally, found his position "very trying".

It was not that Captain Waller did not know what bad machinery was: his flotilla had been just as ancient as those old American "four-pipers". He accepted that as part of the problem. This is what the most qualified of authorities, Admiral Cunningham, said when Captain Waller and *Stuart* (with one engine completely out of action) left the Mediterranean Fleet:

> We on the Mediterranean Station much regret that H.M.A.S. *Stuart* has to leave us. This gallant ship has achieved an unsurpassed record under the command of Captain Waller. In all major operations of the Mediterranean Fleet she has played a leading role and no call for a difficult duty has ever been in vain. To keep this old ship operational and efficient, the work of the Engine Room Department has been above praise. The departure of this great little ship and her gallant crew is a loss to the Mediterranean Fleet.

Hec was great enough to make the absence of one rusty, faulty ship a loss to a great fleet. Again, after the whole devastation of World War II, with all its galaxy of heroes, and after Admiral Cunningham had become Admiral of the Fleet, as Viscount Cunningham of Hyndhope he found it in his heart to pay this tribute:

> Hector Macdonald Laws Waller will always remain in my mind as one of the very finest types of Australian

officer. Full of good cheer with a great sense of humour, undefeated and always burning to get at the enemy, he kept the old ships of his Flotilla—the *Stuart*, *Vampire*, *Vendetta*, *Voyager*, *Waterhen*—hard at it always. Greatly admired and loved by everyone, his loss . . .

And the ship was suited to the man.

The first great climax of her career had come around the Battle of Crete. They were desperate days, calling forth resolution and devotion. The man and the ship had to watch companions die and suffer. The cruisers *Gloucester*, *Fiji* and *Calcutta* (*Perth*'s navigator was a *Calcutta* survivor) were sunk, with destroyers *Juno*, *Greyhound*, *Kashmir*, *Kelly*, *Hereward* and *Imperial*. Battleships *Warsprite* and *Barham*; aircraft carrier *Formidable*; cruisers *Orion* and *Dido*; destroyers *Kelvin* and *Nubian* were all damaged beyond local repair. Cruisers *Perth*, *Naiad* and *Carlisle*; destroyers *Havoc*, *Kingston* and *Nizam* would be out of action for a while. Those were the sorrows suffered by the intimate family of the Mediterranean Fleet. Well over two thousand men were dead.

The father of them all, Andrew Cunningham, had concluded his dispatch thus:

It is not easy to convey how heavy was the strain that the men and the ships sustained. (Notice that the Father makes no discrimination between his children, the men and the ships—this is sailor-thinking.) Apart from the cumulative effect of prolonged sea-going over extended periods, it has to be remembered that in this last instance, ships' companies had none of the inspiration of battle with the enemy to bear them up. Instead they had the increasing anxiety of the task of trying to bring away in safety thousands of their own countrymen, many of whom were in an exhausted and dispirited condition, in ships so necessarily overcrowded that, even where there was opportunity to relax, conditions made this impossible. They had started the evacuation (Crete) already overtired, and they had to carry this through under conditions of savage air attacks such as had only recently caused grievous losses to the Fleet.

There is rightly little credit or glory to be expected in these operations of retreat, but I feel that the spirit of tenacity shown by those who took part should not go unrecorded.

More than once I felt the stage had been reached when no more could be asked of officers and men, physically and mentally exhausted by their efforts and the events of those last fateful days. It is perhaps even now not realized how nearly the breaking point was reached, but that these men struggled through is a measure of their achievement, and, I trust, will not be lightly forgotten.

That was the end of his dispatch, but, writing in his Odyssey, he says:

So ended the Battle of Crete and a disastrous period in our naval history—a period of great tension and anxiety such as I have never experienced before or since... But with it all was an intense pride, which was fully justified, that our seamen had never flinched in standing up to conditions almost beyond human endurance. At the back of my mind, however, there was the disturbing thought that those at home apparently failed to appreciate what our ships and men had endured.

After this, Admiral Cunningham had the humility to suggest to Admiralty that perhaps they would like a

"Near-missed", Battle of Crete, 1941

change in command; he would not be annoyed, "as it may be that the happenings of the last few days have shaken the faith of the personnel of the Fleet in my handling of affairs". Had he but known it then, every man of the Fleet loved him, all the more for what he had done to them—he had shown such an implicit faith in them and they could not have let him down. They knew, too, that he would have been on the bridge of every ship he sent out, if that were possible.

John remembered the last line of a signal the Admiral had made then: "We must outlast him (the enemy). We have to stick it out." That had made a profound appeal to them. If ever a man was loved in the grand Elizabethan manner by a whole Fleet, it was Andrew Cunningham.

Once during those hectic days, in a moment when they took a brief gasp of breath, *Stuart* lay alongside *Perth* in Suda Bay, Crete. Both ships were dirty, stained and strained from constant action and keeping the sea so long. *Stuart* was oiling from *Perth*. Gun muzzles were charred black. Hollow-eyed, sleepless men dragged themselves about to attend to the needs of the ships. George, on the bridge, passed the time of day with some others on *Stuart*'s bridge, which was abreast and a little below him. One of the fellows there, with a grimed, brown face and a blue woollen skull-cap pulled down to the top of his ears, in a thick roll-neck jersey, his trousers pushed into his leather seaboots, rolled a cigarette. He spotted George, "Got a match?" he called.

"Yeah, catch, Mate," George replied casually as he threw his box across. "What's the Skipper like?" he asked to make conversation.

The man caught the matches. He was sturdy and tired-looking. "Not bad," and there was a flash of teeth as he grinned with a puckish humour: "but some don't think much of him." He lit his cigarette and threw the matches back. He picked up an old monkey jacket and turned to leave the bridge. And then George saw, on that old jacket, four torn and tarnished gold rings. "It was old Hec himself," George chuckled; "it was the first time I had seen him."

"No flannel about old Hec," Ken said.

Andrew Cunningham and Hector Waller were cast in the same mould: men would follow them, suffer, and be glad about it. These were both men made by Fate for those ever-recurring Saint Crispin's Days of human affairs.

When *Perth* left the Mediterranean, C.-in-C. made the signal: "I am sorry to lose *Perth* from the station. She has been with us in most stirring times and goes home with a proud record of good work; I wish you a safe passage and a happy home-coming."

4

With this ideal combination, the tragedy was that Captain Waller was ham-strung. He had to sit there without a chance to use the ship as she cried to be used.

Already she had been straddled with enemy 8-inch salvoes eight times in succession. To be hit while engaging is one of the calculated risks of war; but to be sitting like a rabbit on a hilltop, chancing that one shot which can change the whole course of an action, was infuriating. They had seen enough of fleet action before to realize the needlessly dangerous position they were in.

However, to the relief of everyone, their chance came. *Perth* had been firing ranging salvoes. At about 23,000 yards the Captain told Guns to engage the four-funnelled cruiser as he could.

"She's still out of range, sir!"

"All right, try the destroyers and get her when you can."

Perth's second salvo landed on a destroyer. This was more to their taste. But the targets steamed into a smoke screen, and she fired some follow-up salvoes after them. *De Ruyter* now led to starboard and they came under heavy fire. The spread of shot was small: "Never more than 150 yards for elevation and less for line," wrote the Captain. They were ten-gun salvoes.

By this time *Houston* had been hit twice by 8-inch shells which, however, did not explode. *De Ruyter* was hit once also without explosion. While the Japanese, with air-spotting, must have had a clear appreciation of the Allied Forces, the latter did not have a clear one of the enemy—still less of any supporting forces which might have been over the horizon.

At 4.35 p.m. *De Ruyter* led towards the enemy, and about this time, too, the rear enemy cruiser was hit. Clouds of black smoke poured out of her up to three-hundred feet high, but she kept firing. As the smoke cleared, a destroyer was also seen to be on fire. *Perth* now came under intense fire from one of the heavy cruisers. This lasted a long time. The fall of shot was seldom more than a cable's length short or over, and the Captain manœuvred the ship to anticipate the enemy correction for range. In the next quarter of an hour, *Jintsu* with her destroyers, and *Naka*, crossing the Japanese cruisers' bows at 35 knots with her seven destroyers, and the heavy cruiser *Haguro* (sixteen ships in all) launched forty-three torpedoes, none of which was effective.

The Dutch cruisers fired at times, but were still well out of range. At 5 p.m. the enemy cruisers checked fire and, two minutes latter, a hit was observed on the leading ship. They then reopened fire. At 5.7 p.m. the leading Japanese destroyer flotilla launched a long-range torpedo attack and the Allied ships turned away to "comb the spread", i.e. present the smallest target. They also ceased firing. Enemy shots were now falling short.

At 5.14 p.m., *Exeter* was hit in the boiler room and lay stopped. She was soon able to get under way again, but could only make 15 knots. Immediately *Perth* went in to screen her with heavy funnel-smoke aloft and white smoke from her smoke-floats on the quarterdeck. She was supported by *Electra* and *Encounter*. *Perth* made 180 degree turns to lay the protective curtain between the enemy and *Exeter*, who had turned out of line to port. *De Ruyter* moved to starboard and *Java*, from astern, came up to support her. *Houston* made a grand 360 degree turn to port. *Exeter* was belching black smoke from the cold oil in her boilers. Fourteen men had been killed. All ships were now firing again. The American destroyers came in to make smoke, and *Perth* then followed *De Ruyter*.

The Allied line was thrown into considerable confusion as *De Ruyter* circled, presumably to protect *Exeter*. The lack of tactics became most obvious. The captains of individual ships were continually left guessing at the Admiral's intentions. Signals were made in plain language by hand lamp or radio. Aboard *De Ruyter* there were a few R.N. and U.S.N. signalmen, upon whom fell the task of relaying the Admiral's unconventional manœuvres to their own ships. It is a miracle that the ships were extricated without collision. John heard the Captain call down the voice-pipe to him, as if preparing him for *any* manœuvre he might be called upon to make, "The American destroyers are now steaming around the *Exeter* in a grand circle. The Admiral seems to be making a death-or-glory march on a follow-me procedure." An American destroyer captain picturesquely put it, "Sometimes the Americans had to fight by guess and a gaze in the crystal ball."

5

When John heard the Captain's voice he was beginning to lose touch with reality. He was fighting an enemy all on his own. Standing by the ship's wheel and idly letting the spokes pass beneath one's fingers—this is many people's idea of what it is like to steer a ship. Under normal conditions, with a ship on course, it is indeed what happens. The ship was steered beautifully and precisely by 250-horsepower electric motors working in tandem on an hydraulic system, which had its powerful and infinitely sensitive fingers on the rudder crosshead with four great rams. Many times John had sat in the tiller flat watching this smooth, faultless interpretation of the Captain's wishes being applied, through the rudder, to the complex fabric of the ship. The whole gunnery platform relied upon this so that it could come to bear on the enemy. He had heard the turning of the four propellers at high speed, and their turbulence roughly slapping the taut skin of the hull with a sound like a hundred distant depth-charges. But now, he was two-hundred-and-fifty feet away from that vital compartment, connected to it only by two sets of thin copper tubing through which glycerine and water flowed. If these were shot away, he would have to move to the after steering position, a small cabinet in the starboard forward corner of the steering engine flat. If the power went off, he would have eight stokers laboriously to pump the great rams by hand.

In the lower steering position his crew was small. Besides himself, there was a leading seaman and an able seaman, both of whom he had trained to do the job as efficiently as

GENERAL APPROX. TRACK OF ABDA
27TH FEB.-IST MARCH 1942
DURING BATTLE OF JAVA SEA AND SUNDA STRAITS

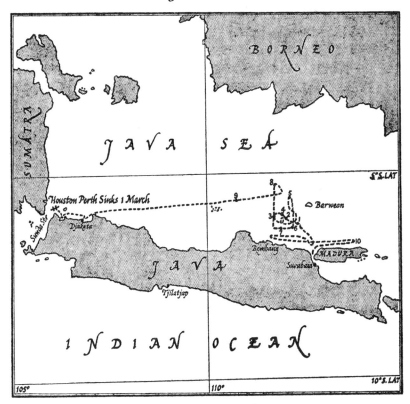

JAVA SEA ACTION

1   4.12 p.m. enemy sighted 27.2.42

2   *Exeter* hit. Later withdraws with *Witt de With* to Sourabaia
5.15 p.m. *Kortenaer* sunk

3   10.15 p.m. *Encounter* picks up *Kortenaer's* survivors thence to Sourabaia

4   6 p.m. *Electra* sunk

5   7.30 p.m. *Perth* and *Houston* open fire

6   9 p.m. U.S. Destroyers to Sourabaia

7   9.25 p.m. *Jupiter* sunk

8   10.55 p.m. *Java* sunk
11 p.m. *De Ruyter* sunk

9   *Perth* and *Houston* to Tandjeong Priok

10 East West over night sweep by ABDA. 26/27 Feb. '42

himself, for at any moment the whole responsibility could fall on either of them. One wrong move at high speeds and in close order could bring complete disaster to the ship. Normally John was at the wheel, with the leading seaman on the port engine telegraph and revolution indicator, and the able seaman on the starboard engine telegraph. There was also a stoker petty officer to effect any mechanical change-overs required. But now they were desperate, and the usual order had gone by the board.

The enemy within the ship was heat-stroke, which, with the rushing of a steam train, irresistibly carries a man to oblivion. With a sounding of an Action Alarm, all lower deck ventilation is shut down so that any fires will starve for oxygen.

The spokes of the wheel were being wrenched and hurled around with such violence now that it looked as though they would be plucked out like carrots. The ship was being manœuvred under full helm, constantly changing engine speeds, the engines rung ahead or astern to turn her in an ever-tightening circle. This technique had been developed in the Mediterranean to evade dive-bombers. It had actually been used by Sir Phillip Boyer-Smythe, then captain, to avoid sticks of bombs which had already left the aircraft. This was all the more remarkable when it is remembered that *Perth*'s turning circle was one of the largest in the Navy. Much of the success was due to the engine room's crew, whose uncanny and instantaneous co-ordination made the ship heel away and the engines pulse with a thrill of life through the whole ship.

"Starboard thirty-five!"

"Starboard thirty-five sir!"

"Slow starboard. Full ahead port!"

"Slow starboard. Full ahead port, sir!"

"Thirty-five of starboard wheel on, sir. Starboard engine slow ahead, port engine full ahead, on and repeated, sir!"

"Ease to ten!"

"Ease to ten, sir!"

"Half ahead both engines!"

"Half ahead both engines, sir!"

"Ten degrees of starb'd wheel on. Both engines half ahead on and repeated, sir!"

"Midships!"

"Midships, sir!"

"Meet her! Steady on two-seven-o degrees!"

"Meet her! Steady on two-seven-o degrees, sir."

"Course, two-seven-o degrees, sir!"

This was some of the dialogue for one simple manœuvre. Replies were gasped out as the wheel was hove around in great lunging movements so that one turn of the wheel, at a single lunge, put on five degrees of rudder. "Hard over" is seven strenuous turns with the strong spring of the telemotor being compressed more at each turn. This meant that the helmsman had to heave around with a concerted swing of both shoulders: bending from the waist and carrying the movement down with the knees bent, then thrusting up again at the other side of the circle on tensed toes, which makes a compact ball of the muscles of the calves and a rigid line along the top of the thighs. It is a quick, smooth movement. With this abnormal manœuvering, the action of the helmsman is more like the weaving of a fighter around a punching bag—crouching, lunging, quick short side-steps, arms jabbing strongly down, boring in then snapping up again. This goes on with sharp grunts and whistlings of sharply exhaled breaths.

No sooner would John report, "Course, sir—" than,

"Port thirty-five! Slow port! Full ahead starboard!"
would come down the voice pipe. Over and over! Time
after time! Urgent yet monotonous and measured, alterations as the ship snaked under the Captain's hand.

But this, in itself, was not unprecedented. At the Battle
of Crete they had sustained thirteen hours non-stop of
concentrated dive-bombing from Hitler's "yellow-nosed
bastards", as they had referred to those special M.E. 110's
and J.U. 8JB's he had called together for the job. And the next
day they had endured a further seven-hour stretch for
which, after 9 a.m. they had only one-hundred rounds of
4-inch ammunition left. Fatty, in the high-angle director,
had received the order, "Only fire when you see the whites
of their eyes!" They had brought the ship's rifles (two-
hundred of them) on deck and ranged them round the
ship in banks of fifty. Each man, with ten rounds in the
magazine and one "in the spout", had fired furiously as
the attackers reached the bottom of their dives. The whole
day had been spent in dodging bombs. John and his crew
had managed it without relief; though they were fit, it had
tired them. But then they had not had such heat to endure.

Now the air was fœtid. It became impossible for the
man at the wheel to handle it and answer the stream of
orders as they came pouring down the voice-pipe. So one
man now stood with his ear at the bell-mouth and his eyes
on the helmsman, repeating the orders as he heard them,
and calling back to the compass platform as they were
executed. The man at the wheel did not waste a breath,
and for the short periods they kept a course, he had his
eyes fixed on the round face of the yellow-illuminated,
tick-ticking gyro-compass card.

This card had become their guide now, in quite another
way. The man steering watched it as if it were an enchanted

moon. Sweat poured in streams over his body—continuous rivers of it running from under his arms, soaking the shorts which was all he wore. Suddenly he would feel his body generate a terrific heat, which rushed out of him: this radiation took the last ounce of energy with it. The yellow moon of the compass card whirled away from his eyes into an immense distance, leaving him spinning in blackness, blind and on the point of collapse.

As soon as the card started to rush away from him, he fell back against the bulkhead and the man on the voice-pipe, constantly on the lookout for this, stepped across, his hand falling on the wheel as the other man reeled away and groped blindly along the bulkhead to the door. There, he called the third man back to the voice-pipe. One thing was saving them: by a freak of chance there was one punkah-louvre left running in the third auxiliary wireless office, just through the door from them. The man on the point of collapse would stagger into the office and lie flat on his back on a bench while the wireless ratings played a cool jet of life-saving air on his face. Above him ships were manœuvering in close disorder, through smoke and gunfire, at high speeds. John realized how much depended on his team's instantaneously carrying out the orders. If that jet failed, or the man on the voice-pipe was slow in taking over from the fainting man——

At the peak of the action, it was impossible for a man to last more than five minutes. Each turn was as hard as any boxing round. The Stoker Petty Officer pulled them out by taking over the starboard telegraphs. Thus, in that important battle in which five nations fought desperately, there were spells during which a young able seaman, who at any minute might faint, held in his sweat-streaming hands—the fate of a whole ship. He had not as many months in the Service as John had years, yet John had pride and confidence in him. Each of them in turn grunted, hove the wheel, sweated and gasped with painful lungs until that yellow moon spun away from him and he slumped against the bulkhead. This was the particular problem of the navigation party below; but all over the ship men were faced with the same problem of heat exhaustion. Some of the engine rooms' crews had been closed up already for seven hours: the temperature there had reached 145° Fahrenheit. Some were brought up and given salt in water.

6

Another hazard the men were now exposed to was flash, that ball of fire after an explosion which runs about with the smooth speed of quicksilver. The chemically treated flash-gear had been cast aside because it had become intolerable. The men cursed at so many immediate things that they had not one curse left for the enemy. The main armament belted out salvoes with measured deliberation. At each salvo or broadside the ship jumped in her compactness: she knew how to throw those punches right from the shoulder—her smallness was deceptive, for she had the punch of a champion. But those punches left disorder in their wake, for the turrets were firing on extreme after bearings with the radical alterations of course. Fittings above and below decks were smashed; boats' planks were sprung and the copper fastenings stood out on their sides like the spikes of a mediaeval war mace. Glass and crockery all over the ship was shattered. The Bridge personnel were at times only a few feet away from the muzzles of "B" turret when it was on an after bearing, and they were taking great shocks from the blast.

It was a period of brisk in-fighting, toe to toe. The four-funnelled cruiser was hit in the stern, and bursting into flames it withdrew. *Perth* engaged the twelve destroyers, while 8-inch shells fell around her. In the remote control in the bridge structure, a Petty Officer Telegraphist was speaking on the phone to Ken, who was below in the main office. A salvo of shell crackled viciously overhead, audible on the phone. "What was that?" Ken asked. "That," replied the telegraphist, "was close."

7

About this time, six to eight large explosions were observed among the enemy destroyers. It was thought that some of them sank. Men on *Perth*'s upper deck at the time said that they could not count more than six afterwards.

Then *Exeter* had been hit. *Perth*'s electrically fired smoke-floats poured out white smoke in a curtain thirty feet high on the sea; and the funnels belched brown-tinged black smoke to complete the swirling screen for the stricken ship. *Perth* heeled far over as she made her one-hundred-and-eighty degree turns at the end of each run, her guns blazing round after round at the enemy, more of which were now seen on the horizon.

"Then a Dutch destroyer came racing down," Darky said. "We saw a torpedo track: it missed us by fifty feet. The after ·5 guns' crews saw the Dutchy and waved him out of it, but of course he couldn't see them. He was just altering course to port when the fish got him amidships. It turned him right over as he blew up. He broke in half and folded like a jack-knife—both ends came together, his bow and stern sticking right up. 'Way aft on the stern part we saw about half a dozen blokes—then they dropped off into the water. She sank in about a minute, I'd reckon."

This was *Kortenaer*. It was the result of a torpedo attack the Japanese destroyers and cruisers had made, launching sixty-eight torpedoes. "Otto" Lund, a young A.B. from the 4-inch gun deck who was on lookout at the time, told them that he had seen other torpedo tracks after the ship had blown up.

Presently they saw a submarine's conning tower on the starboard bow. The ship was swinging, and she engaged it with 4-inch on the starboard quarter. S.2 mounting got seven rounds away, four with the right gun and three with the left. The rounds were hastily grabbed from the ready-use lockers. "It was so sudden," said Darky, "that we were pinching rounds from one another to get into action. We had been using H.A. for the aircraft, now we had to go for the L.A.D.A. for this bloke. We lost sight of him as he passed the stern, but P.2 picked him up on the port side until he crash-dived."

Commander Eccles of *Edwards* said of this period, "It appeared that the striking force had suffered heavy damage and the enemy was pushing home an attack to drive us east."

The Japanese made a destroyer attack to finish off *Exeter*. *Perth* engaged a cruiser supporting the attack and drove her back into the smoke for cover. *Jupiter*, *Encounter* and *Electra* counter-attacked. *Perth* engaged destroyers through smoke-gaps and for several minutes was under their fire, but they were driven off, some of them damaged. Young Otto, new to the sea but thrilled with the events taking place right before his eyes, had told them with an excited voice and shining eyes, "I saw five Jap destroyers

At 17.15 Kortenaer torpedoed

come outa the smoke, like bats outa hell, on our starb'd beam. When they got clear they turned on an opposite and parallel course. I heard the bridge range-taker call fourteen thousand yards and all the ships opened fire on them. I reckon we sunk three. Then our destroyers, the R.N. ones, vanished into the smoke after them, firing like mad. By Golly it was wonderful! I yelled out, 'You bottlers! Give it to them!' "

Exeter was now ordered to Sourabaia with *Witt De With*, who had damaged her stern with her own depth charges as a result of torpedo tracks and a submarine she had sighted.

Meantime the ships steaming between *Exeter* and the Japanese were drawing the fire off her and hitting back. *Perth* engaged an 8-inch cruiser at 21,000 yards. Soon they were on the target, pumping in several rapid salvoes, two of which hit. There was a great disturbance aft, with volumes of pinkish smoke and a molten fulmination. The 8-inch ship, with her companion, sought cover in the smoke. When the smoke cleared, the bow of the damaged ship rose in the air and then settled back. *Perth* then lost sight of her, not knowing whether the sea or only the failing light had swallowed her up. But a cheer went through the ship as the Torpedo Officer broadcast what they had seen from the bridge.

8

As the destroyer attack was launched on *Exeter*, the Admiral had ordered the Allied destroyers to counter-attack. *Electra*, *Jupiter* and *Encounter*, who were widely separated, attacked independently. This was a daring and exciting move, for they had to tear through the smoke on the chance of meeting the enemy, almost certain to be in superior force, on an instant's warning.

Electra, vanishing into the smoke, met three Japanese destroyers, which she engaged at once at 6,000 yards. She hit the leader four times before the enemy were obscured by the smoke; but at this moment *Electra* was hit in the boiler room, lost steam, and lay stopped with her steering gear smashed. A heavy Japanese destroyer appeared and opened fire. *Electra* could only reply with her guns in local control, since the director was disabled. She was hit again and again and, one by one, her guns were put out of action. Abandon ship was ordered. Other destroyers moved in and strafed her with machine-guns, hitting many survivors in the water. She sank at 6 p.m. Fifty-four survivors were later picked up by Allied submarine S.38.

Jupiter rushed into the smoke and found two Japanese destroyers which she engaged briskly until they disappeared. *Encounter*, too, was playing the nerve-wracking game among the smoke. She briefly engaged a destroyer through a smoke-gap. The enemy then appeared to have retired so that, with no more targets to be found, the two ships rejoined the Allied line.

During this mêlée *Perth* sighted two mastheads above the smoke. It was impossible to tell whether they belonged to friend or foe; so, with the 6-inch armament trained upon them, *Perth* waited expectantly. "As soon as they showed the first bit of hull we knew they were Nips," Fatty said, "so we let them have it—three bags full."

9

Darkness was drawing on. *Houston* reported to *Perth* that all the 8-inch ammunition of her numbers one and two turrets was expended. All she had left was what remained of the outfit of the damaged number three turret. This had to be transported from aft forward—an arduous and slow job with projectiles weighing some two hundred and fifty pounds each. They would have to be manhandled—a ticklish task in a moving ship. This fact was passed on to the Admiral. By now there were no enemy ships in sight. *De Ruyter* led away to the north-east. "Presumably," thought Captain Waller, "to skirt the escort groups and get at the convoy." They were travelling at 22 knots, the American destroyers tagging along with them. "We followed the main body, not having the slightest idea of his (Doorman's) intentions, and still only a vague idea of what the enemy was doing."

De Ruyter's short-wave radio was defunct, and only hand-lamp signalling could be made. *Houston*'s voice-radio to American destroyers was off the air also.

Thus, after a couple of hectic hours, ABDA Force had lost two destroyers sunk, one 8-inch cruiser and a destroyer damaged and withdrawn to Sourabaia. In return it was thought that they had inflicted considerable damage on the enemy, but the exact extent was not known. Ken said that the Captain claimed for *Perth* two 8-inch cruisers sunk or heavily damaged, and two destroyers sunk.

"I'm sure we got more destroyers than that," Fatty, Blackie and George maintained.

"But the Captain could only claim what he was sure of," Mr Wyatt said.

The strength of the enemy was still unknown. The Japanese, because of continuous air-reconnaissance, could play hide-and-seek over the horizon with their opponents. There were certainly several formations to deal with. The Dutch Admiral was at a great disadvantage; but he seemed to lack a plan.

It was now dark. At 7.27 p.m. *Perth* sighted and reported four ships on the port beam, range 9,000 yards. An aircraft flare was dropped on their starboard side, throwing them up in silhouette to the Japanese. At 7.33 p.m. *Perth* opened fire, then *Houston*. Starshell were fired, but fell short. Captain Waller observed a row of explosions in one of the enemy ships and, thinking that these might be the launching of torpodoes, he turned away and the other ships conformed. Shortly afterwards the cruisers re-formed; then *De Ruyter* led them on various courses, still with the apparent intention of intercepting the convoy.

It was now 9 p.m. Commander Binford, commanding American destroyers, retired to Sourabaia. He was compelled to do this because all his torpedoes were expended, his fuel state was critical, and any force he could expect to meet must be superior both in gun-power and speed.

The remainder of ABDA was steadied on a westward course for about twenty minutes in close column without a zig-zag. Then suddenly, from right astern in the column, there was a tremendous explosion accompanied by a brilliant flash. *Jupiter* had blown up. She flashed to *Java*, the next ahead in the column, "*Jupiter* torpedoed." She finally sank at 1.30 the next morning. This is one of the tragedies of war—*Jupiter* appears to have been blown up by a Dutch mine in a field laid that afternoon. Headquarters ashore had failed to inform these ships, which were fighting under enough unfair handicaps already.

The rest of the ships turned north without rendering assistance, in accordance with the Admiral's express orders. At 10.17 p.m. they passed through a large number of survivors. In *Perth* they could not decide whether they were

Japanese or Dutch; they knew they were not English. They proved to be, incredibly enough, survivors of *Kortenaer*, the destroyer which had broken in half and sunk at once with only half a dozen men visible on her deck. Now, after five and a half hours, 113 (including the Captain) were picked up by *Encounter* out of a complete crew of 150.

"During this whole period the Allied Force was being superbly shadowed by the Japanese aircraft," Captain Waller wrote. "At 2250 another aircraft flare appeared overhead, and shortly afterwards a line of six calcium flares in the water straddled our line at right angles. This happened every time we steered a new course, and it was soon obvious that our every move in the moonlight was being reported, not only by W/T but by this excellent visual means. The enemy's disposition of forces must have been ridiculously easy."

Shortly before 11 p.m. *Perth* and *Houston* sighted two cruisers on the port beam at the same moment. *Perth* opened fire on them and both ships replied. Their shooting was very accurate, but the rate of fire was slow. *Perth*'s second and fifth salvoes were observed as certain hits, and another was thought to be. The ship which was hit opened rapid fire with star shell, which fell short and formed a blinding curtain between the opponents. One Japanese shell had hit *De Ruyter* on the quarterdeck; one had also hit *Java*.

De Ruyter turned away ninety degrees and *Perth*, thinking she might have sighted torpedoes, followed her. This manœuvre was only partly executed when the whole of *Java*'s stern blew up with a violence that shook the exposed personnel in *Perth*. She lay stopped, heavily on fire; it was obvious that she could not last long.

Then, within minutes, *De Ruyter*, just ahead of *Perth*,

went up in an appalling explosion of flame and searing heat, which was felt in *Perth*. "I thought it would fry us," Fatty said. "It was so close you could smell burning paint and a horrible stink like burning bodies."

Perth only narrowly avoided disasterous collision by the swift action of the Captain. "Hard-a-port! Stop port!" he called into the voice-pipe. Almost instantly the machinery was acting like a reflex of the Captain's mind. Before John had repeated the order, the wheel had been hove over to 35 degrees, the port engine telegraph was at Stop, and the reply gong from the engine room was rung. *Perth* just scraped by the port side of *De Ruyter*. Almost as quickly, *Houston* altered course violently to starboard, and total disaster was avoided.

Only two men from *Java* and seventy from *De Ruyter* survived. Admiral Doorman lost his life. In *De Ruyter*, ready-use ammunition exploded among the men endeavouring to abandon ship. It is generally thought that torpedoes caused the loss of the two Dutch ships, the Japanese cruisers having launched twelve torpedoes as they were engaged.

Now, of the fourteen ships that had steamed out of Sourabaia at 2.30 p.m., only two remained in a condition to fight. It was not yet midnight. The Admiral's verbal orders to his captains had been that, should any ship become disabled, she must be left to the "mercy of the enemy".

All this happened in barely seven hours.

II

Captain Waller was now in command of the last remaining ships. He made an appreciation of his position. He had one undamaged 6-inch cruiser and one 8-inch cruiser with no guns aft and its ammunition seriously depleted. He had no destroyers. Day and night he had been efficiently shadowed by enemy aircraft. He could only guess at the opposing forces; but he thought there must be six cruisers and possibly twelve destroyers. He suspected submarines in the area. He saw no possibility of getting at the enemy, for his approach would be well advertised and there were plenty of enemy destroyers to screen the convoy. "I therefore had no hesitation in withdrawing what remained of the striking force and ordering them to the pre-arranged rendezvous after night-action—Tandjeong Priok," he wrote.

This day is call'd the feast of Crispian:
He that outlives this day, and comes safe home,
Will stand a tip-toe when this day is nam'd,
And rouse him at the name of Crispian.
He that shall live this day, and see old age,
Will yearly on the vigil feast his neighbours,
And say, "Tomorrow is Saint Crispian:"
Then will he strip his sleeve and show his scars,
And say, "These wounds I had on Crispin's day."
Old men forget; yet all shall be forgot,
But he'll remember with advantages
What feats he did that day: Then shall our names,
Familiar in his mouth as household words,—
Harry the king, Bedford and Exeter,
Warwick and Talbot, Salisbury and Gloster,—
Be in their flowing cups freshly remember'd.
This story shall the good man teach his son;
And Crispin Crispian shall ne'er go by,
From this day to the ending of the world,
But we in it shall be remembered,—
We few, we happy few, we band of brothers;
For he today that sheds his blood with me
Shall be my brother; be he ne'er so vile,
This day shall gentle his condition:
And gentlemen in England now a-bed
Shall think themselves accurs'd they were not here,
And hold their manhoods cheap whiles any speaks
That fought with us upon Saint Crispin's day.

Henry V, IV, iii

Part 9

SUNDA STRAIT

I

TANDJEONG PRIOK was quiet as they secured along-side in the afternoon of February 28th, 1942. It was Saturday. The place was strangely hushed and deserted. The exhausted ship's company were infinitely depressed by the lack of spirit there.

Just before he left the bridge, Captain Waller had a short talk with some of the men there. He ran briefly over the plot of the action with them, pointing out where he had claimed the two cruisers and the two destroyers. This gave satisfaction to men so proud of their ship. As the Captain turned to leave the bridge, he said to George, "How are your ears now, Able Seaman Yew?"

George explained; "I made a bloody idiot of myself last night. The blast from 'B' turret on after bearings made me punchy—I couldn't hear a thing after a while. I went down and grabbed a bit of supper. When I got back on the bridge, I told them I was all right—and I started to talk. Next thing I know, a bloke's alongside of me shouting in my ear to shut up. But I can hardly hear him. Y'see I'd been shouting at the top o' me lungs, thinkin' I been talkin' normal. A man gets wet, don't he?"

After the ship had secured, only those absolutely necessary remained on watch. The rest, dirty, hungry and tired, hardly knew what to do with themselves. Some just dropped where they were and sank into a bottomless sleep. Some indulged in the relaxing luxury of a hot bath. Some talked of the events of the past day and night with the animation of a nervous energy that had not yet died down. They were glad of this breather, even though they knew they were not out of the wood yet. But they were glad, also, to be still afloat after what they had seen. They blessed their ship and gave her full credit for their deliverance. They were almost superstitious about her luck.

The men knew that there were un-numbered Japanese ships north of Java, closing in. They wondered what they would be called to do next.

"This joint stinks. They are going to *give* the place away!" many of them said. Both ships needed ammunition for their main armaments, but none was available. Both needed oil-fuel: *Perth* could get only 300 tons. This still left her 50 per cent. below capacity. A reserve of oil must be kept here in case any of the Allied destroyers should come in, their fate at this time being in doubt.

Preparations were being made to blow up installations and warehouses ashore. The canteen store was to be blown up by some Tommy Sappers. "Hop in and get a basinful, mate," they called to *Perth*'s men, across the wharf. The men leapt over the side of the ship and were soon bringing back all sorts of things, but mostly cartons of cigarettes. One, more knowing, managed to get a case of whisky. The Commander was powerless to stop all this, and when he saw how it was, he was not inclined to. Opportunity was taken to embark stores which were addressed to Victualling Officer, Singapore. There were also some three dozen rafts made of balsa wood, each three feet square. These were taken for their own use. When Blackie saw John loading them into the port waist, he said, "That looks bloody lovely, that does!"

"They might come in handy," John explained.

"That's exactly what I mean," Blackie replied sourly.

An American history, alluding to this moment, said, "Admiral Helfrich would not concede defeat. The indomitable Dutchman planned to assemble the remaining Allied Forces at Tjilatjap."

At about 5 p.m. a Japanese plane entered the harbour as cheeky as a sparrow. He was greeted by small A.A. fire. The observer, standing in the rear cockpit, machine-gunned some small craft outside the harbour. *Perth* met him with 4-inch fired at a low angle over the rooftops. This drove away the intruder and broke all the windows in the vicinity.

"The bastards are on us again," Blackie exclaimed in disgust; "they'll have a nice welcome for us somewhere, you'll see!"

At 5.30 p.m. the Captain sent for John Harper, his navigator, and there in the company of the captain of *Houston* (Captain Rooks) said that they had orders to proceed to Tjilatjap, through Sunda Strait. H.M.N.S. *Evertsen*, a destroyer, was to accompany them. He proposed to avoid air attack by keeping about two hundred miles south of Java, and to approach Tjilatjap during the hours of darkness. They would have to travel at moderate speed, as it was imperative to conserve fuel.

Shortly after 7 p.m. the two cruisers slipped and started out. Through lack of tugs, *Perth* damaged one of her starboard propellers against the concrete wharf. A signal was made for *Evertsen* to precede them out of harbour, but she replied that she had neither orders nor steam. She was told to obtain orders and follow. Once clear of the harbour, they went on to 22 knots and zig-zag No. 10. *Houston*, five cables astern, conformed. The ship's company was closed up to Action Stations, then, after clearing away, was relaxed to Second Degree of Readiness, which is not more than ten seconds away from Action Stations. With the ship steadied, the Captain went to the broadcaster and spoke to the officers and men throughout the ship. "We are bound to Tjilatjap. With a bit of luck we should reach there tomorrow."

Later, a signal was received reporting an enemy convoy of about ten merchant ships, with two cruisers and three destroyers, moving eastwards at 4 p.m. It was not thought that this force would contact them or bother about them.

2

In a quiet lull, the Captain went to the after end of the compass platform, abaft the director control tower. The door into the tower was ajar. This was a scandalous little corner strewn with watchcoats, "goon-skins", cocoa "fannies" and dirty mugs. Here odd men could catch a nap. The crushed and trampled coats gave off a dank, pungent odour. The mugs which were seldom washed, were thick with dark brown, greasy "ky". The smell and feel of these things were as comforting to the men as the bosom of a mother is to the nestling babe.

Captain Waller came in among this mess. "Any ky, lads?" he asked.

"Yes, sir," George answered, "but the mugs are a bit chatty."

"Do *you* drink out of them?"

"Well, yes," George grinned sheepishly in the dark.

"Then I don't think they'll poison me. I just feel like a mug of ky." He held the dirty mug while George poured the thick, fatty cocoa into it. When he put a desert-spoon of sugar into the cup, it floated on the viscous brown surface until it was stirred in. The Captain sipped it and said, with an exhalation of pure enjoyment, "Good stuff, this!"

George told them how the Captain stood and yarned with them for a while. He had a friendly shot at George about the time in Suda Bay when he had asked him what the Skipper of *Stuart* was like. "There was no doubt about it—Hec was a man."

"Like when I went into his day cabin a few days before," John said. "I went in to correct his clock. The minute hand came off. I said that I would send for the E.A. to fix it. He said, 'It's all right, Chief Quartermaster, I'll fix it.' He was sitting at his desk, working over a model of *Stuart*. 'I like your models, Sir,' I said. 'I like the ships,' he said—he'd got his fingers round the bows of *Stuart* and his eyes on the rest of the flotilla of models on the mantelshelf—*Voyager*, *Vampire*, *Vendetta* and *Waterhen*. There was something about that 'I like the ships' which I don't think I'll ever forget."

"He could fix anything," Fatty said. "One day the plumber was trying to repair his sea-heads. Hec said, 'Here, give me a shot.' And, blow me down!—he had it fixed in a few minutes."

"And he knew his signals as well as any Yeoman," Jacky contributed. "I was on the bridge reading a ship one day, and I could hear someone reading another somewhere behind me. 'Course, I'm supposed to know what's going on, so I called over my shoulder, 'Who the bloody hell you reading?' And a voice comes back, cool as any killick buntin'-tosser, 'That bastard over there, Yeoman.' I nearly swallowed me signal pad, it was Hec."

3

The Captain had received a reconnaissance report that Sunda Strait was clear of enemy shipping. Therefore it looked as though the force could slip through into the Indian Ocean before the jaws of the trap snapped shut. The escorted convoy, moving on an opposite course towards Java, would be too far away; and, anyway, the escort would not bother about them at this stage. Nevertheless, the ship remained at the highest state of vigilance, for this was the Captain's normal policy, to which the ship's company were disciplined.

At 10.45 p.m. the ships were steaming steadily on a calm sea beneath a clear sky and a large moon. The extreme visibility was six or seven miles. Babi Island light lay on their right 1½ miles away; and on their left streamed the coast of Java, dropping away into Bantam Bay, then returning out to St Nicholas Point, which at the moment lay away ahead on the port bow. This was to be a critical point in their history. The Captain had been led to expect our own corvettes on patrol.

"At 2306, when in position 5° 50′ S. 106° 10′ E. (approx.), a vessel was sighted five miles ahead, close to St Nicolas Point," wrote John Harper, the navigator, in his report to Naval Board. This vessel was challenged, and made an odd reply on a greenish-coloured lamp. The challenge being repeated, the vessel turned away, making smoke. Her silhouette showed her to be a Japanese destroyer. Unknown to them, she had launched nine torpedoes.

The forward turrets opened fire at once, and the ship swung to bring all guns to bear. The alarm rattlers gave out their urgent call to action. All men were on their feet and closed up in a matter of seconds. A number of observers claimed that this first target was sunk. More destroyers were sighted to the northward. The first enemy report was: one destroyer and five unknown. It was later amended to: One cruiser and five destroyers. But this was only a beginning.

4

From then on, the ship was completely under Captain Waller's skilful hand. He manœuvred her as if she were a polo pony. Never were the men more highly keyed to action. A fey spirit had taken hold of them—at last the Captain was free to act on his own initiative; they asked no more. They knew that this could be the end, that only a miracle could save them. But they found themselves strangely alive, eager and exhilarated.

"I cannot attempt to estimate what force was opposing us. During the action a large number of destroyers engaged us from *all* directions; at least one and probably more cruisers were engaging us from the northward, and one officer reported sighting a large number of vessels in close formation, probably transports." John Harper wrote. He was an officer whose observation was limited by his responsibility for keeping the ship in navigable water while the Captain manœuvred her. The coast was close aboard and the sea strewn with islets, reefs and other hazards. His responsibility was great.

Admiral Cunningham, after the Battle of Matapan, wrote:

> However, calm reflection in an armchair in the full knowledge of what actually happened is a very different matter to conducting an operation from the bridge of a ship at night in the presence of the enemy. Instant and

momentous decisions have to be made in a matter of seconds. With fast-moving ships at close quarters and the roar of gunfire, clear thinking is not easy. *In no other circumstances than night-action at sea does the fog of war so completely descend to blind one to a true realization of what is happening.*

That they were against overwhelming odds was certain. Some thought there were two forces through which the ship later passed, dividing them north-west south-east. A general estimate was five cruisers and ten destroyers. Some in good positions said there were as many as twenty destroyers. Several months later, some of the crew were told by Japanese of the convoy that there were fifty-eight ships: this number was found to include at least two heavy cruisers, a light cruiser with ten destroyers, and another destroyer. Also, closing them from the north, were four heavy cruisers, an aircraft carrier and other destroyers.

There was an aircraft overhead. Broken cloud and moonlight made cloud-shadows on the sea, to play a game of confusion with islands and ships. It was a situation for the coolest head and the quickest eye.

The four turrets went into independent control in an effort to engage the ring of enemy which beset them. Six-inch guns were firing at point-blank range, the gun-elevation being only two degrees at times. In an hour, each gun of Blackie's turret fired 136 rounds. The others must have fired much the same. The 4-inch fired star-shell and L.A.D.A. at destroyers racing in. A flotilla of destroyers closed them at high speed. The Local Control Officer, a Petty Officer, on the 4-inch gun deck directed his battery at this threat. "We could only see the leader—the rest were screened in smoke. We loaded L.A.D.A. and went into rapid salvoes. We concentrated on the leader. I yelled, 'Never mind the others—get the *leader!*' We got him all right. That's the one ship in the action I can personally vouch for. I would swear to that one on a stack of bibles a mile high. O' course there, we hit plenty of others—how could we help it? It was point-blank a lot of the time. We expended all our L.A.D.A., so then we fired star-shell into them—short fuse, point-blank. You could see the hits, but I don't think our side four-inch sunk any others. We *may* have, mind you, but of that one I'm sure.''

As the action progressed, the enemy destroyers were gradually able to press in until they could illuminate *Perth* in the revealing glare of searchlight beams and put her more at their mercy. The lights were engaged at once. But they were continually shifting targets. The tactics were to expose the beam of one light for a few seconds to bathe *Perth* stark against the night; then that beam would be folded back within the iris shutters and another, elsewhere, would take its place. Heavy shell-fire criss-crossing them tore the sea to shreds and raised white monuments caught in the beams of light. These white columns made by the fall of shot rose like the lower teeth of some fabulous monster, and it was as if they were fighting the action on the vast, wet floor of its mouth with the snapping teeth biting closer and closer.

Houston was hit first and caught fire around the bridge. After this, her main armament was not observed to fire. She had started the action tragically short of 8-inch ammunition, having only the remainder of the outfit of her after damaged turret—50 rounds per gun. It was possible that this had already been expended. But her lighter guns blazed defiantly on, and tracer could be seen curving away in flat trajectory, showing the closeness of the encounter.

In the midst of that mad mêlée, *Perth* remained untouched. The bridge was alive with that tense excitement which men experience when giving their best, self completely forgotten. Targets loomed, were engaged, were lost. More came. Reports poured in to the Captain, and his voice became the voice of the Ship herself.

"Green three-o, cruiser! There, Guns, there! Let him have it!"

"Red seven-o, destroyers! Starb'd twenty! Quickly, you'll miss 'em."

"A beautiful opportunity, Guns, a beauty! Give it to 'em!"

"Red two-o! What's that? There! See there! Come on, get that armament round and *open fire*! Red, one-five-o! Green one-seven-five! Get the turrets split up, Guns, and engage independently!"

"Torpedoes!"

"Starboard thirty! Full ahead port! Stop starb'd!"

"Midships! Half ahead together! Two hundred revolutions!"

"Steady as you go, Quartermaster!"

"Island there, sir! We're a bit close to the land."

"Right, Pilot. Starb'd twenty!"

"Torps, how are your mouldies?"

"Sir! All tubes ready!"

"Stand by, I'm altering now! Port twenty! One-five-o revolutions!" And the ship began to rake across the numerous targets with her outward tubes. After tube first, then one by one the four torpedoes slid out of their tubes with a flash-driven leap towards the dark turbulance of the turning, twisting ships, the contra-rotating screws running cold on air until the igniter fires and super-heated steam drives them on for a high-speed, short run to their targets.

"Starb'd tubes fired, sir!"

"Good! Port side now! Stand by!"

"How did you go, Torps?"

"I lost two, sir!"

"Good work!"

The Torpedo Gunner, behind the tubes in the torpedo space, observed an aircraft carrier or tender and two destroyers hit. Not only had the torpedoes hit the enemy, but they had also removed a hazard from the ship. The captain continued to fight her at an unsurpassed pace. The whole ship was alive with orders streaming out and information streaming in, like the blood pounding through the heart of a human body. The glare of searchlights; the flash, blast and roar of her own guns; tracer ammunition stitching light across the sky; phosphorescent wakes entangling; ships on fire; star-shell festooned in short strings in the sky—all these confused the evidence of one's own eyes. Brilliance and blackness struggled for supremacy. Smoke trails hung jumbled like curtains in the flies and wings of some immense stage. When star-shell illuminated the area, Fatty said, he did not know that there were so many destroyers in the world. The Torpedo Gunner said he counted eighteen, attacking in three groups.

Unknown to these two ships fighting to the death, a Japanese General, Imamura, had already been blown out of his ship. Two headquarters ships were now sunk, but he managed to get ashore alive.

An attempt was made to cover *Houston*'s defenceless stern. And now, at last, *Perth* began to take hits. The first was in the forward funnel: it cut the steamlines to the sirens, adding a scream of protest to the night already overcrowded with other noise. At just about midnight the Gunnery Officer reported to the Captain that the 6-inch ammunition was almost expended. It was then that Captain Waller decided to try and force the passage of Sunda Strait.

"Full speed ahead both engines! Port twenty."

He was heading the ship down past Toppers Island in the mouth of the Strait. Two cruisers and two destroyer flotillas were barring the way. The engines were rung ahead: John was just snapping on the last turn of the wheel, and the rudder indicator on the bulkhead above him was just flicking over to Port 20.

Then it happened—with the ship travelling at 28 knots.

6

The ship took a terrific blow below the water. The crash and the roar shook her, leaving a strange silence in their wake. Some vital pulse had stopped.

Eighty-seven torpedoes were loosed at *Perth* and *Houston* in that hour, and now the first one had hit.

It struck between the forward engine room and boiler room. The whole of the forward engine room's crew, including the Engineer Commander, was killed—except one. The damage control office and crew were wiped out, with all the vital nerve-endings there: the officers and petty officers and chiefs, skilled in the immediate appreciation and the repair of damage, were gone in this one explosion.

John, at the wheel, was thrown violently against the bulkhead. As he struggled back, he saw the gyro-compass card spinning around in spasmodic, stupid circles. The master gyros had been blown from their gymbals.This must have been obvious to the Captain, standing there by the voice-pipe with one arm around the brass pillar of Pelorus, the navigational gyro-repeat on the compass platform. As the torpedo struck, the Captain said, "That's torn it!"

On the 4-inch gun deck was young Otto Lund, who only yesterday had seen his first action. He had enjoyed every minute of it. The excitement and the spectacular chaos of the Java Sea had been marvellous. He was so glad he had come to sea—it could not have been better in Nelson's day! And now, this night-action with all its speed and brilliance was even better. He was running, with a long round of fixed 4-inch ammunition in his arms, from the ready-use locker to the breech of the gun. "It was like being at the pictures," he said, "only it was the best picture I ever saw. Then all at once—*kerummph*! The first fish. It sat me fair on my arse with the projey across my chest. I sat up and looked about. Suddenly it all looked different. 'Christ!' I said, 'this is serious!' And I was scared stiff after that."

The ship lay with her speed cut and every instrument which depended on the gyro useless. The guns kept banging away in local control. Both the forward 4-inch mountings were wiped out to a man. The after ones got away their last rounds. It was star-shell now; then they even fired the practice projectiles that were on hand. The now frightened Otto yelled, "What do we use after these?" An older voice came out of the darkness, "Rat the bloody spud locker."

They had been fighting just one hour when the first torpedo hit, and the Captain ordered, "Prepare to abandon ship!" Their luck had been phenomenal to have lasted so long. This, the first crippling blow, had put them completely at the mercy of the enemy. The last few rounds of 6-inch were fired. A few minutes after this hit, the Navigator called the Captain's attention to a torpedo streaking toward the ship on the starboard side. It hit the ship in the forward magazine. The magazine was empty: but the

H.M.A.S. Perth—the end

explosion jammed the hatches of the 4-inch magazine, trapping the men within.

Then came the order: Abandon ship!

It was passed to all quarters. The broadcast system, to the lasting satisfaction of Ken, Chief Telegraphist, carried this piece of life-saving information to all parts of the ship. John, on the other end of the voice-pipe from the Captain, heard the order from his own lips. So they began to leave the lower steering position. The others had gone up, and John had his foot on the bottom rung of the ladder when he heard a hail from the mouth of the voice-pipe. He went back to answer it.

"Lower steering position! Chief Quartermaster!"

"Leave both engines half speed ahead—I don't want the Old Girl to take anyone with her." This was the Captain.

"Aye, aye, sir! Both engines are half speed ahead now, sir!"

"Good!"

"Compass platform!"

"Compass platform."

"Do you require anyone to stand by the telegraphs, sir?"

John had no conscious thought of being heroic or dramatic in saying this. *Someone* would have to do it: it was normal routine. Strange that he should not be bitter now because it looked as if he would be the "bunny". It was not heroics, for there was no agonizing struggle to reach the decision. But he realized that he loved the ship: he knew now with an absolute certainty that men love ships with more than trite phrases—with some deep fibre in their beings.

The Captain's reply came back clear and imperative,

with all the warmth a father would use to tell a silly child to do something for its own good.

"Get to buggery out of it!"

Those were the last words the Captain ever spoke to John.

7

"Abandon ship! was now amplified to "Every man for himself." It cancelled all other drills. It meant exactly what it said. Water was pouring into the ship from two large, jagged holes on her starboard side. She was beginning to heel over. She was receiving more and more shellfire as the enemy ships closed in. A shell, passing the flag deck, decapitated a young Yeoman of Signals. The Ordinary Seaman's mess deck was hit, leaving a gaping hole near the waterline. The aircraft catapult and crane were blown into the port waist, totally wrecked and tangled with each other.

The glare of searchlights was constant, though coming first from one ship, then another. She was encircled now: from bow and quarter she was being pulverized. The pom-pom ready-use locker on the flag deck was hit and exploded, killing many. One man had his shoulder and arm taken off, exposing his lung. He managed to get in the water, but died there. Another had both arms taken off and drowned. "A" turret's crew came out of the gunhouse on to the forecastle and started to cut the floats adrift. A salvo of shell wiped them out. One was seen floating dead in the water later.

"B" turret's gunhouse crew came out on to "B" deck and were releasing floats when shells killed them all but one. Desperately this man worked his way aft by the bridge structure to the boat deck abreast the second cutter, where he sat down on the lower boom fast in its crutches. Men were gathered about the boat, clearing away the falls for lowering. The gripes had been cast off, and some had scrambled up the net over the griping spar into the boat. The lowerers stood by with only two lowering-turns on the staghorn. Fatty, who had taken charge of the lowering, was now looking about before giving the order to lower away. He saw the man sitting on the boom. "Hey, Fishcake!" he called the man by his nick-name—"Come on! Hop in, this is the last bloody liberty-boat tonight!"

The man moved wearily in the odd, half-crouched, sitting position he had taken. His arms were folded low across his body. Fatty moved across, to hear him say, "Don't worry about me—I've had it. I'll go with the Old Girl. Don't bother about me. There's nothing you can do."

In the beam of a sweeping searchlight, Fatty saw that the man on the boom was almost shot in two and was holding himself together with his crossed arms. He was the father of six children, and he sat there having to face the fact that he would never see them again. He was about to die, leaving his wife and children for ever. But he spoke without a whimper—"Don't bother about me. I'll go with the Old Girl."

8

When the first torpedo struck the forward engine room, it blew up the deck above into the workshop flat. In the Electrical Artificers' workshop there were three of the action electrical repair party. There was a blinding flash and they were drenched with water, the lights went out and they were left in a black pit. They flicked their torches on and stepped out of the door. The big torpedo gunner's mate vanished. The others checked and saved themselves just in time. They could see that their companion had fallen down into the destroyed engine room through a yawning hole made by the explosion. They were able to find their way precariously around the edge and escape to the upper deck.

John, coming through the torpedomen's mess deck and up the ladder into the sick bay flat, found an awful carnage there. The deck was littered with bloody, dead men. Most of them had been wearing white clothes. The red and white had been so predominant that, later, he could not help comparing it with strings of ceremonial flags, which are made up of red and white bunting. The party was over and the flags lay in a jumbled heap.

He found several men there, mostly stokers from the fire and repair parties, who seemed to be stupefied with shock: they did not realize that Abandon Ship had been ordered and the ship was sinking. He told them, but still they took no notice.

"Captain's orders!" he shouted. "*Get out!*"

He had to repeat this several times before it sank into their dulled senses. He grabbed one of them who had a torch and led him into the starboard waist, calling "Follow me!" to the rest. In the shelter deck he found their way blocked by a great mound of fire-bricks and debris which had been blown out of the fiddley, probably by the first torpedo. Luckily there was just enough room for them to squeeze on their bellies over the top, between the heap and the deck-head—otherwise they would have been trapped. The port side was already blocked by the collapse of the crane and catapult.

Once in the waist on the upper deck, they came under the glare of the searchlights. This helped them to find and

throw the balsa rafts over the side. When they had jetti-
soned all the life-saving gear they could find, John called
to the others, "Hop in, fellas, or we'll miss the last tram!"

John knew that he should jump into the water because
of the danger of striking wreckage head first; but when he
saw the sea so green and clear in the penetrating beam of
the searchlights, he dived. He wore only a pair of blue jean
shorts, a pair of sand-shoes without laces, and a leather
belt carrying his service knife and a small marline spike in a
leather sheath. He left the shoes on the surface. The worn
leather belt had burst as his stomach muscles jerked taut
when he sprang out as far as he could in his dive. Swimming
over to one of the small balsa rafts, he lay half-across it and
he watched the ship draw away from him.

"Both engines are half speed ahead," he thought.

9

He lay there on the raft, which supported him from his
chin to his groin: this position probably saved his life. As
the ship went past, he saw that the quarterdeck was
crowded with figures. He knew why they could not leap
into the water there and get clear of the ship: they would
be in danger from the four great propellers. Only if they
jumped from right aft could they be safe. He could see
them silhouetted against the white beams. Sharp and quick
they moved, like ants.

Across the sea and under the sky came a great roar. From
under "X" turret a huge ragged geyser of shattered water
spouted skywards, ringed with debris and oil-fuel. The
right and left 6-inch guns of "X" turret jumped their
trunnions, and each gun was left pointing outwards from
the other. The ship gave a violent nervous twitch. Against

the ice-white light the mass of milling figures shot into the air, turning over and over like acrobats or tossed rag-dolls. Some fell into the sea; some fell back on board; some alive, some dead. Jim, standing on the after side of the ·5-inch machine guns, was thrown high in the air and dropped on the forward side of them, feeling like a bit of pulp with all the wind knocked out of him. Blackie dropped into the wake of one of the propellers. The turbulence tumbled him over and over like a ball bouncing down a gutter: he thought, that he was going straight to the bottom and that the thrust would hold him there until he drowned. At last, with busting lungs, he broke surface.

The shock-wave of the explosion travelled its devastating path outwards, killing all who were immersed in the water within a certain radius, crushing their insides as a depth charge crushes the pressure hull of a submarine. Those, like John, lying on some support, felt a terrific kick which made them gasp painfully from its sickening effect.

The raft had saved his life so far: but he was suddenly appalled at the amount of shellfire falling amongst the survivors. On the ship, too, pieces could be seen flying off as salvoes exploded with wicked flashes all over her. He wondered how his party had not been wiped out when they came on deck. Near misses and direct hits were taking heavy toll of the men in the water, whose cries came to him out of the blackness between the lightbeams: often men were dead before the sound had died. John could only lie in the water and watch and hope.

It was pitiful to see the ship now as she lay there helplessly, being blown to pieces. But he could not suppress a feeling of immense pride in her. So much of John's memory was in that ship—so now he was filled with ideas of her which refused to die, even though *she* was dying right before his eyes.

Now she was swinging in a smooth wide turn to starboard. The Captain was still on the bridge, with the Navigator. The ship shuddered dreadfully again as a fourth torpedo hit her in the port side forward, sending up an avalanche of water. John Harper, the Navigator, and the Captain had removed their coats and were inflating their lifebelts.

A salvo of shell hit the base of the director tower on the bridge. The crushed, bed-odorous goon-skins and watch coats, along with the dirty mugs and cocoa-fanny, were blown into the black void of the disturbed night. The Navigator can recall nothing until, about an hour later, he found himself in the water with the centre of his ear missing and a deep furrow leading across his cheek to it. He had been half-an-inch from death.

The Captain stayed on the bridge.

10

John lay on the water watching the ship, trying to burn this last memory of her deep into his mind. Between himself and the ship he could see the round, black heads shown in relief on the light-streaked water. They undulated with the heaving surface. The ship herself was brilliantly lit: stark and white with a pure, ethereal quality.

After the fourth torpedo, the starboard list came off her and she heeled slightly to port. She always did carry this slight list to port. Then, with the way still on her, her bows gently dipped to the surface, then further. Her four propellers came clear of the sea. Three of the shafts were now broken, but the fourth was still turning. She went down for all the world as if she were steaming over the horizon from them.

"She did not sink," they said, "she *steamed* out."

In the Captain's day cabin, as the ship settled in the water, the sea had poured in and risen. It covered the Captain's desk. Then it crept higher, swirling in the darkness there. It reached the level of the mantelshelf and sent a ripple along it. Five model ships floated off: *Stuart* leading, followed by *Voyager*, *Vampire*, *Vendetta* and *Waterhen*. A faint echo came above the splash of the sea—*I like the ships*. And five little ships sailed out into the darkness of the cabin in search of their Captain, lying dead on the bridge.

Part 10

THE WAKE

I

SEARCHLIGHT beams still swept the water. *Houston* lay fixed in them. She was on fire about the bridge and after-part, her main armament silenced. A small gun was blazing away furiously, the curving tracer giving a rude defiant gesture to the enemy. But she could not last much longer, she was being beaten down by weight of metal. Water spouted thick and high around her like headstones in a cemetery. Torpedo hits added white monuments bigger than the rest. The peculiar, flat, rolling echoes of the guns played the funeral march in this wide black battle-theatre. Slowly U.S.S. *Houston* heeled over and sank, quenching the raging fires within her, at about half an hour after midnight. Her men felt about her as the Australians felt about *Perth*.

On the black surface of the midnight sea swam the remnants of the ships' companies. The deadly concentration of gunfire, which had killed and injured so many of them, had ceased. They floated on a sea littered with thick, black oil-fuel, which luckily did not catch fire. The cries of men in distress and pain came thinly through the night, like the noise of a whimpering puppy in a noisy street. Men in panic, fearful of death, called on God; others, with jubilant profanity, showed their gladness at being still alive.

An oily head greeted John in the gloom, "Watcher there, Dirty!"

"Well, look who's talking! If it's not Beau Brummell himself."

"Who else you seen?"

"Both directors got out—the T.S. and the Lower Steering."

"The After Engine Room—Shell Rooms and Lobbies—they got out."

"Don't think the forrard ones would—they copped it."

"Listen to that mob over there—they seem to be having a hell of a skylark."

Voices came across the water with rough laughter.

A Japanese ship burned on the water, showing the glare of her fate over the narrow horizon of the swimming men. To the northward, another action began: it was brief and unequal. H.M.N.S. *Evertsen* had at last managed to raise steam and follow the two cruisers. She reported them in action, and was then attacked by two enemy cruisers. She was beached in a sinking condition, but most of her crew were saved.

The actual damage done by the two Allied cruisers will probably never be known with certainty. The Japanese admit almost no losses now. But at the time, in Serang Cinema where most of *Perth* survivors were being held, Slim of the 4-inch gun deck and C.P.O. McConnell, the Director Layer and Chief Boatswain's Mate, were interrogated by a brittle-tempered, pistol-and-sword-flourishing Japanese officer who spoke fair English. "What battleship was there? What other ships?" They told him two cruisers. He kicked them in an attempt to loosen more information. But they could only repeat what they had told him. This made him contemptuous and furious: with that peculiar, hoarse spitting-shout which some uncouth Japanese manage like a ventriloquial trick, he said, "But *two* could not sink *fifteen*! What battleship was with you?"

A report published in the *Syonan Times* in 1942 stated: *In the terrific battle in Sunda Strait many ships on both sides were sunk. It must be remembered, however, that the lighter Nipponese ships were fighting against a superior force which included a battleship.*

The *Japan Times* made a similar admission.

2

Soon after this last bit of action, the men lay on the sea looking up at the high forms of moving vessels. Destroyers were bearing down on them. Some started to swim away in panic. But what was the use? It was impossible to guess the exact course of the ships in the dark. A searchlight beam flashed across this Sargasso of survivors, swept together by some current along with oil-fuel and wreckage: it revealed the crests of waves with high-lights, their troughs as black pits. Were the Japs going to machine-gun them? Someone muttered hoarsely, "For Christ's sake, get it over!"

The destroyers came among them with engines stopped, their upper decks lined with Nipponese sailors looking spotless in white suits. They appeared to be searching for their own survivors. One *Perth* rating was taken on board—probably for questioning and identification, they thought. One man, with overstrung nerves, called, "Help! Take me aboard! Help!"

"Shut up!" growled half a dozen of his companions.

From the bridge of the destroyer near them came a cool, sardonic voice speaking well-articulated English: "We bloody good boys now, eh, Aussie?"

"Well I'm ——!" they said among themselves.

Their search over, the ships drew off with a short kick ahead on their engines to give them way. Then, with engines stopped, they drifted clear, their coloured stern-lights growing smaller as they went. A column of troop-ships, looking as high as Spanish galleons, sailed on past them to invade Java. Their bow-waves hove the men up and down like cheering spectators. Overhead a twin-engined aircraft, with navigation lights on, flew low, weaving a pattern with the stars.

3

Then the sea was quiet at last, except for a few thin cries from men drowning somewhere in the dark. Men, some-times almost within touch of each other, were in different worlds. Here a crowd joked profanely, finding comfort in insulting and being insulted by each other. But close to these men, and unknown to them, a man gurgled his last desperate breaths as oil-fuel entered his lungs and he died, forsaken and alone. Many must have gone like this. Badly wounded men clung to wreckage or floated in their rubber lifebelts, trying not to complain: lightly wounded men sometimes made a great fuss.

The sole survivor of the forward engine room was a stoker, who had been blown through the engine room hatch into the workshop flat by the explosion of the tor-pedo. Somehow he had made the upper deck and entered the water as the ship was almost awash. Now he lay on a raft naked—terribly naked, for he had no skin left on his body, the explosion having flayed him in an instant. Blind instinct had brought him away from the ship. Next day he was picked up by a lifeboat some of his shipmates had

found: it had been ferrying survivors to a Japanese destroyer. These survivors, before climbing aboard, had been
made to take off all their oily clothes. The boatload with
the flayed stoker aboard approached the destroyer and
the men threw away their clothes. An air attack being
imminent, the ship left them—naked beneath the blistering
sun. At last darkness brought some relief. They hoisted a
sail as the wind rose, and ran before a storm, southwards
along the Strait. In the darkness they could hear the cries
of men still swimming, being swept down towards the
Indian Ocean. It was all they could do to hold the boat on
course in their exhausted condition, and they were haunted
by those pitiful cries fading in the darkness astern. The
stoker had been laid across two other lightly wounded, to
keep him off the rough, ribbed bottom of the boat.

A young Reserve Lieutenant had been complaining of
his back, injured by shellfire in the water. He died after
dark. The Padre, who was in the boat, gave a short simple
service, and they passed the body gently over the side. At
3 a.m. the boat grounded above Labuhan: the men
clambered ashore. From time to time, when asked, the
stoker had replied that he was all right. Now they found
him dead. He had been dead some time. On the beach, in
the coral sand, they dug a grave. When he was placed in it,
he would not fit—it was too narrow, for he had died with
his knees up. He was taken out and the grave widened. One
of the men in the boat told John how the Padre, weak
from exhaustion and shock, stood tottering over the grave,
steadfastly giving the burial service. Once he collapsed, but
got back doggedly to his feet and went on. He collapsed
again—this time into the grave on top of the dead stoker.
They helped him out and, though he was at the end of his
tether, he went on with a noble devotion to his calling and

inner convictions. This was the man who, through the building of the Siam-Burma Railway, remained just as devoted to the men and the practice of Christianity.

4

On another raft a man lay down and did not paddle. The others wanted to know why. He apologized and said, "I'm sorry to be a nuisance—you'd better put me off." Later he died, and when they turned him to slip him into the sea, they found that most of his back was shot away. Many died on the rafts.

One man Fatty met in the water had already abandoned ship, but the fourth torpedo had blown him back on board. He was lucky to have been lifted in this freakish way and not to have been crushed by water-pressure. Another had lowered himself over the port side of the quarterdeck on a fire-hose which was still connected to the rising main. He had lowered himself right on to the port forward propeller —but it was stopped!

The first exhilaration was passing. Men were quieter now, as they had to grapple with the problem of staying alive through the hours of darkness, and beyond. They began to think of sharks with some uneasiness, though they did not express their fears: they kept telling themselves that underwater explosions and oil-fuel would keep the sharks away. But they were by no means sure. There were no more explosions—and there was plenty to tempt the sharks. They thought, too, of the reputation of these Java seas.

Yet there was only one case reported of a shark having been seen. Shortly after daybreak, a dozen men were sitting on a small raft, their legs and feet over the side in the water. The black dorsal fin, suddenly appearing, cut the water about ten yards from them. At once the men on that side drew up their legs, causing the raft to cant.

"What the bloody hell are you doing? Trim the dish!"

Each side took their turn to lift legs, yell and be yelled at. The shark cruised about them for twenty minutes or so, then drew off.

Into the funnel of the north end of Sunda Strait flowed the survivors, the wreckage and the oil-fuel. Their dead floated down with them too. Together they were swept southward to their various fates. Some got to Toppers Island: the rest were drawn relentlessly on. Dawn lightened into day. Again there was the desperate struggle to reach the land; but the south-bound current tore most of them away, even as they were about to reach out and grasp security. A Japanese destroyer picked up some two hundred. But many met their doom down the length of the Strait. Of the 682 men in the ship that night, only 229 returned to Australia after the war.

Part 11

LIMBO

I

As the days went on, the patience of the boat's crew wore thin. Hunger became acute, thirst an evil obsession. But they still talked of the Ship. Thirst may bring hallucination, but hunger brings clear thinking; and John found himself nearer the world of Spirit, detached from temporal things.

One middle watch John was at the tiller. The nightly storm had passed in the first watch. Out of its wildness they had been drenched, caught a little water and had a drink. They had shivered until dry. The boat was sailing eastward on a light breeze. All was quiet on an easy sea. It was dark and starlight. There was no moon. This was no new setting for John—over a period of fourteen years, he had stood many middle watches: so this was a nostalgic time for him, taking him back to the first adolescent watches he had kept, in which the depth of night at sea had made a tremendous impression on him.

His thoughts now were revolving about his sentiment for the Ship; and a voice was speaking within the vault of his mind.

"No useful movement. Rolling boat and slatting sails. No wind. No catspaw. No ripple. Only oily, heat-reflecting sea-surface with no horizon. Pale, scorching glare of sky with the faint smoke of clouds, dim and distant. No birds. Only shoals of small fish, striped and coloured in shoals beneath the keel—cool and clean in the light-speared depths.

"Lively little darting fish: clean, cool and wet; mocking ten men: parched, scorched and hungry. Filthy men, unshaven and unwashed, whose skins are thickened with sunburn and stained deep with oil-fuel. Skins filthy and engrained, beards and hair matted with it. Unkempt hair dry and dead and coming out in one's hand.

"Lively little fish with nice striped clothes and coloured waistcoats. Immaculate little fish mocking men without clothes: men in dirty, oily rags, bits of old canvas, or pieces of plaited native mats. Men who scorch and swelter in them by day; and, soaked and sodden with rain, shiver in them by night. Rain which blots out their only guide, the stars, and drives them blindly far out to sea or toward the dreaded surf.

"Ten men. Listless. Sapped by heat and calm. Patience dried up by the maddening, nerve-racking roll, roll, roll and roll. By the lurch and slat, slat and flap of the useless sails. Sails doing no good, but slatting themselves to pieces. Thirst increasing. The sense of heat becoming intolerable. Always three sitting up at the tiller and sheets. They curse for a wind. Pray for a wind. Raving, muttering, or silent.

"But there is no wind. Not all day. It is the same each day. No wind. No bloody wind at all.

"The boat has no comfort—only hardness and heat."

God knows, John thought, we get mad enough about the wind and the boat at times. But we still talk unashamedly about our feeling for the Ship. And the voice in his head went on:

"The face of the sea indeed seems changed—lust for money and power is driving ships and men harder, bringing bitterness to the world. The criminal selfishness of a few

Becalmed

has made them utterly destructive. It seems nothing can survive this stupidity which spells doom to the human race.

"Yet, there still remains the enduring quality of love in the hearts of simple men. Perhaps this is the rock upon which world-madness will always eventually smash itself. Such love is revealed in men's feeling for their Ship.

"To the sensitive the Ship is a meeting place of ideas, and the sum of its ancestors—that long line, from the first man on the first log, of countless men who have enjoyed and endured in humility and steadfastness, driven by that same inarticulate urge with which the fist log was launched. The relation between Man and Ship is born of common experience, from the whimsicalities of daily commonplaces shared; there is the service, the cursing, the inconvenience of it all, but also the inevitable response and compliance one with another. This nurtures love.

"Here, in a boat south of Java, the truth is evident: here are ten men whose immediate troubles, though grievous, do not submerge their affection for the Ship, which they had watched as she sailed for the Islands of the Blest, achieving, with her dead crew, an immortality beyond that of flesh and steel."

Now that the Ship was gone, John felt inexpressibly glad to have been with her to the end.

2

The voyage went on, with monotony and frustration. Being no more than human, they sometimes gave vent to their aggravations. Tempers flashed, but died just as quickly after a few minutes of acetylene-jet heat.

Darky came in for a period of nagging from John. Darky was foresheet hand in John's watch. John had not known him well on board, but assumed that, because he was a

very well-built A.B., he would know his boatwork. But
Darky was a Hostilities-Only rating, whose boatwork had
been nothing more than a couple of picnic-like excursions
at the Depot. So, when John gave orders couched in nautical terms, Darky did not understand. John thought he
was coming the "old sailor" and swinging the lead.

One day, tired of having to sail blind almost every
night, Mr Carr was endeavouring to fix the lamp in the
compass. The box of big boat matches was useless—one by
one they failed. They decided to try a signal flare. Mr Carr
held it while the end was pulled off, and after some difficulty it was struck. It flared in the bright day like a miniature molten sun. Darky was below the thwarts, lying
down in what shade he could find, when the flare exploded
and a piece like a phosphorescent fist landed right on
Darky's naked stomach. There was a sizzling, and the
acrid smell of burning flesh: Darky's yell of agony rent the
calm, scorching air of the Indian Ocean as he leaped with
the convulsive movements of a new-landed fish. Then,
suddenly, he was gone over the side in a desperate attempt
to rid himself of the burrowing incendiary stuck on his
solar plexus. It came away, and the others quickly dragged
him dripping from the sea. All they could do was to take a
pad of the rags the Chinaman had given them at Labuhan,
saturate it in kerosene and lay it over the wound. The
injury kept Darky out of the Red Watch for the rest of
the voyage, his place being taken by Jacky.

3

After the first night's storm off Java Head, they had
endured a succession of days and nights which had gradually worn them down—maddening calms all day, and
storms in the dark when they were blind and could not

see the compass to tell them where the dreaded surf
lay.

"Only some arch-bastard like a Jaunty or a Chief Buffer
or a Jimmy could think this up," growled Jacky. "You
get all the wind you prayed for but when you get it
you're —— blind!"

Their remarks tended to become more and more unprintable as time wore on. It was simple, angry profanity,
though to some it would have sounded like gross and endless obscenity. The two officers did not join in this uninhibited display of mess-deck language. Mr Carr consciously
refrained from expressions at which he was no novice:
his life in the Merchant Service had naturally made him
as proficient as anyone in the boat; but his position as a
representative of the Ward Room and, in fact, as senior
person in the boat, laid upon him, he thought, an obligation of restraint. Mr Wyatt, still not out of the Gun
Room, had become inured there to naval bawdiness. Now
and then the repressive hand of the Ward Room was
lifted from the Gun Room: the Commander extended
their "pipe-down", allowing them to celebrate with the
lid off. The despised Snotties and Subs, who had been
treated with a traditional sadism as a sort of healthy conditioning, were given a freedom which they proceeded to
use with such vigour that hardened shell-backs felt their
ears shrivel, appalled at the hoarsely shouted ditties roaring
up through the Gun Room skylight. But now Mr Wyatt
was prim. Things became "an awful bore", or they were
simply "bloody" . . .

"Wrong move one night," Fatty said, "and we're gone
—Davey Jones and meals for the little fishes."

"We *could* finish up on a reef, too, one night."

Blackie said, "And I bet, if we did, we would hit it at

about ten knots—just when we'd be skiting how good we were doin'."

"Gives me the Willies," Jacky remarked, "tearing around in the dark, not knowing where we're going, and listening for the surf. I feel my ears stretching out like a bloody giraffe's neck."

It was perhaps this nerve-racking ordeal which caused Mr Carr to announce one day from the helm, with unexpected asperity and an edge of authority on his voice, "We'll drop that in-and-out word from now on. There will be no more swearing in the boat!" Mr Wyatt looked plainly gratified. Despite its oil-streaks and fair, fuzzy stubble, despite the dirty ears and tarry-looking hair, his face appeared full of cherubic virtue and aggravating self-satisfaction. The rest of them only half-believed what they heard.

"Aw, sir!" complained Jacky, "it's only mess-deck talk."

"It's not fitting to talk like that when we could meet our Maker at any time."

"Gawd!" muttered Fatty to Ken, "What next?"

Oh well, if Mr Carr wanted to meet the Lord in full marching-order, it mightn't be such a bad idea after all. They'd tag along. But it was bloody awkward for fellows whose tongues, for years, had been oiled by these very words.

"If anything more happens," Jim said in an undertone, "it'll be prayers." This thought shook them, for though each had offered up earnest prayers over the past month, the idea of public prayer threw them into a panic.

Later, George said that the Lord, seeing their misery under this imposed abstinence, reminded them that He was around and opened their lips again.

4

They had been sailing east on a south-east wind. This was the first time they had had wind during the day. Thirst and hunger nagged them; and now, sailing off shore on a comfortable breeze, they could see the green hills of Java looking like an Eden of Promise. The thought of fresh water from a running stream was tantalizing. Fresh fruit held more promise than a freshly bathed harem. But between them and their dreams lay a mile or so of broken surf, seething over reefs which extended along the coast eastwards as far as they could see. They looked for signs ashore to tell them that somewhere there was a channel in.

"There's a hut over there!" Jacky called from his position by the foremast. His quick signalman's eyes had picked up this speck against the speckled backdrop of foliage. "Looks like a canoe or something pulled up on the beach."

"Well, there'll be a channel," Blackie said dogmatically. "Have a look round!"

"Look! Over there! There's a break!"

Cautiously they closed the surf-line, which was in deep water.

"Hundred-fathom line would run right up to the reef here," Fatty said. This made it easier for them, as there would be no outlying rocks to dodge. Once the lazy rollers broke on the first line of reef, they seemed to shoot ahead with incredible speed, running in swift and low with an exultant hiss, reaching the shore a mile away with scarcely diminished momentum.

"They wouldn't muck about," Jim said; "they'd take the bottom right out of the boat without stopping her."

This added more tension to the approach. The thought struck John, "What if we get in and can't get out?" Nobody stopped to consider that. A wide opening appeared before them.

"That'll be it," called Blackie, fully confident, "put the helm over. I'll con her in."

The helm was put over and the boat fell off to port, making an easy run in with the wind just a little abaft the beam. The rollers ruled a line across their vision of the shore, giving them only a glimpse of their path for about a hundred yards ahead. On either side they could see the combers savagely breaking, and they steered between the boiling seas.

"Lucky to find a break like this, lads!" Mr Carr sang out with comfortable satisfaction.

"A little more to port!" called Blackie.

"It's been worth it," George chuckled, "just to see old Bug-whiskers smile."

"Steady," called Blackie to the helm, ignoring this insult. "Port a little . . ."

Then, suddenly, he yelled in a way that froze everybody's blood, "Luff! Luff! For Christ's sake, luff! Get her out of it! Reefs right ahead! Just under the water—they'll tear our guts out!"

And there, suddenly revealed, were jagged remnants of rock stretched right across their path. They were almost about to drop on them. The rocks stood sabre-like, thrusting up from the trough of the wave which, in receding, had drawn them from their scabbards. "It was like a spiked bear-trap," Blackie said later.

Mr Carr thrust the helm down; Ken, on the mainsheets, sheeted the sail aft with a run to give impetus to the turn. The boat shot round to seaward on a starboard tack, and then, encountering an insweeping roller, checked and hung helplessly in irons. The sails were flapping, not drawing. The mast shook and rattled in its clamp, kicking at it's heel in the kelson. They were now in real danger. The flapping sails were giving them sternway, while the incoming swell forced them further towards the broken water and the reefs. Nothing would live long in that mile of broken water repeatedly smashing itself against rock after rock.

"Oars!" shouted Blackie. But already the others had snatched at them. The bow-hitched lashings were wrenched undone, the oars cascaded with a rattle across the thwarts. They were snatched up and wielded like gigantic swords: brought down on the gunwale, rested for an instant while each man shipped his crutch—then, with a flick, each oar leapt into its crutch. Those on the port side pulled frantically; those on the starboard held water, pushing vigorously against the looms to hold them there and turn the boat.

All this time the boat was drifting to leeward—closer and closer to that first breaking line of surf. There, graphically visible, lay a ruled line: on this side of it was Survival; on the other side was Death. Each rower, with his back to the bow, faced this critical line. They knew that their lives depended on the force they could apply to those ash oars in the next few minutes.

The boat came around at last and they could set her on the port tack. But the rowers knew that they dare not stop. She could never extricate herself by sailing alone—the boat's leeway could still murder them. They pulled on with a kind of demented energy, fighting for every inch they gained. It was agony. That first burst of energy had been prodigal, with no thought of the next moment, as long as they could keep on this side of the fatal wave-crest, which seemed intent on sucking them back as they had

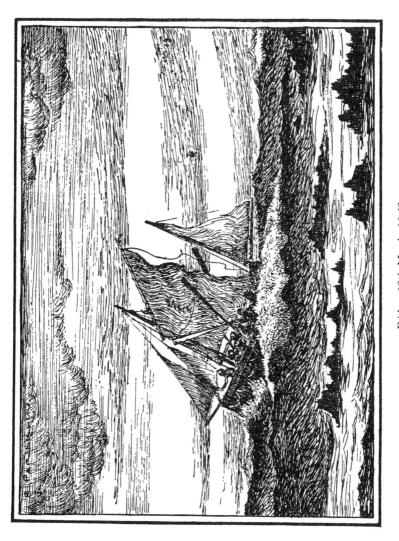

Friday, 13th March, 1942

seen ants swept down a slope of running sand even while racing against it. Now they were exhausted. They gasped, and their chest-cages felt as if a captive vulture was biting his way out. Their ribs, where they joined the spines, seemed to be tearing away as they sucked in painful gulps of air. Their muscles had become hard and bunched, refusing to flex. The oars were turning malign in their grasp, trying to wrench and break their wrists. The tossing sea snatched itself away from the blades, in a judo-like attempt to throw them back and crack their skulls on the thwarts. Everything fought to drag them back over that one wave-crest to their doom.

Stupidly, stubbornly, they kept on. "No! No!" was obstinately repeated in their minds: they did not rightly know, what they meant by it—only that they were denying the wave its final victory. As they drew away, the supreme effort was replaced by a no less difficult and persistent one, which they found more painful because it seemed harder to justify, now that the most urgent necessity was past. They watched the distance, and at last they were able to put the boat about again on to starboard tack. To their immense relief they found that the wind had veered south, so they could now steer south-east. The rowers collapsed where they were, draped grotesquely in positions normally impossible to hold for more than a minute. None of them denied that he had been scared. Only Mr Carr, serene at the tiller, looked unruffled. His absolute lack of distress made the rowers feel all the worse. Fatty, wild-eyed and panting, muttered, "Look, the leader of the Purity League!" He had never got over the coolness of Mr Carr when he had placed his hands on the gunwale, back at Sangieng, and said, "Well, how many'll she take?"

5

Gradually they recovered. Ken was back at the main-sheets and Fatty on the foresheets. The boat was sailing reasonably well, but Mr Carr thought it time for a little more perfection.

"Petty Officer Arrat!" he called. Fatty stiffened. "Get that turn out of the fores'l!"

"Aye, aye, sir," grunted Fatty and, looking up at the head of the sail in question, he saw that the first foot or so was twisted. Fatty lowered the sail, unmoused the calliper-hook through its cringle, and overhauled the halyard through his hands to take out the turns. This done, he re-moused the hook and re-hoisted the sail. It went up beautifully clear, but as soon as Fatty seized the hauling part and hove it with a half-turn around the thole pin on the thwart, the head of the sail spun into the selfsame turns.

Malevolently, but silently, Fatty went through the whole evolution again. The turns still persisted. Once again he repeated it: but, at that last necessary haul, the turn maliciously spun in again. With saint-like forbearance and inhuman self-control, Fatty called, "Turn's not in the halyard—it's in the roping of the sail. Won't be able to get it out."

Now it may have been that Mr Carr was a Merchant Sailor and he still carried something of the competitive pride of Service into the Navy. It may have been that Mr Carr was so big and handsome sitting there, with his level brows beetling, and his commanding hawk nose over firm thin lips and square chin, he looked like a child's dream of a hero-pirate. Or it may have been that Mr Carr's chest was not aching, nor his joints and muscles cringing from further effort, nor was his trachea a raw, red road down which each breath marched in hob-nailed boots.

He said, "What it wants is a *sailor* up there!"

Now all the salt water which had flowed over or under Fatty in his fifteen years of Navy seemed to explode in superheated steam. Nobody could ever recall just what Fatty said. It burst out suddenly, and beneath the eruption they all sat stunned. It was an inspired diatribe born of this particular moment and the brittleness of Fatty's nerves. Spoken at any other time, it would have reduced by court-martial Fatty from a Petty Officer, three Good Conduct Badges, Long Service and Good Conduct Medal, to a badgeless Able Seaman. If every word had been completely unintelligible, the meaning, by pure force and appropriatness of sound, would have been unmistakable. It said everything that was in Fatty's outraged soul.

Jacky sat entranced, realizing one fact: beneath the searing breath of this outburst, the Purity League was completely atomized and dispersed forever. Both the officers realized that sailors will be sailors, even when going to meet their Maker. But to the relief of everyone the air was cleared, Mr Carr's autocratic-seeming self vanished and they saw him as one of themselves again.

6

They had decided that they would continue south-east as long as they could: it gave them easting, and sea-room away from the dreaded coast. They compared their shore observations with the atlas, which luckily showed the mountains in a French hatchure method, so that it was possible to form a good idea of a mountain's profile from it. There were three of these salient features which they could now use. It was not difficult to triangulate these points of reference and get a pretty accurate idea of where they were. It put them about 200 miles east of Java Head. This was a pleasant surprise after their constant feeling of frustration and the daily calms.

"Another eighty or ninety miles and we'll have sailed off the atlas," Mr Wyatt remarked.

"Do a Columbus for it and sail off the edge of the world," said Jacky.

"This slant o' wind's too good to miss—let's hold it while we can. It's all good easting," John said.

"The best we've had," Fatty agreed.

"Hold it all night, if we can."

"Come back to the land tomorrow so that we don't run out of atlas without a landfall for departure," Mr Wyatt suggested.

"Tjilatjap's just beyond the edge of the atlas, isn't it, sir?" Jim asked Mr Carr.

"Yes, couldn't be far away. I should think it would be the next light in sight."

"That's where the ship was bound for. Wonder what it's like?"

"Was a Yankee naval base, they reckon."

"Might still be."

"Some bloody hopes!"

"We don't know, anyway. If we're going to get anywhere, we shall need something more than these starvation rations."

"I'm so weak, I couldn't pull the skin off a rice pudding," George said.

"Well, if Tjilatjap's been a naval base, we might get a better boat—one that will sail," Jim suggested.

They discussed it, and Tjilatjap seemed to hold great promise. Nothing could be worse, they thought, than the way they were being played about with in this unhandy boat. Only Blackie grumbled about the idea. *He* didn't see why they should go in; what if the Japs were there? But the others dismissed his fears as his usual form. Looking back later, they could not but think that it was some premonition which caused Blackie to be so morose over the idea. But it was decided that they go in and have a look. All they had to do now was to find Tjilatjap, somewhere just off the edge of the atlas.

At last they had an objective—not this mucking about in eternal calms. Again the complete logic of making for Tjilatjap occurred to them. The ship had been bound there: so there seemed an obligation upon them to get there still—as if it were an important mission to fulfil before they were free to pursue another. John thought it curious that, though they would possibly be sticking their heads into a trap, they still decided to go in. Yet he, like the others, was drawn to the place. What if the Japs were there? He had a picture of ten prostrate, oil-stained bodies, with ten separated heads gazing vacantly at a squat little man wiping his heavy, bloody sword. These squat little men, their feet planted firmly on new conquest, would not be victims of indecision. Any contact must be perilous. He was reminded of Emperor Jones of Haiiti being lured to his fate by the incessant beating of jungle drums. So the drumming of an idea was leading them in to Tjilatjap.

7

They settled more comfortably in the boat. The fresh southerly wind enlivened them. Gone was the Purity League; but they had less reason to curse now there was an objective in their minds: the calms that had caused them alternately to sulk and rave were now behind them, they hoped.

John had a copy of a *National Geographic Magazine*, which had been found in the wooden lifeboat with the chartcase. The white clay surface of the highly glazed paper was now powdery from salt water and exposure: some of the print and illustration was dimmed. He had been able to read about Professor Piccard's Stratosphere Ascent; but when it came to the lush, verdant fields of a United States County, the prolific abundance of produce heaped up in colourful display, the groups of happy, care-free girls and young folk all so clean and well fed and unworried, John was so exasperated that he threw the magazine away. There were times, too, when they had watched the clean little well-dressed fish swimming leisurely in the cool emerald shadow of the boat, thrust down into the clear light-speared depths of a glinting glassy sea, and found themselves overwhelmed with dis-taste for the oil-scumminess of their bodies and hair.

George said, "We won't even be able to tell about the wicked black sharks' fins follerin' us all the time. Not a bloody shark! Not one!"

"Who's going to believe that those little fish down there, not big enough to eat, were twice as horrible to look at as man-eating sharks?" Jim snarled.

"Just one fin! If only we could see one fin! Then we could easily exaggerate and say that we had dozens follerin' us."

"I think we should give away this shipwrecked-sailor business: there's not one thing we've been able to carry out that's in the drill-book for shipwrecked matelots," Jacky said.

"No sharks," said Fatty. "But there *was* a school ot

porpoise in the middle (watch) the other night. Frightened seven-bells outa me. Snorted like pigs all of a sudden in our wake—out of the dark without warning. Then they shoved off."

"No sharks: no unexpected rescue; no black tongues, swollen and hard as leather."

"Mine's coming on," George said.

"No eating each other."

"Coo! That'll be the day," Jacky interrupted, "Fancy taking one bite of any o' this scraggy mob!"

"No beautiful sheilas on a desert island."

"No sex! That's crooled it! Pack up!"

Mr Wyatt unexpectedly joined in the conversation: "The worldly hope men set their hearts upon turns ashes —or it prospers."

"What's that?" Jim asked.

"That's Omar, the sail-maker," Ken informed him. "He was a wake-up to all this business."

From time to time they had taken turns to plunge into the sea—off the bows, to be dragged aboard at the stern. Though they had seen no sharks, they took no chances: they stood by with boat-hooks and beat the water with flat boards. But there were no sharks. "If there *was* one," Ken said, "I wouldn't bother about him eating me. I'd eat the bugger myself."

The days had been of monotonous pattern: desultory talk, long silences, aggravation from this or that, a continuous feeling of enervation; crawling under the boat's cover, stretched across the spare mast lashed between the two others, dodging the heat, smelling the stench of mouldering grass-mats. Idle, dream-like, and utterly useless days.

Now they were sailing south-east. At dusk, away to the

south, a great line of cloud moved up. It was like an immense rolled-up curtain, white on the front curve and black underneath. It came up like a steam-roller. The wind freshened, so they topped the mizzen and secured it. Fatty stood up and pointed dramatically; "Look!" he said, "we'll cop it now."

"It's a line-squall," Mr Wyatt exclaimed.

Flaws of wind swept across the water, hardening the sea and clipping the tips off the waves, leaving a trail of white scars. The blue trade-wind day changed abruptly to steely grey and green: from steady breeze to gusty uncertainty.

"It's on again," Jim said.

"What do you expect?" growled Blackie.

"Roll, you bastard, roll!" Fatty said: "you'll get tired before I will."

"Rocked in the cradle of the deep," said Mr Carr.

The squall approached them ominously enough: they watched it, trying to estimate something of its force.

"A line-squall, eh?" mused Jacky aloud. "I'm glad you told us what it was, sir. It's kinda better to be hit by a line-squall than just another bloody storm—y' get them anyday. Line-squall! That sounds real tiddley!"

Luckily they only got the lash of its tail, for it veered northwards and passed them by: but they had half an hour's lively commotion and some bailing before it was past. The sky cleared to scattered cloud, the stars shone. It was sufficiently clear to set a course by the stars. The breeze remained light and steady. About midnight they judged it safe to go about and head in for the land. It would not be possible to raise the land before dawn. They were going in to make that last land-fall on the atlas.

Dawn came, and the land hove in sight an hour later. There was a point with the land stretching away to the westward: nothing to the eastward. They thought it was Madasari Point.

"Not far off the edge now," Mr Carr said.

They sailed in on a dying wind. It was clear and hot. They sailed north until they sighted low land ahead, passed Madasari Point, and then turned east. A headland appeared, behind which they thought was an interesting bay— Maurits Bay, they later discovered. Further east, it plunged north. This gave them hopes of a place to land; but the inlet only led to a vast swamp. The wind died, so they carried out this part of the exploration under oars. It made them realize how weak they had become: they could merely paddle the boat with a slow, weak rhythm. It was lucky that the sea was glassy calm, for they could not have pulled in a seaway. There being nothing more to discover here, they pulled off-shore and, boating their oars, lay there as still as the sea and air about them, waiting patiently for a wind to take them eastwards.

Late in the afternoon a light southerly breeze set them slowly on an easterly course. They were well satisfied, for it allowed them to steer parallel with the shore: it was a cliff-like coast, with no sign of outlying reefs.

The wind, being light, called for a more careful trim of the sails to get them to draw without spilling. John was setting up the mizzen halyard to take a wrinkle out of the luff when he found it had fouled in the sheave at the mast-head. "Halyard's foul," he said. He thought someone would volunteer to clear it—one of the younger ones: but nobody did, so John had to go up the mast himself. Half-way through that short climb, he thought he would never make it. The muscles of his arms were bunching uselessly; his legs gripped much tighter than necessary. He knew this was wrong; for if climbing is not done easily, you don't go very far. That was all very well in theory, but he was afraid that, if he didn't use all his strength, he would never get there now. Shame and a silly desperation drove him to the mast-head, where he hung on, exhausted, while with one hand he cleared the halyard. He came down again with a pained, slow dignity. Back at the stern bench, he took a small pull on the halyard, passed a bow-clove hitch around the strongback, took a slow deep breath and said, "She's right now."

He sat down without another word, amazed at his unfitness. A week or so later he was talking it over with Jim, who said, "When I saw you climb up there, I wondered how you did it. I was so weak, I didn't want even to get off the thwart." John thought it had been just as well that they did not know too much about one another's condition.

Dusk came, then darkness; and there, almost dead ahead, fine on the port bow, was a lighthouse flashing. Timing it, they found that it flashed once every minute.

"Tjilatjap, I'd reckon, lads!" Mr Carr said.

"We can steer on that. We don't need the stars or compass tonight," Fatty said. Ironically enough, there were stars all night. They sailed steadily through the dark hours, and dawn brought them the sight of the thin pillar of the lighthouse on top of a bluff. During the day the wind shifted to the north-east, so they had to sail well past the headland before they could go about to steer for the entrance. At 3 p.m. they headed in for Tjilatjap.

Part 12

TJILATJAP

I

As they came under the bluff upon which the lighthouse stood, they realized that they were in the flood-stream of the incoming tide. Just past the lighthouse they picked up the first of the channel buoys, then another and another in regular succession, sweeping past them. The strong, fast-flowing stream pulled the buoys over on their sides so that their conical tops all pointed in to Tjilatjap. The muddy tide was taking them, and there was just sufficient wind to give them steerage way. They thought that they would be making at least five knots over the ground.

"The fastest we've ever gone," Blackie said unhappily.

"This is it," Jacky said. "No going back now!"

"Hope we've done the right thing," said Darky.

"Without instruments we could never get far to sea. We would have to keep to the land," Mr Carr said.

"You can bet your life that, where ever there was a landing, there would also be a village and some boongs to give us up, or top us off," Ken added. "Remember Labuhan?"

"Yes, we are apt to forget these things," Mr Wyatt remarked.

"Well, if we can get a better boat, and if we can get some provisions—" Jacky began.

"And *if* we can get away with it," Blackie concluded.

"I reckon we'll just have to take things as we find them," George said practically.

There was a feeling of expectancy, and there was some anxiousness—some doubt. They had begun to think of a few sinister possibilities. What if there *were* Japs there? They were helpless to turn back now. What if this fast current swept them up right to the feet of the enemy? What would be the mood of this capricious foe? They knew only the evil reputation given him by propaganda. Would they find him boastful, vain, gloating and cruel? Would he be pompous and savage, eager to show the two-handed swing of his Samurai sword to his Indonesian serfs? Or would he be playful and prefer the amusement of some torture from his vast traditional repertoire? These were thoughts that each man, with good reason, kept to himself. They kept saying that they were looking for a better boat, and food. But the feeling arising from being in the grip of this flood-tide was a psychological one of being already captured.

They swung around the bend of the channel and were now heading west. The whole of Tjilatjap harbour lay before them. It was obvious at once that destruction had got there before them. Half a dozen ships lay askew on the bottom in the middle of the long estuary-like bay.

"Bombed!" George exclaimed.

The ships lay drunkenly to port and starboard, only one on an even keel, some showing no more than bits of super-structure, masts and tops of funnels. Some in shallower water exposed riven hulls as well. Masts were missing, funnels twisted bizarrely. So scattered and turned were they, that they had an air about them like that of a group of Pieter Breughel's mediaeval mendicant cripples. Further ahead, on their starboard hand, were the wharves where

the warehouses had been. Now there was only chaos and
disaster in which no salient feature stood save two wrecked
cranes looking like a pair of broken-necked wading birds,
silly and dead.

"They've certainly done this place over," Ken said.

"She's flattened," Jim agreed.

"Might give us a better chance to find something among
the wreckage," Mr Wyatt suggested.

The harbour of Tjilatjap is formed by Kanbangan Island,
which is twenty miles long and only two or three wide at
the broadest point, lying close against the shore of Java.
At its western end the island is separated from Java only
by a swampy region: at the eastern end there is an estuary
nearly a mile wide. The flood-stream now flowing so
strongly was running to fill the swamps. Tjilatjap was three
or four miles from the lighthouse.

"Get on that mob over there," Jacky cried, pointing to
the shore of Kanbangan on their port hand. There were
hundreds of men moving along a road in both directions.
"Wonder what they are? Dutch or native troops?" Among
them, here and there, could be seen figures in khaki. They
were too distant to be seen clearly.

"Who're you kidding?" Blackie asked, already convinced.

"Think we'll keep to the starb'd side of the channel,"
Mr Carr said.

"Bloody good idea!"

As they proceeded up the harbour, the destruction of the
wharves became more apparent. They could see some
derelict American aircraft about, scattered in the same careless manner as the ships.

"Bostons," Ken informed them. "Yank planes."

They continued watching for a likely place to make

Tjilatjap Wharf, 1942

their boat fast, and to look at the lie of the land. The wharves were high and there were no boat-landings. They had to get a line over a bollard ten feet above them. One of them was able to climb up and pass a stern-fast. The sails were dropped, the boat left ready for getting under way again. At last they were all standing on the wharf, looking curiously around them. They felt the wharf heaving strongly as they took their first steps ashore.

The wharf-piles and decking were charred, and in some places burnt away altogether. Wharf sheds had collapsed in a twisted heap under the great heat of fires. In some, the whole galvanized roof structure had sunk intact to the ground as the heat softened the supporting pillars, which had buckled like the knees of a mortally wounded stag: the twisted steel girders gave the impression of still writhing in death agony. Over the sandy plain thousands of drums of oil were scattered in grand disorder. Bamboo buildings showed black gaping holes where the matting walls had been blown out. Tiled roofs were denuded, except where an odd tile or two hung precariously on the skeleton of rafters.

Then, just across the wharf, they sighted two Dutch officers in green uniforms with peaked caps. With them was a Javanese, also in a green uniform. The Dutchmen came across out of curiosity. "Good afternoon," and "G'day," said the boat's crew. "How do you do?" came the reply, in English.

"Good, thank you. We're glad you speak English."

"Who are you?"

Briefly they told of the sinking and the boat voyage. Then they asked, "What happened here?"

The Dutchman shrugged with a suave sadness, "The

place has been bombed. For two days they came over and
there was nothing to stop them. You can see they did it
pretty thoroughly!"

"And now?"

"We are prisoners."

"But the Japs, where are they?"

It was then that they caught sight of something they
had not noticed before. The Javanese in the green uniform
wore an arm-brassard: white with a red ball on it.

"He brought us down to look over this mess," the
Dutchman explained. "We have to bring corvées down
tomorrow to start to clean it up. Look! Along there—
and down there." They followed the direction of his taut
finger. They could see Japanese soldiers with rifles. A short
distance off was a guard-hut with some soldiers lounging
about outside it. They carried only side-arms.

"Stand-by guard," Blackie guessed.

"Well, chaps?" Mr Carr said quietly.

"Goosed!" Jacky commented.

"Get in the boat and get out of it," Darky said.

"With that pro-Jap Javanese waiting to top us off and
make himself popular with the Nips?"

"And the flood-tide to take us *further* up?"

"What are the Japs like?" they asked.

"In the camps so far, they have let us alone. But down
here round the wharf, they are a bit trigger-happy."

"They beheaded an Australian airman this morning".

"A Jap guard was killed two days ago and that has made
them jumpy. They said the airman must have killed the
guard, because when he got caught he could not tell them
who did."

"Nice bastards!"

"I don't think you would get far if you tried to escape

now," the Dutchman said honestly. "This Javanese fellow is—they all are—very pro-Jap just now. He has heard us speak English to you—that will be enough for him. He will be waiting for you to make a move."

"These wharf guards don't sound nice bastards to get mixed up with. I don't want *my* lolly carved off!" Fatty said grimly.

"Who does?" asked Jim.

"All right, let's go out in the boat and get machine-gunned," said Blackie.

"If we took you to the Capitai," one of the Dutchmen suggested, "you would stand a better chance. There are some officers there."

"Are they any better than these monkeys?"

"Capitai? What's that?"

"Some of them are better. Capitai is what they call their headquarters."

"Oh, I see!" George said. "Generals and all that."

"Bring me a General," Jacky said: "I'm not satisfied with the way this war is being run."

After some deliberation they decided that they would go with the Dutchmen to the Capitai. At this stage they saw no value in being liquidated by some fanatical soldier wishing to cover himself in glory for the approval of his ancestors. They were not at all happy, just the same. What they knew of the Japanese was scant and not reassuring: it was propaganda, designed to make people in comparative safety hate the enemy enough to continue to prosecute the war without further hesitation. But it was not designed to comfort those, like this boat's crew, who were about to come under the immediate influence of this enemy. *They* were about to find out at first hand. It was an education which was to continue for some time and, in the end, though much more enlightened, they were just as bewildered as in the beginning.

The Dutchmen had come to the wharf in an old 1930 model Capitol Chev. tourer. The top was up but there were no side-curtains. The Javanese drove. One Dutch officer and five of the crew went in the first load. In about half an hour the car returned for the rest. They passed across a stretch of open plain, upon which the almost complete devastation of the port was evident. Fires and bombs had combined to destroy so much planning and preparation, and to show how ill prepared the Dutch had been. These men were now left behind to bear the humiliation of it. Their captors would rub it in mercilessly, holding them up with sneers to the rest of the Oriental world as examples of Western bluff, bluster and empty promises.

Once more they found reason to love their ship. In the midst of this humiliation there burned a sustaining, comforting thought—they had fought with their ship to a finish. That was good enough for them. They would let all this bloody rot from these silly little bastards go over their heads. They were proud to be *Perth*—she had given them more than the Imperial Japanese Army could take away.

They passed off the bare plain and went along a smooth dirt road completely shaded with coconuts, mangoes, and other trees with which they were not familiar. It all looked pleasant enough until they came to the shops. These had been gutted by looters just like Labuhan. Then they pulled up at a substantial building which, they were told, was the K.L.M. Headquarters in Tjilatjap. The first five were already formed in a loose knot on the semicircular gravel drive. The second five joined them.

"What happens now?" Jim asked.

A Japanese corporal came out and there was some attempted conversation with one of the Dutchmen. At length a Javanese woman interpreter was found. The Australians spoke to the Dutchman, he spoke to the Javanese woman, she spoke to the Japanese Corporal. It was a laborious business, making the sailors feel rather like cattle up for slaughter.

The feeling was not alleviated by an incident they witnessed while they waited. A terrified blackman, whose eyes were wide, white and wild in a grief-stricken face on which tears gleamed, came in bearing a large suitcase hoisted high on his shoulders. The side of the case had been slashed with a sword, and its viscera of brightly coloured silks hung in festoons. One entrail of this stuff hung just by his face, catching his hypnotized eyes and filling him with horror. The wretched blackman was marched in between two wooden-faced little soldiers with sloped rifles and fixed bayonets. Another with a drawn sword walked in their wake. The tragic party came to a halt a few yards away, opposite the sailors. They heard the Japanese language being freely spoken for the first time: it seemed like the noise of caged and discontented beasts—savage, animal sounds, grunted from the gut, forced from swelling throats; sometimes hoarse, sometimes shrill. They talked as if they would be at each other's throats at any second. The phrases sounded more like insults than conversation.

After what seemed to be a short, vicious harangue from the corporal, the soldier with the drawn sword shouted, "Hai!" He turned to the escort, snarling an order with frightful savagery. The party turned left. "Sp'ts'!" he spat at them, and they marched down the drive around to the back of the building. The look on the blackman's face was so piteous that, after he had marched off, it still hung there, disembodied, before their eyes. There was a sharp volley of two shots, the distant rattle of rifle bolts, and the incident was closed.

The sailors looked at one another not daring to voice their thoughts, while the long-winded consultation went on. It had passed out of their hands. They watched the Corporal intently, trying to guess what was in his mind. He sounded uncouth, overbearing and angry. It seemed that this volatile, thick-set, short man would explode at any moment. Nerves on edge, the sailors could only await the whim of a man who gave the impression that he had conquered Java single-handed.

"What a stupid, bloody way for a man to finish up!" Jacky muttered.

"Makes you weep!" Ken said.

"That little oaf up there is deciding whether we live or die!" said John.

George's humour did not entirely desert him, "Well, *he* thinks he's the King, anyway."

"King Kong!" snarled Blackie.

Eventually the Corporal came down off the porch and approached them. They were in two ranks, with Mr Carr on the right. He called them to attention. They all stood like wooden dummies, trying to mask their mixed feelings—fear, born of the undecided future; contempt and hatred for the broad flat face, the black almond eyes, and the bared, good, white teeth. The Corporal's expression was enigmatic: his face showed glimpses of cruel triumph, contempt, and as he came in front of men head and shoulders taller then he, a flash of fear turning instantly to arrogance. They had little doubt now what he intended to do with them: it would be so simple to impress the Javanese

339

with the absolute power and superiority of *Dai Nippon,* and the worthlessness of the West. It seemed there was only one thing he could do. He stood back and looked them over. His face became a mask devoid of all emotion. Only his narrow eyes moved right and left over them. They felt sure a decision had been reached then behind those dark little slits.

He turned and remounted the few steps to the porch again. He drew himself to his full height: he looked down on them as if he were savouring the fact that he was once again taller than they. Half-extending his right hand towards them, palm down, he made small raking movements towards his body and called loudly, "*Oi!*"

The Dutchmen interpreted for them. "He wants you to follow him!"

So they trooped up the steps, through the double doors. At the end of a short hall they found themselves in a courtyard with a wide, tiled verandah around it. In the open centre was a fountain set in a rectangular pool surrounded with potted palms. The pool was dry. They crossed this and, at the end of another short passage, came out on a red brick courtyard at the back of the main building. At one side, in shelter, some Javanese women were preparing food. The smell of it and the wood-smoke tantalized the starving men.

Here the corporal paused and in a high, sing-song voice called, "Oi, Oi! Mutugoi! Mutugoi!" That was how it sounded to them. Three or four Japanese soldiers came sliff-sloffing in slippered feet: their trouser-legs were unlaced at the calves, and they wore broad woollen cholera belts about their waists outside their trousers. Their short, sturdy, brown calves and their smooth torsoes were bare.

The corporal gave some rapid orders in Japanese. The

soldiers vanished, to return shortly with clean towels and soap. They moved ahead of the sailors to a smaller enclosed courtyard in the middle of which stood a well surmounted by an iron pump. One of the soldiers slapped the pump a couple of times with his hand as if to draw their attention to it, then he commenced to pump. The others brought buckets and signalled for them to wash. Jacky and George jumped in without hesitation.

"This is better than being shot," gurgled Jacky from under the surging pump-stream.

"Well, I'm scuppered!" Fatty said. "You could knock me down with a crowbar!"

3

Their spirits rose and they skylarked a bit. The soldiers seemed amused, too, as they continued to pump water and fill buckets. The women, passing the entrance, gazed in curiosity at the strange naked figures of white men as black as Malays. The sailors lathered and lathered with the soap, feeling the sheer sensual pleasure of it intensely. They were looking forward to a brisk rub-down with a towel—and then to be clean once more.

But they were disappointed. After they were dry, they felt the same cloggy, thick-skinned feeling they had come to detest. It was another three weeks before they were able to lose that oil-fuel scum and to perspire normally again. When it did come away, it was in a thick putty-like substance which they had to scratch off with their nails: unexpectedly one day, by a well, they found it would come off. They eagerly began scraping it from each other's backs: but it was still three days before they were rid of it all.

After this they dressed. Beside people with real clothes, they were scarecrow figures. Two of them had cut up a piece of old, yellowed and mildewed sail for loin-cloths. Two had blue combination overalls without sleeves, torn and oily. The rest were in shorts, once blue or white, but now nondescript oily rags. Jacky had a banana-leaf coolie hat, and Fatty had a straw one, while Jim wore the Robinson-Crusoe-boat-flap piece John had made. These headpieces had been passed around to the watch on deck in the heat of the days at sea.

Thus garbed, and trying to preserve some dignity, they were led back to the red-brick courtyard. A small round table was placed against one of the verandah posts, with cane chairs about it. The soldiers had withdrawn. Ten large dinner plates heaped with steaming white rice were put on the table, together with a dish of pickled cucumbers and a plate of thick-sliced bully beef. The woman who brought this to them, smiling, motioned them to eat. They started with all the reluctance of a pride of starved lions.

After their meals of the past three weeks, this was an Arabian Night come true. The biggest meal they could recall over that period had not been more than three good mouthfuls. While they were eating, some glasses of strong, black, unsweetened tea were placed before them. But they soon ran into trouble.

"Gawd, I'm full already," Jim groaned, disgusted with himself.

"Me too," Darky said; "me stomach's like a football."

"Wouldn't it?" George said sadly. "When y'can't get scran, you would murder your mates for it. And when you *do*, y'can't eat it."

"I think we must attempt to eat it," Mr Wyatt said. "These people have given us food, and they may take it as an insult if we don't eat it all."

"That's right," Jacky agreed. "No good getting these blokes mad now—just when they look like treating us good."

So they grimly persevered, stuffing the rice into themselves. As a result, their shrunken stomachs and inactive digestive processes would undergo the most acute agony. Just at the moment, however, they were concerned not to offend an enemy whose kindness and cruelty stemmed from an unfathomable whimsicality.

Presently, three bottles of beer were brought.

" 'Struth," Jim exclaimed unbelievingly, "next it'll be caviar!"

"I have heard," Blackie said, "that the Orientals often treat prisoners well before they execute them."

"Will you shut up!" Fatty barked roughly. "Time enough to think about it if it happens—don't want to go bloody-well batchy brooding over it."

"I don't think they're going to do us over, now," John said.

"How do you know?" Blackie insisted.

"I don't," John answered. "But what I believe has saved us is the fact that we came in from the sea."

"Well, why don't they finish off what they tried to do in Sunda Strait?"

"Because I don't think they look at it that way. These people live very close to things like fire, famine, earthquakes, floods, typhoons, tidal waves and all that. They're close to the sea. They're almost a race of fishermen. Now we turn up, and to them we're survivors from the sea."

"What about our propaganda? Lies?"

"Could be," Jacky said.

"No, not all lies. I guess we'll find that out, all right. But for the moment they're thinking of us as survivors rather than prisoners—we're not in uniform, and we look pretty harmless."

"We've been lucky—for the moment," Ken remarked.

"Let's leave it at that and let tomorrow take care of itself. We can't do anything about it, anyway."

They had eaten and drunk everything put before them —even the pickled cucumbers, which would take grim revenge. A soldier came back and enquired if they had had enough. He used that mysterious pantomime of language with which people of diverse tongues and ideas somehow make themselves understood.

They patted their stomachs, licked their lips in a savoury gesture like theatrical cannibals, and said, "Good! Good! Plenty! Plenty!"

"Takusan-ca?"

"Good! Good! Plenty! Plenty!"—trying to outdo Nippon in native politeness.

Then the soldier led them back to the inner courtyard with the fountain. There, in one corner, they found bed mattresses laid out: some were double and some single. The Officers had a single mattress each, while the ratings doubled as necessary. They sat there yarning and getting used to their novel circumstances. By ten o'clock the place was dark except for the night-lights.

Throughout the night they heard the guards being changed. At intervals a guard would sneak up quietly with a torch and count the sailors. Sometimes he had to make several counts. His anxiety would grow, so that he counted aloud: "Ich, nee, san, yon, go . . ." His voice rattled on, revealing his perplexity, till at last he reached "joo" and, with a sigh, crept away. Once he came close and gently pulled the blanket over the naked stomach of a sleeping sailor.

4

They had not slept nearly as well as they thought they would on these soft beds. The motion of the boat was missing, and its hardnesses to which they had grown accustomed. Mosquitoes whined viciously and bit them. Besides, they had lost the habit of prolonged sleep. They heard the metallic clip-click from the heels of the guard on the tesselated verandah and corridors. The heavy meal twisted like iron within them. It was a restless, fitful night, and they woke in the first light of the short tropic dawn.

They fossicked to find a toilet. Here some of them began to suffer the trials of bodily re-adjustment. Tissues were torn and muscles were cramped in a supreme effort to break constipation. Tears and the sweat of pain were their only reward. Some days of this agony had to be endured, together with a frightful colic, before they could get back to normal.

"These are the heroics y'don't get medals for," George said.

"By God," Mr Carr said, "the horrors of war have got nothing on the horrors of eating again."

Seven hundred and fifty years before, a chronicler of the Third Crusade tells of the army of Frederick of Germany: he had been drowned fording a river; but his men, after near-starvation, reached Antioch: "His army, arriving at Antioch after many long fastings, gave way too plentifully to their appetites, and large numbers died of sudden repletion."

Plates of rice were brought to them, with a little bit of chutney, as they sat around wondering what was to happen next. Again, though knowing more about the consequences now, they had to force the rice down. The eating of plain

Into the smother

rice as a staple diet is something that takes a little practice, especially for Westerners.

Presently, Mr Carr was sent for by the Japanese Captain. A mild, gentlemanly Javanese acted as interpreter. The questions were simple and direct. Mr Carr was obliged to give only the name of the ship and the names and ratings of the men: he also gave a brief account of how they had got from Sunda Strait to Tjilatjap. He was told that they would be placed in a prison camp, to which they would be taken by the interpreter. Five minutes later, they were fallen in and marched down the dusty road.

A mile down the road, they were halted outside a camp among groves of coconut palms. A Dutch Officer, who was called out, entered into conversation with the guide: the guide came back and apologized to them. "They cannot take you—they have too many already." On they went to the next camp, where the same happened. At the third camp they were received, simply because the guide marched them in and left them there, without any questions. There was no Japanese administration at these camps just then—evidently the Dutch officers were on some sort of parole.

"A home at last!" said Fatty, sighing largely.

Ken said, "Admiral Helfrich's remaining Allied Forces are at last assembled at Tjilatjap."

Part 13

POSTSCRIPT

1

H ERE began three and a half years of hope, disappoint- ment, sickness and suffering, with hope always strug- gling up.

In June they left Jacky in hospital in Tjilatjap (he finished the war in Java) and went to Bandoeng. In November, Mr Carr and Mr Wyatt were left there while the rest proceeded to Makasura, near Batavia.

Then in January they were taken, through Singapore, to the never-never of Siam, where they worked a year and ten months on the Burma-Siam Railway, just thirty-nine kilos from the Three Pagoda Pass on the Burma-Siam border.

Blackie died there.

They were brought back to Tamuan near the junction of the Kwai Noi and Menam Rivers. Jim, George and Darky were left there as sick men. Ken, Fatty and John, being pronounced "fit", a relative term, were sent to Singapore for trans-shipment to Japan.

The short voyage from Singapore to Japan lasted seventy days, from July 1st to September 8th, 1944. It was not without incident. The ship caught fire and burned for two days before it was brought under control. On entering Manila Bay there was a submarine scare, and the rest of the convoy was sent in while their ship steamed in a wide, slow circle, as bait, while the submarine was hunted with small surface vessels and an aircraft. Typhoons within the harbour delayed their coaling. Two hours after they eventually cleared Corregidor, outward-bound, two ships immediately astern of them were torpedoed.

Two days later—Friday 13th—they encountered a typhoon at sea. It was nasty, because the ship was completely open forward: Nos. 1, 2, and 3 hatches had no covers and were wide open down to the lower holds. There was only one lifeboat, into which some Japanese soldiers, terrified by the ship's violent rolling, jumped; whereupon the boat scooped up a breaking sea as if it were a soup-ladle and nearly drowned them all. Just as terrified, they jumped out again. Loose gear ran amok, some of it heavy castings of derelict winches.

The ship had previously been burnt and bombed in Singapore, so the remains of her bridge had had to be shorn off with an oxy-cutter. There was a wooden jury-bridge aft. The decks had dropped from the intense heat of fire, and long box-girders had been welded to the deck to stiffen her, but no effort had been made to replace the hatch beams. In the heavy rolling—men in the 'tween decks saw the sea above the coamings—the welding on the girders parted and came undone like a zip fastener. She was then in grave danger of breaking up and foundering. A group of three small islands gave them shelter until the worst of the storm had blown out by the next day.

It cost the convoy five ships, and three more could be seen on fire. The two thousand prisoners this inadequate ship carried were understandably anxious until they reached Moji, where they were sold on the wharf like slaves in batches of 150. The sailors' party was taken across the Inland Sea to Ohama. Here Fatty, Ken and

John spent twelve months in a coal-mine, the instability of which caused further anxiety.

2

Interestingly enough, Ohama placed them almost equidistant between the two fateful bombs of Hiroshima and Nagasaki. John saw the cloud of the Nagasaki bomb rise out of a clear sky to the south. Its great columnar anvil, soaring into the sky, was something he had not seen since that "greatest show on earth" in Sunda Strait. It puzzled him, but eight days later came the explanation in a Manila newspaper dropped on their camp by American planes.

They felt, on reading the newspaper, as Rip Van Winkle must have felt on awakening. Their first impressions of what had happened out in the world from which they had been locked were headed by three remarkable phenomena —(1) atom bombs; (2) jet propulsion; (3) ball-point pens. And, to them, the last was by no means the least remarkable. About October 1945, all the boat's crew except Blackie returned to Australia.

3

This story closes just before they entered the prison camp in Tjilatjap.

As John looked back along the brilliant tropic road down which they were marching, he saw a great archway formed by the soaring trunks of palms. Under this they had just diminutively passed. As he looked at the light-live sky between them, it seemed as if some vast invisible doors, hinged on the palm trunks, had swung shut.

He was conscious at that moment of having left a familiar world and having entered this new one as a stranger. He was walking into it almost as, thirty-two years ago, he had entered the greater world now behind him. He was nearly as naked; he was bigger and dirtier; he had lost his original innocence; but he was as a babe new born. In the place of that pristine innocence, what bulwark had he against the menace of the future?

He felt that it would be something derived from the ship and the boat. On the surface he could only show failure—a ship defeated in battle, a boat voyage which had ended in capture. But he would be for ever grateful for the breathing-space which the voyage had given him.

Would anyone believe that he had been across the Styx and passed through a world of illuminating enchantment? that he had lived with the soul of a ship and the soul of the past? Not likely! They would call such a notion sentimental rubbish.

But, as those invisible doors closed, he knew that he was arrived at a place which would sort out truth from rubbish. He found that, mixed with a natural fear of the unknown and the evil reputation of his captors, he had a vague feeling of eagerness for this new experience. Here was the test.

A line of Shakespeare had occurred to him on the closing of those invisible doors:

"Thus must I from the smoke into the smother."

EPILOGUE

As the ten ragged boat's crew walked into captivity, one of them was carrying a bundle. It contained some tins of pemmican, condensed milk and a few ship's biscuits. They were wrapped in the small triangular foresail which they had found on the beach at Princes Island.

After they had been in camp about a week, they felt that the ship and the boat needed some memorial. John took an indelible pencil, and drew the ship and the boat on this sail. Over the drawings he lettered: "To the memory of the gallant ship H.M.A.S. *Perth*". The ten signed it, then hung it on the wall of their room.

The sail was left behind at Bandoeng and became only a memory to them. But, incredibly enough, after the war had ended a Dutchman sent the sail to Jacky in Australia. Jacky passed it on to the Royal Australian Navy. Later, there was added to it a list of all the names of the ship's company. It now hangs in the Royal Australian Navy Memorial Chapel, Flinders Naval Depot, Victoria. It occupies a Memorial Bay of its own. A spontaneous gesture, made by ten sentimental sailors in their captivity has thus become a permanent memorial to the ship they all loved.

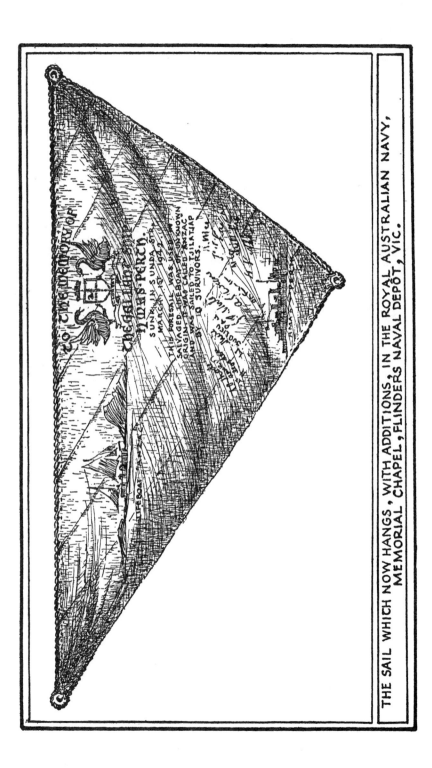

THE SAIL WHICH NOW HANGS, WITH ADDITIONS, IN THE ROYAL AUSTRALIAN NAVY, MEMORIAL CHAPEL, FLINDERS NAVAL DEPÔT, VIC.

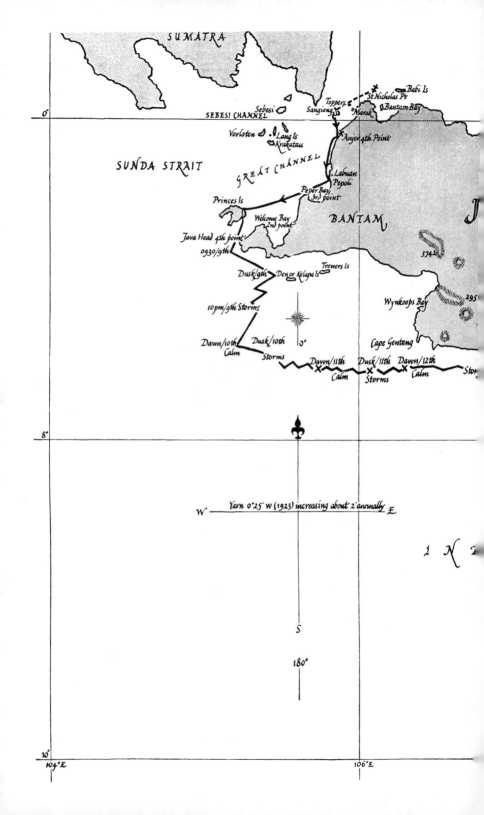

SUMATRA

SEBESI CHANNEL

Sebesi

Babi Is

St Nicholas Pt

Toppers

Sangiang

Merak

Bantam Bay

0°

Verlaten

Lang Is

Krakatau

Anjer 4th Point

SUNDA STRAIT

GREAT CHANNEL

Labuan
Pepoli

Peper Bay
3rd point

Princes Is

Welcome Bay
2nd point

BANTAM

J

Java Head 4th point

574

0930/9th

Dusk/9th

Den or Kelapa Is

Trowers Is

10pm/9th Storms

Wynkoops Bay

295

Dawn/10th
Calm

Dusk/10th

Dusk/10th

0°

Cape Genteng

Storms

Dawn/11th
Calm

Storms

Dusk/11th
Storms

Dawn/12th
Calm

Stor

8°

Varn 0°25′ W (1923) increasing about 2′ annually

W

E

1 N 2

S

180°

10°

104°E

106°E

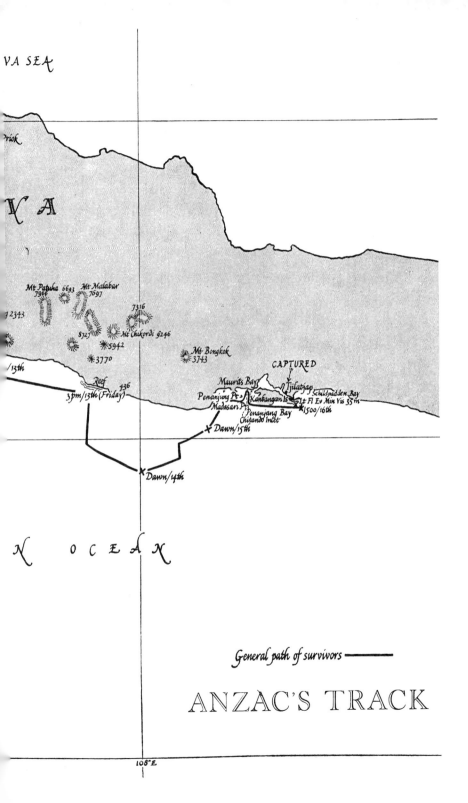

VA SEA

*riok

J A V A

Mt Papuha 6693   Mt Malabar
     7966   7697
12343   7316
        8727   Mt Chikordi 9246
           *5942
       *3770   ⁂ Mt Bongkok
                            3743   CAPTURED

/13th   ↓ Tjilatjap
        Reef   Maurits Bay   Schildpadden Bay
         736   Penanjong Pt   Kanbangan Is   Lt Fl Ev Min Vis 35 m
3 pm/13th (Friday)   Madasari Pt   1500/16th
                                 Penanjang Bay
                               Chitanda Inlet
                            ✗ Dawn/15th

                    ✗ Dawn/14th

ᴎ   O C E A ᴎ

General path of survivors ———

ANZAC'S TRACK

108°E

INTO THE
SMOTHER

RAY PARKIN

by the author of 'Out of the Smoke'

INTO
THE SMOTHER

A Journal of
the Burma-Siam Railway

RAY PARKIN

Author of
OUT OF THE SMOKE

1963
THE HOGARTH PRESS
LONDON

Disease or oldness or sword-hate
Beats out the breath from the doom-gripped body.
From *The Seafarer*. Translated by Ezra Pound

For
WEARY
(Who knows so much more
of all this than I)

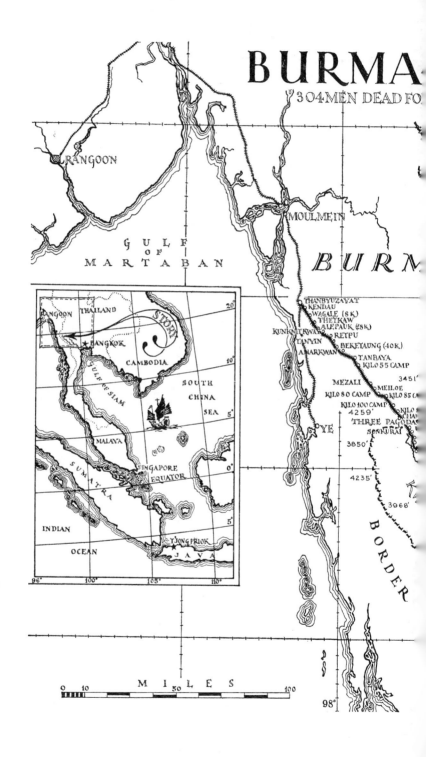

BURMA

304 MEN DEAD FO

RANGOON

MOULMEIN

GULF
OF
MARTABAN

BURM

THANBYUZAYAT
KENDAU
WAGALE (8K)
THETKAW
ALEPAUK (18K)
KUNKNITKWAY
RETPU
TANYIN
BEKETAUNG (40K)
ANAKKWAN
TANBAYA
KILO 55 CAMP

MEZALI   3451'
KILO 80 CAMP   MEILOE
              KILO 85 CA
KILO 100 CAMP
4259'   KILO
              CHAN
THREE PAGODA
YE   SONKURAI
3850'

4235'

BORDER

3968'

98°

Inset map

RANGOON THAILAND   20°
         STORM
BANGKOK
         CAMBODIA   10°
              SOUTH
              CHINA
GULF OF SIAM SEA   5°

MALAYA

SUMATRA   SINGAPORE 0°
              EQUATOR

INDIAN   5°

OCEAN   TJONG PRIOK
         JAVA

96°   100°   105°   110°

M I L E S
0   10   50   100

SIAM RAILWAY

H MILE : ONE DEAD MAN EVERY 17'6".

RAY PARKIN '61.

THAILAND
(SIAM)

CONTENTS

Foreword

This is a story of just one phase of captivity with the Japanese; but it is an experience complete in itself—some fifteen months of building a railway through a jungle, during which survival became the paramount thought.

It was originally written as a diary to capture that passing moment and hold it before it had slipped from our memory for ever. The original diary was written under daily headings which have been dropped; but a strict chronological order of events has been preserved, and each entry was written without any knowledge of what the next day would bring. Also, with the exception of editorial cuts and corrections, this is just as it was written then.

This adaptation has cut the original diary by more than half. In doing this I have been careful to keep the balance of the what-it-was-really-like. It has not been shortened for sensational effect. Every incident related here is an example of the then normal state of things. For this reason I have omitted some things which, though true, would tend to exaggerate the impression. This account can be taken, I think, as the average story for most of us on the Railway.

I have alluded to some of my own sicknesses only to show something of the incidence of it amongst us—a clinical report of Everyman, as it were.

I have waited this long to present it in order that circumstances may not be distorted by prejudice. I hope now it is possible to see more calmly these words which were first written in the Siamese Jungle in 1943–44, to describe our daily lives while building the Burma–Siam Railway for the Imperial Japanese Army.

This was a strategic railway to shorten the lines of communication for the Japanese armies in Burma and India. Their sea communications were being badly mauled. It linked two existing rail systems—the Rangoon–Ye line in Burma, and the Singapore–Bangkok line in the east. It began at Thanbyuzayat in Burma, and ran south-east through the Three Pagoda Pass into Siam. It joined the Singapore line at Bampong, 421 kilometres or 263 miles away.

Engineers advising Imperial General Headquarters said the work would take five or six years to complete. But the railway was urgently needed. The military authorities ordered it to be finished in eighteen months. It was made the responsibility of the Japanese Southern Army Railway Corps, commanded by Field-Marshal Terauchi.

Coolies had been recruited; but this was thought to be insufficient. It was suggested to Imperial General Headquarters that prisoners of war should be used. Several forces of these were sent in, and started building from both ends simultaneously, about October 1942. Prisoners were informed that they were being sent to rest camps in the mountains, where food and conditions would be better. As a result, many of their sick were taken with them.

330,000 workers took part in building this railway. 61,000 were prisoners of war. Japanese engineers stated that the railway involved the building of 4,000,000 cubic metres of earthworks; the shifting of 3,000,000 cubic metres of rock; and the building of fourteen kilometres of bridges. All in a period of twelve months.

It was all done by incredibly primitive means '*after hastening for six or seven months*', to use their own words.

This 'hastening' was the notorious *Speedo*, which killed thousands. Tokyo insisted that the work be completed by August, 1943. But, to quote again, '. . . *as however, the rainy season of 1943 set in earlier than usual, the conditions of the jungle from April onwards worsened and the victims of the work gradually increased. Confronted with these bad conditions, the Imperial General Headquarters at last postponed the target date for two months.*'

In October the two ends were joined near Neike, some 302 kilometres from Bampong.

Apart from ill-treatment (and almost overshadowing it) starvation, disease and the wet season were the great killers.

The Allied War Graves Registration decided in 1946 that the dead prisoners of war totalled 12,399. Of the 270,000 Burmese, Tamils, Javanese, Malayans, and Chinese, the dead are placed at 72,000. But it is realized that this could well *under*-estimate by 20,000.

Lord Russell of Liverpool states that the dead prisoners of war totalled 16,000; and that the Railway cost 64 prisoners and 240 coolies dead for every mile of track.

This story would never have survived but for one man— Lieutenant-Colonel E. E. Dunlop, A.A.M.C., now Mr E. E. Dunlop, O.B.E., M.S., M.D., F.R.C.S., F.R.A.C.S. He took charge of my Java and Thailand diaries and drawings at Tamuan, Thailand, when I was sent to Japan in 1944. By this time we knew that Japanese communications by sea were very uncertain. I realized, also, the impossibility of further concealing these records from the Japanese, with the detailed and repeated searches we would have to undergo. If I held on to them, they would certainly be lost one way or another.

Colonel Dunlop ('Weary' to all who knew him) volunteered to take care of them. At considerable risk, he eventually got them back to Australia in 1945. He says it was no trouble. Those who know Weary would not expect him to say anything else.

I would like this story to be for him.

RAY PARKIN
Ivanhoe, 1961

I

Departure

WE ARE on our way—but nobody knows where. The Japanese have told us we are going to the hills where food will be plentiful, and where we will regain our health. We have had nine months of the Japanese, now.

We are a mixed bag. Nine months ago, with nine others, I became a prisoner of war as a survivor of H.M.A.S. *Perth*, an Australian cruiser, sunk in action by superior forces in Sunda Strait. At Bandoeng in central Java, we joined with an Australian Machine-gun Battalion, a few R.A.A.F., and a hospital unit headed by Lieutenant-Colonel E. E. Dunlop, A.A.M.C. He is now our C.O. and is known to all as 'Weary'. As Dunlop's Thousand we were shifted down to Makasura, just outside Batavia, to await transportation—even as our forebears awaited Botany Bay.

Nine months of captivity has made us adapt ourselves to new conditions in ways not always pleasant. We are in the hands of an unpredictable enemy who has already, in sickening fact, shown us the power of life and death he holds over us. We are an unlovely lot to look at; but we have all come to this state together and have gained a tolerance, as it were, of intolerance.

*

It is Monday, January 4th, 1943. Yesterday we had a final faeces test and a chicken soup supper. Everybody was issued with a mosquito net. We suppose, therefore, that we are going to a malarial area and that, for the moment, we are more use to them alive than dead. It was an evening of saying good-byes to those we were leaving behind: friendships, newly grown, cut down again. We did not sleep, but only dozed over packed kits, being bitten by the bugs of Makasura.

At 2 a.m. we moved off. It was pitch dark and moonless with stars. At first it was silent marching, past the dim little yellow lights scattered in the black of the bush, past sleeping houses. At last we struck a better road and a tram track. Marching was easier. We started to sing: *Jingle Bells*; *Dolores*; an Ambonese song we had learnt (why long for two wives when one is too much); *Sixpence in My Pocket* (which of course we hadn't) and a few other odd tunes. But no sad ones. It was mixed singing and whistling, or da-da-da-ing when you didn't know the words.

A darkened electric train took us quickly from Meester Cornelius to Tandjeong Priok. We got out at the same time as another trainload of Dutchmen. It was still pitch dark, despite the newly risen sickle moon. Silent dockland was only dim shapes studded inanely with deep yellow lights having no radiation of their own. Our lines snaked and concertinaed drunkenly along, following the loom of figures in front. We arrived through the gates onto the wharf.

A full nine months ago, across the watery square before us, H.M.A.S. *Perth* had berthed. From there she had sailed, fought, and sunk—sending seven of us on this unpredictable journey. Now, in the same berth, another ship lay sunk on her side.

We passed other groups of Australians, but could not talk with them. The wharf was packed with prisoners, Dutch and Australian. The guards told us we could have some breakfast. We ate a bit of dry rice and a boiled egg (own expense)* we had brought with us. It was now breaking daylight. Our ship rode high alongside the wharf. She was a normal tramp with raised forecastle and flush deck; of about 5,000 tons, and riding nine feet above her Plimsoll mark. As we were boarding, a lovely

---

* The Japanese paid those who were able to work wages, not direct but into the Regimental Fund. Purchases made by an individual were from a canteen we ran ourselves and against his credit in the fund. Twenty per cent of each man's wages went to the Sick Fund, for only workers were paid. When possible milk, eggs, etc. were bought for the sick. Pay was according to rank—about fivepence a day for a private.

two-masted schooner came bowling into the harbour on a three-quarter wind.

At the foot of the gangway we were sprayed with formalin. The first sprayer sprayed our left sides; the second sprayer, on the opposite side, made us turn around and he sprayed the *same* side again. At the top of the gangway there was an officious-looking soldier with an important-looking satchel. He was directing the single file of incoming prisoners.

We were sent to Number 3 hatch. As we went past Number 2, we heard a hail. It was from two *Perth* survivors we had not seen since the ship was sunk. It was an ordinary seaman and a telegraphist.*

Looking down through this hatch was a bit of a shock. In the 'tween decks, right around the hatch square, there was a shelf at half-height. Prisoners were crowded into this and on the deck beneath, like dogs in a dog show. The decks were covered with plaited grass mats. On the mats crowds of men sat tailor-wise, with their knees to their chins and their heads pushed forward, straining to see the passing men silhouetted against the sky above them.

We went on aft to Number 3. Here were two booby hatches. At the bottom of the ladder we encountered an agitated Japanese who seemed deadly afraid that the situation would get out of hand. As each man stepped off the bottom of the ladder, he had to jettison his pack. With a *Hoosh!* from the worried Jap he scuttled into the low hutch-like shelf.

We sat and contemplated our lot. In a space ten by twelve feet, twelve men were crammed with their packs. But as more men came down, those on the shelves were pushed further and further back. At last there was no more room—even the Jap had to admit that. The late arrivals stood out in the hatch square.

Looking about them they could see the rest of us, monkey-squatting in bas-relief against the black shadow of the shelf behind; above them they could see the deep hatch coaming traversed with heavy iron beams supporting the hatch planks,

* Both subsequently died on the Railway.

Embarkation Tandjeong Priok, 4.1.43

except for one section forward. Through this they could see the smoking black funnel, the samson posts with the derricks and gear draped from them—but nowhere could they see a place for themselves. The 'tween deck was fifty feet wide and about eighty long. Four hundred and fifty men had been crowded in here. And twelve feet across the after end, amidships, was taken up by the stoker crew.

There was a rattle of winches and the thud of berthing wires being thrown down. Soon we could tell from the slight rolling that we were under way. Some became squeamish. It was about 10.30 a.m. Somebody said a Japanese soldier said that we would be eight days at sea. At 2.30 p.m. we got a meal of rice and potatoes that had been brought from Makasura. It was dry and unpalatable. We were close-packed and the fetid heat kept everybody sweating; all our clothes were soaking. Everyone was saving his waterbottle, too, for we did not know where the next water was coming from. Some time during the afternoon we were given about a quarter of a pint of weak, black, sugarless tea. Most of us still had some personal rations (a boiled egg or some green peanuts). We nibbled these when we could muster the energy.

At 7 p.m. the ship issued the next meal. It was rice and soup with a peculiar flavour: the meat with which it was made was tainted. The heat and fug had given us all a splitting headache. Bickering and grumbling went on. There were a couple of roll-calls for which they tried to make everybody stand, but it was impossible. More grumbles. At last we all crawled back in the darkness again. At 8 p.m. a couple of Japanese officers came into the hold, took a brief look around, and departed.

Shortly after this, Colonel Dunlop made the following announcement: 'I have asked the Japanese for small groups of men to be allowed to exercise on the upper deck. This has been refused as, I was informed, the voyage is of short duration. Two days. The destination is Singapore.' Then, a bit later, 'Men may go on the upper deck, two at a time—but don't stay up there and stop others.'

Lighting was now reduced to a few dim yellow bulbs. Men

returning to their shelves did so by trial-and-error or instinct, treading on soft, sweaty bodies. It rained, and the men in the square got wet. When the downpour had almost finished, the crew pulled the tarpaulins over the hatch. This spilled the many, many gallons that had gathered in the folds on to the men below. The men in the shelves slept a bit more contentedly, knowing that others were worse off.

It was a night of darkness and heat and drugged stupor; of entangled bodies which flung unconscious arms and legs athwart each other so that, on awakening, it was hard to tell which limbs were your own. You were conscious of having far too many arms and legs, all of which were sweating profusely. The air was heavy and moist. At 7.30 a.m. the men began to crawl about. We were allowed to go for a wash, ten at a time. The remarkable thing is that we were allowed to use *fresh* water. We were able to fill our waterbottles.

Last night the rats were busy. One came from behind and bit my arm and then scuttled away, either from disgust or alarm. Others had toes nibbled. I had a sock full of green pea-nuts. The rats ate the toe and half the peanuts. They had the advantage over us because, when we settled down to sleep, we were stowed in on our sides so closely that it was impossible to turn over. Despite the hardness of the deck, you slept on one hip all night.

On deck, I could see what was probably Banka Strait and Sumatra. High and dry on a reef or bank lay the wreck of a ship—a typical three-island merchantman. This is where Robin and Mary and Missus were sunk and Missus saved the children. Their mother had been killed in the bombed ship.* They had been part of the fleeing multitudes of helpless women and children from falling Malaya. We will probably never know what happened to them, living or dead.

Men play cards, argue, talk, read, sleep or sit, just watching others. Some wangle extra time on deck and stop others getting up at all. There is the ever-present selfishness of man stealing his fellows' privileges.

* See *Out of the Smoke*.

Yesterday was clear with a breeze and the sea was light green, with broken water. This morning there was a low overcast, which has lifted to a high overcast this afternoon. We get little breeze in the hold, as the wind is ahead on the starboard bow and we are aft. The queue to the latrines lasts all day. At 1.30 I had my turn and managed to get a swill at the bowl under a wooden tank. Dinner was at 2 p.m.—rice and dark soup.

The fact that we disembark tomorrow has kept the voyage tolerable. Apparently the Japanese don't do much better than this when they travel. This afternoon I drew an impression of the hold.

The Hatch Square, 5.1.43

Night came and the hold drugged us to sleep until the 'Wakey, Wakey!' from our sar-majors, and the animal growlings from a couple of guards, woke us up. All we could do was to sit up for a couple of moments and then droop down again. It was 7.30 a.m., but breakfast was not until nine o'clock; however, the never-ending queue for washing and 'wanting' had already begun. The Japanese word for the latter is *benjo*. Each man, except a few schemers, gets only a few minutes on deck each day; but the heat and the perpetual sweating are our salvation. Buckets of tea and hot water were passed down before breakfast. Some had been passing dixies through the hatch coaming to their mates on deck—it is just possible to do this if both men stretch to their limits. This morning a Dutch aluminium dixie without a handle was being passed down full of boiling water. The hand of the man below was burnt, and he snatched it away. The whole lot was up-ended over the head and shoulders of a near-naked man below. He danced, clawing his face, and the skin came away like sodden tissue paper. And now, at dinner time, they are still passing dixies down.

We have doctors and other officers in the hold with us—there is no distinction. With the wind the way it is, on the bow, we get cinders from the funnel into the half-open hatch. These have found their way into the eyes of a number of men. But apart from this, and the burn case, we have had only one casualty—a man who fell down the hatch and has a broken rib.

It is strange to think that in this hold are 460 separate lives, travelling so close and yet so apart. We sit sprawling about, filling in time with yarns, books, cards, or dozing and thinking. This present filling-in of time is odd, because it is only a filling-in of time between other periods of filling in time. And the strength of men to endure seems to be either their selfishness, or their faith in those at home—the hope that they will find, when they get back, the same places waiting for them in the homes they left.

We made contact with other *Perth* survivors today. More have survived than we at first had thought. We have jotted down more names. But we also heard of many more known to have been killed in the water after the ship sank, and more murdered by the Bantaam natives after they got ashore. Out of our 682 it looks as if 309 became prisoners in the Cycle Camp (Batavia). Add to this our ten of the boat party. But we still have a long way to go before we are out of it.*

*

Another night has gone and at dawn a lighthouse is in sight.

* Fifty died as prisoners of war; 229 only returned to Australia in 1945.

All forenoon we have been steaming through islands and islets which ring Singapore. Some of them are only rocks with a bit of scraggy foliage like the cactus gardens one puts on the window sill. We are followed in by a smart-looking Japanese tanker. Otherwise, shipping is limited to a few junks and small boats.

We are now flying the red and white pilot flag and waiting with other ships in the roads. Some are discharging into lighters. One is flying her 'numbers', i.e. four flags from the International Code of Signals. We can make out Japanese guards aboard her. The land we can see on the starboard side is steep, red slopes, patched here and there with dark green growth.

Now the guards have chased us down out of it. They are always doing that; and we are always coming back, like froth from a boiling saucepan. We sit with our kits packed and wish we were out of it, wherever we are going. Where? Bangkok by ship? Thailand by rail? Or somewhere. Take your pick— we don't know.

*

We berthed at Keppel Harbour at 5 p.m. While we were waiting to leave, a few of us sat in the half-deserted hold and watched the rats peek out as they fossicked for scraps. There were also giant cockroaches like young tortoises.

On the wharf, as we formed up, we could see huge piles of scrap iron—plates of demolished oil tanks, flattened-out car bodies and the like. It all looked like a deliberate desecration of the pomp and complacent pride-of-possession of the defeated and departed. There are a few new brick buildings— long go-downs—but there is still much evidence of the bombing. We could see a Blue Funnel ship with her stern bombed and burnt out, and not moved since the occupation. There were two very fine Japanese ships too, as if to rub in the new superiority.

We were formed up in groups of fifty on the road and given a meal of rice and pumpkin soup. Soon, some Ford trucks arrived. Thirty-five men and their packs were shoved into each small tray body. But there were only enough trucks to take half of us. The rest of us began to march.

We passed a mountain of loose coal. On the top were some Chinese coolie women. They were small and dressed in neat, blue, starched jeans: three-quarter trousers and a straight coat reaching just to the knees. Over this was a neat apron shaped like the lower half of a keyhole. On their heads were caps which fitted in a flat flap folded back in a loop over the head and tied: nun-like or Dutch-like. These were red in contrast to the blue of the rest of the outfit. The women were quite brown and smooth and there was something of the textural quality of a Vermeer painting about them. They wore flat-soled sandals with cross straps; their well-muscled and shapely legs showed beneath their trouser bottoms down to their small semi-naked feet. There was something striking about their well-formed diminutiveness on top of that great heap of coal, each carrying a yoke from the ends of which hung two shovel-shaped baskets which only just cleared the ground as they moved.

As we passed through the customs gate some one said, 'Any man got any scents, perfumes, cigars, jewellery, furs or other dutiable articles to declare?' But nobody had.

We were halted opposite the railway station, a very fine building. Here we were at the mercy of a moustached and frenetic Japanese transport officer. With a concentrated intensity he would say in English, as he formed us up into fives: 'One, two, three four, five!...' On top of 'five' he would wail, '*Hurree-ee up!*' Then he counted the fives in Japanese, '*Ichi, nee, san, yon, go, roko, shitchi!*' *Shitchi* multiplied by *five* makes thirty-five—one truck load. His black-gloved hand would fall with the speed of a guillotine, cutting us off, and the whole bunch of us was hurled into the truck by the simple force of his explosive, *H-O-O-O-S-H!*

With this sound we were shot through Singapore. Across bridges and over canals where junks crowded at all angles asking to be drawn. We went past Raffles Hotel. Buck Pederson laconically remarked, 'They tell me that the Japs are preserving it as a shrine to their victory.'

Then we ran out of town into low hills of coconut-strewn countryside with steep little knolls and steep-gabled grass-roofed native huts. At last we came up with a huge jail—Changi. But we went on until we came to a square. We had to hang about here a long time until we were handed over to the British administration. Then we marched on in the dark to our billets.

As we went, we passed by a shanty town bordering the road closely on both sides. 'All slummy and chummy,' Buck said. From inside the hovels of this ramshackle jumble a few yellow lights dimly glowed. Outside some of them stood the proprietors, looking like prosperous tramps on top of a trash heap. Not much was said between us, although they were English and Australian. They appeared to eye us a bit suspiciously—perhaps it was that we were new here, and felt the newness.

At last we came to a big two-storey concrete barracks and were told to make ourselves at home on the ground floor. In the dark, Blackie and I stumbled over a double bed without any mattress. We both flung our arms about it and cried childishly, 'It's ours! It's ours!' Before we went to bed we had a meagre portion of rice and black tea. Then we had a bath under a fire hydrant and felt clean again. We slept as if on a wrecked ship, because one leg of the bed was shorter than the others.

So, at the end of the first leg of our journey to somewhere, we are in Changi on Thursday, January 7th, 1943.

II

Changi

THIS camp is too big to take in all at once. It is like the
Mecca of all prisoner of war camps. It is hilly and pleasantly wooded, and takes up the whole north-eastern tip of
Singapore Island. It is scattered with large two-storeyed concrete barracks which are sharp reminders of the better days that
were. It is called Changi.

There is a strange remoteness about the place to us. We have
been used to small camps with the Japanese always close and
inquisitive; for nine months we have been living with them
breathing down the backs of our necks. Here, there is only one
count parade a day—at 5 p.m. After it is over the Japanese
disappear. Though very pleasant, it seems suspicious and hard
to get used to. We don't see much of the guards for the rest of
the day.

We are Australians arrived among Australians here; but it
would be idle to pretend that there is not an unfortunate feeling
between the prisoners of the Seventh and Eighth Divisions. It
is a rivalry which, under these conditions and the circumstances
of capture, has extended to suspicion, jealousy, accusation and
counter-accusation.

From the point of view of the Seventh, they think the Eighth
were soft, pampered and over-publicized. The Seventh had
been pinned down in the Middle East fighting the Vichy French
Foreign Legion in Syria. They were being blooded; and it had
irked them to pick up copies of the Australian *Women's Weekly*
and read the glamorizing articles on the Eighth and their
excellent conditions. They read of the Eighth having sheets and
servants, while they were shaking sand and scorpions from their
blankets. They had spoken in bitter, defamatory phrases of it

all. At each fresh aggravation, they say it all again. Only the Machine-gun Battalion and some of the Pioneers of the Seventh had been landed in Java to be a bluff and bait for the Japanese. The Machine-gunners were without their weapons, which were on their way to Australia in another ship. Java had collapsed and they had been left like mice in a trap. They resented this because they had not had one good fair crack at the enemy. It has made them touchy because they wanted to be proud.

The Eighth's point of view assailed us within a day of our arrival. It has swamped us. When we met fellows, they poured out their tales with an urgent compulsiveness beyond their control. Both divisions at least seem to have this in common: each considers itself to have been sold out. But this has not united them; instead, each is so sensitive of its own humiliation that it is suspicious of the other.

Here in Changi now, overwhelmed with these recent stories, I think the Eighth feel theirs to be the greater tragedy. There had been such confusion as the Malayan Campaign became a debacle that, within the division itself, internecine frictions, suspicions and doubts were at work. I have heard such stories of valour and devotion, endurance and ingenuity, guts and gore, inexperience and stupidity, defection and cowardice, irresponsibility and criminal negligence. Nothing appears to have been held back.

Some told of having to watch the Japanese build up across the narrow straits of Johore—unmolested, because it was forbidden to fire the guns for fear of giving away their positions. There are stories of not being allowed to fire on the tower or the Administrative building of Johore, which was being used as a most effective observation post by the Japanese. It is said that one officer *did* open fire—and was court martialled. They say that the Engineers worked all night to turn a large naval shore gun to bear on Johore; but permission to fire was never given. Ammunition was strictly limited to a few rounds per day, and these only to mobile guns, not fixed positions. Ironically, the ban was lifted just after the Japanese had captured some

60,000 tons in one dump in the north, as well as other dumps to the west. This curtailment of fire within sight of the enemy has led to the bitter cynical catch-cry, still echoed, here, DON'T ANNOY THE JAPS, CHAPS!

On Singapore Island they had had to fight an enemy who had complete possession of the air and sea around them. They were isolated on a small island which, even then, Higher Policy had decided to abandon: reinforcements had been diverted. Assistance was not only cut off by the enemy, but denied by our own side. They had fought sleeplessly for days on end, as the enemy gained foothold. They had to fight with Confusion as a powerful ally of the Japanese. They fought disjointed engagements without contact on either flank; with visibility little more than a bow-shot; over ground which was swampy, defying trenches and emplacements; with broken communications or none at all; with officers vainly trying to guess the overall situation and with no clear picture of the immediate one; with conflicting orders based on bad guesses and futile hopes. They fought naked under a sky in which the red ball of Nippon always seemed to be over their heads directing artillery fire, or shooting them up. Many of these men had just stepped off transports: many of them had only stepped into the Army a very short time ago. Many had never fired a rifle before, even in training, nor knew anything of Tommy or Bren guns. They were pushed in here and there as reinforcements or as odd units, at a moment's notice. Many carried only ammunition—somebody else had the guns. Plans changed hourly in the overwhelming flux; commands changed frequently.

They fought in a situation stacked against them from the start. Political Authority was expecting these men to make the enemy realize that Singapore *was* impregnable. It seemed amazed that the enemy had not taken its word in the first place. This expectation is reflected in the messages from General Wavell and General Percival as late as the 10th and 11th of February respectively—only six days before surrender, when the situation must have been obvious to an on-the-spot observer, and when any thought of reinforcing the island had been abandoned.

Wavell's message reads:

It is certain that our troops in Singapore heavily outnumber any Japanese who have crossed the straits. [The emphasis is mine.] *We must destroy them. Our whole fighting reputation is at stake, and the honour of the British Empire. The Americans have held out on the Bataan Peninsula against heavier odds; the Russians are turning back the picked strength of the Germans; the Chinese with almost complete lack of modern equipment have held the Japanese for four and a half years. It will be disgraceful if we yield our boasted fortress of Singapore to inferior forces. There must be no thought of sparing the troops or civil population, and no mercy must be shown to any weakness in any shape or form. Commanders and senior officers must lead the troops in and, if need be, die with them. There must be no thought in the question of surrender. Every unit must fight it out to the end, and in close contact with the enemy.*

Please see that the above is brought to the notice of all senior officers and, by them, to the troops. I look to you and your men to fight to the end and to prove that the fighting spirit of Empire still exists and to enable us to defend it.

Signed: A. P. Wavell, General, Singapore

Percival's message reads:

In some units troops have not shown the fighting spirit which is expected of the men of the British Empire. It will be a lasting disgrace if we are defeated by an army of clever gangsters many times our inferior in numbers. The spirit of aggression and determination to stick it out must be inculcated to all ranks. There must be no further withdrawals without orders. There are too many fighting men moving about in back areas. Every available man who is not doing essential work must be used to stop the invader.

Signed: A. Percival, General A.D.V.H.Q. G.D.C. Malaya

Several of the men have showed me copies of these messages, and they told me that, if this battle had been fought a century ago with swords and bows and arrows, there might have been some sense in them. They said that they must have been dreamed up by someone thousands of miles away.*

Yet, even at this stage, men were giving some reality to the facile rhetoric of the great. Men and officers were sacrificing themselves with desperate resolve to prevent complete disintegration. Men were walking down the mouths of enemy guns while a platoon or section disengaged and reformed. Things were done which should make orators stop talking, and weep. One man was hiding, surrounded by Japanese. He saw them brutally bayoneting his wounded mates. Completely reckless with rage, he rushed one of the Japs with his bayonet. But the Jap was on higher ground and his rush carried him on to the point of the enemy bayonet. It entered his neck below the chin and, narrowly missing his jugular, came out at the back. He flung himself sideways off the bayonet and, flat on his back on the ground, drew a pistol from his waistbelt and shot the Jap dead. In a fury he jumped up and shot another five. He then threw his empty gun at a machine-gun's crew. They must have thought it a grenade, for they scattered. He fell into a duck pond where he lay under some overhanging stuff and played dead until the battle had passed him by. In native clothes he regained his own lines by dusk, and collapsed.

There are enough stories of this sort to let the orators know that 'the fighting spirit of Empire still exists'. But there are limits to what the greatest fighting spirit can achieve. It cannot always be a panacea for political folly.

There are also incidents of men's ruthlessness on being forced to look out for themselves—undisciplined men reacting in savage disgust to the way they thought they had been treated. In the disappointment of defeat—a defeat thrust on them equally by both sides, they thought—they looked for, and found, scapegoats. This unit did not fight; that one left another's flank uncovered; this one withdrew without orders; those officers were weak; these other ranks were undisciplined and ran. They

* It is interesting to note that Wavell received a cable from Churchill on the day he issued the above order. Comparison will show the order to be little more than a paraphrase of this; Percival's is but a fainter echo of it.

assert that Raffles Hotel was the headquarters of Japanese Intelligence, to which our officers went and unwittingly reported over 'stingas' to pretty ladies.

All this, and the selfishness which grows in a useless prison existence, has now had nearly twelve months to eat into them. They feel unjustly condemned by the terms of Wavell's message. They feel they have been condemned by an outside world and cannot utter one word in their defence. They *know* the lack of reality in the terms of the messages, but they are afraid that by the time they are free nobody will want to listen.

The Machine-Gunners and Pioneers of the Seventh have Syria and a victory to their credit, which has softened this final defeat a little; but the Eighth have faced a defeat, it seems, ordered by Fate from the start. They had been assured by voluble statesmen; propaganda had laughed at the enemy as a funny little fellow who put up his umbrella and stopped his battles when it rained. The enemy had attacked white superiority at the heart of its Impregnable Fortress and found it was guarded only by a paper dragon covered with brave words.

*

Our Java party is dressed in rags, for our clothes have been cut to a minimum by wear-and-tear and the Japanese. Changiites are well turned out. There is a high standard here which is taken by their officers to be synonymous with morale. The Brigadier is preserving an *élite corps* which is being trained with broomsticks. It is said that, at an opportune time, it will re-capture Singapore. The Brigadier is not going to be caught napping, and he is demanding a high morale as evidenced by the dress of the whole camp. We must appear to him as a deliberate affront. In our rags and with our close-cropped heads, we have suffered his wrath. He has proclaimed us to the whole camp as The Java Rabble. He has ordered our immediate improvement, and deplores that men should have fallen to such a low state; but he has not offered us the means to improve our condition.

Our C.O. has made repeated requests for boots and clothing,

which we know exist here both in stores and in private possession. But all our requests have met with refusal or silence. This
has sparked off much hard and unjust feeling between the two
sides. We are wearing our badge of disreputableness with pride.
We tell the well-dressed that they have much to learn about
this P.O.W. business: their day will come, we say.

We know from some of the men of the Eighth that the Dutch
coming through here have promptly received boots on request.
This is galling enough; but we also hear that the first Dutchmen
spread the story that there were *two divisions* in Java, and they
did not fight. This probably provided the Eighth with the very
scapegoat it was looking for. It perhaps explains why 'Java
Rabble' has been so viciously hurled at us. We love the Dutch
no more for this scandal.

Last Armistice Day, there were fifty survivors from H.M.A.S.
Perth in this camp, passing through from Java. They only moved
up to Burma a week ago. A few were left behind, sick. One of
them told us this story:

'The Brigadier had organized a march-past for Armistice
Day. Somehow the Japs allowed it. We thought it was a funny
thing to celebrate in the middle of the war in the middle of a
prison camp. Anyway . . . the Navy decided, if it was on, we
would be in it. We were a bit scruffy and some of us were bare-
footers. Most of our boots flapped a bit. Our bits of Dutch
uniforms didn't fit too well, either. But we got under way at
last, the Gunner in charge. We put on a real Gunnery School
show. When we formed up at the head of the column, there
were screams from everywhere. "Get to the tail of the column!"
But not the Gunner! No, sir! He said, "I've been twenty-five
years Navy and *I know* where we belong—we are Senior
Service." He quoted King's Rules and Admiralty Instructions.
They tried to talk him out of it. He just stood there, they
couldn't shift him. I thought, "By Golly! We'll have to keep our
yardarms clear after this!" '

'So we led the whole mob. When we got abreast the saluting
base, the Gunner roars, "Eye-s-s . . . *right!*" and he snaps up to
a real tiddley salute. On we go—eyes right, arms straight and

swinging up, and all that. We would show them how to march. When all at once there's a cry like a wounded bull from the Brig. "Who *IS* that man giving *ME* the Japanese salute? *Report to me at once!*" Well, the Gunner doesn't bat an eyelid. He wheels us round behind the base, stands us at ease, and waits. At last, after they have all marched past, His Nibs comes over to us. You should have heard the blast he dished out to the Gunner! He finished up with something like, "Explain yourself, sir!" The Gunner stands to attention like a wooden dummy, Pusser-like. He looks straight ahead and says, "Sir, I have been twenty-five years in the Royal Navy. I gave you the salute of the British Navy—I am sorry you should know the Japanese salute better than ours." Well, did that start something! The Brigadier said he *knew* the Gunner had given him the Japanese salute—he had *seen* him. Don't deny it! The Gunner maintained it was the only one he had used for the last twenty-five years. Eventually some of the Army officers convinced the Brigadier that there was no difference between the two salutes.'

'Anyway . . . that's what happened. . . . You wouldn't read about it, would you?'

*

The Java Rabble is like an irritating flea crawling over a large, well-fed body. But many of the men here, despite official decrees, have given us boots and shirts.

Our little band of Navy was invited over to a concert— a P.O.W. version of *Cinderella*. Cinderella was an ex-Navy Sick Berth Attendant. Afterwards, the concert party took us backstage to a little party. It was a wonderful night. It did much to compensate for all this other ill-feeling. It made me reflect on the danger always arising when any clique is formed—and cliques seem to be one of the commonest things in human affairs.

We are only passing through, so this is just a passing impression of Changi.

*

Now we are gathering up our miserable possessions and standing-by to move on. During our short stay here we have left seventy-one in hospital. We have made many friends at unofficial levels: new ones, new-found townies, friends of common interest, friends of friends, those who know this or that relation—or just friends. Now it is time to say good-bye to them.

Five more Navy joined us—I will write of them later.

Our C.O. has written the Brigadier this parting message:

Two weeks ago my men arrived in a pitiful condition in this camp from Java. You have done nothing to alleviate their needs—tomorrow at 8.30 they leave in the same pitiable condition: bootless and in rags. You have done nothing.

This is Tuesday, January 19th, 1943, here in Changi.

III

Journey to Thailand

At 10 a.m. we boarded motor trucks at Changi and were taken to Singapore railway station. We passed some of those neat little women working in a quarry, red and blue against grey. Over the harbour there was a slight mist and a grey sky making the junks and shipping a fine study. There was a Nipponese destroyer in the roads.

About 1 p.m. we left Singapore by train. There are twenty-eight of us to each closed iron truck, which is quite crowded. There is a guard to each truck. Just before we left, the senior hand of each truck was sent for and briefed by our officers under instructions from the Japanese. This is what we have been told:

'The Nipponese soldiers are not here to guard you. They know you are gentlemen and will not try to escape. They are with you to protect you from the natives, who will rob you. You are warned, when you get to Thailand, to be careful of the natives there. They will rob you. They are thieves—be especially careful of your boots.'

The whole train is in the charge of a Nip sergeant. There are twenty-six cars and two of them are open.

The first twenty miles was crossing Singapore Island to the Causeway. We passed some large oil tanks which had been bombed—crumpled like brown-paper bags of water dropped and burst on the ground. Some more of those red-and-blue-clad women were at work with chunkels and shovel baskets, digging up a pipe line.

The Causeway showed where about 100 feet on one side had been destroyed in the retreat. On our left, as we passed over, was the Administration Building of Johore (some said it was the

Sultan's Palace), a big square building with a large square tower. There were no distant views for a long while as we went through the green walls of interminable rubber trees.

The trucks are hot, hard and rough. Someone said that the wheels are square. We are jolted against each other and the hard walls. At midnight, at Gemas, we had our first meal since leaving Changi this morning. It was rice with a flavoursome tang, which was probably some taint or other, but does give us a welcome change from the monotony of just rice. The rest of the night was spent in awkward attempts to sleep.

*

Just after daylight, about 8 a.m., we pulled in at Kuala Lumpur where they gave us some rice and curried water. The day has been almost as much stopping as going, but we find the breaks welcome to ease our cramped, dirty and sweaty bodies. As the train pulls in to a halt, we all swarm out and make for the water tower. The first one there pulls the chain with the ring on the end of it, and from the large canvas hose hanging down the water pours. We all push in like a rugby scrum, to get under it. Not all of us can, but the outside ones form a milling wall, at which the annoyed guards kick and punch and beat to get us back to the train. By the time they have succeeded, those in the middle have had a good swill. Nobody takes any clothes off—we are not wearing that many.

*

Until late in the afternoon we still had to look at the rubber trees; but the view changed slightly then, and we could see some of the tin-dredging plant, which appeared to be abandoned.

After a bit of mountain country we came out on a great plain of swamp and dredge waste. Kota Bahru is about in the middle. Along the line are signs of the war that was: hundreds of wrecked cars with a few military ones thrown in; scrap iron in the shape of dredger parts heaped up; and, once, the fuselages of twelve Nip fighters.

At 9 p.m. we arrived at Ipoh and had some rice. On we went, half of us sitting up until 3 a.m., while the others tried to stretch out. Then we changed over. At 6.30 a.m. we arrived at a place on a large river or estuary in which we could see some shipping and a tug. We think this was Port Prai. We had some breakfast there and went on to Sungei Putani, where we stopped.

As well as the scrum we form at each water-tower stop, we also try to wet some tea. Our truck has managed to scrounge some, and one man takes it along to the engine where he asks the drivers, who are not Japanese and can generally be persuaded to let us use one of the cylinder drain cocks. With a bit of luck there will be enough water to do the trick. It is often oily, but not enough to put thirsty men off drinking it. There is practically no provision made otherwise for drinking. Not all of us always get to the water tower, so sometimes we get a mess dixie of water from the engine and, using a piece of rag the size of a handkerchief, we manage an all-over sponge with this pint of oily warm water.

*

We ran out of the rubber trees and came on rice fields which flanked the line for miles across the plains from before Alor Star to Pedang Besar. At intervals, rising sheer out of the flat country, are outcrops of rock, wooded, and scarred with reddish gravel clay.

*

We have crossed the Thai border and the country has changed —in foliage, that is. There are clumps of thin-stalked bamboo, whose broad leaves blow back in the wind like lancers' pennons —like the hair, as I now remember it, of my six-year-old daughter when she runs to meet me. Rice fields are golden, green and rust; there are islands of palms and fine old trees with fuzzy young growth on their writhing limbs. There are more streams, too.

We left Pedang Besar about 5 p.m. and I think this is where

we entered Thailand—though some say it was after we left Alor Star. But after Pedang there is no trace of English lettering on the railway stations. It is now in Siamese, which looks like Hebrew, and is sub-titled with Nipponese or Chinese. I have looked at the consignment card on the side of our truck, and I find we are 'From Syonan to Bampong'. I think there are still a couple of nights ahead of us. We are getting sore and sick of this lurching iron box, which all but cooks us by day, and freezes us by night.

*

Our guard is a sad, taciturn figure who sits in the open door-way day and night. We could tip him out in the dark, any time, but that wouldn't do much good. We all feel a bit sorry for him. We gave him a drink of our tea, but he spat the oily stuff out and apologized for not liking it. But he seems to enjoy it when we have a bit of a sing-song, and not to mind our raucous voices.

*

This morning, as we get further into Thailand, the scenery has been good. The bamboo clumps are more numerous—splendid fifty-foot stuff with fine lacy leaves. There are long swaying palms with ladders fixed into their trunks—for the collection of palm sugar, I think. The paddy fields stretch across the plains like a sea; but there is no water in them. Mountains suddenly stand up in razor-back ridges from these plains which are level like the waters of a flood. The sea-like impression is increased by the islands of trees and palms scattered about, giving the country this flooded-out appearance. Some of the rocky out-crops are so sheer and sharp (100 feet or more) that, in the sunlight with the hard blue shadows on them, they look like cathedrals or old castles.

At last we are getting near our destination.

*

At about 7 a.m., in the half-light, we got out at Bampong,

after a cold, cramped night. It was grey and still as we left the station to form up outside. A silent saffron-yellow robe moved like a ghost along the deserted street and went to the door of a low house with his begging bowl. We were given a hand of six bananas and told to get into the waiting trucks.

*

By 2 p.m. we are some sixty miles along a dirt road which was covered all the way in six inches of fine white dust. The Japanese drivers wore gauze masks. Our sweating bodies were caked with it and our noses almost blocked. After four days in the train with very little food, we didn't like this. We got out of the trucks and walked through the thick dust for three-quarters of a mile, and then crossed a rickety bamboo bridge over a fast river. Here we are waiting, and I am writing this by the side of the road.

*

We arrived in this camp, Tarsau, at 6 p.m. We were counted and put into a flimsy two-rail bamboo compound. We were not allowed to wash, although the river was quite close. Caked with road dirt, we lay down under the stars for the night. It was bitterly cold and frosty moonlight when we were called at about 6 a.m. We had a meal of rice and dried salt fish, with a splash of black tea. We had worn all we possessed to try and stay warm overnight. We could get no water for our water-bottles and, since the day before, we have had only one quart.

Light was breaking at 8 a.m. when we climbed into the trucks again. In low gear we ground our hair-raising way along a jungle track which climbed so steeply in places that we had to get out and push. The vehicles looked as if they would tip over backwards. We passed several parched, miserable camps of English.

'There's your canteen, boys! Cop the luxurious layout!'

The trucks climbed along the ridge of a mountain chain* through miles of bamboo—thorny bamboo with long canes

* These mountains rise 3,000–4,000 feet.

bristling with four-inch spikes. At last we got out and climbed down a cliff-like hillside into a camp two or three hundred feet below. As we were going down, digging in our heels to save us from a headlong descent, we met a party of Englishmen coming up the hill and staggering beneath bags of rice. Although there were two men to a bag they had reached a state of exhaustion which made them look like wild-eyed madmen. One fellow sat on a bag, deadbeat. He sat with an uncaring tiredness and didn't seem to notice us.

'Heavy, mate?' one of us said sympathetically.

He looked up with dull hatred on his face and said, 'That's *all* it bloody well is!'

We got down to the river and found a half-cleared patch of jungle. Clumps of bamboo were roaring in flames and there was a tremendous crackling as bundles, eighty- to one hundred feet high, collapsed. There is not a hut or tent to be seen. We camp on the ground until we can build something: fortunately it is the dry season.

We were all formed up, kept waiting long enough to make us both curious and impressionable; and then, from the direction of the English camp, came the Camp Commandant. He was a young, sleek, Japanese officer who looked us over like a schoolmaster receiving a new crowd. He was affable; he spoke of fine things like honour. He cut quite a good figure up there on the mound of earth from which he spoke. He was Lieutenant Hirota, and from his interpreter we got the following information:

He was glad to see us and he was gratified that we had come such a long way to help him. He respected our character. His orders must be obeyed. Disobedience was heavily punished. He was sorry there was so little food, but he would try to improve it. He was sorry, also, that the camp was unprepared. As soon as possible it would be built.

And so we were welcomed and accepted as part of this community of Konyu, a place somewhere in the heart of the Thailand jungle. Each man dropped his pack on the most likely looking bit of dust and called it 'home'.

We were allowed to go to the river in batches at 6 p.m. It is a large fast-flowing green stream, flanked by dense jungle and high banks and cliffs. Feeling a little better, we came back and were given a small poultice of rice cooked in the hurriedly built kitchen.

The 'kitchen' is simply earthen fireplaces scooped out to rest the iron *kwalis*, or cooking pans, on. Our rice contained some of the earth—but it was a start, and better than nothing at all. Before we finally bedded-down, we had to evict some scorpions and snakes. Some would not leave until killed. When we woke in the morning, we had to kick a few more out. Again it was bitterly cold. Daybreak is at 8 a.m. We were up by then and had some plain rice and a mouthful of tea. Then we went to work clearing the jungle.

*

It is the dinner break and, as the meal does not take long to eat, I am writing this up now. Our party here was the first of the Java Rabble. We are waiting for the rest of them to arrive today. Here they come now! We reckon we are old hands— we have been here twenty-four hours. So we are jeering the new-comers. They are staggering as we staggered yesterday, falling over roots and kicking up dust and coughing.

'Pick up your feet!'

'Keep your sections of fours—don't straggle!'

'You don't have to work until this afternoon!'

'Good camp this, tobacco grows on trees. Look out! There's a *Craven A* coming down now!'

A gust of wind has loosened a batch of yellowed leaves and they are tumbling down. The Japs had told us that, where we were going, there would be plenty of tobacco; but of course there is none. The lads are smoking leaves.

*

We went over to the English camp for bags of rice this afternoon. It is a dry, bare, spiritless place. Many are sick. They told us that only twelve per cent are fit for work. They have been here three months and their claims of dead range from eighteen to sixty-four. They think we look well fed and very fit.

The name of this camp is Konyu 3. We are here to build a railway which is to go from Bampong into Burma through the Three Pagoda Pass. It is no good letting our imaginations work overtime. Of course we are wondering, but we are trying to take things one day at a time, and be thankful for each dawn.

It is January 26th, 1943. We have been on the road from Batavia since January 4th.

IV

Konyu – January

WE ARE now building our camp. Clearing is going on all day. Fires burn, smoke curls; the trees are blue cut-outs on a blue ground, and the greens of the bamboo are a sunny yellow. The laciness of their leaves against the sky is as fine as that of a bride's brand-new nightdress. Axes ring, trees crash, and bamboos are torn out of their clumps with the noise of ripping thorns. Men call, 'Oh-h-h . . . HO! H-a-a-U-U-LL!' as they drag and work. They are stripped to hats, boots and shorts. They are red and bronze and moving: dark in the shadows, and rich in the sun.

Above and behind us to the north runs a high, jungle-treed ridge in the greens, browns and reds of the Australian bush. Its sharp edge shows against the white cumulus which just crowns it: the clouds seem to climb no higher in this dry season. South, across the river in its deep channel, lies another mountain. The river is a branch of the Menam and is called the Kwai Noi. To the south, other prisoners are at work on banks, cuttings and bridges, bringing the railway up from Bampong. Eventually it will run westward into Burma, on to Moulmein or Rangoon.

There is much to admire in the country. In spite of our situation, there is something here which is giving my heart a lift: perhaps it is the much good against which to contrast our little evil, giving a sense of proportion.

Monkeys pipe high on top C and sound like the rotary sirens on tugs or destroyers. There is bird music, but we don't often see the birds. At dusk there are graceful flights of geese and heron, and others I don't know. During the afternoon, as the sun swings to the southward, the camp is back-lighted. The green and blue trees are ringed with an edge of green-gold

Kwai River at Konyu January, 1943

light, and the smoke is a floating luminous powder. The clouds, too, have shadowed hearts and haloed edges. Large leaves float, capsize and tumble continually earthwards, lazily, on to the beds of men whose camp is rows of gauzy mosquito nets strung up like the buildings of a city on bamboo poles. Great vines writhe and twine and grip the tall straight-columned trees, whose pink-grey trunks blend against the blue atmosphere. The grip has grown so tight that in places there is a bulge of strangulation.

In the night the trees are lighted by the rich ochre glow from the many fires. They stand drawn perfectly in monochrome by firelight on the blue-black ground of the farther unlighted trees which show as pitch against the faintly luminous sky. The line of the mountain across the river shows its shape only by obscuring the stars. The stars are clear in a faultless atmosphere. At the edge of the clearing, two clumps of bamboo, rising nearly one hundred feet, converge symmetrically in a great curve. At the moment they are simple lines of highlight on black, and they make a perfect Gothic arch.

Beneath this great arch, as the fires illuminate it, a few bamboos, broken, have fallen in from the sides. This gives a strong suggestion of the pattern of a stained-glass window, whose motif is inscrutable. The altar is simply the diffused light hung low on the curtain of smoke. It is majestic and the black depth of it all is full of religious mystery. The blackness, the depth, the height, and the remote stars above is the Presence of ... whatever it is man longs for. You can go to sleep with this feeling cuddled in your blanket ... or you needn't.

And this is the area in which 320 cases of malaria have recently occurred; where only twelve per cent of the English are fit for work; where jungle sores fester and won't heal; where dysentery is a scourge; where food is scarcely on the subsistence level; where work is hard. But it is no good hating these things. *It is no good hating at all.* That could kill you. The sight of beauty, patience coming from it, and thoughts of loving friends at home —these, I am sure, matter more.

*

We have complained about the rations to the Japs and they
have made the suggestion that if we put the sick on half-rations,
those of the healthy will thereby be increased—and the sick
will die and no longer bother us. The present daily ration is:
rice, 23 oz.; oil, 6 oz.; sugar, 6 oz.; salt, 13 oz.; vegetables as
available. This is how it starts on paper, but it bleeds away as it
gets to us. We get three bags of rice per day for 875 men. That
is 720 pounds, of which one-quarter to one-third has already
gone to the weevils.

Tobacco shortage is causing bad temper and much bickering.
Heat, hard work, shortage of tools and too many people trying
to get them, add an enervating confusion to the days.

Four more died over in the English camp yesterday and today. We are getting sore throats and tongues, which are the
first signs of avitaminosis brought on by deficiencies of diet. The
doctor told me that there are a couple of hundred like me. All
we have is permanganate of potassium to use as a mouth wash,
and the hope that the rations will improve. Avitaminosis causes
ulcerated throats and mouths and lips; skin complaints like
tinea in the crutch and scrotum, and a rough skin called
pellagra. This is showing after only five days here.

*

Just after dinner a three-foot-six-inch green snake with a
diamond-shaped head slid across one of our beds and was
killed. This morning one of the chaps found a little golden snake
coiled at the head of his bed. As he touched it the coils tightened
and it was rolled out like a compact little barrel. Large centipedes are constantly being killed, and we have caught a number
of deep green-blue scorpions between six and seven inches long.
The claws are about the size of the top joint of my thumb. One
fellow picked a succulent root which looked like a dahlia tuber,
and bit into it. It set his saliva glands racing and saliva flowed
freely from the corners of his mouth. That was about 11 a.m.,
and it went on until nearly nightfall, but he seems all right
today. On the hillside, which is rocky, men are cutting some
'clean-skin' bamboos about two inches in diameter. As it is cut

it slithers down the rocks and over other cut bamboo, like a man down a ski-run. The bamboos are cut at an angle with the machetes, making them sharp like pens. One man below had his thigh transfixed with a slithering piece.

With food so scarce, men are getting fishing lines ready— safety pins, stripped-down canvas ground sheets and the yarns plaited together.

*

We seven keep pretty well together, but don't live in each other's pockets. We have made many friends.

George is an able seaman who would now have been a leading seaman if we had not been sunk. He has dark, curly hair; a fresh boyish face with a sharp, straight nose which is tip-tilted at the end. He is about five feet ten inches, and a good footballer. He joined the Navy at the outbreak of war. George has partnered with Jim.

Jim is shorter, smoother and not so dark. He has a beautiful pair of shoulders over narrow hips and light legs. Drill has not taken from him all of that smooth, slouchy movement born of circling on the wrestling mat. He is more intense than George, and his whole attitude seems to imply that he intends to outlast this experience—as if he were facing a challenge on the mat.

Darky, an able seaman, on the other hand, is playing lone wolf. He is a 'hostilities-only' rating. Since we have been prisoners he has been content to go his own way. He is very dark and balding, with smooth olive skin; strongly built, of medium height, and with a genius for conserving energy.

Ken and Fatty are two permanent servicemen. Fatty is a big-chested seaman petty officer whose bulk and strength are enveloped in a deceptive roundness. He is fifteen stone; a good swimmer who has swum in the three-mile cross-Derwent swims in Hobart, and won several of them. He will expend any amount of energy in the water, but once out of his element, he reserves it. He is a natural comic, and fooling is expected of him. On- and off-stage he plays the wide, blue-eyed innocent, and he has become very popular with the army fellows. But he has a temper of great force when crossed. He has had fourteen years of Navy and was in charge of our anti-aircraft armament in the ship.

Ken, with whom he has paired, was our Chief Telegraphist. Ken is dark with deep-set eyes, broad forehead, straight high-bridged nose, broad jaw and straight firm mouth. He stands almost six feet, with wide square shoulders. He, too, is an excellent swimmer, but his shape is a complete contrast to Fatty's. He is quiet and serious, with a dry sense of humour. He, like Blackie, joined the Navy when he was fourteen years old.

Blackie and I have partnered. We are both seamen petty officers. He and I have been together from ship to ship now for the past seven years. We were made leading seamen together and, later, petty officers together. That was in the flagship in 1935. Fatty, Blackie and I spent three years in the Naval Depot as seamanship instructors. Ken and the three of us commissioned H.M.A.S. *Perth* in Portsmouth in 1939 and were with her till she was sunk.

Blackie has got a wry sense of fun—when things go right. But he is also very serious, especially about his comfort and dignity, both of which are hard to retain under these conditions. He is black-haired and short; compactly built but not big. He has a swarthy face beneath his beard, in which he takes a great pride, but which makes him look older than his thirty-three years (which is the average age of the four of us). We have all served round about the same amount of time in the Navy.

*

I mentioned that five extra Navy men joined us in Changi. Four of them were youngsters, the other was an older man and a re-entry into the Navy on the outbreak of war. He and the young ones had been part of the majority who had become separated from us when the ship was sunk. Over 200 of them were picked up by a Japanese destroyer and later transferred to a troop transport, the *Somdong Maru*, from which they saw the disembarkation of Japanese invading Java. After some days they were taken ashore and imprisoned in the Serang jail and cinema, where treatment was mean and rough. It was there that they learned that the Japanese thought we had sunk fifteen of their ships. In September they were sent up to Rangoon via Singapore by sea. These men were part of the sick stragglers left in Singapore. When they had seen our little bit of Navy arrive, they wanted to join us, but we were only able to wangle five of them.

The older man, about thirty-five, is a Telegraphist, married with four children. He is a dark, quiet, slow-moving Scot with a dry and lively sense of humour. The young ones had all joined the Navy after the outbreak of war. There is Otto, Izzy, and Bob, who are young seamen; there is Roy, a Stoker Second Class. These we treat with a heavy and affected paternal supervision. As Fatty once said, to sink them, 'Listen you young scrogs! I've drunk more Pusser's ky than you've seen ocean!'

'O.K., Dadda,' Izzy said in his cheeky way.

Izzy comes from Wooloomooloo, a suburb of Sydney, and he had been brought up more by the roving gangs there than by his parents. His father died when he was young, but his mother had done her best.

'My Old Lady was too soft,' he told us. 'She'd never say boo to me. I'd come home molo [drunk]—I was only a kid the first time. And she never said a word. She cried, but she didn't go crook at me. I got on with sheilas, and when she saw lipstick on my shirts, she said, "I hope you behave like a gentleman." What a giggle! Poor old lady—she'd *never* know! Sometimes I'd get real crook and she'd have to change the bed clothes—never a word—I'd feel a bit of a louse.'

Otto came from the West and had two parents.

'My Old Man won't stand no nonsense. A boot in the stern or a clout on the lug that'd make you deaf for a week—no funny business with him. Do what you're told or else! Catch *me* coming home drunk—he'd *murder* me!'

'Huh! Make a sissy outa you!' Izzy sneered.

'A *sissy*!' roared Otto. '*You* don't look like no Tarzan to me, you shrivelled-up street urchin. I'll run you, jump you, swim you, fight you—anything you like—*any* day!'

There stood Otto. Blonde, six feet of bony muscled body, looking like a Great Dane puppy with big bony hands and big bare feet. Even Otto's whisper was big. Izzy lounged: small, hard and dark—skinny-tough, with a nasal voice that was often pitched high in disbelief or insolence. The big lolloping puppy and the tough terrier.

'Neither of you had better start any Tarzan stuff,' Fatty growled like father bear from his blanket in the dust. 'If you want to try yourself out, try *me*. I eat scrogs like you for breakfast.'

Otto and Izzy are just eighteen; Bob is twenty-one. He had been in the reserves at the outbreak, and was sent to guard a wireless station near Canberra. At last he was granted fourteen days' leave, when he had planned to get married. The first week of his leave had been all excitement and preparation. 'I was about as happy as a man could be,' he told me. 'A wonderful girl—we'd been to school together and grown up together—real mates. Then, what do you reckon? I get a recall telegram on the day of the wedding! The wedding's at five o'clock and I've got to catch the seven o'clock express. We had the service—at least I got married—and a bit of the breakfast . . . but that's *all*! I grabbed a taxi and just made the train.'

He had come south from the wedding in Brisbane and joined the ship in Melbourne. We had sailed to the West—there was a mine-laying scare, a couple of ships had been mined in Bass Strait. While the ship was in Fremantle, Bob got a telegram to say that his wife had acute peritonitis. He sent permission to operate, but we sailed north to Java before he heard any result. And we didn't get back to find out, for we fought the Battle of the Java Sea and were then sunk in the Battle of Sunda Strait. Bob said, 'You know, Chief, I don't know whether I'm a widower or a husband.'

Roy is a stoker—an engineer, he'd say—and is inclined to be a bit of a snob because of what he considers his family position. From him we learned that his family had money, and a fine home at a very fashionable bayside town on Port Phillip Bay. We concluded that he had been spoilt. Otto could not stand his affected manner.

'Come off it, Cobber! Don't come the la-de-da guff with us. You're only a common matelot like the rest of us.'

When Roy told him he had £3,000 in the bank, and a car, Otto's eyes popped wide in a kind of awesome respect, but only for a moment. 'What! Three thousand quid! Yes you have! *Like smoke!* If you had three thou' you'd be an Admiral, not a greasy stoker. Don't come that with *me*!'

Otto stood naked except for a G-string and a battered old Dutch straw hat. He stood just beyond the shadow in the hot dust which had blackened on the sweat half-way to his knees. His big splay feet were half buried in the dust. Izzy was slouched against a sapling in a pair of too-big dirty shorts which hung from his hips, leaving his navel high and dry. They drooped below his knees and made his legs look even more skinny. On his head was a Glengarry cap with the flaps hanging each side of his face like a bloodhound's ears. Roy sat on his bed in the shade, hatless, with dirty feet and legs and a pair of shorts like Izzy's.

Izzy's life in the asphalt jungle of Wooloomooloo had not prepared him for this one. He frankly confessed he hated scorpions. 'You don't get them in the 'Loo. I wish I was there now—coppers or no coppers!'

Blackie said, 'That's all right, Izzy, you don't have to worry about *them*. Just get a crooked stick and draw three crooked lines around your bed. Then you start off with the *right* foot and step in between the lines from the outside. Real slow. Each time your foot comes to the ground you say, "Abracadabra", until you are in the centre. They won't cross those lines.'

'A-h-h . . . Dinkum?'

'Honest Injun!'

'Haugh! . . . You don't catch *me* like that!'

And tonight, as we were shaking out our blankets, we heard Otto's whisper like a rumble of thunder:

'Hey! Izzy's drawing them lines round his bunk!'

They settled down in their beds which are bamboo slats in the dust; Otto and Izzy began to talk confidentially, but they could be heard quite clearly.

'Why did you join the Andrew, Izzy? Did you get a sheila into trouble or something, and have to blow through?'

'Na,' Izzy said, unoffended. 'I just wanted to join. Get about a bit. I wasn't gunna walk around the world with the foot-sloggers—a man doesn't want to be a snail, walkin' everywhere with your house on your back. You can see the ships all the time, looking down from the 'Loo. I used to think it'd be good—oh to go to the sea in one of 'em.'

'We didn't see much of 'em in the West,' Otto told him, 'but my dad used to buy me books—you know, those Wonder Books of Ships. And he'd take me to see the ships when they came in. I used to love it. All the blokes with their white dickey fronts pulled across their chests, and their tiddley jumpers with U-fronts nearly down to their navels. They all looked real tarry-ropes to me.'

'Every finger a marline-spike, every hair a rope-yarn, and every drop of blood Stockholm tar,' Blackie broke in good-naturedly. . . .

I have stirred the fire to write this last bit. They are quiet now. The sky is brim-full of clear bright stars. As they twinkle, I think of scattered crushed ice catching light. It is so quiet I can almost hear them clinking on the brim of Eternity.

This is the last day of January, 1943.

And now to turn in.

V

Konyu – February

WE ARE very short of rice containers, so a small party of us—
Ken, Fatty, Blackie, Jim and George and myself—have
been told off to make baskets. I can think of no other qualifica-
tion we have except that we are sailors and can therefore tie
a reef knot. Fortunately we have two soldiers with us. 'Old' Ted
is a farmer and far more resourceful than we are: I don't know
what we would do without him. Arthur, too, is from the bush.

Ted is tall, raw-boned, red-faced with tiny blue veins in a
network on his shiny-skinned cheekbones. He has cornflower-
blue eyes, a thin-ridged hook nose and the straight set mouth of
a confirmed pipe smoker. He speaks slowly in the way of a
thoughtful man, but without stammer or hesitation. He is
sensible, pleasant and unassuming, seeming always like a man
among boys when he is with a crowd. Arthur is big-chested,
medium height; blue eyes and a pointed nose. His brows
beetle a bit with typical outback seriousness; but his deep voice
can rise to a high belly-laugh of fun. They are the best of work-
mates and we are a happy team.

We are thrown completely on our own resources for raw
materials. They say, 'You are sailors,' just as if it were 'abracadabra'.

Just twelve months ago we were on our way to Sourabaiia
with a hastily formed naval force of four nationalities; but
today we went into the Siamese jungle to find the right vines,
bark and bamboos for baskets. We searched for the bark, which
we knew grew on a tree with seven-pointed leaves; but, to our
botanical confusion, we found most of these deciduous trees
bare. However, at last we located one. Now we are restocked
and happy.

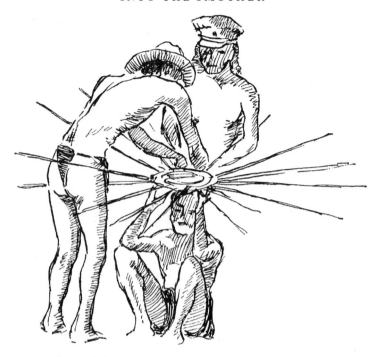

Blackie, Arthur and Jim begin the bottom of a basket at Konyu

This little game seems too good to last. This time last year had seen the beginning of a strenuous phase of our naval careers. It was the culmination of our highly specialized training in precision machinery, higher mathematics, drills upon drills, and all the ramifications of a great service, to condition us for bloody battle at sea. We found bloody battle and fought for three days and nights until the ship went from under us.

Now, we are at work on the beach—a long, willow-edged sandbank down by the river. We tether the canes for our baskets to the willows, to soak in the water. Ted splits and trims the bamboo slats—an unenviable job which results in many razor-like cuts and splinters. He never complains, but works with a perseverance the rest of us are incapable of. He also makes some very good two-stranded rope from bark. He says he has made miles of it on his farm for hay-binding. The rest of us work on the canes and vines, arguing about this way and that, because we are such novices. But we get on without friction.

Jim and George have discovered a bed of clams in a reach a little way upstream; so they slip away in the forenoons and come back at dinner time with the haul. In a private alcove in the water under the willows, one of us cleans them during the afternoon. We put them on the fire when we get up from work and, about 9 p.m., the Navy band, with Ted and Arthur, eat this life-saving food. They are tough and taste a bit like tripe, with a suggestion of mushrooms.

*

Other things are being eaten here too. Today a seven-foot king cobra was caught in a heap of bamboo. He had a fine hood which spread about nine inches across. He was chopped into three and hung up. Tonight the two air force chaps who caught him were cooking him over their private fire. By the time they began to eat, they were already surrounded by the curious and hopeful. But only a couple of the most intimate friends were privileged to taste.

When caught, the first blow of the axe had taken several feet from the cobra's tail, but his head stayed up and his hood spread until the next blow took it off.

*

This morning is *Yasume* day. So far the Japanese have given us a *Yasume* every Sunday. Reveille at 7.30 a.m.; 8 a.m. work; 9.30 a.m. breakfast. And the rest of the day is free except for ration parties. While we were in the breakfast queue Fatty blew up in a rage of disgust. There was only plain rice and, as we presented our dixies, we received a very small portion. The mess-servers said this was all right, since it would leave more for the 'back-up'. (Back-up is A.I.F. for left-overs.) But there was no back-up; and while we waited we had to witness:
1. The mess-servers and their mates getting heaped-up dixies.
2. A *full* bucket of rice and a bucket of tea going over to the

W.O's—ten, plus two batmen. This was thirty men's rations.
We have also seen a bucket of soup going over—fifty rations.
All this in the face of visible malnutrition, avitaminosis and the
added probability of death from diseases not normally fatal.

Although there was no back-up, the men dived into the
baskets to scrape the remnants from the sodden sacks in the
bottom. At this Fatty's gorge rose: 'A bit of *plain rice*! And they
steal *that* from you!'

*

A rumour is around that some of our rations have been sold
to the English. It may not be true, but the damage is done.
Food is an ever-present problem; but with a lot of self-discipline
one is satisfied with a small cup of plain rice and a half a cup of
burnt-rice water. Without this discipline you torture yourself.
At dinner and supper we get Chinese radish water called 'soup'.
Every three or four days we get 100 pounds of meat (including
bone) for 875 men. It makes a thin soup for the majority; but
it is not re-assuring to think what privilege and perks have
taken from it.

Those with avitaminosis get one egg a day from the regimental fund, and have to buy another for seven cents. Bad
cases get two eggs. Hunger is a physical nagging and each meal
brings burning dyspepsia.

The eggs are the best buy. These eggs have a long history
before we get them, because they are gathered from the paddy
fields where the ducks lay them, and may not be discovered
for some time. Many we get are already sun-cooked on one
side and stuck to the shell. After discovery they still have the
long barge ride up the river. So that, as well as being sun-
cooked, some are quite black in patches and some are wholly
rotten. The joke about the curate's egg being good in patches
is a simple fact here. I have eaten eggs from one end as far as
I could towards the other, being stopped at last by an unassail-
able blackness. Sometimes a man breaks an egg and we all
have to clear out until he has buried it. But we know that eggs
might save our lives and that is why we face the blackness.

Already there are 222 cases of avitaminosis, ninety of them severe.

*

Last night, against the indigo mountains across the river, the blue camp smoke hung in horizontal strips like the gossamer cob-webs in an old haunted garret by soft candle-light. Will we be the ghosts to haunt this jungle one day?

*A ground spider (here
one-third). It weighed
quite heavy in the hand*

We caught a ground spider today. She was a good hand-span across and weighed quite heavy in the hand. She had ten legs—probably the front two were thickened antennae—and her maw contained two black claws as big as a cat's. She had her young wrapped in a white silk bundle-handkerchief. We cut this spherical purse open and there were a couple of dozen young there. When we teased her she made a spring from about nine inches in front of my foot almost up to my knee, which I withdrew.

Many varieties of butterflies billow about in clouds. Down by the river I saw a red-headed kingfisher flashing in amongst them.

The weather continues hot; the hills are a warm green-madder with a soft fuzziness which belies their thorns. The dying leaves are ochre in the dry sun.

*

We have a couple of small iguanas, about three feet long, running about the camp. Sometimes, when these lizards are panicked, they run up a fellow's leg, mistaking it for a tree of refuge: then there is a wild dance until they separate.

According to Dutchmen here, the animals of this country are elephant, tiger and many fowl, but especially snakes—king cobra and python among many others. The pythons, they say, are most unpleasant because they lie in wait overhead and drop in coils on the passing victim. Our ignorance of this country is pretty complete, so we are the victims of a hundred little fears. Fires are kept going all night. This is by Japanese order. Tiger fires we call them.

*

Our latrines are simple enough, being large pits covered as best we can with bamboo having holes with detachable lids. The urinal has a distinctiveness of its own. Its architect and builder is Bob Fox, a small dark energetic man, no longer young, who in civil life is a builder. He has taken a twenty-foot piece of large bamboo some six inches in diameter, and scooped out holes between the divisions somewhat like a flute. He has demolished the bulkheads in it by thrusting a smaller piece of bamboo right down the centre. It is set on two forked sticks with one end higher than the other and it drains into a vertical pipe set over a hole in the ground. It is known as 'Bob Fox's Piccolo', and fifteen men can play it at once. Hordes of black bush bees and gorgeous clouds of kaleidoscopic butter-flies frequent it.

*

Last night after we had turned in and the fires were crackling among the murmur of men talking, Otto's voice rose in a hoarse 'whisper' to Izzy which carried clearly for twenty-five yards.

'I took a sheila out in Fremantle a couple of times . . . she was all right, a good sort. I only knew her first name. After a week I asked her what her other name was. She told me it was *MRS* something and her husband was in the A.I.F. Do you think I felt a big ——? A real *louse*! All the fun went out of it—

you feel dirty. I didn't want to see her any more. But she started to tell me she was in trouble. I panicked. I felt real crook in the guts. I said we'd see about it. I didn't know what to do. When I told my Old Man, he said I was a fool—should be more careful who I took up with (as if I could know!)—said there wasn't much I could do; being the sort she was, she was probably lying anyway; not to see her any more. By Golly! I was more careful after that—put me off for a long while.'

'Ah—' Izzy said, 'I don't worry about 'em. If they are silly enough to come at it—that's *their* business, they should know how to look after themselves.'

'Well, I didn't feel so hot for a long while—even when I think of it now.'

*

Last night the sergeants were paraded before the Adjutant, a major. He strongly criticized the falling-off of morale. He commended the W.O's and blamed the sergeants. We saw a little bit of red, because we think the W.O's simply pass on the orders verbally and leave the dirty work to the sergeants, who live with the men. We think, too, that the officers have got out of touch with the men and can only wave the Manual of Military Law at them in an endeavour to intimidate. This only produces a violent reaction in the men, who become even more bloody-minded on seeing the officers vaunting privilege and neglecting responsibility. Often they seem more concerned with traditional niceties of the parade ground than in facing the vital situation of survival with the men: this is not to detract from some officers, who have from their own pay, given food and money to some of the men. And the doctors are, in all things, impeccable.

But it does seem stupid to have this parade-ground stuff thrust on us as a 'morale builder'. These men are not disciplined, in the naval sense; but properly led they are as good as any men in the world. We are hoping that time will heal this breach, but at the moment it doesn't look like it. The men feel that, in facing this situation, the officers have half-a-head start on them and are using authority to their own advantage. I hear it said every day.

*

Yasume is drawing to a close and I have recorded these things that are happening to us; but tonight I will look at the fire-lighted tree again from my bed in the dust, and it will soothe me. Each night I think how beautifully this old tree goes out and merges with the night.

By daylight it is a solid tree, branching in two, and then branching again and again until the smallest twigs are reached. At night, illuminated by the fires beneath, there is more—the radiating rhythm becomes striking. The homely old trunk is divided in two a few feet above the ground, reaching to the east and west; then division after division until the maze of twigs becomes a harmony of direction reaching strongly up and on, into the night, in sharp, beautiful, little highlights pencilled so fine against the sky like an exquisite pain, until the slender-ness is nothing. Yet, invisible but palpable, this rhythm goes on high above the black filigree-tops of the high bamboo. On to the emptiness of space. The populous emptiness filled with this rhythm—this omnipresence which is somehow the very essence of what Man, in his ignorance, fear, superstition, dilettantism, piety, through science or urged by an inexplic-able inner force, has attempted to define. This is the simple sermon of an old tree, so hard to make clear, but so easy to feel: *here* and *now*.

*

Another *Yasume* has come around. I am plagued with the ever-present and recurring trouble of P.O.W's—a sour stomach and its petty magnified miseries.

Reveille at 7.30 a.m. Blue-black and starlight. The sliver of moon had set before midnight. The battalions were fallen in and set to work clearing and thatching huts. Our little basket party moved down to our 'workshop' on the river. There we had our weekly *soap* bath. There is no lending of soap—each man jealously guards the little he has. I don't even share mine with Blackie. It is a piece as big as my thumb and dried as hard as bone, which will make it last longer.

After the bath we stood naked around the big fire we had lit. We stood in the red, glowing cave it burnt in the grey river mist, like smugglers, shivering and baking by turns. Outside the glow, all was grey, swirling, steamy mist which rose from the river as if it were boiling. All night it must have been boiling up from the warmer water, and the cold dawn found the valley and hillsides wreathed in banks and layers of filmy, obscuring whiteness. Columns and puffs kept rising from the river's swift skimming surface.

This is dawn in the valley of the Kwai Noi at Konyu. Dark and cold it starts. The sky pales, but the mist interferes with the clear light, and the east is opalescent. Out of this opalescence the calm crown of the indigo mountain rises. The sky turns red and white—like the pinkness inside an oyster shell. The coming of day, in fact, is like the opening of an oyster shell, long deserted. The greys and iridescence maintain this illusion as, alongside that indigo mountain-top, the great disc of the sun appears with the fine quality of fire struck from a moist shell by a low sun. The disc is not a precise circle, but has a mobile edge of fire—liquid, deep pink, bright.

The baboons go on cat-calling and screaming as they have for an hour or more, filling the jungle with larrikinism. Brief flights of birds are seen, and their songs filter through. The mists slowly melt, and gradually the river stops steaming: it will be another hour before the last wisp has gone. Then Day will have forgotten Night.

*

A hot day. The jungle grows still and dry. The bamboo hangs motionless in the glaring sun and you feel, if it should move, it would rasp in the dry air which is filled with the dust of men moving in the clearing. This fine alluvial dust, which arises wherever man moves, covers all our possessions. We breathe it constantly and it aggravates our throats, which grow raw because we lack vitamin A.

*

9.45 a.m. was breakfast and *Yasume* had begun.

Four of the five huts have been completed. We are under cover at last, though one battalion is still under the stars.

There are constant rumours born of fond hope and vague fears. 'After fourteen days move back to Bampong for big *yasume.*' 'We are to be replaced by Japanese soldiers.' It is sometimes hard to know how to treat rumours, especially when they voice your dearest wish. I don't believe them; I don't disbelieve them. Something like when you take a punch or a bone-breaking hold—you roll with it a bit.

*

Izzy has a gramophone and about a dozen records he has lugged all the way with him in a sort of religious fervour. I say religious fervour, because his Fats Waller records send him into that kind of ecstasy. But it is good to lie back at night and hear even this thin scratching from the worn needles.

*

A word about the rigmarole of morning parades—how long this sort of thing will go on, I don't know.

Out in the dark at 7.45 a.m. Somebody puts some bamboo on the fires and there is a flare of brightness in which the first-ups stand shivering. The quarter warning goes. Some more turn out. Then the five-minute warning. And Austin Fyffe's voice comes clear, with the intonation of the Hebrides, across the clearing. Austin is our Sar-major. He was a Captain, M.C., in World War I. But for this war he has put his age back and joined as a private in the A.I.F. We like Austin a lot: but his voice makes us grumble about falling in before we should. Stumbling among the treacherous bamboo stumps, the crowd go on parade. P Battalion comes from the bush on the opposite side. Overcoats, sweaters, long pants, shirts, shorts and a few hardy ones in singlets.

Before the final fall-in is sounded, the whole parade is silent and waiting—except the officers, some of whom play on privilege to be a bit late. This always causes bitter complaints from the men. The whole parade waits in two lines of battalions facing each other. Each battalion is divided into sections of forty men each, with a section commander on the right of each one. The men are five-deep, with fifteen paces separating the facing battalions. They wait.

The trees rise on tall straight trunks, high above the dwarfed men. They are hazy near the ground from the smoke of the all-night fires which still glow like little burning towns seen over the horizon. A few pallid stars glim. The R.S.M. calls the parade properly at-ease and reports them to the Adjutant who calls the parade to attention. Then in a changing-of-the-guard voice: 'Officers take post!' Again there is a rumble of discontent. Then the parade is reported to the Colonel by the Adjutant. 'Stand at . . . *ease!*' and we all wait for the Japanese to come along and count us in sections.

They come.

'Parade . . . atten-n-n . . . *chur-r-nn!* To the front . . . *salute!* . . . *Down!*' The Adjutant takes the guard to O Battalion and our Battalion Commander calls, 'Duty section . . . *number!*' After they have numbered he reports, 'Duty section . . . forty on parade . . . all present!' The guard compares it with the statement held before him by the Adjutant. And so he passes from section to section, saluting and being saluted. Absentees are accounted for by verbal report here and a counting of heads later. *Benjo*, hospital, orderly, etc. After both battalions have been mustered, the two or three guards take a formal 'To the front, *salute!*' and go.

The Adjutant stiffens again after his slightly obsequious trailing of the guards. He calls the parade to attention, dismisses the officers and warrant officers, and calls for Battalion Commanders to take over.

The Battalion Commander quickly turns us over to the

Sar-major who tells the Section Commanders to break us off for mess parade. At long last, here is someone with the courage to say, 'Break off!'

It is just light enough to see the bamboo stumps, and there is a helter-skelter rush of men to the mess-point with the tinny rattle of mess dixies and spoons and mugs which have been brought on parade. It is an animal rush and each man is self-centred. If he is first to the mess-point, he is first for the back-up. This turns him into something as voracious as a gull on an offal heap.

*

The other morning . . . Tea is no longer tea. It is burnt-rice water called rice coffee. But it is boiled, and only boiled water is safe to drink here. Because of a lack of utensils, we get a very meagre half-pint for breakfast. A small grumbling group, feeling sorry for themselves, said, 'It's an insult giving it to us—it's only good for washing your dixies in!' So they went without and washed their dixies in it.

*

This afternoon Weary Dunlop came over. He is our camp C.O., but primarily our doctor. He came over to ask me if he might read over the account I had written of the night the Germans declared war on Greece and blew up the Piraeus of Athens. He was there too. We talked for a couple of hours. At the outbreak of war he had abandoned the plan of his career, which he had been following for fourteen years, at the request of the Commonwealth Government who asked him if he were free. Being a man who never refuses a request for help, he gave up a great deal to join the A.A.M.C. When the war is over he must slowly climb back in a catch-as-catch-can world and, I have no doubt, the Government that so eagerly sought him will as eagerly forget him. He tells me that all his life he has been a scoffer; but he knows the conventions at which he has scoffed are the necessary weft and woof for the many, and he respects that. But I know he is a most kindly and gentle scoffer—except at the unrighteous. Here is a man who shoulders his own

420

burdens so that they will not worry others, and then heedlessly piles on his own shoulders the worries of anybody who comes to him. He is a man the Japanese have already tortured several times; but about this he says nothing. I heard of one session they gave him. They put a thick pole behind his knees and then made him kneel, holding heavy stones so that the pole acted as a fulcrum to force the knee joints apart with the whole weight of his body (this is called the 'knee-spread'). In addition, his bare knees were pressing into sharp gravel. For eight hours he was like this, and he did not hide from me the fact that it was painful; but, he said, the return of circulation was most embarrassing for, when he tried to stand at last in front of his torturers, he 'stumbled like a silly fool'.

The men would do anything for him and are proud to be with him. I am sure it is his presence which holds this body of men from moral decay in bitter circumstances which they can only meet with emotion rather than reason. He is a big man— some six feet four inches of him—and a most skilful surgeon : a simple, profoundly altruistic man, with a gentle, disarming smile. This selflessness, this smile, command more from the men than an army of officers each waving a Manual of Military Law. When we move, Weary always tries to carry all his surgical gear and books. He has to be bullied to part with any of them; and then, like as not, you will find him carrying something for somebody else.

He told me that, two nights ago, he and a major were sent for by the Japanese Commanding Officer in the English camp. They made their way over a very hazardous track in the dark, to find the Jap sitting up in bed with a mouth organ. They had had to spend half the night sitting up listening in forced admiration to the murder of *Auld Lang Syne* and *Home Sweet Home*.

*

A Japanese soldier said, 'In three months, all men home— Nippon in Nippon; Australie in Australie. Honourable peace— no one win.'

*

The nights are very cold—colder it seems at full and new moons. Before going to sleep we talk, listen to the gramophone, or sometimes educate Otto. He is quite serious. He is trying to master words—something he has not bothered about before. Now it fascinates him and he likes most what he calls 'tiddley words'. Also he keeps pumping us for sea poems, sea songs, sea terms and anything about the sea. He was speaking about his ideas on the subject of marriage, and he told us of a dream he had yet to fulfil. 'You'd get the right girl and all that, of course. . . . Then I'd get her in the kitchen . . . buy her a bag of flour, and all the gear . . . and then I'd say, "Make cakes"— you know, just like you signal the destroyers to "Make-smoke". Then out'd roll the cakes like the smoke—tons of 'em. And I'd woof 'em as fast as she made 'em. I reckon being married 'd be all right.'

Otto always seems to be speaking on impulse, as if his ideas explode outwards as soon as he gets them. If a young lady sighted some of the butterflies here, she must say, 'How lovely! How *gorgeous*!' Now when Otto gets filled with exactly the same emotion, he yells out, 'Look at that bastard! What a *corker*!'

*

The baboons are creating a racket in the mornings still.

In some ways this is an odd country to Antipodeans. The Dry Season is in the winter, and the autumn comes at the *end* of that winter as the leaves drop off the trees. The trees are bare and wintry while the sun scorches down from right overhead. Then, all at once, spring shows up as a number of trees burst into bud and blossom—bright lemon-yellow blossom. In the clearing there are three of them, and on the hills among the bare trees, there are more. Some of the trees are bursting in bright red little leaves as brilliant as flowers. Another has a red blossom somewhat like a coral tree which, like the japonica, flowers before it leafs. So don't ask me what season it is.

*

422

Something has happened to us over the past twelve months—primitive emotions of survival have emerged. Somebody brought up the subject of sex with a sort of disinterested curiosity. We have all decided that Sex is out and Hunger is king.

*

'Old' Mac, a small blue-eyed Irishman looking older than his years, was a mess-server today. He was ladling out the rice coffee, but only giving each man a quarter of a cupful. One man pulled him up. Mac snarled back, 'That's all you want—I only wash my dixie with mine.' The other day Mac got two pieces of meat in his soup. 'Hooray! You've won at last!' the fellows cheered him. He turned on them bitterly and told them to leave him alone. 'If you don't,' he threatened, 'I'll throw the bloody lot away!'

Tobacco is about in limited quantities and tempers are a bit sweeter.

*

This afternoon all the yellow blossom blew down in a gust of wind. All that is now left on the trees is the flower stems—little knobs with bristly whiskers on the ends. Imagine a flowering peach—only yellow—with a fifty-foot trunk, flowering at ten in the morning, and all the petals blown off by four in the afternoon.

This brings us to the middle of February. By the time I do my chores I will be ready to drop dead for the night on my bamboo bed-boards, which are rougher than anything man has slept on since the Neolithic age.

*

Our jungle experience is just a month old. It may seem that the incidence of malaria, dysentery and avitaminosis is excessive for just one month; but this is, in fact, the last month of twelve in captivity.

There are the chronic malarias, and many new cases as we

are more exposed to it here. Some stomachs are more suscep-
tible to fluxes than others, and dysentery gets them first. We
all have almost constant stomach upset of one sort or another.
Continued hard work and little food contribute to it all.

In many ways this month has been a shake-down to new
conditions which, according to a dozen rumours, could end
quite soon. These rumours are born of the it-*can't*-happen-to-us
state of mind.

*

Several nights ago Weary Dunlop asked me over to the
officers' lines for a cup of coffee at 9 p.m. We wandered along
many channels—Greece, Crete, the Greek people, Matapan;
Man's destructive ingenuity; his amazing resistance and
adaptability; Wells's *Defeat of Homo Sapiens*, Olaf Stapleton's
First and Last Men; the brain operating at the same time as
centre both of emotion and reason; on to observation, and the
association of ideas rather than accurate memory; whether the
Caucasus or the valley of the Euphrates was the cradle of Man;
the Middle East, Lawrence of Arabia; Masefield, Kipling,
Conrad—and by then it was 11 p.m.

Just at that point Doctor Corlette came straight from the
hospital tent and the two of them discussed the condition of a
patient. It was decided to operate. The officers' mess table was
bamboo on top of four posts set in the ground in the open. A
huge bamboo fire was lit. On the table, with the aid of a hand
torch, Weary carried out a major operation on a perforated
duodenum with only a canopy of trees above him. A Japanese
officer witnessed the operation and was much impressed. He
asked Weary how he came to have so many instruments. Weary
replied, 'I have carried them on my back for the sake of the
men.' This was a pointed criticism of the Japanese attitude.
Now the patient is convalescing well. The basket party was
called upon to make a bamboo back-rest to offset the chances
of pleurisy.

*

Nature is getting on very well here in spite of our rude intrusion. The bare dust of the camp is splashed with fresh emerald leaves springing from hacked stumps and roots. I am collecting more and more varieties of butterflies. I have plenty of helpers and the underside of the hut roof is covered with dozens of them, each on a bamboo sliver, waiting to be painted.

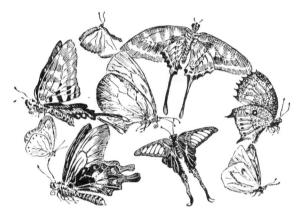

Part of a butterfly cloud

I was surprised by one of the guards with my butterfly book open on my lap. He inspected several of the drawings myopically and tried to scratch one off with his nail. I had to explain they were only drawings. 'Gooda! Gooda! O.K.! O.K.!' he said, but I was very glad when he went. I will keep them out of sight in future. There have been several cases where an artist has been led on with the promise of an easy job, or a feed, to draw for them. And it has not been long before he has been told to draw dirty pictures. From my own observations it seems clear that the guards seek sex amongst themselves.

*

The yellow-flowered tree whose mustard petals fell in a day was a fresh mass of bloom the next. And by nightfall the petals were all gone again. As I was having a swim last night, a fine golden-headed pheasant flew across the river and into the trees.

*

425

We have had our first concert here. It was in a very good setting. A fire burning over a ton of wood at once, cast great light and heat on the audience, sitting on old bamboo mounds, which formed a horse-shoe towards the performers.

Up on the hillside, a long zigzag of burning bush outlined the nearer trees. As the fire crept along the ridge, the loud reports of the water-filled bamboos exploding in the heat were like the skirmishing of infantry.

Up the valley to the eastward was the smell of rain as a wind sprang up, and the little spherical seed-pods of the yellow tree came down like hail—plopping in the dust until it had changed to green. The thatch on the weather side of the huts blew up like the capsizing feathers of a seagull, tail to wind.

Our first concert had coincided with our first rain. More wood was thrown on the fire until the flames were ten feet high and the sparks shot up like intercepting fighters against the bombing of the rain.

The concert went on. *Things ain't the same since my man Bill's 'ome from war*; the Far Eastern Brothers' lowdown on the Malayan Campaign—*frightfully* 'General-Staff'; a duet of two strange fellows: one, tough with a beard, was the tenor, while a boyish-faced, small-framed slender youth was the baritone; *They'll be coming round the mountain when they come*. Refrain: *They'll be dropping thousand-pounders when they come*; *Yeomen of England* and *Old Father Thames* (in excellent voice); a duet of a Scot and an Irishman with *The Little Yellow Idol*. Then, finally, a very good violin played while the rain streamed off the player. *God Save The King*, and it was over.

*

I have decided to give the butterflies my own names as I draw them. Blue Midnight, Moss Queen, High Priest, Jacob's Coat, Little Piccaninny, Sepia Ballerina, Crinoline Girl: they help to take your mind off sore feet, bellyaches, malaria and all that.

*

There has been a general agitation to know what has happened to the Regimental Funds which have been built up by taking twenty per cent of our Japanese pay. The Officer responsible has suddenly become indisposed, but promises a statement in a couple of days. Simultaneously there has been the sudden appearance of a few extras from the cookhouse.

No Japanese rations have arrived for a number of days. What vegetables there were have been finished some time, and we are living on plain rice and any eggs we can afford. These are literally life-saving and could be the one thing that pulls us through. At present the river is easy and the barges can come up. But we wonder what will happen in the Wet Season. We can see evidence of the height the floods reach here.

This brings me to some punishments handed out by some of our own officers. Two men were 'crimed' for smoking after the five-minute warning for parade. The punishment was a *week's* stoppage of Japanese pay: in fact a week's badly needed subsistence. I know the men have been cantankerous and unruly. On occasion they have shocked our prudish naval ideas on discipline; but leadership has not been perfect either. We are all fellow prisoners of a common enemy. The Colonel told me that some of the officers have said, 'The men are not worth bothering about.' And he has been saddled with this unhappy state of affairs. The doctors and two of the executive officers stand out like giants above the frightened self-seekers. I can only hope, as they play god over the men, that *their* god is of the same vindictive character.

*

This is the last day of February—Sunday.

I did not sleep after midnight. My back and legs ached and the top of my head was lifting up and down like a boiling kettle. At such times my febrile brain fills with racing thoughts. In a way I find it a kind of compensation, for you never know what will turn up next.

The night was the silence of great space overlaid with the breathing of many sleeping men and sporadic sounds from the night fires and the jungle; the explosive wheeze of the toc-ta lizards and the double xylophone donk-donk of a night bird; towards dawn the squawk of a peacock or pheasant; an hour before dawn the scream of the baboons.

The fires continue to explode loudly; on the hillside the bush-fire gives a burst of musketry and for a moment you think deliverance is at the door. But it is only the fires making drifting smoke through which the moon must climb, blood-red, until she turns frosty pale above the haze.

I got up at daylight, as miserable as a bandicoot, with my head ringing like an anvil under a hammer—ring and thump, ring and thump. I went to the sick bay and the doctor suggested malaria. I did not want malaria, so I suggested T.A.B. reaction as we had had an inoculation a few days before.

*

Of course it was malaria. For the first three days of March I was miserable with aches and pains; then I was put in hospital with malaria and a bit of dysentery. The 'hospital' is a bell tent, and we sleep on the ground with our feet to the centre. Ken is here with me. The most effective part of the treatment is that we are left more or less undisturbed in our misery. But I cannot complain, for there are men near me who writhe in agony a lot of the time.

*

Weary Dunlop came to see me this morning with his stethoscope dangling from his neck. He, too, has been ill. 'But,' he said, 'I am back in the trade again.' He talked of a spot along the river about which he had spoken before. It is the English cemetery by the hot springs and overlooks the river. He said he would like me to make a sketch of it some time. Then he went on to tell me this little tale about it.

'An English colonel,' Weary said, 'was showing me the site and almost bursting with pride, like a jolly old sexton. "There are just twenty-nine graves," he said, "but with *terrific* scope for more." ' Weary's eyes twinkled, 'I could see that, for before us was most of Thailand. And then, almost as one would ask another, "Are you a Roman Catholic or a Protestant?" he turned benignly to me and said, "Would you . . . er . . . would you care to . . . er . . . *share*?" ' Six foot four of Weary bent forward in patient, polite attention as, with a disarming smile, he asked, 'Is there room?'

'Of course!' he burst out. 'First, I want to fill over *there*.' He chopped off a tract of land with a downward movement of both his arms parallel. '. . . and then, *there*! . . . then, over *there*! . . . but over *there* . . . I think I could fit you in.' He was completely lost in professional enthusiasm.

*

A couple of little things have happened over the past few days which have caused friction between some of the officers and men. One lieutenant ('Two-pip artists', the soldiers call them) withheld our midday drink. We get only half a pint per meal and work all day in the dust and heat. We went from breakfast until the evening meal without an issued drink because this officer complained that some of the men had not returned a couple of the tins to the cookhouse after breakfast.

A jeering line of men at the meal parade told him what they thought of him, inviting him to come out and work with them in the afternoon sun. Then, at the evening count parade, we had to listen to a long harangue from the Adjutant telling us we didn't live up to his idea of parade-ground soldiers. Standing like a ramrod and talking like a guards' major on a peace-time barrack square, dapper and clean shaven, in khaki drill which his batman had washed, he criticized men who had worked all day in the heat and dust. He went further and nagged them about 'disgusting habits at the latrines'. Now many men with dysentery spend much of their waking time in weary, weakening pilgrimages and sometimes take books for simple distraction. This was the 'disgusting habits' he was alluding to. He would not be surprised, he said, if some men took their *meals* there! In his eagerness to erect a monument to this inspired speech, he coined a phrase. He said the *benjo* was becoming a club for the 'crap-happy'. Well, the monument stands: he is now known as 'Crap-happy'.

*

Today I watched two monkeys, mother and son, skylarking in the bamboo. They were silver-grey, and graceful with long tails. We are seeing more birds now. Toucan pass overhead, usually about sunset, flying east. There is a powerful whirr to their wings as if they were creaking doors. This may be a croak they give as they beat their wings. Their red-blue heads and bent, goitrous necks remind me of the pouched florid faces of whisky tipplers.

*

There is one patient in hospital who is an example to us all. His name is Bookman, one of the Machine-gunners. Some say he is a half-caste aboriginal, others that he is a throw-back. But he is a fine intelligent chap with a ton of guts, whom everybody up here calls 'a bonza bloke'. He has dysentery and cannot leave the latrine for any length of time. He is harrowed, weak and bedraggled. When he can, he simply rolls himself up in his blanket by the latrine, in the strewn fire-ash which is spread for hygiene. This morning Major Moon, one of our doctors said, 'How are you this morning, Bookie?'

'Not too bad, sir . . . only twenty-nine times last night.'

Men bitter, cantankerous, pompous, jealous, afraid . . . then, men like Bookie.

*

The diet is still meagre. A cup of boiled rice and half a pint of burnt-rice water each meal. Twenty-three bags of rice came over the other day. It had been swept from the dirt floor of a decayed hut and is full of dust and rat droppings. If we had washed it we would have lost too much. The eggs for the men in the lines are rationed to one per man, but the officers' canteen representative took 250 for fifteen officers. An officer's batman told me that he had been all day without touching plain, boiled rice. Breakfast: fish. Dinner: meat and eggs. Tea: rice rissoles. The only meat the men ever see is a rag, sometimes, in the daily soup—*never* more than one and a half ounces. The ration for the camp is about sixty pounds, including bone. What angers the men is that the officers, as well as not having to work, get so far ahead of the men all along the line. I am quite sure the Colonel and the other doctors don't know what is going on there.

*

There is a rumour that we will be moving to another camp, twenty kilometres up the river.

*

This is Wednesday, March 10th. I am feeling pretty fit again, despite the rations. I saw a pheasant today fly into the trees, and I noticed that his tail had five or six white eyes, like

The duet, Konyu camp concert by firelight. February 1943

a peacock. This day last year we were becalmed in a lifeboat some seventy miles S.S.E. of Java Head, in the Indian Ocean, and only saw one bird.

Today is some sort of a *Yasume*: some say it is in celebration of the Russo-Japanese War. Whatever it is, I have used it to make a painting of the duet by firelight at the concert the other night, and another of a long-tailed, window-winged butterfly which one of the fellows brought in.

Now there are ninety in hospital—fifty malaria and forty dysentery. If we have to move there will be 300 unfit for marching: 'no boots' or in hospital.

We have just received confirmation of our move—we go tomorrow.

VI

Hintok Road – March

IT WAS 11.30 a.m. before we moved off. First, we had to get up that Hill on which men on ration parties had collapsed. There is a road there now, but many of us were fresh out of hospital and the day was well advanced in dry, sapping heat.

At the top we were allowed to rest. We had sweated freely during the climb, but as we flopped down, sweat spouted, like blood, from every pore. It was strange to see the skin spring into thousands of tiny, rushing rivulets. While we waited we saw a small phalanger glide past our heads. Only about nine inches long, it was like a fragment of the remote past. After ten minutes we moved on.

The road followed a narrow, elevated strip winding just below the serrated spine of a mountain chain. To the south were other jagged ridges of dark, stained granite resembling the sheer faces of organ pipes. It was a bamboo jungle, but in one swampy part there were a few patches of palms. In bare, burnt-out patches, some flowers—little, white irises with a pure, orange streak on their tongues—had sprung up from the recent rain with just their heads out of the soil. They grew in bunches, back to back, in half-dozens. But there was no foliage yet. Bugs and butterflies lined the route to watch us go past.

We arrived in the new camp at 2 p.m. and were given a fish soup, and some tea which really tasted like tea. I sipped mine with a spoon, to relish it. Then we were given tents, eighteen feet by twelve, and we put them up. Twenty men to a tent. We cut logs and covered them with a bamboo deck on which we put our belongings. It had rained on the way and been thundery. We were glad to have some shelter.

Chaps from Timor, the 2nd/40th, are here and we have

433

eagerly swapped tales of camps and conditions. Our first impression is that the food seems better, perhaps it is simply that
it doesn't taste mouldy. There is an order in force here which
was also issued to English at Konyu. It states that, whenever
eggs are fried, the yolks shall be broken to prevent any profane
resemblance to the Nippon flag, of course, we have now
christened the 'fried egg'.

Another early impression is the woe-begone manner of many
of the Dutchmen here.

We went to bed crowded, but much more content than one
could have thought possible. It could have been the change,
and an expectancy of things—be they what they might—just
around the corner.

*

With the night fires still casting a glow up to the tree canopy,
reveille sounded. There was a hoarse, 'Huh! Ho!' from the Jap
guards and a shrill imperious whistle from the Dutch. Then
Austin calling, 'All Out, O Battalion!'

We dressed in the dark and paraded at 8 a.m., and went
straight to breakfast—pap, with a splash of tea. Immediately
we formed in the queue for our work rations, gulping down
breakfast to make room for them in the same dixie. Plain rice
and two small vegetables, and rice rissoles.

At 8.45 a.m. we marched out to the site of the railway. The
first few hundred yards of our way was across a short flat valley
which looked as if it would be a swamp in the Wet. It lay between two escarpments. We climbed an arduous zigzag up the
southern one, and up a rock wall for the last sixty feet on a rope.
It was granite and limestone, pocketed with crystal quartz.

Once over the top we went down a long slope between scattered boulders and bamboo. It led toward the river. We
followed the furrows made by elephants hauling out teak logs
when the red, clayey soil had been wet. Dried out, these
elephant pads made good paths. It was another two miles to
the railway clearing.

Here the timber had been felled. We turned elephants and

dragged it clear to the sides. The clearing was thirty metres wide, and each hundred of us have to clear a stretch 150 metres long. It was what the Japanese call a finish-come-back job, and, as new brooms, we finished quite early. The size of the logs we could move by single-minded effort surprised and pleased us. The alternative was laboriously to chop them up. The cicadas were kicking up a din and our heads rang with them. We sweated and became covered with black bush bees, who drank our perspiration and encouraged other species to do the same.

We started for home up the long two-mile hill, through a maze of boulders, and finally dropped, almost vertically, on to our camp. The bamboos among the boulders are small and 'smoothskins'—no thorns or canes. Blue-green, emerald, lichen-coloured, cane-yellow and odd purple patches; crisp, brush-stroke leaves, pencilled stems—it is like walking along a Japanese scroll painting.

When we got back to camp one of our officers ordered our tent to be moved to satisfy some military exactitude in him. So, tired, and dirty and with foul tempers, we set to re-pitching it. We had a very small evening meal. Thunder and heavy rain clapped down on us.

Another 200 from Konyu arrived in the middle of it. It rained all night and we got a bit wet in the tents. One of the half-built huts the new arrivals were in collapsed, and they came crowding into the already crowded tents. Just before dark, an eight-inch armoured centipede, red and rampant, was chased in among us by the storm. As a dismal omen, another Dutchman died: the thirteenth in seven weeks. But, to us, his death was only of passing interest.

*

By morning the rain had flooded the kitchen and splashed red clay and soot into the shallow *kwalis* cooking our watery rice. This made a gritty meal. One mug of pap and one of weak tea. Pap is at least ninety per cent water, so we start a working day on two ounces of solid and eighteen ounces of water.

Fifty of us, with forty Japs, shouldered machetes, axes, and theodolite and went over the escarpment to the railway clearing. We kept on through the dry, unshaded monotony of parched, dead bamboo leaves and bare trees. After five miles we struck north until we came to a mountain-side of massed, shelving rock—split and upturned like big axes and chisels. Loose boulders became a hazard for the next man astern.

We spent a hot forenoon here, surveying and hacking down bamboos and trees in the line of sight. It was an almost sixty-degree slope; our feet ached and our haunches tired, playing mountain goats. Our leather boots were treacherous, while the Japanese were nimble in rubber ones. By dinner time the effort of keeping up with them left us shaking with hunger and fatigue.

After a brief break, we were at it again for the rest of the afternoon. We were hot, weak and hungry, and feeling a little sorry for ourselves. So, it was easy to fall into a mood of homesick loneliness—here in this inhospitable city of ants, millipedes, centipedes, scorpions, bees, wasps, butterflies, dinning cicadas, and grasshoppers, in which man is completely dispensable.

At times like that you get a feeling in complete contrast to that of singleness with nature, and to the feeling of beauty that comes with it: the feeling that this life of the bush is in everyone and everything, which seems to be a guarantee that this life of arduous stumbling, of harassed thinking and inevitable doubting, of honest trying, is something worthwhile.

*

This day began ominously. The pap issue was small and the dinner ration light. We had a long march to a new part of the railway and began work on cuttings and embankments. Hard at it all day in the sun, we found ourselves by dinner with our waterbottles dry. The soil was filled with roots and rocks, and the tools were bad. Tempers grew shorter as men grew thirstier.

Our boss was Billy the Bastard, a small walnut-hard man with a lean, baboon face. He is a Japanese sergeant. His alternative title is Billy the Pig. All day he and his men had been nagging us with hoarse and shrill: *Speedo! Speedo! Hurree uppoo! Hurree uppoo!—Pickee! Pickee! Changee, changee! Basketo, Basketo-oo!* It was almost 8 p.m. when we got back. The rice issue was a little smaller than usual. We demanded an officer present: Justice! Fair Play! Humanity! was the demand of the exasperated men. There had been enough nonsense, enough parade-ground rubbish! An officer came: two officers! They were heckled without restraint. The men were out to show their temper; a temper to which the officers had been blind and which had been aggravated by a number of things: the morning's rush, breakfast, tidying tents, dinner ration queues, the count parade and the work parade.

The count parade is before breakfast and dinner queues, and the impressive ceremony cuts down our time for more vital things. The officers, on the other hand, with less to do than most, claim batmen—while the men don't get time to wash their rags—so that finally, when the Adjutant stood neat and well groomed before the dirty men and announced in tough disciplinarian tones, 'Men are coming late on parade. An N.C.O. will be placed on the left to mark any man late. The late-comers will be marked A.W.L. and will forfeit a day's pay!'—someone shouted, '*Pig's arse you will! You try it!*'

Then there followed a few assessments of some of the officers by the men. 'Bloody good boys! You ought to get out there and try swinging a pick for a day. Don't you take *our pay*!'

This is the first demonstration the men have made. So far the officers have been able to use 'normal army channels' to delay and block—seemingly to preserve their own little privileges. When the parade broke off there was an air of satisfaction among the men: they had expressed themselves.

The next morning we got more pap than we could eat at one sitting; the dinner ration was, compared to the usual, 'full and plenty'. It will take more than a Daniel Webster to convince the men that this was coincidence. A major went out with the embankment gangs to see the conditions. He did a good job. He argued with the Nip engineers, and went very close to a bashing.

They told him to clear off back to camp, but he refused. In the end he hopped in to help the lads get finished. It may not sound much, but this was the man, I am told, who had no courage in action, and little moral courage at other times. The talk tonight is not of our rights and wrongs—but of this man.

*

Out with the surveyors again over the rugged rock slides where we drove the last peg at the 156 kilometre 320 metre mark. From this peg we had a fine view of the Kwai Noi winding away in the distance below. The thin coiling of its green-blue, unreflecting surface could easily have been smoke curling through the trees. The tree-tops seemed soft and feathery. Some leaves were bursting out in reds and greens: here and there a splash of blossom or fruit; red fruit in trefoil bunches; pale lilac blossom, like acacias. But, in the main, the top of the jungle was a sea of new leaf-green and the mauve-pink of bare branches. The near hills showed vertical rock slashes and jagged ridges: in the distance the blue mountains rolled away to the horizon.

At dinner we lit a fire to scorch some dried fish for the Japanese. This was over and we were finishing our rice, when a slithering rustle brought a hooded cobra amongst us.

'Snake!'—But the Japanese did not understand.

'Cobra!'—And they moved as one. The snake flattened his hood, but the axe severed it. In fifteen minutes, enemy and allies were sharing the modest five feet of the unfortunate snake. It was like strong rabbit. While we were sucking our teeth with a kind of holy satisfaction, Buck casually remarked, 'And *that* is what will happen to a *tiger*, if he's silly enough to come this way.'

*

A day of tree-felling at the 150-kilometre peg. We had thirty metres by 150 to do, marked by red flags on bamboo poles, half-way up a steep rocky hillside. The trees grew out of the rocks and their roots seemed to have split them. They were teak, mahogany, coral, acacia, kapok, and others I had no idea of. There were plenty of traps. We started at the bottom to avoid crushing anybody below and to avoid a tangle: the vines in the branches often will not let the trees fall. Then came the tricky part: picking the right ones to free, and dodging quickly when they came; for they never fell true, and brought down tops from nowhere. When they hit they bounded downhill like something alive. Blackie was lucky, he had his shirt torn on his back by a close one. I just had time to give him a quick shove. We were back in camp by 3 p.m. and hardly able to believe it. I have done my washing, bathed and shaved. This is a most painful process with my one rusty razor blade and my knob of bone soap. I shave only my sideboards and neck, leaving what the Navy calls a 'torpedo' beard, Lenin-style. But this is as much as I can endure, and tears of pain stream down my cheeks.

Now I am able to catch up on this diary. I have been taking it out each day to work, but there is only fifteen minutes for dinner. Some of it I have written by firelight, and some while standing waiting on the count parades. I have not been able to catch up until tonight when, with honourable blisters, I think I can make it.

*

I remarked some time back that sex was now only of academic interest, if at all. Hunger is our main concern. Almost all our dreams are concerned with food. The *fact* of food: seeing shops filled with it; seeing someone cooking it, and so on. But one thing is common to all the dreams—*none of us ever gets to eat this dream stuff*. Something always happens. For instance: I had just bought a great pile of cream and mocha puffs, Swiss pastry, chocolate éclairs, etc., and it was all on the glass-topped counter before me. But when I felt in my pocket for the money, there was none. The wish and the reality are always struggling, and reality always wins.

*

Coral trees are bursting out in a rich blush, and a few clumps of yellow orchids are showing up on the trunks of the trees.

There are some handsome birds too, which we have not seen before. They have coal-black coats and fly in scolloping swoops into the branches, towing, on long thin stems some eighteen inches long, two black fanlike feathers with white eyes, like a decoy.

*

We have several sorts of shifty customers with us. They will do anything to escape work, which means that others, by having to do their share, work themselves to death. There is one, a sar-major who in civil life was a barrister. He has never worked manually in his life and says work is only for fools. He boasts that he has never had to work since he joined the Army. He has either pulled strings or paid others to do it—even his latrine fatigue. He is proud of his soft white hands. Being in the Pay Corps he is our canteen wallah, keeping a few books and eating at our expense. Once he was caught for a survey-party, and everybody gloated. But too soon: he got out of it.

There is another one too. He is dark, balding, fit and thick-set—a talkative advertising man who continually justifies himself as a man of principle. He fell in today with the no-boot party. Austin said, 'I was told you have a pair of boots, Kaley.' 'Oh, yes, I have; but they pinch a bit.' His bag was searched and they found a *second* pair of boots. He said they belonged to another man, who denied it. Then he said it was unfair, he was being victimized.

*

Coming home, tired, after a day's work we really can get self-centred. The great winding red-clay road, glaring with brown-paper dryness, is a stomach-draining pull without shade. The pale green, unblinking bamboo leaves are like blind mirrors, between which the sky shows deep blue—almost purple— and against which the mountain in shadow is a taunting, cool indigo. The painful impression of heat is in its nearness—its pitiless glaring, drying our bodies to tinder. The heat presses its boring fingers on eyeballs, making them ache; sweat splashes over eyebrows into eyes.

440

Climbing the Hill in the heat pulls the shoulders forward and keeps the eyes glued to the ground a few feet ahead, shirking the prospect of so long a climb. And then there is this damnable struggle between physical agony and the eye for beauty, which, I am sorry to state, filled me with a desire to see all beauty in Hades. I could not cope with it. That is fatigue; but it brings a sound, death-like sleep.

*

One of the great problems here is boiled water. We dare not drink anything else. Filling waterbottles from kerosene tins is wasteful. Major Woods has built a machine for doing it. It is an all bamboo affair: a large bamboo at the top with ten spigots in it. The bottles are filled and the spigot closed without wasting a drop. A man with a tin of boiled water keeps the large bamboo reservoir topped up as the bottles are filled. There are at least 800 men to fill their bottles after work each night, and the water-boiling party have their work cut out.

The same ingenious major has harnessed the miserable creek, which flows through here, by building a dam above the camp to raise the level. From this dam he has piped water to a shower, through large bamboo pipes on trestles. This shower is a raised platform of bamboo, some forty feet by thirty feet, above which are suspended three long bamboos, each perforated at intervals. The water constantly flows into these from the dam some 200 yards away, supplying more than a dozen showers. There are benches around the sides to put your gear on. To be able to bathe under running water is second only to eating and sleeping. And we are very grateful to the Major.

*

The rains are bringing the jungle rapidly to life now. Hooded lilies, several iris-like orchids, wild ginger and banana (which bears no edible fruit), clumps of orchids in the branches of trees like corsages of yellow jonquils. There are waves of perfume in the bush which we sometimes walk into. Cinnamon, chocolate, and one honey-sweet like clematis. Sometimes the

441

early morning dew on the dry bamboo leaves smells like the Australian bush—or is it just nostalgia?

On the rock escarpment, several hundred feet high above our tents, we watch large black baboons drop through the trees in careless, breath-taking drops of twenty feet and more, coming up with a smooth lazy swing. If a branch breaks, they simply discard it and take hold of the next one.

Near the camp we now have the donking of thirty bamboo elephant bells: a sound identical with our night bird. Today, tree-felling, a chap put his axe into a bamboo and was attacked by a swarm of irate wasps. His whole body is red and swollen and he is pretty sick.

*

We have been clearing rock after blasting on our section. It was picks, crowbars, shovels, chunkels and baskets as we struggled with the broken rock-spoil between the new, raw, white limestone walls of the cutting. They reflected the heat and glare, almost cooking and blinding us.

As we climbed the Hill tonight, a great straight imperturbable teak stood in the heat, unmoved by our struggle. But this morning, as we were going down, it was a different picture. The bamboos were a cool blue-green, dark and clean-shafted. The road was streaked across with rich brown shadows. Beyond, across the valley of the river, in the morning sun, the huge smooth mountain ridge was absolutely pink with, here and there, little splashes of emerald and viridian as if wet. It was so easy to look at going down; so different from that neck- and eye-cracking climb back.

*

Rumours are still with us. 'Build three more kilometres and go to Saigon.' 'End of April, all men go Saigon.' 'American airmen no gooda—boom, boom! Kill many Nippon.'

*

After tea there was the prospect of *Yasume* tomorrow. Lights-out was not sounded, and we talked around the fires. There was

442

a thunder storm. Then Herb Smith, from his tent, sang *The Road to Mandalay*. His splendid baritone echoed fully under the drenched canopy of the forest. At the phrase *and the dawn comes up like thunder*, one of the fellows said *that* was something you would *never* see—how can it *look* like *thunder?* But it made me think of what I had seen only this morning. It was a cool morning in a misty, rugged landscape which rose and fell like a rough sea. The hot sky was daubed with salmon-yellow mackerel clouds. The big smoky-blue ranges beyond the Kwai Noi river were like sullen sharp-crested waves seen from the height of a cliff through the mist of spume and spindrift. The heads of the trees just beneath us, in whorls of light- and dark-greens, with bruises of red, were like the surge of wrack on a rocky coast. A couple of the closer ridges were the green of transparency—close and huge, about to break.

*

I feel quite healthy, though I suppose a normal man from civvy street would not find it hard to push me over. My hands are rough, hard, cut and blistered. I keep telling myself that hard work, of *itself*, is fundamentally good: one of the basic necessities and conditions of life. This can stimulate a mind not dead to hope. I try to tell myself, what I lack in food and comfort, can be made up from all that is sheer Nature around me.

Yesterday Weary refused to let the 'light dutymen' go to work, saying it was sending them to their graves. He was forced to hospitalize them, a compromise which automatically stops their pay. As a reprisal the Japanese have, today, ordered the officers to make up wood and water parties and sink latrines. The men have not a great deal of sympathy with most of the officers, but over the doctors it is different. When we came in and saw Weary digging in a latrine pit, I think at a word from him we would have moved over to the Guard House and flattened it.

*

The toll of work and starvation is beginning to show up here

now, if reports we get are right. In one camp, eighty-five have
died; in another 300 are down with dysentery. Cholera has
already been reported upstream, after a few showers. There was
a sit-down strike in one camp because the sick had to work and
there were no canteen facilities: they had to stand all night,
and at 11 a.m., went out to work without food. About every
hour they were beaten with bamboos. The English major was
beaten very badly with a sword scabbard.

*

The railway is becoming a reality now. All the clearing is
finished, the surveying done, and we are now to build the banks,
cuttings and bridges. Big pressure is being exerted, and more
and more are being forced out to work. The railway is mapped
and already they are said to be at Tarsau with the rails. But
there is a great deal to be done here. I have heard it said that
the project is manned with 150 men per kilometre. They are
working down from the Burma end also: the whole length of
the line seems to be going ahead simultaneously. We are beginning to wonder what will happen in the Wet Season. These
small rains have already given us a sample.

*

Last night there was a very heavy atmosphere and rising
cloud flickered with lightning. By 10 p.m. the storm broke and
rose to a booming shriek, plucking at everything on the ground.
We were glad our beds are raised on logs. Gusts of wind
threatened to take the tent bodily over the 400-foot wall at our
backs. The storm reached a crescendo with incessant blue-white
lightning and short, brutal crashes of thunder. The tent was
filled with an atomized spray which wet us through. I used my
gas cape to protect my drawings and diary. A large branch
dropping like a huge dart, pierced the next tent and quivered,
firmly imbedded, in the ground between the feet of the inmates
whose disgust could be heard above the thunder.

Daylight told us a more detailed story of what had happened.
The storm had cut a swathe half a mile wide. The general

effect was of giant straw washed across a tufted field by a flood. It must have been a 'twister' to have made such a flat path of devastation, winding back and forth across our only road and completely obliterating it in places.

We were given axes at the railway and began to cut a road back to the fork at the top of the Hill. This was to allow the elephants to get down to the workings. We met eight of them at the top with their loads of water in bamboo bottles.

On the way, we came across a tree from which saddle cloths for the elephants had been cut. It was a red barked tree which had been cut to a depth of two inches and completely circled and stripped in two places six feet wide. The cloths were hung nearby to dry. A number of these are packed on top of the beasts before the rig goes on, which is secured by martingale and crupper, but no girth. This is the same kind of tree we stripped for lashings and ties for the baskets.

The fork, which is the junction of the road up the Hill and the Tarsau-Konyu-Hintok road, was reached and from here we began to cut our way back to Hintok.

Trying to cut sprung and springy bamboo, and hauling it from a tangled chaos of canes, vines and locking thorns, is exhausting work, and even the Japanese had to give us rest periods. It is during these periods I try to write, while looking at what I am writing about. All the smallest creatures of the bush seem to have been upset, and have become unfriendly. At the moment, sweat-covered, I am a mass of walking, crawling, nipping bush bees. They cover my hands as I write.

Clumps of bamboo which stood eighty to a hundred feet high yesterday, with each stick as thick as a man's thigh, now lie uprooted and flat on the ground; or twisted and bent like reeds at points from ten to forty feet from the ground. Their engineer-designed, strong, tubular structure is split and flattened, like ribbon, by a force of wind hard to imagine. They are laid along the path of the storm as if to say, 'He went *that* way!'

Bamboos tell a clear tale, but the trees seem incoherent. Big ones have been torn out by the roots and each lies with several tons of soil still clinging to it, sticking into the air ten or twelve

feet. Trees with twelve-foot girths have snapped like matches—
the crowns torn off them, like so many flowers picked between
finger and thumb. Some, crashing, have taken others with
them: some hang like robbers, swinging on vines from other
trees.

We have to be careful cutting into bamboos which are full of
wasps' nests. Jim and George have already been attacked. The
bamboo barricades are the toughest job: whole clumps of them
have been pulled up by the roots like reeds. Clumps which
were twenty feet through, now lie as walls twenty feet high.
Ninety men have been chopping all day and only now, as I
write in the late afternoon, is the first truck coming through.

*

An ox-cart convoy of Thais stayed all night in the camp. The
carts have huge, heavy, wooden wheels with *no* metal fastenings.
But they don't seem able to carry more than a couple of bags
of rice. Among the Thais was one small young women whose
black hair was American bobbed. She wore a straight-topped
bodice of white, a pair of blue trousers, and she had bare,
muddied feet which matched her raven black hair. She was

Thai oxcarts Hintok Road camp. Drivers prepare evening meal

neatly made and stood leaning carelessly against one of the big wagon wheels. A very nice picture: but she was spitting betel freely at her feet.

*

Our Navy band is split up a bit just now. Blackie and Roy are in hospital with dysentery. Jim, George, Izzy and Otto have wangled a job in the Nip kitchen. Good for them as they can pick up some extra food; and the young ones, especially, need this. Last night Otto brought some Jap stew over to me. It was very rich by our standards—meat, fish, beans, pumpkin and pickles. I ate it, but the richness demanded payment of me. Ken, Fatty, Bob, Blackie and myself usually manage to get on the same jobs, out on the railway.

*

Last night, after the storm had quietened a bit, we passed the time 'just supposing'—just supposing we were at home doing some of the things which are quite normal here. Like sitting down at the side of the road and removing our only garment— a G-string, or a ragged pair of shorts—and hunting out some of the more troublesome lice. It made a bit of fun to cook up these situations—especially to listen to Otto's loud laughs.

*

For the time our lives are centred upon the Embankment. It is a long curving affair secured by a high knoll at one end and reaching out towards a bridge at the other. It will be about twenty-three feet high and is known as the Seven-metre bank. Basket by basket, *tanka* by *tanka* (bag stretcher), we carry the earth which has to be scratched from between the rocks in the jungle, tramping it out to the slowly forming bank. It is real coolie work, and the monotony can only be offset by private thoughts and observation.

Lately big pressure has been put on the work. They want the bank by the Wet Season. It is at the 150-kilometre post. All day, each pair of men carry load after load with a bag stretcher.

Pick up. Carry twenty-five yards or more. Up the bank. Dump. Walk back . . . on and on. The way is along tortuous paths which constantly change as the soil-hungry diggers search further and further afield. Some of the unscrupulous take some of the narrow bridges of earth we have left between the boulders. The diggings are a succession of ponds full of tadpoles and covered with frog spawn. In the next hole to us they dug out a twelve-inch centipede whose head was almost the size of my thumbnail. The slimy earth bridges twist and turn on themselves and are treacherous to bare-footers carrying soggy loads. All the time there are hostile shouts from the Japs. And, in the monotony, there is nothing more grating than unintelligible noise.

Each man has to move one cubic metre a day. This may not sound much, but under these conditions we find it plenty. I manage to scribble a bit of this in the dinner breaks, and find that it helps.

*

The Japanese are addressed as George, Charlie, Claude, Eustace, etc. The sergeant, Billy the Pig, is a slightly reformed character; but his underlings have taken upon themselves his shed bastardry. They have no idea of pace and try to get us to work at one that would exhaust us in an hour. We cruise at our own speed as best we can. There are many phonetic sounds the Japanese do not have, and they seem to rely on grunts and roars belched from the belly and chest. The men's tempers are at their lowest ebb at the end of the day after an hour's grinding walk to the camp and it is then, when they are formed up in five rows for the count parade, that they use the grossest insults on our masters.

Our lot is made a little easier now with a cup of rice coffee as we come in—for we have had only a quart of water all day. After a shower we are torn between the cry of our bodies for rest and the nag of maintenance jobs on them.

*

Today it has been particularly bad. We got mixed up with a lazy crowd of low morale, who cloak their laziness with an affected patriotism that they will do as little as possible for the enemy. It doesn't trouble them that what *they* don't do will fall on their mates.

When we should have been finished and away, we were caught in the rain with more to do. The viscous, red mud clung to our feet like lead, and we slipped dangerously with our loads. The poles of our *tankas* got slimy and our fingers ached from gripping them. Afterwards the guards found more for us to do, felling trees for ramps. When we went home in the rain— a strange set of soggy, ragged clothes props—I had parted company, at last, with the seat of my rotten calico trousers. At the count, men dawdled and sulked like children just to get their own back on *somebody*. They blamed the Japanese, and punished themselves.

We got back to the lines only to find that eight tents had been taken—ours among them. Just the platform was left in the pouring rain with all our gear on it sodden with rain. One hundred and sixty men looked like having to spend the night in the rain and were not happy about it. But I was lucky, for Buck Pederson, who takes a special interest in my drawings and diary, was in camp when they took our tent, and he had taken them out and put them in another tent. I was very relieved— for I place a great store by these things. I feel if I can get them back the experience will not be entirely wasted. Memory is not enough.

*

There are odd hazards all about us. One man stood on a five-foot-six-inch banded krait—a very deadly snake. It struck at him and missed, and was eaten for its trouble. One lunch time a man was bitten by a scorpion, or centipede, or snake: I heard three versions. Whatever it was made him vomit but he is still alive. There is also the danger of blasted rock. In the open you sidestep the stone as it comes down. But if you are in the trees you only hear it ripping through leaves and branches.

I saw two bamboos cut as if by a scythe, and dived behind a tree like a man who values even this miserable existence. The elephants were halted nearby while some shots were fired. They stampeded—luckily not through us—and were only brought up after three miles.

*

As we came down the Hill, the valley of the Kwai Noi and its barbaric railway were wrapped in a comforting, cotton-wool mass of fog. We were well over a hundred paces from the bank by now. The nearer boulders had given up their last earth, and we had to endure a long carry along difficult tracks. It was a regular, funeral tramp, of corpse-like monotony. It was a heavy overcast day—too heavy to sweat much in. The simple fact of picking up the stretcher, and the strain of weight on one's arms, clogged the mind to a sodden mass like the earth itself. No thought in the mind save . . . Drudgery . . . Oppression. . . . At such times we are silent as ants. Often, for the life of me I could not tell you what my thoughts are and I am conscious of nothing, save of my feet jolting up from the ground.

*

A dull day with grey half-light—indigo, green and sepia. Whitish rags of low cloud skirting across the mountains, tearing themselves on the ridges. It is humid and we are hurling rocks down the hillside. Scraping them out with our hands, crowbars, picks and shovels. We strain on great ropes, for all the world like the slave pyramid-builders of Egypt. Our overseers are small, swarthy people. I think of Sabatini's Sea Hawk and how, on impossible food in the Spanish galleys he grew thews of steel. I think that all *my* thews grow is tired. But it is quite remarkable how the general health has stood up so far. We are not supermen. We are short on temper. Sides are taken by the have's and have-not's, the will's and the will-not's. But we are not dead yet. We are diligent ants, heaving and pushing great lumps of rock which, if they had broken loose, would have squashed a dozen of us. Self-preservation has brought a bit more interest to the job. Also, despite our slave state, we do gain some satisfaction pitting our will against the inorganic—some vanity is served.

*

Contributions to the Regimental Fund, except for the sick who are not paid, have been increased to one-third of our pay, due, I suppose, to the rising cost of dying. So now I have to work two days to get enough to buy a pencil to write this with.

*

On the way out to work we saw four bullock carts and four frowsy Thais sitting on their haunches eating rice from small bowls, with thin long dark fingers. One, an old thin crone with craggy brows and high cheekbones like smooth walnuts, stood with his tattooed back towards us. It was a pattern of straight, horizontal and vertical designs, in a dull blue, which also covered his chest and arms. One of his companions was a boy. All had slept in their narrow carts during the wet night and looked mouldy and mildewed.

*

Our rations have been patchy. Although some meat and dried Chinese cabbage has come into the camp it is not for us. We are told that thousands more prisoners will be coming up through this camp and the provisions are for them. One night, a basket of onions, three baskets of pumpkin, and two of dried cabbage came in. The Japanese took the onions, two of the cabbage and one of the pumpkin; this left us with two of the pumpkin for 8oo.

It continues to amaze us how we stay alive and go on working. It is the eggs. We cannot thank the Japanese for these, but I suppose we should appreciate their unusual humanity in allowing us to spend our pay on them.

Some say that, because of this underfeeding and lack of clothes, we may be paid our normal subsistence pay by our

Service, after the war is over.* As our clothes fall apart, we try to salvage enough for a simple G-string. As far as the Japanese are concerned, we are expected to exist only on small quantities of inferior rice. Hi-jacking from the Japs gets us a bit of meat and cabbage. The actual total issue per man over the past ten days has been twelve ounces of vegetables. Coming home to-night I was, as ever, ravenously hungry. I was thinking, grate-fully, of my plain rice ration. When we got back to the engin-eers' for the count, all we could smell was the aroma of Nip cooking. It was torture.

*

Our food when the weather is wet is not improved by con-ditions in the cookhouse—a shallow pit some fifteen feet by thirty, without a roof or wall, and with only a skeleton-frame. On either side are the shallow, hemispherical *kwalis*, iron cooking pans, each about four feet in diameter, set over dug-out fireplaces. Their rims are almost flush with the gritty red earth. The rain beats down through the smoke-blackened rafters, splashing sooty flakes into the *kwalis*. The beating rain also bounces up from the red, soot-blackened mud, spraying it into the tepid rice. Soon the floor of the kitchen is under water for the cooks to slosh around in. If there is too much rain, the water rises and puts the fires out. That we get anything under these conditions, is something of a wonder.

So far we have had only a few hours of rain at a time. As our tents go, one by one, we pack more and more closely into the rest. What will happen in the Wet?

*

Today we received the sickening news that there is six *tons* of mail at Tarsau. Of course it *must* be all rot . . . but, it *might* be true.

---

* This was never paid by the Australian Government.

VII

Hintok Road – April

THE day dawned—the first day of April—shrouding the mountain with low cloud to the tops of the trees in the camp. It swirled and, for an instant, revealed the great peak above us—still with a veil about its waist. Austere and delicate, it might have been a Japanese picture.

It was certainly a Japanese picture that was etched into our minds that day. All Fools' Day! The top of the mountain and the tops of all mountains, and all hope, vanished for the day. The white obliterating cloud came right down to earth and wet us through as we waded on the hour's march through thick mud and patches of slush to our job on the railway. My aching stomach turned, in its turn, to water. The job was the same: one cubic metre, one man. The rain drenched us all day. The red earth stuck to our shovels and we had to scrape it off them into our baskets, as we cursed and sweated with ill temper. Many bare feet and falling bodies were sliced by the razor-sharp split bamboo and jagged stones buried in the muddy tracks.

Never, up till now, have I felt so helpless. I think I must be the most dismal of the lot. Content to see us sacrifice our mosquito nets for scanty clothing, the Japs are even taking our tents now—one by one. The only thing we can be certain of having over our heads tonight is the continued threat of further deprivation.

At work we could only move at one-third of our normal pace. But we still had to finish our quota. We were hit with sticks, our faces were slapped, and we were kicked for nothing more than having fallen down with a sodden load of earth. The guards' tempers had gone with the weather.

Because I was sick on the job, Billy allowed me to *yasume*—but for no more than half an hour—and then I had to work through the dinner break. He said sick men didn't eat. All about were great piles of newly felled bamboo which were covering valuable earth.

Billy wanted to get at that earth; so he calmly told another miserable wretch and myself to burn the bamboo—the sodden, green bamboo. When we recovered and told Billy that it wouldn't burn, he screamed and bashed us half unconscious. We scrabbled about, close to the ground, for something a little dry, under something, somewhere. We must have found it, I suppose, for at last we got a flame and built a fire that would have burnt the Devil himself. Cut and torn by thorns in the search, we staggered about feeding it, and got half-cooked. Then we stood away and shivered.

When at last in the gloom of drowning day we started for home, we climbed the big Hill on all-fours. It seemed a miracle how the elephants had got down that day, but their bucket-like footprints made a stairway for us in parts. We arrived back smeared to the waist, and our arms to the shoulders, with the black road mud.

*

Weary's legs are bad—ulcers and beri-beri swelling. But he keeps going all day at the hospital. This affects all the fellows in the camp. They feel for him and worry about him. Many of them try to think of some ruse to keep him off his feet; none has been found.

Malnutrition troubles are attacking everywhere. Eggs have not been coming up, so we are beginning to feel the full weight of the inadequate Japanese rations. A few days ago a few came up, but only enough for two per man. There is no doubt in my mind that eggs will make all the difference to our chances of getting out of the jungle alive.

*

Tonight we had a stump concert with community singing. It

is fine to hear men rise out of their dejection with *Pack up your troubles in your old kit bag!*—when they have no 'fag' nor 'lucifer' to light it with. And to hear them sing without self-pity. Herb Smith sang *At the end of a dusty road.* This was the song he sang the other night when we came in dead-beat. There was a grand yellow sunset riding on the back of a thunderstorm. There was the rumble of thunder; the first big drops began to splatter on the leaves of the trees above us. Bert was ploughing down to the showers, naked except for his torn boots. His voice came fine and clear with a volume which echoed under the tree canopy. *At the end of a dusty road!* And every man who heard the sheer spirit of this man's singing felt his own uplifted too. Never, I feel, will I hear a song like that anywhere in the world. It is a song that will keep singing to me all my life.

At night the blue smoke of fires makes cardboard cut-outs of the trees. But the sun, rising, draws the curtain of night *down* (not up) and lights the world. This impression is caused by the shadow of the mountain ridge which, as it cuts through the smoke, seems to descend slowly before the rising sun. The floor of the stage is twilight blue and the fires are gold, lighting up the greens and browns and reds of the forest. The curtain is down, and vanished into the earth as we stand on the work parade.

*

The day turned hot. A pitiless sky scorched us with the brightness of polished steel. All afternoon it was drip, drip, drip, from eyebrows and nose-tip; a steady stream running from under our arms until the whole body, including our finger tips, was dripping. On the long tortuous Hill, the sun burning with an individual intensity into each man's back, I felt the heat in a way which bored into my very brain, filling my weary mind with its parching presence. I helped Blackie back and he went into hospital.

It is common for men to collapse on parades and have to be carried to hospital. Often Weary himself carries them over in his arms as if they are babies. Down they go with malaria, dysentery, exhaustion, and the like. Feet, cracked and swollen with the scorching earth, are a constant nag for everybody—but we have to keep walking on them.

*

For the past week, amid all this misery, I have been having a daily peep into a crystal of fantasia. At one point on the Hill there were several little convocations of small, delicate, long-stemmed, perfectly grey toadstools—each bunch standing on the summit of a few pats of elephant dung. They stood gracefully awry on the khaki-green of the digested bamboo leaves—as fairylike as Titania herself. Somehow, in the morning silence, they seemed to sing a small pure song of perfect innocence, as the stars sometimes do at midnight in the still bush.

But, at last, they have been destroyed by the many careless ill-shod feet that go to work with me.

*

Weary has brought me a very strange insect which points a long, strong finger at the promiscuity or ambitions of its many forbears. It is green, yellow, blue, dappled, lined, patched, but it has a red body. Its proboscis is a remarkable upturned horn of red-lake, curving forward as long again as its body.* I hope to make a drawing of it.

Will-o'-the-wisp beetle

Tomorrow forty-eight men are to be evacuated back to Tarsau or beyond. They are to be over thirty-eight years of age and chronic cases of exhaustion.

*

* It was a Will-o'-the-Wisp beetle.

One of the things that makes me see red these days is grumbling and bad temper: I lose my temper too. On the job there was a crowd of howling pessimists. I attacked them with profanity and told them to smile: why should we make ourselves miserable when the Nips will do it for us! 'You can't smile with this pack o' bastards,' they grumbled. 'Well,' I came back hotly, 'you bastards are not helping any other bastard to smile.' Surprisingly, they kept quiet after that.

The topics of conversation include jobs, business and possibilities after the war; motor cars, motor bikes and experiences with them; but very little is being spoken about war experiences. There are endless speculations about the course of the war, and the rumours we are constantly subjected to. The time of our release is a big question: already there are those who feel they won't live to see it. There are hopes, fears and fancies about our homes after we return to them. Hopes and fears entangled: the fear of optimism being unfounded, and the hope of having pessimism disappointed. In the main, expectations seem to be conditioned by the fear of being made a fool of if they don't come off. We try to avoid tempting the gods, and remain in humble supplication.

*

The weather continues unsettled. Often the days are hot with a hot, pale sky flying a few high mares' tails. Just over the surrounding mountain ridges rise a few white anvils of cumulus. They let out great claps of thunder, but the sun stays bright and scorches us, unaffected. We continue to scratch the earth from around the rocks to build the banks. It is as if the Wet were a baying animal impatiently waiting over the horizon to be unleashed. Every so often now it has sprung over the mountains, snarled at us, and been hauled back again.

We returned to camp. Two men had fallen sick on the job, one more collapsed on parade and fifteen cases of dysentery were admitted to hospital. Only thirty, not forty-eight, went back to Tarsau. There is a rumour that some mail and clothes are back at Tarsau for us.

At 7 p.m. a heavy storm broke and branches landed dangerously among the tents. One man was knocked unconscious.

*

Some days ago I wrote about the shadow-curtain being
drawn down to earth at sun-up. Now, with this, comes a buzz
and drone like a waiting audience, but from the air fifteen or
twenty feet up. It is the high-pitched drone of thousands of
bottle-green blowflies that hang in the sunlight and follow the
mountain shadow down to earth. As we stand on parade, waiting, we are twenty feet deep in shadow and the high undulating
noise puts a roof of sound over our heads.

*

On parade tonight it was announced that No. 1 Nippon said
that he regretted the shortage of food; but after troop movements had ceased, food would improve. This was after Weary
had taxed him about the grave deficiencies of our diet.* Weary
added that the officers and himself were very, very pleased with
the conduct of the men under these terrible conditions, and
that, if we kept this spirit, we would see the game through to
the end—which he hoped would not be long.

*

The Japanese say that the first train will be through in 147
days' time. There have been movements of Japanese troops
passing through the camp in the past few days. This morning I
got an impression of about 200 of their squat, square figures,
padding along through the mud with bamboo poles on their
shoulders, on which were slung rice bags and dixies. Their
silence and uniformity made me think of mass-thinking (or unthinking) Martians, or Gammas from the *Brave New World*.

*

Someone has said (on reliable authority) that some of the

* See Appendix attached.

officers have cornered a bag of *catchung-idjoe.** This is a very rich life-saving food under these conditions, and very bitter things are being said by the men.

*

It was crystal clear this morning and the mountains looked extra close. The sun is not too hot and is tempered by a thin cloud layer. But it was cold last night. Some men wore shirts on the job this morning. Men wear an amazing assortment of rigs—mostly only the absolute minimum. One man wears a real diaper, put on in the approved Truby King way.

*

Today a Jap said, 'All Thais marchee, marchee.' This is too enigmatic to unravel—but it may mean something.

Although dawn was sunless today, there was still the high collective droning of the blowflies as we stood on parade. Perhaps it is not just the sun's light they seek up there—they may be sensitive to the infra red rays which would still come through.

*

We had *catchung-idjoe* tonight in the soup, which seems to make the story of the officers cornering a bag doubtful. Still, that is how it goes here, life is just as much a matter of what a man thinks as what actually happens. Men's minds and perspectives are under pressure, living close together on the borderline of starvation. So, between the officers and men (or indeed, between this group and the other) suspicion and disparagement are constantly exchanged.

It is surprising how narrow our minds get, from fatigue and discomfort. On the way back to camp I pass many interesting things among the insects and flowers. But my mind will only think of personal things like the heat; my aching arms and thighs; the ache in my big toes at the end of the day; the sweat running off me and collecting the dirt; the battle to get a water-

* *Kachang-Hijau* (Malay), green-peas.

bottle of water when everybody else is also scrambling for it. So I stumble on a bit faster to get back sooner for this quart of boiled water which will have to last me until tomorrow night, no matter how hot the day. I think of some scabs of gummy, burnt rice I may get from the bottom of a rice basket. Will I get enough rice? I am as hungry as a horse but dry rice is all I ask. I think of the bliss of my knobbly twisted bamboo bed and when I shall lie down for the first time since before dawn. There is the nagging of odd jobs I must do, when all I want to do is lie down. And, as I get to the top of the big Hill, I look out and see between the strong brown and green tree forms, the lovely blue of the rain-washed mountains with the sun back-lighting them. But I cannot absorb it in a real way. I know it is beautiful—but what does beauty signify? We each go home, thinking first of that Hill—to get it behind us; then of the arrival in camp and the chores to be done. And then, of the climax of sleep—as if in the arms of a voluptuous woman one sleeps with night after night in utter content, thinking, on arising, only of returning again.

*

There are strange new noises in the night—frogs, I think. One rises like the scream of wind through rigging for about four minutes, and then *diminuendo*, followed by the rasping croak of thousands of batrachian throats in all the ponds and puddles of the jungle. There is also another I can't make out, for all the world like the squeak of a dozen ungreased ox-cart wheels.

*

As we finished work today, the sky puckered up in the west. No sooner were we at the top of the Hill than a great earth-obliterating cloud of close-knit rain came in a great, grey sweep over the mountains and valleys, and beat us all wet, wet, wet. Pouring from every channel in our naked bodies, it filled the boots of those who had them.

Jim and I were in the lead and, in a moment, we were ankle deep in the black slush of the road. A couple of motor trucks overtook us and we shifted over to let them pass. Just as the front wheels of one had passed him, Jim slipped back into the deep wheel ruts. Desperately he tried to pull his legs up and claw his way clear with his hands. The Jungle was too close for me to help him, and I could only watch . . . but the back wheels *just* scraped the side of his foot. Then we both laughed, shakily.

*

It is Sunday, April 11th, and the 2nd/3rd Machine-gunners say that it is just two years since they left Sydney for the Middle East. We were patrolling in H.M.A.S. *Perth* near the toe of Italy. But, today, we all went out to the railway and pushed part of the 152-kilometre embankment up another metre.

Just after dinner there was a cloudburst and in less than an hour every man was up to his knees in brown water, trying to shovel earth from under it. The side of the steep bank was almost impossible to climb: we were hanging on by our toe-nails. Sheets of water lay over the whole workings—even the slopes. A load of earth became a sodden pancake refusing to unfasten its gluey stomach from the stretchers as we tipped them over. Falls were frequent and painful. Curses and laughter were mixed, for there seemed to be some peculiar stimulus in the very boisterousness of the weather. At 3.30 a Nip officer came along and stopped the hopeless task. We all gave a rousing cheer—even the Nips smiled. Going home, each man had to use two sticks, ski-wise, to try and stay on his feet.

As we were being checked in back at camp, one of the rock gang came in alone. On his head was an Australian felt hat. His body was white and his hair was red—*all* of which was plainly visible because the only other article of clothing he wore was one Japanese rubber boot and a sock. In one hand was the remaining muddy boot and sock; in the other, a bamboo staff. Across his streaming back was slung a battered haversack. He looked like some wild prophet fresh from fasting and come to make a revelation.

*

Back to work today in the quagmire of yesterday. The white mist on the valley floor was curling in columns as from a slowly cooling cauldron, and it was foggy over the embankment. They tried to make us work harder to make up for yesterday, though conditions were nearly as bad. Tempers were short and spirits were low. Crawled back to camp at the end of the day and fell into bed, unwashed.

*

Another day of driving. Fell dead-beat into bed. Awoke about midnight, tired out from being endlessly driven to work by the Japs—even in dreams.

Wrote up this diary while standing waiting on parade to-night. I also watched four monkeys monkeying in the trees on the vertical escarpment above us. This morning I discovered that termites had eaten half the brim off my straw hat, and some of the crown.

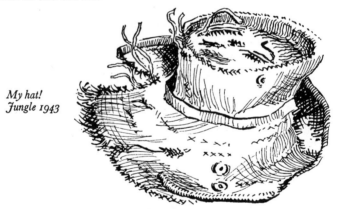

My hat!
Jungle 1943

Jim is pretty sick but still working, and Otto's feet are bad from more than fourteen days working on them without a break. Sweat rash, aided by low blood condition, is starting brutal ulceration. Armpits, chests, crutches and legs become holed. It is not nice to watch these things and wonder when one's turn will come—these complaints seem inevitable for all of us. So far I am lucky, but I don't want to tempt fate—so I don't mention it.

Men are coming in, full of fever, and have to be helped to hospital. There has been trouble between our doctors and the Japs about whether certain men are sick or not. Fourteen sick men have been sent out to work. Things are a little quieter now.

*

Some vegetables and a bullock* came in last night—the first I can remember for a long while. Also, the Nip No. 1 informed us, 'Mail come veree quick. Three days. Veree soon. Clothes, boots—fourteen days.' This bores us but we cannot stifle a sneaky hope that it might be true.

*

Yesterday, Colin, a thin fair young army lad who has been working with me, was very sick with fever. He straightened up from his pick for a moment and a Jap grabbed him by his ragged trousers and shook him. When he could get a word in, Colin said to the Jap, '*Beoke!*' (sick). So the Jap led him away to stoke a huge fire like a blast furnace. At 1 p.m. *maccan* was called. Colin came over to get his rice, but the Jap chased him back to the fire yelling, 'Sick man no-eat! *Ba-ge-e-era!*' So Colin stoked until we went back to camp. I helped him home, and into hospital.

I suppose we could be asked, 'Have we suffered much?' 'Suffer' is a dangerous word here just now—it can induce self-pity. 'Endure' is a better word, it is not so negative. Enduring can give an aim, a sense of mastery over circumstance. I have seen so much self-conscious suffering and men dying from self-pity. But perhaps it is easy for me to talk now when I have my health. When my turn comes, what then?

*

Meanwhile the jungle is growing fast. Vines are leaping with bright new green leaves a foot or so across. They are heart-shaped—some are like two hearts alongside each other. Trees are blossoming. One purple like lilac, and growing like a giant

* A beast kills at 100–120 lb. only.

ti-tree. It is heavily flowered. The flower has five petals in a symmetrical circular device. There is another blossom almost identical with a flowering eucalyptus—the bloom has a tassel two inches long. This falls early and leaves white cups with red bases. Other flowers are springing directly from the earth without their foliage. Some are like gladioli. Bamboos are leafing thickly now. There are more bird calls; monkeys call like Swannee whistles—flutelike on a slurred scale. All nature moves and has its being, and we seem to sit on it like a scab.

*

The perversity of men is strange. We have been having one spoon of brown palm sugar on our pap each morning. This was bought with our canteen fund. This morning there was none. Just because of this a lot of men would not draw their breakfasts, and went without. They would sooner go out to work breakfastless because in some vague way they thought they were being cheated. There were two buckets left over!

Four Englishmen at Tarsau have been shot for attempted escape. They must have been the four we saw being taken back the day after the big storm. An Englishman has had his neck broken by a falling tree at Konyu, and has died.

*

At last the embankments are finished on our section. This is Sunday, April 18th. On Tuesday we go 'hammer-and-tap', which is rock drilling with eight-pound hammers, for the blasting of the cuttings.

The roads are still deep in slurry and slush and it is daily routine to wade out to work through it. Butterflies swarm everywhere along the road. Each day my ignorance is shown up. Take the many kinds of brown and brownish butterflies. They confound me, for I hardly ever see one now with more than four legs. I thought that any fool knew that all insects had six legs.

Tonight one of the fellows brought in a ten-foot snake ready skinned for cooking. It made a feed for him and the many friends he suddenly found he had. Another group had bagged a four-foot iguana which they cooked and smugly ate while we looked hungrily on.

*

We have been issued by the Nips with a limited number of rubber boots. It is Monday 19th, and after fifteen hard working days this is a *Yasume*. I spent a very good night with the knowledge of the embankments behind us and, if not brighter prospects, at least a change. I dreamt of my family, and talked with John and Jill—they are growing up.

The new job should be better. The boots available are too small for me—but there is a slight chance that I may get a new hat to replace the almost ant-consumed one.

We use any bit of rag here until it rots with sweat or mildew, or is eaten or falls apart. The bandages at the hospital are no better. My shorts are always wringing wet to put on in the mornings, because the sweat-salt in them takes up the atmospheric moisture of the night. When they are dry they are stiff with it and feel sandy.

Today we each had to make a bamboo watercarrier. Now that the elephants are gone, we must carry these out to the job full of water for drilling. It is no good to drink because we can only drink boiled water. In the heat it tempts us just the same.

*

There was an incident over at the Jap Engineers' the other day. An Australian was working there in the cookhouse. They called him *Sanski*, which means 'stoker'. He kept their cooking fires going and also those under the forty-four-gallon drums filled with water for their bathing ritual. He had become very familiar with his job and gained a lot of confidence. He cheeked the Japs and got away with it. Then he took to arriving late. At last, one morning, when he arrived the Jap cook took away his breakfast and said, 'You sleepoo . . . *yasume* . . . no gooda!' Sanski replied, '*Bagoose* [Malayan for very good] . . . *very gooda*!' At this the Jap lost his temper and swung at him with an axe. Sanski turned the blow and the Nip cut his own arm. He looked aghast at the sight of blood—*his* blood. He rushed in for his rifle. But Sanski rushed for the jungle. Sanski did not come back until he thought that the Jap had cooled off a little. When he decided to return we watched the Nip standing on one side of the bamboo palisade fence with a bamboo club ill-concealed behind his back, and Sanski standing on the other side with the fence between them. At first Sanski refused to answer the Jap who was beckoning him confidentially. But at last he had to go to save worse trouble: he took a beating and was sacked. It was really quite understandable because, only the day before, he had incurred another beating for coaxing a trusting Nip into a scalding bath tub by telling him it was just nice and warm. There was something in Sanski's stars, surely, which must have protected him from such fatal impulsiveness as the Japs can so readily show.

*

Yasume is coming to an end and I am writing this by the flickering light of a fire. The day faded beneath a blazon of colour as vivid as a medieval pageant. And this was appropriate, for we are living under a law which gives us no more rights than the serfs of those times. To the East, above the indigo ridge, stood a long line of cumulus heads like so many armoured knights' helmets at a joust—steely grey and dead white against the background of high, soft cirrus shot with yellow-grey light. In the West six banners of red-and-purpled stratus hung still on the glow of the disappearing sun. With the coming darkness, the knights' heads slowly sank back and fainted in the ghostly light of a veiled and watery moon. A few lances of lightning—silent and flickering. And a sprinkle of rain which amounted to nothing.

At the concert the crowd of drab, skinny men sang *Advance Australia Fair*, making it ring convincingly in the bush and in our hearts. But it was like a song from the remote future: so far back in time were we in the hands of a feudal army.

*

Hammer and tap. Hintok, April 1943

So, Tuesday. Out we went on to our new job. Some with new rubber boots and straw hats; most of us with eight-pound hammers. A hammer is easier to swing than a pick, which jars in hard earth and rock. Catch the rhythm of the hammer and it is almost somnolent; for you stand in the same place all the time, balanced between both feet on uneven rocks. You strike squarely on the head of the steel drill. Clink! Clink! Clink!— squarely, or you bone-jar your mate's hands as he holds the drill, lifting and turning with each strike you make. The white limestone we pulverize at the bottom of the hole puffs and spurts in little clouds on our near-nakedness, wet with sun- and work-heat, and makes us itch.

Every now and again, we lift out the drill and scrape the powder from the hole with a wire scoop. Then we pour in a little water and let the drill drop back. It runs down with a peculiar metallic and watery resonance, hitting the bottom with a glug of finality. The water, as we clink, clink, clink away with the hammer, turns to milk, then paste. Soon all the moisture is taken up and it is time to clear the hole again. Slowly the hole sinks—twenty centimetres, fifty centimetres or a metre—depending on how they want to blow the rock. About dinner time the charges are put in; we take shelter; and the rock is blown up.

We are working on the western side of a steep north–south ridge overlooking the valley of the Kwai Noi, beyond which lines of steep mountains roll away. It is further back towards Konyu than the embankment. The railway will run along the shelf we are cutting, and out on to the seven-metre bank we have just built; then over a bridge to a rocky spur beyond the ravine.

To get to this site, we crawl through bamboo and rocks along a steep hillside which becomes very slippery and dangerous after rain. The bamboos lean out over the slope and when the track is wet we have to swing from one bamboo to the next like trapeze performers. As we swing, the thin brown papery bark is torn and twisted by our grip, and the smell of squashed bugs (so familiar to us all) strikes our noses. Silverfish, too, come to grief this way. This is the home of silverfish.

*

I found and ate a few jungle grapes today. They are not big; red, but black when ripe. Coming home we passed six elephants and a loose baby which swerved and nearly trampled us.

During the dinner break a stray cow wandered by. By 3 p.m. it had been killed and dressed. Nippon presento-ed it to us;

but later he took it back. While waiting back in camp for the check count, one of the fellows said, 'If they are human, they will give us most of it back.' I said, 'If they are human, they will keep the lot—our blokes would! We have been robbed by our own messmates—it seems to be an Army rule! Why expect the Nips to act any different?'

I had addressed this remark especially to a racketeering W.O. My blood was up, for this man was wearing a new pair of Nip rubber boots. Even though our orders were that no man was to have more than one pair of boots, this man also had a good pair of heavy leather boots *and* a pair of good shoes *which were kept polished*! He had grabbed a pair of rubber boots and someone was now walking bare-footed because of it. I would like to take the matter up, but I know I would be told to mind my own business, as I have been before. There seems to be a sacred cult of 'perks', where army supplies are concerned, to which one must bow. Only an 'outsider' questions it.

*

A Norfolk regiment marched through on their way up-country. They left Changi five weeks ago. We asked them about the mail. They said that they had not received any *since they had left Changi*.

*

The other day while we worked I hung my dixie up on a bamboo cane in the shade. At the foot of the bamboo I noticed a couple of interesting fungi. Each was a white phallus six to eight inches high, with a sulphur-green bonnet like a rocket. The bonnet had a red frill under the brim. When I came back for my rice at midday, this frill had expanded and dropped to the ground in a delicate and fleshy net like a gas mantle. On expansion the red had diluted, displaying a pink hem to the ground, and gradually paling to a creamy colour as it went upwards to the bonnet. There was, perhaps, a maypole effect about it; but, to female-starved men, it had something of the allure of a veil dropped from a hat brim. It smelled like carbonate of soda with a whiff of almond—even at a range of several yards.

'Gasmantle' fungi 6"–8" high before and after dropping its mantle

This afternoon the rain came. Roaring and hissing like an express train, it swept down on the roof of our forest, striking our ears minutes before it struck us. It made the trip back along the hillside track treacherous, especially as we were handicapped with bundles of steel drills almost six feet long.

*

Kaley, one of the habitual loafers (that is one who loafs on his mates, not the Nips), was tackled by a Nip for not working. To put himself right with Nippon, he said that he could not work on *pap* for breakfast. He gave the impression that he was being cheated out of his rightful food. The Nip took his meaning—now we have dry rice for breakfast and not pap. Pap had been decided on by the whole camp as best for breakfast for two main reasons. First, it takes less uncooked rice for the same bulk—though needing extra water, of course. Also, there is some chance of getting it hot. Secondly, in the rush of the mornings there is no chance to masticate dry rice properly; and the rice saved goes to swell our dinner ration when we really feel we need all we can get.

There has got to be another way out, if we are to live. So, I am being stupidly gullible—I am believing, more and more, in my Psychic Inductance theory. I am trying to find out how many vitamins there are in beauty. I am beginning to understand, as a purely factual statement, *man shall not live by bread alone*. The bush is full of 'every word of God'. I think, perhaps, that faith and hope are a couple of unclassified vitamins. I don't mean faith in any dogma—but in what I see in the life of the heart of the bush.

*

Major Moon, a doctor, has spoken straightly to a Nip No. 1 who was in the camp—particularly about food and washing facilities. Now there is to be a soap issue, they say.

*

Tonight, crowds of Malays, Chinese and Tamils are struggling up the muddy road with all they have in the world—a few paltry bundles—on their heads or backs. They are coming up from Malaya and have to march right through to Burma. 'No food,' they say, 'only two-t'ree pound rice each week, little salt. Ipoh, no food. Ride a little way in truck . . . clothes taken away —no see any more. March about twenty-five miles a day.' Most of them don't know where they are. We begin to think this dovetails with a story that we are moving out in twenty-five days and the Indians and Thais taking over. Night comes down grey, warm and dripping, in the darkness of a moon not yet risen, and the poor devils have at least eleven kilometres to go to Kinsayok, their next camp.

*

Fatty is in hospital with beri-beri. There are 180 there now— and many working who should be there.

This morning on parade it was announced, 'By Nipponese order, black-out will be observed from 10 p.m. tonight. This applies to all fires.' The other night men thought they heard explosions, but could not be sure. Then a large number of bullock wagons came up from Tarsau with small arms ammunition. Some of the Thai drivers told us, 'White man—boom, boom, boom!' Bampong had been raided by allied planes. One ox-cart was blown up.

It appears that today is Good Friday—April 23rd.

*

At lunch time, as we were moving up into the trees for the midday blasting, we heard excited cries from the Japs, 'Speedo, speedo! Ah-hoiy-hoiy! Speedo, *SPEEDO*!' We took shelter in the usual way—behind a tree, facing the blow. But at once we realized what was happening—*three* positions were blowing together, and we were completely enfiladed. No matter how we sheltered, we were still exposed to two lines of fire.

The stones and fragments came ripping through the treetops, cutting branches and lopping bamboos like scythes. The sounds stopped. Jim felt a whoosh past his ear. Then I felt a terrific thump on my back, to the right of my spine, and just below my shoulder blade. It made a sound like a bass drum which made men twenty yards away look up. My thoughts became confused: I let out a loud derisive-sounding animal whoop I was powerless to stop. I remember a fellow looking up at me with a curious expression on his face as if he thought this was the end of me. All the wind was knocked out of me and I was painfully trying to get it back with unrelated gasps and wheezes no human should make.

Blackie saw the stone hit me. It bounded off down the hill one way and knocked me on my face the other. It appeared that this recent bit of Thailand, blown on an approximate course of S.S.E., had flown higher than all the rest without touching anything until it came to me. There its trajectory, and my immediate outlook on life, were changed abruptly.

They took me, clinging to the slippery surface of the sloping path, to where the next gang had their explosives tent and a bit of a first aid kit. I felt that I did not want to move any part of me from the waist up, in case something broke or fell out. But I was able to eat my rice: that cheered me up a bit. When I got back to camp I was put in hospital for the only treatment—rest.

*

I had an uncomfortable night, but there was no rushing about this morning in the mess and dinner ration queues, nor crawling out in the dark: almost worth getting hit.

We receive our mail on the 29th—this is official information. But will it be official fulfilment? Last night one of the Nips with our gang of drillers gave me a few sweet biscuits—as a *presento* for my injured back, he said.

More Tamils went through last night. They stopped for a few minutes and had a poultice of rice on leaves to eat. One Tamil said that he had had only one issue of rice in six days—I suppose he meant uncooked rice. He also said that many had died on the way up here and that Changi is now empty of Allied prisoners. Japanese Marines are there instead. It was said that there was a large concentration of troops at Ipoh, moving this way.

*

There is a rumour that 1,000 Australians from Changi are marching up with kit. They are supposed to be due here any day now. Buck Peterson, in a mood of irony, wonders whether all the pairs of boots and trousers they didn't give us are heavy, and whether they will still be the same parade-ground soldiers when they get here, as when they so looked down on our close-cropped heads and called us the Java Rabble.

*

This is Easter Sunday and Anzac Day: April 25th. This morning there was a service and Holy Communion in the hospital lines. It was taken by a visiting English padre from one of the nearby camps. The Japs allow him to move about a bit.

He is a gaunt man with an auburn beard, a soiled shirt and shorts, half hidden by his stained surplice, below which you can see his mud-stained and untidy socks hanging over heavy muddy boots. The heavy boots make his legs look stick-like.

473

About his neck hangs a soiled stole of white with tarnished gold crosses embroidered on it. His voice has a suppressed English clip to it.

The service struck me as hurried and jumbled. The sermon, though poorly and incoherently expressed, seemed to have something. It was the message of Christ's body missing from the tomb. This was the most dramatic way, said the padre, that Christ could tell men that death was not final. He went on to say that it was the 'divine' in us that went on. Though I could not accept this dogma, I thought I saw the glimmer of an idea with which I could agree. It was almost identical with a statement by Professor Wilson in his *Miraculous Birth of Language,* in which he describes the emergence of mind, and its ultimate self-conscious shaping of its own destiny, as part of an organic process. The padre called this emergence from nature a return to God.

*

In the night about 240 Australians of the 2nd/19th Infantry arrived in camp. They had marched from Tarsau with their packs and were pretty well dead beat. They had slept at a campong along the road on the previous night. One of their officers came in exhausted, leaning on Weary and Major Greiner (our Battalion C.O.), who carried his gear between them. He would have fallen over if he had kicked a matchstick, Buck said. Four of our fellows went out and carried in one of the men who had collapsed. Two of them were without boots. As they carried the man shoulder high on a stretcher, his heavy booted feet were between the faces of the bootless as they slipped and staggered.

*

The issue of Jap rubber boots has helped a number of men. But some have been given boots that are too small, or their feet are too bad with ulcers, cuts and festerings, to wear them.

The new crowd tell us that they have been five weeks at Tarsau, and that the food is reasonably good there. At Kanburi there was too much for the limited utensils. This tantalizes us because we seem to be always *just* beyond the end of the supply line.

*

The hospital lines are, on the whole, relatively cheerful. Perhaps this is because we take so many things for granted. Here, as I see it, now, is one of the things we take for granted. The dense rain, heavy overcast sky, and a shallow sea of black mud, with rips and tunnels this way and that, give the place the simple unreality of a necropolis of living-dead. A figure of six foot three inches emerges from between the gleaming wet tents. He is so thin that every bone in his body shows. The two bones of his fore-arm stick out painfully at his wrists, and the two rows of carpals and metacarpals in the backs of his hand. His fingers hang long and thin, punctuated by the knobs of articulation. Swinging at the end of stiff, bent arms, with sharp protruding elbows, they look like two small stiff faggots. His shoulders are sharp with emaciation and the studs of the acromium process, where the collar bone meets the shoulderblade, stick up like bollards on a wharf. His collar bones jut out, like bent iron bars, over a chest cage which might be that of a dressed fowl in a delicatessen. The navel sits on an odd little hemisphere low in front. On either side bony hips flare like the rim of a jug. His thighs are bones, with strings of haunches running down the back, from the shrivelled knot that was once a round buttock. A knee cap sticks out in front like a piece of spiked armour. Below this, the long thin, knife-like shin: it, too, has strings instead of muscles. Legs not unlike those of a fowl. Long, bony feet, right-angled, are splashed past the ankles with the mud and excrement through which they walk.

This is a man. A man who walks naked in the rain to the latrine. Side by side with other wretches, yet alone, he crouches like a dog without a kennel in a bitter wind. He is helpless and racked with violent spasms. Dysentery reduces both body and spirit. In the rain he must crawl there and return to soiled blankets, to lie weak and helpless, without removing the mud of his beastly pilgrimage.

This comes to us all in turn. Men watch each other in silent understanding. What they see is ludicrous, but they don't laugh. Our main troubles (always omitting starvation) are malaria, dysentery exhaustion, avitaminosis, tropical ulcers from cuts and scratches, blisters, chapping and blood poisoning. But so far there have been no deaths in our group.

*

The new arrivals have given us much to talk about and speculate on. They have had mail and we are gleaning bits of news of home. There has been an all-round pay rise. It seems the mail should catch us up soon. But do our people know we are prisoners? Or do they think us dead? Will the letters be able to find us? All mail so far received has been a year old.

*

I gave up my place in the hospital today to a newcomer, and I am back in the lines. A tiger fence is being erected because the blackout now forbids tiger fires. Fireflies have made a spectacular debut: their clear, liquid, bright flashes spark amongst the trees at night.

*

One of the newcomers told me that they had 140 pairs of spare boots when they left Changi, but they had been taken by the Nips at the railway station. This among only 240 men: how many, we wonder, would there have been among 8,000?

Tonight about sunset, 200 Indonesians marched into camp and rested in an exhausted heap. At 11 p.m. they marched on to Kinsayok. There will be no moon tonight until around 2 a.m., and some of them looked pretty sick.

*

At 9 a.m. this morning a mixed crowd of English—Argylls, Gordons, Manchesters, Sutherlands, etc.—marched in. They had been in Thailand since October 1942 (last year). Of 800, only eighteen have died. Tonight at dusk more Dutch came in. They stayed an hour and went on. We hear now that 10,000 are to come up in the next fortnight. Tomorrow, we expect 300 Australians and Americans from Java. This period of movement must mean something big. Perhaps it is the big push to get the railway through—but we can't see how they will be able to work when the Wet Season really sets in.

*

First thing, the Argylls and Gordons moved out. A couple of our fellows' packs have been stolen and the birds of passage have been blamed. One of the Sutherlands said to us, 'You want to stick close to your kits—some of the men with us are the scum of London.' One pack that is missing contained a man's wallet, money and a ring. We think it is an inside job by some one who knew what he was taking, and who reckoned to throw the suspicion on the transit men.

*

I was talking to a 2nd/10th Artillery gunner today. He told me that the 2nd/19th were a fine crowd and saw some real action on the Peninsula. He confirmed the story that they had been allowed to fire only ten rounds a day out of brand-new twenty-five pounders. They could have laid Johore flat, he said, while the Nip was there. One officer did open fire and was severely reprimanded. From their O-pips they watched the Nips place their artillery and disembark troops from the train for two days. In the first twenty-four hours the Japs put over a quarter of a million shells in barrage. As an eye-witness, he said he believed this. They, themselves, had begun in the north in a position they had been preparing for five months; but they used it for only *one night*, and then withdrew forty-five miles down the Peninsula. He said they abandoned—not destroyed— more ammunition than they used. However, they did one good stunt, he said. It was on the bridge of the Endau river. All one night they raked and pinpointed the Nips who had landed on the east coast and formed up along the river. He thought that they must have killed thousands of them. Then they blew the bridge with fourteen pounds of jelly; but the Nips built another, three miles to the westward, in three days. After that, he told me, it was retreat and abandon arms: after ninety miles, they were back on Singapore Island where they were bitterly disappointed by being denied the use of their own guns. He said that any effective action seemed to be continually blocked, and he does not understand the affair at all, although he was there and fought through it. They had arrived in Malaya eleven months earlier, in high hopes—and their destiny was *this*. He said a Nip propaganda paper carried the headlines, DID THEY COME ONLY TO SURRENDER?

This man is a big raw-boned, simple and genuine man from North Queensland—from the interior. He said his first impression of Singapore shocked him. The morality had upset his simple ideas. He is one of the best types that Australia produces and would rank with the best soldiers of the world. Who betrayed this man? Sitting here in the jungle, I wonder if history will answer this question honestly, or justify what they have done to him.

*

Fellows keep bringing in odd flowers from the jungle in the hope that I may get around to painting them. Now the lilies are rolling in. They have forms like arum lilies. One has a hood of deep purple madder fading to streaked variegations at the top edge. Over this dark richness are spots of Naples-yellow about a quarter of an inch in diameter, mottling it completely. From the centre soars a long spear-topped spike as high again as the hood. This is yellow at the bottom, merging to cream-pink at the spearpoint.

Butterflies are in clouds and each cloud seems to be of three or four kinds. They settle thickly to drink at damp places—urinals are a lure. I have seen them settle so thickly that some of them have walked across the tops of the hundreds of close-packed upheld wings, and the butterflies beneath took neither notice nor offence. I caught a small snake today who had just swum the creek. He was a speckled black with an orange band just behind his diamond head. He had swallowed a frog: I could tell by the bulge in his vest. I stroked the frog out and got a grand idea of the distension of a snake's jaws when he swallows. The frog came up unmarked, but dead.

*

There have been 700 hospital cases since we came here: 1,000-odd since Thailand.

*

Tonight, 300 Dutch troops marched in. The white Dutch are generally held in contempt by the Australians who say they lack guts. Tonight there was a heartening exception. After lights out, when all his mates were sleeping exhausted, a Dutchman from a transit party began singing. It was as if he had said, 'Be damned to this misery. I will sing. I will forget it.' While I listened, I, too, forgot. Soon after he stopped, the crowd of them were roused out to march another thirteen kilometres.

*

Izzy has been working at the Nip kitchen, but now he has gone to hospital with malaria and Jim has taken his place. Jim has to get up in the dark to start the day's work. He has put three fireflies in a matchbox with his wrist watch. In the night the flashing bugs make the face of the watch clearly visible.

Another 1,000 English in transit arrived at dusk. They rested and were given some rice. One of them struck up an impromptu sing-song with his piano accordion. Our music-starved fellows flocked around and swelled the noise.

The feeding of transit troops keeps our rations low because the Japs concentrate first on getting their supplies up—after that they think about ours. The early Wet Season has curtailed supply movements. A cow was killed for us today. These beasts are very small and poor: this one yielded only forty pounds of meat—luckily it had bones with which we could make soup. This forty pounds of meat was spread among 800 of us; that is after the various perks were supplied to those with this or that position of advantage. When there is no beast (and that is mostly) we get water with dried Chinese radish boiled in it.

*

When transit troops arrive here they are pretty well done in —particularly in the wet. It had rained about the middle of the afternooon, when in marched a band of Englishmen. They looked in pretty good shape and were led by a man who carried his haversacks in good order. Though he was neat, there was just that amount of disorder to betray an efficiency of purpose. His figure was ample and his round face was red. He carried neither sword nor pistol, nor even cane. He carried something else, which I saw him wave a couple of times—and I think it had something to do with the morale of his band. These men came in in quiet good order, after having been for some time on what others who have come through have called 'death-marches'.

I first saw them a little distance away, the Colonel in front with what appeared to be a stick some four or five feet long with a kind of pennant on the end. It could have been a regimental colour, only it was nondescript. A couple of times I saw him take a few quick paces to the side and sweep the pennant through the air with a circling flourish, as if he were playing drum major. When he got nearer I could see his face carried no pretentious scowl of authority, but rather a boyish enthusiasm, and the pennant he was swinging was a *butterfly net*.

Weary introduced me to him because of my nature drawings. Afterwards he apologized for 'hauling me up like a tradesman'. Colonel Johnson was a real colonel from *Inja*. He looked healthy and at the height of enthusiasm. He told me he was collecting butterflies and orchids *en route*. He spoke as if the war and the Japanese were incidental formalities, like customs inspectors. He rattled on enthusiastically, hoping I would be able to paint some illustrations for him—he seemed to forget that it was becoming more and more difficult to do this. I said I would try to do something for him. He also answered some questions on things that have been puzzling me. The bird that goes donk! donk! in the night is an Asiatic nightjar. The big bird with swishing, creaking wings is a hornbill.

Tonight the butterfly-hunting colonel and his party moved on, so I had no opportunity to draw for him.*

*

The Japanese tell us that it is impossible to get more rice up for us; yet there is plenty in the store for the transit troops. They are concerned wholly just now with the movement of the prisoners, Tamils, etc. They have received some pretty stringent orders from High Command somewhere, about the importance of the railway. I hope this means that their sea lines of communication into Burma are being well cut up by our forces.

The scarce rations are bringing trouble in their train. Scrotal dermatitis is more frequent now, causing much pain and discomfort.

There are twenty-three in our tent now: five Japs live in tents the same size. I have hauled out the flaps at the end and live outside under them.

*

April closes with my own private fairy tale. Jim had brought me some fish and seaweed soup from the Jap kitchen. Now it may have been this, or the fantasy of the butterfly-hunting colonel, or both; I don't know. But I dreamed this last night of the month away and they were beautiful dreams. Maybe the lilies played their part, too. The adventures in the dream I don't remember clearly. There was a romantic Ruritanian land, replete with castles and decorative countryside. Pink towers, draped with great white lace nets reaching to the ground, spun a fairy pattern like dewy spiderwebs in the bush

* Colonel Johnson returned after the war and I believe has since published a book on the Butterflies of Siam.

against the rising sun. (Remember the gasmantle fungi?) And my dream-state accepted it. The whole night was a pleasant Wizard-of-Oz-ish one, made warm and companionate for me by my wife's happy presence.

Lilies—endless variations on a theme :
Colour, form, marking and basis anatomy

VIII

Hintok Road – May

IT IS Saturday the first. My shoulder is still out of action. It nags a bit; but what nags more is wondering if it will simply heal, or turn into a tropical ulcer and eat my back off. Every scratch brings the same worry.

There is still the rumour about that O and P work-battalions are to move back on the 25th of May. We don't really believe the Nips, but still . . .

*

Last night a crowd of rock-clearers came in late and were standing about at the galley, getting food and talking quietly. All at once there were some low growled insults and two fellows started fighting. It was pitiful to see them knocking each other about, and the wild staggering of their weakened and tired frames. I walked in between them and they stopped—and I think they were very glad.

*

Two battalions of English and Scots are staying here to-night. Among them Fatty and I found an able seaman who had been in H.M.S. *Ajax* when we had been chummy ship with her in the Med, and who knew Fatty. He told us some of the news he had received by mail. Mines have been lifted round the invasion beaches; England has had only a brown-out since July; suits are without lapels and have only one pocket—each man allowed only one suit. He also confirmed that four men had been shot at Tarsau for attempted escape, some weeks back. At one stage their crowd refused to work because of poor rations and the whole camp was paraded, including the sick and officers. They were marched around and around until the healthy decided to go to work for the sake of the sick: they went back and finished a section. After a ten-day *yasume* they were marched up here.

Three hundred Australians from Changi also came through. Their spirits were high and we exchanged greetings. One chap, loaded down, still carried a trombone tied across a bundle on his chest. They had been marching since April 18th.

One of our fellows saw his brother—but they were kept apart by the guards, and could only sit and watch each other across the road.

*

About 600 Dutchmen came through today. One of the guards said, 'War over in four months.' The winner was not disclosed. This guard said he had been a radio-announcer and had swum in the Berlin Olympics.

*

Blackie is going downhill again. Each night he comes in, he says that he cannot stick it. He goes on and on to convince himself just how impossible it is. We get mad with him, but Fatty says he is not fit to be argued with.

Otto is being affected too, because he has been hero-worshipping Blackie for some time now. He has been sticking close to him to get all the stories of the Navy he can. Now he is listening to Blackie saying that no white man was ever meant for this. As a result, he is ready to chuck his hand in. He needs someone to crack jokes with about it, to learn to laugh at himself again.

*

I was speaking with Doug Draper today. Doug is a regular R.A.A.F. warrant officer—an armourer. He has served long enough for his long service and good conduct medal. He is a stocky man of medium height, brown complexion and light blue eyes which can flash with authority, or plain enthusiasm. He is a very steady man who takes our present lot as part of what he signed up for. This is just what he told me of their show in the Malayan Campaign.

R.A.A.F. Hudsons attacked a forty-ship convoy in the Gulf of Siam, and blew up an ammunition ship. One Hudson dived at a cruiser and let go a stick of bombs across her stern at fifty feet. After that—he had been doing 312 m.p.h.—the pilot knew nothing more until he regained consciousness alongside one of the wheels from his kite. He was being supported by his Mae-West. After fourteen hours paddling about, he found a deserted native canoe. An armed Nip launch approached but he lay doggo. He tried paddling with his hands, but it was no good. Two days later he was picked up and taken prisoner by the Japs. The squadron had given him up for dead.

The attack on Kota Bharu began at 12.30 a.m., December 8th, 1941. The expedition's barges were halted on the delta of the river by two companies of Dogras and Hyderabads in pill boxes only half manned.* Luckily our kites on the drome were already bombed-up (Doug had taken this on himself, without orders), and the nine Hudsons and two Brewsters took off without warming-up. Each bomber carried four 250-pounders. For the night they claimed three ships hit, one cruiser badly damaged, two other ships, including the ammunition ship, sunk.

On December 7th a flight-lieutenant, acting on a hunch, had made a recce over the Gulf of Siam. Sweeping low to identify a large convoy, he had been fired upon. He reported this Japanese convoy back to H.Q. and was told, in substance, 'Rubbish, we are not at war with Japan.'

Kota Bharu fell after nineteen hours fighting. It was straffed from 9 a.m. onwards. The last attack launched by Allied aircraft was at 4.30 p.m. By which time we had lost two 'upstairs'; one came back u/s with landing gear shot away; and another crash-landed. The drome was evacuated under the smoke of attack and demolition at 7.30 p.m., with the Nips only 80–200 yards away. A cruiser came in to bombard the exit road: just too late.

* They were all killed, later.

Doug's unit moved back to Singapore and carried out further demolition. Their officers had cleared out, and no provision was made for their escape. But he picked up a small ship, the *Wang-Pu*, and got to Palembang. Again he went through the same story of demolition. His C.O. was evacuated in a plane; when the men asked what provision had been made for them, they were told that they could walk. How far? Two hundred and sixty miles to Oosthaven! They managed to get a 'drome service-truck by pocketing the distributor cap, and got to Oosthaven just in time to pick up the *Yomah* for Tandjeong Priok. They rejoined their squadron at Semplak, where they just beat the Nips out of it. But they were caught at Kelajati.

*

Izzy came out of hospital yesterday and went down to the Nip engineers' kitchen for his job back. Jim flared up at him. He called Izzy everything. Izzy whined back, 'Well, I'm entitled—I don't want to go out and work in the jungle.' Jim had to be held back from bashing him.

'You —— !' he fumed. 'What about the others more sick than you have been—*they've* got to go out while crawling bastards like you (with a good pair of boots, too) stay in. Why don't you take your bloody turn. . . .' and then words failed him.

Then Izzy whined that he had no cigarettes. He was given one. Jim had brought up a dixie of rice from the Nip kitchen to share with us. Izzy scooped this up and disappeared with it to the hospital lines. After a while he came back with a packet of Red Bull cigarettes he had traded for it. Some defiant, cheeky streak made him flash the packet and light one up in front of us. I had, at that moment, an awful feeling that there was none he would not sacrifice, without conscience, to his own survival.

*

Nippon demanded that thirty men be discharged from hospital. Fatty and I were discharged. My shoulder has set like a

rock and I cannot move it, nor my neck. I am given a red tag
to signify that I am only to work in camp. Doc. Corlette
apologized, but said that the least sick had to be put out.
But in my case he used a bit of applied psychology on the
Nips. I have nothing to show but a bit of swelling, but the
doctor got some bandages and swathed me, under the arms,
over the shoulder and around the chest like a mummy. When
we were paraded at the guardhouse for work, the corporal
asked me what was wrong. I simply pointed to the bandages.
He was most impressed, took away my red tag, and shooed me
off to my tent for the day. I could see Doc. Corlette give a
sardonic leer behind the Jap. It is this twisted smile that has
endeared him to the men who call him *The Gangster* because of it.

*

There has been some promise of better food. Last night eggs
were delivered: one per man. More tomorrow, they say. Also,
three black pigs: one of them was killed tonight for us. Nevertheless, the strongest of men are reaching their limits and collapsing or going to pieces.

Ted Sorrell's case is typical. Ted helped us making rope, etc.,
for the baskets, back at Konyu. He worked without complaint,
though we urged him to see the doctor; but he always thought
that there were others worse than he and he didn't want to take
their place in hospital. But now he has *had* to go in. His stomach
has gone to water, and won't serve him. His mouth is a nest of
ulcerous yellow blisters. He has jungle-sores on his legs, which
are breaking down badly. 'Do you know what is wrong with
you, Ted?' Doc. Corlette asked. Ted looked at him question-
ingly, waiting for the correct diagnosis. So the doctor gave it,
'You're totally buggered—not a thing left.'

*

Down at the hospital I ran into George Page, our bugler.
George's thin face is crossed with straight black eyebrows, and
sports a Lenin-beard and a hooked nose: above it a very high
forehead, with a centre Mohawk's crest of hair. He is a small

man. His left leg and right foot were bandaged. He was hobbling along on a staff of bamboo, grasping the stick with both hands, and hopping painfully. On his feet were the remnants of boots, with the sides cut out to accommodate his painful feet. I looked at him and he grinned ruefully. 'George,' I said, 'I reckon we are getting a preview of ourselves about thirty years from now.'

*

I saw a fly on a branch emerge from its chrysalis. I watched its wings grow from small, opaque, fleshy buds; expand to soft, opalescent leaves; then finally, become firm, filmy and window-clear, and about one and a half times the length of its body.

*

So unused to food had we become that last night's pig gave almost all of us violent stomachs. For some time we have been living on plain rice and 'seaweed' (dried Chinese radish) soup.

Take Blackie, as he comes in from work: his bedraggled un-kempt beard accentuates his misery; he is quite skinny—his waist and buttocks have fallen away; his cheeks are hollow as his dark ringed eyes; his arms are only half their former thickness.

*

Several rock-drillers have noticed that their sores seem to clear up a bit with the limestone dust they get on them. So a cardboard box of the powder was brought in to be tried out at the hospital. There is also some clear jelly being made from the thin, heart-leaf of a ground vine. It is pulped in cold water and strained through muslin. The Dutch say it is good for dysentery.

*

At 5 p.m. there was a shower. Cloud increased; steady rain fell; darkness became vivid with blue-white lightning. I looked up the hill and, with each lightning flash, from nothingness to

livid revelation, all the figures on the latrines jumped into
sharp relief. It told the common story.

*

Spent the day unpicking bags. The yarn is used to tie sticks
of dynamite together. A large number of trucks passed carrying
provisions.

Blackie is taking a bit more interest. I cooked a three-egg
omelette for him, Otto and myself.

More columns marched through at dusk: a movement seems
to be building up. More and more, too, are those groups of
three: two supporters and the man they support. It often looks
as if all three support each other.

During the early hours of the morning I heard some Japanese
troops. They came through at the run, singing some swashbuckling military song to let us know how high their morale is.
They began a few hundred yards before reaching us, and went
on for a little beyond the camp.

*

Back to work today, clearing at the 153-kilometre mark. This
was the first part of the railway we worked on. Then, the leafless bush rustled with its own dryness; now it is lush and wet
and dripping, pierced here and there by blinding blobs of sun.
There were two lilac-coloured trees which, at first sight, could
have been mauve flowering eucalyptus. They stood in rich
colour against the dark olives and emeralds and the powdered
depths of indigo shadows, giving them weight like cumulus
clouds.

We climbed the wall of the escarpment at the back of the
camp, and dropped down the long slope on the other side
toward the river. We wound through huge, plate-leaved vines
whose leaves were heart- and shovel-shaped; wild ginger; wild
banana; many kinds of lilies; low-leafed things with mauve
pansy-like flowers.

Some of these big, dark lilies are saurian, I'll swear. They
stand fat and still and gleaming, naked, without a leaf of their

own, looking almost carnivorous. And then you suddenly come on a small, white lily that is as Lilliputian as the others are Gargantuan: simply a yellow, cherubic phallus with the white pennon of a long thin petal peeled away from it. There are carpets of small, starred flowers. One has four petals in a compact square and grows plump-down, flat on top of two diametrically opposed begonia-like, torch-flame leaves of red-and-green variegation. One is something like a wild primula. Here and there are spider lilies growing in clumps with long, gracefully down-drooped petals; and upstanding stamens with loose, little, clog-like tips to them.

The track is now only kept open by the traffic on it. When we got down to the embankment we found it amazingly overgrown. There are some bamboo clumps already seven to eight feet high. Broad-leafed creepers were crawling all over it, looking voraciously carnivorous. We had to clear away logs, some of which had been felled some time, and we had some difficulty in breaking them free from this young, reclaiming jungle.

We had only one Nip with us and, through the day, we conversed in that inexplicable way of people without a common language. We had a little Malay and less Japanese; he had a little English and some Malay; we both had arms to wave in international semaphore. He was a pleasant little bloke whose heart was not made for hate. He led us back to camp at the end of the day in single file, singing us most of Bing Crosby's songs. He said he liked Bing's singing very much. He and I finished up singing a duet of *When Irish Eyes Are Smiling* and *Home Sweet Home*.

*

A crowd of English marched in to stay the night; some Dutch and Australians marched straight through. Over the past few days we have had visits from two fairly high-ranking Japanese officers. They were both *horrified* at our food and rice coffee. Five small pigs and some vegetables came in today. We have permission to kill two pigs tomorrow.

Doug Draper brought in the rumour that we must be out of this camp in four days. Someone else said that we move between the 15th and 18th (this is the eighth). The wish to get out is so strong that we grasp at each straw. Some of the 2nd/40th went *back* in trucks yesterday. Blackie wishes harder than all of us, I think. He *tries* to believe we will get out; but when he repeats the rumour, you hear his voice sink with pessimistic lack of faith in what he says.

*

This is Sunday, the ninth. *Yasume*. When we got up it was daylight, not dark, as usual. I collected some wild ginger stems to cook with some *catchung idjoe*, onions and rice polishings. We have been promised better rations to the tune of two pigs every second day, a bag of *catchung* every four days, more veg, and salt increased from three to fifteen pounds a day. This is for over a thousand men. We are to be allowed to write home again soon—the usual four alternative sentences.

*

Back on hammer and tap today. It was a clear, dry morning, the atmosphere having no effect on the distance. Beyond the morning shadows we were working in on our hillside, rose the broad, smooth ridge of the mountain across the valley, glowing in a deep chrome-green; on the very distant mountains, organ-pipe rock scars showed pink with amazing clarity, against the dun-olive of their trees.

In the afternoon it turned hot, and we worked in the white glare of the newly cut limestone. We had to keep powdering our hands with rock dust to stop the dangerous slip of the hammer handles in our sweat-streaming hands. Our arms and bodies were running rivers.

*

When we got back to camp we found our sugar part-stolen. We are all sure it is Izzy. We told him that if we caught him we would half-kill him. This won't stop him, I feel, as he will only take the stuff when we are miles away at work. I think he feels safe to go on. And I don't think he really has the power to stop himself.

*

The Japanese have demanded that an impossible number be discharged from hospital to make the work force up to 700. There are all sorts of crocks out at work today—men with useless legs and feet, and septic sores.

Blackie is back in hospital with dysentery and exhaustion. I cannot but think back to the Blackie of 1937, when we were instructors together in Flinders Naval Depot; how well padded he was with flesh and satisfaction: then, he used to say that I was mad to push a bike ninety miles to Melbourne and back on week-end leave; to run cross-country with the New Entries twice a week; or to do apparatus work and wrestling in the gym. He was always telling me that he was fit enough for anything that might come along: he didn't need to go on with all this tom-foolery. But I was never so sure of myself. I can remember when running that last mile cross-country, or the last few miles of the forty-five-mile race a few of us made of the Monday morning return to Depot, that forcing of endurance out of a body I always felt was so inadequate. And, with all this, I remember a vague feeling at the back of my mind that I was preparing for *something*.

When reveille sounded this morning it was quite dark. Black trees were beautifully drawn against a sky of brilliant stars. The lower parts of the trees were glued to the black cut-outs of the encircling hills. Flickering over these like gun flashes was distant lightning without thunder. The long ghost of the thin valley mist lay along the whole valley. About 9.30 a.m., it slunk away like an unwanted guest whose discretion has just dawned. For a while the chrome sun shone bright on the tree-tops below us. Then a low, flat, broad, corrugated cloud-ceiling hauled itself over us and we were glad of its tent-like protection.

*

The jungle continues to flourish. The wild banana is flowering and the stiff red spearpoint shows crimson against the
young green of its fanlike leaves. They grow only five to six
feet high. There is a bush with foliage like a peony and a
flower like a small black-and-red cauliflower, some two to
three inches across, which grows in the crotch of the separating
stems. The rocks, besides tenacious vines, also support rock
orchids—neat, pale green and sienna things with little hoods
and cups like sensuous lower lips. And there are flowers which
grow a trumpet beautifully spiralled and variegated.

. . . wild banana flowers

What a difference coming home tonight, after weeks of
gleaming black slush. Now sun and shade are splashed over the
baked, crocodile-cracked surface which is smooth to a polish in
parts. There was an unusually warm wind in my face which I
have only noticed previously before rain.

*

Our job is just smashing a hammer with muscular force on
top of a man-held drill. Because of fatigue, you have to concentrate. The head of the man holding the drill is only a few
inches from where the hammer strikes. If you wander, or relax

those tired muscles, there can be a split skull—we have had one already—or maybe a finger taken off. One of the fellows had his ring-finger taken off today. Another has had his, temporarily, saved by an operation. We focus our mind, moron-like, on the small top of that banged and split steel shaft, trying always to hit it squarely lest 'feathers' fly off and bury themselves to the bone, like bullets, in our near-naked bodies.

*

When our kitchen was to be inspected by a high-ranking officer, the Japs backed in a whole truckload of vegetables and supplies. After he had gone the truck drove off with the whole lot.

*

Otto is out of hospital, but by no means ought to be. The hospital chits are now marked by our doctors: *Discharged (date). Driven out to work by Japanese order.* The death certificates of the English who have died at Konyu were marked *Died of (disease, etc.) and starvation.*

I am concerned about Blackie and Otto. Blackie is more of a skeleton than I realized. He has only to lose his grip now and . . .

Otto continues to pay Blackie a kind of unconscious hero-worship. He seems to be satisfied *as long as he is like Blackie.*

*

While I ate my rice at dinner I watched two sepia-bronze beetles with yellow antlers. They were trying to roll a ball many times their own bulk. There was intense teamwork as they forced it up a slope, almost at forty-five degrees and strewn with debris. The beetle on the downhill side stood on his shorter forelegs and thrust up hard with his back ones, which were equipped with two sharp hooks. This made his position like that of a man standing on his hands, with his feet up against a wall, wheelbarrow fashion. His mate, who was larger, was on his hind legs, back uphill, working with his foreclaws like a man dragging a bale of wool towards himself with a bale-hook.

They had already gone twelve inches with this perfect sphere, which they had carved out of human dung. How long these little fellows had been working, I don't know. (Bob Lee told me he had seen two of them work for three days on a sixty-degree slope—repeatedly tumbling down after getting half-way up). When I went closer, the uphill beetle froze, making the smaller one below lose control. Frantically, he tried to stop the runaway. At last it brought up against a small stone, and the little chap froze too. Their precious cargo made me ponder Spinoza's definitions: (roughly remembered) Good, or right, is that which will be useful to us, and therefore we want it; bad (or wrong) is that which is of no use, and therefore we don't want it. So, the beetles and I were on opposite sides of Good and Bad, which, I suppose, keeps Nature in balance. When everybody wants the same thing we end up like we are now.

*

We now have Nippon bridge-builders in camp, and they have no connection with the guards or engineers already here. They seem to have a little more ritual. In the mornings they come on parade and chant and grunt some form of creed or oath. Then they do P.T. on Swedish lines. In their mess-tent, which is a fly without walls, I saw them stand and chant the same thing; before they sat down to eat, they removed their caps and gave a profound bow.

They have a crowd of Chinese from Singapore with them. We are not allowed to contact them. They wear shallow-crowned straw hats, straight-up-and-down coats, and pants of blue cotton. Some of them look old and withered. They live beyond the hospital lines, towards the creek. These, plus careless transit troops, do not help our camp hygiene.

*

As I am writing this the Officer of the Nip guard is punishing his men. Some of them were caught by the *orderly dog* pinching meat and cooking it. He bellows and bashes, and orders them to carry out marionette movements to subdue any independence they may think they still possess.

*

We have given the Japs we work with various nicknames: indeed, I don't know the proper names of any of them. Happy is straight from the seven dwarfs; Smiler should have been another one: he is, perhaps, more western in temper than the others; the Lizard has sleepy eyes; the Crow, alias the Croaker, has a crow's voice; Billy the Pig, whom I have already mentioned, for all his faults seems more straightforward and predictable than the others. Gertie, also the Bitch, is a petulant cook with a whining voice; the Fly, somehow, looks like one; the Fox is more concerned with his own comfort than the Nippon war effort; Tubby is a fat, lazy, little cook; O-Kayké (from his favourite phrase) is a Disney character the talent scouts have so far missed; Willy-the-Wop is a little gangster straight from Damon Runyon. These are the ones we have most to do with.

*

The crowd who marched through tonight said that they were the twelfth of thirteen trains coming up from Singapore. From the camp funds we have bought fifty-two small cattle. Thirty of our worst sick have been sent back to Tarsau.

*

A fine day, with a great rainstorm sweeping up the valley, chased by thunder. A liquid sky with flying, dark grey rags tumbling above the obscuring rain-blur, which robbed the mountains of light, and inked them in blackly, or smudged them out altogether. The unique thing about this storm was that it sliced our bowl of the sky exactly in half, like a pudding on a plate. The northern half of the hemisphere was clear blue; while the southern half boiled like a world in the making. We stood under the blue sky, but in the shadow of the storm.

*

We are getting a few more eggs now. When asked by a passing major how many sick we had, the Colonel said, 'Six hundred suffering from beri-beri.' There are bad cases of swellings, but mostly skin breakdowns: tongue, lips, mouth, throat, scrotum, etc. One fellow's leg looks like a case of elephantiasis. It is so swollen that the toes have almost vanished into his foot, drawn clear of the ground above the ball of his foot. He still has to go to work.

*

Ted Sorrell is really bad. His arms are like flower stems. His lips and mouth are just one festered blister and ulcer. His body has nothing left on it. He sits waiting for foments, panting and shaking in a sweat of weakness. And this was once a healthy farmer over thirteen stone.

The Japs seem to be getting a little of it too. A high officer was over there, I believe, to find out officially *why* they were falling sick.

*

Just before we went out to work this morning, 400 English and Australians from Java and Changi marched in. Some of them we knew well at Bandoeng and Makasura. Bubbles Elliot, a young able seaman from *Perth*, is with them. They are camped across the creek and we are forbidden communication with them.

Tonight Bubbles came up to our tent and gave us some news about themselves. At Changi they had been 600 oddments of various forces. They were fed all right while the train was in Malaya, but after crossing the Siamese border, they spent one stretch of forty-two hours without food. At Bampong they were put into the jail, which was filthy with excrement at almost every turn. Of the 600 to reach Bampong, only 151 got to Tarsau. The men who fell sick had to make the half-way stations as best they could; then they were brought on by truck to the next camp. They marched for seven consecutive nights, resting and doing camp duties by day. When they heard of the march ahead, many of them 'wogged' almost all their possessions—including, in some cases, the boots that had been given them. These had been a mixed blessing because of bad fitting, and the state of the men's feet. I saw one fellow tonight with both big toenails, yellow and lifted, so that you could have pushed a pencil under them.

*

At the hospital tonight I talked to an American sailor from U.S.S. *Houston*. He said that in their final action (The Battle of Sunda Strait) they had not been closed up at action stations. He had been awakened by gunfire. Dutch information had told them that the Strait was clear. 'I was sleeping topsides by a gun, when I was wakened. That was the first I knew: about half our men were asleep.'

*

A night's rain introduced the new arrivals to the camp. Their tents are only the *linings* of old E.P.I. tents—*complete with flyproof windows in the tops.*

*

After we had drilled our 140 centimetres, we had to return some drills to Konyu. This took us back to the old camp-site. Already it is overgrown with vines that grab at your feet and legs as you walk. The attap* has been taken from the huts; but the skeletons are being broken up as the deliberate hands of the invading growth seizes them, bone by bone, and squeezes them until they break.

*

There was an incident out at No. 5 rock party today. A fellow was beaten with a shovel and a bamboo; according to one account he had been worked to exhaustion. Another eye-

* Attap is a kind of thatch used on huts in the East. It is made from palm leaves—nepa, sugo, coconut, etc. The blunt end of the leaf is folded over a thin piece of split bamboo some eighteen inches long in two overlapping layers. This makes a piece some eighteen inches by a foot or so. They are tied on to the rafters or batten in overlapping rows like tiles.

witness said, 'One of those S Battalion blokes—he was asking for it.' (S Battalion are our latest arrivals.) I was talking to Major Wearne yesterday—a fine type of regular army officer, quiet, steady, high morale, and a just disciplinarian—who said, 'Some of the fellows get a sort of reflected glory, thinking they are living on the verge of death. But just the same, it is amazing how the chaps have stuck it so well.'

*

It is fourteen days since *Yasume*; yesterday Billy said, 'To-morrow, tomorrow. No haviga finishoo. O.K.-ga?' We asked him what work we would be doing when the drilling finished. He said, 'Bridgeebuilda.' Today he said, 'Bridgeebuilda O.K.-ga? Nei? Hamma men number haviga samma samma.' So, some of us will be drilling for a while yet.

At 11 a.m. 300 Jap troops marched through with full equipment. One of our guards said that they were going to fight the English in Burma.

*

S Battalion have a colonel with them. This, I think, will relieve Weary of some of his burden and leave him freer for the heavy responsibility of the hospital.

Tonight this colonel was giving a pretty straight talk about men coming late on parade and holding everybody up. He used a few 'bloodies', but no more. Hardly had he finished speaking, when a private in front of me turned and said, 'What do you think of a Colonel talking like that—'bloody' and 'f——' and 'youse c——'. If a man was to talk like that to an N.C.O. he would be matted.' For a moment, I couldn't get the drift of what he was saying. I came to the conclusion that the man had taken such offence at what was being said, that he really believed he had heard those words. It made me wonder how many things we read and hear—stories by one who was there—are already coloured by this unconscious translation in the mind of the teller.

*

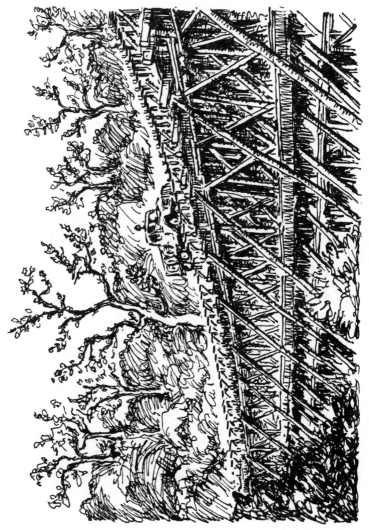

3-tier bridge on Hintok–Konyu section. Rock blasted trees are just sprouting again

The camp is a quagmire, mud on everybody and everything
—in tents, on the bamboo bed boards, splashed up our legs and
taken to bed with us. All night the rain beat on the rotting
canvas roofs, beating its way through in a fine spray, which
made us wet and soppy. No dry place to come back to.

*

This is Sunday, 23rd. We ate our breakfast in the dark,
standing in the rain. To cap a wet night in bed the mud
squelched between our toes.

'I wouldn't send a dog out in this. . . . I'd even give the pigs
clean straw!' a young farmer said.

But, out came the Nips in capes, and off we went. It presented
a challenge to the bare-footers, as if some devil lurked beneath
the gleaming, uneven surface of dirt and water. The men were
strung out like so many bundles of sticks, with rags flapping
about them. One man wore a hat and a torn pair of canvas
boots—otherwise he was like Adam, an Adam with a waterbottle strapped around his middle: blotted and smeared with
mud, he walked like a prophet of old with a long staff.

All day we were wet and dry by turns. The weather is not
cold, but we often feel chilled. We drilled the rock in the rain
on the rocky hillside, often enveloped in the drenching gloom
of drifting cloud. Sometimes we were above the first layer and
below the next. The heat and perspiration of our bodies com-
peted with the rain.

We came home the back way to dodge the road; but we had
to use two ski-sticks each to keep on our feet. The descent down
the escarpment became uncontrolled sliding, over smooth hard
mud, studded with sharp rocks.

*

The Japanese have a special brand of humour. They gave
twelve light-dutymen a light job. It was to roll a forty-four-
gallon drum of petrol out to the compressor: eight kilometres
along that black road of slush—down that Hill which, day

Breakfast—rice in the rain and rain in the rice. Hintok Road, May 1943

after day, wet and dry, has half-killed us—then down a deeply mudded jungle track.

*

Monday, May 24th. Empire Day! What a thought of inspiring mockery to us, sons of Empire. We became wakeful before reveille, and wondered why they had let us sleep so late. It was 9.30 a.m. Word was passed that the transit troops were being searched by the Japs. Nobody was allowed outside the barricade, and a guard had been placed at our gateway.

Yesterday Middy lost a gold watch which had been presented to him on going overseas. This, through repeated temptation of hunger and nakedness, he had refused to sell. Middy—just twenty years old—is a young colossus from Western Australia, six foot two inches and, even now, fourteen stone. Had he caught the thief he would have murdered him. Somehow the Japs had got wind of it and this search was put on. Over the fence I could see the prisoners standing ankle deep in the mud and fishing out all their belongings for inspection. Much of it fell in the mud, and showers of rain swept over them.

When we went on parade at 10 a.m., a new Nippon order on stealing was read out. The Nip officer said that whosoever committed the offence within his jurisdiction would be shot, if found.

*

We had been sent up the road to collect wood for the kitchen fires when, round the bend, we heard a commotion as if the great Panjandrum himself were presiding. Then the cause came into view: a troop of young Japanese soldiers. They were shouting as they heaved some small two-wheeled carts loaded with their gear. Low in the shafts of three of them Timor ponies toiled, splashed to the bellies with mud. The other six carts were man-drawn. The men struggling with these looked as if they were wading waist-deep in the road. Someone said that they ate the horses as they needed them. They were bound for Burma: young, new, and still brash with that traditional,

unquestioning Japanese obedience. Watching them made us feel
a little better.

*

Down at the showers, I met a doctor I had known back in
Bandoeng. He is the M.O. of the new crowd over the creek.
He asked how I was doing, and then went straight on to say,
'You look pretty good—you must be one of the fittest men in
camp.' I half-heartedly denied this, because it caught me
between flattery and a desire for sympathy.

*

Otto complains of little things he once laughed at. I try to
barrack him out of it—and Blackie too. Tempers are frayed.
Jim, Fatty and George have nagged and snapped at each other
until, now, there is a tacit agreement of silence between them.

*

My feet are not too good these days because of the wet; and
the ulcerous sores on my shins are troublesome. Bandages will
not stay on because of the taper of my calf. However, I have
been able to use the leaves of a ground vine, which are very
thin. By licking them well and placing them over the sores they
stick and keep the insects out. If they get torn off by the undergrowth, I can usually find more.

There is a lot to grumble about; a lot to be disappointed
about; a lot to lose our tempers over; but there is also much to
marvel at. For instance, the loyalty of a man's body—to watch
a sore heal itself—to feel that pain is not so much a tragedy but
a process. There is a fascination in trying to help it consciously,
to try and break down any internal resistance to recovery by
trying to quell devastating emotions like bad temper, hatred,
fear, lust, envy.

*

After I came in today, on my way down to the showers, I saw
a mosquito net strung up over a bamboo table. On it lay
Sergeant Stevens with his head between Major Corlette's

504

hands. The doctor was talking quietly to him. Weary was bent over the sergeant's open abdomen, swabbing and cutting with quiet, steady concentration. The anaesthetic had been a spinal and the patient was looking straight up, his eyes slowly opening and closing.

*

The new camp over the creek is not faring so well. They have no sergeant nor Nip officer—only a power-drunk corporal who is playing dictator.

Rumours about moving still come thick and fast, although the 25th has passed.

Tamils have joined the Chinese bridge builders and they have begun to drive piles at the end of seven-metre bank with a primitive thirty-four man, hand-worked pile-driver.

*

On the way out through the hospital lines, I dropped in to see Fatty and Jim, both in with malaria. Fatty is almost stone deaf with it. I mentioned Blackie to them and they said he had got so that they don't care to go and see him. If they try to cheer him up he doesn't like it.

Even Otto told me, 'I had to come away the other night— he would have had me howlin' if I'd stayed. He told me I was thin and how I was a fool to be out working—I oughta get in hospital—I didn't like it—it made me feel up the putty.'

*

We hear that there have been some thirty deaths from cholera in a camp towards Burma. Tonight we were inoculated. Two days ago one of the Chinese died, and some said it was cholera. He was cremated on a bamboo platform.

*

While we were working today the gang next door blew without warning. We looked up to see hundreds of fragments of rock in the air, coming our way. One was a foot across, high in the air and curving right down on us. I leapt up a rock, slipped, and the sharp surface gouged out an ulcer on my shin, giving it a clean start.

*

Last night, in the half-light of a rainy evening, a little procession passed by. The leader was in saffron yellow robes. Under his right arm he had a package, and, upright in his left, he held an oiled paper umbrella. He padded along at a good gait. He was immediately followed by a small boy, also under an umbrella and with a small package. Then followed another man in tan robes with a splash of yellow. He, too, had his umbrella and his boy. Lastly came a man whose robes were tan only. He had neither umbrella nor boy. Over the wet shining mud-puddled road they padded on, rather like swans, gliding forward. The leading priest went with the unconscious press of a man with weightier things on his mind. The others had to keep up with him.

*

Izzy was skulking in the bush today, away from his job. He was caught, with a couple of others; they were bashed and then made to hold thirty-pound rocks above their heads for some time.

*

Just as we were finishing work today a great blinding rainstorm came over from the west, blotting out the mountains in succession until we could hear the giant hiss and beat of it on the tops of the trees across the valley a mile away. I came home the back way, through the foliage tunnel of a track, with the water flowing swiftly down it. It is not a popular track, but I prefer it to the road, for which I am developing a phobia. Tonight I was conscious of a sensuous pleasure walking in the rain; warm with exertion, feeling the pull of the hill against my leg muscles, and the drive of my arms back on the ski-sticks. Bow-waves of water feathered away from my sliding feet. When

I got into camp, I walked straight under the showers as I was, except for my hat.

But when I got to my tent, there—absorbing the sky, in the middle of the pouring rain—was our bed platform with our belongings on it, but no pack. I searched amongst the sodden mess and could not find it; my mind paralysed with red fury at the thief who had taken my diaries and drawings, which could be no good to anyone.

Just as I was about to give way to an open show of misery and anger, Buck Pederson came over and said, 'It's all right—I saw them knocking the tent off, so I got your stuff. It's with mine under this tent flap here.' I thanked him dumbly. He went on, 'If you don't get them drawings back somehow, we've wasted our bloody time up here.'

Buck is a machine-gunner and comes from Queensland. He lost his mother early in life and was still in his teens when his father died.

The world of the Depression conditioned him to live by a set of rules which had been ruthlessly thrust upon him, though we may well raise our virtuous eyebrows. He had a shrewd, native logic, and decided that if the rules were good enough for the privileged few, they would also serve for the many who needed them more, because they lacked privilege. Buck said that because the law allowed the few but forbade the many to utilize the rules, he had had some brushes with it. 'We had to apply the rules surreptitiously,' he said. He used the last word ironically, to show a contempt for what he called a *phoney economy*, in which the poor were blamed, called lazy and shiftless, because they had become a nuisance at a time when more attention was being paid to the pound than the person.

'We left Brisbane when we couldn't get a job—things got real crook. We humped the Bluey and hit the track. I jumped the rattlers and rode the rods. We went all over the joint: we had no plans—just drifted wherever there was work, or a feed. There were plenty of decent jokers, but there were some hard ones too—bloody hard. The coppers were down on us. As soon as they would see a new face in a town, they were down on it.

Told us to move on, said they had enough trouble. I reckon I would have been in most jails in Western Queensland and the Territory—and quite a few in New South. Sometimes it was a good way to get a bed. We might'a' got a bit drunk sometimes—but mostly they just *vagged* us.'

Though Buck was without pretensions, he was not without pride. It was an unconscious pride, a pride in his core, which had nothing to do with vanity. This peculiar pride and honesty moved him in all he did, and, if he should betray it, it gave him an unflinching awareness of what he had done.

His close-cropped head showed bumps and scars and little bald patches like a plainly written history. There was a Teutonic heaviness about his face which, at first sight, gave a hint of brutality; the heavy frontal bone of his forehead, the height and massiveness of his cheekbones, the scarred nose with broad nostrils and tip, the thick, almost loose, lips: all these, in repose, tended to be lifeless in a brutish way. But Buck has a heavy voice and slow smile. When he laughs, the laugh is deep, but does not carry far outside him: as if you are hearing only the overflow from the deep caverns of laughter within. But it is a rich overflow. Even when Buck gives a derisive laugh at somebody or something, you feel that he is only laughing at the recollection of a situation he has been in himself.

He is solidly built with good shoulders and a thick worker's waist and back which has robbed his muscularity of any athletic look. But there is a lightness to his legs and thighs which accentuates the slogging that has gone into that slightly humped back. There is something of the light draught animal about him, and you never forget that he is one of the work horses of society. In some degree I suppose Buck has committed almost every social offence except murder. But he is still whole and balanced, with the knack and insight to give meaning to many things normally beneath one's notice.

As loyalty is his unbroken rule, so is he a good mate and, at heart, one of the nicest sentimentalists. It was as something of a sentimentalist that he joined the army. Knowing that he was a scallywag he had expected severe discipline to bring him into line. He wanted to become part of a high morale. Instead, he told me, he found weakness above him, and despised it.

'I'm not so crooked on being a prisoner—but I *am* savage at the sergeants and W.O's and some of the officers. They let me get away with things: they were weak and went to water when you cut up rough. I expected it tough. But there was too much favouritism and crawling—it makes you sick! When we were told we would be surrendering, I wrecked my rifle under a truck: I was crimed for it and they stopped my pay. We *deserve* to be here!'

*

At 11.30 p.m. we were awakened.
'Come on there, all out on parade!'
'What the bloody hell for?'
'Never mind! Nip orders.'
'What is it?—a truck, I suppose.'
'Curse the dirty yellow bastards!'
I was just awake from a sound sleep. Those few words vividly flooded my mind with a world of black mud. I was indignant at discomfort and injustice. I was almost on the point of conceiving it a matter of the Empire's honour that I should *not* go. A small sore on my foot became the wound of a hero: none could expect me to go with that!
'How many do they want?'
'Fifty—Come on, you chaps!' Austin called out. 'Turn out! They are waiting!'
The men, calling from their dark tents, reeled off causes and reasons—as I had done—why they should not go. Three sar'-majors poked about the tents, digging men out. Each man had to be called by name, or he lay a silent corpse. Excuses were annihilated and grumbling men dragged out. I decided that I would go, and not make excuses, if directly called—*but not unless*! I would wait for the hand of fate to drag me out; and I lay wide awake and morbidly expectant, unable to think what the conditions of the road might be. I knew quite well I was being a coward, and I didn't care.

All around me they went on digging out—but not me. Both the apprehension of going, and disgust at my weakness, had put a little lump in my stomach. But I still lay there.

'Come on, Kaley! What's the matter with you? Sick?'

'Yes, Austin, I am.'

'That don't matter a bugger, come on! What's wrong with you?'

'Diarrhoea.'

'So has everybody! Come on!'

'I went and saw the doctor when I came in—I was late and went to his tent. I've got a sore foot. I had a bamboo thorn in it. I had to go to the R.A.P. with it.'

'That doesn't matter—get out!'

'No.'

'You won't?'

'No, Austin.'

'You refuse duty?'

'Yes, Austin—in this case, I definitely do.'

'Just what I would bloody-well expect from you—I've never expected anything else as a matter of fact. You lie there while your mates go out and work. Just the dirty rotten trick I'd expect from you. Why don't you get up and tell the Major you refuse duty!'

'I'll tell the doctor—that's who I'll tell!'

'Yes you will. . . .'

And Austin went away burning the air.

I was lying there while my mates were up. They wanted fifty: they almost had them. I had volunteered before when others had held back. No. I would stay until directly called. No excuses: Kaley had sickened me of that. Just the same I knew I was too weak to get out and face it. And I got out of it.

I could hear the unfortunate fifty squelching up the road toward Konyu, with only a dim, wet gleam to guide them. There had been four too many. They were broken off. One was a neighbour of Kaley's. I could hear Kaley start a long, self-righteous justification of his actions; and his reasons multiplied as he talked, like the accelerated bisection of microbes in a culture. It made me sick because I knew I was just like him. And I knew, if it all happened again, I would still do the same.

I don't think my conscience would have kept me awake, but fate sent the bugs as a substitute. They bit my face, neck and ears; they bit my back, legs, arms, ankles, feet and hands. I lashed back and was soon enveloped in the peculiar bitter-almond smell of crushed bugs. If I said I have a hundred bugs in the bit of mosquito net I use as a pillow, I would be short-tallying. They are also in thousands in my bedboards, pack, blanket and everything else I possess, and they are all as hungry as prisoners of war.

About 5 a.m. the working party came back, muddied to the ears. A lot had had their canvas boots destroyed in the sucking mud, and come back bootless. They had had to get a bogged truck out, and it had taken them all that time. The cooks managed to give them some rice coffee: Kaley was awake and got one of the workers to make another trip to the kitchen and bring him back a cup. He took it, telling the man he couldn't know how badly he needed it.

*

Today there was a close shave on the job. I was at the dynamite hut when I heard a cry from up the hill, and heard a log hurtling down over the rocks through the bush. Those who could not see it became anxious. Jim Thatcher, a broad-shouldered R.A.A.F. sergeant, looked up and saw a fifteen-foot log leap an eight-foot rockshelf right above him. Just at the right moment he side-stepped and got off with only a bruised arm.

I have come to the conclusion that sailors are not made for mud.

This closes the wet, but not very merry, month of May.

IX

Hintok Road – June

TUESDAY the first. Rain all night. There was as much rain water as rice in the pap we ate at breakfast. Then out over the slippery mountain to work. We belted away with the hammers in the rain and at last got warm.

At 11.30 a.m. a Nip came to the end of the cutting and sounded an air raid hooter. They were going to blast. The fact that I had already been hit, and my previous experience of sirens, found me a bit jumpy: especially as they made no move to get us away.

From above us on the rock-cropped hillside came a panicky cry: '*Look out! There's a log on the way down!*'

Someone else took up the cry. '*Look out! There's a log on the way down—they can't stop it!*'

'*Where?*'

'*What's wrong with the dopey bastards! They'll kill a dozen men down here! What's wrong with them up there?*'

None of us below could see past the ledge above. All we knew was that there was a log on the way.

Then No. 2 gang blew the rock. The ground where we stood vibrated. I jumped for cover: I was *very* jumpy. We could side-step those pieces we could see. Most of them went over our heads, but a few of the larger pieces fell amongst us.

When it was over, and the log had hit a rock and stopped, those below relieved their shock in a stream of bitter abuse at those above—telling them, in lurid detail, that they were worse than the Japs.

*

I have been delirious with malaria: for three days I could

not quite get back to the surface of consciousness. The whole world seemed to be in the next room and I could only dimly hear it through the walls. The form of the delirium was linked with our work. I have mentioned somewhere, how, when we take the drill out of the hole to clear the powder from the bottom, we then pour in some water and let the drill run back to the bottom. This it does with a peculiar, liquid, metallic ringing, striking the bottom with a glug that is almost a *glu-ng-g* and a grunt. While I vaguely heard the world in the next room, my gullet seemed to be wide open and a drill constantly running up and down with a ringing *glu-ng-g*, to the bottom of my stomach. Then it would be withdrawn, giving me a dismal nausea, until, with a ringing and a clunk, it was down again. I was very glad when the world came in from the next room.

If the weather is depressing in the lines, it seems infinitely more so from the hospital. To have to crawl out, sick and in the pitch dark, in the mud of a week's continuous rain to find the latrine is work for a qualified navigator, rather than a sick man. Who, on his return, feeling like an unwanted and beaten dog, with the muck of the journey on him, has to go to bed filthy. He will try to curl between the leaks, and rest. But not all of the sixteen men crowded into the tent can keep clear of the drips.

On my first night, a man died of dysentery. Another lingered a while until a haemorrhage took him. As I was seeing the doctor, I saw his bier go by. Six men stumbled along a greasy path through towering bamboos, dark and green and dripping. The body was on a bamboo stretcher which twisted with each lurch of the bearers. The corpse had its feet wrapped in a soiled blanket; its head and body were covered with a dull, worn gas cape. They went in grim, silent, awkward progress until they were lost from sight—a drab little cortege taking with them a drab, thin, little body mysterious with death. We heard the notes of the Last Post in the distance, sounding as if they were being played under water.

Numbers of men have been going down during the past few days with food poisoning. What, among the few things we get, could be poisonous? Some say the dried meat; some say the dried fish. One of the victims came into our tent. He had the figure of a famine-victim, the appearance of a filthy tramp, and the face of a crucified Christ. He collapsed on the bedboards beside me and lay writhing, filthy from the road and the falls he had taken.

*

On Thursday night our mail-messengers came back from Tarsau. 'So sorry—big mistake—there is no mail for you.'

*

We have been told that K, L, and M Battalions, in nearby camps, have been told to be ready to move to Saigon on the 18th. Also that the Thai government has pleaded with the Japanese to have all prisoners out before the Wet sets in. What we are getting now, I am told, are the Bamboo Rains. This is a lighter period before the Wet proper. It is a fitting title because, just now, bamboo is driving out and down: its root shoots are searching out. They are conical and two to three inches in diameter. The Chinese peel them and boil the pithy centres. Our stomachs just burn when we try to eat them.

*

The English across the creek are having a bad time with their power-drunk corporal. One hundred men get only a bucket of soup; thirty a bucket of pap. At times, twenty or thirty have to go out to work all day without dinner. Already, out of 410, 162 are hospital cases—in less than a fortnight. And one day thirty of their hospital cases were ordered out to work.

*

I was wandering out miserably to the latrine in the rain, when a thought struck me. I was oppressed by the squalor of the camp; our desolation; our separation from our families; the blankness of our future; the mud; the rain; the lack of shelter . . . on and on . . . until I checked myself.

Before me rose a picture, a similar picture, of the wet, washed-out squalor of the bag- and tin-shanties in Happy Valley (Sydney) beneath the bleak winter blanket through the years of '31, '32, '33 : the bags, the tins, the props and the patches beneath which families had to live on starvation level. Now, we, by circumstance of war, are put in our Happy Valleys by an enemy with no cause to love us. But the Happy Valleys and the Dudley Flats, and the rest, were places we had put *our own countrymen* in; and, for good measure, we had kicked their women and kids in with them. Some of those men are here now because they decided to fight for the country which did that to them.

*

Next to me here, is a young country lad from S Battalion. He lives near Young, a large inland town of N.S.W. He talks a lot about farming and it comes out in a slow drawl, in one long and toneless stream. What he loses in slowness he makes up by cutting all punctuation and word-spacing. He swears little—generally using emasculated synonyms—but when he does it comes out mixed quaintly with 'jollys', 'gollys', and 'blesseds'. He has the stubborn dogmatism of people who have decided early in life what they will believe for the rest of it. For instance, he knows that those who suffered and went hungry in the Depression did so because they were lazy. 'There are plenty of rabbits in Australia,' he said.

*

Discharged from hospital : the Japs only allow you three days for malaria.

The weather has become a minatory presence seemingly bent on getting us. We have stopped thinking of our release—only of when we will get out of this jungle and its incessant wet. We talk about it as if it were the end of the war : as if it were complete salvation in itself. And that is what it would be. The roads are all but useless; our supply line is chancy; food is difficult to cook; rations are lower. Our canteen supplies, which have been an actual life-saver, are now rare.

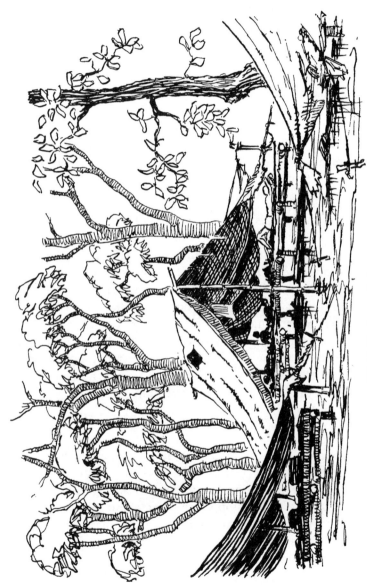

Hintok Road camp during wet season

I have been talking to Weary. He told me he felt a keen disappointment in himself. He had been working all day at the hospital and was late getting back to the officers' lines for his night meal. Two eggs a man had arrived in camp. But for his faithful messman, Weary's two eggs might well have been eaten by one or other of his less scrupulous messmates. However, as he arrived back, the messman brought out his meal: a plate of dry rice with two fried eggs on top. He told me that when he saw those 'beautiful golden eggs', he was affected with an emotion as strong as if a dear friend had come to deliver him.

He said he had to take the meal out and eat it in an appropriate cathedral-atmosphere under the trees. But, just as he was about to take the first mouthful, he saw two skinny Tommies from the camp over the creek, being goaded back under the burden of a heavy log. A Japanese guard was shouting hoarsely at them. As they passed him, they staggered and fell flat on their faces in the mud. Weary said he got up and said a few things to the Jap. Something in the big man's subtle presence must have affected the Jap, for he left the Tommies in Weary's care.

Weary attended to them and talked to them. And, as he stood talking, he became conscious of the food in his hand: those beautiful golden eggs. The Tommies' emaciated frames made him feel guilty. But Weary's ever-watchful messman, Happy Houseman, had his eye on the Colonel—knowing him too well.

'Now, you look here,' Happy said to the Tommies, 'we don't get eggs every day, you know! Mostly it's just rice and seaweed soup—same as you. These are the first we have had for a long while. The Colonel would have eaten his by now—only he's working hard in the hospital lines all day. He needs them more than you do. You eat them, Colonel! Go on!'

Weary said that Happy's voice was like the Devil in his ear. At that moment he was torn two ways: but the Devil had whispered a very good reason. Weary went to his pack and scraped together a few biscuits and some palm sugar we call

goula-Malacca (rubbish he called it, then) and he got some sort
of a feed together for them, even though they were due for their
own meal when they got to their own lines. He watched them
eat what he had given them, and then go.

'Then,' he said, 'I ate those awful eggs. . . . That's the difference between an ordinary fellow . . . and a saint . . . I
suppose.'

*

It was a hard working day, after malaria. I was still quininc-
drunk. A small party of us had to go from No. 5 to the river and
bring back four forty-kilo boxes of cement. They turned out to
be barrels, so heavy that several times we broke the wire upon
which they were slung from poles. It was teeming with such
tropical volume that down on the floor of the valley jungle,
where we were, the noise above us was deafening. There was a
hissing roar as the big drops hit the overhead leaves and bounced
sound in all directions. And it was so dull beneath the trees that
the outer daylight, which we glimpsed from time to time
through the leaves, we swore was actually sunlight. A couple
of bets were laid on it.

The river camp is occupied by the gangs working the com-
pressors and jack hammers. It looked as forlorn as ours. It is
perched on a bank sixty feet above the river which is now a
broad, brown, swirling mass with low bamboo islands infesting
the slow backwaters.

The trip back was hard. The strain of having to keep our
feet, two-abreast, on the narrow, dished track; the vines sawing
at the ulcers on our shins; the curses; the petty hate; the loss of
temper. It was 4 p.m. before we got back to our rice. It was
9 p.m. before we finished for the day.

*

A Nip officer visited the hospital and one hundred with bad
feet and legs were sent out to work. Some of them came home
very late—between 10 and 11 p.m. At least one of them had to

crawl the last mile. No one was with him. Several times he just lay flat on his stomach in the mud to rest.

*

Rain all night. Slept pretty well between the drips, but still wet this morning. Had another trip to the river camp. We went for blocks, tackles, rope and dog-spikes: uncomfortable things to carry. We are getting logs ready to build some bridges.

Three or four 'sold out' (collapsed) on work parade this morning. A couple more had to be carried up to the work parade. Weary carried one. He insists on this carrying.

When casualties are brought up, they are sat on a big teak log which we call the Wailing Wall, at the edge of the clearing. Weary tells the men to sit there, no matter what the Japs do, or say. Their usual practice is to approach these sick men and bellow, '*Kurra!*', with the threat of death in their voices. The man is usually so shocked that he stands and takes a few paces forward. As soon as he does that, the Jap soldier considers him fit for work, and he is sent out.

Now, when the Jap bellows, Weary looks at him disarmingly, picks up the man like a baby and stands in front of the Jap with him, and says, 'This man can't walk, Nippon.'

The English sick were being paraded again as we went out. One of the fellows fell over a stone cutting today and was pretty badly hurt. One of S Battalion had a fit on the job and went into a delirium. The doctor said it was cerebral malaria.

We are very late home again, and I am just managing to scribble this with a bit of light from the fire: I'll have my rice later, for I can eat that in the dark. Because of very limited time these days, this writing must become even more scrappy.

Some eggs came in tonight and the Nips paid for them: can't make it out. Tonight there were 300 in hospital, despite the drastic clearing out by the Japs.

*

The last shred of my boots has left me. We worked on a bridge span until 9 p.m. Then we had to make our way back through the jungle track without a moon. Luckily the track is narrow and the bamboo and tangle grow close each side, so that, if you get off it, you are soon brought up short. I would rather this than the road, which is now thigh-deep in parts.

Sergeant Harris did not come home at all. He said he would rather sleep out with the tigers and go without food, than face that trip back in the dark. Billy the Pig waited at the top of the escarpment for the last man to come over. He called, 'O.K.-ga?' over the cliff, as each man went down the tree trunk with the steps cut in it. He sat there like a faithful baboon, asking each man if he were the last. He held his cigarette lighter with

Oriental bamboos make gothic arches over English dead. Hintok River camp 1943

its puny bud of flame to guide us where to go over the edge.
He came down last.

I went over and, as I stepped off the tree-trunk ladder, I
slithered dangerously down the greasy track in the dark. I was
really anxious about slicing my foot on an unseen tooth of rock.
But I could not stop myself.

I got to the bottom and started to wind my way through the
trees of the swamp—just where it snakes in a strong 'S'—when
I came abruptly on a lantern burning on the ground. There was
also a fire being kept going in the rain. Five men were digging
in the swampy ground with slow, weak, noiseless movements.
Near them were five stiff, angular corpses each with its head
and shoulders in a rice sack: the rest of them was naked. They
were English dead. I asked one of the gravediggers what they
had died of. Starvation? His black-bearded skull opened on a
white-clouded tongue and scummy teeth. He looked up
glumly, and then burned with a short, flaring heat. In bitter,
sullen hatred he said, 'Rice . . . bloody rice! . . . That's what
bloodywell killed them!'

*

It has been a hard week. A few days ago two English, an
Australian and a Malay died. There has been an outbreak of
cholera at Konyu: three deaths a day. Three more English
died today. We have had our first case of cholera here. One of
S Battalion drank unboiled water out on the job. He was
affected by 3 p.m.: ten hours later he was dead.

*

My own petty troubles loom large and nag me. I've had
malaria again and have a poisoned leg about three times its
normal size. I am a bit full of it at the moment because, tonight, I came home over a very slippery track, bootless, with
the mosquitoes eating me alive—and carrying a naked, cross-
cut saw across my bare back. It made me nervous.

*

Jack Ward was beaten up by Happy and the Surveyor a day or so ago. He was beaten because the American-trained surveyor understood more of what we said than he was meant to. We were saying what we thought of the Japanese at that moment. He was beaten with bamboo, fists, and finally, a crowbar. He is lucky to be alive. Happy was beating him about the head and shoulders with the crowbar. Jack was fending off the blows with his arms, as well as he could. Weary of this frustration, Happy drew back the bar like a bayonet and made a short-pointed lunge at Jack's groin. It would have finished him, but something stopped Happy carrying it right through. I have noticed before that Happy does not lose his temper as completely as do the other Japanese. He is a boxer: unusual, I think in the Jap, who seem to be a biting, scratching, screeching lot when it comes to a fight. I think this gave him that fraction of control that saved Jack. He finished up very sick and sore just the same.

*

For the past week the rains have gradually cleared and it seems as if the Bamboo Rains have petered out and we may get a bit of a dry spell before the real Wet. It is not encouraging to look forward to the Wet and cholera; yet both are inevitable and there will come a time when we will be facing them.

*

The Japanese are really applying the pressure now. The rumours are that we will still be moving back on a certain date, but work must be finished.

The English camp here is most dismal. The morale is low. They have little sense of hygiene: they wash their mess gear in the creek *below* our showers, under which men with dysentery wash.

*

We are tired, tired, tired. Our bodies cry with a silent screaming of fatigue, and their cunning defeats our vain intelligence.

The body schemes only for rest and is prepared to break every concept of honour to do it. We hope that the 29th will bring *something*.

*

We are now working on the foundations of the second bridge. The first one is finished. These bridges are short things of seven or eight trestles linking one knoll with another, around the side of the mountain. The cuttings are put through the knolls, or spurs, at rail level. Then we cut a ledge at a lower level, between them, and put a trestle bridge on it. These follow the ups and downs of the ground, and Japanese whims. Some are bolted on to concrete and some are not. All this is done with a frightening simplicity, and the complexity of difficult calculations is dispensed with, so that the job can be pushed on at greater speed. Many different sorts of woods are used in the bridges, so long as each log is the right size. They vary from indestructible teak, to kapok which dries out quickly as light and as soft as balsa-wood. Apart from normal difference in their mechanical co-efficients, I cannot but think of the different rates at which these logs will be digested by the termites.

Most of the building is just plain bullocking and very exhausting. The Japs we are with have no idea of rigging. To them the breaking strain of a rope or wire is only when it breaks. After a few hair-raising accidents, a couple of the sailors amongst us said we would show them. This has saved them breaking so much gear, and it has also saved our lives and limbs. Smiler, with whom it is possible to talk, and even pull his leg, said, 'O.K.! O.K.! O.K.!'

*

Blackie has had his beard trimmed. This may sound trivial, but it gives me a ray of hope for him.

The food seems to have improved slightly. We now have a very small piece of dried meat or fish with our dinner ration.

*

Fourteen men of No. 2 gang did not show up all day at work. At night they were rounded up as we fell in to come home. Some of them gave other fellows' numbers to the Japs. The innocent men, despite their protests, were beaten. As usual, the tempo of the beating increased as the Japs' appetites were whetted. It was fists, bamboo, pseudo-Judo, and boots and clogs. Clogs danced a wicked fandango on the skulls and faces of the men, heel and toe. In the heat of it a clog would fly out of the mêlée of half a dozen Japanese wreaking vengeance. Two men were knocked down and their dysentery-infected stomachs poured out as they were heedlessly kicked.

*

Thieving has increased with the pressure, and the tempers of the men rise hotly at every new offence. Men are low in energy; but often, just when you think a man's spirit should break, some thin, resilient string holds it together. The man you have despised comes good.

*

On parade tonight, a Japanese order was read out. It said what a great work we were taking part in. How pleased Nippon was about our willing and cheerful working. The railway was of great importance to the Japanese and *must* be completed. We were called on for great and glorious effort so that the Emperor would be justly proud of us. It would mean much hard work, but it must be completed at all costs. Nippon very sorry but—many men must die.

*

I had to give up swinging the hammer today. My poisoned leg, the ulcers on it, malaria, and a craven stomach drove me to it. Billy doesn't like me any more.

With this recurring malaria—we are never really free of it —we are just hanging on with ringing heads full of quinine. My head rings all the time like the high-pitched humming of telegraph wires on a hot summer's day. It is light too, like a solitary little white cloud on the same hot day. Hundreds are like me.

The ringing carries with it a partial deafness, and this, in its turn, produces an isolation from the world about. You feel that your mind is a closed circuit, not quite making contact with the world outside. Perhaps a goldfish in its bowl, being carried from one room to another, would feel something like this.

Many say that their heads ring all day against cotton-wool walls inside. They don't want to think; they don't want to listen: just go where they have to go, do what they have to do and, at last, get back to camp and fall onto their bamboo slats.

With me it has a peculiar reaction. The isolation of deafness creates its own sounds: thin, distant-sounding music of astounding clarity—but *so* thin! This seems appropriate enough, for the music is from the past: it is the compulsive music of the bugle. Upon the slightest provocation, or on none at all, bugle-calls sound in my head . . . over and over . . . another and another: one tailing the other, or hogging the stage and playing on and on like a little boy showing off. Each call drags in its own wake memories of all the places I have heard it before.

For fourteen years now, ever since I first joined the Navy, I have been chasing the demands of a bugle. The first night I heard Sunset, the First Post and the Last Post; nostalgic, haunting, romantic. The next morning there was the cold awakening at 5.30 a.m. to the Reveille, the harsh blast of Out Pipes, followed by the ruthless demand of Both Watches. For fourteen years they have never stopped for me: no wonder they play now! I have just reckoned it up and, on a normal peace-time day, between 5.30 a.m. and Lights Out at 10 p.m., there would be forty-five calls demanding this or that. War has increased this number.

Liberty Men: Hobart, Melbourne, Sydney, Brisbane, Perth, Suva, Tahiti, New York, Portsmouth, Durban . . . and all the rest . . . but, for some reason many times in Jamaica. Kingston . . . Our first war stamping ground . . . a friendly and earthy place . . . black people without illusions . . . and the Liberty men receiving their last instructions before landing: '. . . Beware of rum and syphilis.'

All at once I hear *Repel Aircraft* . . . dusk in the Mediterranean . . . the twice repeated call: *There's a bomber over there! There's a bomber over there!!* Two Italian torpedo bombers low on the water in the dim dusk that is now almost full night . . . we have been closed up to Stand-to-the-Sunset for almost two hours— we were just about to fall out . . . the lookout just fluked them in his glasses . . . a quick wheel order . . . turn into the spread . . . and they miss us . . . sheer luck.

Liberty Men goes again, but right on top of it *Both Watches*— fooled again . . . no going ashore this time . . . stream P.V's instead . . . the ship is rolling heavily to an Atlantic swell just outside Halifax, Nova Scotia . . . steep rolls, almost gunwales-under . . . your weather leg is bent double and your lee one stretched straight to keep you up . . . a thick fog closes your world to a small room of sight and sound, within the circular glow of the yard-arm group to help us find the maze of gear . . . we roll right down to port and the ocean swell heaves up almost to our feet and is shot pea-green with the incandescence of electric light . . . there is a splash, and both paravanes are slipped . . . they run below the water just outside the ship like submarine ghosts, and the towing wires hum on the shoe which grinds on the stem as the ship plunges deeply, forging ahead . . . the fo'c'stle, cleared of men now, washes down all night in the great licking swell. . . .

*

There was a new man in our party today. Now, Billy has a ritual about a new face on his jobs: he always hits it and snarls at it. He seems to resent any intruder in our tight little clique. As we arrived on the job, we were fallen in amongst newly barked logs which were still slippery with sap. Billy had a thick piece of bark like a cricket bat in his hand. As he walked along the front rank, he saw the new face, and he hit it with the piece of bark.

The man reeled backwards on to the slimy log, slipped off it, and fell to the ground quite groggy. Before he could recover, Happy, Billy's lieutenant, jumped in and started to kick the fallen man about the head and shoulders with his rubber boots. He kicked the man unconscious and went away obviously feeling pleased with himself. In the turmoil of starting work we managed to drag the man under a bush where he could recover.

A little while later, six men were bringing a log down the slippery hill. The man was in the way. They stopped the log and a couple went to move him. Happy screamed that they were to stay with the log. They pointed out that the man was in the way. Happy said to drag the log over the man; but some others quickly dragged him aside.

Then Billy saw him. He must have thought, 'One man *yasume! Damme-do-no!*' He hauled the man to his feet by his hair. It was not far from a forty-four gallon drum of water at the dynamite hut. He dragged the man over to it and soused him in it. Then he slapped the man's face, back and forth, with his hand. More splashing, and more slapping: groggily the man began to revive.

The reviving man came back to consciousness shaking his head up and down and saying, 'Thank you, Thank you,' as if Billy were an angel of mercy. Billy pushed him staggering down the hill to work.

*

There was a lot of bamboo drill today: we all caught it. I got a kick on my ulcerous shin from an impatient Nip. The pace quickens. We erected four trestles and dragged all the timber for them from the jungle. It was after 10 p.m. when we got in, with only a shaving of moon to come home by. I did not bath nor lick my wounds, but tumbled straight on to my bed.

And, as soon as I was asleep, there were the bloody Japs waiting for me, and they worked me until reveille. The biting bugs lent reality to the dream. Each morning we feel more tired than the one before.

*

527

We are looking forward to the 30th to see what will happen. This is Sunday and there are three more days to go. How we are hanging on, I don't know. I think the doctors are a bit baffled too. They have to send out men who are totally unfit, and somehow those men stick it. You can still hear occasional snatches of song: even at reveille, in the dark, in the rain.

*

We have two cases of cholera in the camp. I have heard that in a camp, just this side of Tarsau, there have been seventy cholera deaths. A travelling Roman Catholic priest was said to have passed the disease on.

It is hard to sift rumour from fact in this crazy life—the more unlikely, the more likely to be true. *For the wildest dreams of Kew are the facts of Khatmandhu, And the crimes of Clapham, chaste in Mataban.*

*

The latest 'official' forecast: 'We move to Konyu in seven days and stay there a month, doing light work. The sick will be evacuated by river from there. Finally, we will move south.'

*

Our second bridge is all but finished. Only two trestles and the corbels remain to be done.

*

Three hundred English have come into camp, and there is a party fixing up a camp near No. 4, down by the river. Are these our reliefs? Now the ground is too fertile for rumours, and men are being panicked by everything they hear: a despondency sets in. 'I can't see us ever getting out of here!'

We are jittery between hope and fear. Tempers are vile over childish things which normally would be taken no notice of. And, yet, bitter and endless though it may seem, men somehow understand how it is with each other.

*

During the day five more English men died of cholera, and two of dysentery. These English are careless. They drink from wayside pools, they wash their mess gear below our showers, their own officers make no provision for getting the men boiled water. Stories of their officers are not pretty ones. They have taken a larger tent than they need, leaving the men much more overcrowded. They are waited on by batmen, and spend their time in self-seeking and self-protection. English cholera suspects now stand at twenty.

*

I slept almost work-free last night and feel a lot better. This is the 30th, the day on which so many have pinned their hopes of a *Yasume*; a move; and so on. But there are no real indications that tomorrow, or tomorrow, or tomorrow will be any different. Where, once, small things gave hope, now they are signs of worse to come.

This closes the bridal month of June.

The Leaf insect—pale green with rust blemishes ; yellow-green on underside

X

Hintok River – July

IN THE dark, before reveille, I was told to pack up: I would be moving down to the River Camp with eighty men.

The track down was as greasy as the inside of a banana skin, and was grooved in the middle, making it impossible not to slip constantly into the centre and tangle your feet. We went out through the English camp. They were digging graves in the swamp as we went past. Near the river it became more treacherous and I came down, with the whole weight of a tent I carried on top of me, and twisted my knee. The coverings had come off my leg ulcers: rubbed raw, they were suppurating down my shins. I cursed, really wanting to weep.

We dumped all our gear in an uncleared patch of jungle by the river. 'All right! That's where you live. What are you waiting for?' the officers told us. They also told me that I was in charge of the party. We cleared the ground, pitched the tents, dug drains and cut tracks. Our officers did not come near us; and the men did not want to work, even for themselves. We got some soup and rice at 8 p.m. I ate in the dark after I had seen the others through, and went to bed dirty. We have had no time to build beds and are sleeping on the ground.

*

Up at 5.45 a.m., floundering around in the dark trying to organize meals. The officers are not interested. We just made it before the Japs grabbed us and marched us out to work as No. 2 dayshift. We carried all the tools to the new job, which is knocking the top off a hill. We have no time to ourselves and it is impossible to take any cholera precautions, such as sterilizing our dixies before a meal. The officers have made absolutely no provision for it. I am having trouble organizing boiled water, and we are often waterless for the day on a hot, rocky hillside. To add to the danger, several hundred Tamils have been camped upstream on the creek we draw our water from. Some men still weaken on the job and drink unboiled water. Generally, when this happens, the crowd howl down the offender.

Our camp site, as God made it, is a good one. It is in the shadow of tall, straight-trunked trees with leaves a foot in diameter. There are clumps of tall, green bamboo making a dapple of light and shade in green and gold. But we don't admire the view much.

I have been meaning to mention my working trousers for some time. Carlyle would not know where to put them in his *Sartor Resartus*. Aprons or trousers? They are not so much a combination, as a sad relic of one, and a poor imitation of the other. They were made as white Dutch recreation-shorts, but cast in a peculiar mould. Imagine the lower half of an egg with two cigarettes stuck out, leg-like, below, and you have the sort of shape they were fashioned for. The umbilical circumference is the greater by far, and it has a tape through it. I had to split the legs up because they were too narrow. Now, time has split them further, right to the waist. The stitching between the legs has also gone, and the garment is now a double, back-and-front apron. I wear a G-string, which is a knife lanyard about my waist, with a piece of mosquito net, eight inches by two feet, draped fore-and-aft.

*

We have a party of Malay Volunteers and odds and ends, here. They are a good crowd and work without bellyaching. Among them are two finely tattooed Indian Army soldiers. One has three four-masted barques sailing around his chest and back; the other has a large angel and two flying birds from his neck to his navel.

*

Forty more came down from the Road to join us. Among them was an aspiring general, so I relinquished my dubious command. My chaps cut up rough about it. But I was only too happy.

Last night there were some Thai barges at the landing. The Nips did some trading—beer was 25c.: women were five ticals.

*

Today, two of our fellows blacked-out and lay where they fell. Nippon walked by, unmoved. We came by with heavy rails on our shoulders and could do nothing. Temperatures of 101 and 103 are common enough. All at once a man blacks-out, or doubles up with sudden pain and starts vomiting.

*

We had rain last night and, although the tent leaked, our home-made slush-lamp (pig-fat and rag in an old tin) gave a long, wobbling, smoky yellow flame that was cosy. I keep this written up at odd times. I now feel that it is an obligation to tell of the times.

The luminous fungi make a strange sight at night. The odd, stencilled patterns of witch-fire hang down from the blackness like ghosts.

*

We are putting in cuttings, and building spurs of embankments out from the hills with the spoil. We are now night shift. At work we are hemmed in by trees and hills; we can see only the ragged tops of a mountain, east and west, sometimes grey, sometimes indigo. Because we see only a small section of the sky, we cannot see the approaching weather. It rained until after 8 p.m., when we sat shivering and ate our rice. Even hard work did not warm us up, and our hands went numb. The diary got wet at first, but I rigged a shelter of leaves for it. I take it with me all the time and scribble into it as I can.

After dark we lit big torch flares and three large bamboo fires to work by. The torches gave a flame the colour of a newly risen moon on a hazy horizon. A velvety plume of black smoke poured up from them. We moved tremendous quantities of rock to try and get warm, but, after midnight, we began to slow down. All we got was a Gargantuan scream, '*SPEED-EROO! SPEEDEROO!*' and other sounds which defy phonetic notation. *Fortissimo* and *crescendo* might be all right for Wagner, but they are too insipid for Molly. Molly—short for Molly the Monk—is a huge, black haired Japanese sergeant of ape-like proportions.

Before daylight we had cleared all the rock. Then we came home along the rain-greased track, led by the elongated rubbery glow of the dying torches which went out before we got home.

*

We were pulled out of bed at noon and spent hours fooling about getting oil and stuff for the flares. Then, at 4 p.m. we marched back to the job for the night. There is every sign of the Wet Season moving in to stay now. On the job we are without both shelter and clothes.

I am in charge of this gang which has sardonically christened itself the 'Dirty Thirty'. We don't even get time to wash. I have to act as go-between for the men, and odd jobs come my way. Today, for instance, I heard a voice call from the jungle. I moved toward it to hear better. A man too sick to move? Colic? Cholera? I found the man: he was in a mess. I told him to clean up as best he could, there were plenty of wet leaves. He said he couldn't. I made a dozen suggestions. All the time he repeated he couldn't. He sat there quite convinced that it was now all my affair. I even had to threaten him to get him up to a tub of water by the blacksmith's shop, then bully him to make him wash himself. All the time he was telling me I was not doing my job. He spent the rest of the night with no pants, and a green Dutch coat tied by the arms about his waist as an apron.

*

The river is rising and covering our spring water supply. The weather is dull with a wetness that gets into everything. Two

Water chain, Hintok River. August 1943

died at the Road Camp—one of cholera, one of dysentery and beri-beri.

Three hundred Eighth Division moved in here today, saying that they were only here for five days and were then going south. It seems this section will soon be finished.

*

Our dirtiness increases with the wet and mildew. At this point, writing close to many deaths and having no guarantee of living on, I must philosophize: to sum-up where I stand in all this. I don't pretend to state it precisely or finally, but my philosophy seems to be working in some practical way. I can give it no precise definitions; I can only suggest that it should be read with what Spinoza calls 'knowledge of the third kind'.

I feel that, in each of us, there is a basic harmony or pattern which may well be the sum-total of the particular ancestral experience of the individual. Anyway, assume the basic pattern. This, the invisible skeleton we are moulded onto, is unconscious,

534

and goes on in spite of plausible explanations, philosophical schools, or religious sects. It is not changed by *them*, though *they* may be by it. This is our real shape; but it is *not* unchangeable.

Now, where this is apropos to the present moment is whether our shape is able to keep constant under conditions of adversity: this is the test of its integrity. It is not a matter of making an intellectual attack on our problems: it is a matter of whether we have that *feel* for things which is our intuitive weapon. I feel, given the chance, which we are hardly given by modern Western materialism, this deep knowledge can outstrip egoistic intellect. And our circumstances can tell us, too, whether we have 'mumbo-jumbo-ed' to some intellectual phantom not worth a damn. It seems to me that in the constancy of this real shape is the preservation of a man. I don't mean, by this, that a cholera germ will have no effect on him; but that he may be helped to fight it.

That is not very clear, perhaps. But what I am doing about it, here and now, is to try and clear away those constipations of a whole spirit: I mean hate, fear, anger, jealousy, discontent, avarice, covetousness, and that kind which comes from vain pride.

*

I was talking with one of the Japs on night shift. He told me that the railway—285 miles—would be finished in a month. In twenty days the rails would be here. He said, 'When railway finish—Engrissoo come bomb! Boom, boom!' I said, 'No bloody good—we would have to stick it up again, then.'

*

It is dull weather, under constantly dripping trees. We stand or work, like cattle in the rain, day and night with only a few rags clinging coldly to us. Beds are always damp, feet always caked with mud so that one sleeps with it six inches up one's legs, which are too muddy to pull under the blanket.

Low clouds, wet and weeping, tear themselves open on

mountain crags, steaming down into the river valley. The night is a procession of rain squalls and fogs. In the fantastic light of torch flames men become stiff robots of attenuated shadow, projected like cubist art upon the swirling screen of fog: as if their solid origin were dead, and this wandering thing, their shadowy soul.

We shovel rock, picking it out with bars and breaking it up with hammers, so that we can move it. We pass it over the side of the bank along a standing chain of men. Nippon, hooded in a raincoat, sits huddled by the fire and is scarcely more comfortable than we are. Sometimes he comes and stands at the brink of the cutting, looking down on us, hoping the work will soon be done, yet making us dig down to the last crack of solid rock so that the drillers will have a good start.

*

Each man, no matter how miserable, looked forward to the hot rice, and pork soup we knew the rest of the camp had had for supper. Camp workers and day workers have had it; now we gloat because ours is still to come and we have worked hard for it. Thirty men stand silently in a single file, impatient with an intense expectation that stills the tongue. The orderlies have a steep hazardous climb—over fifty deep, slippery steps up from the river. They could lose the lot in the dark and wet. At last the mess orderlies came back. Three buckets of sugarless pap, and no drink!

The cook had coolly told the orderlies that there were no late meals! He had given our meal away as back-up to the camp duties. We all wanted to murder some one. I shook an officer, demanding to know more about it. I said, dramatically, that thirty men had been robbed of a meal that could mean the difference between life and death; but it stirred no sympathy in that officer. He was responsible, but *he had forgotten!* The men abused him unmercifully, and I didn't care to stop them. At last, he gave us a spoon of sugar each and promised to do something about it. He could not have been more Japanese in his attitude.

In the morning at 9.45 a.m., after the men had had only a few hours sleep, they were hauled out to peel veg for the soup they mightn't get. The Q.M. reprimanded me for complaining over the stolen meal. This was a bit too much for me. I could see in my mind, a tight little group, safe in camp, looking after themselves and making sure it would not be them who would die: let the lesser breed do that. I could have abused him then with the grossest insults. But all I said was, 'It's a pity you don't have to swing a pick or a hammer alongside some of these sick men sometimes. If this is your Army form, I'm bloody glad I went to sea!'

*

I have been given ten extra men today, but the names of only nine. The officers can't tell me who the other one is—but I have to produce him to the Japs, tonight. I told them a few elementary things and did not improve my relations with the Orderly Room.

*

The daily blasting along this section is terrific, like a war approaching. The long trestle bridge the Tamils were building has collapsed like a house of cards. It now lies flat, with the trestles intact. The rails are in sight from the 150-kilometre peg. Rain continues and the river threatens the cookhouse. Some barges came up today and we were able to get some canteen supplies from them. Food has improved a little.

*

I am lucky. The Dirty Thirty are not a bad crowd to work with. Our yarn-spinning in the tent has pulled us together and we have a little *esprit de corps* of a tattered sort. I have managed to get almost all of them to tell some tale or other. But, as these men are soldiers and farmers, they keep at me for sea stories.

We work a little game on the Japs. As Number 1, I am expected to drive the men for the Japanese. So I yell at the men in a rough overbearing manner and the Nips think I am, '*Yuroshi* [good] Number 1.' But the Japs don't know that what

I am yelling at the men is a string of awful insults about our bosses and their ways, what we think of them, and what we would like to do with them. But it has practical results, for when I ask for a man to be allowed to *yasume*, sometimes they allow it. The Nips on this job are relatively tame, if handled rightly—and that is a big strain off our nerves and tempers.

Just the same, I have noticed that, in our present state, we *must* growl; so, if the men are not venting their tempers on the Nips, they fall into argument among themselves.

*

It was a long shift from 4.30 p.m. to 7.30 a.m. We had taken no meal with us. At midnight the Nips called, '*Oi, Oi! Michie, Michie!*' I told them we had none. They wanted us to send back to camp for it. I spoke with the men and we all decided that we would rather go without than risk losing it over the greasy track in the dark.

We got back to camp in the morning and, after only three hours sleep, we were hauled out by our own people and put to work on camp duties. I protested, but got nowhere. I think that we are being cut down to size by our Orderly Room for having been too outspoken.

The cutting we are working on is supposed to be finished to-day, and the rails to be here in two days. They say the steam train will be here in twenty days.

There were nine new cases of cholera at the Road today, and there is a strong rumour that all except the choleras will move down here in two days.

Captain Bret Moore has gone to Tarsau for mail: we are always shuttlecocks between hope and fear. Only this minute, through the tent walls, I could hear a sentence spoken by a Jap being repeated, 'Speedero, speedero. Thirty more days and all men come back.' First, we have a siding to put in at the Hintok station. By that time the big cutting at the Kinsayok end of this section will be completed. Right on top of that, comes the rumour that we will then be pushed into Burma.

*

A crowd arrived down from the Road today and the camp was a hive of news and rumours. No more sick are to be discharged from hospital; they are to be sent to Tarsau. The Road will be a cholera camp. There are now thirty cases. Three died yesterday and one, so far, today. O and P Battalions are moving *up*. More recent arrivals are moving back. The Colonel has complained. The story goes that Java troops are lucky they have been treated as well as they have, for the Japs consider them, not as British, but as mercenaries. One can only speculate where that one began.

*

We went to work at 7 p.m. It was a different job: to help put up the collapsed Tamil bridge. It was a crowded, noisy scene. Men stumbling about in the dark, hauling logs or tailing on to derrick falls and purchases, by yellow torchlight. The sheaves in the blocks were constantly clogging with mud and sticks, defying any effort to move them, until we scraped them out again. We worked the whole night and did not get back until 8 a.m. It was like the Tower of Babel—Tamils, Chinese, Malays, English and Australians; and the Japanese herding us about, shouting the common local pidgin, and underlining phrases with bamboo rods.

It rained until about 3 a.m. and the Tamils took large leaves, a foot to eighteen inches across, and tied them over their heads like Quaker bonnets, with bits of vines under their chins. Otherwise, like us, they were practically naked. When they work, they make a din something between an Oriental New Year and an Irish wake. This noise seems to take all their skill and energy. But they maintain a seething activity through it all.

We were plagued with bamboo lice which crawled over us in thousands and bit us everywhere, but especially about the face and neck. The rain and the damp and, probably, the Tamil uproar, seemed to stir them up. They fly and, though they are microscopic, they have a vicious bite.

Going back the men were so tired that they cursed the Tamils as obscene boongs, only because they were talking a tongue the men did not understand and it jangled their nerves.

*

I am back on day work, at last. I was detailed to take out fifty men. It was a day of bedlam amongst deep, black mud and the black bodies of noisy Tamils.

The river is rising fast and the cookhouse was only just saved by calling out all hands to move it from the swirling waters. There is something about this large surging stream, so swollen with menace, as if it would be glad to sweep away the lot of us and go on, chuckling and tearing at its banks with malicious satisfaction.

*

I went over to the hospital to see Otto tonight. He is a mere skeleton; his eyes are sunken and ringed with a wide band of withered, black skin. The tissue-paper skin of his head is pulled in ugly creases over the clear insertion of his lower jaw into the skull; the bridge of his cheekbones, just above this, is indeed a bridge of the limits of suffering. He looks like death. Very simply, he promised me he would get better. 'This is not the worst thing I have had to put up with,' he said.

I came away feeling guilty, for I am relatively healthy. Except for malaria clinging to me all the time, my troubles are only mechanical. My body does not look very different from normal: the soft layer on top has thinned a bit, that's all.

*

Today was fine with a wind change to the north-west, after days of sou'easters chasing loose cloud up the valleys to envelop mountains and pour their insides out on us.

During the forenoon, two men collapsed with malaria. I was able to get them *yasumed*. During the dinner break two more went down with stomach trouble. One of them, I was certain, had cholera; he could not walk. The others could only shuffle with the greatest difficulty. I haggled with the Nip corporal all

Two malarias with a cholera. Hintok, July 1943

afternoon to be allowed to send them back. He roared and swung at me with whatever he had in his hand at the time— shovel, bamboo, or hammer—but I moved discreetly and none of the blows fell solidly. At last, about 4 p.m., with a couple of petulant blows, he said they could go. I asked how many men were to take them in. He said, none: the other sick could do it. I said they couldn't. He swung again, squealing, *Baka-eer-oo!* Then he said they could crawl. I could move him no further.

I got the two malarias standing up, and then got the cholera between them, with his arms about their necks. They made a wobbly tripod. I asked the malarias to see if they could get him to the end of the cutting, about 500 yards away, where there was a cave. They could leave him there, and go on into camp for help. If none came, we would pick him up as we came back from work.

I watched them go—the two malarias, with the cholera about their necks. They were bowed and sweating with pain and concentration, trying not to collapse. The man with cholera was limp between them with his head lifelessly on his chest, hanging like a crucified man. His knees were buckled and his feet dragged. His trousers, which were ripped across the back in two places revealing his skinny, fouled buttocks and stringy thighs, were unbuttoned at the waistband, and, as the others dragged him along with slow, shambling gait, his pants kept falling about his knees. The two men had to stop and pull them up before they could go on. One of the malarias reached over to pull them up: they wobbled, then, they all fell over. Slowly they dragged themselves up again and staggered along the cutting until they came to the cave. Later the stretcher party, making their fourth trip, came out and picked up the cholera.

*

Although the mail arrived yesterday, we did not get it until tonight. I received three from my wife, dated June, July and August last year. What they meant to me is not easily told.

Unfortunately, not all letters the men got did the same. One man got a letter to say his wife had been killed in a car accident. Another found out that his wife had gone off with a man who, she said, 'had the courage to stay in Australia to defend it'. Another man got a letter from a well-wisher saying he ought to know that while he was away, his wife was being unfaithful all over the town. Another one was told in a letter from his wife that there was a new baby in the house, and he was not the father.

*

Five died of cholera last night and Bob Costin was one of them. Because Bob has always been so cheerful and alive, this came all the more as a shock. He never knew whether he was a widower or a husband—whether his wife had recovered from that emergency operation. When the mail was being given out Bob was already on a stretcher being taken over the difficult track to the cholera-camp at the Road. On the twisting and jolting stretcher he suffered the pain and outpourings of cholera. He apologized to the carriers for being a nuisance. At last they got him there. A messenger with the mail arrived soon after with three letters for Bob. But Bob was dying, and he never read them. He died with his wedding unconsummated, and these letters from his wife unread. He never knew that he was not a widower.

*

I have a new job today, which is a bit of a break. I am *Maccan Boy*. I wait in camp and work under the Nips and, at about 11 a.m., I pick up their dixies of freshly cooked rice and take them out to the Japs on the job. This saves them eating sour rice, as we have to, for dinner.

Billy is down with malaria, but he still supervised the digging of a kitchen I had to do, before I went out. I noticed the great number of scars on Billy's close-cropped head—like hieroglyphics of his past. When I got back to camp at about 4 p.m. with the empty dixies, Billy gave me a packet of Red Bull cigarettes and said, 'O.K.-da! Come back house.' This meant that I could go back to my tent. There is something childlike, sometimes, about this ogre. One of the other Japs here in camp today was Willy the Wop. He is also known as Noisy, because he seldom says a word; he does not like the army and does not mix much with the others. He has only been known to hit a man once. He is entrusted with the simplest jobs.

*

A report has come down from a camp up the river: they have had 300 deaths in three days. Even though it is a Dutch camp, this sounds exaggerated to me; but it indicates the general conditions and the depressed atmosphere we live in. Many of the Dirty Thirty are now dead.

There is a private aspect of this cholera plague. Naturally, no man knows when his turn is coming, and I don't think there is a man here who does not think that it could be any day, any hour. He sees it happening all the time. So he watches anxiously, and if what comes away is white, he can be fairly sure it is cholera, and he feels a shadow pass over him. When he goes out in the night and watches, it will *always* be white—in the moonlight. So he lives with uncertainty until daylight.

*

I have just turned out my pack, which is sodden. My drawings and diaries seem all right—I keep them well wrapped, but I have to watch for mildew. The pack is alive with hundreds of bugs, and the stitching is white with nits. The bugs I killed and evicted, but it is impossible to get all the nits.

The river is so dirty that distilling water takes a long time. This is done on an apparatus made by the Heath Robinsons of the camp, from stuff they have scrounged and stolen, chiefly from the Nips. The distilled water is used to try and save the lives of the choleras. An intravenous saline drip is given to them. Because we cannot make enough here, two men travel back and forth to the Road all day. They have made their last trip for the day as late as 4 a.m. They each carry two bottles in haversacks. They are young men with exceptional stamina. Even so, they are given some of the offal and the blood of the slaughtered beasts to keep them going.

*

I am still Maccan Boy. There was very heavy rain last night. Many decided to go without breakfast. They stayed in until called out to work parade. I asked Billy, 'I wait house?' He wagged his shorn head in assent. So here I am writing this until it is time to take out their rice.

I am back, after going out to the job with the rice. I made my way through the Tamil camp, my hands full with seven dixies, my waterbottle at my belt, and my haversack and dixie across my shoulders. I felt my way gingerly through the four inches of slush for a firm footing on the hard, greasy bottom. I felt my way close around the bole of a tree.

But I forgot the waves in the ground caused by the radiating roots. My feet shot from under me and I landed on my back, my waterbottle imbedding itself in my hip. From behind my ears to my heels I was submerged in unthinkable Tamil slush. My arms had instinctively shot into the air to save the dixies of rice, so that I had no hand to save myself from the mess. There was no chance of washing then. I boiled inside, caught between indignation and plain misery. When I got back at 4 p.m., I got rid of what the rain had not washed off.

*

The colonel in charge here told the men on parade last night that beards were not regulation in the Australian Army: men with beards were to remove them. Those without razors were to borrow them. Razor blades are rare and rusted—nobody would think of lending them. Our camp-officers stood by the colonel: sleek, shaved and bathed, wearing washed shirts, shorts, and good leather boots. They faced dirty, gaunt men with rags of beards and rags of clothes, who were very tired and who had not had a chance to wash. They let out a frank, abusive growl. The colonel roughly called them to order and told them that their discipline was disgraceful.

*

A Nip was killed at the compressor cutting. A stone was dislodged from the top and rolled on him. I said to Buck, 'I suppose the wet loosened it.' Buck shook his head, 'I know the joker,' he said.

*

Tonight the men were slack in getting out on parade at *Tenko*: they had only just come in from work. The sar'majors were calling out, 'Shake it up, there! On parade 17 Company— On parade 25 Company! Move out there!'

From the tents came ironical cries. 'Tell the colonel that I'm having a shave!' and, 'hold the show up, old chap. I must shave!'

*

Maccan Boy again. My feet are troubling me more. I had a restless night with the throb and itch, and it is hard to tell which is worse. They are severely cut, but dressings for them are out of the question. The cuts get on as well as they can with the mud packed tight into them. The tenderness almost screams when my feet strike split bamboo, sharp sticks or rocks—or bamboo thorns.

About fifty men were hastily gathered together yesterday and sent back to Tarsau. Roy was one of them. He has constant dysentery and his legs have broken down with ulcers. He was not strong to begin with.

*

On my way back with the empty dixies today, I met the distilled water messengers. They told me Otto was dead and had been burned last night. Only Jim and Mac were there for the Navy. Somewhere up there, in this grey-green jungle, a fire burned and in the smoke was Arthur Lund, able Seaman, R.A.N., with his few pitiful effects. He followed Bob by only a few days—I don't know how many, for each day is just another one until it is all over. But, for Otto, it is either all over, or it has just begun. Otto, here, was a willy-nilly soul; so much wanting to find his way when he talked with me so earnestly. True to youth, he could scoff and disbelieve the things he had not experienced, yet he would say it would be *beaut* to have some of those things. He had hoped that they were in his future. At the last he must have wondered what it was all about: whether it was easier to live or die. He had told me he would resist to the last; but, underneath, I think, he was the simple creature of a fate he believed all-powerful.

The orderlies told how Otto, under the wearing strain, had bawled them out and told them to leave him alone. He tore out the intravenous drip. 'What's the use?' he said. Weary had tried to tongue-lash him back to a will-to-live. Meekly then, Otto had said, 'All right, Sir, I won't go crook any more.' Nor did he. Later, he quietly pulled out the tube, and died. This thirteen-stone boy, who galloped the rugby line, died a shrunken skeleton of five stone—no more. He was not yet twenty.

*

At 10 p.m. last night stretcher bearers were called out. Somewhere back in the jungle came the notes of the Last Post. The babbling murmur of the camp stopped and all the men outside stood still. When the last notes of the Cavalry Reveille had faded, almost with a sigh the murmur started up again. The acrid smell of the pyre drifted across the camp and, in the smoke, another man was gone.

*

Today as I was taking the seven dixies out, I stopped by the side of the track. In the shallow top compartment of each dixie was an omelette. This was too much for me, and I thought it too much for them. So, taking my spoon from the band of my hat, I lifted the lid of each in turn, and carefully trimmed each one. I heard a noise and looked up: there was a Jap ten yards away. I slipped the lid on, fumbled my spoon, and made out

I was getting a fresh grip on the handles. I was sure he had seen me, but I was brazen. It was our carpenter, and he knew me. I gabbled, '*Yasume-ca?*'

With sad, droopy eyes, he said, '*Beoke* [sick] *Takusan beoke* [malaria].' I gave him his dixie. He said, '*Arigat . . .*' and touching his head, muttered, '*Damme, damme*—no gooda!' and stumbled away.

*

My feet were worrying me when I got back. I have to probe them in several places with a safety pin to relieve them. I went over to the R.A.P. to bathe them in a bamboo basin, and I was late parading with the gang when they came in. The corporal whined, 'YOU! No gooda! *Damme, damme! Bakaeer-oo!* Maccan Boy no gooda! *Ashita*, changee, changee.' So I got the sack, and a bashing about the head.

*

Kaley is buying up food like a plutocrat, with his looted money. He is the best-conditioned man in camp. Yet he hangs about the sick bay and gets in at every opportunity. He uses any means to do it. Back at the Road, he was buying specimens of men's stools and being admitted to hospital with dysentery.

*

I have noticed something that seems to have crept on us. I have heard men on the job ask somebody if it has stopped raining. Several times I have had to take a second look myself. We put out our hands to test. We begin to understand how cattle feel.

*

Two more died last night. These men had been constant mates. They had shared their whole war together. They ate together and shared everything they had. They were partners on hammer and tap. They caught cholera together and died in the same hour; they were cremated on the same pyre.

Though cholera still kills, it seems to have lost some of its dreadfulness, as patches of sunshine slow the death rate.

*

Today is fine and hot. I get deadly tired, especially my legs. It was very hot swinging a pick on the rocks, and it magnified our tiredness. Then came the rain. At first it was refreshing. But the wind came and chilled us. And the tracks home were the last straw. I had been congratulating myself on my improved feet, when I ran my foot along a buried piece of split bamboo: in a moment, my big toe was kippered. I suffered more mental than physical pain.

*

Today I worked alongside a young marine who had been present at the sinking of *Prince of Wales* and *Repulse*. He told me of one man washed down a quarterdeck hatchway by a torpedo explosion; washed forward, through the mess decks and up through another hatch to a gundeck. He said it took six or seven minutes. The time may be exaggerated but the rest might well be true. He also told me of something he saw while he watched the *Prince of Wales* sink. He was watching a Carley float with seven men on it. They were paddling hard, away from the sinking ship, with their backs to her. Behind them the *Prince* was slowly heeling over toward them; while they were shouting and singing in ribald relief at being clear of her. The flooding ship sucked water back into herself. Slowly the unknowing survivors were being pulled back—still singing. Over, and over she heeled until the tops of her large funnels levelled with the sea, and the water rushed in. In one great gulp, the seven singing survivors were swallowed.

In *Repulse*, the engine-room crew had been trapped. Some of the boiler-room's crew climbed up inside the funnel which was very hot. At the top they were stopped by steel mesh they could not loose. He had heard them being burned to death as he watched.

'Robby' his mates call him. He is tall and pale, with a black curly beard. He told me he had escaped from Singapore on a sub-chaser, with a party of forty-eight. They hoped to make Java, refuel, and go on to Australia. They had been sunk by a Japanese cruiser near the southernmost island of The Seven Sisters, near Banka Straight. There was a rear-admiral, an air vice-marshal, a lieutenant and an Australian telegraphist among them. The telegraphist went mad, and was eventually left at Changi. The three officers died. Only twenty-three were left alive after five months isolation with very little food. They found a bag of rice and salvaged some tinned stuff from their wrecked boat.

'It were a proper fever island,' Robby said with a grin. 'It were enough to make anyone barmy, that island were.' At last they built a raft and ten of them set out for help. The Nips picked them up, and came back for the rest. Robby told me he had been in the Service about six years. He likes it and intends to stay and finish his twenty-one years.

*

As he was telling his tale, some one cried, 'Stand fast!' We all stood and faced the cortege of one Bob Lee, slowly shambling with difficulty along the elephant-churned track. Behind them came George, the bugler, with his cornet, looking as if he too belonged on the other side with the dead. The corpse was straight and stiff: face-down on a bamboo-and-bag stretcher, wrapped and tied in a rice sack. Feet-first and sharply down-pointed, in rigid calm he went. The shape of the wasted body was revealed in straight, rough sculpture, as if Death had re-chiselled it.

It was the only death today—the last of July.

XI

Hintok River – August

I AM LIGHT duties because of bad feet. Light duties—we were given a trip to Hintok Road to bring down Engineers' stores! The rain started as we set out and made the track treacherous again. The mud and cold water seem to ease my hot, throbbing feet. Blackie came with me.

Hintok is practically a ghost camp, now. We ate our rice in the old Engineers' hut, which is rotting and leaking. We lit a fire inside it, and stopped shivering for a while. Blackie and I had to struggle back with a couple of large tents slung on poles. I was afraid for Blackie, in case he fell with this weight on him— he is so thin that, if it happened, I thought his legs would break like carrots. So I kept the load closer to my end of the poles.

We had to haul our load hand over hand up the cliff on the way out. Just before we got there, we passed the English cemetery. At first, there had been a rough attempt to put a wooden cross at the head of each grave. But, after a time the exhausted grave diggers, who were often the very next to be buried there, had only put so many sticks on each mound, to tell how many lay beneath.

We got back to camp about 5 p.m. There, Doc. Reece, the English doctor from the Road, told me to come over and he would put a dressing on the gash in my big toe. I stayed and talked with him for some time. He told me that, of the original 470 of his English, 120 had died since they came to Hintok. Eight more had died since they had come to the river. He estimated that, along this whole project, there would be 15,000 dead prisoners.*

*

---

* Lord Russell's final estimate was 16,000.

Rained all night. Reveille went with no one wanting to get up. Breakfast was only pap; there was nothing to drink because it had not been possible to get the water boiling. The dinner issue of rice was cut in half because, in the rain, the open fireplaces could not cook it in time. It was the heaviest prolonged rain we have had so far.

Slowly the trees showed themselves against the steel-grey sky of the dim jungle dawn. It was cheerless, and the men kept turning their minds away from having to go to work. Fall-in sounded. Some still sat about in the leaky tents; some of us got out. Wet and miserable, we stood waiting on parade. Okada came out and told us to *yasume* until the rain stopped. So, now, we pray it will last for ever. It gives me a chance to write this up.

*

There is a story that 50,000 coolies are coming up.

The Tamils have a way of their own with cholera patients.

At Hintok River camp the Tamils build a shrine over an anthill. An old tin on a bamboo with a couple of joss-sticks, and a lime impaled on a tin trident

A rough shelter of bark or leaves or rags, about two feet high, is put up out in the bush and the man is left there, in it. In a shirt, but without trousers, he lies there on a bag or the sodden ground. He stays there to die or crawl back, if he gets better. When they die they are left to rot, and contaminate the whole valley with cholera.

*

Spent today in a dirt-cutting which the rain had turned into a morass of red clay. Newly dynamited stone chips were all about it like pieces of glass. The coarse hair roots of the bamboo cut like steel wire jags. The bare-footers spent the day sucking in their breaths and cursing.

Slithering down the track on the way home, I took the top off my little toe with a split bamboo. It now matches the one I did yesterday.

*

The tracks have become a morbid phobia with us. I have tried to puzzle it out. It seems to be a question of our vulnerability to nature: the tracks are a symbol of it. Man is vain and proud, liking to overlord creation. I remember how, out sailing or walking, I used to revel in wind and storm. I always had oilskins and woollen clothes and stout boots. At the end of the battle I would have a hot bath, a rub down, and a shift of warm, dry clothing—and a good meal. How brave I was!

But not any more. I am vulnerable. I squeal. Every little thing seems to be able to defeat me. Twigs attacking my feet, make me cringe; overhanging bamboos bang my head and rouse my silly temper. Even in our tents there is mud and water, shrivelling and festering my feet and drawing flies. Our comforts are snatched away: we are vulnerable—raw.

*

My feet are quite bad. I was put on light duties again. This proved to be both a misfortune and an experience. I was with a party of fifty, most of whom had bad feet. There were a lot with malaria who should have been in hospital. Of our fifty, only forty-three at last got to the job. One was taken back with cholera. Two more did not get there until 11.30 a.m. because of their feet.

First of all the Crow beat them; then Happy beat them. He punched and slapped them heavily; he hit them around the neck and head with an inch-thick, solid bamboo; he threw them to the ground with ju-jitsu trips. While one of them was on the ground, he got a blow which split his scalp. He was only down for a minute, but when he got up there was a pool of blood four inches across. The two beaten men helped each other away to the pits where they had to dig.

The Crow made me cover the blood with a shovelful of earth. But one of the men was still bleeding. We tried to get permission to get him back to a doctor. But they seemed afraid of having the blood-stained men seen. 'Washee-washee!' they screamed.

Unfortunately, the wounded man argued. Happy got furious and gave him a few powerful punches; then he stood and took a hard, two-handed swing with his heavy stick. It caught the man behind the neck, and I heard the sinews crunch. It lifted him off his feet and flung him down an eight foot bank. He just missed being impaled on a sharp bamboo stake at the bottom. He lay there, unconscious, for five minutes. The Nips kept calling to him roughly, 'Up-oo! Up-oo! Speak-oo! Speak-oo!' At last he got up and staggered to his pit.

*

We were working alongside a crowd of Tamils. They worked in gangs of twenty-five. When they had finished their task, they came and squatted on the new-heaped earth of it. They jabbered like excited monkeys to their overseer and the Japs. When they were sent home, they went like a crowd of kids just out of school.

Their midday meal was rice and soup. They had no dixies. Instead, they picked big leaves. They piled the rice on to these and then, as the soup was poured on to it, they kneaded it quickly in. Holding the leaves level with their mouths, they slurped it in, using the fingers of their eating hands like chop sticks. Before the meal, a man with a bucket of water (not boiled) lightly splashed each man's eating hand. It was a ritual.

*

George was with me out at No. 1 Cutting, shifting earth and rock. Just before dinner he collapsed in terrible pain. We pulled him under some bushes a little out of the rain.

By 2 p.m. I talked the Nip into letting me take him back into camp. I hung him over my shoulders, but my feet made me very unsteady. When we fell, I had to strain to let him down as lightly as possible. Every now and again the pain would seize him unbearably. I held him while he squatted to do the simplest thing. When the spasm exhausted itself, we went on. This happened a number of times.

George and I live within a couple of miles of each other in Melbourne. I spoke of the places we both knew so well, and of what we would do when we were back. George said he didn't think he would see them again. I got him to Doctor Corlette, who said it was a kidney colic and put him in hospital.

*

At work today, passing out lumps of rock along a human chain, I could not keep standing and had to squat. The flies tried to eat my festered feet, so I had to keep them buried in the mud. After a fortnight of this, I had had enough. I went to the doctor.

He said my feet did not look as bad as some of the others. I said I knew that they did not look as bad as some of the others, but for the moment, I had come to the end of my pride. I have seen feet here so ulcerated, blistered, cut and swollen, that they don't look like feet any more. Apart from the normal cuts and blisters, my feet have grooves running around them exactly like worm-eaten wood. I told the doctor that, no matter what they looked like, they had beaten me. He put me in hospital.

Now I feel like a malingerer: the prisoner of a cunning body.

*

Izzy has been down with amoebic dysentery for over a week now. His face is wizened and old. Horizontal lines run across his face and forehead, drawing them down at the outside. It is an expression of immobile, clown-like sadness: a slightly re-laxed mask of the grotesque grimace of Tragedy—but more tragic because I know this old and harrowed face is barely twenty years old.

I went over to the hospital lines today to see him. He had just staggered from under the flap of the grey, mildewed tent which hung in strips and holes, letting in the rain on the miserable sick beneath, and stood, swaying, a dirty grey-yellow figure, ankle deep in mud. His G-string hung slack, exposing him, and his legs were streaked. The worried look had become desperate, disgusted, and hopeless. He was black with mud down one side, and was looking about in a vacuous panic for a bam-boo (the only bed pans available: cut about eighteen inches long and open at one end). I got one for him and held it while he sat on the six-inch hole with trembling knees. His face screwed up; his body quivered and shrunk in agony. His eyes opened and rolled shut again. I had to stand behind him and steady him with my hands under his arms and the bamboo between my feet.

He shook each time his skinny little body knotted up, and he groaned with a low intensity that made me feel hopeless. It was raining, and this helped me to wipe him down. Then I carried him back to his split bamboo bed, four inches above the mud. I pulled the remnants of a dirty blanket over him and sat on the end of his bunk.

He opened his eyes.

'How are you, Izzy?'

'Not bad,' he said with a weak whisper.

'You'll be all right. You'll get over it—just try and stick it.'

He gave me a weak, grey smile and faintly shook his head, as if he had entered a realm of understanding I should never know.

'Yes, you will,' I said with crude attempt to shake off this feeling of inferiority. Another weak smile denied what I had just said. 'You *must* be getting better.'

'I don't think so, Chief. Yesterday . . . fifty-one times . . . today thirty-nine . . . so far. . . .'

Not twelve hours of the day had gone.

'. . . bamboos are awkward . . . fall off . . . bloody mess . . . disgusted . . . don't bother about 'em always.'

'You'll be all right—just hang on.'

It came out automatically: just to comfort *me*.

Again he gave me that strangely calm look. His head was a shrunken skull covered with wrinkled parchment like a mummy: it was no bigger than a decent sized fist. He had become a shrivelled relic before he was dead.

'You'll get back to the 'Loo and the sheilas there.'

He shook his head. It struck me that the grimace of anguish stamped into his face, now robbed of mobility, might have been the look on his mother's face when she had seen him come home drunk.

As if he had read my thoughts he said, 'This way . . . the Old Lady won't know . . . think I'm a hero . . . better like this. . . .'

I started to break in. '. . . . better like this,' he said.

*

I went over to the officers' lines today. Talking with an officer I was able to see something of how the officers live, in much cleaner circumstances, having plenty of time to themselves (excepting the doctors). It was pretty obvious that they had better access to the canteen supplies. This officer spoke to me of his diary. He must essentially see the show from a different angle.

My story is from the point of view of the men. I suppose it is bound to be partial. On certain things the officers have more information. A lot goes on of which we are not aware, and which we are too busy with our own affairs to think about. It would be hard to write this without some injustice to the officers. But it would not be true to say that the men have not felt bitterly towards the officers—sometimes with just cause.

*

An officer has been sacked from Quartermaster's duties. There was a question of a bag of *catchung idjoe*, 1,000 limes, and some bags of sugar that never got to us.

We had a boot issue today, but there were only four pairs for each section of thirty men. Yet, of those for our section, two pairs were given to men who had leather boots and had never been without boots for a day. All we can do about it is to curse foully those we think are responsible. I have tried to get some justice done, but the rackets are too tight. There seems to be a gang who are thoroughly organized for their own preservation. I would not exaggerate if I said that some of these men are as heartless as the Japs about the fate of the ordinary man here. At least the Japs have the excuse that they are our enemies, and they come into the open with their cruelty.

*

Weary has been down from the Road a couple of times. He seems in good health and high spirits. This, in itself, is a tonic to the men. It went around the camp when the workers came in, 'Weary's been down, and he looks well.' He is a symbol and a rock to us.

*

This is Friday, 13th. Two choleras died last night. One of them was Pinkie Bookman, a half-caste aboriginal. Ever since Konyu, he has been an especial victim of dysentery, but he has always been quiet and uncomplaining. The doctors, particularly, held him in high regard. This morning the Last Post and Reveille played him on. 'Poor old Pinkie,' they said, 'What a bonza bloke!'

*

Out to work on the compressor embankment. This has to be finished for the steam train which is due soon. The rails are through, but only barely good enough yet, for the motor trains. The steam train is said to be held up just now by a collapsed embankment between Tarsau and Konyu.

We were very late home, taking in all the picks, shovels, bars, baskets and hammers. The Jap officer said, 'All these men *yasume* tomorrow.'

Five motor trains were held up here this morning. They were loaded with sick. A large flat rock had slid down on to the track. A heavy wire rope was parted trying to haul it off. At last it had to be drilled and dynamited. There will be a lot of this sort of thing.

*

The Japs gave us a *yasume*. But our camp people preyed on us. When I brought the men in last night, I told the Orderly Room that we had been granted a *yasume*. 'What-ho, you can unload the barges tomorrow,' they gloated. This came from men who don't have to go out daily and face the Nips on the job; men who are better fed at our expense; men who complain all too loudly against the inhumanity of the Nips. We call them the White Nips.

*

Ken and Fatty are in the wood and water party, a pretty hard working lot. But Fatty says he would rather work hard and not have to face the Nips all the time. They also get a little extra food.

The doctor had said that Blackie must eat, in spite of diarrhoea. Ken and Fatty take him some of what they get, in an attempt to get him to eat. But Blackie says, 'What's the use?' Fatty bullies him comically, and they both give him pep talks. I have been with him too much, my words no longer have effect.

Ken and Fatty have built themselves a little bark hut, with a bunk on each side you can just squeeze between. Fatty told me that, once, after he turned in, he had been disturbed by a scratching sound which he could not make out. He thought it might be some swamp crabs cutting the bamboo with their claws. It was a fortnight before he found out what it was. Although Ken was a bare two feet from him in the dark, it had taken Fatty all this time to discover the scratching was Ken receiving the B.B.C. news through a small radio he had made in an old rusty jam tin. The senior officer in the camp was the only other person who knew of its existence, and he got the news from Ken. Ken, as our chief telegraphist, was well trained in keeping secrets. Of course, having mentioned this once between ourselves, we never referred to it again; nor did we get any of the news, except what came back to us as rumours. It is safer for the operator that nobody knows.*

We are always hoping for, and talking about, a possible move out. We have seen a lot of others go. No. 5 Bridge and No. 1 Cutting are finished. Of our original thousand there are about 450 in hospital and only 150 available for work just now.

*

I was out on No. 5 Bridge today, driving dog-spikes and gauging the track. It is one-metre gauge. It was a good job, calling for moderate skill in driving the spikes to pull the rails a little this way or that. Until now the track has been virtually ungauged, and only light traffic has gone over it. To look down the track has been like looking at two farewell streamers rolled out at random on a road.

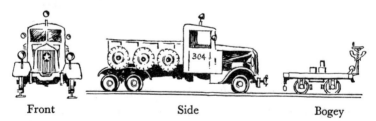

Front   Side   Bogey

Dual purpose diesel trucks with interchangeable pneumatic and flanged wheels. Bogey (right) when linked with another by rails, makes flat-topped cars to carry sleepers, rails, personnel. These were used until track was fit for steam trains

There have been a number of derailments; it is remarkable that anything has stayed on the rails at all. The motor trains are six-wheeled trucks with interchangeable flanged or pneumatic wheels. The wheels not in use bolt on the side of the truck.

* In the original diary this was only cryptically mentioned.

They are diesel, based on German design. The cars are simply bogeys, spaced with rails bolted into place, and with a few planks to carry passengers, who have to hang on for themselves.

*

Today I got the coveted job of *flag-man*. I sat on a rock at the end of the cutting where the line comes out in a curve on to the bridge. I was there to stop trains running down the men working on it, and I had a red flag and a green flag. I flagged three trains in the day. I was able to write this up between showers. I have an old respirator-haversack and I can keep the Diary separate in the back compartment. It is well stained, but remains legible.

*

I went to bed with the usual mud-caked feet. The passageway of the tent is ankle deep. Sometimes in the night, I wake up and feel that both my feet are in plaster casts; the heat of my feet has dried the mud. I sit up and peel them like taking the jackets off roast potatoes. I pull them up under my blanket, and feel the luxury of it.

Then I am visited again and have to get up. I come back with my feet in a fresh plaster cast that is still wet.

*

Izzy is dead. The boy we often called a lying, thieving larrikin is gone. From somewhere, in his last weeks, he produced an endurance and courage I greatly admired. He died better than many.

*

Again I am flag-man. I began the day as No. 1 of the gang. This is because a number of the erstwhile Number 1's who have always pushed themselves forward for the job, are now trying to get on the Tarsau list. These are fellows with good boots and more clothes than the rest of us. They are of the boot-racket and the *inner circle*. But when I got here, Billy handed me the flags.

I now had a chance of talking with some of the large crowd of coolies going up the line. Chiefly Tamils and Chinese from Singapore, they had walked most of the way. One Chinese told me that it was one month since they had left Singapore. I asked him about conditions in Singapore. He said succinctly, 'No —— good! No rice. No work. All men hungry. All men leaving. Nippon still there. Very small food on way up.' I could not but feel a surge of sympathy as they filed past, straggling, and those far behind, limping. There were old and young: some were only children of eight or nine. There were crippled and malformed; some, starvation had made ludicrous with skinny lankiness, buck teeth grinning sadly from sunken cheeks, beneath protruding eyes.

There were at least a thousand of them: they passed end-lessly. In some groups there were spurts of speech sounding like chiding or sobbing; some were silent. Now and then one of them would throw me a *good morning*, and perhaps a phrase of English. China, India; India, China. Men with luggage; men with nothing; army packs, buckets, baskets, cases, boxes, kerosene tins with lock-up lids, bags, bundles of blankets—or only a bundle handkerchief; strings of dried eels on bamboo poles; or flat, dried fish swinging in the wind like signs outside an English pub. Rice in buckets or baskets, cooked for the day's meals—carried on heads, under arms, on shoulders, on backs or in hands, or from bamboos shared between two. Some bundles were all bedding; others had none. Some carried nothing at all. Some carried only a coolie hat: one man had nine on a string, and not another thing. They wore army odd-ments, ladies' blouses, sarongs, barely sufficient G-strings. Men. Men. Males. Men without women.

Then, all at once: a woman! Unspeaking and seemingly alone among them all. I could see no one interested in her. Then more and more men, leaving no clue. A long way back came an old gaunt Chinaman, seeming older than he was—but old, nevertheless. At his heels was an old woman with a look of sorrow and steadfastness in her wise old eyes. I was struck by the fidelity of the pair. I knew nothing of them, but there was that bond which appears between some men and women seen together. It is impossible to ignore it: it is too precious.

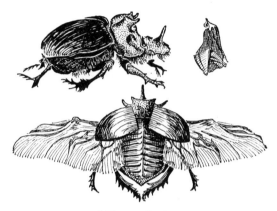

Rhinoceros beetle
crawling like a lumbering tank on rough ground
wings extended for flight and looking like a grand coat of arms
showing how wing folds on back under coverlet

This drawing is just about half size

XII

Alone – August

THIS is August 22nd, and I have been detailed for a job on my own. There is a stranded Ford truck on the road near Konyu, which belongs to the engineers. Until now there have been two men minding it: one Australian and one Englishman. I have been sent to relieve the Australian. Each man makes a trip back to his camp every four days for provisions. There are strict orders that the truck must always have one man there.

It was a long trip up and I am writing this while I wait for my first meal to cook.

As I came out, I passed more Tamils and Chinese walking up the railway. One story of this mass migration is that Singapore is being cleared to avoid famine and rioting.

I turned up the mountainside before I got to Konyu. I had been told that if I followed this creek, I would save a mile or so. It was very precipitous, for the creek tumbled down over twelve-foot boulders. With my pack, and no boots, it was slow climbing. Eventually, I came to the road. Here, I found more Tamils and Chinese marching up along a road that is a silent, unflowing river of mud.

I arrived at the truck and the Australian was all packed and ready to go. He gave a brief, *so-long* and vanished. The Englishman also went. I asked him about his relief. 'Dunno, mate,' and he was gone.

So here I sit alone in the Siamese jungle: my only weapon is an axe with a split-off handle, eighteen inches long. I have brought some rice and *catchung idjoe* with me. Apart from that, I have two pieces of dried meat (stinking); four dried fish (banjos, because of their shape); some sweet potatoes; and some dried potatoes. The condition of all this stuff is doubtful because it has been wet. There is also a little coconut oil and some salt and pepper. My cooking utensils are a quart-billy, and an old biscuit tin. A creek flows close by, but I must boil all my water.

I am no cook, but here is where I learn. I boiled a piece of the dried meat and poured off the rank stock; then I mixed it with my rice and *catchung idjoe* and a scrape of curry powder I found: this disguised it well enough.

I have no matches, and the fire was only grey ashes when I came to use it. The others went so quickly that I have had to fossick the camp to find where I stand. I have reset the cover over the back of the truck where I sleep, and the camp is ship-shape enough for the night, but there will be plenty of work tomorrow.

It is coming on dark and I feel at peace. I have boiled water, had a hot bath, and planned what I intend to do tomorrow. I sit on my blanket in the back of the truck, writing, as darkness comes down. There is no out-look here. I am completely hemmed in by a wall of bamboo with stiff green hands. The leaves are pointed and splayed, as a man's hand thrusting into a glove. Behind the green hands are the dark, cavernous recesses from which pour mosquitoes in hordes to drink my blood.

The crows are noisy, tonight. Two large black ones sat on a bamboo and eyed me with what I thought was professional interest, as I ate my supper. There are other birds which I have not seen yet. One of them has a note like a thrush. The only other sound is the croak of lizards and the small rush of the creek. Darkness is almost complete and I feel content, in a deep way that my brain is too tired to reason out.

*

The sun is setting on another day and the night insects are tuning up, like a big orchestra. I have been abroad since day-light, and was up once during the night to put a log on the fire. If it goes out, I am sunk. I am like the primitives who have to carry fire with them wherever they go. I have no way of making it.

After breakfast I went into the jungle to get solid wood for the fire. I cook with bamboo, but need the heavy stuff to keep the fire going all the time. It is awkward with the splintered handle of the axe which blisters and cuts my hands. And, as I wear only a G-string, the mosquitoes eat me greedily.

I dug out a pool at the spring, where the water is clearer, but just as unsafe. I bathed and put my few mildewed belongings out in the sun. In the jungle I found the skeleton of a man who had died alone. He wore a sarong. I knew he wouldn't mind, so I took it for myself. I don't know what he died from, but I have washed the sarong well and spread it in the sun. I have been told that ten minutes' sunlight will kill a cholera germ.

I also built a pool in the creek by pulling stones from the bottom and building a dam with them. Now there is a gravel bottom, a clean flow, and a good depth for bathing. I have no real idea of the time, so I work and eat by guess. At dark it is bedtime.

I was able to make a watercolour of a plant like a multiple Venetian pole this afternoon. I have seen a lot of flowers here I should like to paint, if I get the time. As I eat or cook by the fire, I watch hundreds of small bronze lizards with a black stripe down each side. I watch them catch and chew flies.

Last night the barking croak of the larger lizards and the shrilling of a million crickets made the night fill with crowd-excitement, which did not die away until the early hours of the morning. Today, until dinner time, the monkeys were cater-wauling like schoolboys. One of them, I think, must have had a good fall. There was a snapping of branches and a great monkey-commotion went up.

The day has been hot and sunny, and I feel so much better being free from camp routine and the Nips. There is time to think and see a little beyond our misery. Apart from a painful crack under my right foot, I feel very well.

As I was writing a while ago, a fine waterfowl with elegant plumage walked by, Pharisee-like, on the other side of the road.

*

ALONE–AUGUST

Another day has gone. I have just finished my supper. I was up with the first glimmer of light, I am living cleaner and eating better—and just now I can think of nothing more to wish for. I made a watercolour of the truck. Even for this I must use boiled water, because sometimes I draw my brushes to a point with my lips. Three brown pheasant came feeding near me by the creek. I sat still, and they had no fear. Now comes a host of hopping, marauding, brown birds with a white slash round their eyes. There is something of the big kingfisher about them. They hop and snatch aside leaves and jab at slow fat worms. They hop from ground to branch, and branch to ground, picking bugs from under the bamboo bark. They move with a continuous, chirping purr. There are a hundred or more in the flock and they move in an extended line, going steadily forward, fanatically snatching and pecking as they go. They have passed by, almost over my feet, without taking the slightest notice of me. The scuffling they make turning the bark and leaves, and their voices, are now fading into the jungle.

I feel a contentment which makes me burst out singing and whistling. I talk to myself, addressing myself as *Claude, Eustace,* or *Charlie,* telling myself to buck up, get a move on, do this, do that. I have ants and lizards for company and, occasionally, a small lizard cocks me a friendly glance.

*

One more day. Last night, after I had stopped writing, I read aloud to myself for exercise. Darkness stopped me. But I was wound up. So I had some small community singing. As I was singing, an air I did not know came out. I could not help it, nor did I know it. It was as if someone were singing through me. This has happened to me in dreams, but never when I have been awake. (Perhaps there are more here than I know about.) Then I brushed-up on the bedtime story I have written for John and Jill: *'When the sun goes down in the old, old west, etc.'*

At last I settled down to sleep, but the rats gnawed at my vegetable-box and kept me awake. My mind turned to my wife. I found myself saying, 'Gracious Lady, I to thee, in this

567

My home, Konyu Road, 23.8.43

mood of reverie . . .' until it became two verses to her. I got up, put some wood on the fire, and wrote them out by the light of Back on my bed, and the children demanded something. Two words, *Tweedledee* and *Tweedledum* (the substitute for John and Jill, I suppose), kept dinning in my head. So pretty soon, Tweedledee and Tweedledum went for a sail in an old oil drum. We got them wrecked; we got them a raft and brought them back with adventure and suffering; and we got them a good lecture from Mum and Dad. Then I got a little sleep.

*

At daylight I was about my chores, firewood, etc. I built a stone bridge across the creek to the pool at the spring. Then I had a shave, outlining my torpedo beard. I don't know how many months it is since I last shaved.

As I was having my dinner, about one hundred Australians ploughed up the road towards Hintok. They had tents, *kwalis* and, the whole lot piled on them, they floundered up the river of mud chanting their very Australian opinion of it. They told me it was 1.45 p.m.

A little while afterwards, a Nip soldier came down the opposite way. He came over to the truck. His two upper, lateral teeth were framed in gold, and both his canines were all gold. His opening words made no sense to me. 'You want me?' I thought he had come about there being only one man at the truck. But it wasn't that. He was with a party of 29 *Orando* who were bringing trucks through. He had wandered away from them on his own. He looked at my bed in the back of the truck and said, 'Wife-oo? *Nie-ca?*' I shook my head. He repeated the question. 'In Australie,' I said. But what he was really asking me was what I was doing about a wife, here and now. I said I didn't want one, I would rather have a plate of rice. He poked about a bit more. I sat down to eat my rice and fish. He sat too. He exercised his schoolbook English. How old are you? Have you a wife? Any babee? How many? Then the conversation died. He sat there, fidgeting, somehow shy and embarrassed. He scratched his groin. '*Bashabish-ca?*' he said. I hadn't the

foggiest what he meant. He repeated it. I repeated my blankness. He made a phallus of his finger and performed a symbol
with his other hand. '*Bashabish*,' he repeated. He seemed in a
state of roused childlike passion, which was strong enough to
overcome his shyness, but not his embarrassment. He was
making a proposal to me. I remembered what Weary and I had
discussed about this back at Konyu. At last this soldier turned
away abashed and disappointed—uncomfortable as a hurt
child.

*

Later in the afternoon five trucks came along. They were big
six-wheel, all-wheel-drive Marmons. On the previous day they
had covered just one mile and a seventh. They were hoping to
reach Hintok by nightfall. They had been six days from Tarsau.
I knew a couple of the drivers: I had met them at Bandoeng,
Java, and had not seen them since.

There were a couple of Dutch drivers also. One had been a
seaman in Alfred Holt's Blue Funnel ship *Polephemus*. He left
Holland before the invasion. He was in Alexandria in 1941,
when we were there also; now we are in the Siamese jungle
together. He spoke of Australians doing far more than the
Dutch in erecting memorials to their dead. (There is a big
wooden one a mile back.) 'We are too afraid of the Japanese,'
he said. 'They tell us to crawl in the shit, and we crawl in the
shit. Well, some day it will be different. We also will be free.
But how long? It may be too long coming.'

I watched them get the trucks under way again. They could
only make headway by passing wire ropes around trees and
winching themselves forward. Sometimes one would bash the
other, to get it moving.

*

Another day. As a result of the storm last night, I had to re-
rig my canopy. I have had to cook all my vegetables tonight
because it was a race between me and the rats. All I have left
is a few potatoes and enough rice for two meals. I don't know
what my crowd is doing about provisions for me: they should

know I am on my own, and am not supposed to leave the truck. I'll try the next camp tomorrow, if nothing turns up.

*

I had to go to the next camp and I was lucky. The Q there gave me some rice, fish, dried cabbage and a chunk of tough fresh meat. I talked with him for a while. He says he detests rice, but he looks fat enough. He said he could eat it if it had been disguised. Being Q.M., he has every chance of doing so. This led me to ramble on about my *psychic-inductance* theory. He said all he could see in it was the difference between eating food with a good or bad grace. For him, I suppose, this is all too true.

I came back and set about my chores, and strained my back on a big log. It is easy to do this in bare feet on greasy ground. As I was heaving the log on to the wood pile, a snake slid past my bare foot. I killed it. Then I was sorry because it was a beautiful thing in form, movement and colour; a translucent sandy-olive, the head was diamond-shaped, greener than the rest, and had red markings. It had a swift, effortless glide as if moving just above the ground—like a smooth swimming fish.

*

At sunset, heavy clouds burst, and it rained most of the night. The rains seemed to have changed: always lightning and thunder with them now. I try to convince myself that it is the beginning of the end of the Wet Season. My shelter here is better than the rotten tents I have been living in all through it. Bugs, too, are fewer, and each day I air my belongings, washing them and washing them.

I am pretty well settled in, and after my chores the chief of which is wood-getting, I can write and draw to my heart's content. All kinds of spiders pose for me in their webs. Down at the creek where I was dhobying on a flat rock, I saw a tawny spider dart out from her fern-leaf lair and grab a black and white swallow-tailed butterfly. She held it down for all the world like an amateur wrestler applying a body-press—legs splayed well out and weight thrown forward on her chest. She injected her poison into the thorax of the fly until it was drowsy.

The butterflies here are the same sorts we have been seeing all the time. There appears to be no particular season. Rather, they seem restricted to certain areas such as river, roads, pools, high ground, low ground, shade, sunshine, etc. There is enough of this sort of thing to keep me busy here for a year.

During the afternoon my back got worse, so I lay down with what I have written of *The Boat*.* But, after thirty-five pages I realized that I was not in the mood to go on writing *that* now. I know, now, that it is hard to write creatively when new experiences are crowding in on daily life. There is nothing to do but let yourself go to a saturation of the present, and it always seems that time is so short. In Java, Laurens van der Post told me not to work as if the Devil were looking over my shoulder—but he seems to sit there, just the same.

*

I have no appetite, tonight. The rain almost finished my fire. I rebuilt it from one coal I found cringing in the ashes. Dull wet weather. Wet wood. Myself as dull as the weather. Saturday is closing into night.

Saturday night! Saturday night in Ivanhoe. People going to pictures and plays. Patriotic performances. Uniforms everywhere. Servicemen *home on leave*! Humanity bricked-and-mortared in security and habit, with some certainty of the future.

Here, it is Saturday night in Thailand. A green, wet jungle and the million plants and creatures I have not yet begun to know and the noises of un-civilization. No cinema. No plays. A few Japanese uniforms. Just the eternal business of survival and escape from pain. Man is *superior*: but has he got a superior faculty for simple *being*? Do his religions give him superior faith to accept Creator and Creation without question? I am sitting here on this Saturday night with my bag of rice, to take

* Since published as *Out of the Smoke*.

my place amongst it all for a while—maybe I will surprise a
secret!

*

Up early again and looking in the jungle for subjects after
my chores were finished. I found some and came back black
with mosquitoes. After I got back I bathed in the creek and
started on what I call jungle tulips. Crimson, they grow straight
from the ground, without foliage. Underground runners spread
them all about the brown, leafmould floor of the bamboo bush.
I have marked a couple more interesting spiders in their webs.
At present I am happier with these subjects—living with them
gives you a fellow-feeling. I got so engrossed with another
drawing that my supper cooked dry.

About 3 p.m. a red fox crossed the road and came quite
close, as I sat still. He was a beauty and I was sorry he did not
stay longer.

*

Had to work hard to build up my wood supply again. Still
no word from camp about provisions. In the afternoon many
Tamils and Chinese went past and there seemed to be more
women and children with these.

Later, seven elephants came down from Hintok. They like
the road mud as little as we do. They meticulously dodged as
much as they could. They skimmed their trunks over the
surface to find the best footing. Mostly, they walked down the
double tyre tracks left by the Marmons. One of the drivers
sang in the high, monotonous, minor key of the East. I could
hear it a long while before they arrived, and it trailed back
long after they had passed.

Just as I was getting the late afternoon meal, I heard a loud
halloo-ing and yahoo-ing coming down from Hintok. Presently
I saw a Nippon soldier on a mud-bedraggled pony, leading a
pack animal along the deeply rutted road. But the shouting was
still coming, and soon, about a dozen more soldiers on ponies
came in with more pack animals. They all dismounted at the
truck and tethered their horses to the bamboos. The horses

cropped hungrily at what bamboo leaves they could reach. The men came over to me as I ate. It was a limited conversation. I found out the time by pointing to a watch. It was half-past three. They poked about the back of the truck and saw my last sketch with the model sitting on a clod of earth on a shovel. They made quite a fuss, '*Yuroshi! Yuroshi!*'

Small fleshy flowers (2″–3″ high) growing in cover. They range from red, through orange, to pure yellow—speckled and plain. There was something 'seven-dwarfish' about them

They stayed about half an hour, smoking by the fire. All were mudcaked and a couple of them washed their boots and puttees in the creek. They showed an uncomfortable interest in my blanket and the few clothes there. I had to do some fast talking to keep them. Their own clothes were thin and patched and torn.

*

I have managed to preserve a pair of shorts and a shirt—by not wearing them. Mostly I wear only a G-string. But now, while I have this feverish cold, I wear the skeleton's sarong and a singlet. My head aches, my eyes ache, my back, hips, and legs take turns at throbbing. My brain won't stop working and I don't sleep until just before daybreak. I think of all sorts of things; make up speeches for all occasions; make up rotten poetry; plan what I will do tomorrow; think over all I have seen, and wonder if and how I will get it on paper; I think I will make it into some sort of a folio when I get it home. Then I realize that I may not get home. Well, I will; or I won't— that's a separate question. They had a search the other day at the Konyu camp. They were looking for maps and diaries and wireless parts, I believe. There is a chap there who draws for a London paper (*Standard?*)*. I am told that he has had his name taken as an artist. This could take him to Japan. I don't want to go to Japan: I want to go home.

*

When I went to my rice I found that I had only enough for one more meal. I went again to Konyu: our people don't seem to be concerned. I got a good issue of rice, salt, dried cabbage and some sweet potatoes and a little bit of tea. This was taken from a chest marked: C-in-C TROOPS. MALAYA. SINGAPORE. It read like an epitaph.

I had to wait for my muddy, pony-riding guests to go before I could make this trip for the provisions. As they left me, they set up a wild din which seemed to belong more to the Steppes of Siberia, or the plateau of Tibet. I don't suppose that the Thai jungle is so remote from those places, anyway.

Coming back, I saw a number of men bathing in a creek: I think they must have been from the hospital. All were quite emaciated: ribs and joints stuck out. The fellows with large heads and small bodies looked the worst—especially with their hair uncut.

I was talking with Weary on this question some time ago, at Hintok. He said, 'You can read any amount of books on starvation, but none of them give the picture we see here . . . that posterior aspect of a man . . . that most prominent feature the rude exposure of his anal ring below the bony tail of his coccyx . . . it seems to protrude even beyond it . . . the gluteals are completely gone and the pelvis looks like flat bony plates with the great trochanters sticking out each side like walking-stick knobs.' That is how men are here now. In all the camps it

---

* It was Ronald Searle.

will be like this. Grace and beauty wrecked; dignity of gait gone, and replaced only by a shambling, dispirited progression.

I was quite dizzy coming back and I had to rest a couple of times. It feels like a good dose of malaria.

*

This morning I woke up faced with the necessity of wood-getting. I recoiled from the thought of using that splintered handle. I put my rice on to cook and started on a ten-inch teak log, which bridged the creek near here. It was about eighteen feet long and I had it in three six-foot pieces as the rice boiled.

But by then the aches had really set in: I could not stand up straight. I made a small pot of tea. In trying to be frugal, I used some of the stuff I found under the seat of the truck. It was mildewed and I couldn't drink it. From then on things seemed to go wrong: I got out of step with the world. The charcoal spattered and crackled, and burnt my bare thighs. The logs would not stay banked on the fire. The more I tried, the more futile I became. Drizzle set in and I stood on a live coal with my heel. I wanted to howl like a kid. My eyes were being prodded back in their sockets by invisible fingers, and my head

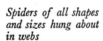

Spiders of all shapes and sizes hung about in webs

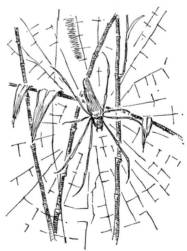

thumped like a beaten anvil. I crawled into the back of the truck with my rice, and lay down. After a while I tried to eat something, but couldn't face it.

After a couple of hours, I worked quietly on a drawing of a spider in her web. I had to cook more rice as what I had was sour. I dumped it in the fire. The fire was no good and the water would not boil. Then all at once, my previous symptoms jumped down off the bamboo on to my back again, and clung there. Each little ache and throb heaped misery on me and I crawled back into the truck again. I ate a few spoons of rice, and pushed the rest away. I spread my wet dried cabbage in the sun and dozed. It rained, and the cabbage was worse than ever. Late that night I cooked more rice, but could not eat it. But I did make a good cup of tea with the stuff I brought from Konyu. Then I spent the worst night of this bout, so far. It rained most of the night. I got up twice to tend the fire. Fever chased cabbages and kings around my head until early dawn when I finally dozed off.

*

This is Wednesday, September 1st, when, in the Southern Hemisphere, spring officially opens. About midday, I made some tea, and then went to Konyu to see a doctor. I was just saved from a blackout as I got there, by sitting down. At the R.A.P. I asked to have my temperature taken. There were two orderlies there, but they told me I would have to wait for a third—the one who took temperatures. After standing about some time, the third man came in and sat down. He said that if I came over to him he would take my temperature. It was 102. I saw the doctor and he prescribed twelve tablets of quinine. Six at once, then two three times a day.

When I got back I cooked a little pap, which I managed to eat, and made some tea. The night seemed especially still and silent: then I realized that the quinine had deafened me.

*

I got up late. I still have a high fever and ache, but I had a better night than the one before. I ate a bit of rice, and slowly made my way to Konyu.

I saw the doctor. He asked me my weight, to prescribe the quinine accordingly. He remarked on my good condition, apart from malaria. I am still more than eleven stone (twelve is my normal).

When I arrived the doctor was operating, cutting out ulcers. One man lay on a bamboo table, with a man at his head, sprinkling ether into a pad on his face. The doctor was engrossed in cutting down the front of the shin into the flesh under the ulcer. He was cutting deep under the six-inch sore, taking off a liberal fillet. When he was half-way along the cut, the anaesthetist, becoming very interested, allowed the man to come out of the ether. The dreadful moans of the patient brought him back to his job. I watched it all through the mosquito net under which they were operating.

*

I awoke feeling better. I got up and put a meal on the fire and, while it was cooking, I went to the creek and had a soap bath. All very quietly though, for I wobble a bit with any effort.

I was sitting, sketching, in the back of the truck when Happy arrived. This is the first I have heard from our camp in twelve days—and it had to be a Nip!

He said, 'O.K.-da! Finish come-back! Men come, truck take away.' He had five fellows with him. They stripped my shelter down. Then some Chinese came with petrol, oil, a spare wheel and a battery.

I ate my dried cabbage, and drank the cabbage-water. I was not looking forward to the trip back, feeling so weak. I was not so sure I could make it. Just as I was about to leave, another Nip came and said I was to wait until tomorrow.

So now I sit in the dilapidated cabin trying to keep my feet out of an open bucket of oil on the floor. I have to see that no wandering Japanese takes it.

It is raining as I sit writing. It recalls an effect of rain that

I have been meaning to record for some time. In the jungle the rain, as rain, ceases at the tree-top roof. Almost all the trees are large-leafed; just below this roof are the interlacing bamboos. There is a roaring hiss as you stand below. The roof leaks and the rain becomes large globules of water, which tumble down with earth-thuds and leaf-splashes. The floor of the jungle here is covered with small seedling bamboos, which look like hands appealing from a grave below the leafmould. Large drops of water, spinning earthwards, hit the young springy leaves and send thousands of them dancing up and down in a grand leaping ballet—so that even the ground seems to leap.

*

Today is the anniversary of the outbreak of war. We have had four years of it. By November, I shall have completed fifteen years in the Navy.

The night passed fitfully. I got up slowly and cooked a little rice. Then Happy and the other Nip came out with fifty Tamils. The truck would not start. They hooked on a four-inch rope. Shouting and struggling, the Tamils slowly pulled it on to the road. When they had it headed for Konyu, Happy and the other Nip shouted as if at a bullock team. But they were drowned by the squealing, shouting Tamils. They lay forward almost on their bellies in the mud, straining as the truck slowly sliced through the slush.

Men sat waiting on what we called the 'wailing logs'. Sick parade outside 'hospital'
Hintok River camp, 13.8.43

I smothered the fire and left my little holiday camp forever.
At last I got back to camp and went to see the doctor. He
started to write hospital but changed it to light duties.

It seems a long while I have been away, and I am slowly
picking up the camp routine.

*

A letter came from Austin Fyffe who is at Tarsau. Roy has
died. His leg was amputated because of ulcers. Amputation is
the last resource, and it is always doubtful whether patients
have the resistance to stand the shock. But a gangrenous leg
makes death a certainty. Blackie is bad, Austin writes, and he
has been evacuated to Kanburi.

*

There is a strong rumour that we are going up to Kinsayok
soon. The pressure on the work has eased, but we still work long
hours. More than anything we still crave sleep. The weather is
gradually getting finer, and the death rate has fallen. Food is
a little better.

Tonight, from his tent in the dark, Herb Smith gave us an
impromptu concert of about six songs. Never could songs mean
more.

*

When we got back to camp after work today, we had to pack
up our gear and shift into already crowded huts. The tents are
being taken tomorrow. The story is pretty strong that Italy
capitulated on September 9th. Even the Nips are saying,
'Italia finish. Soon all men shake hands. War finish-da.' And
they seem pleased. I suppose they are as sick of it as we are.

Herb Smith sang again. *White Dove*, *Trees*, and *Dusty Road*.
The last is especially popular—it is close to the present and it
gives us heart.

*

Today Smiler got me to draw him some monkeys and elephants on cards for him to send home. He told me that we are

going to Kinsayok, but not to work on the railway. 'Changee—changee Indian. Australie *yasume.*' He said also that the camp commandant there was a Christian.

It is just fourteen days since I got back from the truck.

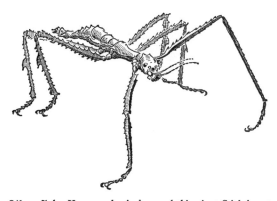

Like a Jules Verne mechanical marvel this giant Stick insect stood while we looked at each other. His body was 8″ long

XIII

Kinsayok – September

FRIDAY the 17th. Departed Hintok and took passage to Kinsayok. Four hours by river barge. The river was impressive. It ran under vast rock cliffs on entrenched meanders. The mountainsides stood back a little, deep in jungle, like waves about to break. In parts, it reminded me of the Culebra Cut in the Panama Canal.

George played on his cornet and we sang some good old ones. *Roll Out The Barrel, Sons Of The Sea, Dolores, Sixpence In My Pocket, The Lights Of London,* and others.

We watched colonies of monkeys climbing in the trees over the water. There were a lot of family groups, and what appeared to us to be family squabbles. We took sides in these affairs and barracked. Some nominated who was ma-in-law, the bullying father, the wolf, the spoilt brat, and so on, cheering and booing them as we took sides. Most of this went on in large fig trees, rather like the Moreton Bay figs of Australia which grow to enormous size.

We arrived at Kinsayok at 4 p.m. and unloaded all our camp gear. At 5.30, a crowd was put to work on a half-built hut. By supper time the frame was complete and it was thatched. Even some bed-platforms had been put up in this 120-foot building.

The camp is spread over a wide alluvial flat. On the other side of the river a mountain drops straight into the water. The rain has made the camp a cattle yard. Many of the huts have sunk to their hands and knees as a result of poor lashings. In places their roofs sag to the ground.

I met Weary, and I stopped to talk with him. He saw that I had fever and told me to turn in.

*

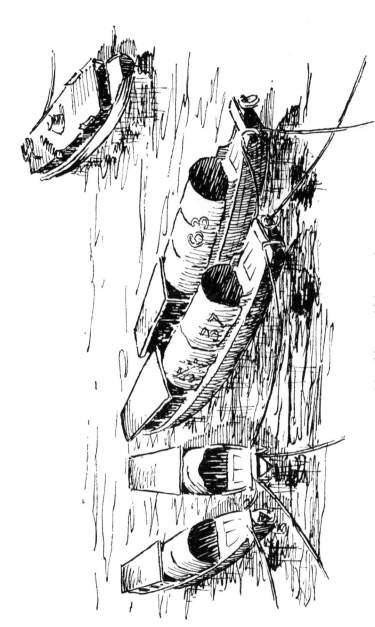

Moored barges with 'pom pom'

Lying alongside me, also with malaria, is Middy, a giant of a man from Western Australia. He has fallen away to a skeleton and shows his big bones clearly. Generally, it has gone hard with big men here.

Many big men, after a certain point, dropped their bundles and died. I am thinking of a tall, barrel-chested man who used to laugh at the work and conditions, and was undoubtedly the fittest man I have seen up here. One morning, in July, we had been to the mess point in the dark and slush for our pap. Most of us stood there in the rain and ate it, not daring to move a step for fear of losing it. But Big Jack never worried. One morning, I took a chance too. He was just ahead of me and turned aside to enter his tent. I had only gone a few paces when I heard the bang of a dixie on the ground, and the smack of a man falling in the mud. The air turned blue with his curses, echoing in the trees. They died away and I could hear the sound of weeping—the blubbering of a child. From that day on his leg ulcers got worse, dysentery troubled him more and more. He became sick enough to be sent back to Tarsau. Later, we learned that Big Jack had died after a leg amputation.

*

Though the wet weather continues we are told that it will be over in a month. Another party was sent back to Tarsau today.

We have been reformed into new battalions, from the remnants that have been gathered together. The Australians are known as Yama (mountain) Battalion; the English are Kawa (river) Battalion. Our original O Battalion (or 25 Company, as it was later called) started out with 450 men; now there are only thirty of us left here. Ken and Fatty are still with me: we are the only Navy left here now.

*

I was dragged out of hospital today along with other *heavy sick*, and sent to work. We worked until late.

There was a parade of bootless. Many, who had boots, discarded them with the hope of getting a new pair. The Japs took all those with white feet, beat them, and sent them away. Then, by one means or another, the whole parade was whittled down to only thirty. Colonel Ichii was then proudly informed that there were only thirty in camp without boots—and that they would soon have them.

Colonel Ichii has suddenly appeared to look into our con - ditions. This is why the sick go to work.

*

This is the tenth day since malaria hit me this time. Weary has kept me in hospital—though I have to go out each day with the heavy sick for half a day.

There is still some cholera among the Chinese and the Tamils. Tonight, coming in from the railway, one of the gangs found a Chinaman dead, his head in a stream. They thought it was cholera. There was also a Tamil under a bridge in the last stages of it.

We were allowed to write a letter card today. I wonder if anybody ever gets them.

*

The Nips make us sing on the way to work. It has become quite an institution. George, our trumpeter, plays us out with his cornet until we are clear of the camp. The songs we sing are *Sons Of The Sea* and other jingoistic numbers. But the favourite is *They'll be dropping thousand-pounders when they come*, sung to the tune of *She'll be comin' round the mountain*. And this, strangely enough, is also the Nips' favourite.

*

Today I got a pair of boots. When we came in from work, we were lined up for a very long while. Eventually we received a pair of canvas rubber boots. Colonel Ichii personally asked me, 'Have you no s'oos at all?' As I looked at him and listened, I could have been watching Warner Oland as Charlie Chan.

The boots are too small and they hurt, but they are boots. Tonight I went to sleep with clean feet, for the first time in months. However, we did not get the boots for nothing. We were told we had to sing for them. To the Japs, a singing man is a grateful, happy and contented man. We sang them a verse of *They'll be dropping thousand-pounders when they come.*

*

My boots were too small anyway, but now, several thorns I have in my foot have festered. My feet are now so swollen that, in the boots, I can only shuffle. The boots are almost bursting—but I keep on wearing them because . . . well . . . it is *something* to have a pair of boots. The doctor has put me on 'light duties'.

*

There is supposed to be a week's *speedo* coming up on the railway. Slit trenches and air raid shelters are being dug. There is some slight Japanese air activity. There is a tale about more mail at Kanburi. Rumours all the time.

And so much for the last day of September.

XIV

Kinsayok – October

F ULL duty.

The jungle is flowering more each day. There is a fine, yellow lily with leaves like velvet. One of the Nips killed a four-foot golden snake. He cleaned it ready for cooking with about six inches of the tail still in the skin. Though gutted and headless, it still squirmed. The Nips grilled and ate it, telling us how it made them strong. One of them grabbed a hammer from a Chinese and started to break stone like a maniac, to show how strong it had made him. And one of them said it was a wonderful aphrodisiac, demonstrating with crude pantomime.

On the way home we each had to bring in a dead stick of large bamboo for the Nip kitchen. Most of us stopped to bathe at one of the clean, fast-flowing streams we have to cross. It is very pleasant and it saves us time when we get back. We wash whatever clothes we are wearing also, and they dry on us, on the way back. There is very little time between mess parade and *Tenko* at 7.45 p.m. I write this up in the dusk after Tenko.

*

Out on the railway at hammer and tap. Today has been very windy—a warm wind, and we hope it is something of the change of season we are all so looking forward to. Other signs of change are increasing: new sorts of flowers—numerous vines of the Morning Glory (Convolvulus) type with white, yellow and blue trumpet bells; there are purple, blue and red flowers also; and bamboos shoot in almost dangerous profusion.

Today the bush bees drank our sweat again, which had not happened all the Wet. The sky is calm and lime-washed with the vapour of fine weather. I sleep better—without that

587

brow-beaten feeling through all my dreams, which is the subconscious reaction to being completely in the hands of a capricious enemy whose *thumbs-up* or *thumbs-down* is life or death to us.

*

I am now working with the sleeper and rail gangs. We load them on to rail cars which take them up-country. They have come this far by river. We work at night and sleep by day. I like this better. With the sun coming back, it is less exhausting. We also work unloading the barges. In conversation with a couple of Chinese, we found out that they are receiving six times as much pay as we are.

With the heavy carrying, I came close to a blackout several times. Then came the pains in my back and legs, and I knew it was malaria again.

*

Nothing seems to happen when one is sick: the horizon of events closes in like the iris of the eye in a strong light.

Forty heavy sick were sent to work on the railway by Corporal Okada. The story has come up from Tarsau that there have been seventy-seven amputations: some fatal. It is said that there will be 600 unless they can get better treatment for ulcers.

Blackie is dangerously ill. I heard no more.

*

They call him Pop: more often, 'old' Pop. I don't think he is old. But he is shortish, portly, balding and sandy-grey. He is blue-eyed, and his face contains that subtle quality called Irish. He lives with the officers, though he is the most unmilitary type in the camp. He has the habit of being lost in meditation, and doesn't always notice what is going on around him. He is a Roman Catholic priest.

Pop carries out the normal ritual ministrations to his flock. I have seen him often in the grey early morning as he stands with the raggedness of a peasant in his smock, before a rickety bamboo altar at early morning mass. I feel, for the rest of the time Humanity looms larger for him than any religious label. With this humanity his humility is complete and natural—like the Irish in his face. Not for him how many angels on a pin's head.

Pop was walking outside the officers' hut today. He did not see a guard there. The Japanese private let out a bellow, '*Ba-a-GEE-ERA! KURRAH!*'

Mildly Pop stood before him: he realized that he should have saluted. The guard shouted and struck him back and forth across the head, so that he went staggering back, zig-zagging with each blow. His lips were cut and his nose bled.

Across a piece of open ground, between them and the Guard Room, a Japanese captain saw what was going on. He went back into his office and came out with a wooden chair. When he got to the scene of the beating, he roared at the soldier, '*Kiotski!*'

The guard snapped at once to attention, as stiff as a dead fish with a curve in its back, and a wooden mask dropped over the fury of a few moments ago. The officer looked at Pop, shaking and bleeding. '*Yasume*,' he said mildly, and dismissed him. Then he turned to the soldier.

'*Ba-GEE-ERA!*' he stormed, and set about him with the chair until he had quite wrecked it on the man. He sent the chair to the carpenter's shop; the soldier dragged himself to hospital to the mercy of Corporal Okada—Doctor Death.

Unloading attap-barges, Kinsayok

As we worked today, I was able to watch some of the moored barges. When I got back I made some notes. There were four of them moored to poles like Venetian gondolas. They were backlighted by the sun, and lay dark on the silver water with the strong grace of swans.

Yesterday, as I worked unloading a barge of attap, I was told that it was made from nepa palm leaves. These grow in swamps: during floods they float away in islands. In ordinary times attap is worth $9 a thousand, but the price has soared since the Japanese began using such large quantities. There is a better class of stuff, I am told, which is made of sago palm.

Some men going back in a steam train said that there was only three kilometres of railway and a bridge to build to complete the railway. They say it will be opened at the end of the month.

*

Flowers are thicker. Yellow bells, blue bells, white bells, mauve bells—brilliant on creepers which smother whole clumps of bamboo and look as big as buildings. There are many new sorts of lilies, brilliant against the different new leaf-masses, or the shadow-caves of the jungle. The nights have been fine and hot and clear. Sunsets are colourful and are followed by moonrise in cold silver. The hours of sleep are voluptuous. Dreams are easier. Life is rosier. I feel that the beginning of the Dry, at long last, has had a tremendous effect. It is now we begin to realize what a huge burden the Wet put on us.

*

On the job, some of the Nips called for swimmers. Sensing a bit of a change, I volunteered. We went to the river to dynamite fish. Our job was about five miles from camp; and we walked at least another five miles to the river.

After walking along the track a while, we hitched a ride in the cab of a steam engine. From this we got a very good idea of how wobbly the track was. The engine had to go very slowly in parts. There is still a lot to be done in ballasting the track.

*

There was a *yasume* from the railway today, but the camp guards found work for all.

In the evening, after *Tenko*, a party of 150 went to Colonel Liley's camp, to a concert there. When it was over we came back along the line in the moonlight.

A couple of new huts have been built for the hospital. Corporal Okada gave a speech, born of the impression the new buildings had made on him. 'The hospital has now been made a new organization—I am very pleased for you. You must do the best for your duty and heal your patients quickly with the new organization. You must all do your best for your duty.' This was to the Allied hospital staff.

A couple of mornings ago, Corporal Okada was complaining bitterly that there were not enough heavy sick for him to work. It is from these that he must draw his work force because all others have to work on the railway.

Weary stood very still, while Okada spoke. He looked down on the Japanese corporal, bending over slightly and fixing him with an intent look.

'All right,' he said. '*You* select some of the men you think are fit and we will examine them and see if you are right! All the time you say, "Why so many men sick? Why so many men sick?" But you never ask, "Why so many men over there?" ' And Weary waved his arm across at the hillside we could all see covered with crosses. 'You never ask that!'

Okada went away without taking any more men.

*

The story has come up from Tarsau about Joe Richards. Joe is a man who has given some very interesting talks on big game hunting and wild life in Africa. Before the war he had gone to India as a carpenter, but soon became interested in hunting. He became a licensed hunter and took regular parties elephant hunting in Africa. At Hintok when we had a mild plague of snakes under our bedboards, Joe was the one to pull them out by the tails. He was quite adept at biting off their heads: a native way of killing them. Now we hear that Joe has had his leg amputated. Normally doctors don't do this until there is no other way: it is never certain that the patient can stand it. But Joe asked to have his taken off. He had come to hate it, he said, for the misery it was giving him. They said that Joe watched them take it off. When it was severed and was being put out of the way, Joe said, 'Show it to me!' He took it in his hands and said, 'You bastard! You won't trouble me any more!'

*

When we got to the railway today, we were told to *Yasume*. Then we were all marched back to camp. There was a cheer, as we all thought we were getting the day off. But when we got back we were all put in the Engineers' yard and, at midday, were marched back to the railway again.

The Engineers were all dressed up and carrying rifles and bayonets. We were told we could eat our rice. But they moved us back from the line to the bush, and made a show of guarding between us and the track.

After a time, a train came past: a steam locomotive and two trucks thatched with attap. In the trucks were the General and his party. We were valiantly being prevented from assassinating him. Even the Nips kept under cover.

*

We hear that the line is now joined. The track-layers came back on a train tonight and told us that there were guards on all bridges.

*

It is Monday, October 25th, *Yasume Day*, and the official opening of the railway.

Tonight, at sunset, the General came back in his special train. The Kempi Tais (Military Police) are in camp with him.

I am taking no chances that they are here only to protect the General: I have planted my diaries, etc.

We received a 1-c.c. needle against the plague today. Okada says it is due here next month.

*

A foggy morning, looking as if it will be a fine day. Last night there was a grand, sweeping sunset. The duck-egg-blue sky was shot through with a pale apricot light which stained the league-long mare's tails high up. Down on the horizon there was a line of bold daubs of stronger apricot and shadow-purple, made by slow cruising argosies of cumulus moving over the shadow-stricken land, which was blueing to black, as if some giant fist had bruised it.

As I write, a man has just exclaimed, 'Wouldn't it? I've even got bugs in my *tobacco*!'

*

Worked with the heavy sick. I feel a bit better, but the doctor has given me another day.

The Kempi Tais are back in camp: we can expect anything.

Thirty Manchesters came into camp today, on their way back. Three hundred of them had marched up past us at Hintok. These few told us that the rest were buried up the river. They were one of the first parties to march through Hintok.

XV

Kinsayok – November

IN HOSPITAL today, Cossy told me something of his life.
'Cossy' is a corruption of 'Quasimodo', the hunchback of
Notre Dame. It is his nickname because he is hunch-shouldered
and small. He is the butt of many jokes. He moves with a jerky
energy and scuttles away with a high-pitched giggle when
someone is having a go at him. (You can almost hear the bells
ringing on his cap.) As a jester, his wit would be provincial
and raw.

In civil life, before the war, Cossy worked with sheep. He
will talk readily of his work with the eagerness of one who
thinks his job matters. He told me all about 2–4–6 tooths, full
mouths, broken mouths, fluke, white worm, bots, etc., etc. He
told me about the prevention and treatment of ills in sheep.
He told me how a drover may hold up the Royal Mail for
fifteen minutes, and other traffic for thirty; how they may not
drove on foggy days. In short, he took me droving all around
Tasmania with him. Gradually, I got him to tell me something
of his early life.

He was very young when his parents died. His brother,
sister, and he went to live with a Mrs B——, until he was
about nine. They lived there with fourteen other orphans. He
said they had a good time. Then, with his brother and sister, he
went to live with a Mrs P——, where there were nine of them.

Mrs P—— was the wife of a sea-going engineer. Though
only thirty-five, she was mentally unstable. He found out later
that she had been syphilitic. Her husband came home only
once a month to pay her, and left again at once. He was good-
natured and would give them two shillings each for the pictures.
But, as soon as he had gone, the money was taken from them.

Their meals were mostly of bread and dripping, or bread and jam.

'Sometimes,' he said, 'she would make a kind of bread stew for dinner and put in potatoes and cabbage—not peeled or anything. Generally it was burnt about half an inch thick on the bottom of the big iron pot. It used to be rotten. But there was one thing—we always got a hot meal on Sunday. We used to look forward to it, too. We were hungry for it all the week. The woman next door used to feed us some cakes and scones through a hole in the brick wall of the wood shed. But *She* found it after a while, and we all got a belting. Boys and girls—the lot! We would get a hiding for almost anything. She used to give it with the handle-end of a razor strop. A few minutes late from school—anything. We lived quite close to the school and we would only get out to go after the first bell had rung. So we had to run like hell to get there in time.'

After ten months of this the neighbours complained to the Child Welfare Department, because of the cries continually coming from the children. A welfare nurse came and found bruises on them all—on their stomachs as well. They were ordered to be removed. On the day they left, they had to scrub the whole house spotless. Then they all sat, dressed in their Sunday best, around the wall of the kitchen—wordless. She gave them a penny each and said, 'I suppose you will all be glad to leave.' None of the frightened children dared to answer.

'At the next place we were treated well,' Cossy said. 'We were all such skinny little weeds when we went there. She treated us all right. She did a terrific business in abortions— but that had nothing to do with us.'

That's how Cossy grew up into a hard-working citizen: small, sturdy, hunch-shouldered, generous and good-natured; and with a sense of humour born of being on the receiving-end of life all the time. Drover, station hand, butcher; a man with a national pride in his Tasmania: a pride which eventually landed him in this hospital alongside me.

*

It has been a dull day with light showers. The railway workers brought in all the tools today. They oiled them and bundled them up. They say the rail work here is finished.

*

This is Tuesday, November 2nd: Melbourne Cup Day. We have run a sweep at five cents a time. Due to certain international difficulties we ran our own horses. The draw was made at dinner time from such horses as *Bludger*, *Waterchain*, *Benjo*, *Corletto* (after the doctor): there were twenty-one starters. I did not draw a horse. First, second and third had already been decided, but nobody knew until the *broadcast* at 9 p.m.

The broadcast was made from the inside of the little library hut. A great crowd gathered and excitement was tense; there were arguments and wild betting to back them up. Bookmakers were calling the odds, and many were completely lost in the reality of it. Nearly everybody rode his horse for the whole hotly disputed two miles. There was a tremendous roar at the finish, everybody shouting the name of his horse. But the *official* placings were: *Starvation*, first, narrowly defeating the *Bludger*. I did not catch who was third. The losing jockeys, although phantoms like their mounts, were accused of all sorts of foul play, so that the others might win. It is still being argued out.

*

We went up to a site by the river near the Kinsayok station. We are building a camp there for some Engineers. The river bank is steep and rocky. One big tree thirty to forty feet above the river leans right out over the water with its roots clutching a huge boulder like the claw of a giant Roc bird: I almost found myself looking in the branches for Sinbad.

A new crowd there told us that, when the 30th Battalion had gone north, 116 died before they had done a day's work, and that the 29th lost ninety.

*

Here is the Nippon *Lights Out*. We heard it so often at Hintok. Despite the fact that it was Japanese, there always seemed to be a strange benediction of ultimate peace in it— even in the cholera season.

Spent the day over at the Engineers', bundling up tools. We hope this is the beginning of the end.

Yesterday was my birthday and today I have completed fifteen years in the R.A.N. My first meal, on that bleak November night in 1928, was curry and rice. No curry today!

*

This afternoon we stoked the forty-four-gallon drums of bath-water for the Nip Engineers. We were under a Dutch corporal working permanently in the Jap kitchen. After the stoking there was nothing more to do. So we were left hanging around with no one to march us back to camp. At last, we attached ourselves to the carpenter's party and went back with them.

A quarter of an hour later, the Dutchman came into our hut and told us that the Japanese corporal wanted to see us. When we got there he was in a bellowing mood. I could see he was putting on an act in front of the others. He singled me out. '*You* . . . Number One-ca?'

I wasn't in charge, but I said I was, to save more bellowing.

'*Arrugh-oo!*' he growled with exaggerated ferocity. '*Damme! Damme!* You go! . . . You no pinish-da! *Ba-a-geera!*'

It is always difficult to make excuses, particularly in Japanese when you hardly know ten words. So, I tapped my head sadly and said, '*Atama concreto!* [Stone head.] Very sorry.'

He tapped my head savagely. '*Ba-a-ge-e-e-ero-oo!*'

I simply repeated what a stupid fellow I was, and tried to look very contrite—and I was getting more sorry every time he hit me. At last he seemed to simmer down and I thought it was all over.

But he had to play the schoolmaster. He took a piece of flat bamboo two inches wide and five feet long. He drew a cross on the ground so that, as he stood, he swung fairly over it. We formed a queue and, one at a time, stepped on to the 'X' to get four or five lacerating whacks across our buttocks and thighs, and back. His aim was wild. After each turn we went around and tagged on to the end of the queue again for the next lot. We all wore only G-strings and there was nothing between the flesh and the bamboo.

As I heard the bamboo whistling behind me, I sneaked my forearms back flat, to take some of the sting out. By now the other Japanese had come to see the sport and shout with laughter at our discomfort: to them it was slapstick. They began to see it as baseball batting practice and they encouraged the swing.

But the slat was no good. Here you are—this is more like it!— one of them laughingly handed the corporal a piece of thick bamboo almost identical with a base-ball bat. It was a piece cut from the butt, where it grows solid. A short halt while he planted his feet more firmly, and tried his swing; he swung, and grinned in satisfaction.

He signalled me to take my place with a laughing *'Kurra!'*

The flats of my forearms went back to check the blow. But I stopped, realizing that the two thin bones of the forearm are no match for the club. I had to lock both hands in front to stop the instinctive warding off. I thought the first blow had shattered my spine, and the second my hip. The rest landed on flesh, which wasn't so bad. Then I limped to the end of the queue.

I watched the others. Two of them put their arms back: each got a broken ulna. After several more rounds like this, we were allowed to go. We were told that it would be more serious next time.

The men with the broken arms supported them on pieces of

flat bamboo held in their other hand. We made a dejected, limping procession going back to camp.

When we had been called out of the hut the rest of the crowd had suddenly gone silent. They had watched us go without a word. Now they looked us over to see what had happened. The bruises were coming up: green, yellow, blue, purple and red— intermingled like the daubs on a painter's palette. They saw that we were all there. They looked at us as we turned around for inspection. Then, suddenly, they all burst into roars of laughter at our coloured backsides.

'Blue-arsed monkeys!' someone yelled.

*

Colonel James, the English C.O., and our senior officer, took me over to the Guard Room as exhibit 'A' to the Japanese Captain of the Guard. He looked horrified and said this was very bad, and he would make enquiries at the Engineers'.

Later he sent for me and, in the presence of the Colonel, I was given an apology from the Engineers by the Captain. 'So sorry,' he said, and went on to explain that the corporal had got a bit carried away and the situation had got out of hand. The corporal is a great baseball player. He said it would not happen again. But I think what really upset the Captain and got us an apology was the fact that this punishment had been dished out by the Engineers instead of the guard.

*

Last night Major Wearne came back from Tarsau with news of thirteen more deaths. Among them was Blackie, who died at Chungkai of dysentery on October 8th, a bare two years after his father. His young wife is widowed, and his son is fatherless.

*

Today a service was held (with I.J.A. permission) for the dedication of our crowded cemeteries here. Wreaths were laid, hymns sung, and the Last Post played. Last of all came the Reveille, somehow suggesting all the unrealized hopes of the dead, and the half-dead who are left. The service was in Dutch and English. I made a wreath from tall grasses and some red leaves that had fallen from the trees.

Malaria hit me again at night.

*

Some mail has been given out, but not much.

As we lie on our bamboo beds, and look up at night, we can see the rafters by the dim light of the yellow, smoking, slush lamps. Rats live in the hollows of the bamboos there. We hear their scratching and scufflings and the nuptial squeals. In the dim light we occasionally see snakes gliding along the rafters to wait for the rats; they wait with beady eyes, grinning mouths and flickering tongues. They wait by the holes the rats have gnawed: they seize and swallow the rats and, by morning, the snakes are gone.

*

Cossy had a small toe snapped by a vicious fish while we were bathing the other day. It has poisoned rather badly. Tinea, too, is a trouble here because it leads to infection. Some had lost legs and even testes, as a result.

A rumour has come up the line that a bridge has collapsed with a whole train on it.

*

The weather is fine and hot and springlike. Already (November 21st) there is talk of Christmas. It is hoped to buy a pig, of about 200 kilogrammes, at a cost of twenty-five cents a man. The interpreter says that there is a lot of mail at Kanburi. It would make a good Christmas present. Much of this Christmas-talk is just like that of the cities. The canteen is sending out *shop-early* pleas.

*

After one hour's work the camp was *yasume-ed*. We had a complete football competition in one day. The finalists—

Hintok and B.D.F.—had to play three matches each. There was a church service after *tenko*. Later, B.D.F. put on their revue, *Tout du Monde*. By our humble Hintok standards it was lavish. It was on a built-up stage in the open, with wings and footlights (slush lamps and home-made carbide ones) but the main light was from the two bamboo fires. The Nips had given a *cigaretto presento* to the football finalists, and filled the front two rows. When the ballet came on, they pressed forward like lecherous old men.

Last night, by the way, eleven Japanese girls who had spent four days at the Engineers' camp boarded the train to go further north. They were dressed in smart western dress with high-heeled shoes; lacquered and groomed, they moved with all the confidence of their trade.

*

We have been at work remaking the road, which the Wet Season has virtually obliterated. In places we can find no signs of it. We have a section, running eight kilometres each side of Kinsayok, to build. This ten miles has to be done in a month. Along the way there are a good number of skeletons of man and beast: some of our road markers have white skulls stuck on top.

*

Owing to the long walk out to the job on the road, there is talk of opening another camp to the south. Each day we walk further and further, and there is less working time left.

On parade each night we are learning Japanese marching songs. George plays the tune on his cornet a couple of times. The Japanese words are read slowly and, a phrase at a time, we repeat them all together in a low rumble. Then at last, we attempt to sing them. When at length we have some grasp of the song we are set marching in a wide circle like Japanese warriors, chanting our battle song—generally we have no idea what it means.

Here is one we sing in Japanese:

INTO THE SMOTHER

Kuni o deta kara ito tsuki zo,
Tomo ni shinu ki de kono uma to.
Semete susuna yama ya kawa
Tota susuna ni chi ka yo-u.

I will not guarantee the Japanese of that, but it is something like what we sing, anyway. Translated, it means:

You know not what month you leave your country,
Self and horse think only of patriotic dying—
Going over mountains and rivers
Arriving at the battle with the blood rushing to your head.

XVI

Hintok Road Again – December

IT IS December 5th and I am just out of hospital after malaria again. The main body of Gore Battalion are going down to re-open the Hintok Road camp. I have been told that I will be Battalion Sar'major of those left.

*

Last night I was suddenly informed that I would be going to Hintok. I am glad of this, for I would rather stick with the survivors of O and P Battalions. A peculiar *esprit de corps* has grown up among our company in which the rogues count for as much as the saints.

At 10 a.m. we marched into waiting trucks at the Kinsayok siding. We ate our rice and a couple of boiled eggs at 12.30. Then we waited until 2.30 for an engine. During the short trip down to Hintok we passed three derailed trucks lying in gullies below.

From the Hintok station we had to cart all our camp gear—tents, *kwalis*, tools, etc., as well as our packs—up the mountain and down the escarpment to the old Road, or 'Mountain', Camp. I came to grief, with a load on top of me, in a clump of ragged bamboo stumps. We had to make a couple of trips. The fireplaces were cut into the earth first thing, and a meal was put on. Some of the marrow and pumpkin seeds of our previous occupation had grown and, with a few small ones we found, we made some marrow *soup*. We all sat, at last, by the light of the fires and the moon, and really enjoyed our rice and marrow water.

But we felt, as we came back into the camp, the shadow of

603

the cholera plague. It is a camp of the dead—the dead who are burnt, but whose memories burn on.

*

The wild flowers are thick and there are many kinds. But, as many as there are, they are dominated by the green walls of the jungle.

A few of us went up to the cemetery. It is a small rectangular area fenced-in with a low bamboo fence, which encloses the terraced rows of wooden crosses, fairly close together. They are close together because under the name, which is burnt on each cross, is the simple word: ASHES. The weeds are tall between the crosses, and a blanket of this season's vines and creepers is trying to smother it all.

We stood, dwarfing the crosses; the trees towered above us; the 500-foot escarpment, rising straight up fifty yards back, made the trees small; and, dwarfing the mountain—the sky.

Tall clumps of bamboo stand up ninety feet, like the quills of a hedgehog, some awry and broken; a few fallen across the graves already. The jungle seems to be trying to hide this little human tragedy from the world.

We stood together there without saying a word to each other; thinking of the once-live bodies that are now ashes here; thinking of the cholera pyres. What *were* we thinking? That it was strange that these ashes should be so silent and unanswering (especially the youngsters); thinking that they would be here forever; thinking that it was good to be alive; to stand there with the hot sun burning on the back of your neck—even to feel the drawing ache the hot earth put into our bare, cracked feet. I think we all thought that we were glad; that the burning sun had never felt so good before.

*

We are making 800 metres of road a day. The camp has quite a pleasant atmosphere, and the Japs with us are not bad.

In fact it feels as if we have come away for our Christmas holidays.

*

Today we linked up with the Kinsayok section and it has been a *Yasume*. Tonight we had a Red Cross issue: the first since we have been prisoners, almost two years. Some say it came through the Thai government. But, such as it is, it is here. My share was a two-inch square of soap. And that, or its equivalent, is what each man got.

The R.S.M. said, 'Each man will draw a ticket on which will be written the article he is to get. No doubling-up, or you will only be robbing your mates. *I know you wouldn't do that!*'

His heavy sarcasm was matched with a jeer.

'Not bloody much! Just you give us the chance!'

*

My foot is poisoned and I can't walk on it.

Today 100 Dutch came in from Kinsayok, and it is now rumoured that we will have to metal the road. This will keep us in the jungle longer yet.

*

Two days later.

I can walk on my foot again: the doctor had to pursue me half-way through the jungle, probing deep into my sole with a scalpel, and twisting it to get the last of the thorn out.

I am working on the road again. In places we can find no traces of it; we are really cutting a new one. It is hard, dirty work, but nothing like the *Speedo*. There is a pale mauve, flowering creeper growing everywhere just now. It festoons trees and bamboos like Christmas decorations. There are several sorts of *blue* bells: powder blue, mauve, and royal blue. Other vines have yellow flowers, some are white with a dark centre, like a passion flower. The hills are turning red, yellow, bronze and gold as the leaves change colour. The escarpment is more beautiful with each successive sunset, when the low light lights it like an opal.

Today we had Funny Pants for boss. He is delighted with the name we have given him. He laughs and jokes and desperately tries to live up to it—even to controlling his temper, which he seems afraid might spoil his name.

*

We are told that we are to have a real Christmas vacation on the 24th and 25th. They are going to kill two beasts a day for the two days. Permission has been given for anyone who likes to go to Kinsayok on Christmas Eve and return on Christmas afternoon. This is because B.D.F. are putting on a concert —a Christmas special. But nobody wants to walk thirteen kilometres each way, and we are hoping to put on a concert of our own.

*

About 2 a.m., four or five planes were heard. They passed over low, going west towards Burma. Joe E. Brown, our wide-mouthed Nip sergeant, rushed about, putting out the fires.

Tonight, our crowd from this tent is sitting around the fire yarning. Each of us took turns to relive our childhood Christmases: the drums, the whistles and the squeakers, that helped to make Australia bedlam. Each tent, tonight, has its own family fireside circle: talking quietly, singing noisily, murmuring or laughing. As long as we remain within the small horizon of the jungle, we are happy enough; but if we sigh for the wider horizons of a well-provided society, then we feel poor again.

*

An argument here is simply a flat denial of all the other fellow says, and answering with preposterous things you expect him to swallow. When there are two, it is even going; but when there are six who keep forgetting the subject, or whose side they are on, it is confusing. Today the argument wandered to which Australian state had the largest percentage of enlisted men. The protagonist of South Australia said, 'Victoria *oughta* enlist more than South Aussie.' 'Why?' 'Because there are more wowsers in South Aussie: they object to war and won't let their sons join.'

While this was going on, I was watching a column of ants. Beneath most of their bellies they carried brown, zeppelin-shaped eggs. There also was a spry, little lizard who has his home near mine. He came out with his fine, knowing, bright eyes and glinting back tapering perfectly to the end of his fine, long tail. His sleek head was cocked and his body was poised with curiosity and anticipation.

He looked up, straight at me, and said, 'Watch this!'

Then he darted in and picked a single ant clean out of the crowd. He took only ants with eggs: sometimes he managed to get the eggs without the ants. These robbed ants would stand bewildered, take hesitant paces this way or that, and wave querulous antennae in utter futility. Meanwhile the little lizard had a feed of eggs. It soon became clear why he darted in and out so quickly. A couple of ants fixed to his tail and bit it speculatively. With a lightning switch he flung them off. He could have murdered many in revenge, but he didn't. He did not kill as sportsmen kill; I liked him because he did not want to impose his superiority on all the weaker things of the world.

Horned lizard; looks at me reproachfully as I make his portrait

*

Yesterday at dusk we caught a bamboo snake, about two feet long, in our tent. There is no doubt that they are beautiful. Why is this beauty so hateful to many of us? Is it because we can't disentangle it from our fears? Why is the snake the ancient symbol of wisdom, when naturalists tell us that it has one of the lowest brain-forms?

*

Two days ago we had to dig our road through an eight-foot high anthill. As we cut through it we got a perfect cross section of an Antopolis whose honeycombed colonies looked like smooth pieces of perforated coral six to twelve inches long.

They are dry and full of eggs and nurses. Towards the centre it becomes damper. In the centre is a large grub, as thick as my little finger, and as long as the last two joints. It is yellowish-white, with bands that constrict it in two or three places, much like an uncooked sausage with rubber bands on it. One end is fairly hemispherical, while the other is concave like the top of a pumpkin where the stem fits in. But, instead of the stem, there is the head and chest of the queen ant. The great balloon is her pregnant abdomen, which is at least fifteen times longer than the rest of her.

*

Fever again.

The officers are building a stage and terracing the hillside for seating. There is to be a concert tomorrow night, Christmas Eve, another on New Year's Eve. When we arrived here it was doubted that we could get one show together. Each night, down by the old cattle pens, the concert party is hard at it until Lights Out.

We try to tell ourselves that Christmas is just another day, but it is not. The habit of the many to celebrate on the slightest pretext, for one thing, will not let men alone. Then there is that mysterious thing called the Christmas Spirit.

I have boiled all my clothes to kill the lice. They are dry again now.

At *tenko* tonight we got a message from Captain Suzuki, Commandant of No. 4 Group, P.O.W.'s, Thailand. He said he had been appointed over us and was happy to be with us in the front line of the Greater Asian Co-prosperity Movement. In the past we had given obedient co-operation, even though life in the jungle was full of distress and hardship. But we realized our position as P.O.W.'s and members of great nations of pride.

There would probably be more jobs to be done in the future, but, realizing the cost of the work in the past, he would apply himself to the recovery of our health and conditions.

*

After midnight we heard the drone of aircraft and the guards had all the fires put out, including the cookhouse. So we had a very late breakfast.

It is Christmas Eve and a *yasume*. But, now, at 10 a.m. there is a needle parade for plague. There is rumour of an outbreak up the river.

I have spent the afternoon making Christmas menus for the camp.

BREAKFAST
Sweet pap
Sausage
Scrambled egg

DINNER
Braised steak, mashed veg., brown gravy
Pork pie
Banana custard
Rice tea

TEA
Roast beef, roast sweet potatoes, brown gravy
Banana oysters
Tea

SUPPER
Jam tart
Sweet coffee

The Christmas Spirit is creeping abroad. Tonight there are fireside groups, community singing and, when Lights Out was sounded at 11 p.m., we all stood and sang *Holy Night*.

The only Nip left in camp is Joe E. Brown, the sergeant. The rest have gone up to Kinsayok. A party went to the river to blow for fish, but got very few.

My legs are stiff from having to hop everywhere because of my poisoned foot.

*

CHRISTMAS DAY. Meals as per menu. How the cooks conjured up this stuff has got everybody beaten.

We held a service at the cemetery at 5 p.m.: the Dutch had one in the morning.

After dinner I yarned with Taffy. He told me again of the sinking of the *Repulse*. He said a torpedo had blown him through the side of the ship: from the engine room right into the sea. He came to forty-eight hours later in hospital in Singapore, badly burned and bleeding from the nose and mouth. There was a stoker petty officer who was drunk on rum. He had a pistol and he told the others in the boiler room to clear out—'If you come near me I will blow your bastard brains out!' He had gone down with the ship. Taffy was the only survivor of his engine room.

Dinner was a big meal: we had to eat it in instalments until 4.30 p.m. because our stomachs have shrunk these days. Now we have that universal Christmas feeling: bloated stomachs and wind.

The concert was a great success. Its object was fun, and we got it with the simplicity the title of the show suggests: 'Fun with F.A.' The stage was good—not just all right. To see the theatre thus extended into the heart of the jungle by the will and effort of a few men (with no musical score, and only a battered cornet) was, to me, very moving.

A show was born from the memories of the men who took part in it. It took the form of a broadcast from a radio station whose call-sign was 'K-U-R-R-A, Thailand—*the call that gets attention!*' The station was competing in a £50,000 prize for the best broadcast programme. Just before the show goes on the air, the char, Mrs Hagsbrush (Fatty) and the aspiring announcer, (the Adjutant, who wrote the show) poison the announcer, Wilberforce Winterbottom. Then these two muddle through by grabbing anybody and everybody to perform. They win by a narrow margin.

Except for Herb Smith's voice, nothing was very good, but every single item was fully enjoyed. Fatty, as Mrs Hagsbrush, was better than West End. The 1880 scene of *Going Down to Bangor* was so convincing as to be uncanny. The dress of Mum, Dad, the Maiden etc., complete with grey top-hats, bonnets, veils, coats, etc., achieved an illusion of complete reality, though they were made of rags.

The heart-breaking, though slightly improper, love tragedy between Ferdinand the Bull and Jessie the Cow rolled them in the aisles. Jessie coyly woos Ferdinand across a barbed wire fence. . . .

At last the show was over with the singing by all of *Holy Night* and *The Maoris' Farewell*.

In closing down the station, the Adjutant addressed the world at large over the dead, make-believe microphone. 'This is station K-U-R-R-A, Thailand—now closing down. From all P.O.W.s here we wish to sailors, airmen, soldiers, nurses, doctors, A.R.P. workers, lighthouse keepers, mothers, wives, sweethearts and children—wherever you may be . . . a *very* merry Christmas . . . and, good night.'

There was a tense silence for half a minute, when only the bush spoke in small clear voices like static. We knew that the sound of these words had only travelled to the wall of the mountain and echoed back to the stage; that we had spoken only to the unlistening bush . . . and yet! . . .

So passed Christmas 1943, at Hintok Road camp.

*

Holidays are over. Back to work on the road today, and we hear that the hours are to be shortened.

Major Greiner told me that Telegraphist MacDonald died at Chunkai a short time ago. Ulcers had run over his foot and leg. Amputation killed him. Six of the original thirteen naval ratings who came here with us are dead. Only three of us are here now.

We called him a 'Bocta' beetle
(here two-fifths size)

Major Woods brought me a Bocta beetle this afternoon and I made a drawing of it. He told me that at one stretch, during the *Speedo*, we went 105 days without a *yasume*.

*

On Christmas Day a truck came from Tarsau. The driver said that there were 9,700 letters waiting to be censored there.

*

We had an easy day over at the Engineers' yard: they are in a holiday mood too. They are preparing some rice-dough concoction for the New Year.

*

Out to work at the quarry breaking stone for the road. Morning shift. After dinner I made a drawing of the horned lizard while he looked at me reproachfully. Then I let him go. But he did not go until he had given me a hard stare and said, 'You should be ashamed of yourself.' I made two drawings of different kinds of mantis.

After this I felt very stiff and weary from sitting yoga-wise over the drawings. But it was not the sitting, it was fever again. I cooked myself by a fire until 9.30 p.m. As usual I talked like a gramophone. Then I went to bed with my mind racing and sleep, when it came, was semi-delirious. This is not entirely bad, for many of these unbidden febrile thoughts are often intensely interesting. And I always feel mentally exhilarated from thoughts that are not ordinary. It compensates for my washed-out body.

*

New Year's Eve. Got up feeling that the worst of the fever had gone.

After supper, I sat over the fire with Buck Pederson and we talked ourselves over all sorts of subjects. Buck is not an intellectual and he never talks nonsense. Whatever he says is always related to living. We talked and said that we would not bother to see in the New Year.

Suddenly we heard the Last Post. All the men about the fires stood, like so many high-lighted dolls against a black curtain. We both said at once, 'Who're they burying?'

I looked overhead and there were the Seven Sisters on the meridian, and Orion's Belt sitting high, also . . . all very bright.

'Midnight!' we both said incredulously.

They were burying the old year of 1943—a burying year. The Reveille wakened 1944. . . . To what? we wondered. Then Buck and I turned in.

Thai trading barge and house raft, Hintok River camp 27.1.44

XVII

Hintok River Again – January

NEW Year's Day, and a *yasume*. Spent mainly in preparing for the concert.

Wood for the fires had to be brought from the jungle. We use bamboo for these stage fires because it is easier to control the brilliance. But it takes a lot of bamboo. So a ruthless court was convened. Any man caught swearing was found guilty without being allowed to defend himself. He was then sent to get wood, or flowers for the performers' bouquets.

Our tent made a pudding. We scrounged some left-over boiled rice, and pounded it into sodden dough. We put in some sliced-up limes, eggs, palm sugar, wild ginger roots and some green peanuts. It was then moulded into a large cannon ball, heavier than Nelson ever knew. In the meantime, Len, a machine-gunner, and the only man among us with a singlet, had to take it off and boil it until we considered it sterile. The pudding was then shrouded in it, put in a kerosene tin and boiled until about three o'clock. This long boiling was more traditional than necessary. I asked Len why he boiled it so long. 'You always cook puddings a long time,' he said. But Buck said, 'Never mind about the pudding, just make sure that woggy singlet is properly done.'

With some wild pumpkin and palm sugar we made a thin jam sauce. I was elected to cut the twelve pounds between the fourteen of us. More impressive than the launching of a liner, more sentimental than the christening of a firstborn, was that first stroke that laid bare the sodden middle. Then we all ate it with a gravity matching that of the pudding. Solemnly we praised it. Politely we smacked our lips over it. There were surprises too. I got a South African threepence in my slice. The others got Japanese sens. Len had slipped them in without saying a word.

Of course, we all enjoyed the concert. It was called *The Sorrowful Sultan*, or *What Price Laughter?* The Sultan had not laughed for thirty years, nor had any of his wives borne him a son. The Court Sorcerer said, when he laughed again he would also have a son. Those who failed to produce this laugh, died: the bait for the attempt was the Princess. It ran for nearly three hours and it was almost midnight when it finished. Again, the costumes were amazing—at a time when the players, off-stage, did not have enough to keep them warm by night, nor respectable by day.

At the conclusion of the concert, Major Schneider, our senior officer, gave us a message from Sergeant Okada (Joe E. Brown) wishing us a happier year than the last. He would be staying with us and would do all he could to make the camp a happy one.

*

Tomorrow, the heavy sick are to go to Kinsayok; the rest of us, we are told, are shortly to go to the River Camp where there is some railway work to do. Another three months, it is said.

*

The few engineers have now gone from this camp. We went over and dismantled their huts for firewood.

This seems to be a festive season for the Nips. They have decorated the gateway of the camp with streamers of bark and foliage, and strung strips of white calico across also.

*

There has been no meat in the camp for ten days now, so ten men went to Kinsayok and drove thirty cattle down. They came back with the story that a Nip officer at a B.D.F. concert had announced that the war would soon be over and that the Nips were thinking of how they could get the prisoners back to their own countries. He suggested, too, that we overlook the past twelve months.

*

This morning we began to take stores down to the river. The jungle is thinning out again. As the leaves fall, Nature's million dustmen gobble up the debris. We made two trips and I brought back an impression of a Thai houseboat there, which is now committed to paper.

*

Broke camp and made a heavily laden trip to the river. It was moonlight by the time we got settled.

The new camp is on a cliff some sixty feet above the water. Getting water up for the cookhouse in kerosene tins is hard work. Major Woods is going to build a funicular lift which will bring up eight buckets at once on a platform on an eighty-degree slide. The runners will be whole tree-trunks, adzed, and fished together. He brought me eleven feet of old wire rope and asked me to make him sixty feet from it. It was like asking for a silk purse out of a sow's ear. But I remembered what I had seen some electrical linesmen doing one day before the war. They had told me that they were putting in an 'electricians' splice'. As a young know-all sailor, I scoffed at this un-nautical method. They had worked with soft wire: this was steel. However, after a lot of broken nails, cuts, and jags, Buck and I have produced just on sixty feet of rope. We stranded it and joined the strands with this splice, so that it will run comfortably around the barrel of the windlass.

*

Last night was a quiet moonlit one. By 4 a.m., most of the noises of the bush had stilled. We were all asleep.

Suddenly I was awakened by a high-pitched shout full of panic.

'There he is! GRAB HIM! GRAB HIM! What's he doing here?'

Major Woods and Lieutenant Wiley sat up as one. In that

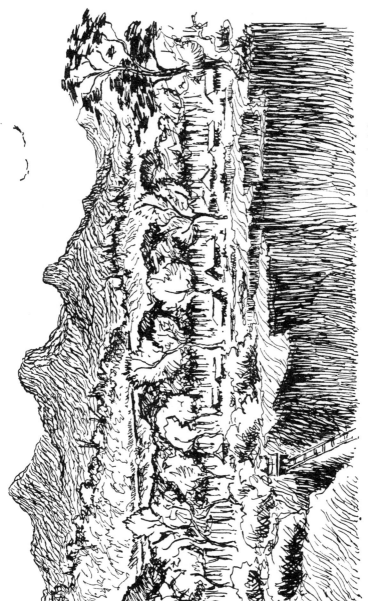

The Hintok River camp on cliffs above river—showing water elevator, and railway on the left 25.I.44

unthinking moment they looked at each other, and sprang at each other's throats.

Even more excitedly now, the original voice was shouting, '*There! Grab him . . . at the foot of Major Schneider's bed! What's that Tamil doing here? Grab him!*'

The two, fighting each other savagely, took no notice. The Voice grew still more insistent and shrill. Major Schneider, inside his mosquito net, waited for he knew-not-what from the villainous Tamil at the foot of his bed. We were all awake now, with prickly scalps and crawling spines. An officer's voice tried to tell the Voice that there was no Tamil there at all. But the Voice could *see* the man. He still could! 'Grab him,' he pleaded.

To make sure the Voice was awake, they shook him, and told him there was no Tamil there. But he was awake, all right. He shouted louder and more desperately than ever. '*Grab the bastard!*'

The other two stopped fighting, realizing their mistake.

At last the Voice was convinced that the Tamil was Major Schneider's cap, coat and haversack hung on a pole in the stark moonlight. The Voice had wakened for a drink and, reaching for his waterbottle, had seen it.

*

In the afternoon Buck, Alec and I had been back to the Road Camp to bring down more gear. At the station we spoke with some fellows from Burma. They gave us some news of the main body of *Perth*'s survivors at the 114 Kilometre Camp. We were told that there had been no deaths among the Australians there: we hope it is true. But in one of the other camps, an air raid had killed thirty Australians and ten Dutchmen.

Alec is a sergeant from the 2nd/3rd Machine Gunners. He and Buck and I have spent a lot of time together right through the show. Alec is short, broad and dark with a smooth, boylike face which is almost always calm and untroubled. But it is not an immature face. There is a great steadfastness through all his easy-going ways. Nothing seems to upset him, except in-justices and rackets. The three of us have found much in

common, outside ourselves, and our observations of Nature
and the world around have given us much to talk and speculate
on because none of us is an expert. But, together, we have
become enthusiasts.

On our way back we watched the way vines spiral around
the trees. In some places they all went left, while in others they
went right. We looked for a reason for the difference. We had
heard that they followed the sun, so that those of the Northern
Hemisphere would go opposite from those of the Southern
Hemisphere: here they went both ways in the same hemisphere. But we knew also that the sun went both north and
south of them, at different times of the year. We found that in
certain areas they would all go left, or right. We found a
dozen theories to fit. Then we found a patch where they went
both ways, so we gave up.

The water lift was tested tonight and it works. The wire will
have to be looked at daily.

Vine blossom : orange-vermilion 2″–
3″. Background shows how vines in-
vade trees and make them appear in
full bloom

The river mist which floats in the valley for an hour each
morning makes some grand pictures. This morning, standing
on the platform of the lift, some sixty feet above the vague
surface of the water, I caught a lovely subject. Below me, with
bows poking out from behind a clump of foggy basket-willow,

was a barge and a scow-like motor boat, with a flat canopy roof. On this roof were more than a hundred red pots in rows, making the only colour in the soft grey picture. Beyond the boats, and resting neither on the surface of the river nor in the sky, was a willowed sandspit on the opposite bank. It was like a soft smudge of Chinese ink on damp paper.

*

The camp at night is like some native quarter in the Middle East. Tents of various patterns are scattered about, and little bamboo huts with attap, or bark roofs and walls, are here and there. There are fires and cooking pots; conversation, chanting and singing; the boiling up of the nightly coffee (if you can get it); pudding boiling; or the making of horrible hard burnt scones of rice dough. All this is only cooking in a different way rice which is already cooked. Figures stand naked by the fire-light over kerosene tins of hot water, bathing and gleaming in streaked, wet highlights, as they move: ruddy against the black shadows.

*

I am getting to a stage again when I can observe things outside myself with greater interest than I have for a long while. The crust of my self-preservative selfishness seems to be breaking at last. For a while at least the struggle to keep alive is not so hard, death is not so imminent these fine dry days when Nature is so beautiful.

*

Major Woods brought me a toc-ta lizard, which I painted. He posed perfectly for five hours after he had buried his teeth in a stick. When I came to let him go he would not release the stick. At last I prised his mouth open and found that he had left his needlelike teeth still buried in the wood.

*

A Chinese in the camp here has been found to have leprosy.

Toc-Ta' lizard with a beautiful golden eye. To hear just seven toc-ta calls is good luck, they say

He was noticed by our doctors at the washplace. We have been warned to be careful in our contacts.

We can write another letter card with slightly different wording. We always wonder if anybody ever really gets them.

*

It is a clear and peaceful day; here and there the unhurried noises of saw and axe and the quiet morning remarks of one man to another; no monotonous piping of plover, nor the flighting cries of parrots, nor the silly screech of peacocks, which Joe E. Brown shoots when they come out to strut on the sand-bank over the river, nor crows' flat cawking; nor have the monkeys started their melodious, larrikin calls of love, fun or anguish.

Just over from our tent, Old Jack, a sar'major, digs in his garden which he has begun because he doesn't have to go out to work. At the moment he has stooped to point out the micro-scopic progress of an onion shoot since last night. He says, of course you can see it!

The hills beyond the river are warm and soft, looking rich with the yellow of dying leaves and the red of sprouting shoots in treetops. The bamboos are still and soaring anything up to

100 feet: they give a deferential bow of grace, which is more in their appearance than character. Their tall plumes of pale leaves suggest a femininity—but, like some women, beneath that lacy charm there are thorns of poisonous spite, split razor-edges which cut to the bone: they have driven men to despair and made them weep.

Now a man is whistling on a barge coming up the river behind a chugging, one-lunged, *pom-pom* diesel boat. Chinese and Tamil maccan boys go past with a gang's meal balanced on poles and swinging in rhythm. From a long way off comes the faint *gruff-gruff*, *gruff-gruff*, of a train up Kinsayok way. Three engines labour up the big hill behind camp with the *clash-clash* of a piston exhaust. As they climb above the camp, they will tell each other with a screech and a tired wailing whistle, that they want to stop. Then they will catch their breaths and raise more steam for the supreme effort. There is fairly heavy rail traffic, especially at night. Mostly troops, I think.

At the end of the camp a rocky hill rises up a couple of hundred feet and plunges sheer into the river on the other side. It is tree-covered and the home of a colony of large, short-tailed baboons. They call to each other and come down to get a better look at us. It does not take much to realize that *we* are in *their* zoo.

*

About midnight . . . clear and moonless . . . Out Fires! Out Fires! The heavy drone of aircraft in wide formations: to the east, to the west, and overhead. To Bangkok! The young men in those planes will hail Bangkok and the east very differently from Joseph Conrad in *Youth*. A Thai said that Bangkok had been raided thirty times.

Today, we sat about over at the Engineers' without much to do. A large, black-faced possum was asleep in a hole in a tree. He was about three feet long to the tip of his bushy tail. When we disturbed him his eyes popped wide open. With undulating bounds he climbed straight up, almost to the top of the tree. At the top he poised for a second, stiffened, then leapt straight out into space. His legs stretched to the four corners of the compass and he turned into a hexagonal kite: he was a phalanger. As gracefully as a paper dart he glided down in a slight curve, losing height and threading between trees until, after about seventy-five yards, he came up on the trunk of another tree, about six feet from the ground. He clambered to the top of it, and took off again. Each successive leap took him further into the jungle.

Part of our diet is now bean shoots which we cultivate on wet bags down by the river. They are very rich in vitamin C.

*

On top of the cliff, Joe E. Brown has had built an idyllic little bamboo hut, complete with surrounding veranda and low garden fence of split bamboo. The whole Pacific could not produce anything nicer. It was a pleasant, easy-going day with the mirror-like river seventy feet straight below us.

About noon, out of a breathless day, came a sigh. A gust of wind stole through the already half-naked trees. A shower of big leaves tumbled down with the hoarse, rustling whisper of one far-gone in dying.

A Thai poling his barge across the river

Some forty letters arrived in camp tonight—all for the 8th

Division. There is also a rumour that we are going to Japan to
work in the coal mines.*

*

It is just one year since we arrived in the jungle.

Buck and I went out to get wood. It was a fine, cold morning
with the red sun breaking through the bloody mist and showing
us the softly lighted tree-tops in the valley below us, as we stood
on the railway. We watched the Chinese gambling with the
Tamils, using cowrie-shell counters. Except that they always
count the shells in fours, we could not make head nor tail of
the game.

In the afternoon Buck, Alec and I went to the sandbank
where we watched monkeys, pheasant, and hornbills. The
hornbills creak even when they glide: I suppose, from their
throats, though the illusion is that their wings are creaking
doors.

*

Tonight the show was *Kannibal Kapers*. There is something
about these shows that no other theatre could give. The stage
is set at the foot of the rocky hill which is the home of the black
baboons, and it makes a natural amphitheatre for seating above
the stage.

The stage is of built-up earth and bamboo, and of the conventional design, complete with wings. Javanese Dutch took
the parts of natives and concubines. Two ukeleles were the
whole orchestra. In the centre of the stage, stood the great god
Ju-Ju, with the sacrificial pot in front of him.

Ju-Ju is cut from the trunk of a kapok tree, with the sap still
in it. But already he has a life of his own. He is complete, with
belly and breasts and prominent navel. His hollowed-out eye
sockets are lit from behind with two slush lamps which also
smoke and add to the supernatural effect. The arms are hinged
to raise with each solemn and spine-chilling proclamation.

The witch doctor and his rival were the comics, intriguing

---

* This was ultimately true for me.

Stage set for 'Kannibal Kapers', Hintok River camp 27.1.44

to get each other boiled and eaten. For the rest, it was a musical which gave the Javanese a chance to sing many of their fine songs.

There was something about this international flavour of the show that affected us all. And we talked about it when we got back to our tents. The harmony of people together: the theatre and make-believe seems to be an important thing to humanity —particularly in primitive states. And here, a mighty effect was wrought between the two big fires illuminating the stage from either side. They crackled and exploded like cannons, and steam and water hissed out of them as the show went on.

*

There is not much work to be done here. An occasional trip out with the surveyors, wood-getting for the camp, and that is about all. On *Tenko* we have a session of Nip army drill. Then, each man has to take a squad and drill it in Nipponese. Nobody really minds it, except those who are always complaining. It is done in a spirit of fun. And Joe E. Brown is tolerant.

By the way, Ju-Ju now sits at the gate to the garden of Joe E. Brown's little hut. He asked if it could be placed there after the concert. He is very proud of it. I suspect, at night in the moonlight, he comes out and sits silently before it, as if it were some remote ancestor.

We are keeping A.R.P. watches these nights in two-hour shifts.

The latest rumour is that we don't go back to Kinsayok, but go down river in fourteen days' time. One of the Japs said that malaria-men did not go to Nippon. This would apply to ninety-five per cent of us.

This is the 31st. We have been out to get wood for the fires at the Dutch sing-song tonight to celebrate Princess Beatrix's birthday. Then four of us spent the rest of the forenoon lazing at the sandbank. This has become a favourite spot. At first the Nips came and found us swimming there. We waited for the storm, but they went away again. Then they came back with tools and built us a springboard! It is about 500 yards up river from the camp landing. Often, when there is a crowd swimming there, and the dinner bugle blows, you can see men push a few sticks of bamboo in as rafts and float down

Survivor of O & P Battalion. Lazy Daze. Hintok Sand Bank 31.1.44

to the camp. When they come abreast of it they abandon-ship and swim in.

Alec went into the bush and brought back a few large, red, camelia-like flowers which had fallen from a big white-trunked tree without any leaves yet. The tree was thick with flowers and, as he stood under it, a whole flock of birds were gorging on the honey from them. They shook a shower of honey-dew on him and he came back quite sticky. Alec said that the honey was bitter, not sweet.

Then Lindy got restless. He heard a noise he thought was a lizard or a broody bird. So he went to find out. After a while, he came back and told us it was a lively little squirrel doe, playing with five bucks. They would pursue her more or less in turn, along some *cul de sac* of a branch. Each assured her of motherhood. Lindy said she was coy and artful, but never indignant. At other points we heard similar noises.

'Well,' said Buck, 'it must be spring . . . at least for the squirrels.'

At night we went to the sing-song. The Dutch supplied sweet coffee and *catchung goulah*, a kind of nut toffee. Most of the show was in Dutch, but the songs were in French, Malay, Dutch and English. As always the firelighted trees enclosed and united us in that strange sentimental way they have. Almost exactly overhead I could see the bright pinpoints of Orion's Belt.

Buck was looking up too. 'The trees are still like wax,' he said.

Vermilion blossom (3″–4″ diameter) of the white-trunked tree. The Blossom comes before the leaves

XVIII

Tarsau Again – February

FIVE days of February have already passed. I have to search around to find out what day it is.

On the first day I had no breakfast and we spent the forenoon on the sandbank. Nor did I have any dinner: I went down with heavy malaria. I sweated all night. It rained and my head and shoulders got wet, but I didn't care. Buck pulled me in out of it. For three days I did not eat. Whenever they rattled the tin for meals, I tried to shut out the sound that was making me heave. At last Buck cooked me a four-egg omelette and I managed to eat some of it. The next day he brought me a little soup. At night one of the fellows brought me some sago. It is almost the most depressing bout I have had.

The strange thing about it is that, over the past ten days, it has swept through the camp. I don't think it has missed a man. Buck was just getting over it when I went down. Our doctor went down with it too, and Doctor Corlette has come down from Kinsayok. We think it is dengue fever.

The days are hot; the valley is heavy with blue bush-fire smoke, and the mountains are shrouded. It rained a little at 9 p.m. and settled the dust.

Alec, Buck and I have been talking over things that have happened. We have all gained a greater respect for the humble body. We are sure that the body is *not* a snare set by the Devil for the destruction of the soul. To have seen bodies trying to go on living; to have seen them trying to repair themselves un-aided; even to have seen them fail, was to learn to respect them. Too much of Man's achievement is outside himself in books and libraries and machines. The old *inbuilt* skills and instincts are atrophying, and man is losing his independence and individuality. He needs a whole city for a slave, while he is a slave to that city.

I recalled this: 'The more things the mind knows, the better it understands its own powers, so much the more easily can it direct itself and propose rules to itself. The better also it understands the order of Nature, the more easily it can *restrain itself from what is useless*.' This was from my old friend Spinoza.

Buck and Alec agreed.

*

We are to be on the train at 11 a.m. on the 12th: the day after tomorrow. We had a plague needle this morning.

*

We are leaving Hintok at last. It is hard to believe. We are dressed in the full glory of the rags we have left. We are lounging about on our packs, trying to get comfortable in the heat. Buck is lying near me with his head in the shade. He is flat on his back in the dust, with his head on his pack and his hat over his face.

'You writing?' his muffled voice comes from under his hat.

'Yes, about getting out of here.'

'You can say good-bye to the joint for me, too.'

'I will . . . and to some of the blokes who are not coming with us.'

'Yes . . .' he said. '. . . but there's *some* I'm glad are staying . . . they were no good when they were alive . . . so what's the good of saying they were . . . just because they are dead? It makes y'sick when y'hear blokes say, "Poor Joe! He was a good feller." When all the time y'know they hated him . . . they're frightened what might happen to them when th die . . . bloody hypocrites!'

Buck's plain honesty trailed off matter-of-factly under his hat. And he was silent again.

'There was a lot of good blokes, Buck,' suggested Alec, who was reading.

'Course there was . . . I was only talkin' about the no-good bastards . . . and now they're talkin' about them as if they'd been decent.'

'You're right there. There's still some of 'em left. I wouldn't like to have their conscience when they get home.'

Leaving is hard to believe. This valley . . . hot and parched . . . the big trees leafless . . . bare like bone . . . it is almost a petrified forest. Crawling beneath are the little saurian relics: blue-black hard-shelled scorpions—slow-moving like old tanks, or like fakes in a monster film; big, red, horny centipedes with a mesmerizing movement in the ripple of rapid legs; and the harmless, coloured, round-backed millipedes running around like painted toy trains looking for a tunnel; scaled snakes glide with a dry rustle. . . .

Come back in a thousand years, where will the skeletons be? If you go into the bush, off our regular paths, you will find some scattered there now. A white, sad skull with a fallen jaw, gap-toothed; a tibia or femur sticking up like a stake; while on unburied bodies, from the bones of the hips across to the chest cage, there sometimes hangs a hardened hide of skin, like a sheet over an armchair. In this grisly shroud are rents and tears, as if the moths had been at work. Through the holes you can see the gone-ness of life as a millipede, finding a tunnel at last, crawls incuriously in.

Many of our men are here in this valley of the Kwai Noi, through which the Railway now runs. They died when this parched, leafless forest was a dripping green cave with a black, muddy floor which seemed to suck men down like quicksand and hold them there until they could not rise again.

The cemeteries in which we put the remains of these men are cleared and neat now. We worked hard to give them that order and a calm, deathlike dignity which was not available when the men died. When the next Wet Season comes the jungle will climb the fence again on to the graves, and hide this sorry little patch forever. Perhaps a bright red flower will bloom and a bird will drink its honey.

*

The men have stopped skylarking. We are all hot and tired and restless. The card games have bored, no longer is a dozing man toppled off his pack into the dust with roars of laughter, or sleeping men's faces tickled with straws. There is not much talk at all.

Fatty said, 'You still writing? Pack it up! It makes me tired to look at you.'

Looking about the near-silent men, I feel that there is something we are all thinking, but that we will never own it. It has been easy to think only of getting out. But I have thought about other things, however distasteful, because I have been afraid of thinking too much of getting out. There seems to be just so much good a man can take these days. Somewhere, remotely inside me, I can feel a little burning thrill, a trickle—like an excitement jumping up and down. But it is distant like a child calling from a long way off, as if you can only see him through the wrong end of a telescope. We are keeping our hopes silent.

I can hear a train whistle in the distance, up by Kinsayok. Another half an hour: it is 6 p.m. All day with nothing to do but sit and think and sweat. It is still hot. I am stiff from sitting and writing. I'll stretch my legs.

The train has stopped half-way up the big hill at the back of the old camp. They always do. They can't hold the steam on the wood fuel. Stick in more wood. Get up more steam. All the engines have asthma and the steam leaks away. Three of them are wheezing on the hill now, trying to store up enough steam to pull the train over the top of the hill and roll into Hintok.

She's over the hill!

Men are getting up out of the hot dust and smacking clouds of it off themselves. Packs on shoulders . . . moving forward. It is 7.30 p.m. The trucks have carried horses into Burma. The acrid dust kicked up as we get in nearly chokes us.

The train is moving slowly out.

In the dusk, among others, we are leaving the young sailors behind forever. But we are glad to be going.

*

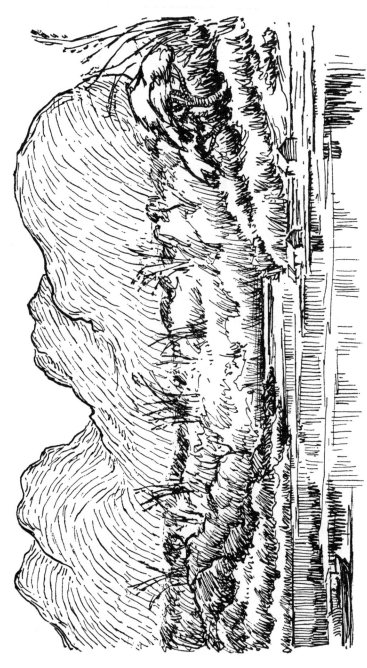

Elephant Hills across the river at Tarsau 5.3.44. The huts are on bamboo rafts (right)

Eventually we arrived at Tarsau at 12.30 a.m. We were lucky, for a big red moon came up out of the smoke over the trees to show us something of the way we had to stumble along from the station to the camp.

Here we were counted many times in that unsure way the Japanese soldiers have. Then we were pushed blindly into broken-down huts with steep low roofs. They had no walls, very little attap on the roof, and half of the bedboards gone. Bugs and lice owned the place. I killed what I thought were four big hungry ants crawling up my legs, but the smell quickly told me that they were bugs. We were fed a meal of yellow rice—Burma rice, they called it—with whitebait, which I ate until my mouth was a salty mess of fins and scales.

About 2.30 a.m., I crawled in with the bugs, and slept on a bare nine inches of split bamboo slats having enough space on either side to fall off. But I can sleep like my tree-dwelling ancestors. I slept well and all I know of the bugs was the strong smell of those that I had squashed in my sleep, and the red lumps where they had fed.

*

This is a big camp of 8,000. Today is a general *Yasume* day. We wandered about finding old acquaintances all the morning.

In the afternoon Ken, Fatty, Jim, George (whom we have rejoined here) and I went over to the hospital lines. The hospital covers a large area with long, scattered huts. It contains from 2,300 to 2,800 patients. It has a mildewed atmosphere of recent death over it. But the old hands say that the death rate is now down to one-point-something, instead of twenty-three a day, not so long ago.

Scotty Thompson, a R.A.A.F. sergeant air-gunner, is in the hospital. We first met him and half a dozen other R.A.A.F.'s back in Tjilatjap. They were captured not long after us. They had flown from the Middle East right into the same trap as we had. Scotty had been a medium-sized, active man with sandy hair: a fast, strong football, handball, and basketball player. He was always cheerful, generous, unassuming, and particularly unselfish. Now, he has not only lost flesh so that his muscles are just so many strings from point to point, but his frame seems to have shrunk to childlike proportions.

At the ends of all these huts, is a small screened-off section with a couple of bedplaces. Here, men are put when they are about to die, so that they won't distress the others. An orderly told me that Scotty had been put out there twice. There had been no hope for him. They had asked him how he felt. 'Good as gold,' he said, 'and it's no good you bastards putting me out here—I'm coming back!' And each time he did.

We asked him how he was.

'Good as gold,' he told us with a voice completely devoid of self-pity. Then conversationally he added, 'Can't seem to put on much weight, though.'

Then Seib, our friend from Surinam in the Dutch West Indies, came along. We had all been together in Tjilatjap. Scotty was very happy to see us all together again, gathered on the bamboo slats of his bed. His face was alight with pleasure: the face that was brown, wrinkled parchment drawn over a shrunken skull; the colourless lips drawn back in a death's-head grin over teeth that seemed a bit too big. His eyes seemed enormous, dark and sunken. But when he said, 'Like old times —all the old Tjilatjap mob together again!' then there was a great warmth in that hideous face and a twinkle in the lack-lustre eyes. We talked over old times, and it was Scotty who cheered us up.

The orderly came around while we were there, with almost the only amenity the hospital could give (and this not always). It was a small saki cup of lime juice. Scotty wanted to share it with us. We all told him roughly not to be so bloody wet. But he wouldn't drink it while we were there, though we told him to. He said, 'It's not very nice drinking when you fellers haven't got one.'*

There are numbers of men here without legs. I have heard that it is estimated that, up and down the line, there have been 1,500 amputations. One story says that the A Force had 500

* Scotty got back and is now the father of a fine family.

amputations of which 400 were fatal. But it is hard to know the real facts.

Joe Richards, so far, is the only one to have mastered the home-made wooden legs the camp workshop, under Weary's direction, has made. Weary has been here a while now—he came down while we were at Kinsayok. Joe has been most determined about getting used to the artificial leg. It has taken plenty of guts. As an example to encourage others, he fitted on his leg and threw his crutches away, refusing to use them again. Joe was the man who had asked to have his leg taken off.

*

This big camp is not so much to our liking after our little holiday at Hintok. Big-city-like it is full of restrictions, rackets, and the like.

*

Rumours. Rumours. We stay. We are in transit. B.D.F. come down tomorrow and we go with them. Nippon on the 27th. Nippon in four months. On and on.

*

During the bad times here, men would collapse on the latrines and fall in. At least one was drowned.

*

It is just two years since our ship was sunk. Two years since we were launched into this. And, as the month closes, there is talk of marching out. We do want to get out of the Jungle. It is not so much the jungle as it is now we fear. It is the Wet Jungle that will come again. We are afraid of drowning in it next time.

XIX

Out of the Smother – A Postscript

NOTHING much has happened until now, Sunday, 26th of March.

We have worked in the jungle surveying, getting wood for the charcoal burner, cutting bamboos, clearing along the telegraph line, and so on. We have swapped yarns with others from other parts of the railway. We have had our bouts of fever.

But now, at 5.30 p.m., comes the order, 'All fit men from Hintok stand by to move in thirty-six hours.'

*

On Tuesday 28th, at 9 a.m., we were marched out to a large bare patch of ground with all we possessed. I had a ragged shirt, the shorts I was wearing, a dirty blanket, a piece of canvas and a few other odds and ends. I had, also, my diaries and drawings: all I really had to show for the past uncertain fifteen months. I had worked hard to keep them going, and I had taken risks to keep them safe.

Now, on a piece of bare ground, the Japanese were going to search us. For all the dangers, I had not been able to bring myself to abandon them. And now it was too late. They were bellowing hoarsely for us to empty our pockets out. Though it was a search, it reminded me of the many times I had mustered ordinary seamen's kits with the duty officer. I thought of all those kits neatly laid out on the spare hammocks. So I took my piece of canvas and spread it on the ground like a spare hammock—and it was about that size. But I slipped my diaries and drawings underneath it. Then, on top, I laid out my miserable kit with some semblance of naval good order. This concealed the bumps underneath.

Most of the others had simply tipped all their gear out on the ground at the feet of the searching Japanese and let them scrabble through it. The soldier coming along our line was pulling things about roughly and growling with Japanese ferocity. As he came to the man next to me, he flung the gear about and came across a tattered book.

'*Nani?*' he squealed, '*Ba-a-GEERA! Book-oo nie! Damme, Damme!*'

He tore up the book in seeming rage and viciously slapped the man's face. Then he turned to me.

I stood with my feet planted on the canvas, with a wooden seriousness on my face and my body strained to an exaggerated 'attention'. This appeals to Japanese soldiers. I stood thus impassively above my mean, but neatly laid-out kit—and my diaries. It was all spread with a candid innocence which proclaimed that it could not conceal anything.

He stopped in front of me, appraising my puffed-up chest and arms stretched like bow-strings at my side. For good measure, I threw him a stiff salute. This checked him while he returned it, and it threw him out of his step from the crawling predatory picnic he had just been having with the other kits. It brought him back to the drill book. He looked a little surprised at my neat array. I didn't budge. He took a step forward. I quailed. I waited for him to snatch something and reveal the bumps underneath. He stopped, with his feet almost on the canvas at the other end.

'*Yuroshi!*' he said, 'Number One—gooda! *Yasume.*'

And he passed on.

When the search was over we marched straight to the station. We embarked in the train that was going to take us out of this jungle. After the train passed Wampo, we began to run down out of the mountains. We watched the Jungle trailing behind our rattling train which hooted hoarsely once in a while as if it were shouting our feelings for us.

This was the realization of a hope. Many had not lived to experience it; none of us felt we could again. But not even the thoughts of the dead—the horribly dead—could still this inner personal exulting.

Once before, especially, I had experienced this feeling . . . almost exactly two years before.

. . . Then, I was alive after a battle and swimming at midnight in a shark-infested sea. Our ship was gone. Our human enemy, the Japanese, had left us to the mercy of the sea. And the Sea was as implacable as the Jungle. The long dark night was spent in this element man could not live in. It was a continual struggle to keep from drowning; there was the continual fear of sharks. It sapped our energy and, given time, the Sea would take us. We swam only to stay alive. We made no valiant struggle. Weakly, we tried to stay only on this side of death. There was no plan, only blind purpose.

. . . With the morning we could see land—distant. The current bore us toward an island. Our weak struggle was renewed and we swam for the land as it came close. But the current that bore us so close now tried to tear us away.

. . . This was our last chance. There was little remaining strength with which to beat the whole impersonal and apparently cruel sea. For many that strength was not enough.

. . . As we reached the shore each man, then, was an island unto himself. It would be hard to forget the feeling that I had at the touch of that beach under my weak crawling limbs; but it would be impossible to feel it again without equal stimulus. I can remember the coarse coral sand between my fingers, the solid compactness of it pressing against my numb knees: the delicious solidity of it . . . to know at last one could be still and not sink or drown . . . to be now alive. We had, by a very small margin, beaten the sea. Nothing that has happened since has ever quite quenched the thankfulness of that moment, two years ago. . . .

Tonight, at Tamuan on the plains of Siam, I lie on the bare earth, under the stars, and listen to the faint rumble of distant thunder which is like the ominous echo of events now distant in the jungle. I feel the bare earth, dry and hard under me, pressing against me in support. I feel that same feeling again.

This time we have escaped the Jungle. For the moment, that

is all we ask—we are out of the smother at last, and I have brought this record with me.

*

We did not go back into the jungle. But George did, and he suffers to this day as a result. We stayed at Tamuan until June, when Japan Parties were made up from the remaining 'fit' men. With others, Ken, Fatty, Buck, Alec and I were taken to Singapore by train, and thence to Japan by sea.

There we spent twelve months in coal mines under the Inland Sea. About a month after the end of the war in the Pacific, we were embarked in a U.S.N. Hospital ship (*Consolation*) at Wakayama, near Osaka. After being 'processed' in Manila by the Americans, we joined H.M.S. *Speaker* (an escort carrier) and were brought to Sydney.

The next day I was in Melbourne with my family again, after nearly four years.

Survivor of O & P Battalion 29.1.44

APPENDIX

MEDICAL EXPERIENCES IN
JAPANESE CAPTIVITY*

By Lieut.-Col. E. E. DUNLOP, M.S., F.R.C.S.

THE fruits of experience as prisoners of war in Japanese hands, though abundant, were exceedingly bitter. Herculean tasks were enforced upon semi-starved and enfeebled captives—for example, the construction of the Burma–Siam railway by slave labour with primitive hand tools. To medical personnel fell the scarcely less arduous task of clearing the Augean stables of sickness. The crude slave hovels used for the accommodation of prisoners were euphemistically termed 'hospitals' when allotted to the sick, and were provided with some slender medical staff. During the days of darkest savagery they were little more than crowded pest-houses where sick were conveniently segregated, though by no means allowed to die in peace.

I have been asked to record briefly some salient impressions of three and a half years of imprisonment in Java and Siam, involving prisoner-of-war command of a number of camps and hospitals, including railway construction camps. The medical problems of the scattered prisoner-of-war groups in the Far East, and the struggles of the medical services against great odds, are of historical interest. The circumstances militated against research or far-reaching discovery but sharpened the unaided senses to greater clinical acuity and necessitated resource and ingenuity of a high degree. It is obvious that many prisoners of war will suffer for the remainder of their lives from disabilities related to their grim ordeal. Those who witnessed their fortitude and unconquerable spirit under conditions of

* Reprinted by kind permission of the author and the Editor of *British Medical Journal*. First printed October 5th, 1946. Vol. ii, p. 481.

great suffering, slow starvation, and physical wretchedness hope that their disabilities will be fully comprehended and will receive generous consideration.

CONQUEST OF JAVA

In Java, as in other conquered regions, medical personnel together with sick and wounded shared in the general programme of attrition designed to teach a sharp lesson to 'criminals' and 'rabble' who had dared to oppose the Japanese Army. All the inmates of an Allied general hospital under my command were ejected at a few hours' notice, and the majority forcibly marched to a fantastically overcrowded native gaol with negligible medical arrangements, where calculated humiliation, gross under-feeding, and savage regimentation were the daily routine.

Only a few medical stores, widely dispersed and concealed, escaped confiscation. Defiance of international conventions was emphasized by the confiscation of Red Cross brassards, along with badges of rank, unit or service ribbons, decorations, etc. Under compulsion all Red Cross markings were obliterated. Mass violence and beatings and some untidy public executions enforced obedience, under vigorous protest. Uniform clipping of the hair to the scalp was required, and the extravagant mass 'salutations' enforced by the humblest of Japanese soldiers produced spectacles not devoid of Gilbertian humour. Medical officers and padres spent considerable time and energy in the task of instructing in Japanese drill and ceremony. There was some alleviation of the harshness of treatment in the British P.O.W. camp under my administration at Bandoeng, where for a few months the prisoners carried on highly organized educational and recreational activity in the teeth of difficulties and-misunderstandings.

Malnutrition and deficiency diseases were rife within six months, pellagra being excessively common and associated in approximately one-third of all troops with distressing burning of the feet. The ration at this time amounted to about 2,000 calories daily. While much more adequate than that in some later camps, it consisted largely of low-grade rice or dried potatoes, and was thus markedly deficient in protein, fats, and vitamins, especially of the B complex. The Japanese paid little heed to protests, carefully documented requests, or demonstrations of cases, but following the official acceptance of the captives as 'prisoners of war' meagre pay for work was introduced. This pay together with some fortunate clandestine negotiation for money on credit enabled us to augment the diet of the sick with purchased foodstuffs according to need.

THE BURMA–SIAM RAILWAY

Late in 1942 the movement of Allied prisoners to Lower Burma and Siam commenced. Soon some 60,000 captives and a larger force of Asiatic coolies were given the gigantic task of cleaving a railway through 400 kilometres of jungle-clothed mountains and oppressive valleys between Thanbyuzayat (Burma) and Bampong (Siam). By the end of 1943 the main task was completed by the enfeebled remnant of the decimated force. Some 15,000 prisoners together with uncounted scores of thousands of Asiatic coolies had perished. While this major tragedy was largely due to calculated official brutality and inhumanity, Japanese medical officers contributed in lending what zeal they possessed to the support of medical enormity in search of further labourers, rather than in a co-ordinated medical plan of evacuation, hospital services, and supply of medical stores.

Indiscriminate treatment of prisoners led to my being placed in command of a working force of Java captives transferred as packed human freight in the holds of a tramp to Singapore, and subsequently by rail for four days in box-trucks to Siam, where in due course they marched into the Konyu–Hintok section of the line in dense jungle about the Kwa-Noi river. Some six months of command of working camps mixed with endless medical work and peripatetic surgery was followed by experience of command of jungle hospitals, including Kinsayok, Tarsau, and Chungkai, before I was transferred in June, 1944, with large numbers of sick of the Siam force to Nakom Patom.

There I enjoyed the privilege of working under Lieut-Col A. E. Coates, A.A.M.C., as O.C. surgical section of this large hospital devoted to men still broken in health by the railway construction in Burma and Siam. The grimmest battle for the lives of men had already been fought in the crudity of jungle areas, and the attitude of the Japanese left little doubt that improved conditions bore some relationship to the changed state of the war and to world knowledge of the treatment of prisoners.

WORKING CAMPS

During railway construction men worked under savage pressure up to sixteen hours a day for months without rest, so that they rarely saw their squalid huts and tents in daylight. Amid thorny jungle and rotting corruption, with ceaseless monsoon rain lashing their bodies and soaking their miserable accommodation, large numbers were soon bootless, with practically no bedding, and reduced to rags about their loins. The heat was in general excessive, and well-nigh intolerable to bare feet in rock cuttings, but the greatest load on men's spirits was the pouring monsoon rain, converting the whole area into a quagmire of evil-smelling mud.

Pellagra, diarrhoea, irritable bladders, and massed overcrowding interrupted rest, and the urge was often uncontrollable as men floundered out into darkness, rain, and mud. Hunger, food deficiency diseases, malaria, dysentery, ulcers, and skin sepsis, and extreme exhaustion were woven into a dull fabric of suffering rent here and there by sharp outbreaks of cholera. Whatever reserves of physical strength or spirit a man might possess were in the long run exploited, so that the stronger suffered longer, only to pay the same relentless tribute in loss of life and broken health.

Apart from some capricious inoculation measures, preventive medicine, hygiene, and sanitation were negligible. Men and tools were grudgingly spared for the most primitive sanitary measures. Such materials as antimalarial oil or chloride of lime were absent or pathetically scarce. Often there were insufficient containers to supply boiled water. Until the belated supply of limited American Red Cross stores in mid-1944, medical supplies other than quinine were farcical. A typical monthly issue for a thousand men, mostly sick, consisted of 6 to 12 bandages, a small piece of gauze or cloth, 1 or 2 ounces of spirit or iodine solution, and a few dozen assorted tablets of dubious value. Non-expendable stores such as instruments and ward equipment, though freely confiscated in the early months, were afterwards only possessed by cunning or ingenuity, since no issues were made. Allied medical personnel were distributed with scant regard to either incidence of sickness or qualifications on a scale of about 1% of strength—doctors and orderlies combined—for all purposes. Where by faulty distribution the number exceeded this slender provision, as in Konyu and Hintok camps, they were compelled to do routine manual work and the sick were deprived of their services.

'MOST SHAMEFUL DEED'

As the working force deteriorated under semi-starvation, diseases, and illimitable exhaustion, ferocious pressure was exerted to secure from sick and dying men increased fortitude in the Japanese Imperial cause. As sickness was regarded as a crime, the sick were given no pay and a reduced ration scale. (Col. Nakomura on assuming command of prisoners of war in Siam in June, 1943: 'Those who fail in charge by lack of health is regarded in Japanese Army as most shameful deed.')

Relentless insistence upon fixed figures of workmen daily, if defied, led to the sick being turned out of hospital with indiscriminate violence. Sick parades were endless, since the wretched condition of the men required daily assessment and comparison. They dragged in up to midnight or beyond, and attendance was again needed at works parades before dawn. Japanese N.C.O.s and privates frequently overruled medical officers and cut short argument with violence.

In the Hintok area works parades were a deplorable spectacle, featuring scores of men tottering with the support of sticks, or even being carried out bodily to meet fixed figures. Men unable to stand were carried, to work in a lying or sitting position. During the grimmer months of railway construction the sick were deliberately persecuted by works supervisors. For example, men with horribly festering bare feet were forced to work on sharp rocks or in thorny jungle hauling logs; disabling ulcers were struck or kicked; those collapsing were savagely handled; and sufferers from diarrhoea and dysentery were compelled to foul themselves working.

The engineer officer of this area, Lieut Hirota, led his men in ferocity by personal example, and on occasion flogging of the sick was followed by their demise. Lieut Osuki, P.O.W. camp commander, stated that he did not care if sick men died, since 'working percentage better'. Lieut-Col Ishii, in charge of 13,000 prisoners, when shown emaciated dysentery sufferers devoid of drugs, commented on the treatment by no food for two to three days with loud laughter and the retort: 'In future no food one week, better!' The pungent protests of medical officers against these conditions need hardly be instanced. Capricious evacuations of sick were by casual hitch-hiking on passing lorries or barges. The weak supported or carried the weaker. Frequently days were spent in transit with exposure and little food. Barges arrived at jungle hospitals with both the sick and the dead in the stench of gangrene and dysentery.

JUNGLE HOSPITALS

Typical of early base hospitals heroically evolved under the greatest difficulties in Burma were Thanbyuzayat, Lieut-Col. T. Hamilton, A.A.M.C.; and 55-Kilo hospital, Lieut-Col. A. E. Coates, A.A.M.C. In Siam, Tarsau, Lieut-Col. W. G. Harvey, R.A.M.C.; Takanoun, Major T. M. Pemberton, R.A.M.C.; Chungkai, Majors Reed, R.A.M.C., D. Black, I.M.S., and Lieut-Col. J. St. C. Barrett, R.A.M.C.; Kanburi, Lieut-Col. J. Malcolm, R.A.M.C.; Tamarkan, Major A. A. Moon, A.A.M.C.; and Non Pladuk, Major Smythe, R.A.M.C.

The conditions at Tarsau and Chungkai hospitals at the time I was first associated with them are illustrative. Each contained a constant population of approximately 2,500 very sick men as a citadel within a jungle city of sickness. The sick lay massed together on bamboo staging in decrepit collapsing huts. Bedding and hospital utensils were largely non-existent. No instruments and very few medicines were supplied by the Japanese. Lack of tools, materials, and fit men combined with overcrowding to create a nauseating lack of hygiene. Bugs, lice, and almost universal scabies infection produced minor torments and florid skin sepsis. Men were too weak to keep themselves clean, and there were few orderlies, or even containers for water.

TABLE I.—*Chungkai P.O.W. Hospital Statistics*

Diseases	1943			1944		
	Total Treated	Died	Case Mortality Rate %	Total Treated	Died	Case Mortality Rate %
Malaria . . .	3,336	67	2·0	1,753	13	0·74
N.Y.D. . .	374	—	Nil	142	—	—
Bacillary dysentery .	734	129	17·5	139	2	1·44
Amoebic dysentery .	1,309	266	20·3	1,113	46	4·13
Enteritis . .	565	19	1·6	414	12	2·92
Cholera . .	134	54	40·3	8	—	—
Diphtheria . .	88	14	15·9	1	—	—
Lobar pneumonia .	26	23	88·5	13	6	46·15
Bronchopneumonia .	32	25	78·1	6	3	50·0
Bronchitis . .	32	—	Nil	47	—	—
Avitaminosis (mixed)	774	257	34·5	397	61	15·36
Pellagra . . .	189	110	58·2	62	10	16·1
Beriberi . . .	335	170	50·7	100	11	11·0
Tropical ulcer .	1,353	37	2·7	1,129	—	—
Other skin diseases .	851	—	Nil	674	—	—
All other diseases .	1,496	89	5·9	795	24	3·02
Grand total .	11,628	1,260	10·7	6,793	188	2·70

The condition of tropical ulcer patients was pitiable, and these wards stank of the hospital gangrene of pre-Listerian days. Rags, paper, leaves, and locally picked kapok and cotton were employed as dressings. The blowflies hanging in clouds about the patients produced maggot infections with far from benign effect. Dysentery and avitaminosis wards were scarcely less distressing. Some crude operating and pathological facilities had arisen from P.O.W. resources. Discipline, supremely high morale, and the pooling of resources in foodstuffs, money, materials, and human ability were even more important than purely medical treatment. A duck's egg daily might be all that was needed to turn the scales of a man's life. Herculean labours improved sanitation and accommodation. Patients were trained as medical orderlies, others were employed in the mass production of improvised equipment, even if they were only able to whittle with a knife on their beds. Sick-welfare money from various national and unit sources was directed into a common pool, and used with the utmost economy in a planned series of standard special diets, or in the clandestine purchase of essential drugs from the Siamese. For example, at Chungkai from January to April of 1944 we raised 38,000 dollars from prisoners' meagre resources, largely from the officers' pay of 30 dollars a month. (On capitulation of the Japanese the rate of exchange was 60 dollars to one English pound.) In addition, friendly sources contributed 3,000 dollars a month. Emetine, iodoform, and other drugs were obtained by the risky venture of selling Nipponese quinine. Emetine cost 35 dollars for 1 grain (65 mg.), and iodoform for tropical ulcers several hundred dollars a bottle.

The relationship of equipment to special problems was well illustrated by the great fall in septic cross-infection after the introduction of a rigid 'forceps' technique, employing large irrigating cans and small portable sterilizers, made from the mess-tins of dead men and heated by charcoal stoves devised from biscuit tins and mud. Even this simple equipment was extremely hard to obtain, and the striking benefits of mass disinfection and scabies treatment involved stealing petrol drums to make steam disinfectors. Intensive surgical measures were employed to drain pus, remove sequestra, and graft raw areas; amputations were performed where necessary. The steep fall in mortality at this stage was most gratifying.

NAKOM PATOM P.O.W. HOSPITAL

This huge hospital situated on the paddy-fields some twenty miles (32 km.) from Bangkok contained as many as 8,000 sick during its most active period. Little was provided for prisoners other than the buildings and some Red Cross stores, but with more static conditions, and comparatively greater material resources for improvisation, the scope of medical work was made to compare with that of a large civilian hospital. Had even the crude facilities of this hospital been made available at an earlier date, great loss of life might have been avoided. Pin-pricking regimentation and constant interference with medical officers and sick, day and night, made the work of the hospital very difficult, and parties of sick were constantly being transferred in the teeth of medical opposition.

Isolated parties transferred in this fashion were employed in railway maintenance, road construction, and bridge repair in areas harassed by Allied bombing, and some suffered terrible experiences recalling the tragic fate of 'H' and 'F' forces during railway construction. An epic story was a six-weeks march of 800 British soldiers for some 600 km. (375 miles) from Nakom Nyak to Pitsanloke carrying their sick on rice-sack stretchers. Due to the devoted work of the medical officers, Capt. C. J. Poh, S.S.U.F., and Capt. T. Brereton, A.A.M.C., only three died on the march.

RECORDS AND STATISTICS

All the diseases of the male adult were encountered, and in addition numerous tropical diseases, even those as remote from ordinary experience as yaws and leprosy. The main diseases are shown in tabular form. Chungkai P.O.W. hospital statistics (Table I), kept by Major A. L. Dunlop, R.A.M.C., are self-explanatory. Where multiple diseases were present only the main disease on admission was recorded. Australian figures (Table II) are taken for my seven working camps, since the records I retain of other nationals are less complete. The average camp population from which the Australian casualties quoted were drawn was approximately 1,000. Usually two medical officers and six to eight medical orderlies were available.

MALARIA

In the absence of adequate clothing, bedding, and mosquito

nets, in jungle areas where there were debilitated troops and negligible larval and mosquito control, the disease was almost universal. B.T. infections predominated over M.T. and showed such phenomenal recurrence rates as twenty attacks in a year. Suppressive quinine in a dosage of 3 to 6 gr. (0·2 to 0·4 g.) daily in my experience was given too sporadically to have noticeable effect.

Blackwater fever was not common—e.g. a total of 17 cases at Nakom Patom among thousands of malarial subjects enduring repeated attacks. Cerebral malaria was not infrequent, and, with no ampoules of quinine suitable for injection, sterile solutions were made from any quinine available. I found Howards' 5-gr. tablets of quinine hydrochloride very effective given intravenously in a dosage of 10 gr. (0·65 g.).

MALNUTRITION AND AVITAMINOSIS

'Vitamins are luxuries,' was the answer of a Japanese medical officer, Capt. Novosawa, to a request for an increase. Pellagra was the most common disorder, and exerted a sinister influence on the course of other diseases. The early symptoms of pellagra appeared after a few months of imprisonment—notably angular stomatitis, glossitis, pigmentary changes, and dry scaly skin. Scrotal dermatitis with erythema and loss of rugae rapidly progressed to exudation and scaly crusting. 'Burning feet', much in evidence after six months, gave great distress at night, the sensation being most marked in the ball of the foot and passing forward to the toes. In some the legs and hands were affected. The circulation in the feet was excellent, but free sweating gave them a clammy feeling. The deep reflexes were hyperactive, and some patients had knee and ankle clonus. Rare cases progressed to spastic diplegia. Amblyopia was seen at the same time as the 'burning feet', and occasionally both conditions occurred in the same case.

Later experience showed the rapid response of scrotal dermatitis and most mouth lesions to riboflavin, 6 to 8 mg. daily for a few days. Nicotinic acid or nikethamide was effective for other symptoms, except the amblyopia. In my experience the diar-

TABLE II.—*Australian Patients Admitted to Author's Working-camp Hospitals June, 1942 to October 1943*

Camp	Malaria	Dysentery	Enteritis	Cholera	Diphtheria	Pneumonia	Bronchitis	Avitaminosis and Malnutrition	Injuries	Tropical Ulcers	Other Skin Diseases	Other Diseases	Totals	Deaths
Bandoeng, Java (June 14–Nov. 7, 1942)	37	129	7	—	—	2	2	17	8	3	25	58	288	1
Makosura, Java (Nov. 7, 1942–Jan. 4, 1943)	14	28	1	—	—	—	2	18	1	2	20	27	113	—
Changi, Singapore, south area (Jan. 7–June 20, 1943)	7	29	—	—	—	—	—	38	6	1	12	16	109	—
Konyu (Jan. 25–Mar. 12, 1943)	166	153	21	—	—	—	3	5	5	7	12	18	392	—
Hintok, Mountain Camp (Mar. 13–Aug. 23, 1943)	916	558	340	93	11	18	38	194	113	209	221	171	2,882	57
Hintok, River Camp (July 20–Sept. 18, 1943)	590	98	56	57	—	1	4	78	38	104	213	95	1,334	25
Kinsayok (Sept. 10–Oct. 23, 1943)	288	17	22	—	—	1	—	2	26	49	31	10	446	—
Totals	2,018	1,014	447	150	11	22	49	352	197	375	534	395	5,664	83
Deaths	—	10	—	63	—	1	—	3	1	—	—	5	83	—

Notes.—1. Most cases of enteritis were of pellagrous origin. 2. The figures bear little relationship to total disease, since almost all troops worked through illness, and malaria and pellagra were almost universal. 3. Where several diseases were co-existent only the principal one was recorded. 4. Avitaminosis and malnutrition column: 50% were serious pellagra cases, the remainder cases of protein oedema and beriberi. 5. The low death rate at this time was quite exceptional, and is in large measure due to the fact that most of these troops were seasoned Middle East veterans of very fine physique. Large numbers, however, died at a later date in base hospitals.

rhoea associated with pellagra was not very evident until the second year of prisoner-of-war life, when it became common and distressingly uncontrollable. Mental derangement was seldom marked, though in the terminal phase some cases showed extreme mental apathy and evinced difficulty in swallowing any food, particularly rice.

Nutritional oedema or famine oedema was excessively common, some soldiers becoming horribly bloated. In severe cases alimentary absorption seemed poor, and deterioration continued despite large numbers of eggs daily. Beri-beri occurred in all forms, though in some instances it was confused with famine oedema. Scurvy and frank vitamin A deficiency were uncommon.

The basis of these disorders will be evident from the average ration recorded at Hintok camp in March, 1943. (This particular ration is by no means indicative of lower levels.)

Average issue per man per day: sugar 16 g., salt 10 g., fresh vegetables (mostly Chinese radish) 23 g., dried vegetables 6 g., meat 16·5 g., dried fish 26·5 g., oil of coconut 3 g., rice 600 g. (poor quality, some musty and almost uneatable).

Many sources of vitamins were tried in the absence of vitamin concentrates, but none was so effective as fresh foodstuffs obtained by money or credit. The whole question of a man's survival frequently hinged on the provision of money from prisoners' meagre resources, and on purchase facilities. Fresh ducks' eggs and the *katchang idjoe* bean (a lentil favoured by the Dutch) were excellent for all purposes. Meat was more expensive; yeast excellent but difficult to produce economically in concentrated form. Grass extracts were freely employed, but suitable grass was rare in the jungle. Jungle 'spinach' was popular. The supply of ducks' eggs for purchase, always hazardous in the jungle, was a major consideration in sustaining life in Siam. Blood transfusions later became a valuable measure in the worst cases of malnutrition, and under all circumstances there was no dearth of volunteer donors.

CHOLERA

The severe outbreaks of cholera were due to squalid conditions and association with Asiatic coolies, who contaminated water supplies and camp areas. Water sterilization often presented great difficulties. The Japanese showed terror of the disease, and frequently compelled the patients to be attended in appallingly unsuitable jungle sites with little shelter —in the hope they would die quickly. One notorious case where a cholera sufferer was shot by Japanese order illustrates this attitude.

Typical cases showed dramatic prostration, with copious rice-water stools, vomiting, husky voice, cramps, ringing in the ears, weakness, and feebleness. As sterile saline and disinfectants were not supplied, many courageous improvisations were made, particularly for the replacement of fluids in the algid phase. Saline was prepared from kitchen salt and spring, river, or rain water distilled in curiously designed stills. In one instance a medical officer employed a drilled bamboo thorn as an improvised cannula, and on occasion the risk was taken of administering saline with boiled and not distilled water. The most severe epidemic I encountered was one with which Major E. L. Corlette, A.A.M.C., and I were concerned at Hintok, where in our own immediate camp of 1,000 men, 150 showed obvious infection, and there were 63 deaths. Hundreds of deaths occurred in the neighbourhood. The cases were nursed under leaking rags of tents, in an appalling morass in the jungle. Some early cases were given intraperitoneal saline injections of several pints. Three stills were hurriedly improvised from lengths of a stolen petrol pipe surrounded by bamboo jackets, and irrigated by water brought in bamboo pipes from a spring. Some 120 pints (68 l.) were produced and given daily through a number of continuous saline sets manufactured from such oddments as our stethoscopes, bamboo tubing, saki bottles, etc. In cases with extreme fluid loss as much as 20 pints (11 l.) were given in twenty-four hours. Saline was very effective in the algid phase, but numbers passed into the stage of reaction (typhoidal state), rosy flush, and fever, or succumbed to other illnesses related to their gross debility.

Hypertonic saline was seldom employed owing to the crude clinical facilities. Capt. J. Markovitch, R.A.M.C., reported favourably on the use of double-strength saline. I found that potassium permanganate, in the usual 2-gr. (0·13 g.) dose as a pill wrapped in a cigarette paper, did not give relief commensurate with the burning discomfort caused.

DYSENTERY

Despite the appalling mortality and morbidity caused by this disease the Japanese refused to recognize its presence and compelled us to refer to it officially as 'colitis', or still more vaguely as 'other conditions'. Amoebic dysentery predominated, but emetine and other specifics were not supplied by the Japanese. The terrible severity of amoebic infections and the great shortage of emetine presented problems dealt with in a separate paper (1946). Liver abscess was an infrequent complication, which under the circumstances required open drainage by the subcostal or transthoracic approach.

TROPICAL ULCER

This disease was highly prevalent in jungle areas among famished fever-ridden subjects exposed to blows and trauma. A distressing feature was massive spreading gangrene with acute exacerbations of spread. Frequently the deep fascia was penetrated and there followed gross involvement of bone, joints, muscle, tendon, vessels, and nerves. The type of evacuation and the practice of flooding ill-equipped hovels with these patients were disastrous. The base hospital sections receiving them became cesspools of 'hospital gangrene'. Waves of virulence spread about the wards, infecting other wounds—e.g. incisions for suppurative bursitis, septic scabetic lesions, and healing ulcers.

Ulcers were often multiple; three men seen in association with Capt. J. McConachie, R.A.M.C., were dying in agony from large ulcers arising from minor skin lesions all over the body and limbs. The pain, of which I have had personal experience, was very severe and caused muscle spasm, so that the lower limb frequently contracted with flexed knee and dropped foot. Natural healing, where the outcome was favourable, took months to years, and often resulted in severe deformity. Mild antiseptics were useless, and for effective action reagents were destructive to normal tissues—e.g. hyd. perchlor. solution 1 in 50, saturated solution of potassium permanganate, strong copper sulphate solution, pure phenol or lysol.

The best measure was removal of all gangrenous tissue by excision and curettage, followed by the application of pure phenol or lysol and a light sprinkle of iodoform powder. The latter was a specific for tropical infection, often effective even with such economy as 1 in 20 dilution. The distressing pain disappeared and the dressing could be left for days; the resulting granulating area was then skin-grafted. With this procedure, early cases could be healed in a month without deformity. The Japanese did not supply iodoform, but it could be bought in small quantities at high prices from the Siamese. It was the most economical of all purchased drugs, and the sight of it brought a glad smile to sufferers.

Many hundreds of men endured the agony of curettage of ulcers necessarily without anaesthesia. Necrosed tendon and muscle required wide incisions in fascial planes and formal excision. Huge sequestra were extracted when they loosened, some constituting the greater part of the shaft of the tibia. At Nakom Patom sequestrectomy was accompanied by large 'saucerizing' procedures. Amputation was often necessary to save life, and some patients begged for it, despite the crude knives and butchers' saws employed. Immediate mortality rates were surprisingly good—e.g. under 10%—but there were associated gross nutritional disorders often evidenced by running diarrhoea and famine oedema. Further depletion of body protein occurred with the copious discharges. Ultimately about 50% of amputation cases succumbed, many of them after good healing. Blood transfusion was a valuable measure. When hostilities ceased, 170 amputation cases surviving at Nakom

Patom, including two with bilateral amputations, were already provided with useful artificial limbs.

Some hundreds of skin grafts in the hospitals with which I was associated showed gratifying results in healing and lessened deformity, compensating for great difficulties in arranging dressings and suitable firm pressure over graft areas. I found that a light dust of iodoform powder over the graft area gave considerable protection against recurrence of tropical infection.

SCABIES AND INFECTED SKIN LESIONS

In some hospitals over 90% of the population had scabies, many with florid skin sepsis. Mass treatment by wards was required, using improvised steam disinfectors for personal effects. Sulphur was largely purchased in a crude form. A very economical suspension with a minimum of oil was made by means of ox bile.

The feet of workmen employed without boots and constantly in mud and water became cruelly inflamed with gross septic tinea. Cure was difficult without rest.

GENERAL POINTS

Mental disorders were surprisingly infrequent, and neurosis uncommon among Anglo-Saxon prisoners. The hostility of the Japanese to the sick made their lot so unattractive that possibly a source of conflict was removed. Notwithstanding this fact, in well-led camps a heroic feature was the routine way men in the extremity of fatigue and debility lined up to take the place or bear the burden of those in worse case. A minor outbreak of hysterical palsies in the last year of imprisonment was predominantly among Netherlands East Indies soldiers. Suicide was uncommon and I personally know of only six cases. Possibly owing to lack of all privacy, and to the debilitating diet, sexual perversion was very inconspicuous. Though some men inevitably became morose and irritable, and quarrels arose, sanity, good humour, and optimism were predominant.

Ingeniously hidden wireless sets and news translations helped in sustaining morale, as did the organization of recreation, entertainment, and mental activities. Astonishing stage effects were obtained with rice matting, bamboos, rags of mosquito netting, etc., and symphonies were orchestrated from memory and played with impressive effect on instruments of great ingenuity. Fertile minds invented most diverting games. Formal religion appeared to have no enhanced appeal in camps of sickness and death. The maintenance of strict discipline was the greatest factor in preserving life and maintaining morale, and this was never questioned where officers set an example in unselfish devotion to duty.

JUNGLE SURGERY

The Japanese with characteristic interest in the dramatic and sadistic appeared to find a surgical operation a 'good show'. Shortly after arriving in the dense jungle in the Konyu area I performed a successful night operation for a perforated duodenal ulcer—on a hurriedly constructed bamboo table, lit by a bonfire and a borrowed hurricane lamp. Following this event I was freely allowed to visit other camps to perform operations, and incidentally effect medical and other liaison. In these areas only emergency operations were performed, such as those for acute abdominal lesions, wounds, and gross sepsis, and usually in the open or under a large mosquito net. Many penetrating wounds were seen from brittle fragments of steel drills (e.g. necessitating excision of the eye), and some severe dynamiting injuries.

In the absence of strapping for extension, fractured femurs were best treated by driving the cleanest nail that could be found through the upper tibia. Thomas splints were devised by twisting wire, and pulleys and cords were manufactured. The Hamilton Russell type of extension was used on occasion. It was found that good healing usually occurred in abdominal wounds, using well-washed hands and no gloves. All instruments, along with such drapings as were available, were sterilized by boiling.

Lack of anaethesia was the greatest difficulty, and it was necessary to perform most minor operations in its absence. Minute amounts of chloroform were obtained from the Japanese and Siamese, and carefully conserved for special procedures. I was able to obtain small quantities of 'novocain' products, and this became the sheet anchor for spinal anaesthesia (1–2·5 ml. of freshly prepared 10% solution in distilled water). With variations of technique this sufficed for almost all operations on the abdomen and lower limb—e.g. gall-bladder surgery and amputations through the thigh. Local infiltration was much less economical but was necessary for the head or upper limb. Lieut-Col A. E. Coates did a most impressive series of 120 amputations of the lower limb at the 55-Kilo Hopsital in Burma, employing a solution of cocaine (approximately 0·75 ml. of 2% solution intrathecally).

Catgut or other suture materials were rarely supplied by the Japanese, and numerous substitutes were used. I found cotton very useful, also silk obtained in quantity by unravelling the parachute cords carried by R.A.F. personnel. The most useful product was a locally prepared 'catgut' from the peritoneum of pigs and cattle, first introduced by an ingenious Dutch chemist, Capt. von Boxtel, working under Lieut-Col Coates. The peritoneum was trimmed in 6-metre ribbons of varying width, twisted on a winder and dried. Sterilization was effected at 130 F. (54·4 C.) for half an hour, after which it was put in ether for twenty-four hours, and finally in 90% alcohol and iodine.

Surgical instruments were most scarce, and ingenious improvisations were made. On occasion razors and pocket-knives were used to make incisions, while butchers' saws and carpenters' tools found useful employment.

SURGERY IN BASE HOSPITALS

In base hospitals the resources in tools, scraps of metal, and cherished oddments were greater, and some quite complex instruments were devised—for example, sigmoidoscopes, bowel clamps, rib shears, Cushing's silver clips and applying forceps, and optical apparatus. At Nakom Patom hospital, where the theatre was reasonably dust-proof and provided with a cement floor, a great range of surgical procedures were carried out under the enthusiastic direction of Lieut-Col Coates, who worked tirelessly at surgery in addition to administration. Major S. Krantz, A.A.M.C., has reviewed the surgical work of the hospital, in which he took an important part. Excluding very minor procedures, 773 surgical interventions were carried out, including such varied operations as brain and spinal-cord surgery, thyroidectomy, gastrectomy, enterectomy and anastomosis, abdomino-perineal resection, cholecystectomy, thoracic surgery, splenectomy, nephrectomy, laryngectomy, orthopaedic measures, and nerve sutures.

Appendicostomy, caecostomy, and ileostomy were allotted some place in the treatment of dysentery. Appendicectomy was carried out for appendicitis in 133 cases without mortality. Operations for hernia totalled 114, the majority being repaired with unabsorbable sutures. There were no deaths, 5 infected wounds, and 3 known recurrences. While it cannot be said that surgical procedures played a major part in the survival of prisoners of war, they represented considerable triumphs over unfavourable conditions.

IMPROVISATION

Necessity is indeed the mother of invention, and while the Japanese were in the main obstructive rather than helpful they paid Allied prisoners the compliment of expecting miracles of improvisation to replace normal supplies. In heart-breaking jungle areas devoid of the most commonplace materials, where even pieces of wire, nails, fabrics, empty tins, leather, etc., were prized possessions, and habitations were made of bamboo and palm leaf held together with jungle fibre, ingenuity was indeed tested.

Astonishing uses were made of bamboo, which served for such varied construction as beds, brooms, brushes, baskets, containers, water-piping, tubing, splints, etc. Timber was obtained by felling trees and splitting with wooden wedges, and used for many purposes, including footwear (clogs). Where solder could not be extracted from sardine tins and the like, water-tight tinsmithing was done by ingenious folding. Sources of hydrochloric acid included the human stomach. Flux was readily manufactured if sulphuric acid could be stolen from car batteries. Leather was prepared from buffalo or cow hide, and thread or string from unravelling webbing equipment, kit-bags, etc. It was necessary to equip jungle hospitals by the work of patients as well as staff, and they were organized in mass-production efforts with all available tools and resources.

Articles made by this 'cannibalization' of effects at Tarsau and Chungkai included urinals, bed-pans, commodes, surgical beds and pulleys, feeding-cups, wash-basins, irrigators, sterilizers, small portable charcoal stoves, disinfectors, stretchers and stretcher beds (with sack and bamboo), back-rests, leg-rests, oil-lamps, brooms, brushes, trays, tables, orthopaedic appliances, splints, surgical instruments, and artificial limbs and eyes (from mah-jongg pieces). The artificial limbs made at Nakom Patom under the direction of Major F. A. Woods, A.I.F., were designed from crude timber, leather cured from hide, thread from unravelled packs, iron from retained portions of officers' stretchers, and oddments of sponge-rubber, elastic braces, etc.

Part of an appeal to camp members at Chungkai was: 'The following articles are urgently needed: Tins and containers of all sorts, solder, flux, nails, wire, screws, sponge-rubber, scraps of clothing, hose-tops and old socks, string, webbing, scraps of leather, rubber tubing, glass bottles of all sorts, glass tubing (transfusion purposes), canvas, elastic, rubber bands or strips, braces, wax, mah-jongg pieces, and tools of all sorts. Nothing is too old, nothing is too small.'

TWO LIFE-SAVING ACHIEVEMENTS

A life-saving measure introduced by Major Reed, A.A.M.C., and developed by Capt. J. Markovitch, R.A.M.C., was the use of defibrinated blood for transfusion purposes. Using soldiers trained as technicians, thousands of transfusions were carried out by simply collecting the blood of a suitable donor into a container while stirring continuously with a spatula or whisk. Vigorous stirring was carried on for five minutes after clotting commenced on the spatula. The blood was then filtered through sixteen layers of gauze, and administered. Much help in the preparation of drugs and chemicals was given to medical officers by chemists, botanists, and scientists. Another life-saving achievement was the production of emetine from a limited quantity of ipecacuanha by Capt. van Boxtel at the 55-Kilo Camp. Sgt. A. J. Kosterman and Sgt. G. W. Chapman did most valuable work in this respect.

Distilled water for intravenous use was prepared in numerous camps and hospitals. Alcohol for surgical and other purposes was obtained by the fermentation of rice with a suitable strain of fungus and distillation up to 90% strength. Grass extracts and other vitamin sources were exploited, and some useful items of materia medica were collected from local natural sources. From these, such products as essential oils—e.g. cloves and citronella—were obtained. Milk and bread made from soya bean lent some variety to the diet at times.

Products of minor importance included ink, paper, and cork substitutes. Major T. Marsden, R.A.M.C., provided an in-genious pathological service with improvised apparatus which satisfied most routine requirements. Colour indicators for pH were extracted from local flowers, and litmus paper was manufactured.

CONCLUSION

The treatment of sick prisoners by the Japanese left almost all civilized behaviour to be desired.

The fortitude and sustained morale of British soldiers under prolonged strain and suffering were most praiseworthy. The toll of long-continued strain and multiple debilitating diseases merits consideration and sympathy in the problems of post-war rehabilitation.

THE
SWORD
AND THE
BLOSSOM

ライバーキン一九六七

RAY PARKIN

THE SWORD
AND THE BLOSSOM

RAY PARKIN

1968

THE HOGARTH PRESS

LONDON

This, in the hope that Man will stop trampling Eden—before Eden tramples him.

Chanting at the altar
Of the inner sanctuary . . .
A cricket priest.

ISSA

ACKNOWLEDGEMENT

I wish to thank Edna Beilenson for allowing me to use the eight *haiku* which have been taken from the four volumes: *Japanese Haiku*, *The Four Seasons*, *Cherry Blossoms* and *Haiku Harvest* (Peter Pauper Press).

The late Peter Beilenson translated with the deceptive simplicity of a fine mind and, to me, seems to sit close alongside Issa, Buson, Basho and the rest in a fraternity which releases the well-springs of the universals of which our lives are made.

R. P.

CONTENTS

GLOSSARY OF UNCONVENTIONAL
WORDS AND PHRASES

Bandicoot: An Australian rodent-like marsupial some of whom are popularly considered to be able to take the tubers or roots of a crop without disturbing the foliage.

Bash-artist: One prone to beating others.

Batchy: Silly, mental.

Battler: Underprivileged worker for life.

Being on: A crisis happening.

Big Smoke: City.

Bimbo: Batman. *Bimbo-ing:* Batman's duties.

Bludger: A parasite. Originally, one who lived off the immoral earnings of a woman.

Bludger's paralysis: Unprincipled evasion of duty or work.

Blue: A mistake, disturbance, fight, etc.

Blue, to: To cause mistake, disturbance, fight, etc.

Bonza: Extremely admirable.

Boss cocky: Head man.

Bring undone: To unnerve, cause the downfall of.

Bunny: Hapless victim, dupe.

Bunyip: Unresolved mythical hybrid animal of Australia.

Bushed: Absolutely bewildered.

Coasted: Took it easy.

Cobber: A mate, special friend. Also general form of address like mate, bloke, chum, etc.

Codger: A man, fellow, person. Generally implying old.

Cop: To observe, collect or receive.

Cop it sweet: To take what is coming without complaint.

Crook: Sick, bad.

Crook, to go: To complain, usually with force.

Dilly bags: Hold-alls.

Dinkum: Honest, true, genuine.

Donor: Girl friend.

Draw the crabs: To attract unwanted attention.

Drip, to: To complain dismally.

Drongo: No good, unreliable disappointing person.

Drum, to give: To supply vital information.

Dunny: A privy. *Like a country dunny:* Isolated, all alone.

Fish: Torpedo.
Front: Effrontery.
Front, to: To face, be brought before.
Furphy: Rumour.

Get on to: To observe sharply, to understand.
Gig, to: To look at with unveiled curiosity. Also *Gig over.*
Grouse: Exclusive, high quality, the best.

Harry-Careyed: Old silent screen star. Rhyming slang for *hara-kiri.*

Irk: Lowly individual (R.A.F.).

Jack, the: Venereal disease.
Joe Blakes, the: Rhyming slang for snakes also for shakes giving the image of D.T.s. In malaria it means the rigours.

Lamasery: A monastery, Buddhist.
Leave for dead: Outclass, outstrip. To desert some one.

Magging: Arguing or talking with nagging irritation.

Off Lolly: Beheaded. Lolly = head.
One-out: Alone, single-handed.

Plonk fiend: Wine addict or alcoholic.
Pom, Pommy: English or Englishman.
Presento: A gift, something for nothing.
Prize, no: No bargain. Worthless. No great shakes.

Rake (of trucks): A string together.
Retread, feet need a: Very sore, worn-out feet.
Ridge: Right. Probably a contraction of the facetious pronunciation *ridge-it.*
Rubberty: Pub. Contraction of rhyming slang *rubberty-dub.*

Scran: Food.
Sent off: To remove without permission, to steal.
Shiner: Black eye.
Shot (shoot) through: Abscond, escape, gone.
Snib: Small catch on a lock to prevent the door from locking when closed.
Strides: Pants.

Take, a: A deception. A person of unsuspected capabilities.
Toey: Anxious, nervous, short-tempered, jumpy.
Tojo: Hideki Tojo, War Minister for Japan World War II.
    Hence a belligerent militaristic Jingo prone to ruthless
    actions.
Top off: To inform on.

Wake-up, a: An awareness to a situation.
Weighed-off: Calculated, accurately assessed.
Whack it up: Share it out.
Winward corner: Lit. nearest the wind, hence closest to danger or
    action.
Wog, the: Malaria.
Wowser: Obsessively Puritanical in appearance, if not in fact.
    A spoil-sport.

AUTHOR'S NOTE

In the Japanese dictionary there is a simple word: *Kuru*, an irregular intransitive verb which means *come*. But the prisoners of war only ever heard it as *KURRAH!*—harsh, savage and insulting. *Kurrah* was the word above all that they hated and feared. The other Japanese words are spelt largely as they were heard by the prisoners. The final vowel is always pronounced. All vowels are short unless double letters or a mark are used.

In the English dictionary there is a simple word: *Bastard*, a noun and adjective which means an illegitimate person; or, of things, unauthorized, hybrid, counterfeit, something ill-conceived. Used loosely it is considered a vulgar word. Here it is used frequently because, in fact, it was. But mostly it carries an accuracy of meaning in the last sense. It was faithfully expressive of the disgust or disappointment felt: a colourful figure of speech using the illegitimate legitimately.

John's philosophy will appear over-simplified—but this is not the place for the un-simplified expansion. Here it only suggests a neglected point of view. But . . . *May I, for my own self, song's truth reckon* . . . on this, a sort of sentimental journey.

The drawings have been taken from John's sketch book kept on that journey.

Ray Parkin,
Ivanhoe, 1967

PROLOGUE

Fever-felled half-way,
My dreams arose to march again . . .
Into a hollow land.

(BASHO)

HE was called Boof, meaning 'ox'. He was big. His name was
Eric Brent, but only official papers said this. Even his wife
called him Boof. Harry was Boof's mate and they had been
through a whole war together. One night Boof's wife telephoned
Harry.

"Harry," she pleaded, "he's got that horrible sword out
again. . . . I'm scared . . . he keeps saying something like *kurrah*
. . . it sounds awful and he keeps saying it."

"I'll come at once, Doris. Don't do anything . . . he'll be all
right. I'll grab a taxi."

The front door was on the snib and Harry pushed it open.
Boof stood facing him, seeming to fill the whole breadth and
height of the passage. He had the sword in his hands and was
making short cuts with it. Boof had said he had been getting
bad headaches, but Harry was startled to see him now—so out
of character. Yet, when he saw Harry standing there he said,
"Hullo, Harry, what brings you here?"

"Just passing," Harry lied. "Here, what are you trying to do?
Trying to take-off Four-eyes or the Ape or the Mad Mongrel or
the Boy Bastard or someone? You'll scare hell out of Doris and
the kid. Give it to me, I'll stick it back on top of the wardrobe—
and for Christ's sake leave it there, if you don't want to scare
'em to death."

"Who? Me? I wouldn't do that—you know it."

"You mightn't mean to—but what do *you* think . . . like a
bloody Tojo."

Harry sheathed the sword and put it back. Boof went into the
kitchen. "Are you scared of me, Darl?" he said out of the blue.

Harry came in just in time to hear, "Of *you*? Me? You great
ox—you know I can cut you down to size any time."

But afterwards Doris begged Harry to take the sword away.

677

She did not know anything about it, except that Boof had told her he had picked it up in Japan after the war was over. He had said that there were dozens lying around. But Harry knew about this one. He got Doris to leave it where it was. "It might upset him if it goes—he might think you don't trust him or something—you know. . . . Leave it, my dear, the old fella's all right —you and I both know that . . . but if this happens again, ring me and I'll come at once—doesn't matter what time."

Harry and Boof worked on the waterfront together.

Several times afterwards Doris had to ring him. He would go right over. It was almost a set pattern which, if Boof noticed, he did not let on. Harry would take the sword away from Boof; abuse him good-naturedly, and put it back on the wardrobe. Boof accepted it, but Harry would always stay a couple of hours. Generally they would open a bottle of beer and yarn over old times.

At work Boof told Harry that he was getting bad headaches. He said he did not want to worry Doris with them. And he was not sleeping, and sometimes he felt sick. He had had a couple of blackouts. The Repatriation doctor had sent him to get glasses, but it had made no difference.

PART 1

SURVIVORS

Congratulations
Issa! . . . *You have survived to feed*
This year's mosquitoes.

(ISSA)

Moored boat, Menam River, Siam

SURVIVORS

I

A CROWD of skinny, unkempt, yellow-brown, bare-footed men were streaming out of the glare of the tropical sun into the long bamboo and attap hut. Their hats were sad with dejected and torn brims: they had been used for pillows for so long, and some had eaten their rice out of them. But, in most cases, the hats were all of half of what they wore: mildewed G-strings or shorts so consumed by time and the rotting mildew of the jungle Wet Season, that they were now ghosts, hardly recognizable, and giving little respectability.

There was a similarity about all these men. It was not of shape, size nor even race. The mark of something unseen was on them all. These men had lately returned from building a railway through the Burma-Siam jungle for the Imperial Japanese Army. Some were still returning. Many would never return because the railway had cost them one man for every seventeen-foot-six of the track they had laid. It was two hundred and sixty-three miles long. Now they were back on the open plain of the Menam-Kwai Noi rivers around Kanburi and Tamuan.

This was Tamuan. There were about a thousand here now, and they were building the camp to take about ten thousand. They were still sleeping on the ground, but it was luxurious simply because it was dry.

Apart from the capricious cruelty of their captors, they had lived a long time with other unnerving uncertainty. At any time during that long and unusually wet season in the liquid man-consuming jungle, disease could, and did, start a lottery with their lives.

Five of these men had come together.

The big man now lay on the dirt floor under a stained, threadbare blanket, shaking like a thick tree in a storm. The four had just come in to their bedplaces near him, to get their dixies for the midday rice.

"Hullo," Harry said. "The old fella's got the shakes."

Each took his blanket and put it over the shivering man.

"There you are, Boof, sweat her out, mate," Harry said.

"Thanks."

"What about a drink, old-timer?"

"Thanks."

Boof's big bare arm came from under the blanket and he drank deeply.

"*Meshi?*" Harry asked.

"No thanks. Whack it up between you."

Boof pulled the blankets up, shaking violently. He was deaf from quinine and in a muffled world of aches. After the shaking would come a high, dry, scorching fever. At last this would break and the sweat would soak his blanket. Then he would sleep like a baby. After four or five days the fever would be almost gone—but never quite. It might hit him again in a month, or even ten days. In the jungle they had been allowed only three days—if there was any room on the hospital quota, which was seldom. Almost always they had gone to work with it, and often collapsed there. Now it was easier. Boof might get five or seven days. He was 'bed-down'. That is, he saw the doctor each morning, got his quinine, and stayed in his hut. But at seven p.m. he would have to go out with the rest to the Japanese count parade, and usually have to stand around for a long time.

On the way to the cookhouse by the river to get their rice Harry said, "You know, Boof reminds me of that great big water-buffalo that little kid washes in the river here. It's wider between the horns than the kid is high, yet he pushes it around and bullies the daylights out of it—and the old buff just takes it all. . . ."

Boof and Harry had started to build the Railway from Thanbyuzayat and had worked down in various camps to the Burma-Siam border. When it was finished, they had come through by rail to Tamuan. They were from the 2/2nd Pioneers. Here they met Buck, Alec and John, who had worked around the mountain section at Konyu and Hintok, in Siam. Buck and Alec were from the 2/3rd Machine Gun Battalion. John was from the Australian Navy—his ship had been sunk off Java in early 1942.

It was now the middle of 1944. This melting-pot of the survivors had brought them together. Whole units had dissolved and the remnants mixed.

Harry led the way down to the river along the narrow dirt track. He was fair, above average height and still pretty solid. A dirty bandage on one leg covered a nagging tropical ulcer that had been with him for months.

There was not much time to get the rice, eat it and get back to the lines for the work parade.

Tamuan was a big camp. It was bounded on the west by the Menam river; a mile away to the east was the road. The north and south boundaries were, as yet, indefinite but they were at least a mile apart. Only the first couple of huts had been put up. They had plenty of work ahead of them to clear the area and build the rest of the huts. All the building material had to be carted from the river on their backs. On the wide alluvial plain the remains of the old paddy fields' low broken walls looked something like ruined forts would from the air. There were groves of banana palms and some patches of scraggy tobacco. Scattered here and there were Thai huts and houses. The Thais had been given three months to get out by the Japanese, and they did not like it.

The whole area was divided up by narrow dirt tracks running north-south and east-west, about two hundred yards apart.

With the short dinner-break over, they were back at work carrying twenty-foot lengths of bamboo in bundles on their shoulders from the river to the building sites. Two to a bundle,

Giant mango trees

they padded their barefooted way along the beaten earth tracks which, sunbaked as they were, drew and swelled their cracked feet painfully.

When they got to the river for another bundle they had to wade out waist-deep to get it. It was in huge rafts that had been floated down from up-country.

They broke some of the monotony by taking different tracks. Sometimes these led past Thai houses. There was one, shaded by mangoes and Jack-fruit and banana. In the cleared space at the back of it, two young women, naked to the waist, winnowed rice with flat circular basket trays three feet wide. Bareheaded, they worked in the sun with the smooth grace and calm of habit. Their lustrous raven hair cut at the shoulder, their pale brown skins lightly sheened, the simple deep colour of their sarongs gave them the quality of porcelain figurines. They moved like reflections in almost still water. Brown and white fowls pecked and scratched in the glittering winnowings around the bare feet of the women. A couple of honey-coloured children played in the shade with a skinny smooth-haired black dog. A patient ox with large, drooping-lidded eyes trudged somnolently around and around, yoked to a shaft which trundled a big stone millwheel over a flat nether one, grinding the rice to flour. In the hot sun the trees were breathless.

As they passed, Buck said, "There you are . . . we call them *wogs* . . . look how silly they are! . . . come out the door, pick some fruit and go back and have a sleep. . . . Not for us: we rush about."

"They've got something," Harry said.

"Oh, don't worry," Buck said, "they won't have it long . . . someone will come along—some efficient bastard will put it on a business basis, and then goodnight all this Garden-of-Eden stuff. . . ."

Buck and Alec were carting together. Alec was shortish, with wide shoulders and a narrow waist. He had an easy-going voice and a boyish face. Buck was heavy set with a thick waist and slightly humped shoulders. His face was heavy with thick brows and lips. Scars showed through his short-cropped hair. He had been a rolling stone knocking about the back blocks of western Queensland and New South Wales. Alec came from a farm in the south. His voice belied the fine temper of the man beneath. Buck's grumbling roughness and biting satire hid the good humour and essential kindness and justness of his character. But John and Alec knew the real Buck. Alec was a sergeant, Buck was a private—both machine gunners. John was a petty officer. They had shared the worst of the Railway together.

When they had gone on a little, John said to Harry, with whom he was carrying, "You and Boof joined together, Harry, didn't you?"

"Yes, John—the old Boof and I have been together right from the jump. Boof was a country bloke, but he met Doris when he was down one time. So he came to the Big Smoke and got married. I knew him a bit before the war. He used to drive a truck and I struck him down at the wharf. Then we met in camp the first week in the army. We went to the Middle East together—finished up in Syria."

"So did Buck and I," Alec said.

"I remember your mob there," Harry said.

"We bombarded there for you at Damour," John said.

"Yes, and were we glad! The Frogs had us absolutely stopped at the river—you made a mess ashore all right. It wasn't long after that we were across."

2

After a silence, John said, "You were telling us about Boof, Harry."

"Don't get me started on Boof, mate! . . . Look, I'd bore you stiff."

"Well have a go," Buck said. "That's what sergeants are for!"

"Get it off your chest," Alec said.

"Funny thing about Boof, he was mad for bayonet fighting. And he was good—real good. At unarmed combat he was as good as the instructors. He could disarm a bloke while you blinked."

"You wouldn't think it to look at him—he seems so quiet and easy-going—never seen a bloke so hard to upset," Alec said.

"Well, there it is. I used to needle him a lot about it. Boof, I'd say, you're half-Dago the way you go for the bloody knife. He'd say, I don't know, Harry, it's man to man—and if you've *got* to kill a man—well . . . you know."

"And how'd he go? Did he get a chance?"

"Well, you wouldn't read about it . . . every time it looked like being on, we got seen-off. . . . The first time we were attacking a fort near Damour . . . walls ten foot thick . . . bare rocky hillsides . . . you know the sort of thing. The Frogs were well in, with pill-boxes and all that. We had fought our way up as far as we could and gone to ground like lizards. We got the order to fix bayonets. We were going to have a go at the pill-boxes. Boof had the section next to mine—we were corporals then, we got made sergeants after the show there. . . . He stuck his thumb in the air ... he was waiting for it ... like an arrow in a bow. But all at once they pinned us down with fire from the fort and the jokers in the pill-boxes bailed out and beat it back inside. Slap inside the gate we could see a couple of tanks giving them support. You should have heard Boof! The air was blue! We by-passed the place eventually."

"You couldn't take any of it easy," Buck said.

"For all Boof went crook then, I don't think he meant it about the Frogs—he was just so disappointed. He's harmless until something really gets under his hide. One night in the canteen, two idiots start maggin' each other ... when Boof's drinking he likes it quiet. He generally talks about home and that ... and you couldn't get two words out to hear for the noise of these bunnies. Boof goes over, grabs them by the shirts just under their chins and almost lifts them clear off the floor— *together*. They weren't little blokes either. He talked to them like a schoolteacher asking them to be quiet ... they started to yap back .. crunch! their heads together. Then he said, we want to talk, not listen to you blokes. And he put them down ... not another peep out of them."

"The Machine Gunners got to Java about the same time as the Pioneers, didn't they?" John asked.

"Yes," Alec said, "*without* our weapons. We'd become bloody infantry. Colossal organization. ..."

"It was over before it started," Buck said.

"Our C.O. told us that Wavell, before he bailed out, had told him that every hour we could delay them was valuable to Australia. ... It was obvious that they did not expect us to hold them ... we were being written-off," Alec said.

"We went in at Leuwiliang and we were supposed to be supported by the Dutch—but we couldn't find out where they were ... nor the Japs either—*nobody knew where the enemy was!* Christ! It was a mess! And I was none too happy about it. The Dutch had blown a couple of bridges, which didn't make it look any better."

"That must have been about the time our C.O. got a phone call from the Dutchy telling us to stick around Buitenzorg and take over all positions the Dutch had evacuated. We came up your way and were on your left."

"Do you know," Harry said, "we got a signal saying, *No*

Japanese landings in Java. Five minutes later one of our platoon patrols watched five Jap tanks drive up to the Leuwiliang bridge from the west!"

"There were some Yank artillery came in there and gave us a bit of a hand. But the whole bloody thing was hopeless," Buck said.

"We had one little show when Boof nearly got his chance. But still we missed. We were making across a paddy field . . . no cover but a few stalks of rice. Two mortars and seven machine guns were on us . . . yet we only had one bloke hit up till then. . . . The officer said we were going to make a bayonet charge of it. . . . I could see Boof get set. . . . One of our blokes stood up and emptied three magazines of his Bren . . . the Japs scattered, so we up and off . . . but in twenty yards, five of the seventeen of us were hit . . . we went to ground again . . . it was coming on dusk . . . they were trying to encircle us . . . but in the dark we were able to get out, dragging our wounded on ground-sheets. But the whole thing had become disorganized . . . they collected us in the end, like everybody else. The Dutch had packed it in and left us on our own like a country dunny."

"But there was nothing you could do—I've never known such a *depressing* time. Boof said, Well at least I thought we had *these* little buggers at the end of a bayonet at last. He knew that he'd never get another chance. He admitted it got him down a bit."

"Java," Buck said, "*that* was a proud page in our history to tell our grandkids about."

3

They were now returning to the river for the fifth time for another load of the slimy bamboo. "If Takamura's in a good mood," Harry said, "this ought to be the last trip . . . that makes about ten miles for the afternoon. . . . I think my feet need a re-tread."

Takamura was in a good mood. "O.K., finishoo . . . campoo-backa." He had not always been in a good mood. Where Alec, Buck and John had been he was known as the Charcoal Burner, for that had been his job. Short, pudgy, and with glasses he had been overbearing and cruel. He had beaten men unmercifully with a professed fanatic devotion to Japanese aims. It had been a surprise to them to have found him now so mild.

When they got back to the hut, they found Boof asleep, breathing deeply and regularly. The blankets were wet. The fever had broken.

"Like a baby," Harry said. "We'll bring his rice back with us."

"Better take his waterbottle too."

The river looked like another Ganges with hundreds of prisoners washing naked and swimming to soak away the fatigue of the hot plodding miles. It was a broad stream and,

Prisoners bathing

at this time of the year, shoalled with many sandbars. They dropped their dixies and hats on the ground as they watched, and walked together into the river. Each wore only a G-string which they washed with themselves and put it straight on again. It would be dry soon after they left the water. They would sleep in it all night.

"Even in this lousy life there are compensations," Harry said. "If only clothes were as simple back in Civvy Street."

It was for a reason that they wore their G-strings in the water. A few nights before, an English captain had been with the crowds of men bathing. He was one of those men who, somehow no matter what the situation, never lose that air of staid dignity. He had given a shocked cry and waded from the water with both hands clamped to himself. Blood streamed from between his fingers. A doctor there attended him. After swabbing away

the blood, said, "Well, I could not have done a better job myself
—you are perfectly circumcised!"

There were other cases when the job had not been so neat.
Small voracious fish would snap at any chance they saw. Many
a man was startled by a sudden tearing of a scab from his legs
or body. Any wounds or scabs attracted them. It was caution,
not modesty, that made them wear the G-strings in the water.

The call sounded for the evening meal, blown by a thin man
with sparse black hair, a hooked nose and a trumpet as battered
as he was.

The meal was rice and a few odd vegetables. The cooks had
made efforts to make it a little different. Tonight there was some
fresh pumpkin, onion, silver beet, and cucumber. It made their
mouths water. It was eaten raw, skin and all, chopped up, a
couple of spoonfuls on top of their rice. They were all so vitamin-
conscious that this was to them a psychological feed as well.

"If only we'd had this up-country," Alec said, "there would
be a few more of us here now."

Harry took Boof's waterbottle around to the cookhouse to get
it filled—no other water was safe. It was a thirsty camp because
the means to boil water were scarce.

4

They took Boof's meal and water back to him.

"Boof," Harry called quietly, "here's your scran."

Boof slowly turned on his back, sweeping the blankets to his
waist as he did so. "Ah, that's better—sweat took the aches a
bit."

Harry pushed the dixie of rice towards him.

"Oh, bloody food! . . . I s'pose I'd better eat it."

And so, on one elbow, he shovelled it silently and mechanically into his mouth. It took determination. Many wouldn't
trouble. But even Boof had to rest halfway through it.

"Here," Harry said, "take a pull at this. I'll get it filled up
again after *tenko*."

Boof drank deeply. He paused with a great breath. "Don't
worry about it tonight, Harry, there's no moon—you'll break
your bloody neck or tread on a snake or something."

"Don't you worry about me, old timer, I reckon I've got eyes in the end of my toes by now." And this was not so far from the truth, for circumstances had developed many new sensitivities in them.

George's trumpet sounded in the distance.

"There goes the quarter warning."

"I'll finish this when I get back." Boof pulled back the blankets and pushed the dixie under a rag at the head of his bed. Then he stood up. He was six-foot-three and, though his frame was gaunt, he was so solidly proportioned that he did not look that tall.

"Here's your hat, Boof."

"Thanks."

They began to move out of the hut. Boof's first steps were slow and stiff and it looked as if he were stopping instead of starting. After they were on parade, there would be endless waiting, never knowing how long. It took little to start the guards on a slapping spree—bad drill, anything.

They began to fall in at the five-minute warning. The Dutch, the English, the Australians formed up in *kumis* of one hundred, five-deep. At last the Japanese came. The whole parade was called to attention with a loud *Kiotski!* from the prisoners' adjutant. He then took a few smart paces forward and reported to the Japanese sergeant taking the *tenko*, the count parade. He was a tall man and known to the prisoners as the Tiger. This seemed to describe his nature very well. He had been in the camps that Harry and Boof had been in. He was an unrelenting man, quick to take offence and act with black temper.

"Watch yourself, chaps, it's the Tiger."

As he came opposite their *kumi*, he took the salute from the section leader. The Japanese private with him, fearful to please, shouted "*Bango!*" and, like rifle-fire, the men numbered in Japanese. *Ich', ni, san, shi, go, roku*, . . . and so on until the last man called *ni-juu*. The private was about to call the hundred correct, when the Tiger roared.

"*Bage-e-e-ra!*" and he strode straight into the ranks, knocking men aside. Nobody could guess what this was all about, but that didn't matter. These things just happened. They had put Boof in the second rear rank to cover him as well as possible. With the long standing, he was bound to sway. Perhaps he had

THE SWORD AND THE BLOSSOM

now. Perhaps the men weren't covered-off properly and the suspicious Tiger thought there may have been a man missing. But they did not know.

Boof stood looking straight to the front. He and the Tiger had met before. The Tiger pushed Boof violently in the chest, but, though Boof was unsteady he had leaned forward just enough to take it. *"Bageera! Damme, damme . . .* you, soldier, no gooda." And he hit Boof about the face with back-and-forth blows with his big knuckly hands. Boof's lip was cut and an eye blackened. But he hardly moved. Still shouting complaints, the Tiger strode out again.

"He's always picked on Boof," Harry said, "because of his size, I reckon."

They reached the hut and Boof sat down on his ground-sheet. "Had your quinine, Boof?"

"No. In my pack. Will you, Harry?"

"Here you are, mate, and take a good swig at the bottle, I'll get some more."

"What about a wash before you settle down? I'll nick over the well and get a bucket," Buck said.

After a stand-up all-over wash, Boof settled down on the ground and pulled his blanket over him. "You blokes had better take your blankets—I won't need them tonight."

"Well, just yell out if you get the Joe-Blakes and we'll chuck them over."

Boof settled down to sleep. Harry went down to the cookhouse to fill the waterbottle. The others lay on the ground on their backs with their blankets only to their waists. As Harry lay down he stretched out on the bare earth and said, "Japs or no bloody Japs, this is a moment of luxury you couldn't buy with money." He patted the smooth hard ground, "Like a cloud."

John lay awake for a while. He watched the silent lightning flickering low and pale over the tree-fringe toward Bankok. The hut had no walls and it was easy to look along the ground to the horizon—as if into the future, or the past.

This was the gathering camp of the survivors, still forming. Just as the remnants of the prisoners were being gathered together, so too were the guards who had driven them. Already there were the Camel, Lookee-up-lookee-down, Snake's Hips, the Mad Mogul, the Mongrel, the Singing Fool, Boxhead, the

Lizard, the Tiger, the Bombay Duck, Four Eyes, Pork Face and Puddenhead. John knew that as long as there were Japanese guards over them they would live with uncertainty and indignity as their daily lot. There was nothing they could do about it.

5

Roads had been dug through the camp to take the motor traffic. It was easy work to put them across the flat plain, through the old paddy walls no more than a couple of feet high. And now the Japanese commandant had decided he would have them all gravelled. About a mile north of the camp there were wide gravel banks jutting out into the Menam river. With bag stretchers they carried the gravel up the steep banks to the waiting motor lorries. On the way to the job most of the men had picked a crimson hibiscus each and stuck it in the band of his hat.

When they arrived at the track leading down to the gravel banks, they passed under a tamarind tree. "Get the spread on that!" Harry said. "A hundred feet if it's an inch."

The trucks had brought their shovels and *tankas* (the bag stretchers). "*Oi. Oi. Mutugoi, mutugoi*, all men one!" shouted a skinny guard, strutting as if looking for some one to push around.

The men began to mutter insults as they went in and got their tools. "Bloody Snake's Hips—Who let him out?" "I'll get that skinny bastard one night without a moon." "Well, watch him today—I reckon he's after blood." "I believe the Tiger stirred them up last night after they got back from whoring in the town."

There was a roar. The Tiger had just come on the scene with an officer. "*Kurrah!*" he bellowed, "*Damme, damme, tak'san sagio! Talkoo nie. Bageera! Sagio speederoo!*"

The prisoners took their tools and went down to the banks where clumps of basket-willow grew. In the channel toward the other side of the river, and almost under the thickly wooded bank, a long low raft of bamboo was drifting past. It was one hundred and fifty feet long and, about amidships, there was a low attap hut outside of which smoked the embers of a fire on a bit of sheet iron. In the bow and at the stern stood two Thais who worked two sweeps vigorously to keep the raft in the channel. The river was broad with skin-smooth straw-coloured shoals of clean gravel and sand. Tamarinds, mangoes, bamboos and the sailing-ship masts of the kapoks grew right down to the water's edge, making deep, rich reflections under the banks. Further out, the water swept in glittering silver and gold about the shoals.

Gravel party

The men shovelled and carried. The Japanese soldiers kept at them, harrassing, screeching, jabbering. This was always with them—it wore them down more than the bashings.

It was still early morning. Opposite, a dirt road ran straight into the river. Some Thai women were coming down to canoes which had clean carved lines and upswept ends. The women carried silver dishes covered with gleaming white napery. The canoes shoved off and paddled leisurely across, and the women got out just above where the prisoners were working.

"That's the grub for the Buddhist priests," Harry said.

"Thought they only had a begging bowl they took round when they were hungry," Alec said.

"There's a lamasery along there a couple of hundred yards beyond the tamarind tree . . . a lot of young blokes there . . . must be some sort of a training joint," Buck said.

"Well," Boof said, "they're giving them the de-luxe treatment."

"Have you seen any of 'em?" Harry said. "I got on to a couple—they're as smooth and sleek as a skinful of lard . . . they shave so close that they're *blue* . . . skulls, faces . . . even their eyebrows . . . not a wrinkle on 'em anywhere . . . I haven't seen an old codger yet."

"Wonder if there's any chance getting in on it . . . do you think the Nips would let me change over on religious scruples?" Buck said. "Wonder what you have to do to join?"

"You have to give up all desire. . . ."

"The Nips and rice have fixed that for me. . . ."

"You have a yellow robe made of rags. . . ."

"That's an improvement. . . ."

"A begging bowl. . . ."

"My mess dixie. . . ."

"For medicine, all I can remember is the urine of a cow. . . ."

"Another improvement . . . where do we join?"

They hove their loads in over the tailboards and turned with the folded empty stretchers back to the river. Under the tamarind, shuffling barefoot through the shade-splashed dust was an old walnut-wrinkled woman, her withered empty breasts lay asleep against her chest. She wore only a crimson sarong. Her white hair was thin and teased, standing away from her thin small skull as if in fright. Her teeth protruded forward so that her lips could only cover them for brief moments when she made the effort. They were brown-black with betel and her mouth and gums were blood-red like a wound. Her lips would purse forward over her teeth while she collected the dribbling betel, then, like blood, she spat a red splash into the grey dust. Her skinny arms and legs moved only by a lifetime's habit. Her shoulder blades, collar bones and ribs, and the knobbly curved spine were as plain as in a diagram. She looked as if she were stripped of all except the last brief moments of life.

6

About ten in the morning, from the top of the bank, there suddenly broke out the brassy clashing of cymbals that filled the air with the shivering edges of ringing sound. Drums beat and rattled, drowning out and being drowned out. Threading thinly through it all came the sing-song, plink-plonking of highly strung oriental strings. All day it went on—it trailed behind them as they went back to camp at night. They wondered what it was all about.

"Sounds like a drunks' all-night party started early."

As they took their loads up they could see more. There was a house, large by local standards, built towards the front of its grounds. In the shade of several spreading trees and a few banana palms, were half a dozen trestle tables covered with white cloths. Food was being brought out on plates and dishes. Children looked as if they were a little better dressed than usual and played about with that subtle interplay which suggested that they were relations. Adults were moving about as if without proper purpose. The noise of the instruments came from the inside of the house.

"What a headache in *there!*" Doggie said.

They found out that this was the beginning of a funeral celebration.

"Perhaps they are trying to wake the joker up," Buck said.

"No chance of burying him alive . . . a thousand quid on that . . . he'll be dead all right when they burn him."

"Be a rotten position to be in," Boof said. "If you were alive, you wouldn't know whether to turn your toes up just to get away from the bloody din . . . or whether it would be worth while coming back."

"Wonder how he died?"

"Someone got the grapevine that he was a head man and he'd been done over by some political mob . . . red-hot on politics out here!"

A couple of ivory-smooth, saffron-robed young priests went into the place together with an older priest whose face showed a few seams of time, but not of adversity.

"Those robes are silk!" Buck said. "Thought you said they had to be made of rags?"

"That's what the book says, Buck, but I suppose a lot of these blokes can make their own rules . . . our blokes do."

Doggie, who always had his ear to the ground for scandal or

profit said, "I was just talking to some of the mob over there, they said this was a political job. . . ."

"We just heard that."

"Yes, but these blokes are saying that it was the boys in the yellow robes were the blokes behind it . . . they gave the orders."

"Wonder what those three are doing in there? Have they come to bury the bloke or just make sure he's dead?"

The din carried on. When they came up each time to the trucks, they had to raise their voices to be heard. Their rice was brought out for the midday meal and they queued up behind one of the trucks for it. The din was unrelenting.

"Sounds like the hit parade on a crook wireless!" Harry shouted.

"This must be the most popular assassination of the century, I wonder if they'll be as glad when I go?" Alec said.

"Get on those two jokers," Buck pointed. "I bet they are the poor uncles . . . they just snoop round . . . not game to talk to anybody . . . but they are doing all right with that grub . . . reckon it won't be long and they'll be sleeping it off in the dust under that mango. . . ."

"That's if the kids don't tear all over them. . . ."

Most of the prisoners went down to the shade by the river to eat their rice.

A couple of barges, well-modelled and made of teak, were tied to their long mooring-poles pushed upright into the sand. By the side of one of them stood a young mother with the water just wetting the hem of her dark-blue pencil-striped sarong. In one hand she held her pink bodice taken off in the noon heat, in the other she had the tiny hand of a toddler who was splashing and squealing about his mother's skirt. Bending slightly forward, her front was in shadow and her well-formed breasts hung forward a little and, coppery, they caught the cool reflected lights from the rippling water.

A few of the prisoners made lecherous remarks.

"Haven't any of you low bastards got any mothers or sisters!"

Boof's voice carried a threat that was heeded.

Shortly after this, another Thai woman came down to the water near the barges. She wore a dark sarong which was tucked close-up under her arms. With one hand at her throat and the other lightly catching her skirt by her thigh, she swirled through the water with a graceful swing of her shoulders balancing the movement of her hips. She stopped when the water was above her knees. Then she commenced to wash herself all over —her face, arms and shoulders, with neat sensitive movements of her hands like two small fans in ritual dance. Then her legs and thighs. Then she sat low in the water and, under the discreet cover of her dress, her hands, like trained serpents, washed the rest of her body with the smooth simplicity of unconscious habit. Then she stood up. Reaching up to the deck of the barge, she took a fresh sarong. Standing just ankle-deep in the water, she slipped the fresh garment over the wet one. With her elbows up and her hands holding it like a cylinder, she slipped the tuck of the old one in a deft movement of a free little finger, and it dropped in the river about her ankles. Then she fastened the dry one. With a comb and a few light caresses to her hair, her toilet was done—all in full view of more than a hundred men.

"As demure as a girl at her first dance," Alec said.

The afternoon passed in the monotony of shovelling and carrying. At intervals, like the sporadic playing of a geyser in a thermal belt, the guards would flare up.

Marching back, they passed a Thai house. It was built on stumps five or six feet off the ground. On the steps sat a young, lean Thai with smooth yellow skin drawn over high broad cheekbones. His arms and body were tattooed with a thick lacework of dark blue, running like veins just under his skin. A clutch of half-grown chickens scratched about. Bored dogs lazed in the dust, hot in the late sun. Children played and squealed and, at the louder squeals, dogs half-opened their eyes, wrinkling their foreheads in effort. There appeared to be more litters of children than of dogs—hardly a year between them. On the step below the young husband, was his young, almost childlike, wife. Both were naked to the waist. Her perfectly candid breasts were taut, elongated and out-thrust. They seemed to invite, almost demand, the whole world to nurture. And it was not long before the world came to suckle. A small, black-headed sepia-eyed boy child, dusty, with chubby bouncing buttocks came to her. He was carrying a naked girl almost as big as himself on his hip. In a moment, both those breasts met this hungry world in mutual satisfaction.

"Disgusting! Bloody wogs!" This came from a sergeant, whose

rectitude and high moral standards he left none in doubt of.
"Look, they're all the same!"

They were just passing another house where a woman squatted, tailorwise, in a skirt and loose blouse. A toddler came
scampering to her, on impulse, without pause, he lifted up the
loose hem of her bodice, groped with both pudgy hands and
buried his face in the warm satisfying comfort that fed him.

Built on stumps

There were plenty to agree with the sergeant. "They don't
know any better—they're just animals."

"Just as well they are not *human* like you sanctimonious
bastards," Buck said.

7

That night they lay alongside each other on the creaking
bamboo slats of the bed platform that had now been built.
These platforms stretched the full length of the huts on either
side of a dirt passageway.

There was the nightly talk before sleep. The conversation would go beyond each little group and become general. It would be only voices in the dark. They talked of the past and filled in some of the gaps they had been too dazed and exhausted to note when the Japs had been driving them through the *Speedo*. Men had vanished without their noticing, or knowing where. They had no way of telling whether they were now dead or alive. Haphazard remarks and hearsay were now piecing it together.

It was a sultry night. The toc-ta lizards which normally wind-up with a noise like a ratchet and then make a succession of toc-ta calls with their outgoing breath, now only gave a tired half-hearted performance as if they could hardly wait until bedtime.

"What about up at Tarsau—when the aircraft used to come over on their way to Bankok? . . . they used to get pretty jumpy and have all the fires put out . . . it was stuffy in the huts, and the blokes would sleep out . . . then the Nips brought out that order, Men sleeping in the open are not to shake out their blankets—*the noise causes alarm and despondency.*"

"What about the Jungle Lion up there . . . remember him at Hintok? . . . the way he used to rant and roar . . . bash artist too . . . reckoned he was pretty good . . . beat his chest like Tarzan and say, Me Jungle Lion! But down at Tarsau he came over to us as if we were his old schoolmates . . . he'd been up to the village and got himself a woman—very cheap, he said . . . but now he was dragging his rifle and looked a proper drop of misery . . . like a kid whose old man's gone crook at him . . . he had the jack . . . he said. Now, me no Jungle Lion—me only Jungle Lamb . . . so we said, Oh ho! and he'd smile sadlike . . . I got quite sorry for him . . . he had changed . . . every time the *Kempei Tai* were about or there was a search or anything, he'd come over and give us the drum."

"What about a couple of those doctors up there at Tarsau! There was one I hated more than any Nip. . . ."

"I know the bastard . . . a bloke came in one night . . . a Pom (and the doctor was a Pom too) he was just about to collapse with malaria . . . I don't know how he got himself there . . . the doctor was all spit and polish in clean khakis—even the brass on his gaiters was polished . . . by his batman of course . . .

SURVIVORS

he didn't give this poor bloke a chance . . . STAND TO ATTENTION
WHEN YOU ADDRESS AN OFFICER!"

"I know him, it's the same bloke . . . this night I was there a
joker comes in from work . . . his feet were swollen, you could
hardly tell where his toes were . . . no ankles . . . they were as
thick as his knees . . . his balls were up like a balloon . . . his
mouth was scabby . . . he had the lot . . . and what do you
think this prize bastard says? The best thing you can do is to
go out and do some work and earn yourself a couple of eggs. . . ."

"They were the blokes that Weary was crook on . . . I heard
he threatened them that if he could help it they wouldn't ever
practice again in Civvy Street. . . ."

"There wasn't many of the bastards but didn't they make it
felt!"

Sometimes the talk split into several groups, each still half-
aware of the other with ears so tuned that at any point they
could enter each other's conversation. On the previous night a
machine gunner had died of dysentery before sundown. He had
not been buried until late this day. Arch, a machine-gun sergeant, was talking in low tones to John. Arch had been a pall
bearer. The padre had said that he could not possibly bury Bill
this morning because it would interfere with his regular Sunday
service. Arch was saying, "Hardly anyone goes anyway." He
was still sickened with disgust. "If ever I had any faith in a
Church, it would have been shattered today. Poor Bill! They'd
only plugged him and tied his arms in front at the wrists, and
tied his ankles together. He was naked on a bag stretcher, with
another bag thrown over him. It's been hot . . . and the smell!
. . . this was our mate, Bill . . . Christ! What a send-off! If he'd
had a mother or sister there. . . . Then the padre says, I don't
think we need remove the blanket—he meant the bloody bag.
. . . It's bad enough our mates dying . . . but when you have to
see them go like this. . . ."

"And you know it's not always the Nips . . . ," Harry said.
"Don't talk to me about misfortune making brothers of us all
. . . not after what I've seen in this lot . . . the good blokes—yes
. . . but the others—once a bastard, always a bastard."

"Believe there's more of our blokes coming down from Kanburi
soon. Might get some more news of blokes we left in the jungle."

"I think my young brother's at Kanburi . . . last I heard . . . ,"

701

Boof said. "I'd like to see him again before we get moved on."

"Where do you reckon our next move'll be?"

"I heard that four hundred from Chunkai left for Japan, and more are standing by," Alec said.

"The thing I don't want to have to do," Harry said, "is to go back up the jungle—maintenance parties are going back, you know."

"They have to. There's still plenty of sick coming down."

"The first time, we just hung on . . . we didn't know what we were in for . . . but next time . . . one more Wet up there, knowing . . . I would not bet on myself."

"Well, gents," Buck said, "that looks like our future: go to sea and get torpedoed, or back up the jungle and cop cholera."

8

For some days they had been working on hut building.

Takamura was one who had charge of them now. On the Railway he had been one of the most ruthless. A Japanese captain, Hirota, had issued an order that prisoners, when frying eggs, must always break the yolks so as not to make a profane image of the Japanese flag. Takamura had stalked the camp after dark just to catch men out. Often, when a man had only just broken an egg into his pan (a salvaged wheel cap), Takamura would give a violent shriek and, running, kick the pan and the offending egg far into the night and the jungle. Then he would punish the man. But now he was milder. He recognized and welcomed them. He said he wanted to be friends.

"You, Nippon, *pinto, pinto.* . . . Bash, bash!" Doggie said. "No gooda . . . no gentleman."

Takamura made a deprecating gesture, "You *damme . . . pinto O.K.-da.*"

"No," Doggie said brazenly, "*pinto damme*, Takamura San no gentleman."

"Cut it out, Doggie, you bloody idiot! We'll all finish up with a bashing."

"No jentoruman-ca? *Damme-do-no* . . . you speak how."

Doggie told him, Takamura had some English.

"You, *pinto, pinto*! Australie no *pinto*. No gooda . . . no boxing
. . . only Nippon *pinto* . . . sporto *nie*. British Empire, one man
hit, other man hit also . . . one man hit only, no sporto . . . no
gentleman."

"O.K.-da. *Ima* Takamura jentoruman, *shinshi, pinto nie.
Ashita: pinto nie. Ashita, ashita: pinto nie.* Now Takamura jentoruman."

And tomorrow and tomorrow, Takamura tried to be a
gentleman the way he had promised.

Thai hut

"There we have him," Harry chuckled. "Takamura:
apprentice gentleman."

That night Takamura and other young Japanese soldiers went
on leave into Kanburi. "It's their whoring day," Buck said. They
came back to the camp shouting and singing drunkenly. "Look
at 'em," Harry said. "Each one's about six feet tall—not so
different from our mob, at that." "Watch them go quiet past
the sergeants' hut," Alec said. But the Tiger came out and, with
one bellow, had them straight and silent in an instant. He roared
again and they ran, to be back in a matter of minutes in full
marching order with packs and rifles. For two hours he put
them through it until their cotton uniforms were wet with
sweat and black with dust. They marched and sang lusty battle
songs; they charged across the bare plain with fixed bayonets
with shouts of *Banzai* that twisted their stomachs. They ran,
chanting songs and panting hoarsely. They were ready to drop

703

with exhaustion when the Tiger, after another savage speech, let them go.

That night one of them sneaked back to his lady love of the afternoon. He was caught coming back after midnight. The Tiger put them through it all over again. It was almost dawn when he let up. "Good old Tiger," Harry said. "Give it to the little bastards—give them some of what they give us."

"It's funny," Alec said, "even though the Tiger's bashed up plenty of our blokes, it takes the sting out of it a bit when he gets into his own blokes too."

"As long as it's not *you* he's bashed," Buck said.

"Well, he's bashed Boof plenty," Harry said.

"And you too, Harry. But it's no good doing your block with them blokes. You've got to take care of yourself—don't let them get under your skin . . . let *them* burn their guts out . . . I'm not going back psycho—not if I can help it."

"Listen to that! Boy, is he getting into them!" Buck said with comfortable satisfaction. "What a bonza lullaby—sleep like a baby now."

"You see, Harry," Boof was saying, "those jokers have grown up their way . . . we can't make sense of it . . . but have you noticed how they get bushed with us? . . . sometimes we seem to be understanding each other . . . then something happens . . . don't ask me what . . . out of the blue they are screaming maniacs . . . something . . ."

"That's what I mean, Boof, they get on your nerves . . . that's what wears you down . . . you never know. . . ."

"I know . . . but I tumbled up in the jungle . . . remember . . . when the Tiger was doing us over about the milk we pinched. . . ."

"Do I! That's *one* thing I won't forget."

"Well, when the Tiger was screaming his head off at us . . . you know how he was . . . you'd have thought we'd spat in the Emperor's eye . . . he nearly broke down with the act he was putting on . . . *that's* when I woke . . . *the poor bastard can't help it* . . . I woke."

"Not much consolation *then* . . . the working-over they were giving us . . . I wanted to murder every whore's son of them . . . I wanted to howl with sheer bloody helpless rage. . . ."

"But you didn't."

"No. I didn't have the guts to."

"Well, I felt I got the edge ... when I knew they could not help themselves. ..."

"But it still bloody hurts!"

"On the outside, Harry. On the outside, that's all ... a few lumps and bumps maybe ... I can't stop them on the outside ... but the little bastards are not going to get inside and unscrew anything if I can help it."

Harry then believed he almost remembered the moment that Boof had tumbled to the Tiger. And he knew that, then too, Boof had stopped the Nips getting inside of *him*.

In the morning they were back on the half-finished hut. Takamura told them how tired he was. "*Ho, gunso kichigai ... shikaru tak'san yonaka sreepoo nai ... damme ... byōke ima.*" The sergeant was a madman who reprimanded them at midnight. They had no sleep. No good. Sick now.

"Takamura San *yasume ima* ... all men *sagio O.K.-da.*"

Takamura drew himself up seriously and faced the ranks of his Number Twelve Party. He addressed them with his mixed language, meaning, "Gentlemen there is no Nippon supervising you when I leave. Work honestly and finish at five o'clock. Those who do not work honestly do not knock off until six o'clock."

Takamura vanished into the trees. The men worked on and, having finished the hut easily, went back to their billets, glad of some extra time to themselves.

They lay back on their bed-slats and listened while the conversation drifted about.

"I don't reckon we'll ever understand these buggers," one remarked. "Look at Takamura ... what he was ... and now, today."

"I still couldn't trust one of 'em."

"What about that English bloke at Tarsau ... the one that got V.D. ... they stood him in front of the guardhouse without his pants in front of everyone. The guards would flick him with bamboo switches every now and again ... poor bastard ... bad enough with the jack, without that ... they made a great fuss about it ... fancy them ... and they get all bloody officious with this poor bloke ... made his life hell ... five days he had

to stick it . . . they gave him a couple of hours sleep each night
. . . they can get so holy over someone else's blue, but shut their
eyes to themselves . . . that's what makes you mad . . . bloody
Imperial Benevolence. . . ."

"What happened to the bloke?"

"They went to get him one morning and he'd shot through.
. . ."

"Did he get away?"

"Yeah . . . when we got out to the Railway, we found him—
a train had gone over his head."

"Poor bastard."

"Yes, but what do you think these yellow bastards turned
round and said then? They said he must have been a brave man
to have faced death like that."

"You never get used to them . . . a man's getting like a neuro-
tic sheila."

Some of the men in the hut were just down from Chunkai, a
few miles up the river. This had been the camp where the worst
sick of the survivors had been sent. Now there was a further
chance of hearing some fresh news of mates.

9

Each afternoon at about five o'clock, a rain-storm would
sweep across the river plain in wind-lashed sheets. This reminded
them all that the Wet was beginning again up in the jungle.
Mixed deep in each man was a fervent wish that he would not
be sent up there again.

As they lay there talking, another storm broke. The huts
swayed and filled with driving spray. The attap blew up like the
feathers of gulls tail-to-wind, and gaps of light appeared in the
roofs. The roof of the cookhouse by the river blew off. Men
watched their own anxiously. A latrine shelter blew away and
the pit filled with water. At another place, the sanitation squad
was changed from mere pit diggers to classic heroes, trans-
formed by a single idea. A half-completed latrine was in danger
of blowing down. Now these men stood braced in the mud,
their shoulders against the bamboo pillars with broad determined hands clenched about them. Ten pillars and ten men—

not, like Samson, wrecking the temple, but saving it. The very importance of their task gave them a classic pose. The hut leaned over while the wind tore at it with rising shrieks and ten taut bodies tensed together, giving visually a kind of harp-string vibration. The rain lashed with a force that made the skin feel cut.

As if at the fanatic call of some faith-healer, some of the hospital patients got up and went out in the rain to wash.

Saviours of sanitation

Standing there gaunt, skinny and naked, going through the grotesque mime of washing made so by weakness and fever, they were as if hypnotized. Some fell down. At last the last patient was helped back to his bamboo platform and the latrine was safe.

John said, "I have seen the caryatids in Greece—but those blokes left them for dead."

"I was thinking what a grouse rugby scrum they made," Buck said.

The rain passed away to a spotting sunset which gleamed in orange and red, making gaudy the remnants of the rain-washed rags of the spent storm. Thousands of frogs set up a harsh din that filled the whole plain. Crickets came in with a shrill treble which bored long thin holes in one's thoughts. Among all this was one basso frog whose voice, all the prisoners said, was the deep note of a love-lorn crooner of the old school. It was unique and persisted strongly above all other sounds. The other sounds were xylophonic notes like the shipwright's caulking mallet striking the polished steel top of the flat caulking punch which drives the oakum into the deck seams—a sound which is a confused plink-plonking on and on, endlessly, until the seams are done and the pitch comes hot, smoking and pungent to be payed in. Above this the philosopher-voice of the great basso made his *AII-OE-UNG-G-G-G*, with only slight, but deliberate, pauses between couplets. This deep electric loudspeaker hum of the *ah-oe-ung-g-g-g* was woven into their dreams to confuse them between sleeping and waking. But, before the sun rose, all was quiet except for an occasional weak trilling cricket.

The men were just settling down to sleep. Suddenly there was a cry, "Look out, there, SNAKE!" Men jumped up in a clatter of creaking bamboo bedslats. "Where?" It was dark and the inside of the hut was black with only the loom of night outside. "Felt him in my blanket as I unrolled it—I flicked him into the passageway, I think." There was a crash of bamboo on the ground. "Relax boys, I've got him."

But they all got up and shook their blankets out again. Snakes were plentiful. Coming back to their billets, men would often find snakes taking shelter in their blankets, packs, or even boots. This was a result of the clearing that had been going on. Sometimes they could see, by the dim light of a slush-lamp, snakes gliding along the bamboo rafters stalking the rats that lived in them. By morning they would be gone.

After the usual grumbling remarks about the life of a prisoner, the Japs, snakes and so on, the men were settling down again. Suddenly there was a series of horrible screams. Men woke with prickling scalps. Half a dozen men were locked violently with terrible cries coming from their knotted centre. One man shot from the mêlée and tore up the centre passageway to safety. All he left behind was a cry to his mate, "Are you all right, Gobby?" But the sounds from the struggling men were not all human. The rest of the men in the hut were sweating.

A man had rolled over in his sleep and his outflung arm had

struck another man in the mouth who immediately had the impression that a great woolly dog was tearing at his leg. He had screamed. The man who had hit him, half-awake only, was transfixed with fear. Yet, in seconds, he had fastened his teeth into the other man's leg *even as that man had dreamed*. And now the man who was biting had taken on the complete personality of a dog. He was barking, growling and snapping exactly like a dog. The others did not know that there was *not* a dog there. They attacked indiscriminately in the confusion while the animal sounds came from underneath. Everybody was shouting. At last they pulled the dog-man out and slapped him sensible. All were now wide awake, shot full of energy by fright. They talked to wear it off.

10

Harry, Boof, Alec, Buck and John joined the water-carrying party. They had so much to do, and were in their own time to do it. The Japanese had about thirty forty-four-gallon drums without tops. Each one was placed over a small earthen fire-place. Every day these had to be emptied and refilled with fresh water, which was then heated for their daily soak by a couple of prisoners. The soldiers, after washing, would climb in and soak in sensuous pleasure. As long as everything was ready for them, there was no trouble.

The water was drawn from a well that had belonged to a Thai house near by. The windlass was a wooden log turning on two forked branches set in the ground. The crank handle was made of a crook of wood where two branches had joined each other at right angles. Time had worn all parts smooth and tolerant to each other like husband and wife. The rope was soft and frayed from soaking and wear. Overhanging the well like a leaning Egyptian fan was a banana palm. From it curved a stick of green fruit at the end of which the spear-point of the unfinished flower arched downwards like a falling scarlet rocket.

The track from the well to the drums was smooth footworn earth. Carrying two buckets knocking against their knees for five hundred yards or so slopped water on the track, each trip making it more slippery.

In the wooden attap-thatched house by the well lived a
couple of Thai families. It was a large one-roomed place with a
sleeping-platform high at one end. There was a brood of five or
six children who had followed each other closely into the world
to mothers who appeared to be still in their teens. But they were
very placid, surrounded by a fecund strongly growing nature

The well

bearing fruit all around them. Red pomegranates glowed on a
small tree. Mangoes, tamarinds, banana, paw-paw and Jack-
fruit overhung and surrounded them, preaching fertility.

One morning two Japanese soldiers went into the house, and
after some time, came out again.

"One of them's Takamura!" Harry said. "Get on him, will
you—he's as romantic as a schoolgirl!"

"More like a tomcat come out of a dairy," Buck said.

Takamura had a white flower in his hand which he sniffed
dreamily as he walked away. In contrast, the other Japanese
went to the well, picked up half a coconut shell, and washed
himself.

They came across snakes on or near the path. . . . Because of their bare feet they killed them whenever they could. A small cobra bit himself when he was hit and went inert. When they put him on an ant heap the tail below the bite writhed but the rest did not. Alec said, "Is that because it was where he bit himself or where we hit him?" Another snake about two feet long had a golden, diamond-shaped head, a bronze back, and along his sides ran turquoise and green beaded scales. His underside was like white mother-of-pearl china. Just behind his head by his large unwinking eye ran a black streak. He was enhanced by an all-over liquid lacquer sheen. But, when they hit him and broke his back, he shrunk to half his diameter, went dull, and his living beauty vanished.

"We broke the spell of life—why?" Harry said.

It rained that night. The next morning they came along the path and Alec called, "Hey! Get on to this!" The snake was now covered by a half-round mud shelter along his full length. Gently they broke part of it away and found it swarming with ants inside. Already the snake had been reduced almost to a skeleton.

"Organization," Buck said. "Our bloody side could do with a bit of that!"

The day was now clear with a hot sun in a blue sky and a high thin cirrus cloud-veil. About ten o'clock the deep drone of aircraft was heard. Distant thuds of anti-aircraft batteries up by Tamarkan bridge punctuated the heavy air. There were some deeper rumbling explosions. The prisoners looked up and grinned. The Japanese ran inside and came out with their rifles, screaming at the prisoners not to look up. The aircraft did not draw off. High above the gunfire more than a dozen big four-engined planes wove vapour-trails, making the sky look like a child's finger-painting. No fighters went near them. They stayed, weaving their four-stranded trails until three o'clock in the afternoon. The word filtered through to the men from the 'canary' (the camp wireless) "The Allies have landed in Europe."

Even the die-hard jingoes of the Japanese looked uneasy and puzzled as if seeing something that could not be. There were a few more beatings that day.

The water carriers were finished and on their way to the

river when they passed what, at first, looked like a monstrous centipede fifty feet long. Over one hundred men were staggering under the load of a fully-grown coconut tree. Poles had been pushed under it and on each side men with cracking muscles shuffled foot by foot. The great clump of root at one end dwarfed them. The Japanese were transplanting it about half a mile to the entrance of their new headquarters. On the opposite side of the gateway they had already planted a twenty-foot cactus which now had plate-sized yellow flowers on it. One of the men who had been working for the day up there had told them that one of the officers had a sloth in a cage. "Poor little bastard," he said, "he looked at me with those for-Christ's-sake-help-me eyes. . . ."

When they got to the river they stopped to watch some Thai children playing. They were naked except for a Roman Catholic scapular each. One boy wore a helmet which made him look like an animated toadstool. Two of the boys had bows with which they shot stones into the river. The bow-string was made of split-bamboo with a slit in the centre that made a neat socket for the stones. While the boys were plopping stones into the river, six canoes drifted down. In the bows of each a half-naked man stood with a folded net gathered in his hands. Then, all at once, with a smooth swing of waist, shoulders and outflung arms, six nets sailed and fell in perfect circles on the water with a soft hiss—like the expanded ripples of a few evening raindrops on a calm pond. "It must be one of the most beautiful rhythmic sights in the world: justified equally by mathematics and aesthetics," John thought.

II

After evening parade, Boof went over to see his young brother who had come into Tamuan that afternoon. There were still deaths in these camps. A couple of days previously two had died of cerebral malaria. Dysentery was still taking them. Some were running down like clocks that could not be re-wound. One man died of cholera and became a reminder of the previous year when even the most sanguine of them wondered if it were possible still to be alive in six months' time.

Creaking, twisting, stretching, they were settling down with a brief sense of luxury only the deprived can know.

Alec turned to Harry.

"I heard you talking to Boof the other night about the Tiger and the going-over he gave you."

"That was over Jimmy . . . he was real crook . . . Boof thought it would help him."

There was a silence.

"Well," said Buck, "are you going to tell us—or aren't you?"

"It was up at One-O-One Kilo camp . . . young Jimmy had been brought down from further up . . . he was bad . . . the doctors didn't like it . . . they mentioned milk . . . like asking for the moon.

"Boof said to me, The Nips have got a stack of it in their store . . . I reckon it's ours really . . . I warned him. . . . We'll get our heads cut off . . . Jimmy's crook, he needs it. If I can get it, he said, they can cut my bloody head off.

"Well, I couldn't see him one-out, so I went with him. That night we crawled through the jungle to their store . . . bamboo and attap, the usual . . . there was a moat of water about six feet to keep the rats out. We jumped it to avoid the noise. We both had ulcers on our legs and crook feet—if you'd seen us jump in the dark like a couple of broken-down elephants on ant-eaten legs. . . . I wasn't too happy. These Nips were all bash-artists. . . . I wondered what they would do if they caught us *kutchi*-ing their stores. But Boof was so set on it he was dangerous, someone had to be with him.

"We blued, of course. We played it too cunning. Instead of taking the cases from the top, we tried to take them from the bottom because for some wet reason we thought it wouldn't be so noticeable. They were stacked about nine high. It was slow. The wire bands got caught. Boof eased the top cases while I worked one out from underneath. As I got a couple out, the others come down with a crash. My guts turned to water. I was expecting something to happen all the time. I died a thousand deaths and froze on the spot. I don't know how Boof felt, but he didn't move either. He froze like a lizard on a branch. But nothing happened. They must have thought it was a falling branch or something. After a bit we picked up the cases and slunk back like a couple of scared Indians.

"The doctor and orderlies were waiting. There were tins of water hot already. We broke the cases open and emptied in all the tins. We burnt the cases and pushed all the tins under in the latrines. We filled them with water first so they would stay sunk. Then we put the bamboo covers on. In the morning there was no sign. All day Boof and I waited for the storm to break. But nothing happened.

"That night, Boof and I went again and sent off two more cases. But we worked from the top this time—no noise. The night after we did the same. We thought Jimmy was looking a bit better. Boof said, We'll go again tonight. I said I had a funny feeling—let it go a couple of nights. It wouldn't hurt. We'd draw the crabs—give it a spell. But Boof was set. I didn't want to go back there tonight. There was a bright moon and we had just been lucky with cloud the other nights.

"Boof said, All right, Harry, you don't have to. He wasn't being nasty—that's not Boof. So I went. I said I thought he was crazy. We got the cases out easily enough, we had that weighed-off by now. We put the attap back carefully, picked up the cases and turned to cross the moat. Just then the moon cleared a bank and made everything stand out. And there, facing us across the moat, were four Japs with fixed bayonets. Not a word. In that light, with bared teeth, they could have been four death's heads. We didn't say a word.

"*Kurrah!* They all screamed at once.

" '*Bagee-eera! Kutchi, kutchi! Kurrah!*' The way they yelled you would have thought they were spewing.

"No sooner had we got there than, CRASH! I was hit over the side of the head with the muzzle of a rifle. It cracked my head against the case I was carrying and I let it drop as I felt the barrel half-way along whack me on the back of the neck. I was down on my knees. In came the boots and rifle-butts. I couldn't tell one from the other. Ribs, kidneys, head and all. I crouched over to protect my groin—you know them. I was feeling pretty sick from the kidney-kicks, and I wished they would knock me cold. But they didn't. The pain seemed to go straight through me like a knife. I wanted to scream, but I think I only croaked. My stomach came into my throat and was squirming there. I wanted to spew. I couldn't. Boof was getting the same as me.

I suppose I was grunting and squealing. But Boof didn't make a sound—I thought he was out.

"Then it eased off. But I didn't care whether they went on and finished the job or not. We just lay there. The next I know I'm being pulled and kicked about. In the distance I could hear, *Kurrah . . . Kiotski . . . standupoo . . . Bageer-eera!* Then I felt a screaming pain in my leg, as if it was being cut off. . . .It brought me right back to the bloody misery they were giving us. One of them had whacked the ulcers on my shin with the flat of his bayonet. We staggered to our feet, picked up the cases and back to the guardroom. We stood all night outside with the milk at our feet. The guard was changed twice and each new guard slapped us and kicked our ulcers, that were now running red and yellow down our ankles.

"We watched the moon set. I've never seen a moon so far away. It was more like being alone on it. At last, over the tops of the trees, the mountains turned pink—like a woman's dress (funny how you think of things like that at times like that). . . ."

"Probably because you don't think you'll ever see them again," Buck said.

"Something like that . . . but I know it was so lovely that it made me feel worse . . . we were still in the valley shadow and you could see the bar of shadow between the light and shade in the air above us. . . ."

"I know," Alec said. "We used to watch it on parade up there."

"In the light just above the shadow, you could hear the buzzing of thousands and thousands of those blue-green blowflies. At last the sun came up and the bar of shadow came down—and every last mother's son of those bloody flies with it. All day they tramped around the latrines, but they seemed to take the day off from latrine-crawling and tramp round us. They ringed our ulcers and started to eat us. They had it all their own way—we couldn't crack a boo or the guards would shout and kick our shins—which was the only time the flies got off. When we started to sweat the little black bush bees came to feed on our armpits, burrowing in. They're little buggers . . . not bad really, but on top of the rest. . . .

"I don't know what I looked like. I only know I felt lousy. I suppose I wanted to shut it out because I couldn't face it . . .

not so much what they'd done, but what was coming. When I looked at Boof, I didn't think I could look as bad as *that*, no matter what. . . . There was a cut in his scalp and the blood had flowed into his right eye, down his neck on to his chest. His right ear was swollen and the left one was torn at the lobe. The skin was off his nose from the bridge to the tip. Both eyes were closed and bluey-black. His left cheek was a greeny-yellow bruise. His lips were puffed up and blood had dried around his mouth. His body was like a leopard only the spots were red and blue and green and yellow. The flies fed on him. His shins, like mine, were yellow, running down from broken scabs.

"Boof wasn't saying a word . . . we couldn't of course . . . he just stood there. But it was a long, long day, believe me. Every now and again there was a yell and a slap and they pointed to the loot—the bloody milk. They love suspense. If they wanted us to turn yellow, I was way ahead of them—I was almost wishing they'd finish me off. But Boof . . . even when they kicked his shins they might as well have been kicking a rock. . . . I reckon Boof, without a word or a move, pulled me back from going over the edge. . . .

"It was well after sunset when they took us into the guard-room and all the guards gigged us over. Some of them pointed and laughed like schoolgirls. They gave us a drink of black tea, bitter as gall. Some rice, we had to eat with our fingers. Then outside again all night. One of the guards slipped us a drink of water. *Mizu*, he said, and let us sneak a bit of a sit-down on the cases.

"The Tiger was away out of the camp just now. What would happen when he came back we didn't like to think. Up to now it had been Saito's party. He was a nice prize little basket—he loved being boss-cocky of the show. D'y'notice how the corporals get more power-drunk than the sergeants or officers when they get the chance?"

"We knew one at Hintok," Alec said. "The camp was just over the creek from us. In three months, out of three hundred prisoners one hundred and twenty were dead—a corporal in charge."

"The next day out came the sun and the flies started eating us again. About ten o'clock two guards with rifles and fixed bayonets marched either side of us and halted. The Tiger came out. He looked at us. He looked at the milk. Then he let go—but with his tongue. It was mixed-up Japanese, Malay and bastard English. Of course, the old Imperial Benevolence came into it . . . this meant that they could fit us for anything . . . I wasn't too happy . . . once they start working themselves up, you know how it is. . . .

"Then he stopped all at once and said *S'p'ts'* and they quick-marched us into the jungle. On the way we picked up a couple of shovels. When we halted out there, the Tiger snatches a shovel off Boof and marks out an eight-by-two square on the ground. He threw the shovel back and it whacked me fair on the shin. It hurt like an electric short-circuit across your brain. I promised I would murder him one day—but I didn't tell him. Then, when he pointed to the square, I wasn't so sure. . . .

" 'Dig-oo!' he said. So we dug. The guards sat on the stumps, but I noticed that they kept their rifles in their hands and pointed our way. After we got down a bit, Boof said, 'This looks like a grave.' I nodded—it seemed worse in words. 'More *takusan*,' the Tiger said. So we widened it. Then he went away, leaving only one guard. But he cocked his rifle, just to let us know. Boof said, 'When the time comes, Harry, we've got these shovels—I reckon we could take a couple with us.' We dug all day. 'They'll be able to put the whole camp in if we dig much more,' I said.

"After dark they brought us a bit of rice and a drink of water. My tongue just blotted up the water, not a bit went down. The guard said, '*Mati, mati*' and vanished. It was no good trying to shoot through. We were buggered anyway—and the jungle at night . . . so we just dossed down in the hole and went out like lights. Next morning they kicked us to our feet and we felt sicker and sorer than ever.

"It was on again. *Bageera! Kurrah! Sagio tak'san! Kurrah!* and so on. We didn't know why they wanted it so big. Boof said they'd work us till we dropped and then off-lolly in the bottom of the hole. We got cagey and coasted. Boof kept me going, just being there, he was so steady. I just followed. It was like having someone else's dream. We slept in the hole again that night. No water or rice this time. This is it, I said.

"We were awake when they came the next morning. The guards were in full order and the Tiger was carrying his sword, drawn. Boof said, 'Get a good grip of the shovel and be ready. I'll watch his sword.' They halted—all proper drill. He shouted and they brought their rifles to the loading position, and we heard the bolts work. I thought, they'll bloody-well shoot us and we won't get a chance! We kidded to be working. *Oi, soldier! Mutugoi, mutugoi! Sagio nai! Kurrah, speederoo!* We crawled out of the hole. It was a bit closer. And we kept latched-on to the shovels. A good swing, Boof had said, would nearly take a man's head off. But they stood us up with the guards ten paces away. We had been caught flat-footed. All at once they brought their rifles up. Then at one word from the Tiger they pulled the triggers. A million years passed—the rifles *had only clicked!* Misfire? *All* of them? I couldn't work it out—and I was in no condition to. Then they shouldered their rifles and moved each side of us. 'You dead-oo,' the Tiger said. They marched us back to camp and let us go. That nearly brought me undone more than all the rest because it did not make any sense. The bastards know how to get at you."

"That's them," Alec said, "they make you die a thousand deaths."

"Sounds stupid, like some kid's game . . . ," Harry said.

"They look at it differently," John said.

"They must."

"You don't think you're dead, Harry."

"Are you kidding?"

"To the Tiger you are."

"*Nani?*"

"You are dead—they can't kill you again."

"That's good."

"Not so good. You're dead because you marred the Imperial Benevolence . . . the Tiger had to do it."

"Well, if he's so patriotic, why didn't he finish the job?"

"You are still needed to work for the Emperor. But if ever any of these Nips do you over for nothing at all, there's no charge because you are already dead. You haven't been let off, you just haven't any rights any more."

"It's like haunting yourself," Harry said. "I wish you hadn't told me."

"And Jimmy got back, of course . . . he's here now," Alec said.

"Yes. And I think that bit of milk might have just given him the edge."

12

They had just arrived from the well when a corporal came out and called, "*Oi! Oi! Soldier, soldier!* . . . *you* . . . *Oi! San Mai* . . . *kurrah* . . . *speederoo, speederoo!*" Boof, Harry and John were sent in to the sergeants' hut to clean it up.

"Bloody bimbo-ing!" Harry growled. "I hate these jobs—its too close to them."

The change, coming out of the strong light into the dimness of the hut, was remarkable. The walls, here, ran right up to the eaves and cut off the outside completely. A church-like quietness struck the prisoners who had lived so long in crowded congestion and noise in half-walled or no-walled huts—or in rotten tents hanging in strips. There was a profound effect on their thoughts —on those feelings that seldom become thoughts. Some call it 'atmosphere'. And it was sharpened by their condition of no-privilege. It was enough to endure hardship and deprivation when they saw nothing else; but given even a mild comparison of comfort, and the feeling of want painfully returned.

On either side of the earthen passageways were cubicles, two steps up, separated by split-bamboo walls. Plaited mats were spread on the bamboo floors. Crooked pieces of branches, dragon-like, were fitted in here and there. Low, home-made tables occasionally held a small bamboo vase and a stem of something. Mosquito nets hung over the beds unrolled on the floor, giving the rooms, it seemed to the prisoners, an unaccustomed privacy—as if they were places of habitual assignation. On the Tiger's wall hung a scroll painting of a branch of plum blossom. On a peg, and hanging across the lower right-hand corner of it, was the Tiger's sword in its scabbard with its sword-knots dangling. The picture and the sword seemed to contradict each other.

"Never get to the bottom of these bloody Japs." Boof said. "They say one thing and do another . . . look at this!"

When Boof saw the sword he remembered how the Tiger had held it drawn when he and Harry had stood with their

shovels. He could still see it glinting steely-bright on its three
equal and harmonious curves. He could still feel the grip of the
shovel in his hand. How could the sword and the picture *not*
contradict themselves?

When John looked at the picture, it gave a fine pain like the
thin cut of a razor which goes deep before you know it, leaving
little on the surface. It was the first real painting he had seen in
over two years. It was said that much Japanese painting is
calligraphic. This branch of blossom was written with an assurance and simplicity that was breath-taking. It was the voice of
rising sap. This was personal in him. All through his captivity
he had carried a small colour box that had been a door of
escape which did much to take him out of himself and his
discomfort. He had heard many theories of art, both plausible
and fantastic. But there was one which he thought was valid.
It was the theory of 'participation' which was an identification
of the artist with his subject in a way that was not just an
empathy but a fusion. It would be stronger in primitives
because they could more readily experience directly without
intellectualization. For them feelings would not have to become
words before they could become action. Participation was an
intuition like the cell's knowledge of all that science has not yet
found out. It was something that John tried to get from painting
. . . a fuller realization of 'being' . . . a quickened awareness that
made simplicity and simple things paramount, and the grand
and celebrated less significant. It was a method of exploration,
not exhibition. This the plum blossom suggested to him.

It was small wonder that he was so affected for, as a prisoner,
he had been living close to these things as had the hermit-
philosopher-painter-poets of the East. It was not the awareness
of the go-getter, but of the richness of sitting still: of the meaning
of a raindrop running down a leaf, or a snowflake melting.

Boof said, "The Tiger's a funny bugger—you wouldn't think
he'd go for a picture like this. . . . I would have thought it
would be a bloody old warrior. . . ."

But, as Boof was looking at the blossom, it reminded him of
his home. Spring frost and morning ground mists. Cows coming
in to bail with slow bovine undulation in the mist-spearing light.
The magpies' clean, knife-clear warbling from the huge gnarled
gums standing like fog-greyed mountains in the big paddock.

Mudlarks piping black-and-white notes thinly down the corridors of time and space imprisoned in the cold morning. The orchard cloudburst of pink and white. The brown and white chickens scratching in the petalfall. The swift, sudden, upswept flash of a pair of jewelled blue, green, red and yellow Rosella parrots lighting on a knobbly budded branch to eat the soft new growth.

"You know, it reminds me of home, somehow," he said.

"The Tiger too, I suppose," John said.

"Do you think he's dinkum?" Harry said. "This, I mean."

"I think . . . probably . . . in a way we don't get on to."

John had found, while up on the Railway, the knack of letting an idea take complete possession of him. At first it was merely a device to take him out of his misery. But it became more—exploring, of itself, uncovered unexpected possibilities in ideas. This excited him. For days or weeks, an idea had taken hold of him, softening misery that was driving other men to despair. It made self less and life more. And now, though much of the necessity for this escape was gone, the habit was formed.

"What is it about the Tiger and the picture and Boof?"

This idea stayed with him for years. All men are woven into their country's past. Different on the surface, but obeying the same laws underneath. Between the Tiger and Boof, there appeared to be a complete contrast. Australia, the oldest continent with a young civilization; Japan, young islands with an old civilization. One stable with leisurely people; the other shaken by earthquakes with a volatile people. One sentimental and formal; the other sentimental and informal—but both quick to defend their sentiments. One drought-haunted and lonely; the other flood- and storm-stricken and crowded. But as well as this there was, minute by minute, the weaving of them stitch by commonplace stitch into a nationality. Ideas in word and print (and, significantly, the distorted repetition of these) stitched each into the tapestry of his history. John thought the difference between men is not so much that of the material of which they are made, but the national stitches that conceal it. Perhaps this, John thought, was at once the difference and the similarity between Boof and the Tiger—the civilized forces which controlled them.

In Boof was the traditional resentment of authority, stemming, maybe, from the echoed stories of the harshly treated convicts; or of the colonists suffering from official bungling and lack of understanding thirteen thousand miles away. Or from an absence of class order which made Jack as good as his master; or at least as good as his natural ability. Yet there was still a strong conformity to a tradition in him.

The Tiger was almost fossilized in his place in the family unit and the feudal order; in his unquestioning allegiance to the Emperor. The discipline of the forces of nature, through religion, showed him that the individual was but a straw in a divine wind.

Boof lived to get back to his family—all that his country stood for. The Tiger now lived to die for his Emperor—as an expiation of his existence.

He was born in the year of the Tiger and his nickname had come from his own countrymen: the young ones over whom he ruled so strictly. He was born about the time when Japanese warships were escorting Australian troopships to Europe. He grew up in an atmosphere of old Japan, although the cities were already fermenting with imported ideas. All these were struggling for political identity in the face of the old order. It had become a surging sea of action and reaction, expression and suppression, full of fortuitous currents carrying Japan on almost haplessly. Yet, even in the cities, much more of Old Japan clung to the people than the progressives cared to admit. This was to make the resurgence of the militarists much easier.

Although it had been used by the Shoguns and Jingos to enslave the people to their war ambitions, the relationship between the Emperor and the people was a profound one of a high spiritual ideal. The close affinity between the Emperor and his subjects is called *O Meta Kara*—the Great Treasure. It is the pulse of *Yin* and *Yang*, the male and female structure of creation. The people are obliged, through prayer and ritual, to assist the Emperor in his medianship with the light- and warmth-giving Sun Goddess. The early temples, *Miya*, were made of wood, undefiled with paint or metal (later permitted by Buddhism). Only the votive offerings and the *Gohei*, strips of white paper from a wand, were visible. In a closet of purest wood there was a case containing 'August-Spirit-Substitute' or 'God's Seed' which was usually a mirror. Some said this to be Amaterasu herself. The Divine Rescript from the Sun Goddess to the Emperor concerned the sacred mirror and said: *Always have this sacred mirror in your palace, worshipping it day and night as my spirit.* In Shinto philosophy the Emperor himself is '*a living spotless mirror*' and *by looking into the mirror we are constrained to self-reflection, purging ourselves of mental distortions.* Thus, *by constant and persevering observation of Shinto rites which preserves the mythological times of the gods and the primordial wisdom of pre-logical mankind, the Emperor cultivates a balanced and perfectly rounded personality despite the overwhelming pressures of technological civilization.*

The Shinto conception of royal coronation differs from that of the West at which an archbishop, a mere *representative* of Supreme God, crowns a monarch. For the Japanese, the Emperor *becomes Kami* in human shape (*Akitsu Mikami*) without any intermediary between himself and *Kami*, the Life Source. *Daijosai*, the taking of the sacred rice: *sacred prince restorative of unifying clarity and sacred word capable of bringing spiritual union* is akin to the Mass, Sacrament, or Holy Communion of the West. The Emperor is the highest Shinto priest, *Sumera Mikoto: Divine prince able to convert all chaotic turbulence into transparent clarity.*

These deep elemental religious sentiments reigned over the people for centuries. It was felt at the family shrines, *Kami Dana*, or at the wooden temples growing out of the countryside in such a way as to be part of the anatomy of Japanese life and religion. The old Shinto was for simplicity and purity. These wooden temples, with a durability of about half a century, were constantly rebuilt by replacement and maintainance. *Naiku*, meaning to keep-the-old-new. Thus the past became the present and tradition was kept fresh: *Ideas do not change and character stabilizes—honour gods, love country, clearly understand the principles of Heaven and duty to man, revere Mikado and obey the will of his court.* There was no defined moral code because '*Japanese consult heart and know right*'.

Emperor Meiji had written feelingly in a poem:

We cherish all nations as brethren sharing divine blood.
Why is the world so sea-tossed with angry waves!

This was something of the Emperor-people relationship.

But, throughout a long history, while the Emperors had been allowed only to cultivate their virtues and minds, the Shoguns had cultivated war.

The Tiger had been brought up in a small mountain village in Satsuma, Kyushu, where people had to work hard to maintain even poverty. Their simple pleasures came from that which could not be bought, and which they did not have to buy—a dictate of poverty. *Mono-no-aware* is an awareness in the Japanese spirit of the transience of all things. In despondency this may bring suicide. But, normally, it teaches an obedience to the laws of nature, making them modest and joining them in common sympathy. *Furyū* is, in them, a state of mind given over to communion with all that is beautiful and creative in nature. This, in spite of earthquake, hunger, flood, fire and feudal oppression, allowed the Tiger's people to watch a moonrise, a tree blossom, or a thousand other things and elevate the watching to a ceremony which was a profound and humble thanksgiving for the mystery of life.

Sitting around the warm and friendly *hibachi*, the Tiger had listened wide-eyed to the stories of Tengu, Futen, the Wind Imp, Raiden the Thunder Drummer, and the Rain Dragons. He heard of great warriors: fierce, yet as chivalrous as the Knights of the Round Table. He had kept crickets in cages which he had made himself. He had flown kites at festivals. These things had bred a deep sentimentality in him, unconsciously born of poverty, of inferiority. And, when it was challenged, his spirit smarted, his anger flared with a righteousness that justified any impulse. So, sentimentality could change in a moment to fierce ruthlessness. This was the swift threatening storm-shadow on a sparkling sea that the prisoners had learned to hate and fear without being able to fathom its cause, because they, too, had a righteousness justifying *them*. In both, really, it was the 'blood-relation' at work that can only properly ever work in prelogical animals—in man it frustrates and complicates because of the Intellect's back-seat driving.

Japanese scholars have tried to justify this relation. Shinto, though denied by many to be a religion, has conditioned the Japanese thought and action in a way that religions do. Its basic difference from dogmatic Christianity is significant. Dr Chikao Fujisawa puts it like this:

Prince Shoto [about the time of Constantine] issued the following edict: *We hear our Imperial Ancestors paid deep reverence to the Shinto deities of heaven and earth. Wherever they dedicated shrines to the mountains and rivers they held mysterious communion with the divine power of nature. So the male and the female cosmic potencies (Yin and Yang) were harmoniously blended and their concordant influences gave rise to a durable peace. Let our ministers with their whole hearts do reverence to the deities of heaven and earth.*

What this saintly prince accomplished was, after all, bold incorporation of Buddhist metaphysics and the cultural texture of ancient Shinto as flesh and blood; while the Christian faith, which had been transplanted to the West from *without*, had *uprooted* the western version of the Way of Kami previously prevailing in Europe. In short, Christianity destroyed the foundation of the folk beliefs indigenous to the Western soil, while Shinto, implicit in the core of Japanese nationhood, was able to imbibe and digest sucessfully the substance of Buddhism, thanks to inherent creativity. This salient trait of Shinto must always be taken into account when trying to grasp the Japanese way of thinking.

It has been suggested that the Japanese work on *intuition* and *synthesis*; while the West works on *logic* and *analysis*. This may be true as a general conclusion and as a pretended virtue for the one or the other. But in simple practice each side mixes them in varying proportions, dependent on the nature of the expedient to be undertaken. So that the black moods of the captors found justification for their black deeds in the precept: *Whatever is, is equally part of divine law. The concepts of GOOD and BAD do not arise. There is no conflict between God and man, nor between man and nature. No moral law, no original sin, no dread of hell . . . the blood relation* [intuition and synthesis] *rules and controls the Japanese.* To the ordinary Japanese, and particularly to the indoctrinated soldiers, they were merely 'looking into their hearts and knowing right' in the immediate impulse.

When the West acted with blood-relation, it was logically justified or hypocritically denied. When the Japanese acted thus, they saw no reason to hide it and therefore it appeared to the prisoners as obvious and self-admitted hypocrisy. This embittered them and made them completely cynical of any genuine virtue at all in their captors.

On the wall of the Tiger's room also hung a few flimsy paper cut-outs. One was of coloured paper which, when folded, became a three-dimensional doll—ingenious, tasteful, simple. Even to Boof, Harry and John it was strongly nostalgic in a world of men and bitterness.

"There's a woman in the Tiger's life," Harry said, looking at the doll. "You don't really know about the other bloke, do you? ... We shoot each other ... get bashed ... hate each other ... bloody well hate—*we're good at that!* ... but this doll brings you back. ... I get the feeling that some Arch-bastard put us both here to kick each other's guts in ... when he says stop, we'll stop ... then the Tiger takes his doll home ... but when they say 'start' his kids and our kids will be at it again."

The Tiger had sat here, silently, looking at the doll and the picture. He had been reminded of an old poem:

> *If there be snow*
> *I call to mind how I crossed the mountain in Shiga*
> *And time after time I brushed aside*
> *The blizzards of cherry blossoms*
> *That settled on my sleeves.*

This very sentimentality, which most people have, is, in time of national ambition, the thing that is used to set them at each others' throats. Into the old traditional way of life the war lords had insidiously entwined their will and power so that the Tiger could not suspect nor separate the specious from the real.

The story of the Black Ships of 1853 had been made sinister. Belching smoke like dragons they had waited to thunder death into Yedo. But, more sinister still, they threatened the thousands of peaceful defenceless sailing-junks that came from the north and west in an antlike lifeline for a country so poor in roads. So the vainglorious assault was only the trick of a cowardly assassin. Thus, to the Tiger, Pearl Harbour became a divine retribution for the intruder. What one side called *treachery*, the other called *strategy*. Curiously, and significantly, between 1853 and 1941, the definitions changed sides *exactly*. And during the transition there was a time of unanimous agreement.

On 8th February 1904, without declaration, the Japanese fleet attacked the illuminated Russian fleet at anchor. They torpedoed two battleships and a cruiser. The next day they again attacked. It was not until the 10th that they declared war. The conservative London *Times* then reported: *The Japanese navy has opened the war by an act of daring which is destined to take a place of honour in naval annals.*

In Japan, the pressures of propaganda reached their height in the thirties. This was *Kurai-tanima*, the Dark Valley, when ancient dreams of conquest were rabidly developed. The fear of Western ideas killing the dream which had been re-affirmed as eternal truth by the Shogun-inspired Imperial Rescripts through the ages, had brought out the old Samurai to take vengance for the Meiji restoration which had overthrown them. Emperor Meiji had proclaimed on oath: *The old and unworthy ways and customs shall be destroyed and the people shall walk along the highway of heaven and earth . . . knowledge shall be sought among the nations of the world and the Empire shall be led to prosperity.*

But now Motoori and Hirata re-interpreted the ancient sacred books *Kojiki* and the slightly later *Nihongi*. The *Hakko Ichiu* principle was adapted from the *Nihongi*. Perhaps no other people have been so well conditioned to accept so completely their country's propaganda. And here, briefly, are some of the things to which the Tiger bowed.

Koda Ha, the Imperial Way—Emperor before all—was made to oppose democratic ideas and influences. It was made to mean all the Generals wanted it to mean. General Araki is an example. He was chief of the *Kempei Tai*, the secret police of the Army. In 1931, as Minister for War, Araki became the idol of the politically inclined young officers with the philosophy of national mystique which asked the nation to revere Japan as a sacred land superior to all others, and therefore destined to rule the world. The Army assumed the right of direct political action. A fanaticism of selfless lives was taught. Araki wrote: *On each bullet and on the edge of every sword the word mercy is written. Yamato spirit is in the Emperor all power, all goodness, all wisdom flows from him to*

the subjects . . . everything depends on our power. With one resolve and with one stroke our object can be accomplished. Whatever that is which obstructs the great plan should be wiped out without the least leniency.
Matsuoka wrote: *I firmly believe in the great mission that heaven has given Japan to save humanity in conformity with the great spirit in which Emperor Jimmu founded the Empire. Japan should take over management of the continent on a large scale, and propagate Hakko Ichiu and Kodo in Asia, and then extend it to all the world. The Empire faces an unprecedented crisis but, I believe, it also faces an opportunity for the Yamato race to make the greatest progress in history. Should we lose this opportunity, we will have to sequester ourselves from the world for at least 200 or 300 years.* And, later: *The Yamato race now stands at the cross roads of its rise or fall. The Manchurian Incident should be termed the start of* construction *not* destruction *of world peace. The Co-prosperity Sphere in the Far East is based on the spirit of Hakko Ichiu or The Eight Corners of the Universe under One Roof.*
Konoye said: *Shining as the sun and stars is the goal of the Japanese Empire. The spirit of universal brotherhood denoted in the* Hakko Ichui *is embodied in concrete form in the Greater East Asia Co-prosperity Sphere. It is the greatest honour and life mission of every Japanese to do his part in its construction. But our movement must not stop at the realization of the Co-prosperity Sphere in East Asia alone. We must prosecute the movement for all time, and so realize peace and security for the whole world, now torn by violence and swept by conflagration.* [pre-world-war II.]
The paper *Chugai Shogyo* contributed: *. . . for the accomplishment of which all conceivable hardship must be borne so that we shall be able to display to the world the glories of our national polity.*
Myamoto said: *. . . The people should be satisfied with the lowest standard of living. The craving for the life of luxury must be abandoned. At this time when the nation is risking its fate, there is no individual any more. What remains is the nation and the nation alone . . . Come rain! Blow wind! We are finally determined to fight the storm.*
The Japanese soldier, dying especially fulfilling the will of the gods, is promoted to the ranks of the higher gods or *kami* and is revered by the nation. As they consider themselves descended from earth gods, there is really no difference between this and the Westerner's expectation of heaven. Behind all these propaganda concepts there lay the whole cosmogony of their religious convictions. The Tiger believed that if this Barbarian challenge

were not met and beaten, there would come a chaos which was the anger of the gods. The Carp upon which Nippon rested would move in anger and shake the unworthy islands to pieces. *O-kaze* the Great Wind would sweep them clean in purification and leave them as a desert.

In feudal times the samurai was at the head of the four classes over the agriculturists, artisans and merchants, in that order. He had the right to cut down any 'rude' fellow. This was a man who, in his opinion, was an other-than-expected-fellow. The law forbade any interference with him in doing it. It was now the Barbarians who were the other-than-expected-fellows, threatening *Hakko Ichiu*.

The prisoners believed the Japanese to be merely mad superstitious fanatics practising cruelty only for pleasure. All the rest was only an excuse—no Christian country would act like this. Probably none of them knew that Kaiser Wilhelm, emperor of a Christian country ruling by the grace of the Western God, had addressed his soldiers thus: *Recruits! Before the altar and the servant of God, you have given me the oath of allegiance. You are too young to know the full meaning of what you have said, but your first care must be to obey implicitly all orders and directions. You have sworn fidelity to me, you are the children of my guard, you are my soldiers, you have surrendered yourselves to me body and soul. Only one enemy can exist for you—MY enemy. With the present socialist machinations, it may happen that I order you to shoot your own relatives, your brothers, or even your parents which God forbid—and you are bound in duty to implicitly obey my orders.*

The Tiger was a committed soldier. He had been photographed in ceremony before he left for the war. Believing as he did in his cause, self-dramatization was natural. He had been made conscious of the ideal of *bushido*, the warrior's way. This is a mantle many men will assume when great purpose and conviction overwhelm them. To the Japanese the plum stands for *courage* and *tenacity*. To the Tiger, the sword and the blossom there were not so disparate. Cheek-turning Christians sing *Onward Christian Soldiers*.

Times of civilized action for survival, John thought, are always times of expediency, when all the imperfections of the time have to be made expedient to the action—and to the excuses for them. Ideal conduct is set aside and the struggle with conscience left until the danger has passed.

True, there appears to be a similar expediency in the natural world. But, to John, the vital difference seemed to be that the natural expediency did not build up in the endless repercussion of recriminations, revenge, and retaliation. This seemed to be the prerogative of self-justifying Intelligence.

John wondered, and he had no way of knowing, how much he and Boof and Harry, like the Tiger, had been exposed to national ideas which had unconsciously conditioned them without rousing criticism or suspicion. While we recoil from our enemy's ruthlessness, we practice our own. If the violent swings of the pendulum of political action and reaction, John thought, are ever to be stilled, then we must surely look to what has made our enemy different and to realize that we are not so much looking at his faults as into a mirror.

The day passed without incident.

13

Ten thousand ducklings had been brought into the camp by the Imperial Japanese Army. They were only a few days old. The Japanese announced that these birds would be raised to supply much life-saving food in eggs for the prisoners. It was done with typical bureaucratic impulsiveness that leaves vital detail to others.

Many ducklings, in a pitiful eagerness to stay alive, died. On the first night they were crowded into hastily built pens on the river bank. They were enclosed at the back by the steep bank, at the sides by low attap fences, and in the front by the river. The little ducks pushed about like a crowd at a football final. A few handfuls of grass had been thrown in to them, but they were so tightly packed that almost all of it was trampled. The heat had given them a frantic thirst and they were in continual struggle to get to the water. All night they fought punily for a drink, or just to save themselves from being trampled to death.

In the morning, the prisoners coming down to breakfast

looked down on the pens. For three or four feet out from the water's edge there was a flaccid sodden raft of the dead—like soft yellow crumpled leather, washing to and fro. On the bank, close to the water, were more—unmoving except for a few twitches of the nearly dead. The eyes were little black slits. Here and there an unclosed eye shone with a small bright spot, giving a tiny view of eternity. The beaks of the sideways-lolling little heads were closed in wide empty grins, sometimes seen in the last looks of the defenceless. The survivors waddled weakly as if speechless with grief. Unsteady, some had to sit. All were innocently preoccupied with survival.

"The bastards!" Boof said.

"How long do you think the poor little buggers will last?" Alec said.

"The quicker the better," Harry said, "poor bastards."

"This lets you know just where *we* stand with the slit-eyed mongrels," Buck said. "They'll blame the ducks for dying."

A Japanese soldier came down to the edge of the bank and looked at his dead and dying charges.

"*Kurrah! Ba-a-a-g-e-e-r-a!*" he squealed. He jumped down the bank to the shallow edge of the water. "*Ba-g-e-e-r-a-a!*" he screamed again as if he were weeping. Kicking, he lashed out with his booted feet hurling the soft bodies out over the surface of the river—they fell like limp, half-filled rubber gloves. "*Damme! Damme! No gooda! . . . Sabotag-oo . . . Damme!*" The dead on shore he kicked far out into the river. Some, not quite dead, struggled weakly for a moment and then drowned. Some, alive, in flat-footed panic could not get out of the way and were squashed under the soldier's heedless iron-shod heels.

As if he were guilty, Buck said, "I shouldn't have said that—I drew the crabs."

"You can always bet it will happen," Harry said, "whenever their Imperial Bloody Benevolence is marred."

Boof said nothing. They were all in the same boat . . . those sodden little corpses were so like some of the corpses of men he had seen die in the Wet of the jungle last year . . . the same emptiness when every bit of dignity is torn off men by the disfigurement of their disease . . . the caricature of death . . . the raw rough nakedness of their burial . . . their incomplete cremation on a sodden funeral pyre in a dripping green jungle.

"Humanity . . . ," he breathed, not quite knowing what he meant. "The bastards. . . ."

When they came back at midday the sun was like a blow torch in a cloudless sky. The ducklings that still lived had been brought from the river and put into squared-out shadeless pens of low attap fences on hard, bare, scorched earth that was too hot for men's bare feet. In the pens, bright little balls of yellow tottered about, their wide-grinning beaks opened and shut like comic clowns. They were gasping for their lives.

When Harry saw it he said, "Gawd strike me dead! How *evil* can these bastards get. . . ."

"Or stupid," Alec said. "They are so wrapped up in Dai Nippon that they think *anything* will work for them . . . the world is theirs . . . they can't see anything else."

"Some day they will," Buck said. "I can hardly wait. . . ."

"If one of them ever *kurrahs* me when we're out of this," Boof said. "Every time they say it, it's one notch further I'm tightened up."

There was not a drop of water for the ducks. Alec called to a soldier in mock jocularity, "*Oi, Nippon . . . duckoo . . . water nai . . . mizu nai . . . all duckoo mati mati . . . speederoo . . . shookoo . . . anata . . . pinto . . . pinto . . . shookoo speakoo, damme, damme . . . mizu speederoo.*"

The soldier sucked in his breath, "*Nani? Damme? O.K.-da.*"

"Wonder if he got the message?"

The prisoners who had finished their rice brought up water from the river in their dixies. They squatted about the pens holding them to encourage the birds to drink. Some, in their eagerness, stumbled over the edge of the dixies and fell into them. The men laughed, "Go on you little beauty, soak it up!" Then three or four of the soldiers came back. Yelling, they tried to push the men out of the pens. But the men made a stand and with pidgin and arm-waving tried to explain that the ducks needed shade and water or they would all die, and then the Tiger would beat them all up.

The prisoners offered to move the pens for them into the shelter of the trees. The soldiers let them.

The next day the orderly officer told them on parade that a Nippon order had been issued. The remaining ducklings were to be divided among the huts and each hut commander was responsible for them. They were to be reported at *tenko* each evening. Any deaths would be regarded as gross neglect and sabotage against Imperial Benevolence. Hut commanders would be punished.

The ducklings continued to die and the men were beaten for it. Twenty-five had been issued to each hut. In one case only nine lived. The hut commander was badly beaten as an example. They were treated as pets by the men, who fed them with what they could. The thousands of iridescent blowflies that swarmed around the mangoes also buzzed low over the heads of the little ducks. But, even as they stretched up on their short legs and stood vainly on tip-toe, they could not catch the flies. They turned their heads up and snapped their beaks like small clappers—all in vain. So the men sat about and caught flies for them.

At night snakes would take some. The Japanese would not believe this, and when a dead body could not be produced, they accused the prisoners of eating them. They said the snake stories were wrong-headedness marring Imperial Benevolence.

"This Imperial Benevolence," Buck said. "If there's *one* thing we've had *none* of from these bastards, it's bloody benevolence."

One night a snake squeezed through between the stakes of an enclosure and swallowed a couple of ducklings. Then it could not squeeze out again. The men caught it and produced it to the Japanese as proof.

"So," said the Japanese, "you have allowed the snake to steal from His Imperial Majesty thus marring. . . ."

"You can't win," Harry said. "They just make you spew. . . ."

14

The five of them sat in the shade on a low paddy wall watching a prisoner in the midday sun doggedly demolishing the two-foot walls of one of the dried-out paddy fields that had made regular rectangular patterns across the plain.

"This won't change him," Buck said.

"They had to do something . . . they couldn't let him get away with it."

"The man's an animal."

"But he'll live where others die," Buck said.

The man they were speaking of was solid, tough and dour, and he had long decided that he was going to live. Others could look out for themselves. Nobody cares about you but yourself. Use, but don't be used—the rest is bull.

He had been caught at another man's pack.

"You bloody thief!"

"You can't talk to me like that."

"Can't I? What are you after . . . my only bloody shirt?"

"Don't call me a thief. I'll drop you!"

"Don't deny it, you shifty bastard—you're red-handed!"

The fight had started. The thief knew his mark. His accuser was a much slighter man and had had a lot of malaria. Cold-bloodedly he drove several hard jabs into the man's spleen and watched him drop in agony. Some men had come in and saw it.

"You bloody louse . . . if he's gone . . ."

"He picked me."

"I bet he did . . . with your weight and size . . . you know he's been crook."

"He shouldn't have started it."

"You deliberately hit him in the guts. . . ."

"I'm not usually a copper," a sergeant said, "but you'll front the Colonel for this."

The fallen man was taken over to the hospital. He was still alive but very sick. There was no sympathy for this man. He had been given ten days' additional hard labour. He had to start before the men got up in the mornings, in the midday break, and after work until lights-out. He had showed no mercy, so he would get none. He took his punishment silently and without any show of emotion. No matter how hard he was driven he gave their sense of revenge little satisfaction. He was prepared to let everything, even mass contempt, go over his head.

"Barring accidents," Buck said, "he'll get back while many virtuous won't—you see it happen."

"What accidents? Like someone doing him over?"

"Could be . . . but I was thinking of Japan Parties . . . see if he doesn't get out of it. . . ."

"Has he got pull somewhere?"

"No, it's just how things go."

"Hullo, what's on now?"

A sergeant-major was calling out, "Japan Parties are posted at the ends of your huts—go and have a look. Japan Parties will parade at fourteen hundred hours to be addressed by Captain Suzuki."

The five of them found themselves in the same party. At two o'clock they were fallen in, waiting for Captain Suzuki. The Japanese soldiers, under the Tiger, bellowed their way among the prisoners shouting for better dressing and straighter lines. *Damme's* and *Kurrah's* and running slaps swayed the ranks. Then there was another yell to get them straight again.

"I wish the bastards would make up their little twisted minds," Harry growled.

The Tiger merely stood severe and silent waiting for reports. After the parade was reported, he grunted "*Yasume*". The prisoners stood at ease while time was allowed to elapse to impress them. Then Captain Suzuki and the interpreter came out of the guardroom. The Tiger roared, "*Kiotski!*" Captain Suzuki saluted a brief acknowledgement and climbed on to a specially built platform. He glanced at a paper in his hand and broke the expectant silence with a high, yet loud and rasping voice. He was neatly uniformed, wearing highly polished long leather boots, belt, and sword. A white open-necked shirt with sharp collar wings laid across the lapels of his tunic gave tone to his smooth brown skin. His cap was tight on his close-cropped black-haired skull. Its narrow peak threw black shadows over his broad cheekbones and full mouth. His glasses glinted as he vigorously shook his head and shoulders to punctuate his phrases.

The prisoners could understand only one word in a hundred and, to them, it sounded harsh and threatening.

"Wonder if they'll ever tell us what's it all about?" Alec grinned.

At last it was over.

"Well," said Buck, "now we know."

But the interpreter now took Captain Suzuki's place and began to read a carefully prepared translation. Captain Suzuki stood beaming.

"You are now being evacuated as prisoners of war from

Thailand to Nippon, where you will be engaged in various kinds of work. Looking back on the past year and ten months you have worked both earnestly and diligently and produced a great achievement in the construction of the Thailand-Burma Railway. The work was energetically proceeded with and successfully completed. For this we desire to express sincere appreciation.

"Your work in Thailand having finished, you are being transported to the Land of the Rising Sun, an island country choicely situated in rich and beautiful scenery. From time immemorial our Imperial Nippon has had the honour of respecting justice and morality. The people of Nippon have the nobility and generosity of spirits. . . . They are men and women of determination, generous by nature, despising injustice in accordance with an old Nippon proverb: *The huntsman does not shoot down the wounded bird.* Such is our character.

"In the Spring the cherry blossoms are in full bloom; in the Summer fresh breezes rustle over the shadow of green trees; in Autumn the glorious full moon throws its entrancing light on sea and river, giving an iridescent appearance of gold and silver; Winter brings a change of appearance: the landscape is covered with a mantle of snow and the scene changes to one of dazzling whiteness. Such is the nature of Nippon.

"The benevolence of this nature gives us an insight into the Emperor's will and induces us to act firmly together in the discharge of our filial and loyal duties as long as we live, in accordance with the example set by nature.

"Go to glorious Nippon with an easy mind, execute your duty in an efficient manner, then our hundred million people will accept you as you are and you will enjoy our Imperial Benevolence. If you have enmity in your minds and oppose our forms of justice, thereby marring the Imperial Benevolence, it will reflect adversely on you for your remaining period as prisoners of war.

"Think over this and rely on our justice, bearing in mind the sudden change of climate and customs in which you will shortly find yourselves, I advise you to take care. I pray for your health, your good behaviour, and, finally wish you *bon voyage.*"

"*Bon voyage!*" Buck said. "What about telling the bloody submarines that! He means *BOMB voyage!*"

The next day they were called out on to the big cleared space of the parade-ground. They were lined up with three paces between each man and five between ranks. Then they were told to throw all their old kit into the centre. They were to be completely rekitted.

"This is a turn-up . . . it's about time the bludgers gave us something!"

"In two and a half years they have given us nothing— only taken it away . . . all except a few pairs of Nip rubber boots between the lot of us . . . no wonder we're almost naked."

"The only clothes we've got left are the ones we haven't worn . . . I've got a shirt and a pair of shorts . . . because I've only worn a G-string all the time. . . ."

"Same here . . . but don't be too sure . . . I put my shirt on the other night and it split across the back . . . rotten."

A few men were taken from each party to some bales the Japanese had cut open. From these they were given bundles of coloured shorts to give out—a pair to each man.

As the men put them on there were jeers, catcalls, squeals, laughter and groans. They were cotton shorts tied at the waist with a tape. They were of all colours: mauve, blue, red, pink, yellow and green; spotted, striped and flowered. They had been made from scrap material. In some, one leg was a different colour from the other. In others, besides this, the front of one leg might be different from the back—spotted in front and flowered at the back. The combinations were endless. From somewhere, from nowhere, came a rumour of where they had come from.

"A bloke told me that these strides came from the harlots of Singapore."

"Get away!"

"Dinkum. They felt sorry for us, they said, and they saved up and bought this material with their own money. Then they made them themselves."

"They did it in their spare time."

"Business must have been bad."

They had begun by abusing the Japanese for the shoddy issue. But now they wore what they were given without complaint, sentimentally moved by the thought that these other outcasts had given them a second thought. But they still gave each other wolf-whistles.

Next they were given a short-sleeved cotton singlet each.

"What about the rest of our gear?"

"Here it is."

More square bales of clothing were opened—green Dutch tunics and shorts.

"They must have picked this lot up in Java."

But it was too small for most of them. It had been made for the Indonesians of the Dutch Army, a small people. Boof, Buck, Harry and John could not pull the shorts above their knees. They staggered about, hobbled, and had to sit down to take them off.

Buck said, "I reckoned it was too good to be true—fancy me owning a pair of pants after all this time. . . . The rich get rich and the poor get poorer."

"Never mind, we'll get a bigger pair."

They cut open more bales but there were no bigger sizes.

"*Ashita, ashita,*" Takamura promised.

"Tomorrow? Honour bright?" Boof said.

"*Ashita* O.K."

But they never got them. Most of them went from Thailand via Singapore to Japan in these coloured underpants and white cotton singlets only.

Men got busy with their packs. With lighted bits of bark or leaves they singed along the stitching of flaps and straps trying to kill the bugs, nits, and lice that hid there. With sharpened bits of sticks they tried to squash them also.

"Give them a week or a fortnight and they'll be eating us again."

"Well it keeps them down a bit."

They had been allowed to keep whatever bedclothes they had. This was not much. Stained and threadbare blankets from which strips had been torn for bandages in bad times; bits of mouldy canvas or split-open rice bags. These they scalded to kill whatever was in them.

Men had been saying goodbyes to mates: officers to men, men to officers, promising to look each other up after it was all over. Certain things were left unsaid. All felt the uncertainty of the passage to Japan. It was as if the Japanese had given a 'thumbs-down' to those selected, some thought.

The men waited, a strange motley dressed in the confused bright selections put together by the compassionate needles and sympathetic hearts of harlots. Their dingy, worn packs were on their shoulders. The Japanese guards came out on to the camp roadway. They were called to attention. The sergeant, inside, was receiving his last instructions from Captain Suzuki. Both of them now came out.

"The bloody Tiger," Harry breathed.

"Of course," said Buck. "It had to be . . . no pants . . . now the Tiger . . . it's *normal* . . . just our usual rotten luck."

The party marched off. The Japanese had given permission for the camp band to play them out. A drum, a cornet, a violin, a trombone, a clarionet and a banjo—all still convalescent from the rigours of the jungle—began to play raggedly but picked up as they went along and the voices of the marchers came to the rescue with the words *They'll be droppin' thousand-pounders when they come* which the Japanese thought was *She'll be comin' round the mountain when she comes.* They marched out the camp gates on to the bitumen road that led to the station.

They passed through the township with its poor broken-down shops and dwellings, and skinny little dogs scavenging hungrily. They were practically hairless, their grey skins scaley with mange, their eyes big and distrustful. Once through the township they turned right, across a rough dirt track that led to the railway line. Among the scattered low bush were dead trees standing spectrally holding out the stumps of decayed and broken limbs. "Like lepers begging," Harry said. On these branch-stumps roosted large black vultures with folded necks looking goitrous and plucked. They stared at the prisoners with baleful eyes and relentless beaks set in bald heads with drooping crimson wattles.

"They look like bloody hanging judges," Buck said.

"Look at them," Harry said. "If we get past *them*, we will be out! . . . with the bloody jungle behind us."

Then Alec said, "We're out!"

They climbed into the bare metal trucks, heated now to the temperature of ovens. They sat in them streaming with sweat for three hours before the train slowly pulled out to take them south to Singapore.

"Well, we got past the vultures. . . ."
"Not by much . . . when you think back."
"No."
"Now what?"
"Sharks," Buck said.

PART 2

THE VOYAGE

Roaring winter storm
Rushing to its utter end . . .
Ever-sounding sea.

(GONSUI)

THE VOYAGE

I

THE journey south was slow. In the iron trucks they broiled by day and shivered by night, crowded thirty to a truck. Half of them only could stretch out at a time. At the change-over, at night, there were always the few who did not want to give up the little comfort they had and give others their turn.

They had one guard to each truck. He sat in the doorway dangling his feet out. He was quiet and inoffensive. There was a sort of fellow-feeling between them and the guard: none of them wanted to be where they were, and they had been through the jungle together. The untidy little guard talked with them about home. *Wifoo? Babee? Hondo? Meshi?* What did they eat in Australie? How could he believe the prisoners when they spoke of the great quantities of food they ate and could get? Steak and eggs, butter, bread, *beeru takusan!* The Australians built up a food paradise to indulge themselves in. The Japanese soldier was disturbed at the fantasy. Its prodigality appalled him; its opulence attracted him. Conditioned to frugality he was uneasy.

"We could tip the little bugger out one night—say he went to sleep and fell out," Harry said. "They leave their rifles laying about . . . be a cinch . . . but you couldn't do it to this little bloke . . . he looks like little-boy-lost."

"See him perk up when we have a bit of a sing. Watch him. Does not understand a word hardly . . . yet he goes for it."

"I think this little codger would rather be where people are singing—no *bushido* bull for him . . . he's cut out to be a short-arsed troubador."

"Last night he says, More . . . *sukoshi . . . yasume nie. . . .*"

"And when we dug up a few more songs, did you see him brighten. *Airoshi . . . arigato . . .* all men sing . . . O.K. *Airoshi, sama* all men shake hands."

"And they dress the poor little bugger up in his sloppy uniform, tell him all sorts of crap, give him a bayonet, shout at him and make him yell *banzais* and buggery to make him hate and

743

kill . . . to make him want to get knocked-off for the Emperor
. . . he should be home with a little sheila, singing to the kids
. . . ," Boof said.

"I hate the bastards, all of them!" Buck said.

"Even this helpless little bloke?" Boof said.

"Not him especially . . . just all of them in one lump . . .
don't separate them out . . . they've got to do what they're told
and . . . remember . . . they will bloodywell do it . . . don't forget it . . . just think how many of our blokes are not coming out
of the jungle. . . ."

"You're right, of course, Buck," Boof said, "but just the same
. . . somehow . . . if you can't recognize a man . . . an individual
man . . . any more, then what have we got? We've got to have
the guts for that, or we are gone . . . like you say they are. . . ."

"Well . . . like that . . . I suppose . . ."

"So where the bloody hell *are* we?" Alec said.

"We're just the bunnies, mate," Harry said, "to do what *they*
say . . . the blokes up in the jungle are just the dead bunnies . . .
what good have all those dead blokes done? . . . tell me that . . .
what did they die for? . . . They didn't die fighting. They died
with their hands tied behind their backs . . . suffering . . . and
in the end *wanting* to be bloody well dead . . . that's how they
died. . . . Buck is right to hate 'em in one rotten lump . . . the
Arch Bastard seems to suit *them*."

"Some top-brass makes a bloody blue and we get written off
. . . but of course he's done the right thing. . . . Just the fortunes
of war you know, old boy! . . . But don't worry . . . we won't
go to waste . . . the battlers never go to waste . . . they can
always be used up by somebody. The Japs got us . . . so you
know, Harry, why those blokes died? . . . They died for the
glory of Nippon and all that Greater East Asia Co-prosperity
shit!" Buck said.

"That's what turns your guts."

After a while Alec said, "Now that we have crossed the border
here you suddenly realize that those dead blokes are up there
for ever."

They came slowly south, waiting for hours, giving way to
every other train on the line. Meals were infrequent—sometimes one, sometimes two a day and at any hour. The rice was
often sour when they got it.

They left Tamuan at 3.21 p.m. on the 21st of June. Nompladok, Peppery, Choomsong, Hadjai, Padbesar, Port Prai, Ipoh, Kuala Lumpur, and at last, Singapore, at forty-two minutes past midnight on the 26th. They were tumbled out of the train and marched up River Valley Road to the River Valley Camp. In the dark it was only bare bug-infested boards on which they slept until daylight. In the morning it looked like a deserted, dried-up cattle yard. The huts were of unsawn poles, rough sawn planks and tattered attap roofs. The bunks were double-tiered along each side of the buildings. Grey, dead wood; bare and treeless earth; grey barrenness—was the prisoners' impression. Even though a thousand men had moved in, the camp still looked abandoned.

Working parties were sent out. One day they came back with a tall story. They had been loading a ship with bales of rubber. Her forward holds had been burnt out. The decks were littered with wreckage. She couldn't last a day at sea, they said; and they didn't know why the Japs were loading her. For the sake of a good joke and to scare the timid, they said it was the ship they were going to be sent to Japan in.

The first Japan Parties had already left from Saigon. But the Allied submarine offensive forced the Japanese to send this and subsequent convoys from Singapore to sneak across to Borneo and along the coasts of the island chains.

One morning the Australian major in charge had them all paraded. He did not waste words. Almost all the quinine had been stolen. He came straight to the point.

"Some low-down motherless bastard has stolen nearly all the quinine. This is as good as a death sentence to a lot of us. You all know what happens without it . . . you've seen and heard cerebral malaria when it gets hold of someone. We all have malaria—even *with* quinine . . . you know what can happen without it. I'm asking any man who might have any idea who this animal is to come forward. None of us likes to be a copper . . . but this is to save the lives of your cobbers . . . your own, too, maybe. . . . It's just been missed, so maybe he hasn't had time to wog it yet . . . don't be afraid of your mates calling you a policeman . . . if anyone does, get a good look at him."

No one came forward. After waiting for the men to talk it over, the major said, "Well, if any man gets on to anything come

straight to me, personally . . . any hour, day or night. If, after
we get to sea and I find the man who did this, I promise you he
will never reach Japan—no matter how well he can swim . . .
I will personally see to it. All right, Sar'major, dismiss the
parade."

"Some of our bastards would sell their own mothers."

"I reckon I could name a dozen who would come at this."

"That doesn't get the quinine back."

"It's gone, you can bet on that . . . through the wire as soon
as it was knocked off . . . it'd be all worked out."

That day they got orders to stand by to be ready to move the
following morning. Originally only 'fit' men free of malaria and
skin and alimentary infections were to make up the Japan
Parties, but at least ninety per cent of the prisoners had
malaria which was with them like a chronic cold. At nine a.m.
on 1st July they marched down River Valley Road through
Singapore to the docks. The city looked drab and depressing.

"Greater East Asia Co-prosperity Sphere," they jibed.

The Japanese soldiers, mooching about aimlessly on leave,
looked lost. People gazed with idle curiosity at the prisoners
marching past in brightly coloured underpants.

"Wonder if any of the harlots will see us?"

"Won't give them much encouragement to see them on this
scroggy, moth-eaten mob."

They marched on to the open wharf and were fallen out.
Guards were placed at each end. The day was overcast. The
prisoners sat looking at the sea and the ship with mixed feelings.

2

There lay the ship that was to take them to Japan.

"It's the bloody ship we were kidding about!"

She was a three-island ship of about four thousand tons. There
were two hatches forward with Number Three between the
bridge and the funnel. But there was no bridge! It was gone—
the centre-castle ran straight aft to the funnel without anything
there at all.

"No bridge," John said.

"Tell me more," Harry said, "you fascinate me."

"Oh, there's the bridge, right aft on the poop. That wooden hut with the square windows."

"Someone said she'd been bombed-out."

"Burnt too, that accounts for her bridge. It was just wood with an iron framework—they've cut what was left of that off with a torch. The bridge and monkey's island is completely gone."

"What was she? A zoo? What's this monkey's island?"

"A little platform right on top of the bridge for the standard compass."

"What do the monkeys do now?"

"They steer from down aft," Buck said.

"Cop that!" Boof said suddenly. "She's an armed merchant cruiser."

"No!"

"Well get on that gun right at the back!"

"Blow me down! *The scourge of the China Seas!*"

There, with the wheels lashed down to the deck, was an old field-piece with its belled, brass muzzle pointing over the stern in antique defiance.

"It must have been disposals from the Boxer Rebellion."

It was a muzzle-loader that could only fire cannon balls of which there was a neat pile on the deck alongside.

"They must think there's a hell of a lot of *bushido* in that thing."

The ship had once been painted grey. Now it was weathered and chalky, with broad rust-streaks and flaking scabs. Patches of her original colour showed here and there: a bit of black and some pink boot-topping.

"Some jokers on the working party said the Japs told them it was caught when they took Singapore."

John wandered along the wharf toward the stern. He was looking for some scraps of paper. All his sketching gear was secure in his pack. At last he found a few old weathered tally sheets on which a Chinese tally clerk had tallied out ten railway trucks during one midnight shift. He had a stub of pencil that was easy to conceal. It was almost two years since he had seen a ship or the sea. For fourteen years before he had been captured he had lived in ships continuously. Now he automatically noted details. All those little things it had been his business to

THE SWORD AND THE BLOSSOM

maintain and work. The ship was riding high in the water.
The top of one of the propeller blades showed in the rudder
recess like a shark's fin. Every joint and corner bled from
neglect.

When John returned, Buck said to him, "No one will believe
you."

Other parties were coming on to the wharf and there were
shouts of recognition.

"Fall in! Get sorted out! Don't get these bastards started—
it'll be bad enough anyway."

"I thought we'd lost him," Harry said.

The Tiger had come in amongst a knot of guards and let out
a roar. They scattered along the wharf, shouting abuse at the
prisoners.

"Look at the mob! Do they think they'll get all them into the
ship. With the forward part burnt out, how much room do they
think is left?"

There were twelve hundred and fifty prisoners to go on board.
They were herded up the gangway with shouts and pushes. On
the way they had to go through a long low cargo shed and each
man had to pick up two bales of sheet rubber. These each had
handles on them made of rolled sheet rubber cemented on each
side like a basket. Each weighed between seventy and eighty
pounds. The taller men could lift the bales clear of the ground
with straight arms, but the shorter men had to struggle along
with bent arms, straining. Some dragged them, knocking their
feet and knees together, making them stumble.

"The dirty yellow bastards! Only *they* could think this up!"

"They lay awake at night just thinking up new bastardry—
that's ALL they do!"

"*Kurrah!*" shouted the guards, "*Baggeeroo! Talkoo nie!*"

They rushed in pushing, punching and slapping the staggering men. Above it came the Tiger's roar. It was hard to tell
whether he was roaring at the guards or the prisoners.

"What do they expect, trying to make us load the ship with
all our gear on. How many trips do they expect us to make?"

"One'll be enough for yours truly—even if he threatens to cut
my bloody head off."

"One of the guards back there said, *Airoshi, O.K. swim-oo.*"

"Lifebelts!"

"Pig's arse! You'd go down like a stone if you hung on to these!"

"No. They float—but only just."

"That bastard couldn't lie straight in bed!"

They did not have to make a second trip. It was all some of them could do to reach the head of the gangway. They had to be helped. On deck, they were pushed forward. Some fell and there was further abuse. As John was over the water on the gangway, a cool whiff of air from between the wharf and the ship struck his nostrils. It was the tang of salt and iron and a little oil. A flood of unbidden memories came with it—of blood, oil and salt water mixed into this same tang.

The men were divided into *kumis* each of one hundred and fifty men. John's *kumi* was sent forward to the burnt-out end of the ship. Precariously they made their way across the boat deck. The deck itself was gone. A few planks only were laid across the remaining frames. Below them heaps of coal overflowed from the bunker to the now open bridge space. They had to go down a steep iron ladder to the foredeck. There were no handrails, and even John, who knew how to turn his feet sideways on a ladder, found it hard to keep his balance. A couple of men fell. They went forward to Number One hatch, just behind the break of the forecastle. Here a wooden ladder led down to the 'tween deck. Below, four guards were yelling and pushing the new-comers back into the far corners to make room for more. John and the others were pushed right back to the bulkhead that separated Number One from Number Two hold. He stood with his back to the bulkhead and alongside the foot of the foremast that came through to the deck there. Like everybody else, his pack and the two bales of rubber were stacked close at his feet. Finally there was a packed mass of standing men.

"They've got us here to muster us," Harry said. "They'll tell us off from here."

The guards seemed to be squealing louder than ever. Gradually there was silence. There were some words between the major, the guards and the interpreter. Then the major, dead-pan, repeated what he had been told. "You are to settle down and make yourselves comfortable. These are our quarters."

"What!"

"That's what the man said. There's not much we can do about it."

"What about the bloody rubber?"

"They say that's to sleep on."

"Strike me dead! Have you FELT 'em—they're like cobbles!"

To get any space at all the men had to floor-off the deck with the bales and finished with a crude cobbled surface on which to live.

"This is bloody lovely!"

"Settle down fellers, the guards are getting toey."

"—— the guards!"

"I'd sooner you than me, cobber."

Finally they had to sit with their knees drawn up. Boof, John, Harry, Buck and Alec had put their two bales on top of each other against the bulkhead and this gave them a sort of seat with the bulkhead for a backrest. Those who could not get a bulkhead position had men in front of them and behind. All had hard feet and knees in their backs, and elbows in their ribs.

"It won't last long like this, that's for sure! By the time a few get malaria and a few get dysentery it'll be a nice bloody mess."

The crowded men were sitting around an open hold twenty feet deep below them with nothing but a four-inch coaming to stop them falling over the edge. There was no guard-rail or rope. John would not dare think of what would happen when they got to sea with the ship rolling. There was only one section of hatch-planks over this lower hold, and that was forward where the ladder came down. So they were, in fact, robbed of living space by this open hold.

This hatch was the smallest in the ship because here the ship narrowed to the sharpness of the bow. The other hatches were more in the 'block' of the ship. There were no hatch-covers on One, Two or Three, which were wide open to the lower holds. Three was the bunker hatch full of coal.

As well as the loss of accommodation from the open hatchway in the 'tween deck in One, the section of hatches that was on there cut off the access ladder to the lower hold and thus stopped any overflow from getting down there to ease the crowding. In this lower hold below was a layer of ingots of tin, overstowed with a tier of casks of latex rubber stowed on end.

It was hard for them to believe that their present condition was real, or that it could last more than a couple of hours. Just forward of the square of the hatch a small space had been allotted to the officers. The rest, including the wooden section of hatch-covers under the ladder, was packed right to the edge.

"How many do you reckon we've got in here?" John said.

"When they mustered, two *kumi* commanders reported to the Major."

"That's three hundred men! That can't be right . . . there's GOT to be a blue . . . ," Harry said.

But the men were there. On board there were one thousand Australians and two hundred and fifty Dutchmen. Six hundred of these were in the forward open hatches.

"There's a couple of things I don't like," John said.

"Only a couple of things! Even for a P.O.W. you must be easy to please."

"That open hold . . . someone will break his neck . . . look at all those blokes crowded along there . . . one decent roll . . . they are not a wake-up yet."

"What can you do?"

"If only we could get hold of some rope. . . ."

"If we don't look after ourselves the bloody Japs won't. Have you thought what would happen if we had to get out of this hatch in a hurry?"

"Three hundred blokes and just one ladder . . . an open ship like this . . . she'd go like a jam tin."

"No lifebelts."

"We've got the rubber. . . ."

"You take the rubber—and you know what to do with it."

"What about boats?"

"I only saw one on the port side as we came down—take about twenty . . . there could only be a couple on the starboard side . . . I didn't see any other davits anyway."

"Those blokes thought they were kidding back in camp yesterday. I hope they are taking a good look round now."

The ship moved out from North Pier to the Outer Roads beyond the mole, and anchored. All day they were kept below. Only men going to the latrines were allowed up. There was one latrine to each three hundred men. Four latrines in all.

About sunset the mess orderlies made their way to the galley and came back with buckets of rice. Serving out the meal in the packed deck was all confusion and complaint. Men were afraid of being missed. They were constantly being kicked and trodden on in the scramble. It was almost impossible to put a foot between the men. They sweated against each other. When darkness came, the goings and comings were blind. There were no lights at all. Even to raise an arm to scratch brought abuse. Men kept pushing away elbows and knees which were sticking into them. About two a.m. it rained. Nobody could move. Those in the square were wet through with all they owned. Rain beat in underneath on others. John, right back at the bulkhead, felt water running down him. It was coming through around where the mast came through the deck. For hours, large drips like the Chinese torture fell on his chest. He could not budge an inch out of the way.

At last dawn broke on a mass of dirty, bad-tempered irritable men locked in an exhausted lethargy with muscles and joints cramped with a stiffness that stabbed with pain. The universal, "What a bastard!" was their good-morning.

"How long did you say it would take us to Japan?" someone asked.

3

As the ship had pulled away from the wharf they had passed a large cargo-passenger ship with a gaping twenty-foot hole in her bow, allowing the slow wash of their passing ship to run in. Like a bite out of a bun, the stem was bitten through well back into the hull.

"Torpedo," John said.

"An encouraging start to our luxury cruise," Harry said.

"What do you expect, at the price?" Boof said.

Two days later they sailed with a convoy of thirteen other ships and three small escorts. They carried a large painted 6 on each side of the funnel.

"I thought it would have been *thirteen* for us," Buck said.

"Well, Buck, now you know we are only half that lucky," Alec said.

There were three small oil tankers, two cargo-passenger ships and a collection of old tramp types with them, but the ship the prisoners were in was in the worst condition by far.

"I wonder what her name is?"

"She'll be *Something Maru* now, you can bet."

"There's only one name they *could* give her. . . ."

"What?"

"The *BYŌKE Maru!*"

A derisive laugh went up. "That's it! That's bloodywell IT!" they said. *Byōke* is the Japanese word for 'sick'.

"Spirit of Sickness, *she's one of us!*"

The guards spent the day in watches on the empty fo'c'sle gun-platform. From there they could look down into the forward hatches and aft, clear to the boat deck, for there was no bridge now to block their view. Meals were now served out on deck and the men stayed there as long as the guards would let them. Sometimes they would let the men stay, but, on their own unpredictable impulse, they would rush from the fo'c'sle shouting *Damme, damme!*, with kicks and flailing bayonets, sometimes jabbing viciously at men's legs and buttocks as they tried to scramble down the ladder, or over the coaming and down the lifelines.

The ship was like a wreck; ragged, rusted gear, broken castings, bits of plating and junk, winch cylinders almost rusted through, great cankers of rust as if the ship had leprosy, the lagging of the steamlines rotted and gapped like ulcered limbs. Because of the crowding, some of the men had found billets among the heaps of coal in the now-roofless bridge space. They were quite exposed to the rain and had tried to rig shelters with gas-capes or ground-sheets. They used the deep-troughed coal barrows filled with rain. Men sat naked in them bathing.

Under the fo'c'sle was an open space. A bench ran along each side of it. On the starboard side was stowed the ship's paint in drums and pots. On the port side was a vice and coils of rope and wire and a few broken blocks and an odd tackle or so. A small 'head' or lavatory was also piled with junk (which is old rope only fit for oakum, strands or yarns). Forward of this, running right up into the eyes of the ship, where the hawse pipes leading the anchor cables out came through its ceiling and went out its sides, was the lamp room smelling strongly of kerosene above the paint and Stockholm tar of the rest. After some haggling and in spite of some roaring ferocity, the P.O.W. doctor was allowed to use the deck of this open space as his hospital. Here

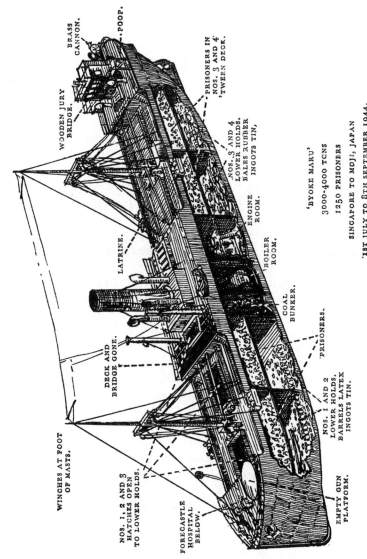

WINCHES AT FOOT OF MASTS.

NOS. 1, 2 AND 3 HATCHES OPEN TO LOWER HOLDS.

FORECASTLE HOSPITAL BELOW.

EMPTY GUN PLATFORM.

DECK AND BRIDGE GONE.

LATRINE.

'PRISONERS.'

NOS. 1 AND 2 LOWER HOLDS. BARRELS LATEX INGOTS TIN.

COAL BUNKER.

BOILER ROOM.

ENGINE ROOM.

NOS. 3 AND 4 LOWER HOLDS. BALES RUBBER INGOTS TIN.

'PRISONERS IN NOS. 3 AND 4 'TWEEN DECK.

WOODEN JURY BRIDGE.

BRASS CANNON.

'POOP.'

'BYOKE MARU'
3000-4000 TONS
1250 PRISONERS

SINGAPORE TO MOJI, JAPAN

'1ST JULY TO 8TH SEPTEMBER 1944.

at least the patients could breathe fresh air though it was often mixed with salt water and rain. Already there were six patients. These did not include the malarias who simply got their quinine, which was now very short, and put up with it. As Buck said, "Malaria's now general issue and you had to muster it every now and again or get crimed for losing it." He said that this was a good idea really, because when your cobber got the wog you got the rice—that way it seemed to go further. He said that without malaria they'd starve.

John and three of his navy shipmates raided the bosun's store. They rigged guard-rails and lifelines around the dangerous hatch square. There was little to secure to and it was pretty meagre, but it now gave them some sort of a chance. They also rigged a series of lifelines to the upper deck to try to offset the hopeless inadequacy of the single wooden ladder. The soldiers were wary of using the lines with the twenty- or thirty-foot drop below them. The sailors tried to show them that climbing a rope was not so hard, that you could soon learn to hold on with your feet as well as your hands. A lot soon got the knack. This helped to break down the dreaded possibility of panic. They also found a couple of straight iron ladders in the wreckage and lashed them into positions for the non-rope-climbers.

"At least an improvement on one ladder for three hundred men."

Then they asked the Australian officers to try to get the Japanese to exercise some abandon-ship drills. It was unlikely that the Japanese in the real event would worry at all about the prisoners. Previous experience had taught them to expect little, but if the men were practised they would be more able to look after themselves. Whether the Japanese intended to leave the prisoners to their fate or not, they did not miss this opportunity to show that there was Imperial Benevolence. They *ordered* it as if it were their own idea, and they got in the way.

After a number of exercises, ignoring the Japanese as much as they could, and by paying attention to what the sailors were trying to tell them, they got a fairly good grasp of what they were up against. It was dinned into them that panic would send them all to the bottom with the ship. Fatty, a naval petty officer, said, "For Christ's sake move quickly—but *don't rush*, don't panic . . . take your turn behind . . . and take your finger out

when you're on a rope—think of your next astern . . . I know
you're only soldiers," he said, keeping up a jocular rivalry, "but
you're too hairy-arsed to act like sheilas . . . don't be like a pack
of girl-guides."

There were no lifebelts, but the Japanese wanted them to
bring up the bales of rubber as life preservers. The guards were
rushing about under the eye of the Tiger. They were rattled.
Then they thought of the rubber.

"If brains was hundreds and thousands," Boof said, "they
wouldn't have two to rattle together."

"What would you do with them?" Harry said in disgust.
"The silly little bastards! Get out of it!"

The men climbing up the lifelines and pulling themselves
over the coaming, the most critical part of the climb, were
being pushed back by squealing guards as they tried to hang
on, breathless, over a thirty-foot drop.

"What the bloody hell?" they gasped.

"They expect us to bring up a bale of rubber too . . . a
bloody lifebelt, they reckon."

"Pig's arse! If I brought up a bloody bale, I'd ram it right up
the little bastard," Boof grunted as he heaved himself over the
coaming and almost fell on a protesting guard, who lashed out,
kicking and punching.

The Major went to the Tiger and talked to him. At last the
Tiger agreed that, in practice, no rubber would be brought up—
only if it was real. After a number of runs and the men really
put their minds to it, it was surprising how quickly they could
get out of the hatch.

The Tiger said at last, "*O.K.-da, O.K.-da. Airoshi*—all men
yasume."

All that the abandon-ship drills could achieve was to get the
men out of the hold before the ship went. With a ship as wide-
open as she was, without hatch-covers, she could go to the bottom in minutes after a torpedo hit. On deck they would have
the option of jumping into the sea or waiting for it to come up
and meet them. There were no boats for the prisoners. In fact
it was doubtful if there were enough for the Japanese themselves. John had had a look around at what boats there were.
On the port and starboard sides, rigged as accident boats—
that is, turned out on their davits and griped to a griping spar—

were two small wooden boats with curling paint and bare grey wood. Their seams were open. On the starboard side, just abreast the funnel, two other boats lay on the deck, unchocked. Their paint curled and flaked too. Even the planks were slightly curled so that John could get the tips of his fingers into the seams. He could see daylight through about twenty per cent of them. No amount of soaking would tighten *these* up. Their buoyancy tanks were battered and loose. If this firewood ever got into the water, John thought, the tanks would float away separately—until they sank, for they were split and pin-holed.

But all this absence of Japanese concern for their safety did not really surprise them. Two and a half years had conditioned them.

4

Gradually they got rid of the bales of rubber. They had gone to a lot of trouble to get rid of the bugs infesting their packs before they had left Tamuan, and again at River Valley. With sharp sticks they had tried to reach the nits, but with only limited success. Now, in the fetid atmosphere of the holds the bugs were breeding at an explosive rate. The rolled rubber sheets of the bales provided a perfect protection and home for them. They would bite viciously in the dark and be gone before they could be struck. The many hundreds killed sent a bitter pungent smell through the hold. But they bred in plague proportions. It must have appeared to the bugs that they had an eternal blood supply and almost invulnerable shelter.

"I hope they get my malaria," Buck said.

At night the men stealthily passed the bales to mates waiting on deck, who sneaked to the ship's side and dropped them into the splash of the bow wave so they were not heard. They left a trail of bales, like some marine paper chase, from Singapore to the Sulu Sea. This only reduced the bugs, it did not get rid of them.

Then the Japanese decided to rid the ship of flies.

"So the Tiger thinks these stinking holds will be sweeter if we kill the flies," Harry said. "Doesn't he know that the flies are the cleanest bloody things down here!"

Each man had to catch ten flies a day. Each night the dead flies were counted out before the Tiger and a Japanese officer. Slapping and unpleasantness arose from a short tally. The day's kill was carefully done away with so that it could not be used again. After a while there were more slappings than flies, and, at last even the Tiger had to admit that they had become too scarce to hunt. But this was many days after the prisoners already knew it for a fact.

They took turns at shovelling in the coal bunkers. Most of them did not mind the two-hour tricks. It was a break from the smell and the monotony of the crowded holds.

On the 6th of July the Borneo coast rose out of the sea to the eastward and they altered course and steamed northerly with the island on their starboard hand. The weather was overcast and sultry. The sea was calm with a low swell over which the ship moved slowly as if on the back of some slowbreathing monster—rolling and pitching slightly in easy combination. Rain squalls swept over them as casually as country people cross their main streets. The days and nights were in low key, the seasons merged, drenching and steaming them by turns. At times an old Army 97 made a laboured, slow and clattering anti-submarine patrol around them, moving as if the air were a kind of invisible liquid glue. It ducked low under heavy cloud like a fly under a ceiling. Offshore, the rain had turned the sea muddy. Trees with bare branches drifted about unfamiliar and lost, having been swept to sea by the swollen rivers.

The ships of the convoy steamed through the muddy waters. On the 8th they anchored in a bay. Some said it was Miri. In the grey morning light, oil rigs could be seen like dark pencil-marks against the watery hills. It was an open roadstead and the anchored ship rolled heavily, lying beam-on to the shore-going sea.

"Wonder why we anchored here?"

"Subs, I bet."

"Sorry I asked."

A rumour went around that they were due in Japan in 1st August.

"D'y' reckon we'll get there?"

"Why? Subs?"

"Them too . . . but the ship . . . do you think she'll go the distance?"

"One thing . . . I can't see any sub wasting a fish on her . . . not while there's anything else about."

"I hope you're right, mate."

Even though they could get a certain amount of time on deck by risking the unpredictable tempers of the guards, most

Trees with bare branches

of the time was spent below. The crowding was eased by this, but the monotony was not. Argument and senseless bickering often broke out. If one slept in the day, then the sleepless night became twice as long and discomfort in the dark seemed to magnify. Tattered books changed hands. Sometimes being read by a dozen at a time—each man passing on the detached page as he finished it. Thus twelve men would be in the grip of the same emotion at the same time. This was sustained by the forceful unprintable spontaneous remarks about the villain or something, like an audience at a melodrama. Some arguments could go on sporadically for days. Sometimes they would build up bitterness between the men as they went on. Then outsiders would come in with, "What about bloodywell shutting up!

Can't you forget it, you're like a pack of schoolgirls magging!
What about trying to act like grown men for a change! The
way you are going on would make a bullocky spew blood!"
This pressure of outside ridicule would generally silence them,
though, often, not without some cantankerous shots.

Sometimes it fell quiet, especially in the afternoons when the
sun had come through and the steaming humidity of rain-
soaking and sweating spread an apathetic stupor. There would
be only some murmured talk. Occasionally a broken-reeded
mouth organ would desultorily try an experiment, as if talking
to itself.

On the starboard side a man was going thump, thump,
thump! almost continually, with short pauses now and again.
The listless listeners' nerves began to stretch, for they had just
decided that it had stopped when thump, thump, thump! again.

"Do you *have* to do that? How much more have you got left?"

"If I'm careful, enough to last to Japan."

"Gawd strike me! Do you expect us to put up with that bloody
thumping till then!"

The thumper was a man who had found a little hoard of
black peppercorns under a hut at River Valley. Now, between
two lumps of iron each day, he would pound the day's supply to
sprinkle in his rice. A little thing like that could change the
never-changing taste of the rice and was prized. Thus part of
this complaint came from envy. If men ever got that little to
change the flavour of their rice, they did not only have it as
they ate it: they gloated over it and savoured it in anticipation.
They went through elaborate and unnecessary preparations like
mental patients preoccupied with an obsession. This man could
have ground his pepper in ten minutes—but he never took less
than an hour, during which he thought only of food: all sorts of
food. And the coarse black pepper was to be the fulfilment of it
all.

There would sometimes be another sound. Then men would
prick up their ears and some of the drowsy would become awake.
This was a metallic clink, clink, clink . . . then a blowing sound
. . . then perhaps a curse that was not too bitter . . . and the
clinking would start again. Sometimes this went on just as long
as the pepper pounder. But the men waited, wishing the clinker
luck. At last successful, the cry "Fire" would go up. "Bring 'em

out boys, there's fire." Cigarettes rolled in anticipation would be lit. At the first draw, men would suck in as if they were trying to fill their boots with smoke.

It was a jungle lighter, an idea picked up from the Thais Only a few were really expert, for it took endless patience. A piece of bamboo about six inches long was stuffed with kapok. This the men got out of the pods of the kapok trees at Tamuan. By holding a piece of quartz or other likely stone close against the top lip of the bamboo and striking across it with a piece of broken file it was possible to produce a spark. Then the operator had to be quick enough to blow that spark into the kapok, and blow until it glowed. Then a light could be taken and it was put out immediately to save it. It took many many sparks generally before one ignited the kapok. The coarse tobacco ('wog weed') was rolled in anything from toilet paper to pages from a Bible. Sometimes even cardboard was split patiently until it would roll. "You don't need tobacco with this bloody stuff . . . you could burn a house down with it," Buck said.

There was no provision for washing. They stayed filthy with sweat, dirt, dust and rust. Grimy, they became irritable and quick-tempered. At night John sat on his pack with his back against the bulkhead close by the foot of the foremast. The fire that had gutted the ship had destroyed the wooden wedges (the partners) around where the mast ran through the upper deck to the 'tween deck below. Through this space the rain ran and splashed right on to John's chest. He could not move to dodge it. He used a small piece of towel on his chest to damp down the splashing on his face which sometimes kept him awake. The towel acted like a wick and let the water run down his side. He also used the wet rag to give himself an all-over sponge. Those in the shelter would ask those who were being soaked by the rain to pass them in a wet rag which they had thrown to them dry.

"We'll finish up with all the diseases in the book," Harry said. "Scabies, crabs, lice—the lot!"

"And if one of this scaly mob bit you," Buck said, "it'd be rabies."

"What's the date, John? You've been keeping it going."

"The ninth."

"Nine days without a wash."

"Wouldn't you guess? Take a sniff, it's beginning to build-up real good . . . just as well there's no lid on this hatch . . . it wouldn't stay on long."

"Get on it when there's no wind . . . you could spread it on bread. It gags you . . . it's like sour honey."

One day the word went around, "You can get a bath in Number Two!"

"How?"

"The rain's half-filled the lower hold."

In the early dawn they went like Indians, dodging across the deck and down the vertical ladder to the hold. The after end of the hold, where the decks had dropped in the fire, had collected more than eighteen inches of water. It sloshed around with the roll of the ship on the bare floor between the engineroom bulkhead aft, and the ingots of tin at the after end of the square.

"Bondi beach," Harry said.

But in a couple of days this was so fouled that they had to give it up. At last the Japanese decided to make some provision. Every second day was bath day. They were allowed only ten minutes to get out of their hatch, each *kumi* of 150 men, and go right aft to the well-deck there. Here one of the crew haphazardly played a fire hose from a deckhouse on to the prisoners below him. With all the pushing and shoving some hardly got wet. Boof and the others quickly realized that there was only one place the water *had* to go—into the scuppers. They dived for these in between the milling legs and with their hands scooped water over themselves.

Permission was also obtained for men to exercise daily on deck in batches of fifty. John took them with a table of exercises the Navy had worked out "for general use afloat by officers and men of all ages. The exercises can be carried out with boots on and where there is very little space." But there were those who, in spite of the need of it, grumbled and said it was an invasion of their personal liberty.

"What bloody personal liberty do you think you have got left, you drongos," Boof said to some of them. "Hasn't it fallen on you yet? Solid ivory, you blokes."

Some said that the Navy had no right to boss them about.

"You've got to give up with some of these bastards, don't

you?" Harry said. "Talk about the Japs! It's *these* bludgers that will do us in!"

All men were under a strain of sickness, hunger, thirst and the ever-present uncertainty of what their captors might do next. It was not unusual for them to take it out on each other. Perhaps, because the real causes of their deeper suffering could not be reached, they lashed out at the things they could, to avoid the terrible and final feeling of absolute impotence.

They continued to steam north along the coast of Borneo. Through the rain they saw tall mountains with their hoary heads buried in grey swirling clouds casting indigo shadows on the thick jungles beneath them.

Awake before dawn, John felt the day coming and watched the hatch opening slowly lighten above him. His mind turned over their situation in contrast, and that afternoon he wrote:

> *The herring-bone feather of flying-fish-flight*
> *Dappling the gleaming smooth skin of the sea*
> *Which scarcely yet breathes; low leaden light:*
> *The day slow-coming, from darkness not free.*
>
> *Low-ceilinged the clouds—that vaporous race,*
> *Whose mother, the Sea, hath given them life:*
> *Come from her bosom to Air, there to trace*
> *The legend'ry monsters fain to run rife*
> *In the phantom brush-strokes of night's dark wind . . .*
> *Clouds, heavily hanging in dawn's left hand,*
> *Wait only earth's turning their colour to find*
> *And hail the new sun come up from the land.*
>
> *In the iron dark holds, cramped men turn and groan—*
> *To add one more day to a thousand from home.*

He called it *Clouds, and prisoners, at dawn.* and dated it Sulu Sea, 14.vii.44.

5

One bright moonlight night as they steamed along and the dense black smoke poured from the poor coal under the boilers, Buck spoke. Looking up from the lower deck, lying on their backs, they could see the square of sky frosted with moonlight in which only a couple of brighter stars could survive, and which lurched drunkenly as the ship rolled. The swirling black smoke came and went across this limited field of vision.

"Good night for subs, John?" Buck said.

"We'd be sticking up like churches against this bright sky."

Sticking up like churches

"And this would be the bloody cathedral with its come-and-get-me smoke," Harry said.

"Just think," Buck said, "this could be our last night."

"Don't stop, Buck," Harry said, "you're good for morale! It *could* be our last hour."

"Well, we know it's on all the time . . . and now at sea . . . it's not just the Japs . . . It's our own side as well."

"No bastard loves us," Boof said.

"Peace *or* war, " Buck said, "where do we stand?"

"Right-o Buck," Alec said, "so this is our last night—what about it?"

"Well, are we ready to go?"

"What are you? A bloody Bible-basher or something? No, NO. I'm *not* bloodywell ready . . . would you mind telling them —G.H.Q. BOTH SIDES," Harry said.

"What I meant was, *how* will we go?"

"I reckon that'll be interesting."

"There's always the chance that we'll be too busy to think about what sort of an act to put on."

"Well, supposin' you got a bit of time?"

"We know Dougie's religious . . . he's cut and dried . . . he'd have to pray or something. . . ."

"Where do you stand, Buck?"

"I haven't cared much . . . could be I'd squeal at the last minute. But if there's a Joker in the sky holdin' all the aces . . . and if I've got any guts left—I'll have to cop it sweet. If it's like Dougie says and they play favourites up there . . . then that's it, for me . . . I know where *I'd* stand in that sort of a line-up. . . . *That* mob ought to know that you can't made a silk purse out of a sow's ear."

"You'll cop it sweet?"

"I hope . . . if I've got the guts."

"I s'pose I'm not much different," Alec said. "You see hypocrites and the shifty blokes running things . . . it's easy to be put off when you can't be bothered anyway . . . we send the kids to Sunday School for the sake of morality—where else can they get it? So we give a few bob and let it go at that . . . but I wouldn't mind a slice of heaven if there's any going."

"It's like the weather," Harry said. "We talk a lot about it . . . but what difference does it make? It's there or it isn't . . . cleverer blokes than us can't settle it."

"Heaven's wishful thinking," Buck said.

"You might be right, Buck," Harry said, "but a nice sweet wish is not a real bad caper. Over the last couple of years I've lived on wishful thinking. From where we stand at the moment, getting back home's just about as far off as a fair dinkum chance of heaven. But, mate, for me, I'll just keep on wishing—and home's first preference."

"What about you, Boof?" Alec asked.

"Yes, Boof," Harry put in. "You go to church with Doris back home."

"Well, it's just there. That's all. Since I was a kid. Like school and Saturday footy . . . Sundays . . . get the cows milked, climb into our Sunday togs, harness the trap and go to church . . . met everybody there . . . I used to like the singing . . . it was a crowd that'd stick ... when anyone was sick, the rest looked out for them ... they stuck ... ploughing, harvesting, bush-fires, floods, raising money for this and that ... they stuck. ... It was like having a town full of uncles and aunts. ..."

"And if we were torpedoed tonight ... how do you feel?"

"Bloody unhappy."

"Why? Don't you think you'll go to heaven?"

"Bugger heaven! I'm thinking of Doris and the baby ... that's the only thing that gets me about this ... and we can't do a thing about it."

"John?"

"I'm with Boof ... it's our families."

The ship moved north uneventfully. They felt like men swimming in shark-infested waters—surely the attack must come.

A lot of them felt an urge pressing them for an expression of thoughts outside their normal thoughts, a strange stirring, touching them deeper than they knew. Inarticulate, they wanted to speak. This life had reduced the separation between the profane and the profound. So much does the ordinary Australian hide his deeper feelings normally, that he loses the means to express them. They looked around for a means that would not make fools of them. Almost without exception they fixed on 'poetry' as the one way to say peculiar things without being laughed at. It was as if behind the shield of rhyme they felt protected from ridicule. Memories. Gum trees, the bush, a township, a state, dogs, kangaroos and wallabies, droving, sweet-hearts, mothers, old fathers, things in which they had roots, that made them Australian, as they thought.

John, no less than the others, wrote his rhymes. It was as if, at sea, these thoughts became clearer to him. He remembered back to a deep impression made on him when he was first at sea. As a new ordinary seaman, he was lookout alone on the after end of the ship—only a phone connected him with the bridge. It was between midnight and dawn—the middle watch—a time at sea when often the human world shrinks to a pinpoint and the earth seems back in the Archean age, still enveloped in Beginning. John had felt this then—as if some vast voice were there. A voice so low in key as to be lost to the human ear which hears only the limited range of obvious squeaks. Yet there was a strange vibration in his being, as if a booming sound, too deep to register, dominated and enveloped the limit-less stretch of ocean around him. As if the deep-breathing sea, the stars reeling to the roll of the ship, the clouds sailing like massed fleets past the bright crescent moon, and even the darkness itself were all obeying, after having heard quite clearly.

Over the years he had tried to tune in to the voice. Vast, omnipotent, omnipresent, omniscient—but with a true god-like impartiality that was eternal justice.

So now, in this old ship, the embers of the old memories were stirred. He wrote some verses of the memories, with a refrain that alluded to the present. For old-time's sake he called it *The Sailor's Sea*.

The flying fish play in the sapphire spray
And flash from the sea—shoals thrice three times three—
Shedding wet round rings from shimmering wings
In the wave's smooth side, as onward they glide
With low skimming flight like swallows at night:
Till all vanish down 'neath the sea-wave's crown
And scarcely a blur tells e'en that they were.

   Oh, the shark steals sly with small evil eye,
   While old Mother Carey awaits the unwary
   And deep Davey Jones will share in our bones.
   But, till one of them gets us,
   Oh, we'll pray the Lord lets us
   Look still on his wonderful wonderous sea.

The porpoise leap high 'neath the pearl-grey sky,
Each making in jade a jewelled cascade
Of bright heaped water chuckling with laughter,
Upswept by the bow which leads us on now.
These sleek shining fish with swashbuckling swish
And short curving arcs have welcomed all barks
Since ancientest men first kissed the sea's hem.

   Oh, the shark steals sly, etc.

The albatross swoops athwart our high poops,
His grey speckled wings wind's harmony sings:
The flight of the bird is the rhythm heard
In the heart of man who yet loveth Pan.

In the bald bird's head is a bos'un dead:
Unrepenting he and drownéd for fee,
E'er prisoned to be 'twixt land and sea.
   Oh, the shark steals sly, etc.

Quick Thresher the shark has risen up stark
To beat down the hull of the old whale bull,
Whose mighty flat tail strikes back like a flail
Raising white squalls recording the falls,
While small fishes' eyes are wide with surprise,
Till Shark strikes him dumb and bites out his tongue—
The old bull is dead and Thresher has fled.
   Oh, the shark steals sly, etc.

Green witch-fire oft plays upon masts and stays,
Like flickering fauns, in tropical storms;
And the ghosts of the drowned among us abound. . . .
All's Life-shuttle Form making woof that's warm
For the mind of man, in brief mortal span,
An illusion sublime—awaiting the time
Of Gabriel's horn! The Absolute born!
   Oh, the shark steals sly, etc.

For man's time on earth is less than his birth:
That Past-Future sea—Immortality—
Will gain scarce a jot from Present's small lot.
Yet it's NOW *that man knows benevolence flows. . . .*
Embrace all beauty—*our sacredest duty.*
So leave all your fears to saints and to seers,
For sayers of sooth can have no more truth!

   Oh, the shark steals sly with small evil eye
   While old Mother Carey awaits the unwary,
   And deep Davey Jones will share in our bones.
   So, till the last trump shall reach us,
   Oh, we pray the Lord teach us
   Ineffable beauty that lives in the sea.

This he dated Sulu Sea, 16.vii.44.

They had passed through Balabac Strait into the Sulu Sea and ran eastwards of the long narrow island of Palawan. As they cleared the end of the island and got into the Mindoro Strait they struck a heavy sea. An unlashed gangway banged violently with every roll, threatening to smash its way through the ship's side. It was found hanging by one end in the morning. The loose litter on deck clanged about dangerously. The ship creaked as if she were about to break. Many became alarmed. But the old ship wallowed stubbornly on as if giving hint of a deeply hidden character that had been underestimated.

Approaching Manila Bay, men felt relief. When they were at anchor, they thought, they could breathe freely again, if only for a time.

There was a sudden hard metallic clang on the hull.

"What's that?"

"The ash hoist—you know how that bangs."

"That's no bloody ash hoist—besides it's not time to get up ashes."

Several vicious crashes were heard and felt on the hull.

"Once heard, never forgotten—it's depth charges," John said.

"Christ! Do you think they'll get us?"

"Not likely while he's being depth-charged."

"I hope they keep the bastard busy."

"He's ours!"

"I don't care whose he is—bugger being patriotic—this is too bloody personal—I'm barracking for the Japs this round."

John climbed to the coaming and looked around. Overhead he saw a twin-engined bomber swooping low, and two escort vessels moving in. Depth charges brutally ripped up the sea. He felt a whack across the back of his head and shoulders. There was a flash of light before his eyes. His hands and legs gripped the lifeline instinctively and saved him falling to the bottom of the hold. The guard had hit him with a bayonet. He slithered to the 'tween deck.

"What did you see?"

"Stars."

"What's going on?"

"They're hunting a sub."

The hunt continued while the convoy steamed into the bay past Corregidor. But the *Byōke Maru* stayed outside, to steam in a wide slow circle. Contact with the submarine had been lost. Two aircraft criss-crossed, searching. The escort vessels sniffed about like terriers. The tension on the prisoners grew with the absence of depth charges. How could they know that the submarine was not getting them lined up?

"We're bloody bait!"

"Makes you feel good, doesn't it?"

"I feel like murdering some bastard—that's how good I feel!"

"I told you nobody loves us."

It was sunset before they slowly steamed between Bataan and Corregidor. The western sky behind them was bathed in rose and pearl. As the anchor took the rattling cable out in a shower of red rust, the ship came up to it and stopped.

"I reckon I'll sleep better tonight, gentlemen," Harry said.

7

It was a grey dawn. They came on deck to get their breakfast. Anchored near them were two ships with gaping torpedo holes in their sides. Another, half sunk, was lying listed and burning on the beach. In a floating dock an old World War I cruiser with three straight cigarette funnels was dry-docked. The great wireless masts were standing intact, as they were before the Japanese came. Before breakfast, in the steely half-light they watched a strange force put to sea. Four destroyers, one cruiser, two battleships and one hybrid battleship-aircraft-carrier with a skeleton deck built over the after turrets and strewn with a motley of aircraft.

"That's the roughest squadron I ever saw—like a Spanish onion boat, a couple of Gypo dicos, a garbage scow and a Peruvian peanut barge," Fatty the naval petty officer said.

"Might be making a rendezvous ... but they look a bit battered," John said.

They watched them steam out in line-ahead past Corregidor.

"I hope the subs are waiting."

For three days rain squalls and gales lashed the harbour, and the shipping, moving in and out of the changing visibility of the driving weather, made fluent life-sized watercolour paintings which caught the inner spirit of ships and the sea with searching simplicity.

But below the prisoners had nothing to admire. The ship's rations were almost gone; the looseness of long starvation forced men to the latrines in the rain and wind. There was the nuisance of those who could not get there in time. The crowding could not be relieved by going on deck. The aching malarias could not stretch out. The depression of malaise was intensified as the enforced half-sitting half-lying made a rack to wring the last bit of suffering out of them.

Coal lighters were brought alongside, but in this weather they could not be kept there. Lines broke one after another. The Filipino coalies were marooned on board when the breakaway lighters were taken back. Because of the sick, not all the rice was eaten. Boof was returning a couple of the buckets to the galley with a little left in the bottom. On the boat deck, he spoke to one of the Filipinos.

"What's it like in Manila, since these blokes took over?"

With simple directness and a strong American accent the Filipino said, "Boy, there's no —— apple pie here now!"

They were half-starved ashore and they had no food on board.

"Here," Boof said, "cop this!" and he tipped the remnants of the rice into the man's straw hat.

One of the cooks told a guard. Three of the guards rushed up and *kurrah-ed* Boof to attention. They stood him up by the break, in full view of the foredeck. They beat him in turns, shouting childish reprimands. They found it hard to reach his face, so they made him kneel. He was kicked in a way that jolted him. He gave an occasional involuntary grunt. They made red and blue welts on his chest, back and neck with their bayonet scabbards. *Kurrah!* they yelled at him. He had insulted Nippon. Nippon was good. Nippon provided well for its subjects. You, a filthy prisoner, have dared to give your filthy rice—you have unspeakably marred the Imperial Benevolence! *Bageera!*

They hurt him, but his silent revenge was in not letting them know. He stood in the wind and rain all that day and night until midday the following day. After the first beating he was subjected to spasmodic spite from the changing guards.

"Those bloody *kurrahs*...one day...," Harry had said when Boof came down. But Boof had said, "Forget it. Cop it sweet and don't let it burn you up. . . . I should have played it a bit more cunning. . . . I thought I could trust that little cook bastard."

"That's no excuse. . . ."

"They don't need an excuse."

Boof needed to stretch out to ease his bruises. John looked down at the lower hold—empty. But the ladder down was

Lighters could not be kept alongside

blocked off by the forward section of 'tween-deck covers crowded with men. He went to the bosun's store and came back with some rope. Making one end fast to the corner stanchion in the deck, he dropped the end into the hold. Then he went down the rope to the bottom. Here he made the bottom end fast so that now a climber could use his feet against the stanchion and, hand-over-hand, walk up or down if he had a reasonable amount of strength. It was not hard for them to get down. They gathered some loose hatch-planks and set them on the port side aft under the coamings so that they were not too easily seen by the guards from the deck. Here there was room for them all to stretch out now. Others followed them but accommodation was limited by the number of hatch-planks, for only with these was it possible to cover the sharp edges of the heads of the latex barrels.

They had saved Boof's rice for him. It was not yet sour. He ate some of it. Although it was all they should get until tomorrow, they gave him their waterbottles and he drank deeply.

"That's better," he said. And, with a few audible groans, settled down on his back. Once he muttered, as if to himself, "The little bastards," and went to sleep.

"How is the old fella!" Harry said.

"Well," Buck said after a while, "Now we can have our malaria in comfort."

The gales continued. Lighters could not be kept alongside. At last the ship had to be taken inside the breakwater where the sea was flat. They had already been in Manila fifteen days now. The rations had dwindled to famine issue. One ration lighter had come alongside but had broken away and drifted well to leeward before the struggling little tug could secure it and take it back.

One night two aircraft carriers left with a convoy. "Things must be swinging our way a bit when they have to protect a convoy like that."

"Seems funny to me . . . who protects the carriers?"

"They might pick up some escorts outside."

"Might."

In Number One men had started to plan to build houses. They talked and argued for hours about bricklaying, carpentry, plastering, plumbing, plans, and layouts. They drew plans. They argued on plumbing costs and what you could get away with. Some quoted by-laws. They even visited men who had been in the various trades before the war. They got quotes for different jobs. This visiting was not entirely a simple affair. If some men were on deck it could be done. But in the bad weather they were so crowded that, for a man to visit, some one had to change places with him. Despite so much friction and discomfort, they managed. They built their houses, pig-headedly holding that their ideas were better than some of the silly ideas that others fell for. They laid out their gardens and planted them —each, again, with his set ideas. Gardening became a hobby and a topic with them.

One feature of all this was the slanderous force they used to deride each other's ideas. A strong outburst seemed to do a man good, it compensated for their constant repression and devaluation by the Japanese. It was instinctive therapy.

John was able to add a little to a hobby he had started back in Java. He had become friendly with an Edinburgh surgeon of the R.A.F. This doctor was a brilliant cartoonist who could turn their every indignity and misfortune into hilarious satire, changing the sting of defeat into belly laughs. He had asked John for some tips on watercolour. In return he had taught John anatomy. John would draw the skinny prisoners and then, under the doctor, he would try to identify this or that lump and bump as bone or muscle and give it a name. (After the war, John learned that this doctor had been lost in a prison ship torpedoed just outside Nagasaki in this same year of 1944.) Now John had borrowed a copy of Gray's *Anatomy* from their own doctor, and was drawing and reading from it. Just as life in the jungle had fascinated and humbled him, now the ingenious body-mechanics fascinated him and made him realize how much had been achieved without intellect.

Men would talk about anything—ignorance was no bar. In fact, the pace of an argument was often spurred on by the dogmatic assertion of sheer ignorance. It made the knowledgeable reconsider just how much they did know. Often there was nothing but nonsense in what they said, but the very violence of their arguments killed apathy, their insidious enemy.

8

The ship was coaled, and it had taken them three weeks. They were anchored in the Corregidor roads waiting for the rest of the convoy. They could see the broken, bombed-out buildings on the crest of the high hump of Corregidor looking like the disordered spines on the back of a defeated monster.

"It is a monument," Harry said, "to a lot of talk."

"The ever-ready bull-dust," Alec said.

Buck growled something unintelligible.

"I will return," Boof quoted, "but not in time for us, my fine be-medalled friend—we'll be in Nippon before you."

"We *hope*." Buck said.

The convoy gathered around them.

"There's some rubbish here all right," Harry said, "but they're still miles in front of us."

"What about this weather?" Buck said. "If we get it at sea, they won't have to waste a fish on *us!*"

Below they looked around at the walls of the hold. Large red scales hung as if ready to drop at the least tremor. There were damp patches around the rivets on the plate-lapping. They bled, and a thin film of water glistened.

"It looks as if her first coat of paint was her last," John said.

They explored over the tops of the barrels. On top of them, in the square, lay two heavy hatch beams fore-and-aft with nothing securing them. Two or three barrels lay loose on their bilges ready to roll to any movement. They jambed dunnage down between the barrels and either side of the beams. "That might hold them a bit," John said, "but not if it gets really rough. Remember, keep your eye on them—if they move they'll squash you like a fly."

That night before John went to sleep, after conversation had died, he lay thinking of the old ships gathered here with them. Old ships were the ways of past generations. Old ships, hulks and lighters had always attracted him. Most of them had been old sailing-ships—an era that, except for a relic or two, was dead. He had developed a strong respect for the men and the things of the past who, with much less, had faced the sea and circumstance. This simple acceptance of life was what kept on impressing him.

Some of these ships were taking scrap iron back to Japan for the mills of war. This had been going on for years. He remembered one day in Sydney Harbour on the quarterdeck of the Australian flagship, awaiting the arrival of the Archbishop of Sydney. He was one of the quarterdeck staff. The archbishop was late. The ship had swung out into the stream and brought her stern close to the passing traffic of ships. A Japanese ship loaded with scrap, looking like a half-sunk log, steamed slowly past. It was 1935. The Admiral had paused his fore-and-aft pacing, taken a brief look at the ship, and paced on. As he neared the waiting men by the gangway he said, "The next time you see that stuff it will be coming through the air towards you . . . just remember that! We'd better have something ready to throw back!"

The incredible assortment those ships carried recalled a past to John—a curiosity about it—about when these now derelict things had been objects of pride. So much of it suggested craftsmanship—the co-ordination of hand and mind, not the mechanical mass-production of now. He saw in this co-ordination an indispensable harmony, within the people, that had maintained a close and vital relationship between the brain and that cell-complex, which is 'us'. This co-ordination was vanishing with 'progress'. John wondered if this change subtly frustrated man's eager and interdependent cells to bring on the depressive moods of a senseless-no-purpose life. Man's inheritance was now being passed on through books and machines and not through his own stream of life. It was Institution not intuition that was now the new brain centre; while separate human brains, losing the hand-hold on their own cells, became merely the sycophant cells of the Institution while Institution is doing away with the necessity of people. John had begun to think of the cell (for man) being the beginning of wisdom: for it knew secrets beyond consciousness. It did not have to tell the brain everything, but could work on its own for the survival of the whole. It could institute action—essential and immediate action—without the brain or intellect ever becoming aware of it. This was what John called stomach-wisdom. And its free, uninhibited action was what he meant by hand-holding of intellect and intuition. Men like Sergeant Arrow saw the key in Intellect alone and in the assumption that the rest was becoming rapidly redundant to be replaced by machine and instrument. There appeared to be an astounding faith in this new synthesis that was taking hold of the world with a fanatic fervour unprecedented in history. Each ship-load of scrap had seemed to him like so much junking of humanity.

At daybreak the ships got under way and crawled out under the overhanging bluff of Bataan to the open sea. The ship felt the swell and accepted it, sliding into the pitch and roll with the habit of a lifetime, which the spirit sustains even as the flesh fails. When the anchor was being weighed, clouds of steam from the worn-out steam-lines' broken joints enveloped the crew on the forecastle head. In the comings and goings of this swirling fog, they looked like a bunch of Elijahs ascending to heaven on a cloud. The windlass hove and faltered as the links of the cable clanked with rheumatic complaint reluctantly over the lip of the hawse pipe to crawl across the deck and vanish wearily down the navel pipe to the muddy companionship of their heaped fellows below—as if they were dreading the next anchoring that would stretch them all out again—wrenched nerve-taut. In the hold, the sound of the steam sometimes came like a thin distant shriek, and the home-coming cable clanked cavernously in the chain locker just through the bulkhead.

"Gives you confidence," Harry said.

"If we ever get to Japan," Buck said, "I'll bare my arse in Bourke Street."

Two days previously they had seen two destroyers leave with all dispatch. Their screws threw out a high white wake and the bows sliced high-curving water as they raced to sea. Four hours later they had returned, their decks crowded with survivors—Japanese soldiers. "That's nice," Alec said.

Now as they steamed past Corregidor, Alec said, "Hooray for our side!"

"I'm a bit with the Japs," Buck said. "Just now I hate the Yanks!"

"Why couldn't we bloodywell walk?" Harry said.

"You sound like the blokes we brought out of Crete," John said. "They were glad we pulled them off the beach—but they said that they would be a bloody site gladder when we put them ashore again. . . . but, after being bombed in harbour I'd rather be at sea and mobile."

"But at sea you stick out like a country la-la—you *know* it's *you!*"

"It's what you get used to."

"But you said *mobile*—this thing's about as mobile as an ant in treacle!"

At River Valley, John had been able to get a pocket compass although it had cost him almost all he had. One of the men who had come into the lower hold with them now lay on a hatch-plank not taking his eyes off that compass. When they cleared the bay they had turned northerly. Wally knew this was toward Japan. But he became alarmed when the ship turned westwards.

777

"Something's up," he said.

"Wal, if you watch every alteration you'll go batchy—the ships are zig-zagging on account of submarines."

"Yes, Wal, take it easy—you make us all jumpy," Harry said.

"As if we're not," Buck said.

"Well did you see the crew? They've got their lifebelts with them."

"Half their luck. . . . I wish we had."

"But they've got little dilly bags on deck too!"

"I don't think I'll bother to pack," Boof said.

"What do you think our chances are, John?" Wally persisted.

"How would I know? Work it out for yourself. I've seen ships get through when you wouldn't give them a dog's chance . . . and the other way round . . . when we expected it, it never came . . . then out of the blue—whack. Does that help you?"

"Pack up worrying, Wal, or you won't be worth a bumper."

Three small escort vessels picked them up outside, and a two-engined plane patrolled overhead. The *Byōke Maru* led the way at the head of the port column.

"We're flagship," someone said.

"Enjoy it while you can, cobber," Fatty said. "We're Aunt Sally, on the windward corner . . . we'll be the first one through their sights. Do you still feel proud? Just hope they don't think this old hooker's worth a fish—that's all."

They were keeping close to the coast and their zig-zag was limited. John and Fatty were on deck, unobtrusively between the coaming and the winches at Number One. This gave them a pretty good view of the rest of the convoy. Thirty ships in two columns. Immediately astern of them were two fine small oil tankers, well-laden and moving ahead with the typical lazy wallow of their kind, foaming water out and around them like half-tide rocks. On their forward catwalks each carried a small single-seater aircraft. They decided that this was probably a bluff for these could not be launched, though the catwalk might look like a catapult from a periscope.

Broken clouds sailed over the bright, ruffled sandy-green water, westward with the wind, racing their dark shadows which slid down the mountainsides like toboggans into the sea and played porpoises on the waves. The sea flowed glidingly past the slow-moving convoy of the overworked and rusted ships. Yet the sea, like a mother, gave them all, equally, a grace and character of movement.

Fatty and John were looking at the high mountains, mottled blue and green with the chasing cloud shadows, when they felt that vicious metallic giant hammer-blow strike through the ship's hull from under the water. Instantly they knew what it was for they had both known it before, but much more intimately. Automatic reflexes started up in them—they had tensed without springing to useless action. Almost at once the roar followed across the water. On their quarter they saw a high column of white water stained with the black-brown of crude oil. Two men in the overside latrines hastily scrambled inboard.

"Fished!" Fatty said.

Less than a minute later the second tanker was hit in the stern. It telegraphed the brutal blow through the water into the hull of the *Byōke* like a cry of kind to kind. Those below were suddenly fearful. The second blow sent alarm through them. They felt trapped. Fatty leaned over the coaming and shouted, "Don't panic! It's not us! They are after the cream!"

Then further shocks, not so hard, struck the ship.

"It's only depth charges! Settle down!"

The escorts were hunting now and tearing the water with their wakes and the ragged eruptions of their charges. A small trawler-like ship had moved in to stand by the torpedoed ships which were pouring black smoke with a lurid heart of licking flame. Boats from the rescue ship were manoeuvring to windward to pick up what survivors they could.

"You've got to hand it to them," Fatty said, "they are good sailors . . . and that's a bloody efficient little ship. . . . I hope she sticks around."

The guards and crew were showing signs of acute nervousness. A couple of prisoners on deck had yelled, "You beaut!" Humiliation and fear in the guards turned to uncontrolled anger. They clattered down from the forecastle-head to the foredeck, shouting. They rushed among the prisoners there with drawn bayonets, flailing them dangerously. There were a number of cuts and bruises as the men scrambled helter-skelter over the coamings and down the lines and ladders to the deck below. Some of them then looked up incredulously at the way they had come down.

"How the bloody hell did I get down here! *I can't climb a rope!*"

Twenty-three depth charges sent their nerve-racking message to the men below. Fatty had told them, "Don't worry! That's keeping the sub too busy to send a fish our way."

On their quarter they saw a high column of water

In seventeen minutes both tankers had vanished. Burning flotsam spread on the surface. Now, except for the normal bang of the waves against their bow, there was a quiet made uncanny by reaction.

The convoy divided. Later that afternoon they anchored in a bay. As the slips were knocked off the anchor, the old cable rattled out with a frantic rush until the anchor found the bottom, and then only in short surges as it checked the way of the ship. As the restraining cable came taut, it slapped roughly against the side of the ship just outside Number One hold, where they were. Each slap sent a shower of rust flakes as big as ship's biscuits from the inside of the scabrous walls.

"Hey! Careful out there!" Harry called. "That's all that holds us together."

"I told you, if we get to Japan, I'll . . ." Buck began.

As the ship came to rest Harry said, "I hope they leave us here—for ever!"

Close inshore were two wrecks. One sunk, the other on her side and burnt-out. There was a small jetty at the head of the bay, and that was all.

In the hold, waiting for their evening rice, Buck said, "Time one of you blokes copped the wog—I feel like a bit of extra *meshi*."

"What about you, mate; don't you think *I'm* hungry?" Harry said.

They had been in the ship forty days now. Each had had his bout of malaria. Buck had only reminded them of the obvious— that their turn must be coming up again soon. Then each would go into his own private retreat, not bothering anybody until he was fit company again. Nobody bothered him except with water and quinine. Food was always offered but seldom eaten.

Water was always scarce. They said they sweated more than they got. Now, after anchoring, some of the men were up at the winches, trying the drain-cocks on the greasy cylinders for any condensation they could get.

"Like bloody castor oil!"

"Rich and rare—all right for a plonk fiend!"

"Any vitamins in grease?"

"Oh, yes! Full of them!"

"No. But dinkum? There might be!"

"Just keep hoping, mate! *Hope*, that's the only thing you are likely to get any vitamins out of!"

Men were always at the winches, for the leaky lines were continually giving little banshee whistles and hisses in the darkness. Men crept up at dawn and tried their luck. Sometimes then a curse would be hurled at the unspeakable unknown who had left a drain-cock open.

By now there were some very sick men who had been moved up to the forecastle hospital. Beri-beri and pellagra were setting in. Some were bad with malaria—one with cerebral malaria who gave strange disturbing animal cries that were horrible to the men in the hold.

"Poor bastard," Harry said. "He gives you the jim-jams right up your spine. I get the feeling that we are all going to finish up just like him."

Men would burst out bitterly against the Japanese. They called for recognition of their sufferings after the war. People would *have* to be told . . . they could have no idea . . . the Japanese should be exterminated . . . they were no good to the human race . . . when people at home learn what we've been through, they'll *have* to do something about it. . . .

"Listen to them, they've really got it today."

"Just as well to get it off their chests before it turns their guts."

"I wonder," Harry said.

"Don't you reckon it's better to get it out of you?"

"Only if you *do* get it *out* . . . but a lot of these blokes are only building up for the next time."

"How?"

"Each time it takes less and less to get them going . . . they are not getting it out . . . they are storing it up . . . in the finish they'll be so sorry for themselves they won't be able to stand a thing . . . say 'boo' to them and they'll be gone."

"You can't afford it, mate," Boof said, "It's a trap . . . join in the fun of hating . . . then before you know it, it's got you . . . you're gone."

"I like a good hate myself," Buck said, "It does me good."

"Because you get it *out* of you, Buck, others don't," Alec said.

9

Once more the cable was coming home, tiredly with a stretched creak that sounded excruciating. The short squealing of the links grinding over the lip of the hawse pipe joined in.

Then it was as if they thumped with unbearable pain across the deck to climb down into the chain locker to pile uncaringly, link on link until, suddenly, the unstable pile collapsed with a short rattle, and they lay in the dank dark: in the silence of death. To the men in the hold the dolorous sounds of the painfully crawling cable made the ship seem very old.

"The next time," Harry said, "instead of the anchor coming up, the ship will go down and lay alongside it."

"Poor old bastard," Boof said. "No one cares . . . only the old know how the old feel."

"Maybe we do," Harry said. "They've made us old a bit early."

The ship slowly turned her head toward the open sea and steamed out.

"Here we go again," Buck said.

"Man the compass, Wal," Boof said.

Those thirty-six hours of safety at anchor made it harder to go now. As if his whole salvation were in the small swinging needle of the compass, Wally would not take his eyes off it. Harry looked up the open shaft of the hold that swung back and forth across the sky. "If she went without turning over, do you reckon there'd be a show of floating out, John?"

"Depends—whether she flooded up . . . or down."

John looked at the grey overcast of the sky. The lighter parts were yellowish as if the air was tinged with a faint dye. The ship began lurching with the creaking they had become used to. Occasionally at the end of a particular creak, there was a hard crack.

"Needs a doctor."

"She must have the wog—that's just how my back goes."

The wind and swell increased and the added sounds in the ship let them know that she felt it.

"She's a stiff ship," John said.

"*She's* stiff! *We're* stiff you mean, to be in her!" Buck said.

"Not stiff that way . . . not like with luck or rheumatics. . . . It's all the bottom-weight she's carrying. . . . In One and Two there's all this tin at the bottom. . . . Three's full of coal. . . . Four and Five have got it all in the lower holds . . . in the 'tween decks throughout the whole ship, there's only the prisoners. . . ."

"This skinny mob wouldn't make up much pudden," Boof said.

"Well, what's this bottom-weight do to us," Wally said.

"It makes her stiff . . . and it'll probably make you seasick. . . . When the sea lays her over, that weight will bring her back so fast your teeth will rattle . . . then up the other side before she can check . . . she'll swing about like a belly-dancer—only you won't like it so much."

"Will she capsize?" Wally asked.

"No, Wal, but before she stops you might wish she would."

"Oh! That's good."

"You say she's stiff when she'll act like a bloody Salome! You matelots always say things arse-up!" Harry said.

"What do you know about *matelôts*? What's a *matelôt*?"

"French for sailor, Wal," John said.

"It's what these navy blokes call each other—and I know, because I lived with a hundred of them up in the jungle—Boof and I . . . off John's ship . . . they had us talking like them in the finish."

The ship rolled and heaved her way on. Water began to bleed through the rivets and plate-seams and form a shining film on the ship's side in the holds. As the day passed, they watched it spread.

During the afternoon John said, "I've just been thinking . . . yesterday was my daughter's birthday . . . the eleventh . . . she's eight . . . the boy will be six in April. . . . I've only seen them twice in the last five years."

"Mine's six . . . she wouldn't be two when I last saw her," Boof said.

"Ah well, me sons, let's hope they won't be too old when you see them again," Harry said.

Men began to get seasick. John and Fatty went up into the 'tween deck and set-up the guard-rails and lifelines taut and secure. They cautioned the men to keep low and clear of the square.

"This is real, you blokes, someone's bound to get killed unless you are *bloody* careful," Fatty told them. "Watch the roll!"

That night the wind became gusty, howling over the ship and then dropping away. Heavy rain-squalls swept over them. Those on that one section of hatches in the square were half-drowned.

They tried to crowd into shelter under the coamings. It was impossible. They were beyond complaining.

In this crowd, beneath the ladder was a man whose hair was only a thinned wisp on top. It was hard to tell whether it was grey or fair, but the tufts over his ears and neck were speckled grey. He seemed older than most of them. He had childish blue eyes in a snub-nosed face that was once round. It was now gaunt. Often he was seen with steel-rimmed spectacles, reading, oblivious to all around him. He had been among the last to come down and he had stayed obediently where he found himself. Younger men had said, "Here, Pop, go in there with the officers." "No," he said, "that will mean that someone will have to come out here. . . . This must be where I was meant to be." He said it as if there were some privilege in it. In vain they had tried to persuade him. "He says he won't take anyone else's place—you can't kid him . . . it's no good."

Most of the men called him 'Pop', but the Roman Catholics called him Father. He was a Redemptorist priest. Under that ladder, all the dust and foot-scrapings of the men going up and down fell on him. The wispy fuzz on the top of his head was peppered with it. 'Pop's Halo' they called it. John had watched him talking and often laughing with the men. Here was a man with with all the unworldly humility of a St Francis, he thought. His convictions were so much genuinely a part of him that he did not conceive of any others. His simple duty was to set people right. To him, God had given explicit and exact instructions for the fulfilment of His will. There was an implicit pact. Not one syllable could he question. There was none of the sophist in him to make him sinister—only wholesomeness and simplicity. They all respected him. Now, as he sat cross-legged in the China seas he was strikingly like some Eastern holy man . . . humble, appearing spiritually grateful for the foot-droppings that taught him the blessedness of humility . . . that showed him his place.

Now he was mingled in this sodden crowded heap of humanity exposed to the strange and boisterous shifts of the weather. For him, God's voice was in this elemental stirring. Within, he listened keenly, as if the Voice were more likely to be heard in human extremity. This quality had made him Redemptorist.

If the air was hot and oppressive, it was not noticed by the prisoners, who had grown used to the sour steaming stench of sweat which hung stale with every breath they took. Now the ship flung them, sweat-streaming and rain-streaming, against each other. It was too dangerous for men to go on deck now. The only latrines were slung over the side. One mis-step, one lurch of the ship, when climbing over the side in or out of them, and there would only be a thin cry like a gull's to mark the fall into the heaving sea—one tenuous tombstone of sound blown away immediately on the wind. Nobody would go. Kerosene tins were passed around grumblingly. A sharp impatient curse would proclaim an accident, with little hope of cleaning it up. The seasick added their groans and substance to the thick pungency. As daylight came, they could see the great black bellies of the low clouds gleaming with a steely sheen as they boiled overhead. The wind increased. The sea, high and confused, was running generally from the south-west.

The ship seemed as if she were driving straight at the bottom when an overtaking sea lifted her stern high and ran forward with her as if to fling her down and stick her stem in the bottom of the sea like a dart. The screw raced, threatening the shaft bearings, until the throttle was cut. She would teeter on the crest then, breathlessly, slip from the wave's grip as it over-ran her. Her bow would go high, as if she were about to fall over backwards. This thirty- or forty-foot rise and fall of the bow left the men feeling that the bottom had fallen out of the world and they, giddy and sick, were going to plunge straight through into some awful pit. If they could only touch something un-moving! But they were blindly suspended in this spinning, heaving iron box. And they did not touch bottom. Their heads would start to come up while their stomachs were still going down . . . pulling away from each other with terrifying speed . . . stretching taut and incredibly long, a thin tortured nerve. Stomachs surged into their throats to be drawn away again *just* before being vomited out. They plummeted in extreme vertigo.

The shrieking wind tore the tops off the waves, leaving a whole wide plain of whirling white scars. Now the sea looked old—incredibly old—streaked with league-long streaming hoary strands of foam tossed violently about like the hair of an angry prophet. The shattered wave-tops were swept across the sea and struck the ship like vast and vicious volleys of musketry. Flying over her, it was sucked into the vortex of the open hatches in drenching salt spray. The stern was lifted, the bow went down, and the wind and sea joined as if to tip her right over. They held her on her side while she stubbornly fought for her life with unsuspected vigour. Her bottom-weight snatched her back just in time, then, rolling hard the other way, her high sides met the sea with a dreadful impact that sent a shudder right through her. For a moment she steadied, the streaming rust looking like a

They held her on her side

terrible wound. But there was no real rest for her. Wave after endless wave marched purposefully at her as if deliberately dispatched by malignant personal force to finish her.

Men fell into helpless paroxysms of sickness. Stomachs contracted, rock-hard. On all fours with misery, men's backs arched: their shoulders rounded up and they collapsed on to their elbows, barely able to keep their faces clear of the deck as they retched. Chests tightened, squeezing the last gasp of breath out of them. Uncontrollably heaving, they were stricken with a horror that they would disembowel themselves through their throats. Their heads felt as if they were being pulled off like a fly's by some invisible giant's extruding fingers. Their tongues forced out, tearing at the roots. Eyes clenched, and then bulged . . . and . . . born of all this agony . . . only a thin string of slime.

Looking up from the lower hold, John could see a line of helpless heads with open mouths lolling over the coaming, with wide staring eyes made unseeing by misery. The sounds were those of wordless animals, forced out—half-screech half-scream —by the violence of muscular contraction. There was a queer groan as the air rushed back into the deflated bodies. They moved helplessly with spasms like the reflexes of a newly dead snake thrown on hot ashes. The noise of some two hundred sick men sometimes rose louder than the storm; sometimes it mingled with the shriek of Tai-feng, the great wind, and the groaning labouring of the ship herself; sometimes it was drowned in a louder shout of the attacking wind and sea. As the men vomited the ship bled through her plates as if a vital plasma were oozing out as she was being trampled to death by the unending horde of waves. It was as if the elements had decided that this was the hour in which life and all its works should be obliterated, and the Rule of the Insentient begin all over again.

It was a miracle that the prisoners were not thrown from the 'tween deck into the lower hold. John continually expected them to come tumbling down in a heap of broken bones—and worse. All at once the ship gave five violent rolls that surpassed anything that John had ever before experienced at sea. Some rhythm of the racing sea, some uplifted crest, some more powerful gust waiting its chance—some extraordinary combination of the attacking elements caught her and threw her on her side, right down to the lee bulwarks and beyond. With her high freeboard this meant that her decks were almost vertical. They thought it was the end of her. Although, at the time, John was lying athwartships on a plank, he was thrown up to his feet and hurled across the hatch. He just managed to save himself by grabbing at the stanchion at the corner of the square, but the force badly bruised his hands. Alec was shot out into the centre. The beams they had chocked snapped the three-by-three inch dunnage like matches and hurtled down to the ship's side. John felt sure they would drive a hole through the weakened plates, but the violence of the recovering roll snatched them back just in time. Now the beams began to slither with increasing speed to the other side. Again the quick roll saved the side. But the careering beams tore the heads out of the barrels, and the loose ones collapsed, scattering the staves and spewing wide the sticky white latex. In the middle of this mess Alec jumped for his life with a fantastic agility born only of life-saving reflexes. It was a

diabolical kind of a sword dance with the murderous beams—
each more than twenty-feet long and weighing a ton. John was
quite convinced that he was about to see Alec squashed like a
fly in front of him—knowing there was nothing he could do
about it. All Alec could remember was, "I just kept jumping."
To do this he had to also dodge the deadly trap of the barrels
that had had their heads torn off. If he had stepped into one,
the heavy beams, in passing, would have cut him in two.

Five breathtaking rolls, each seeming greater than the last.
John caught himself saying, "One more and she's gone!" On
deck the loose castings were crashing about, breaking themselves
and upperworks to pieces. Luckily, a lot of it went over the side.
John's eyes shifted with tense anxiety between the fantastically
leaping Alec and the deck above him. Surely, at any moment,
that groaning mass of men there must come hurtling down to
almost certain mangled death. It was as if he were merely
waiting for it to happen to those helpless doomed men up there.
The beams would finish them off. But they did not come down.
Their limp helplessness saved them. They lay in an inert,
uncaring, tangled mass—locked, like those ants which cling
together in a hollow sphere to roll buoyantly across small
streams, or link netlike, to reach out to pull the edges of leaves
together to sew. This mass was locked in a flat mat of helpless
misery that could not rise—that had no wish ever to rise again.
Unconscious of the mess they were in, but dimly feeling a deep
desire to be free of all the trouble of living. They were not weak-
lings, for they had lived through much. But their years with
dysentery, fever, hunger, ill-treatment and the sores of debilita-
tion had left them at this moment, with no memory of any goodness at all. They had the dangerous dream of the peace of death.
It was as if only the age-old sea knew how to defeat these men
after the jungle, disease and the Japanese had failed.

By a strange paradox their lives were now in the hands of
another tortured and neglected thing that had suffered callous
adversity also. This ship, that with some mysterious wisdom,
knew the strength of weakness. They had cursed her high freeboard as a submarine trap. The Japanese had not loaded her
down because she was weak. And now this freeboard they had
cursed was keeping solid water from filling the open hatches.
The finest ships dread stove hatches in typhoons and hurricanes

(or less)—they fear for their very lives. Yet here was this decrepit ship with hatches that had never been closed, wide open, in the grip of a typhoon and refusing to recognize that she never had a chance. She wrenched herself this way and that—*just* avoiding, time after time, some huge exultant oncoming sea with a seething crest hissing confidence, streaming it in the wind like a battle standard. One wave would throw her over for the next to catch her helpless and overwhelm her. But she was able to fling herself up again with amazing energy. So violent was the action that the four big girders, welded along the upper deck to stiffen her, were ripped of by the distortion as she writhed free of the fatal grip of the sea in these five rolls. The welding split like a zip-fastener coming undone, and the girders were flung loose across the deck and over the side leaving havoc behind them. The bottom weight that was saving her was straining her dreadfully. The men had become conscious that their lives depended absolutely on what this ship could stand.

John gave no thought to the Japanese navigating the ship. He knew the fight for survival had been taken out of their hands. It was solely the ship's fight now. Her engine power was so depleted, the wheel so futile against this elemental conspiracy, that there was only one thing left to depend on. It was that hypothetical thing scoffed at by the sceptics: the inner spirit of the old ship herself. Whether it was there or not, whatever you called it, however you denied it—everyone now relied on how this profane pedestrian rusted iron tank (or girder, if you will) behaved. If this lump of material had no soul, but, when your life depended on it, and she saved that life, then it was pardonable to think she had. And now, unaided by man (more particularly, *unimpeded* by man) because it made no difference what he did with engines or rudder, this inanimate, inarticulate, unprepossessing lump of cankered iron continued to float and keep them all alive. If her actions were only doltish mechanical ones, it did not seem so to the prisoners then. Every roll or pitch, every rise or fall they felt as a deliberate action of this Stoic structure. With every crashing shock they became anxious for her.

In moments of crisis, of extreme danger such as this, there is an affection for objects that share it with us. We are vividly aware of their place and meaning in our lives. If we call it 'soul' perhaps it is because they have surprisingly revealed some quality that is more palpable and touching in them then, than it is in everyday humans. This interpenetration of man and matter is not recognized or is ridiculed in the West. A great religion might call it idolatry though two early protagonists drew attention to sermons in stones, and consideration of lilies.

With uncanny patience she endured

Nor do the materialists believe in it, they might call it superstition for, to them, 'other things' are to be enslaved or exploited. And yet, John thought, this interpenetration is a simple ingredient of *any* 'reality'. What struck John now was her simple undauntedness, her straightforward courage without flourish in the face of one of the greatest furies that can be set against a ship. With uncanny patience she endured: unshaken in spirit by the insensate vandalism of the roaring sea, or the shouted insults of the wind that made her reel. This tolerance and acceptance seemed to John to strike such a deep consonance

with an inner principle of universal survival that he was prepared to grant her a soul. In that a soul seems to be that essence
of virtue which remains after its material origin has dissolved,
now, to John, this ship in this struggle was distilling some of that
enduring essence.

But, not trusting her, five terrified Japanese guards had
rushed into the port lifeboat swung out over the side on her
davits. As if to admonish them, the ship rolled on her side
holding them out in the boat as in a ladle, to a leaping wave-
crest that ran curling forward and swamped it, almost washing
them out and filling them with terror at being drowned where
they sat. Then she heaved herself back again, holding them up,
ridiculous, to the sky like five witches on a ducking stool. They
scrambled out of the boat and ran for shelter amidships. The
boat streamed water like a sieve from every seam, showing them
that it was more suited to punishment than salvation.

Ships must know something, John thought much later. In the
typhoon of 17th December 1944 (this same year) the well-
found Task Force 38, Admiral Halsey's Third Fleet, found itself
in the worst of the storm for five hours. Seven hundred and
ninety men were lost overboard, killed below or trapped in
sinking vessels. Eighty were badly injured. Three destroyers
capsized. Cruisers and aircraft carriers were heavily damaged.
One hundred and forty-six aircraft were destroyed. All these
ships had fought the storm with powerful, man-controlled
machinery—and they had suffered. But one destroyer's engines
broke down and took herself out of the hands of men. She
drifted out of control in the boiling seas, and *she sustained virtually
no damage.* John liked to think that the little ship knew something.

In 1939 he had been in a hurricane off Bermuda in a cruiser.
She had been swept from end to end. Gear was carried away,
boats were smashed. The wind even tore at the running rigging
and frayed it out like rag into a mass of streaming 'Irish pend-
ants'. The wind-speed recorder had smashed against the far
side, beyond its limits, and thrown all its red ink over the graph.
Ashore the wind had registered 136 miles per hour—this was
on the edge. John considered this storm to be just as severe.

They had been in it now for more than six hours. They had
lost sight of all other ships. Each was now somewhere struggling
alone. They watched little spurts of water forced through the

plates as she twisted. When those girders on deck had carried away, the ship had every appearance of breaking up. The chief engineer told the captain that, unless the ship could find shelter soon, he could not be responsible. The pumps were overworked and failing and the hull itself was doubtful.

The typhoon had driven them northwards and they were now in the vicinity of a small group of islands called Mabudis, part of the Batan Islands. Mabudis is three islands which form an equal triangle, the centre of which is a sheltered anchorage. In a blind world of thick spume and spray, with visibility down to nothing, they had been carried past other islands that could easily have been their graveyard. One long island, Itbayat, had for several hours been under their lee. It could only have been a quirk of current that had kept them off this dreaded lee shore. They could have ended their lives being tossed about like rag dolls in the exploding surf between the teeth of the black rocks on the hungry coast. It was as if they had heard the baying of the triple-headed Cerberus in anticipation of what Harry described as a 'cargo of old bones and dirty livers'. It was like some ancient sea of Greek mythology: one of the illogical gods had turned them clear with an impulsive forefinger towards the shelter of Mabudis. The wind had eased enough for steerage way to be got on the ship. With the wind and sea on her quarter she yawed toward safety with the unsteadiness of exhaustion.

The ship anchored, enclosed by three islands in a flat fallow field of water—wind-ripped as if growing short grass. Beyond, between the islands, the open sea rushed past like horses with streaming manes. The islands were conical with rounded tops. On them grew clumps of pines and bushes, but mostly smooth grassland. On the lower slopes were some squared patches of ribbed red soil where the plow had been. Small thatched cubes of farmhouses looked no bigger than a few scattered pebbles, as if they had rolled down from the summits and stopped just short of the beaches. Grey sky dissolved into wet smoothness, grey-green sea was edged with leaping whiteness at the openings. The islands, which rose green-ochre with indian-red scars and wet sepia rock outcrops, surrounded and dwarfed the high-sided battered ship, wind-rode at anchor. Her wet sides glistened, still bleeding red rust as if freshly grazed by the hard sharp-scraping skins of swarming sharks. The flaws of wind from the outside storm made tentative grabs at her, and she yawed to her anchor like an old frightened horse.

The galley fires had been lit again after enough of the storm damage had been cleared away to allow it. The first meal in almost thirty hours was being boiled. But it was mostly thirst which plagued them—especially the sick. The winches had already been drained—but there were now two less. These had been smashed by the runaway gear at the height of the storm. The sick under the forecastle-head were now in an awful mess. The paint drums had come adrift and burst. The helpless men, lying on the iron deck in their sodden blankets, found themselves swilling in red oxide and grey paint. Their blankets mopped it up. They could only lie there and get covered in it too. They slid about in it, crashing into the ship's side or the legs of the benches in a helpless heap. Long suffering made them uncaring. Occasionally they would push a pot or drum away, out into the open deck if possible where, they weakly hoped, it would be washed clear over the edge of the world. Now an effort was being made to clean up these sick men before the paint dried hard on them. It was not easy, because most of them did not want to be disturbed—they could think of nothing but the blessedness of just being still again after being so terribly thrown about for so long. The unbelievable peace of being still was everything to them now. They were afraid that the malignant hand that had so constantly flung them about was still there. It had become a presence. But they were wiped off. Their blankets were squeezed out and hung to dry like cardboard. Their close-cropped heads and eyelashes were paint-matted. It would have to grow out.

The chocked boats on the starboard side were matchwood, but little of them was left on board. The boat in which the guards had been ducked was gone. The gripes, broken, hung like two torn dirty hair ribbons. The chain slings of the boat hung lifeless, each with a broken piece of the boat's keel clinging to the clenches that had refused to let go. The decks had been swept clear of all the iron debris that had littered them in Singapore. This tidiness was sinister, a grim reminder. They were beginning to realize the miracle of their escape, even as the sick felt the wonderful stillness of the world.

When the rice and the rice-water at last came, all drank but many did not eat. The seasick were too exhausted. And, with an irony they had come to expect from fate, those who could eat had plenty, yet though they ate their fill for the first time in months, it was very little more than they usually ate. The years of starvation had made their stomachs small. To be tempted, to give in to the desire to wolf down too much, was to invite a torture as terrible as anything the Japanese could come up with. And the rice would be sour before they could safely manage it. "How's our rotten luck," Harry said. The day had been the thirteenth of August.

10

At eight o'clock the next morning they weighed anchor and steamed out from between the shelter of the islands. The sea was still rough but going down. Away to the eastward there was a pall of smoke billowing skyward with an energy that was an evil omen for the ship at its base. Misty rain drew a curtain over the dismal incident. Later they learned that five ships of their convoy had been lost. One, with English prisoners, had run ashore in a rocky inlet on Itbayat. She had become a total loss. The prisoners were taken off two days later by Japanese destroyers. Two other ships had caught fire and burned out. Two went without a trace—probably gulped down by the maw that yawns between two hard-driven seas . . . a momentary glimpse of a masthead or funnel like a drowning hand . . . posted missing. . . .

They fell in with another ship and an escort. The following morning they were steaming in line ahead along the south-west coast of Taiwan. The mountains rose massively, close on their starboard hand. The whole was washed in with one big brush in a single colour boldly with subtleness on wet paper. The grey sky was swept in with flowing volumes of clouds and dripping curtains of drizzle enveloping the dark mass of mountains whose weight and immovability was not concealed by their water-blurred edges. Broad, flat horizontal brushstrokes made the wide sea's surface. Sweeping through the drizzle, roaring past them continually at mast-height, was a grey two-engined bombed-up aircraft. Approaching with the roar of engines in crescendo until overhead, suddenly at this moment in all this wet greyness, two balls of red flashed over them from the wings of the bomber. But they vanished instantly as if no colour at all could endure in this enveloping primeval grey world.

At five o'clock that night they anchored for two hours in a southern port of the island. Instructions were received from a shore motor-boat and they proceeded north again. The next day dawned blue and bright with a fresh wind, a sparkling sea and a cirrus sky. Late that afternoon they anchored in the outer road of Keelung. But at eight p.m. they shifted again and made fast to buoys in the inner harbour. That night almost the last of their rations were cooked. There would only be enough for a thin pap breakfast. After breakfast the day was a hungry one. But on the following day a ration-lighter came alongside. That night they had some bamboo shoots with their rice. They ate them eagerly, but suffered awful heartburn that night.

Two days later two Japanese destroyers came in, their decks crowded with prisoners. They had been taken off the *Asaka Maru*, the ship that had run ashore. They also had three prisoners from a ship that had foundered. They were found clinging to a raft, the sole survivors.

The harbour was crowded with shipping. To John it was a vast maritime museum. Steam vessels with slim hulls, raked masts, thin elegant funnels—even a couple with chain funnel-guys and rigging—cargo-passenger ships, now troopships, were festooned with airing blankets spread on a thousand bamboo poles, and crowded with eager noisy troops with hardly room to stand. John doubted that he would ever see such a collection again.

On their fourth day there, a Dutchman died of cerebral malaria, complicated by pellagra. His body was taken ashore. This was their first death, which was remarkable. There was, in this crowd of skinny miserable-looking men, an inner toughness that gave no evidence of its quality except in the fact that these men were still alive. None of the indomitable qualities which we are led to believe typify characters showed at all. Instead was what appeared to be a complete contradiction of all this facile formula for psychological insight.

On the fifth day at Keelung, they steamed out of the harbour.

Wally anxiously watched the compass. He was disturbed by a series of westward alterations. Nobody was allowed on deck. At six o'clock that night they found themselves back again in Keelung.

"What would they want to do that for?"

"The subs are too thick, Wal. They are afraid of ramming one."

But the next morning they were under way again, headed eastward toward the Ryukyu Islands, a chain which hangs like a necklace over the huge protruding bosom of China bulging into the China Sea, and runs right up to Japan. Now they were only two ships without escort. It seemed that they were expected to get there by stealth, from island to island and rock to rock.

The weather was bright with an intense blue sky streaked boldly with high free cirrus which used the whole sky to swirl in. They were now across the Tropic of Cancer and into the steady sea-chasing trade winds. It was flying-fish weather and they leapt in glistening wet shoals, streaking like drops of dew that were late and were hurriedly taking up their places before sun-up.

To the westward of them lay the old tea-ports: Foochow, Woosung, Hankow, Pagoda Anchorage and the rest. There was the impossible Min River negotiated by the tea-clippers, unthinkably dangerous, aided by nothing but wind, puny mid-nineteenth-century tugs, and a captain's heart (which had to be very young to risk it). From these ports came the fanatically laden clippers with all the impatient haste of pride and profit. With never a backward glance, they spread sail after sail and raced half the world around to London and other ports, in as little as one hundred and two days in 1850. On the way, they offered sails and spars, lives and limbs in supplication to the gods of Wind and Chance that they might favour them. The merchants profited much, the sailors little. Yet each year plenty of them came with enough devotion to the sea, and enough human frailty of swelling pride to face these elemental gods who, like the merchants, took their percentage. The presence of these ships was so strong to John that his mind was full of skysails, moonrakers, watersails, ringtails, stunsails, courses, staysails, spankers, spencers, and all the rest flying from masts and yards like man-made clouds impatiently dragging the slim hull after them like children rushing to a picnic racing their own shadows. He felt that the *Byōke Maru* was now among these long-dead ships—yet they did not seem dead, only invisible.

The weather took hold of the prisoners and brought them to life. The life that had been beaten small by the typhoon, the rain and the sickness. The malaria-ridden sap in them was quickened by this sudden spring, like a hope expanding in them. The gods had taken their percentage—five ships—perhaps now they would be satisfied and let this old ship pass on to Nippon, where there were also many more gods. Surely the toll must have been paid! But they could not forget that all along this route men were lurking under the surface with orders from Washington to get *their* percentage.

Washing was still difficult. They craved to be clean even as they did to be free from hunger and thirst. The leaking bottom of the hold, in one part, almost bubbled like a spring. One of the men deliberately took a piece of three-by-three dunnage and pounded the hull until there was a hole and the water flowed freely in. They called it the Village Spring and, in a never-ending stream, came to cleanse themselves as if it were a new Lourdes with miraculous power. It lifted their spirits. But, after three days, Boof and the others below with him were suddenly surprised by the guards in the 'tween deck roughly ordering the men off the hatch planks over the ladder leading down to the hold. There was the wooden rattle of planks being pulled aside, and then short Japanese legs appeared on the rungs. Two guards, the captain, the chief engineer, the carpenter and the bosun came down. They began to search. Soon there was a '*Ha! Oi! Damme, damme!*" as the Village Spring was discovered. The carpenter rounded off a big wooden plug and drove it fast into the bottom of the ship with a maul. The guards started to squeal and roar. They drove the prisoners out of the hold, beating them as they were clustered at the foot of the ladder waiting their turn to go up. They had to find themselves a place again in the 'tween deck.

11

On the 30th of August they anchored off Naha, on the southwest corner of Okinawa. Here, along a dusty airstrip, aircraft took off in red clouds and passed low ahead of the ship before climbing. Ashore they could see only some low buildings oxided with the dust, and a wireless mast. Late on the following after-noon they continued north for five hours and anchored in a small bay in the dark. The stars were reflected clearly in the calm black bay but, as the anchor splashed clumsily into the water, the stars scattered away like a frightened shoal of small fish—cautiously coming back as the water calmed.

In the morning they came on deck for their rice and burnt-rice water. They loitered there in the bright morning. A couple of men had a kerosene tin on a rope and were dipping water up from over the side and washing themselves. Some were still hopefully trying the winches for oily condensation, although others had been there already. In small groups other men were sitting about naked, with their shorts or G-strings in their hands. They were intently hunting lice while they talked. The lice were invisible until they had eaten, and then a small bloodspot showed in their transparent bellies and betrayed them. The marks on the men showed that both the bugs and the lice had already eaten. "Tally-ho! There go the little bastards!" one of the men said without raising his head. "I reckon they're Will o' the Wisp, out of Scarlet Pimpernel . . . with a touch of Dracula."

There was some contentment in the morning for the prisoners. It was September the first—to those antipodeans it was the first day in their spring, and they felt it in a jaded way.

Alec and John were leaning over the bulwarks looking into the pale-green translucent water. It looked absolutely still, but in the depths was a mysterious movement—undulating, yet spasmodic like the movement of an amoeba under a microscope, or protoplasm pulsing life. This movement only became evident to the watchers because of a blue, diamond-sharp glinting within the great body of the water—as if the sea were filled with millions of loopily sinking spangles, each glancing back the brilliance of the sun now cooled in the green sea to that of the glittering stars on a moonless night.

"*Coruscating!*" John said. "You couldn't get a better word for it in a million years! Ever feel like that about a word, Alec?"

"Sometimes . . . when I go to describe something and a word comes just right. . . ."

John had felt like this about a particular word before. The Seventh Cruiser Squadron was anchored in Salamis Bay, off the Piraeus. It was a fine bright day early in April. They had just come in from the Battle of Matapan. It was a particularly fine

There was some contentment in the morning

bright day—Psyttaleia Island with its lighthouse lay on the water like a gem: trees, bushes, rocks and the earth itself mingled their colours like an opal. To John, then, the air itself had a visible, palpable quality. It intervened and broke the steely cobalt of the zenith into a softer powdery cerulean. He felt as if the air were charged with all the atomized past of Greece. As if the Battle of Salamis had left all its combatants suspended spiritually in time and space here. He told himself that he was being too gullibly subjective. Or, he wondered, was he being receptive to some subtler reality? He got it down to a more acceptable conception: the air seemed full of sparks that were moving *just* too fast to be properly seen—only sensed. With this feeling of the invisible sparks, came the word: *scintillating*. In the minds of many down through the history of this country, he thought, this surely must have been a quality that had affected thought and action. That night the Germans blew up the Piraeus from the air. An ammunition ship, the *Clan Fraser*, was hit and burned. Drifting, flaming lighters acted as fire ships on all the captive vessels of the inner harbour. A ship anchored in the next berth to them was hit directly by falling mines. By the time the smoke cleared and the last of the debris had fallen, this ten-thousand-ton ship had vanished. The white-hot ammunition ship made a perfect incendiary when it exploded at 3.15 a.m. and turned the whole port into a pyre on which Scintillation was consumed in flame and smoke. The next day a vast oppressive pall of slowly drifting smoke, ceilinged at a few thousand feet, stretched from horizon to horizon like the dark Teutonic influence that caused it. It spread medieval gloom beneath which small specks of humanity, antlike, fled dispossessed and bereaved in sadness and horror. For the time, Scintillation had been overcome.

Now, as Alec and John watched the water, they saw dimly in the depths beneath them six smooth-swimming sea snakes like ropes of muted emeralds gradualy becoming clearer as they rose almost to the surface. In the coruscating pale-green water their scales glinted in dark and light bands.

"That looks like fairy-tale stuff," Alec said. "You wouldn't expect to see it in real life. If it were night instead of day, and we were looking up instead of down, you'd say they were swimming in a green sky of stars. . . ."

"It gives you the impression . . ."

"Like something happening a million years ago?"

"Like in the Garden of Eden . . . somehow makes time seem small. . . ."

They watched the snakes for almost quarter of an hour, until they slowly sank out of sight again.

"Did we see them . . . or did we dream them up?" Alec grinned.

All that was left was the pale sparkling bay, the clear sandy beach meeting the sea in a softly hissing fringe of white-water lace below the green bushes of the shore. All was quiet and obedient under the light-riddled blue of the sky.

After a while, Alec said, "This Garden of Eden business . . . what you were saying . . ."

"I'm working on it."

"Some blokes say they can't remember anything any more . . . they don't know how they will get on back in Civvy Street."

"It's a funny thing . . . with me it seems clearer than ever . . . sometimes I feel that I am very close to . . . something . . . but for the life of me I could not tell you what . . . sometimes it is as if my thoughts are being dictated to me. . . ."

"And your Garden of Eden?"

Alec was alluding to something that had started a year or so ago in the jungle. Men had been arguing about original sin.

"It's like beer and cigarettes . . . they pick on the things you can't do without, and then they slug you for it . . . and make you pay," one of them had said.

Dougie had said that sex must be original sin because Jesus, who had come to save them, was born by immaculate conception —without sin. And it had been Dougie's Bible that John had borrowed to read for himself exactly what had been written. He thought it was nonsense to think it was sex, for along this the stream of life flowed. Yet the fig leaf loomed so large in people's minds.

The serpent said, ". . . for God doth know that in the day ye eat thereof, then your eyes shall be opened, *and ye shall be as gods*, knowing good and evil."

To John, it seemed that men had since then believed the Serpent: *to be gods*, one way or another.

It had suddenly struck John that *this* was the very sin the old writer had cautioned about. Yet he seemed to be a lone voice whose allegory had been subverted to the Wish.

This was something of what he was telling Alec now. "The Garden of Eden was the state of the world before words came. . . ."

"Words?"

"Yes, words . . . they are the dividing-line between Eden and the outside . . . Eden is still with us . . . we saw it in the jungle, in those sea snakes . . . but we were not in it. In Eden *action* is the only knowledge—not *words*. The only knowledge in Eden worth a damn is that which can *reproduce itself* . . . that which is written into the cells themselves, not in books.

"Adam is the animal of words—Intellect, newly born and full of brash confidence . . . the little boy after his first day at school. He says Eden is for the birds—and he lacks the sense of humour to see that this is really true. He only stays alive because of his inheritance from it—he couldn't live a minute without the 'blind' workings of chance. Eve is Intuition, his only interpreter of these 'blind' workings. But Adam says she is only a rib. God tells Eve she is going to have a tough time with this know-it-all Adam. But Adam will never really forgive her; for his own self-esteem he will have to discredit her because, in Eden, the female holds the male like a cocked gun and only *she* can say when the trigger is to be pulled. This is Adam's shame. So he hides his shame with a fig-leaf and a pious pronouncement. And, to God, he *blamed* Eve. This was the first self-justification of Intellect and the first swing of the deadly pendulum of intellectual 'good' and 'evil'."

"Well, and what's all this come to, do you think?"

"Very bluntly: Man dreams of becoming God. He decrees right and wrong and acts on it. But he has built a house of confusion in which many 'rights' and 'wrongs' fight each other to the death. This flaming sword is like the Tiger's sword that hung at the bottom of his picture: it is the symbol of the dream of conquest—even to godhood—that man has. . . ."

"And?"

"Now the universal heresy is to proclaim *this* as original sin."

Here the guards came and drove them all below again, as the ship prepared to get under way.

The next day another Dutchman died of beri-beri and pellagra. He was buried over the side—farewelled by a miserable little crowd of his countrymen who looked as if they almost envied him. George played the Last Post on his trumpet. The broad flat splash of the bow-wave made it sound like a thin cry in an infinity of darkness. The corpse, tied in a blanket, slid stiffly off a tilted hatch plank, made a small inaudible splash within the spreading bow-wave, and was gone. With weighted feet it sank to the bottom to stand like a lonely exotic statue amid teeming other-life—a piece of abandoned redundant humanity. The ship rolled slowly on.

12

It was night. The only thing not black was the faint loom of the overcast sky through the square of the open hatch. Men became indistinct blobs only if they moved against this faint light. Otherwise, all were of one ink filling the hold. The old war-torn derelict ship lurched sullenly across the uneven sea, as the waves slapped the empty holds with hollow drumlike bangs. She creaked and strained like a hastily built coffin being carried on tired shoulders. And coffin she might well become, crawling over the submarine-infested waters where the Americans were concentrated to cut off all supply to Japan. She had nothing to rely on but luck. But they tried not to anticipate. Harry had said, "If we have to die—for Christ's sake let us try and make it only once!" But they knew for a sober fact that this death they might have to die could well be just beyond the next wave. It made them think about where they stood. Some wondered what their hopes of heaven were; some, what would be the price of their sins; some, believing it was over when you are dead, wondered what memories of themselves they would leave behind. Many wondered why they had lived at all. They wondered what would happen to their families. They felt despair. What purpose? they wondered again. These are times when men become islands unto themselves—each with his own special geography.

Buck had raised the question one night when they had spoken on the spur of the moment. And just now it seemed more pointed. He lay in the dark in the creaking ship with the others, most of whom were now asleep. He had a high fever, which made his mind burn bright. So it would burn until the sweat came hours later. *Then* he would sleep. He felt as if he were in his coffin being carried into the limbo of it-didn't-matter-what. With a certain sort of detachment which comes at these times, he found himself looking back, as it were, at what we variously call 'life'.

As he had told Alec, it was as if a separate voice within him spoke in dialogue. The sea, the darkness, the familiar sea-and-ship movement, a sharpened awareness of life that was not just human—and now, the final irony: that the most probable death that awaited them would come from their own side to win freedom for their families who, with the same blow, would be made fatherless and widows—these things focused John's mind on the great So-what?

At this point the Voice began the dialogue.

"You were telling Alec about what you thought Eden was—now what you were really saying was that what you need outside your skin with which to get food and shelter (like what you need outside your head to beat boredom) is a weakness which complicates life and makes you more vulnerable ultimately—through the genetic chain."

The Voice went on, "That is only part of pre-intellectual wisdom that Man, in his short two million years, has almost completely unlearnt."

"What a system," John said, "with wars like this one just to try to balance things up. How much time has man got left?"

The Voice said, "Even if head-wisdom were superior to stomach-wisdom, there is something so incontinent about it and its frenetic pursuits that it does not have time, nor wit, to remedy the faults it creates while trying to evolve its own generative independence."

"What is it?" said John, "Why does man think it is possible?"

The Voice said, "Theist and atheist differ only in incantations to abstract a divine right of action for themselves. From it springs the patriotic fervour of the Tiger. But the same principles have set the Australians through a complicated chain of circumstances of action and reaction, as enemies against the Japanese. It has filled them with the same holy fervour as the Tiger . . . . . . each is RIGHT . . . each is caught."

"The Tiger and Boof," John said. "You know . . . somehow I feel, that without all this . . . if they were on a farm together . . . but now they have been given parts . . . parts they were not born to . . . and they've got to act them out, or, in the world's eyes they'll be traitors . . . they have no choice."

The Voice said, "Just as stomach-wisdom tends to atrophy in civilization, so does any intellectual thought linking back to it.

There is no new wisdom except that it would be now new if the old wisdom were heeded."

Then John remembered what Buck had said when Sergeant Arrow had hotly denied this suggestion of childishness in man.

"That's bloody rot," Arrow said, "about man only being guided by his wishes. He analyses with intellect and reason. Reason is what makes him superior to all other forms of life. It conquers emotions and we are rational and logical—this way we can discover purpose and bring it about—you've only got to look back over the last fifty years."

"Balls!" Buck had burst out. "You brainy half-smart bastards all talk clever . . . you kid each other . . . talk's only a smother . . . the world still ticks the way it always has . . . one proverb covers the lot of you: *A standing prick has no conscience* . . . just think it over before you talk big . . . anything you want bad enough you'll take *and make it right*. That's why we have wars and depressions. . . . Reason! My arse!"

The Voice said, "Perhaps Buck had a point there . . . you remember how Herman Melville said at the end of *The Bell Tower*, 'So the blind slave obeyed its blinder lord, but, in obedience, slew him'."

"What a mess," thought John. "What's left to believe in? Has man turned out to be a cancer crawling over everything and living off it until it dies? Forests, animals, the earth itself—the Japanese Army plundering China, laying waste, issuing forged currency and forcing it to be honoured . . . is this *only* Japan marching? It is hard to believe that there will be a last-minute reprieve . . . life is not like that, ultimately it is just. But if man is on his way out, where then lies Purpose? Is all that is left to be a hopeless cynicism?"

"Do you remember," the Voice went on, "not long before the war, you went into the country by car with your family. You had stopped for lunch. It was early autumn after the driest summer for fifty years. The bushfires had been disastrous. It was the year of Black Friday when Melbourne, and half the State, did not see the sun because the smoke made it like night at noon. As far away as New Guinea the sunsets told of the fires two thousand miles away. Where you had stopped, the rolling paddocks were dead, dry grass, and their ridges made an encircling horizon in a bleached-bone world. Scattered about like headstones the big ring-barked gums were standing smooth satiny skeletons of whitened wood. Close by the car the tall dead grass leaned its straw stalks over toward the hard baked earth. White sulphur-crested cockatoos screeched in the scaffolding of the dead trees with a cry like a shrill and angry protest at the harshness of the season—at the apparent onset of death everywhere. At the time something struck you about this scene . . . you were uneasy somehow because man had no place in all this . . . if the drought killed all humanity, this would still go on . . . there was an underlying rightness about even this which took no count of man. . . .The dead grass nodded forward in seeming somnolent satisfaction somehow sure and secure in the future. Its head was full of seed and the seed was full of knowledge. This knowledge was not fantasy: it was wisdom carefully stored over hundreds of millions of years. Tested, it was life-action—not words. Significantly differing from human knowledge in that it did not contain ambition nor an unrelenting desire to revolt against necessity. Man seems to despise lack of revolt; the grasses seem to know revolt as something futile and fatal. The grasses neither toiling nor spinning, have encompassed folly, misfortune and necessity, fire and drought and being eaten. They can die contentedly before the next generation is born, yet bequeathing it a complete inheritance of complete knowledge—*all* that it needs to know. Unquestioning of purpose, it is a complete fulfilment of it. To attempt more than *to be* is to propagate uselessness even though it leads to the flattering belief that the life-force in us is the total god-force which destines us to recreate the world nearer our own narrow conception. It is sad that religions have seen fit in the past to partition the New World to allow men to march in without conscience or compunction but with an assumed God-given destiny to destroy whole tribes and take their lands. This is not past. As in the past man subverted his religion to his avaricious wish, now, with his new religion, Science, he has partitioned all nature from which to wrench secrets with half-knowledge and thus become the greatest vandal ever known. The early reliance placed in celestial nepotism has been carried forward to entrench man in his follies like a spoilt child—to wax his ears against the wisdom of the rustling grasses pregnant with *all* that *is*."

John lay in his coffin looking sadly out, "Wherein lies hope?

Wherein is that which justifies faith? Man is bent on bigoted hara-kiri . . . where is hope?"

The Voice said, "*Blessed are the meek* . . . this is all you need to know."

Tomorrow would be the sixth year of the war.

"In other places," John thought, "on the outside, men are watching the growth of machine and technology with fascinated pride—the victor growing more confident, the gradual defeated feeling more the impact of man's victory over things. The old hunt was being quickened . . . what then would Victory mean?"

Already the loom of light in the hatch square was growing paler. The sweat broke and John was drifting off to sleep as if he were drifting out into eternity.

13

They continued north, drawing closer to Japan. Passing the islands one by one like beads on some Oriental rosary. Each increased a strange curiosity.

So far, since they had been prisoners, this Nippon had only been that incomprehensible thing which had sent so many fanatical, exaggerating soldiers pouring down over the Asian continent and sea like ants from their nests, marauding and seizing everything in their path. It was the home of these short, squat, flatfaced men who were untidy, often to them ludicrous with simian shuffle and incongruous habits; but who unerringly struck deep fear into them because of the authority of absolute brutal power that was answerable only to itself.

But, in those seas, islands rose before them with another spirit that could not be linked with the human one under which they suffered. It was of life-becoming, like a young green shrub in spring. Red soil and green growth spoke the story of strong earthy beginning. The greens told of the potential and permissible emergence of living variety in all its tender indefatigable resilience. It was a silent but inescapable reproach to brutal human belligerence and assumptions.

These islands from Taiwan to Kyushu had stirred imaginations in the past also. The Japanese thought of Japan as a silkworm spinning out of its mouth, at Kagoshima, this thread of

THE VOYAGE

islands southward to Taiwan. In ancient times it had been given the name of Okinawa—the Long Rope. The Japanese called it Ryu Kyu, but the islanders themselves called it Loo Choo—the Sleeping Dragon, possibly from the dormant volcanoes there. As each island was passed, John felt curiosity grow. Okinawa, Kume, Le Shoma, Oki no Erabu, Toku no Shima, Amami O Shima, and then that small scattered group of bonsai islands Tokara Retto, looking as if they had been blown out of the broad caldera of Yaku Shima in that distant cataclysm that had left this circular scar above the sea. This volcano, with its head and shoulders blown off yet still more than six thousand feet above the surface, was like a persistent pristine finger-mark of the creating Sun Goddess, Amaterasu herself.

"Wonder what they'll make us do when we get there?" Buck said.

"Couldn't be worse than the jungle."

"Don't bet on it!"

"Some one said salt-mines."

"That sounds like our luck—if there's nothing worse."

"Foundries . . . coal-mines. . . ."

"With our luck, it will come from the bottom of the barrel," Buck said. "I'll bet . . ."

Just then a small square of wet paper flew, batlike, above the hatch. The fresh cross-wind blowing over the opening sucked it down. It swooped like a diving kite. A second later it was stuck on Buck's cheek like a large, badly-placed postage stamp. Clinically he peeled it off and held it, looking at it intently.

"There you are," he said. "*That* says it all! . . . it used to be just a funny saying . . . it was ridiculous because we thought it was impossible . . ."

Knowing what he had in his hand, the others knew just what was on his mind.

". . . but now it's the plain bloody truth! *We couldn't shit in the ocean!* . . . that's how stiff we are . . . that's where the slit-eyed bastards have got us!"

It was a piece of used toilet-paper that had stuck on Buck's face all the way from the overside latrines. Prolonged starvation had brought on a looseness that, in the words of one of their doctors, was 'after the second year distressingly uncontrollable'. These box latrines had been replaced after the typhoon had

809

swept away the others. Four only for twelve hundred and fifty men. So, against better judgment and of necessity, the windward ones had to be used. If the wind were on the beam (across the ship) as it was now, it struck the ship's side making a strong up-draught which at deck-level was snatched across the ship and sucked into the vortex of the open hatch as it passed. Therefore a man would feel this go up his back, as if the hand of fate were deliberately rubbing in his misfortune, and follow the wind into the hatch. Buck had remarked this phenomenon with the pithy phrase. Sometimes, when a piece of paper followed, some one would say, "Hullo . . . he wants a bloody receipt for it!"

They passed Tanega Shima and crossed the twenty-odd miles of Van Diemen Strait and anchored off Kagoshima. Just four hundred and ninety-five years and fourteen days before them, Francis Xavier the Jesuit had landed there to bring Christianity to the pagans. Within a hundred years the Japanese reacted strongly. They had been made suspicious by the internecine rivalry of the Christian orders and nationalities—and especially by a remark of a wrecked Spanish pilot who boasted that the mighty power of King Philip's overseas empire was largely due to the pioneering work of his missionary friars. With a brutality quite typical of both the East and the West at that time, the Japanese suppressed Christianity in Japan.

But, in 1853, the West came back again with more persuasion than religion, although they acted as if at the behest of God. Kagoshima again received their attentions. The *daimyo* of Satsuma was on his way back from Yedo along the Tokaido in 1862. It was customary to give a *daimyo's* train absolute right of way under the pain of severe disapproval. Foreigners had been requested to keep clear of the Tokaido this day. But, 'contempt-uously and with no waste of courteous language or sympathy for national troubles', some refused. Two Americans, van Reed and Schoyer, while riding, met the train. They filed aside and passed without hindrance. But three Englishmen and a lady came by also. Mr Richardson, an old China hand, 'knew how to deal with these people'. He disregarded warnings from his companions and rode into the procession. Incensed retainers reacted to this insult by hacking at the party with their swords. Richardson was killed, the others wounded, but the lady was not touched. This was called 'The Richardson Affair', and one year later seven English warships came to avenge the insult. The city of Kagoshima was laid in ashes. Foundries, mills and factories, the beginnings of a new civilization the West was forcing on them, were destroyed. In addition, one hundred and twenty-five thousand pounds sterling, and three Satsuma steamers were extorted at the cannon's mouth as a fair price for the loss of Mr Richardson. 'Having accomplished every act of retribution and punishment within the scope of the force', they retired.

The Tiger knew about Kagoshima . . . and Shimonoseki. Here there were English, French, Dutch and American combined to force the strait and destroy the defences. No state of war existed. Again they pointed the cannon and, as well as severe shore destruction and consequent murder of the population, they extorted $3,000,000 Mexican. This was for 'indemnities' and expenses. The American expenses were less than $25,000, but they took $750,000 plus interest.

All this was done to a proud but helpless people.

William Elliot Griffis, an American, who taught for four years in the Imperial University of Tokyo, 1870-74, was so moved by what he saw that he wrote:

> During my stay of nearly four years in Japan, several Europeans were attacked or killed; but in no case was there a genuine assassination, or unprovoked assault. I was led to see the horrible injustice of the so-called indemnities, the bombardments of cities, the slaughter of Japanese people, and the savage vengeance wreaked for fancied injuries against foreigners. There is no blacker page in history than the exactions and cruelties practiced against Japan by the diplomatic representatives of the nations called Christian—in the sense of having the heaviest artillery. In their financial and warlike operations in Japan, the foreign ministers seem to have acted as though there were no day of judgement. Of the Japanese servants kicked and beaten, or frightened to death, by foreign masters; of peaceable citizens knocked down by foreign fists, or ridden over by horses; of Japanese homes desolated, the innocent men and women, as well as soldiers, torn by shells, and murdered by unjust bombardments, what reparation has been made? What indemnity paid? What measures of amelioration taken for terrible excesses of bloody revenge at Kagoshima and Shimonoseki? What apology

rendered? For a land impoverished and torn, for the miseries of the people compelled by foreigners, for the sake of their cursed dollars, to open their country, what sympathy? For their cholera and vile diseases, their defiling immorality, their brutal violence, their rum, what benefits in return? Of real encouragement, of cheer to Japan in her mighty struggle to regenerate her national life, what word? The only answer of the horse-leech—for blood, blood; and at all times, gold, gold, gold. They ask all and give next to nothing. For *their* murders and oppressions they make no reparations. Is Heaven always on the side of the heaviest artillery?

This much the simple people of Japan had known, but the prisoners had not been told. Neither did the face of nature record it. They looked across the green water to Sakura, the island that blocked off the head of the gulf. It was a volcanic cone three thousand seven hundred feet high. From its peak, right down to the sea on its western face, there was a single crazed sheet of bare volcanic rock—solidified lava, looking like the shell of some fabulous tortoise that bore continents on its back. Sakura had erupted in 1913 and spread this smooth stone plate of armour over the mountain. It was strongly pink with escaping oxides.

"There's something about this place that gets you in spite of the little buggers," Harry said.

A small junk with slatted white calico sails forged past the ship—close-hauled, with the speed of a dhow. The segmented sails were being pulled with an invisible force as if in their ancient form was a pact with *kami kaze*.

They weighed anchor at eight o'clock and steamed down Kagoshima Gulf in the silver and black of bright moonlight. They anchored at ten-thirty but were under way again early in the morning, northward toward Nagasaki. An Australian died on this day. The first of the voyage—sixty-eight days out from Singapore. Dysentery and pellagra had been his pall-bearers. He too slid stiffly over the side to stand alone and straight fathoms down until, picked clean, his bones would lie more leisurely in a little heap.

That night they hove-to in the outer roads of Nagasaki. A boat came off from the shore with a medical party. It was a dark night with close, broken clouds consistently hiding the moon behind their bright edges. Only an occasional star looked through. The medical party set themselves up on Number Four hatch. Above them an electric cluster-light sent down a wedge of yellow light like a big slice of cheese standing on the deck, and the men the rats infesting it as they moved in and out of the beam.

It was a glass-rod inspection. They had long since left prudery and pretence behind. This was not what bothered them. The

Right in the middle of a Hiroshige painting

slightly rolling ship, the poor light and the deep shadows were all against a good clean painless execution of the test. The men were instructed to drop their trousers as they came up, and to pull them up as they went away. Instead, they simply took them off and walked up and away without them. "Who wants to be hobbled up there with the ship rolling!" It was an anal swab with a glass rod. The smear was put on a glass slide and placed in a container with the man's number on it.

Because of the handicaps there were painful gasps and curses. And there was the usual gross ribaldry to turn indignity into humour.

"Don't struggle—they can make you do anything, except love the child."

"Don't be too sure about that either, mate!"

The next day they anchored in a bay that put them right in the middle of a Hiroshige painting—it was already idealized: a perfectly polished sea plain; reds, greens and greys; mountains, rocks, islets and twisted pines. It looked like one of those temple gardens of contemplation which show the universe in miniature.

On the following day they anchored in Moji roads. The day after they went alongside and came ashore and stood on the open wharf to find out what would happen to them. At one end, without shade, five sick men lay on the concrete. Some others tried to give them shade with their bodies. These standing men looked at the sick and spoke an occasional broken sentence to give an encouragement they felt no confidence in. Or they offered them a drink or a smoke.

They looked at the *Byōke Maru*, riding high against the wharf on the full tide. It was strange now to look at her from the outside when so often they had thought she would be their coffin. The typhoon had taken almost every last shred of paint off her. Red-raw she lay quietly.

"Doesn't look much, does she?" Boof said, "but she's got guts."

"It's not the show ponies . . . it's the ordinary things . . . ," Buck said.

"How long has it been?"

"Just seventy days today."

PART 3

THE MINE

Felicitations!
Still . . . I guess this year too
Will prove only so-so.

(ISSA)

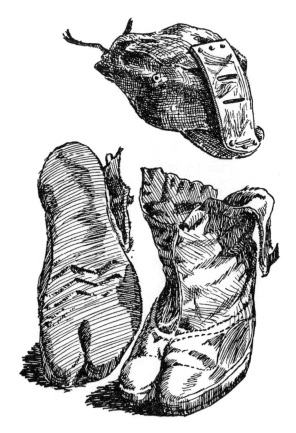

Mine cap and boots

THE MINE

I

T HEY waited on the open concrete wharf in the hot sun.
Almost all waterbottles were empty. Japanese civilians
gathered together with the guards and decided what was to
become of them. The Tiger was there.

"Look at him, he's only a little fish in a big pond now," a
prisoner sneered.

The prisoners, too, had lost something. They had been
seasoned jungle workers, toughened and without illusions,
expecting nothing and prepared for anything; but now they
were in a new strange place and did not know what to expect.

"Maybe we'll miss the Tiger at that," Harry said.

"What's going on?" Buck said.

They were fallen in.

"The slave market begins," Boof said.

Two *kumis*, with Boof and the others in them, were marched
away to a couple of hulked sailing-junks which lay alongside
waiting for them. Their masts were gone and the decks had
been torn up to make them open barges.

"Coal barges," John said.

"Don't go down the mine, Daddy," Harry said, "there's
plenty of bastards on top."

They went across a plank and down a rough wooden ladder.

"Drier than the *Byōke*, anyway."

They sat on their packs. Some stretched out using their packs
as pillows. On deck against the sky stood a Japanese. He spoke
to them in American so smooth that they forgot he was Japanese.

"My name's Tanaka . . . I'm the interpreter. You are going
over to Ohama on Honshu . . . over there, about fifteen miles.
The Ohama Mining Company hopes you will be very happy
there. You'll find things different here . . . and I guess you
won't be sorry," he finished pointedly.

Baskets of bread were passed down. There was one small
bread roll for each man. "Bread," the rice-fed men said unbelievingly as they bit into the first bread for over two years,

"Japan will do us." They were told that the bread was cooked by the British in the camp they were going to.

"Good on the Poms!"

It was cooked every second or third day, when they could get the flour for which an equal weight of rice was deducted.

A cloud of black smoke swirled over the open hatch and cast a glowing shadow. Slowly the two hulks were drawn away from the wharf by a small panting tug trailing a vigorous plume of black. Tanaka squatted on deck and talked to the men below. He was an American-trained dentist attached to a small hospital near the camp. The mining company used him as their interpreter. On a visit to Japan just before the outbreak of war, he had not been allowed to leave. He saw George's battered trumpet strapped to his pack.

"What about hitting something on the trumpet, fella?"

"When I get this bread roll down, mate."

"O.K.? You fellows sing? It'll be a couple of hours before we get anyplace."

"I hope we win the war," one of them said.

"Why?"

"So's we c'n eat bread instead of bloody rice!"

George played the old favourites. The sentimental and the profane: the softly sweet and the bawdy boisterous were all equally part of P.O.W. sentimentality. They made a stump concert of it. Some sang solos. Some recited stale old stuff they had heard a hundred times, listened to again in comfortable habit. George played some solos with a bit of triple-tonguing that always brought a cheer. Tired old improper jokes were told and laughed at, much like parents doting over the antics of an only child.

John watched the sky swing above them as they rounded the Moji signal station and headed eastward into the Inland Sea. He went up the ladder and looked across the shallow sea with its changing colours. He looked at the blue-and-green hills on both sides of Shimonoseki Strait. Most of them were only four or five hundred feet high—one cluster over near Chofu was nearly a thousand—but all had the spirit of bigger mountains. "They're *bonsai-ed*," John thought. It made him wonder if the Japanese had formalized their landscape or whether the landscape had formalized the Japanese.

"I've been *Shinto-ed.*"

In the wake of the tug they headed east. Ahead of them, a twin hill notched the horizon. This was Ryuo San, pine-crested and four hundred and forty-one feet high. Their camp was in a small hollow on its seaward face which was turned southward. The shore wind made the sea choppy as they came alongside the mine jetty, making the buoyant hulks lurch and bump against it. They had to jump, and they were awkward—their legs had been ship-bound for seventy days. The exaggerated concern of the mine officials for their safety contrasted strangely, to them, with past treatment. It made some of them call patronizingly to the Japanese, "All right, Pop! Keep calm— don't get anything in a knot—we'll make it."

It was about four o'clock and the day was warm. They straggled up the hillside to a flat open space that could have been a baseball pitch dug out of the side of the hill. With their backs to the sea, they faced a group of mine officials, older men with a mildness that surprised the Army-conditioned men. They were dressed in black civilian clothes that were so common as to become a sort of quasi-uniform for the whole Japanese people. There were also two guards there—a corporal and another in shabby washed-out uniforms. They did not wear leather Army boots, instead they wore the black split-toed rubber boots which all the men seemed to wear.

At the edge of the ground, behind a single-railed fence, stood the women and children of the village. Some in drab, bloomer-like trousers and wearing blouse-like coats; some with broad black *obis* and, slung across their backs, wide-eyed babies with the wisdom of innocence in their stare. Toddlers and teenagers stood there too, clean and shining in their unworn years. All looked at the prisoners with frank, but not rude, curiosity.

To men, new out of the vortex of war and its relentlessness, this was something that affected all of them except the mean and soured. It was strange that this exotic place, which had been only a legend to them a few years ago, was the place that had bred the men they had learned so to hate. And yet, in this very place, the sight of the women and children immediately represented to them, not the spawn of the enemy, but the human family—so forgotten among so many submerged values.

They were welcomed and told that this place was Ohama.

Hama means seashore. They had come to help to produce coal. The company was very happy to have them. They would be taken to their quarters where they would be able to rest after their long journey. It was hoped that they would soon be fit again.

The corporal took charge of them. They tried to march well —perhaps out of pride; but also, perhaps, out of deference to those women and children that they should not witness human decay.

The camp was surrounded by a high wooden fence topped with barbed wire. They marched through the open double gateway. On the left, just inside, was the guardhouse. There was a sentry on duty. But the sergeant and the rest were there to see the prisoners come in.

"*Kashira hidari!*" and all the prisoners' heads and eyes snapped to the left. And they had their first look at the sergeant, a tall black-jowlled man with broad shoulders and a rangy body. He scowled ferociously back at them.

"Another Ape," Boof breathed, recalling a sergeant who had driven them hard on the Railway through the *Speedo*.

"*Bageera! Talkoo dame!*" he shouted with a terrible force.

When they had received the order *Na-oru!* and were past, Harry said, "I reckon you would be *dead* right, mate!"

From the gate it was downhill into the camp. At the bottom they were halted and issued with numbers in black on little white calico tabs to pin on themselves. They were taken to rooms by the British already in the camp. There were one hundred and fifty English, Scottish and Welsh—mostly Royal Air Force with some anti-aircraft gunners. There was a striking difference between these and the newcomers. They had been here now for two years. They were satin-white and their muscles could be seen moving under their thin skin. They looked fit. But their faces had a lifeless sullen quality. Behind their eyes was a kind of wilful unseeing, and their mouths seemed set in perverse resignation, as if their monotonous confinement had so narrowed their minds. To the Australians they appeared restricted and self-centred, if not self-pitying. The British said the Australians looked brown, fat and well-fed. The Australians assured them that they bloodywell weren't. Their 'fat', they said, was the oedema of starvation. Some were worse than others. One man was fifteen stone. His knees and ankles had vanished in one ugly sausage shape of a leg. He had difficulty in walking. All of them were surprised how unfit they had become on the voyage.

From the gate it was downhill into the camp

That walk up the hill, and the short march to the camp, had found them out.

The two-storied, unpainted wooden buildings, long and narrow, flanked a single-storied one. This centre one contained the dining-room, the cookhouse and, at the end nearest the gate, the Japanese offices. The two-storied ones were dormitories. The rooms on each floor were connected by a corridor down one side. There was a staircase in the centre of the building and another at the end where the *benjos* were. The *benjos* were the toilets. They were not *gofujo*, honourable impurity; nor *habakari*, impoliteness; but simply *benjo*, motion place.

Fire was feared as an ancient enemy. These bare, thin, pine-board buildings would burn like a box of matches once started. But there were no hoses, for only a small water-service came into the camp, and in winter this was often frozen. Outside the huts were small concrete tanks of water not much bigger than bathtubs. Inside, at either end of the corridors, were two large half-barrels of water and a few buckets of sand. In the barrels swam small golden carp not an inch long. At intervals along the corridors were lifelines of coir (coconut fibre) rope, coiled and ready to be thrown out of the upper windows in case of fire.

They jostled in the passageways as they went to their rooms. One of the two-storied buildings was filled with the Australians and the overflow shared the other building with the British. In each room a Britisher was acting as room leader to show them the ropes. There were a hundred things they wanted to know. They did not want to put a foot wrong, they said. The rooms seemed luxurious to them. There must be a catch in it. After sleeping in mud and rain, in dust, on bare dry earth, on corrugated bamboo, on lumpy rubber and bare iron in dank holds, this seemed "like being allowed to eat anything you liked—the night before you were hung," Buck said.

There were ten rooms on each floor. Each room had twelve *tatami* mats. These were each about six feet by three. Japanese rooms are made to take just so many mats and each makes a bed space. *Tatami* is rice straw plaited an inch or so thick on to a wooden frame and is springy. At the head of each mat, by the wall, were twelve neat piles of bedclothes that astounded them. Each contained a thin padded mattress and a cotton-filled top cover. All were new and of beautifully flowered materials that seemed like silk to them. Their own mildewed bits of blankets and canvas showed them what they had come to. Alongside these fine-coloured covers they felt uncouth. On one wall was a high shelf of scrubbed wood. On the other side of the room was a deep open space across which, waist-high, ran another shelf. Their spare clothes had to go on the high shelf and be meticulously folded. On the other went their toilet gear; and on the floor under it, their boots, lined up like guardsmen. But, for the moment, most of these items were non-existent. Teeth had been cleaned with the frayed ends of bamboo; soap they had not seen for more than a year. To talk of spare clothing to men who had travelled from Singapore to Japan in only multicoloured underpants and cotton singlets was to talk philosophy to a tiger. They were allowed only the barest necessities in the rooms. Footwear had to be taken off at the door. This was a sensible Japanese custom that saved the *tatami* from being cut up, or dirt from being walked in. Packs and other stuff were taken to a store and locked away. This kit store was a billiard room which the mining company had provided but which the guards forbade. The men had to watch their rough packs piled on the table itself. No cut-throat razors or knives were allowed; no pencils or paper. John managed to hide some behind boards, with a pencil that, during searches, lay under his tongue.

They managed to borrow some soap and converged on the bathroom. This was a square building behind the cookhouse, and joined to the boiler house. The boiler was fired by old timbers from the mine, and it supplied steam to the bathroom and cookhouse. The bathroom had a concrete floor with a fifteen-foot square in the centre sunk some three feet and now filled with water into which a steampipe blew, heating it. A square lip about a foot-high ran around the bath's edge. Scattered along it were square wooden dippers which the naked men used to wash themselves with. The Japanese way was to wash off and then climb into the bath and sit on little wooden stools up to your neck, and soak in the hot water. But the American and Dutch doctors they had there forbade this because, they said, it would spread skin diseases.

After the bath the Australians went back to their rooms feeling clean, warm and satisfied. They sat in luxury on their *tatami* mats and soft bedding. It was more than two and a half years since they had really lived indoors.

"I just don't believe it," Harry said.

"Well, Buck, what about it now?" Alec said.

"Right now I wouldn't call the king my uncle . . . I just couldn't be bothered being miserable," Buck said as he lay back on the richly flowered mattress with his half-grown hair and patchy stubble he had tried to scrape with a rusty razor-blade.

"Buck," Boof said, "you look like the King of Siam on the dole without his harem."

"You can keep the harem . . . just leave me the mattress . . . I'll trade you ten wives for a small chunk of soap!"

Jock Geddes was their acting room-leader. "It will be all right tonight . . . they won't say anything . . . but you are not supposed to have your bed down until after *tenko*, unless you are nightshift."

They fired dozens of questions at him, about the camp, the mine and the guards.

"On the whole they are not too bad. The *Shookoo* is all right, but the sergeant stands over him and makes him do things he wouldn't do otherwise . . . he's an old school teacher . . . a Japanese gentleman really . . . he's not cut out for this . . . but the bloody sergeant keeps him up to it."

"The sergeant . . . that big black bastard . . . the Ape . . ."

"Yes . . . we call him the Ape . . . the corporals are not bad, but like the guards who are local civvies, they are frightened of the Ape and this can make them proper bastards too . . . watch the Mamba."

"Who's the Mamba?"

Just then Tanaka came to the door and smiled in at them.

"Well, you guys, settling in all right? I guess this is better than Siam."

"You're not kidding, mate, what's the catch?"

"No catch . . . these people are not the Army . . . you'll find them all right."

They forgot he was Japanese. He seemed so frank and spontaneous that they trusted him. At one time he even used the phrase 'these little yellow men'. He left them to visit the next room, and went from one to the other putting the men at their ease.

"A good interpreter's half the battle."

"I wouldn't say too much in front of him, just the same," Jock warned them.

"He'd be all right, surely . . . he's Yank!"

"Yes, and he's Nip too . . . he understands too well what we say . . . you can't get away with double talk with him . . . he knows all the slang . . . watch him!"

"But the way he spoke here!"

"That's to throw you off . . . he listens outside the windows some nights . . . you know how thin the walls are . . . we've had blokes beaten up, and we know it's him."

A bell rang and there was a hoarse shout.

"Grub up! Come and get it or we'll throw it out!"

The dining-hall was a long cement-floored room with three rows of wooden tables and stools, bare and scrubbed. At one end was a counter to the kitchen. Here the rice was weighed out dollop by dollop: just so many grammes each. This was arrived at by weighing the whole meal first and dividing by the number to be served. To make sure that there was enough to go around, the answer was slightly reduced to allow for what stuck to the tub and so on. As a further precaution each scoopful was slapped on the scales in a way that made sure they tipped. It was tipped into the waiting dixie before the scales had a chance to bounce back, and the man's number was crossed off the list. As well as the rice there was a small measure of soup on this night, and it smelled exceptionally savoury to the new men.

"Meat!"

"Horse . . . horse guts!"

"More flavour than snake, anyway."

"We get about thirty pounds every third day or so . . . sometimes."

There was also an apple a man.

"Bread, soup, fruit, sit up to tables on a seat," Harry said, "We're IN!"

"Don't bank on it, chum," a passing Welshman said sourly, "or you'll be bloody disappointed, man!"

That night they did not sleep as well as they thought they would. Tossing in the night, with the others restless also, Harry said, "I miss the discomfort."

2

They now had new tricks to learn. There was the close contact with the guards and their punctilious insistence on salutes and bows and dress and rules they had not yet learnt.

On the first night at *tenko* they had paraded and each room was reported to the duty Japanese. It left them hoping that they would never have to try to make that mumbo-jumbo report themselves. When Jock had given the report, they had looked at him as if he were Einstein.

"You'll pick it up," he assured them.

"Like buggery," Buck said, "not as long as my ought points down."

They had listened to the approach of the rounds. Cooped up in the rooms now, they felt uncomfortable. The guards answered the room reports with hoarse shouts and grunts, not unlike the roars of British guards on parade. But to the prisoners it sounded uniquely Japanese. Each volley came one room nearer, like an approaching threat.

"Are they always like this?" Harry muttered to Jock.

"Sometimes, but I think the Ape is trying to impress you blokes."

"We're impressed," Buck said. "He can knock off now."

Then suddenly the Ape was at the door with the duty guard and the prisoners' commanding officer, adjutant and sar'major standing dutifully behind him. In the room the men were lined up.

"*Kiotski!*" Jock shouted.

The Ape stiffened.

"*Kerei!*" shouted Jock again from the taut position of attention. All men bowed stiffly together, from the waist with backs straight and eyes fixed on the floor ahead of them.

Grasping his sheathed sword with his left hand, the Ape returned the salute with his right hand, for he wore a cap. He looked them all over closely. His eyes hesitated a fraction of a second longer on Boof. The Ape had been the biggest man in the camp. For an instant his eyes narrowed and his mouth tightened.

"*Na-oru!*" and they jerked upright again. Jock made the room report. "*Suing: juu-ni mai. Geko: nash. Gunsuing: juu-ni mai. Mai kits: nash. Sushin: nash. Imasitu: nash. Tanko shotai: nash.*" (Room total: twelve men. Absent: Nil. Parading: twelve men. Men short: nil. Sick in room: nil. Camp hospital: nil. Mine party: nil.)

The duty guard was looking at the board just outside the door. It was a wooden board with rows of small hooks on which small wooden *tenkens* hung, each with a man's number on it in Japanese. This showed where he was supposed to be: Room, Walk, Dining-room, Benjo, Camp Work, Mine Work, Bathroom, etc. Now the guard was checking to see all the tickets said the same as the report. If some one had forgotten his ticket there would be trouble. The guard called "*Hai!*"

Jock gave another *Kerei!* and then *Na-oru!*

The Ape saluted and grunted, "'*Sme!*" and they stood at ease as his iron-shod heels measured the distance to the next room.

The next fourteen days were spent getting ready for the mine work. They were taken for walks along the Inland Sea past the little rocky point with small twisted pines clinging to it, toward Motoyama where there was another coal-mine with more prisoners working there. But they had no contact with them. They were surprised to find out how hard these walks of only a couple of miles had become. They realized how ship-bound they were.

They were issued with mine working-clothes. A pair of split-toed rubbersoled boots; a pair of black hessian-like trousers which reached just below their knees; a short black coat of the same stuff, with sleeves reaching midway down the forearm; and a miner's cap with a composition piece on the front to stick the lamp into. Lastly they were given a thick rubber belt to strap the battery on their hip. Their numbers on the white calico patches had to be worn at all times. Each man had his photo taken wearing his number, and these were stuck up on a board in numerical order at the guardhouse.

"Have you seen the photos?" Buck said one day. "What a collection! . . . not a smile in a cartload . . . our cropped skulls . . . we look like death warmed up . . . bloody murderers, the lot of us . . . you could hire any one of us to haunt a house— any day . . . when I got on to mine, I frightened myself."

In the camp the Ape kept them on the jump by making sure he had the guards on the jump too. They had to put up with petty persecutions over saluting, matters of dress, leaving rooms without changing *tenkens* and so on. There was slapping and standing to attention for hours outside the guardhouse with sporadic abuse and humiliation. And they were pulled out at all hours for periods of drill in saluting and bowing, because someone had not saluted properly. The Ape was making sure that they knew who was the real boss. The old schoolmaster officer somehow just had to stand by and watch all this abuse without lifting a finger.

"I don't believe he could," Harry said, "the Ape would top him off . . . say he was collaborating with the enemy, or some bushido bull . . . it's the system, I reckon."

Sometimes after *tenko* at night they were made to kneel on the hard boards of the corridors with the guards moving up and down behind them to slap indiscriminately at the least waver or whisper. Sometimes they made them hold their arms above their heads as well. It was a peculiar situation where the Ape and his underlings could thus take their spite out on the prisoners, while the officer, who was otherwise genuinely concerned for their welfare, was powerless to stop it.

They were taken out of the camp on surface working-parties "until you are fit to go underground," the officer said. They dug roads and tracks under a mine foreman. Sometimes they carried old mine-timbers from the mine yard for the kitchen and boiler fires. Their foreman's name was Tomito San. He was a quiet, steady well-built man in his forties, about five-feet-ten, direct and manly. He treated them as men, but not weakly. They liked his straightforwardness which never varied. To be with him after the frightening unpredictability of other Japanese they had met was pleasant indeed. They liked this man. So, instead of Tomito San, they called him Tomato Can. They were sure he understood, yet he did not resent it. He had been an athlete and held boxing medals—unusual for a Japanese then.

"You know," Harry said, "he's one of the most handsome jokers I have seen—Nip or anyone else."

The day came to be taken down the mine. The *Shookoo* himself led them. They were split into three shifts, and each went down separately. Each man drew his lamp and battery at the lamp room, where girls attended to the battery recharging and issuing. They were a gay crowd and ready for a joke. The men threaded their rubber belts through the lugs of the batteries. They were 'wet' batteries filled with acid. The wire from the battery went up their backs to the lamp fitted in the front of their caps. They made their way to the mine entrance. Above it was a small shrine to which some of the miners sometimes bowed before they went down.

The entrance was a hole going down toward the sea at a steeper angle than that of the hill. By the time they reached the shore they were below it. The tunnel was a wet log-and-mud stairway. After some time they came to the junction of another tunnel, also coming down from the surface. It brought the coal

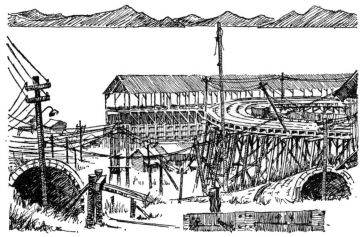

The entrance was a hole going down toward the sea

trucks and the flat cars with the timbers. A rake of empty trucks came rattling down on the end of a steel cable. On the front was a noisy miner riding it like a cowboy and shouting *HAKO!* . . . *HAKO!* giving warning to get out of the way. At the bottom he unshackled the empties and shackled on a rake of full trucks. He gave a signal on an electric bell to the distant *makki* driver on the surface and away he went like a retreating echo *HAKO* . . . *Hako* . . . *hako* . . . thinning with the metallic clacking of the wheels over jointed rails. There was very little room between the sides of the trucks and the walls.

"What do you do if you get caught in the Drift with a rake coming?"

"Hug the sides between the timbers and make sure your feet don't slip . . . or you'll be under the trucks . . . a Nip lost a leg a couple of months ago."

They went through the dimly lit tunnels. Along the centre, overhead, a pair of wires carrying 110 volts for the lighting ran from timber to timber.

At long intervals were small yellow globes giving a weak jaundiced glim to the dark dank timbers which carved thick slices of jet-black shadow out of the air. Water seeped and flowed over everything. The lighting wires were patched and joined so that no piece was more than twenty feet long. Many of the joins were bare, some were wrapped around with yellow insulation tape the ends of which hung down at varying lengths, dripping water. Often they were up to their ankles in mud and their knees in water. Water flowed in streams in drains at the sides of the drifts into sumps where the electric pumps worked continuously to keep the mine workable. They learned the value of the split-toed boots in this slippery place.

The *Shookoo* through Tanaka, who did not like being below, pointed out the danger spots in the roof, bad timbers, and so on. "Be careful at all times" was what he kept saying.

They saw some of the British down there.

"Watch'er, Lofty. Watch'er, Jock. Watch'er, Jimmy. How's she go, Di?"

"You'll be sorry."

"Resign while you have the chance . . . don't sign the dotted!"

"Stay on top."

"Go sick . . . break a leg."

"There's no future in it, man."

Often they had to crouch as they went. With heads thus bent forward, the peaks of their caps prevented them from seeing upward. They would brush the dangling dripping insulation-tape hanging from the lighting. Then there would be a violent galvanic jolt in their necks, and sometimes a blue spark would jump from the peak of their cap to their nose. They would be knocked suddenly sitting in the mud as if from a deliberate blow.

"What a bloody joint," Buck said, "I told you!"

They came to the surface again, not very sure. *Yasume* day was on every tenth day. Then the shifts changed over. After the next one, in a few days, they were to start digging coal. Three shifts, *Ichi Shotai*, *Ni Shotai*, and *San Shotai*. Morning, afternoon and night. 6 a.m. to 2 p.m.; 2 p.m. to 10 p.m.; 10 p.m. to 6 a.m.

"I can hardly wait," Buck said.

It was autumn—blue skies, warm, light breezes. They had just finished their morning meal and lined up for their mine ration—a small portion of boiled rice deducted from the other meals. Each had been issued with a *bento hako*, a food box, which was small and light with dovetailed corners and a lid which tied on. It was ten-to-six as they lined up on the roadway between their

Up to the gate

dormitory and the dining-room. The sar'major called their numbers with free remarks about characters and pedigrees of the late ones. He did not want any trouble on the first day. Satisfied that he had them all, he marched them up to the gate, halted them, turned them into line and, saluting the duty corporal, reported them. Then a private called their numbers with a forced bellow that mutilated the sounds and made it very hard for the men to guess which was their number. Their numbers were in the two- and three-hundreds. There are several alternatives for the Japanese numbers. For instance: *yon* for *shi* because *shi* is associated with death and is often avoided—just as the cultivation of camellias was in early days because the heads fell so easily, just as did people's heads then. And there were others. There were mistakes which brought bad-tempered shouts of *bageera* and *kaneera*. They were glad when they were turned and heard the order *S'p'ts'* which was *sapatsu* meaning 'forward'.

At the mine they filed past the window at the lamp room and drew their lamps from the girls, calling their numbers. Some said, Robert Taylor, Spencer Tracy, and Charlie Chaplin. The girls giggled, for those names were more familiar to them than the men guessed. They also made jokes in Japanese which kept the men guessing, but both laughed together. The men liked the girls for no other reason than that they were pleasant and wholesome.

"Makes you feel more human," Buck said.

They were now in the mine and going down the seemingly endless flight of muddy log stairs taking them under the sea. They had been split into gangs and each had picked up its 'gaffer', a term the British used to call the timberman who had charge of them.

"Good little sorts," Harry said. "You wouldn't mind them for sisters."

"I know what I'd like them for. . . ."

"So do I. . . . It's bastards like you that get us locked up at night."

"A-h-h, they're only slit-eyed wogs. . . ."

"No wonder they called us barbarians . . . it's bastards like you . . . they could have called us much more . . . you're twisted, mate . . . crook on the world because it's not all your knockin'-shop . . . you never grew up in the head."

"I . . . who do you . . . why . . . bloody wowser . . . you're *pro-Nip!*"

"I still say they are good sorts . . . too bloody good for *you*. . . . Now, want to make something of it?"

"You know bloodywell I've had malaria . . . you big blokes . . ."

"Pity the wog didn't take your blood count down enough to get your feeble mind off the old business."

"You're *hard* . . . no . . ."

"And you're dumb . . . shut up and look at the scenery."

"What scenery?"

They were going down in single file and their lamps shone on the back of the man in front, or made flashing highlights and blacks around them as they turned. There seemed to be no end to the long procession of square timber arches.

"Are we pointed toward Australia?" Buck said. "With a bit of luck . . . think they'd notice if we went a bit too far?"

They were carrying the timberman's tools between them. Buck had the saw, *noko*, which cut when you pulled it, not when you pushed. Harry had the light miner's pick, *tourabashi*, with a blade one side and a stubby hammer on the other. Boof had the *eoki*, the hammer-headed hatchet. But the gaffer carried the tin *tenkens* himself.

"He doesn't trust us," Jimmy said. Jimmy was the English pickman with them. The *tenkens* were imprinted with a number in Japanese so that a tally could be kept of what they sent to the surface. They would be stuck in a special hole in the ends of the trucks to be pulled out as they dropped down to the tipping ramp. Each truck held a good cubic metre.

"They've got more confidence in me than I have," Buck said.

Jimmy spoke to the gaffer as they went along. "*Suki San, tenken takusan-ca?*"

Suki held them up. "*Takusan . . . Konnichi sagio takusan . . . san-juu-go.*"

"Thirty-five bleeders . . . he says tonight plenty work."

They pantomimed fatigue and sickness. They told him he was Nippon not Hitler. Boof said, "*San-juu-go damme-do-no!*"

"Strike me! Hark at old Boof, he's getting the lingo like a native."

"*Sukoshi presento,*" Harry said to Suki, not to be outdone.

"*Nani?*" Suki said in mock horror, "*Sabatagoo . . .*" After a while he said, "*O.K.-da . . . go . . . O.K. ca?*"

"Five . . . not bad, for a start," Jimmy said.

"Why? Will he give us more?"

"No . . . But there are more ways of skinning a cat."

"Shifty, eh . . . Jimmy you surprise us colonials. . . ."

So they said to Suki, "*Airoshi, bagoose!*" (throwing in a bit of Malay).

"*Airoshi, Suki oto san,*" Jimmy said.

"*Arigat'* "

"What was that?"

"I said, lovely—Suki our daddy."

Boof laughed a deep laugh that made Suki grin. "Listen, you mob," he called down the line, "don't you call us bastards anymore—we got a daddy!"

A little further on Boof said to Suki, "Good on yer, mate—you'll do us." But Suki did not understand.

Suki stopped and stepped aside. He took the *tourabashi* and dug a little hole in the wall behind the timber and buried the five *tenkens* there. He did it shrewdly with a nice mixture of caution and confidence.

"He's done this before ... he's as cunning as a *benjo* rat," Harry said.

They came to a wide junction in the main. This was where San Coda and Ni Coda divided. They kept to the left into San Coda. There was a striking difference between these two branches of the mine. Although the whole mine was under the sea, the water that ran through Ni Coda was fresh, while San Coda was salt. The pumps were constantly going. If the sumps silted up and were not cleared then the pumps themselves were flooded and submersible portable pumps had to be brought in for the emergency. It was a poor mine and probably only the war kept it open. There seemed to be more maintenance than production. Even now, with things 'normal', they waded considerable distances along rails with the water over their knees. The slippery bottom held unexpected bits of wire and metal which penetrated wet rubber boots as if they were butter. Many a poisoned foot started this way. In the parts where the roof was low they had to stoop and be careful to dodge those gleaming, dripping ribbons of insulation that dangled down like so many little snakes ready to strike. When they forgot, these galvanic little serpents bit without hesitation. The lighting was dim, rather mapping out the mine than illuminating it—putting a faint glow on the blackness without lighting any objects within it.

They came to the last 'dip' where the rails doubled to allow the shunting of the full trucks past the incoming empties. It was dry today showing a thin layer of silt, for it had not long been pumped clear. They started to climb the last hill to the end of San Coda, near which was the heading they were to work on their first shift underground.

The Hako Boy had just shackled on a rake of empties. Outside each heading on the way up, he would leave a few, but the majority would be left at the conveyor at the top. Several times during the shift the full ones would be dropped down and more empties brought in. Electric winches, called *makkis*, hauled up and lowered down the trucks on a wire rope.

Some of the men asked the Hako Boy, "*O.K.-ca? Hako-sampo?*"

"*O.K.-da. Speedero.*"

A lot of them climbed in the trucks and crouched low.

"Silly bastards," Jimmy said. "Someone'll get killed one day ... there's no headroom in places ... it only needs one timber to be broken, or a bit down, and it'll tear into the tops of the trucks before they could yell out."

Without waiting to see all men aboard, the Hako Boy rang his bell twice for the go-ahead and the trucks jerked away with gathering speed, rocking and clacking over the uneven rails and fading almost at once to a distant receding noise. As they walked on, at short intervals they could hear the sound of the bell in the distance (One: *stop*. Two: *go*. Three: *back*) as the Hako Boy dropped his trucks off and raced on. He was eager to get rid of the whole rake so that he could snatch some time on his back on a comfortable platform he had built of *shimbuns* alongside the *makki* up there. He did not seem to pause an instant until he finally flung himself down on his bed—at about the same speed as he rode the trucks up the main.

They came at last to their heading, after walking for a full thirty-five minutes. It branched to the left from the main. Eight trucks had been left for them. So far the heading had gone in about thirty yards. It was new. This meant that, for the time at least, they would work in relatively good conditions. But time and pressure would alter that.

Jimmy went in, looked at the coal-face and at the roof, quickly sizing up the situation that meant nothing to the newcomers.

"Just as I expected, those irks are always dripping about others, and they leave it like this ... no timber ... not a spoonful of coal ... trouble is we will never get *them* following *us*."

Suki looked at it. "*Damme-do-no,*" with a rising moan of tragedy that finished with a little squeal of disapproval. "*Bageera!*"

"Pack o' bastards," Jimmy said. "Well, it's experience for you—we start from scratch." He turned to Suki. "Timber ... more *ich' hachi shaku* ... *O.K.-ca?*"

"*O.K.-da* ... *hachi shak'*."

"Back down the main a bit, chaps, there's a few on the side ... pick a good one ... *hachi shak'* ... a *shaku's* the same almost as our foot."

"We're learning," Harry said.

"With this shifty crowd ahead of us you'll learn *all* the tricks ... but from the wrong bloody end."

Harry and Boof went for the timber.

Jimmy took a *tourabashi* and started to cut into the side walls to get a good bottom and a snug fit for the vertical legs called *ashi*. The top cross-piece was the *ari*. Jimmy also trimmed into the roof to make a good fairway so that when in place, all the timbers would be squeezing firmly. They measured the legs and Suki, from long practice, cut them at just the nice angle for set so that the *ari* would slip on to them with its angled notches at the ends. Jimmy took the *eoki* and was busy making wedges while Suki was cutting with his pulling saw. It was not long before these men mastered the art of timbering. They found that even among themselves they used the Japanese terms naturally as words of immediate significance.

Boof and Harry came back. "Had to carry the bloody thing with our chins on our knees like a pair of camels ... a man needs to be suffering from duck's disease to get around this place." As they dropped the log, Harry said, "Well ... there she is, China ... eight wet slippery *shakus* ... you know what to do with it ... I suppose ... I'm not being rude, Jimmy, only I haven't the foggiest—and it's too wet for firewood."

Jimmy put a couple of saw-cuts in it near the ends and then shaped the notches with the hatchet.

"You'd made a good shipwright, Jimmy," Alec said.

"Nothing in it, you'll soon catch on. . . . Right ... now ... see if she fits."

Two held up the legs and two pushed the cross-piece up. Jimmy and Suki watched it critically. "Push her in."

Boof and Harry grunted. "I think there's a bit of the world in the way," Boof said.

"Right . . . hold her away a tick," Jimmy said, chipping at the roof. "Now try."

"One end," Harry said.

"Drop your end a little, Boof . . . hold it . . . this bit here . . . now try."

"Almost, not quite . . . it's on, but not right across."

"It will . . . just a bit more *yakki* out of here . . . there . . . push . . . like a glove."

Jimmy turned the *tourabashi* around and gave a couple of good blows with the head. "Home," he said. "Home like a draft-dodgin' civvie . . . hardly needs the wedges—but we'll put them in to save trouble later . . . you'll be surprised how she moves down here." He drove the wedges on the inside between the cross-piece and the uprights, forcing it hard against the roof.

"Nothing in it," Alec said.

"They don't all go as easy as that . . . you'll see."

"Phew! It's stuffy down here . . . always like this? Dead clammy!"

"I'm sweating like a pig."

"No air," Jimmy said. "Always like this after *yasume* day . . . be all right when we get the pick going—that'll give us a bit of air."

He took up the pick from where the previous shift had left it and gave it a couple of bursts like a machine gun. He looked at its point and said they'd want another one next shift.

"*O.K.-da*," Suki said.

"We start from scratch, fellas . . . no coal down . . . no timber . . . and it won't be long before we've got to lay more rails . . . the throw-back's getting a bit long . . . but we won't stop now—there's enough of us for a double throw to the trucks . . . well . . . here we go chaps—only thirty trucks to go."

"Don't this timbering business count?" Harry said.

"Just a bit of handicap they throw in . . . I'd better knock down a bit of *sumi* instead of maggin'."

The trucks were spragged with a bit of timber in the wheels above the points of their heading at the junction. They released a couple, dropped them down, and pushed them in. It was up-hill into the heading, it always was, so that the full trucks came out by gravity. On the wet rails they usually had to sprag a wheel to stop the trucks taking charge and getting away, or tumbling.

Jimmy, pale and small, his cap lamp throwing a circle of light on the coal-face, was hard at work, totally engrossed. His coat was off and with every movement of the heavy pneumatic pick in his bent arms his muscles kept coming and going under the thin skin like a boxer's. The bridge of Jimmy's nose was not quite straight, his teeth were good and large. In his black pants,

Jimmy's nose was not quite straight

crouched there boring into the coal, it was not hard to think of him in similar boots weaving before an opponent in a rope ring with the same intent expression. That is what had unstraightened his nose. He was stronger than many more powerfully built men.

"Our little Jimmy's a take," Harry said. "He'd be a surprise for some blokes I know."

"We're lucky," Boof said. "There's a lot of Poms I wouldn't like to be with . . . you wouldn't feed some of them."

The pick was roaring like a motor-bike and the point gave off a chattering ring above the roar. It filled their narrow cavern and shouted conversation sounded as if it were coming from very far away. *Pickonomi* was the Japanese for this pick. They had accepted it as just its name. But later when the fleas in camp bit and multiplied they could see how the Japanese had named it thus. The pick vibrated and jumped about as the air-driven piston hammered up and down as lively as a flea. *Nomi* is the word for flea.

At last Jimmy stopped the pick and put it down. Wiping his arm across his forehead he said, "That's a start."

Suki had hung the *tenkens* on a piece of hooked wire at the side, but now there was no sign of him. They poked the wire of the *tenkens* through the hole in the end of the truck. "Now all you have to do is fill the bastards—thirty of them," Jimmy said. He said 'bastards' with a short 'a' like the Americans. The Australians said it as if they had borrowed the first syllable from a Merino sheep. "Oh, I forgot . . . take your lamps off. . . . One'll be enough if you hang it up . . . unclip the tops, else we won't have a light to take us out."

"Where's Suki?"

"He's all right . . . he's left it to us . . . tools are here if we need 'em . . . he'll be back a couple of times, maybe . . . he's got a cubby hole in an old heading somewhere . . . give him a go and he won't bother us . . . better like that."

"Won't we see any Japs?"

"Oh yes . . . keep your eyes skinned for Okada . . . he's the shift foreman for San Coda."

It was a double throw-back from the face to the trucks. Boof heaved it back almost to them, and others filled. From time to time they changed about. With a spragged wheel they took the full ones down and pushed the empties in. It went pretty smoothly. But after a number of shifts they began to see some of the things that could go wrong. Many parts of the mine were on the move because it was overworked. They got the tale from somewhere that this mine had used German prisoners of war in the First World War. They had no way of knowing how true this was, but they accepted it.

"The wheel's turned a full circle now," Harry said. "It's *our* turn *ima*."

Over a long time, headings had been driven everywhere. Old disused mains were collapsing and flooded, filled with old logs and fallen earth. Now, the new headings kept cutting across these. Digging through solid ground is relatively safe because it will support a roof and timbers only have to be put in every so often. But, going through a collapsed heading is only penetrating a heap of rubble that collapses like clay as it is dug into. So they had then to creep forward an inch at a time, trying to hold the roof up with *shimbuns* which were rough-sawn flat pieces. Timbers had to be put almost alongside each other instead of from four to six feet apart.

But, without ever encountering these honeycombings, they still suffered from their effects. The coal lay in bands or strata of about six feet or less. But not in horizontal layers, for the folding of the earth's crust turns them into undulations that we can see on the surface as synclines or anticlines. The weight of the earth and sea above press down on everything below. If there are spaces there then, on the slopes, this terrific downward pressure is deflected sideways. This movement distorts, presses down and out, and breaks or buries the timbers. The trucks cannot pass them. New timbers have to be put in. In some places, after making their headings a full nine feet high at the start, within a month these had been pressed so low that the trucks could not clear the roof which had come down. This meant cutting a new roof, and replacing all the timbers. The cutting-out of enough of the old timber to make room for the new was a nightmare. It was exasperating sawing and hacking at wet, stubborn wood that had been driven into the clayey rock and which, though loose, refused to give itself up.

Though it was hard getting coal, there was some satisfaction in it when things went normally. But these other continual handicaps seemed to bring all the satisfaction to nothing. It was not so much that they wanted to produce coal for Nippon, they just wanted to feel they were getting somewhere. Much of the horror of being a prisoner was from this treadmill feeling. Like a slow internal bleeding, it was draining them. Some worried about it a great deal, wondering if, when they were finally freed, they would have any initiative left. Others countered by doing as little as they could get away with as a wholehearted enterprise. Doing nothing became a positive end in itself.

"A lot of them are just bludgers, anyway," Harry said, "but others will get sucked in if they are not careful . . . and finish up real bludgers like the rest . . . when they get back they'll reckon the world owes them a living . . . playing the 'Old Digger' racket round the pubs . . . I was a prisoner of the Japanese . . . they did

terrible things to us . . . you wouldn't believe it, Sir (real crawly)
. . . could you spare a couple of bob, I'm on the pension . . . I
can hear 'em now!"

"Some of the First War diggers used to make me spew," Buck
said. "But there'll be a new crop after this show . . . doesn't take
a pro. to work that out."

"Right-o, Buck, chuck some more of that black stuff into that
truck before *you* get bludger's paralysis too," Boof said.

Sometimes, when the roof had pressed low and before they
retimbered, there was just a narrow slit left between it and the
top of the truck to shovel into. This called for a nice bit of
specialization. *Impey* was the Japanese word for shovel. To get
the coal to leave the shovel in a nice flat sheet and sail it into the
truck without losing any on the lip outside was something to be
cultivated. Harry said, "You know, I've developed a real
ingenious *impey* . . . just like posting letters . . . think I'll give
exhibitions when we get back."

"Oh, do!" Buck said. "It should thrill the crowds."

They had almost finished their eight trucks, but Jimmy said
to leave one empty in the main.

"Why?"

"You'll see when the Hako Boy comes down to pick up the
full ones."

Soon they heard the high-pitched voice of the Hako Boy
shouting at the entrance of the heading. "*Oi! Oi! Carabaco . . .
damme-do-no speederoo . . . Speederoo!*"

"Right," said Jimmy. "Now I'll show you about the empty
truck. Cut those trucks off there . . . that's enough in them."

They took the full trucks down to the main to the others they
had already placed below the points. Above was the long rake
from the conveyor that was worked by some fifty Koreans. They
had already filled twenty trucks. But this one empty was now
between these and their own, stopping the Hako Boy from
connecting them up and rushing on his way.

Jimmy said, "Buck and Alec, you come with me. Boof and
Harry, make out to push the empty in, but tumble it on the
points and give us a bit of time."

While the Hako Boy was fuming around Boof and Harry who
had got the empty off the rails, Jimmy and the others went up
along the rake into the darkness. "Right, now here you are . . .

take a couple of these *tenkens* . . . pull out theirs and put in ours."

"You shifty bastard, Jimmy, I'm proud of you."

They had to dig down the end of the truck with their hands to clear away the coal so that the wire could be pushed in. It was all done quickly, at the cost of only a few fingernails. Then, when they got the all-clear, Harry and Boof, with an apparent supreme effort, got the tumbled *hako* back on the rails and pushed it clear into the heading.

The Hako Boy said, "*Kichigai, damme damme!*"

"What's he say?" Boof asked.

"Crazy, no-good."

"He's half right."

The bell went, the shouting man and the rumbling trucks diminished down the main.

There was no gas in the mine, so smoking was allowed. The prisoners were issued with five cigarettes a day at this time. They called them *kinchis* and they were allowed to take only two down the mine. It did not matter that there were no matches, for a simple lighter had already been devised: a piece of wire stuck into a piece of wood. The 110-volt lighting in the mains provided many bare patches without insulation. They simply placed the wire directly across these bare patches, making a dead short-circuit which quickly made the wire glow red-hot. It was then pulled off and the cigarette lit. Above the point where the light was being taken from, all went black until the wire was pulled off again. Everyone knew when somebody was getting a smoke. If it took too long the unseen and unheard in the dark would give way to rhetorical profanity, urging him to bloodywell hurry up, "He must be making toast!"

"I must try this when we get home," Boof said.

"Not at my place, my good friend," Harry said.

Some could get the wire hot without any wood. They held the bare wire that was a bit longer to take up the conducted heat. The trick was to make sure that you contacted both wires at *exactly* the same time, then no electricity flowed through you to earth. Getting it off required a quick flick, or you became part of the circuit. To be able to do this gave one a bit of assumed prestige. One thoughtless man, getting himself a bit of esteem, carelessly put his wire across a *makki* circuit—440 volts.

Luckily the violence kicked him clear on his back into six inches of water and discharged him. All he got was burns.

Suki came back some time later. "*Hako numeroo-ca?*"

"*Juu-nana*," Jimmy said.

"*Nani?*"

"*Juu-nana . . . sagio takusan!*" (Seventeen . . . work much!)

"*Hako chiisai-ca?*" (Hako small?)

"*Hako okii!*" (Hako large!)

"O.K. . . . *meshi, meshi.*"

They put down their tools, sat down on the coal heap or a log, wherever it was a little drier, and opened up their *bento hako's* and began their rice. It was a very small ration, but they chewed it slowly and made a meal of it. Suki pulled out his carefully wrapped chopsticks and began to shovel the rice into his mouth from his upheld box. Occasionally he would stop and, with a neat, deft movement, pick up a piece of pickled *dikon* from a small bowl and slip it into his mouth.

This was often a time of conversation between the prisoners and the timberman. They talked of his home life, he asked about theirs. They talked of the war and how it was going. These miners were not zealots. The rights and wrongs of the war were never mentioned. They seemed to accept the prisoners as part of the war, like themselves. War was just there—like flood, fire, famine, storm, earthquakes, taxing overlords and plague: for centuries the ordinary man had had to learn to get along with them as best he could—this was *not* fatalism, it was practical adaptation, a lifesaver. Maybe the gods or the devils sent these things, who knows? So these men were without hate. They did not like their own army at close quarters. To them it was an overbearing bureaucracy always taking for itself and leaving the civilians and their families very little—and this as a favour. Nor did they like the *B-ni-juu-ku's* (B29s) that were coming over now and bombing and burning them. When they spoke of them they showed fear but not hate, for they came like the typhoon and earthquake. Does one blame the wind?

"Fatalistic bastards," Arrow had said, "Just puppets—they can do what they like with them . . . that's what makes them so dangerous."

John had not argued. But surely there was more to it than this. The bamboo bends with the wind but is strong. The grasses are eaten and are trodden down and burnt in drought, but they multiply. Somehow, in this submission, this acceptance was the real strength of the people: the vestige of primeval wisdom still living. Since Eden, man had found more and more ways to exploit this non-resistance. It had become the hallmark of the

Shrine above mine entrance

sucker. But John could not forget how the *Bōyke Maru* had recalled the sermon of the grasses to him. Although these people were the enemy, something deep within him made him admire this quality, this characteristic. It seemed to him then that wars, poverty, exploitation and power-politics sprang from a neglect or loss of this quality. He liked these simple men. After all, if one wants a friend in adversity, the one who puts up with it rather than the I-demand-my-rights kind is the better mate.

Jimmy went down to the main and got a light. Buck borrowed it off him when he got back, so did Suki. Suki got out his little pouch containing his pipe and tobacco. The pipe was a *kiseru* and had a stem about six inches long and a silver bowl the size of a salt spoon. From his decorated metal container he took a pinch of tobacco and, between his thumb and forefinger, rolled it into a little pill which he slipped into the bowl. From Jimmy he got some hot ash which he held on the palm of his hand. Cupping it and turning the bowl on its side, he brought the tobacco to it and drew deeply until it glowed. In two or three draws the tobacco was nothing more than glowing ash. But he had another pill ready. Tipping the hot ash into his palm by a little puff through the pipe he recharged the bowl. With the same movement as before, he lit it.

"Get a long way in a long time, that way, mate," Harry said.

"*Nani?*"

"I said, it's good . . . *Airoshi*."

"I don't know," Alec said. "There's more to it than that."

"Yeah, saves tobacco," Boof said.

"No, you have a look at the way he does it . . . those actions are pretty cunning . . . smooth . . . you wouldn't have to be ham-handed . . . reckon there'd be a bit of satisfaction being automatic but never missing . . . something like those blokes in the Middle East we used to see in the cafés . . . the blokes with the strings of beads they used to work round and round in one hand . . . get what I mean?"

Suki smoked about six small bowls and then carefully put the *kiseru* into its sheathlike pouch. He put it back in his pocket with the tobacco container.

"*Oi, kuke, kuke! Sumi takusan, hako takusan!*"

"Start," Jimmy repeated, "Plenty coal, plenty boxes."

Jimmy was working away, enveloped by the rattly roar of the pick. He kept glancing at the roof. Suddenly he stopped, looked intently at the face and jumped back, calling, "Look out!"

Boof, who was shovelling at the face, jumped back with him. The coal shivered and almost at once exploded into fine pieces. It burst out for four or five feet leaving a heap of coal ready-made against the face.

"That's all right," Boof said. "Made to order."

"All right if you don't get caught in it," Jimmy said.

"What caused it?"

"Pressure . . . went too far without a timber."

"How'd you guess it was going?"

"You get to know . . . hear something different . . . see a little bit of coal jump . . . little things, you know . . . can be dangerous if you are not quick enough."

"Had many accidents?"

"Not many . . . 'bout three months ago a heading came in and trapped three of our blokes . . . I suppose you've been told —but, if anything starts to fall in . . . don't try to run *out*, or you'll run right into it . . . The face is where the solid support is—always run to the face . . . it will hardly ever come in right up to there."

"What happened to the jokers?"

"They got to the face and there was enough space left . . . bit of luck . . . the air pipe came down but didn't break . . . they were able to keep the air up to them . . . three days before they got them out . . . in the dark, they said, they didn't know which way up they were after a while . . . you just can't tunnel through a fall . . . keeps coming in . . . they were a bit hungry when they got out. They gave them a few days off and fed them up . . . Billy Evans said it was worth it for the feed. . . . Di Dougie and Dougie MacArthur were the other two . . . they said Di spent the three days worrying about his donor back home—they were unchurched and now he doesn't think she's being true . . . what's he expect . . . he's no prize himself."

They found, as Jimmy had said, that it was easier to work without their lamps on and the heavy book-shaped batteries hanging on their hips. They got used to having the minimum lighting. Their world became one of blackness faintly etched with wet gleaming highlights here and there from a corner or a timber's edge. The faint glow at the mouth of the heading from the weak lights in the main was enough to lead them out with the full trucks although all else was a bottomless black. The merest adumbration of objects was enough for them to be able to move about with tolerable ease. But the pickman wore his lamp because he needed the light to see better where to drive his pick and to keep an eye on the roof.

The batteries became a nuisance because the acid spilt from them. If they had to do much stooping and bending with them on, then the acid would run out on them and burn. Luckily, there was always a good supply of water to wash down quickly with. But, with the most care, it was not long before their trousers were rotted and falling apart on the hips. These had to be constantly patched with any bit of rag they could lay their hands on, even the sleeves out of their coats. They had to be indecent before the Japanese would give them new clothes. The guards made a lot of fuss, accusing them of sabotage and neglect. But the Japanese themselves were, during that time, probably the most patched people in the world. Garments were patched and patched until the original was gone and the patches formed a sort of second-generation garment. But the prisoners did not have the skill, nor the tools, of the Japanese. They had only makeshift gear. Threads from fraying blankets, or bits of canvas, bits of string, wool from no-longer-recognizable socks—often a needle was no more than a thin piece of wire. With these materials and indifferent skill, the results were unique.

Because the batteries did not get enough time on charge between shifts, or because the girls got them mixed and issued the wrong ones, or because there were not enough of them, or because their life was almost spent anyway and they could not hold a charge, the lamps died early. It was not uncommon to see sixty men stumbling out, tired and irritable, behind one or two lamps that were fading even then, and it was a race against time. They cursed as they slipped and were jolted into profanity by fright when a wet dangling piece of insulation became a conductor and gave off a blue flash which cracked their necks with a spasm of shock. This was a time when patience ran out, when they wondered if they had slipped out of the real world into one which had no norms.

Boof said he wouldn't be surprised if a leprechaun showed up. But nobody ever reported one—even with an Oriental cast. But there was one wraithlike figure that never seemed to take on a plain reality. This was the *benjo*-man, whose job it was to bring down empty pans and take the full ones back to the surface. These were not sent up by rail, but were carried by this silent, ever-never-present little man in the black coat and trousers of innumerable pale patches. Never stopped, moving always with a swift, short, flat-footed stride over mud and obstacles as if they were not there, he carried the two pans at the ends of his bamboo pole with a smooth sedateness as if the Mikado himself were inside. Nobody ever heard him speak, nor anybody speak to him. They said he had to make so many trips a day, but he never seemed to knock off. Perhaps he had no home. Perhaps he was working out his *karma*. Perhaps he was in another life, separated from this one only by a thin transparent wall of time —on the next turn of the spiral. They did not even remember him wearing a lamp. Mystery was added by the fact that no prisoner ever found any of the *benjos* with which he played his ceaseless put and take.

Instead, they used the headings or mains fallen-in, piled high with broken and discarded timbers, and flooded. They looked like bare entombed primeval beaver dams, long forgotten. Not beaver, but rats lived there and took over the job of the *benjo-*man. They sat around on logs, watching, wrapped in long fur with large and shining eyes, and a look of doglike gratitude in the beam of the cap lamp. Their reflections were ghosts— transparent in the clear, limpid water that showed the fine silted bottom like a crystal. Beyond the beam of the cap lamp was a profound, silent blackness of such compelling quality that it was easy to imagine a whole new world being created from it. It had the inscrutability of Beginning. And, from this Beginning came life in exquisitely fine white filaments, more like a subtle imagined feeling than a thing. These lay themselves on the dark, wet timber as lightly as starlight on a leaf at midnight. Their stark whiteness seemed a complete renunciation of the dark—and yet here they had their being where there was no difference between black and white. Here, John thought, was wonder at its most wonderful: great beyond comprehension, simple beyond science. Were the filaments here, or not here? Life or not-life? Were *these* the threads that joined the tangible to the intangible? Was there, conducted along these threads from the mother-blackness of beginning, the stuff that made all-life? Did it come like this to our intuitive awareness? Was he looking at a point where the world-controlling wisdom of the cell was being born?

Despite the sweat, aches, exhaustion, plain discomforts and exasperations the work of the mine brought them, this wonder did much to lessen them for John. Many hated the mine with all their being. But now, to John, these places below the earth, below the sea, where man had taken what he could get and abandoned with unconscious ingratitude, became significant with a shrinelike quality. Here the unquestioning rat-priests lived like unspeaking monks about their business. Here in the blackness lay these filaments of the promise of life-to-come-again on the wet logs and stones as altars—a token of the only eternal life that matters, and a reassurance against the dedicated vandalism of man. To John, as in the heads of the grasses, here was another confirmation of a faith that could keep a man sane, even grateful, in adversity. A faith that needed no words and no personal favours.

The last three days of each month were a *Speedo*. All effort then was for coal production at the expense of maintenance. This was a time of vital statistics on which the whole month's production returns were based. The first part of the next month would be all maintenance. So the months went by, coming and going endlessly in and out of the dark nether world to the bickering prisoner-existence of the camp.

4

On each of the monthly pay days they assembled in the dining-hall and were paid by shifts. Mine officials attended out of what seemed to be a paternal interest—as if they assumed that among the prisoners and the employers there should exist an *esprit de corps*. The prisoners were sceptical, thinking this just another bit of Japanese duplicity, and remained suspicious always. For good work, *presento's* of soap and cigarettes were made. The prisoner received his gift with a perfunctory bow which was returned often with a genuine smile and occasionally a handshake. The guards present had to tolerate this but showed their disapproval by petty insistence in bullying voices on matters of drill. Later they would patrol the corridors looking for the slightest opportunity to 'even-up'. Here they saw, closer than ever before, the contradictory-seeming sides of Japanese character.

The mine officials seemed to accept them uncritically. They

had issued a number of *shirushi-banten, happi* coats. This meant, literally, a marked coat. It was a kind of livery which may have a family crest on its back signifying the donor, in the form of an ideograph or monogram. It was a loose coat worn over regular clothes. Theirs had a five-pointed star-flower in white on a black coat. On the white emblem were crossed *tourabashis*, the

Happi *coats*

badge of Ohama coal-mine. For a Japanese to receive one of these was a privilege which pays respect to his loyalty and acknowledges his service.

The Japanese workers in the mine also accepted them un-critically, showing only polite curiosity and some fellow-feeling. These miners seemed to have retained much more individuality than any of the guards or soldiers they had met. The resurgent dream of the militarists was less to these people than their pre-occupation with the daily effort of living.

They received their pay in pay envelopes notated entirely in Japanese: their number, days worked, total pay, cost against cigarettes, and net pay.

John brought an envelope home with him. *Sam-biaku-ni-juu-nana* (327) Days worked: 24; Total pay: 8 yen, 30 sen; Cigar-ettes: 2 yen 46 sen; Net pay: 5 yen 84 sen. But there was little to spend this money on. The canteen only opened on pay days. Tooth powder which seemed like marble dust in an envelope;

an occasional toothbrush or razor blade so rare that they were virtually non-existent—this and nothing else. For a short period there had been a kind of substitute tea. What it really was they never found out. But, brewed in boiling water, to the Australians it became redolent of the water of a sluggish creek into which eucalyptus leaves had fallen thickly and soaked black on the bottom. Nostalgia flavoured it.

Camp fowls also suffering avitaminosis

Their staple ration was only rice, despite slight additions. Cooked, it was a total of three teacups a day. Officially the scale read—Mine workers: 860 grammes a day; Surface workers: 720 grammes a day; Camp workers: 520 grammes a day; Sick: 420 grammes a day. The mine workers got four issues a day. The meal before going below was split and a small portion taken to work. Sometimes whale blubber came in and was rendered down and the oil mixed with the rice. The remainder, which the whalemen used to call 'fritters' and which they used as fuel under their try-pots, the prisoners called 'crackling'. It was put out on trays.

"Crackling! Come and get it! If you've got the guts!"

There would be a thunderous rush down the wooden corridors and stairs. Men would soon be squabbling like seagulls over it—seldom without a fight.

Sometimes they got green ginger roots. These they sliced thinly and poured hot water on. Meal after meal they would pour the hot water over the same pieces. As the flavour became more fugitive their taste became keener in pursuit. One lot would last them four or five days, after which the pallid remains would be eaten.

A few tangerines also came in. The pips were chewed carefully. Some ate the skins unceremoniously at once with the pulp. Some traded them. Others performed a fetishlike ceremony with them. John saw a major who did not have to go out to work spend a whole afternoon slicing some skin into the finest shreds. He put them from one container into another. He turned them over. He cut them finer yet. He picked them over again as if he were counting them. It was as if this orange peel had taken the place of his lost battalion. He had started cutting at two o'clock. That night, when he had collected his small portion of rice, he mixed the peel into it with the exactitude of a military manœuvre on paper. It took him more than an hour to march it all, in small hand-picked squads, down his gullet.

Salt was scarce. Surface workers in the mine yard kept a fire going all day down by the seawall. The old mine-timbers gave them plenty of fuel. Over the fire was a kerosene tin of salt water kept boiling and topped up. By the end of the day it was allowed to boil dry and the residue was scraped into their dixies. It was grey and had rusty streaks through it, but half a pint of salt got them thirty cigarettes. Men had stopped smoking because cigarettes had become better currency than money.

Food-consciousness was general. In some it had reached a morbid state. On *Yasume* days they had plenty to do. Camp chores, wood getting from the mine yard for the boiler house. They had clothes to patch, worn boots to mend. They bathed using a little more soap. They went through the agony of a shave with gapped and rusty blades. The jungle beards had been ordered off by the Japanese. Hair, too, had to be kept short. If it was long enough for the guards to pull it was too long. The guards with strong nails could manage to pull very short hair. There was only one pair of clippers in the camp. These were drawn from the Adjutant. When the clippers were out, the word went around and a queue formed. One man sat on an upturned tub and the next in line hacked away with the blunt

clippers which pulled as much as they cut. At last, either the
hair was short enough or the victim could stand no more. Then
the next man took his turn. Patchy white skulls showed through
the tufted and plucked heads.

Clothes to patch, worn boots to mend

"Gawd! Gabot Cook himself wouldn't be noticed amongst
this lot!"

Gabot Cook was a fictional Tasmanian convict who turned
cannibal.

The British and Australians had grown into a common
community. That is, what they had in common was slightly
more than their differences. There were still Pommy bastards,
and mookin' Orstrilians. They had a general idea of the war
situation. Before they had left Thailand, the Australians had
known about the Normandy landing. When they arrived in
Japan, they heard about the hold-up in Arnhem and found the
British in Ohama very pessimistic about it. The Americans were
creeping closer to *Akitsu-shima* (this land of joined dragonflies).

Each day a copy of *Mai Nichi*, the English-language newspaper, was placed in the *Shookoo's* office. Although it was sent in for the prisoners by outside authority, the Ape forbade it to be let out. But the copies were not destroyed, they were kept on the office shelf. The two prisoners, who were sent each day to clean the office, read what they could of the latest and took the bottom copy away with them. Thus the pile never grew larger nor less.

Uncertainty and impatience raised questions that nagged for answers. If Japan were finally invaded, what would happen to them? In the final death-or-glory stand which the Army said they would make, they could only expect a swift thumbs-down from their captors.

"We're not out of the bloody wood yet," Buck said.

They felt that the end of the war was approaching but, without melodramatics, it might well be a race with death itself. They were reminded of how close to the wind they were sailing. Men would go down with a routine sickness that they had weathered a dozen times before. But they would die, and the death spoke inwardly to each man.

5

They were night shift and asleep in their rooms. John awoke abruptly. There was a deathly silence, as if, while he slept, all sound had been murdered. It was time for his hourly pilgrimage. On the hour, like monks to prayers, their bladders took them down the long corridor to the *benjo*. John crawled out into the cold, leaving a hole in the bedclothes like an empty tomb. He looked out the window. The world had turned white. Hillsides were covered with smooth virginal white. It was as if some religious hallucination had taken him to some ethereal place. It would not have surprised him to have seen a flight of angels gliding in virginal robes in purposeless adoration of the vacuum. The snow had thickly covered Ohama with a pure sexless mantle. On the whiteness, in black calligraphy, the pines wrote a strong protest against this suffocating sterility. The houses too, roofs obliterated, showed here and there the man-made walls which added their square protestation to that of the trees. In the trees: sap. Within the walls: blood. From *these* the world would regenerate in spring . . . not from the chilling angelic purity of the snow. This thought flashed through John's half-awake mind as his incontinent bladder drove him to the *benjo*. He walked as two people: the detatched and the dispatched. He went back to sleep with these vague half-formed thoughts.

December and January brought the cold to these tropic-conditioned men. They were quite ungrateful for it. They shivered and, in bed, curled up into hard unmoving lumps holding the warm to their bellies like a child with a stolen toy. Some, on *Yasume* days, even refused to leave their beds for meals. The temperature stayed around 17 degrees Fahrenheit. They became eager to get down the mine, where it was so much warmer. The west wind howled across the sea on to them. It had travelled right across the frozen steppes of Siberia gathering up every gelid particle on its way. It jumped across the Korean Strait and blew them all down their necks. When they came up from the mine, wet through, they would have to stand about in this vindictive wind for sometimes nearly an hour, waiting for the last men out. With bare legs and thin short-sleeved coats and wet canvas boots they stood hunched, hugging themselves and shivering. The power lines were loaded with ice and down-pointed icicles in rows like the teeth of the wind itself.

They marched back to camp with cracking joints. After the afternoon shift it was almost midnight before they got back. The concrete bath would have little more than a film of water on its bottom. The water pipes would be frozen and the steam pipe cold. It was pitch dark, with only the ghost of night outside looking disinterestedly through the window squares. Blackout precautions were complete. They would wipe off the coal dust with icy wet rags and pull on their camp clothes and make their way to the dining-room. Here there was one miner's lamp for the whole place, and it was placed by the scales. In a silent queue they filed past, sliding their dixies on to the counter and waiting for their rice to be dumped in impersonally by the server who slapped it on to the scale so that it went down with a bang.

"There . . . that's it, matey."

"Now you see it . . . now you don't . . . you bloody juggler!"

Each man would make his way up the dim aisles between the tables and find a place. There was not much talk. They were tired. Their minds fixed on the waiting bed, and the shortness of the night. They chewed resolutely on their rice to make these few spoonfuls into a meal. Their champing jaws measured it out chew by chew, as if to cheat the cheat at the scales. Not one grain of rice escaped in the dark. The last time their spoons scraped the plates they knew as sure as fate that they had captured the last grain. But they always took their plates or dixies to that lone lamp—only to prove what they already knew. An amazing acuteness had come to their proprioceptory sense— the first to be given to them in their embryonic state and now resensitized to such vital purpose. They washed their dixies and went irresistibly to bed, lured, like wingless moths, by the black flame of sleep.

After the evening *tenko* they had fifteen minutes of exercises to keep them fit against the cold and colds. By Japanese order they stripped down to their trousers only. The exercises consisted merely of free and violent arm-waving, body-swinging and foot-stamping in the cold air. At the same time, they had to SHOUT at the top of their lungs. The guards went up and down the corridors making sure that this Bedlam remained at its peak. At first, feeling foolish, the men did not know what to say. So the Japanese led with various hauling cries. *Cor ... Nor ... OOSH!* Or, *Ich ... ni ... san ... HOOO!* Or, *OOO ... ISH ... AAAR! OOO ... ISH ... AAAR!* But soon the prisoners got the idea. It became self-expression for them, and the buildings became one great confused shout of vile insults against the Japanese—clear only to those near, but safely lost in the general uproar which was increased by gusts of laughter. Later they admitted that this method of warding off colds was not as silly as they had first thought it.

They were also subjected to morale-building on the subject of frugality. This inferred that their ration was more miraculous than microscopic. A story appeared on the notice boards in each building. It concerned a German boy whose family were so poor that they could not afford the usual foods. They ate only turnip tops and the things that people usually throw away. He never had any boots. But, bare-footed and turnip-top-fed, he became remarkably strong, full of endurance and intelligence. At school, by hard work, he rose above the others, went on to university and became a brilliant doctor. At athletics he made the others look novices. He wrote a great thesis on the enormous benefits of vegetable peelings and turnip tops.

"What do you think of it, Buck?" Boof asked. "Believe it?"

"Course I do! But do you think the bastards'll give us any?"

The men had torn strips from their blankets and sewn them across the backs of their raggy singlets. Old socks had also been soled with pieces, making *tabis* of them. All clothes were worn to bed. They had been given a Japanese Army tunic, a pair of trousers, and a light duffle coat. One of their troubles was to get their working clothes dry by the following shift. Often they had to wear them wet. A colonel visited the camp and ordered another blanket per man. He also ordered additional Oriental beef (soy-bean) as there was no other source of oil or fat for them. They got some beans, but no blankets.

The men now ignored the orders of their officers about the large bath. After washing off they climbed in and sat up to their necks on the small wooden stools. "Stoke up the bloody boiler! Blow her in!" they would chant. It was the only time they were really warm. It became a scandal centre, a gossip club and a raconteur's platform. With only their heads sticking above the water, they sang—looking like a small sea of John-the-Baptist's heads. It was a day-time thing only. The afternoon shift came back to just a few inches of cold water in the bottom. Next to getting some sleep, the comparative warmth of the mine made it the next best place. The cold in their rooms made them cringe.

6

A new conveyor was going to be opened. Boof and the others were sent to begin it. The way in that night was a wet one. At one of the dips, a hundred yards or so of the main had been flooded within a foot of the roof. They had to go through it. They took off their batteries and held them above their heads with their *bento hakos*, and waded up to their necks in water. Their chins skimmed the surface just a foot or so below the timbers of the roof. When they came to a dropped or broken timber, they had to sink their mouths below the doubtful water.

"You know," Boof said, "I don't think the Union is very strong in this mine—the delegates are not very active."

"I don't suppose," Harry said, "the delegates want to be seen walking around without their heads."

They walked out of the water on the other side, streaming.

"Like Captain Nemo's mob after 80,000 leagues under the sea," Buck said.

"Anybody cop any wire?"

Nobody had. But when walking in water there was no chance of seeing anything below it. Many sharp broken bits of wire were imbedded in the mud. The first they would know was a sharp stab right through their rubber soles. Often they hoped it would poison and give them a few days off. The fresh water of Ni Coda also caused 'foot-rotting'. Men would watch the festering condition develop hopefully. But the Japanese simply shifted them over to San Coda, where the salt water effected a gradual cure.

They walked on, draining off as they went. The timberman was just as wet as they were. At last they halted. They had come to the top of the drift. They put their food boxes in a safe place. The timberman began examining the wall. A short way up, the *makki* was in its niche on the opposite side. Some empty trucks had been left up here for them.

They took their clothes off and wrung them out.

"That's *my* bath for the day," Buck said.

"What if it's not pumped out when we go up?"

"Then it'll do for tomorrow too."

The timberman took his *tourabashi* and started to pick about at the wall. The *yakki* began to fall in a heap about him. "O.K.-da," he called. They dug a hole into the wall, about eight feet square. They shovelled the clayey *yakki* into the empty boxes and dropped them down for the Hako Boy to pick up. The hole was squared out and lined with stout boards right up to the roof. Then, on a platform, they continued to dig straight upwards. Instead of *yakki* they were soon digging into black coal.

"*Sumi!*" they said. "Another seam."

In ten days, with the other shifts, they had dug to the top of the seam, and driven out horizontally about sixty yards. The first hole was now boxed in to become the chute with a chopper door at the bottom to fill the trucks by. Alongside the chute was a narrow shaft with a ladder up which they climbed to the work above. A conveyor belt now ran along the tunnel they had driven out and it was powered by an electric motor they had hauled up into position. Then they dug out at right angles to this conveyor, throwing back the coal on to the moving belt that carried it to the chute. They were making what they called a 'ball-room' as opposed to a straight narrow heading.

About fifty prisoners worked this new place. After a while the throw-back to the conveyor became too long. The ballroom was getting too large. It was not timbered like headings because it was too wide in all directions. Instead they kept putting in small poles as props. On top of each they put a piece of flat *shimbun*. They cut the props a little long so that when they drove them vertical by banging the bottoms across, they were then tight. They put them in at five- or six-foot intervals. Soon they were in the middle of a small leafless forest. It became bigger with sinister recesses of blackness speared vaguely by the jerking flash of traversing cap lamps which jumped their beams from post to post. And lurking here, in the dark, was the demon of force.

The creaking world above them started like some awakening giant flexing himself. They felt like fleas in his bed—afraid that at any moment he would turn over and squash them. The props started to bend and snap with loud pistol-shots—sometimes quite close together. They replaced the cracking timbers, but they began to break almost as fast as they replaced them. They were new to this and it made them nervous. Some quietly, some with loud abuse of the whole Japanese system. Some showed no visible concern. But none was unaffected by the snapping props and creaking roof.

At last the Japanese called for the men to shift the conveyor up to the face. This would then feed into the conveyor at right angles to it that fed into the chute. They were told to stand with their backs against the face while the roof was collapsed. This seemed the last straw. Their nerves were not as good as they had thought. But there was nothing they could do. Admittedly, they could have run out down the ladder by the chute and waited in the main below. But they did not want to make fools of themselves. This is a kind of self-immolation almost as strong as the much-talked-about self-preservation. This was the self-preservation of an integrity. They watched fascinated, with their backs pressed against the coal-face. Some had to go among the lines of props and knock them out, working back. All the props were knocked out now except those close to the face. They now waited for the roof to collapse *between them and the entrance*. This was to be kept open by a line of thin poles along the other conveyor.

At first nothing happened but the nervous fidgeting of the tyros. Then there was a deep low kind of creaking and the first huge piece of roof fell. It was as big as a house. More and more, breaking as they fell, heaped high. Over this heap the roof continued to hollow itself upward as if clawing its way up to the sea bed. It seemed as big as the inside of the dome of St Paul's, London. They remembered that the mine, at one point, was only seven metres from the sea floor. Was it here? Would they be drowned without a chance—totally irrecoverable? Not that that matters to a dead man, but at the moment they were not dead and it seemed to matter. The prospect of being squashed flat and fossilized for millions of years seemed the worst possible kind of imprisonment. They stood, rooted, watching the roof falling at the edges and doming like a mouth above them as if preparing to swallow. Chunks fell within six feet of their rooted rubber boots and staring eyes. Then it stopped. Occasionally an odd lump detached itself and fell with a heavy thud—dull, like the contented rumblings of the earth's stomach.

"*Oi! Oi! Kuke . . . kuke . . . starto!*"

The ballroom was once again a narrow alley along the face, joining the other alley at one end, which was the way out. It was not the place for a fast getaway, for there was barely room beside the conveyor belt to put your feet, and the obtruding timbers made it a squirming way out. It gave them a feeling of being cornered. They began shovelling again and the conveyors rumbled and clanked monotonously on.

Two accidents occurred while they were there. Once, the whole place flattened right in. By a miracle it happened *between* shifts. The other accident was more nearly fatal, and perhaps more miraculous. This time the whole roof collapsed just as the men were making their way out. All at once they found themselves in a tumbled and bruised heap mixed up with their shovels in the chute. The whole roof had evidently come down simultaneously and the complete displacement of air had simply blown them along the only escape—the only way the air could get out They could never really get blasé about the conveyors. The theory was all right. The domed-out roof would support itself like an arch in a bridge. But they always felt that the Japanese worked on far too long. Standing with this cataclysmic-seeming force heaping the collapsing world at your feet with no apparent reason to stop until you were completely buried, was something they never quite got used to.

"It's no joke," Buck said. "You stand there and when the first lump comes down . . . all at once you remember . . . your sins come up . . you reckon this is it . . ."

"But I didn't think you believed," Harry said.

"Listen, mate, when you're frightened enough, you'll believe anything . . . this business finds you out."

Sometimes they would take a turn down at the chute, filling the trucks. The wooden door of the chute was lifted to let the coal flow. It was pushed down like a guillotine to shut it off. Sometimes a lump of coal stuck and the coal kept pouring out, burying the wheels and sometimes the truck. Meantime they fought the blockage with shovels and curses.

"This must be real crook coal," Harry said after one struggle.

"If you listened to Buck," Boof said, "you'd reckon it was no good for anything but to fill the Japs up with from the wrong end."

The trucks were full at the moment and the chute empty. They were just considering having their rice when, down the main, flashing among the dim overhead lighting they saw a cap lamp jerking about to the slippery, floundering gait of someone coming up. It was Okada the shift second-in-command, looking as if he were wading with the aid of the stick he always carried. This was his badge of office. He no longer carried a *tourabashi* like an ordinary timberman. Nor did he wear the black clothes, but a lighter coloured tunic and trousers. The tunic had four pockets and the trousers, below the knee, were bound with puttees above his black, split-toed boots.

"*Moshi, moshi.*" He greeted them looking into the two empty trucks they had just placed.

"*Nani? Carabako-ca? Damme-do-no,*" Okada said.

"Chute *carabako.*"

"*O.K.-da. Meshi-ca?*"

"*Ima,*" Harry said, "We're going to have it now, old cock."

They opened up their boxes. Okada sat down and took out his *kiseru.*

"He's a real Nip . . . no cigarettes for him," Alec said.

How many boxes, he asked. Sixteen they said. *O.K.-da*, he said. He asked them if they were married. Children? He told them of some of the simple things of his home and family. He compared with them. Okada San was unconsciously Japanese, unlike the self-conscious soldiers who had bullied them. He had a wife and three young children. He had had to get a few days leave from the mine. He told them it was for him to go and make arrangements for a house for his father. A small house. This was the custom. Old, old custom. The eldest son provided it. Others sometimes helped, but eldest son made sure, he said. He was now content. It had been done. He had gone to Tokyo where most of his family lived. He said the *B-ni-juu-ku's* had destroyed much. Bad. Fire rained down. Fire they feared since old times. America no gentlemen . . . they had sunk hospital ships. This was bad.

They told him the Japanese had sunk the *Centaur*, one of their hospital ships. He said this was bad indeed. He found it hard to believe. He shook his head . . . he was puzzled.

What would happen if Japan lost the war?

Japan cannot lose war . . . many gods . . .

They mentioned *B-ni-juu-ku's*. . . .

He nodded sadly, with the Japanese way of being able to say yes and no at the same time and mean it, like seeing two sides of the coin at once, he said that if Nippon defeated and Emperor profaned much honour would be lost. Honourable death would be all that remained.

"*Hara kiri?*"

He nodded, from the shoulders as if bowing to the inevitable with tragic acceptance.

They said he didn't mean it.

Nippon would, he said.

More coal rattled down the chute. They had finished *meshi*. Okada sat silently. They could see his world crumbling about him.

7

It was Christmas eve. One more turn below and they would have two days off. They were on afternoon shift and were now at the gate being counted. They concentrated so that they did not miss hearing their number, no matter how the guard mutilated it. There was always great relief when it was over and they were marching to the mine.

By saving the five *kinchis* that each man received daily, until they had twenty-five, they would be able to buy a plate of rice with some tid-bit added. *Daikon, mesu, sayu,* seaweed, crab or squid. Perhaps a couple of small chopped pieces of pork. They would have arranged with a timberman to bring it down. Although the rice was not much, these timbermen did seem to take a pride in the little tid-bit their wives had added to it. It showed John how the genuine simplicity of these people allowed them to enjoy the so little so much—how their lives were so easily enriched by small things. People to envy, he thought, not pity. For just as it took so little to gladden them, so it took just so much more to sadden them. This faculty, this secret of riches, is, he thought, one of the first casualties of an opulent society.

Boof had twenty-five cigarettes on him inside his mining jacket.

The Mamba was one of the duty guards. He was a civilian who extended himself to please the Ape more and more. He feared the draft. If he were called up to serve his Emperor, he hoped the Ape would find him indispensable. So he went out of his way to enforce and even anticipate the big square-shouldered sergeant's every whim. This was why he was so hated by the men, and feared because they were helpless. Toady-like he had sensed the tension between the Ape and Boof. The Mamba had watched the Ape looking at Boof. Now he went deliberately to Boof and ran his hands over him. Boof did not move a muscle. The Mamba's hand stopped, then pressed.

"*Kurrah!*"

He seized the overlapping lapels of Boof's black coat and pulled them open. The cigarettes fell about Boof's feet.

"*Kurrah!*" he shouted again.

Boof bent down and picked them up. Then he stood straight again. The Ape came over and stood in front of him without saying a word. The intensity of the look made Boof wonder. He was about five paces in front. Quick to see an advantage, the Mamba stepped in again to shout insults and to punctuate his remarks with kicks at Boof's shins. Boof might have been a stone temple lion for all he showed. This goaded the Mamba further to beat Boof's face and body, as Harry said, "Like a bloody little schoolboy doing his silly little block."

The shift could not be held up forever. The Ape made signs for them to be moved off. He held out his hand to Boof for the cigarettes. To Boof's surprise, he gave him two back. This was the number they were allowed to take down the mine. It would seem that the incident was closed.

Down below, Boof had been sent with a little timberman called Koko. Koko San was small even for a Japanese. But his shoulders were wide enough and his muscles knotty like the outside of a walnut shell. His teeth were prominent and crooked, his nose broad and flat. His eyes were quite large. He was bandy. He was quiet, shy and likeable. He was one of those people in whom, you are sure, there is no evil. You trust them. You would not hesitate to help them. They are perhaps what you would like all mankind to be. There was that indefinable quality of Eden that animals have. As they walked down the sloping steps, Koko San in front, it seemed that he came hardly as high as Boof's waist.

"Look after him, Boof," they called.

"Don't lose him."

"Where'd you find the Oriental leprechaun, Boof?"

"Give him back to the Irish."

"I'll look after him," Boof said. "He's worth two of some of you useless bastards. He'll do me for a *tomadachi*."

Koko San used his *tourabashi* as a walking stick. With its head in his hand he padded industriously along, unaware of what was being said. He was thinking his own thoughts. Perhaps of his wife and two young children, whom he hoped would grow up like their mother who was beautiful. And, by beauty, Koko San meant graciousness and kindness and a courage to face life with unquestioning steadfastness. Ever since he had married her he had felt a joy and an assurance that he was indeed a man—but he kept this shyly to himself.

At the store he handed Boof a shovel. "*Impey, O.K.-ca?*"

Boof put it on his shoulder and made a pantomime of buckling at the knees under the weight. Koko San laughed like a child. They stood close to the wall to let some flat cars go past loaded with timbers. Snow lay thick upon the logs. On impulse, Boof scooped up a double-handful and made a snow ball. Then he threw it at the timber opposite and watched as it hit squarely, and blossomed for an instant as a white chrysanthemum then vanished for ever—but he carried the picture with him. "The first snowball I ever threw was under the sea in Japan—that'll be something to tell the young one."

Koko San led him on a long way, to parts of the mine he did not know existed. At last they came to a cavelike space after going up a ladder. It was timbered but had been pressed low. It could have been an old abandoned conveyor. For twenty-five yards Boof crawled after Koko San. But, where Koko San was on his knees, Boof was on his stomach. They came out where it was a little higher. Here Boof could kneel up. And here they dug all night, Boof squatted on his haunches, Koko San on his feet but bent over almost double. Boof wondered what they were doing. Even outside the army, he thought, the human race does so much that is useless. Here he was in a little black hole under the Inland Sea—it could be the centre of the earth—with a little likeable man who could not understand two words of his language, and Boof scarcely more of his. Their countries were at war and in the few short hours they were here below probably thousands of their countrymen would be killed by each other in the indiscriminate path of violent explosion and frying flame. This night, on the surface here in Japan, women and children like Koko San's beautifying family, and old men like Okada's father, would die in the cause of saving the world. This likeable, unquestioning, hard-working little man could be a grief-stricken widower by the morning. But he kept on working as if he and Boof were the only two people left in the world: as if they were of one race, one faith, one hope. At some time during the night Koko San called a halt for *meshi*. They sat down, Boof's head almost touching the roof, and with room only one way to stretch his legs. Koko San looked at Boof's plain rice. Shyly on the end of his chop stick he offered Boof a little of his chopped pork. Politely he urged the other to taste it. His wife, he said, was a very good cook. They carried on a halting, partially understood, conversation, often repeating and repeating. Though the words were not understood, Boof felt strangely that he had understood far more than *was* said. Koko San spoke words that

Boof did not understand, and yet he became understood. Boof thought back to his father's farm. Maybe this was how animals know—when you see two horses nodding and cropping together.

At last they came out. He now felt he knew Koko San, but he never found out what they had really been doing. He always thought of it as some sort of a supernatural meeting between him and Koko San. Like on the Willow Pattern plates—those two stubby birds being the souls of lovers flown up . . . well he and Koko San had dug down instead.

When they came out, Boof was very glad they had left it no longer. The timbers on the way out were now a full six inches lower than when they went in. He did not think anybody would ever get in there again.

Near the surface they stopped at the pumps and washed off in the swirling rusty water which felt warm. They returned their lamps and waited for the rest of the shift to come up. The snow was thick and the west wind was an invisible cold knife. They stood shivering and welcomed each latecomer with a curse as if they would like to see him hanging lifeless like the long icicles from the overhead power-lines. It was after eleven before they scrunched their way back through the snow. They were counted in. They could hardly wait. Impatience and brittle tempers goaded them. Would there be any hot water in the bath? What would the rice issue be like? Bed! And they were just about to march off.

"*Sam-biaku-ni-juu-ku!*"

"*Hai!*" Boof shouted back.

"*Kurrah!*"

Boof stood in front of the Ape sensing what would happen. He was made to kneel with his bare knees on the coarse iron-stone gravel where passing feet had slushed away the snow. His knees were numbed with cold, but bullet-like pains shot through his legs. They made him kneel up straight and forward with his arms above his head.

The shift had gone. Now the Ape looked at him intently. The Mamba jumped on to Boof's shoulders, balanced for a minute grinding Boof's knees hard in the gravel. Then he sprang upwards, kicking as hard as he could, to land just in front of Boof with the seat of his pants right in Boof's face. He laughed.

The Ape went in and went to bed. But before he did he left orders. He spoke with the bellowed grunts of authority which threatened that if they did not see to it, he would have no hesitation about putting them in Boof's place.

Boof knew what he was up against. *Whatever is, is equally part of divine law. The concepts of Good and Bad do not arise. There is no conflict between God and Man, nor between Man and Nature, no moral law, no original sin, no dread of hell . . . the blood relation rules and controls the Japanese.* Boof had never heard these words, but he knew them from experience. There were now depressions in the bones of his knees and the skin was broken. His cold arms felt as if they were trying to hold up a block of stone. The cold gripped his back like a claw. There was the plain enduring of the pain that still went on.

He thought his arms sagged. He thought he pushed them up again. He couldn't have. A harsh *Kurrah!* and a kick in the stomach came from somewhere. This happened several times. He felt himself shivering. He heard Japanese voices, and then laughter. There was a scrunch of boots behind him, then a kick. Wait for it, there would be another. Instead he felt something soft spreading over his back. It ran down like knife cuts. More cuts ran down his chest. His back seared and his stomach muscles jumped rigid and stayed knotted until some of the pain went. He heard another *Kurrah* and a *Bageera* and his wrists were seized and his arms pulled roughly up again. Twice more during the night they threw hot water over him.

"*Takusan samusa-ca? Damme-do-no. Ima O.K.-da.*"

They threw the hot water over him to warm him up. He did not know how hot it was nor how much he was burnt. Boof kept his eyes closed to try to concentrate on nothing. A couple of times a guard prised open his lids with his finger tips and peered closely as if looking through a slit in a fence. And then he laughed explosively.

Once, when this was done, Boof noticed a faint greyness of the pre-dawn. The smooth low ceiling of the sky could not be seen. The camp was still asleep. This morning they would sleep in. It was Christmas morning. A little later, it seemed from miles away, he heard young voices singing *Annie Laurie*, then *Home Sweet Home*. They were being sung in English but with a Japanese accent. Then he heard a pleasant little jingly Japanese tune.

"It's the kids," he thought.

The snow-covered hills rose above the camp fence. Five rows of barbed wire ruled black lines on the white beyond. On and between the lines, like quavers and semiquavers, stood the black notes of six bundled-up children between twelve and six years old—each singing clear thin notes into the cold still morning, songs they had learned in school. They had sung from the hill before to the prisoners. Some had called them cheeky little brats, but most of the men encouraged them. The children were well-meaning and polite. The men enjoyed the quaint corruptions of pronunciation. The children had known that this was a day of religious festival for these men with large noses, so they had got up early to sing to them.

Boof listened with his eyes shut.

The day came quietly, grey over a white world. The Ape came out from the guardhouse, bare-calved and in unbuttoned trousers. His boots were unlaced and his open shirt hanging out. He yawned, stretched and looked across the landscape. He gave a couple of grunts. The guards were already bellowing at Boof to straighten up.

"*Sam-biaku-ni-juu-ku!*" the Ape called.

"*Hai!*"

"*Kiotski!*"

Boof concentrated his will. He rose slowly to his feet, almost as a mountain might. He thought he was steady, but he was swaying. His eyes were open, but one was black where a misdirected kick had caught him.

"*Wakare.*"

Boof dragged his arm to a salute. The capless Ape gave a curt bow in return. Boof started to walk away. After half a dozen steps, without being able to feel his feet or legs, he fell in an uncontrolled sprawl.

"*Bageera,*" the Ape laughed.

Boof picked himself up clumsily, like a man with two unbending wooden legs, and made his way down the hill into his room. Harry was awake and jumped up to help him in.

"Get my coat off," Boof said. "Be careful, I think it's stuck to my back."

"The dirty little mongrels," Harry said as he saw the skin and blisters sticking to Boof's coat and coming off with it.

"They chucked hot water over me."

"Look at his knees," Buck said. He and Alec carefully started to rub some circulation back into Boof's legs. As the circulation was coming back, Boof said, "You blokes are worse than the Nips."

The bell at the guardhouse clanged rapidly to rouse the prisoners to Christmas morning 1944.

"Merry Christmas," Buck said.

Boof stood with the others on the count parade. As soon as it was over Harry got the doctor. Nobody said what they thought about the knees. They could become a death warrant. Legs that have been broken down so often in the jungle, legs that grew on a body starved over a long time, were not a good risk. The Ape said that Boof was not sick so that he went below again with the shift after the holidays. But below, the timbermen were sorry and allowed Boof to lay up there while the others did his work.

In spite of the Ape and his lackeys, the *Shookoo* tried his best to bring Christmas spirit to the day. They queued in the biting wind for *presento's* just before dinner. Each man received five extra cigarettes, half a small sweat towel, and five dried persimmons on a string. The persimmons had been given by the schoolmaster *Shookoo* out of his own poor pocket. For dinner they had rice with soya beans added, and some bean paste soup with some horse offal which made it quite savoury.

"Knocked over in an air raid, you can bet—that's all the meat we are likely to get from now on," Harry said.

"Don't look a gift horse in the mouth," Alec said.

"Mate, if we had to look at *this* gift horse . . . it wouldn't be his mouth."

"You can't put me off," Buck said.

The mining company had provided one bottle of beer between each two men. In the dining-hall at dinner they toasted with beer.

"Merry Christmas . . . to absent friends and families."

"To next Christmas out of the clink!"

"Never get out . . ."

"Be years yet . . ."

"Don't make me . . ."

The pessimists and the optimists met head-on and it was a topic of speculation for the rest of the day.

Christmas passed. The New Year came . . . 1945.

Some said it would be over this year. Some said it wouldn't.

8

The cold weather continued through January and February. Air raids grew more frequent. Many nights were spent in the

A shelter entrance

shelters, which were dug into the side of the hill. There were two of them. Each had two entrances dug in, joined by a tunnel that was the shelter. Black curtains hung over these entrances. Inside, two small carbon filament lamps gave a weak light. They were packed in five deep and only some could sit down. The rest stood, cold, weary and sleepless through the long nights that were often from ten or eleven at night until four or five in the morning. A couple of times they were there until eight o'clock—which was long after the raiders had gone. It seemed a kind of revenge the Ape took on them. During this time the guards carried loaded rifles and fixed bayonets. One manned a little tower at the foot of the flagpole. From the flagpole, day and night, flew a tattered Japanese flag. The fly was frayed out

From the flagpole, day and night

until it had reached and eaten into the red ball. There was a guard at each shelter entrance.

When the warning came, somebody always went first to the kitchen and got a live coal. Sometimes smoking would be allowed in the shelters, but at other times the guards *kurrah-ed* and *bageera-ed*. But somehow the light was always kept alive and, sooner or later, someone would light up again. Then there was more bashing and, as they could not get into the crowded shelters, the guards hit those they could reach although they had nothing to do with the offence. This caused dissension among the prisoners, especially among the non-smokers who had been hit. They said if a man was meant to smoke he would have been born with a chimney in the top of his head—but this was not where they told them to put their bloody cigarettes.

On the alarm each man grabbed what clothes he could pile

on and his blanket. They poured out on to the roadway, each with his especial hand-picked bouquet of words. Some took books on the remote chance that they might get under one of the lamps. Books had come into the camp with the stamp of the *War Prisoners' Aid World's Committee, Y.M.C.A., Geneva, Switzerland.* John's steady companion was *The Philosophy of William James.* He had, at first, thought these occasions ideal for abstract contemplation. He thought of Chinese philosophers, high in storm-tossed mountains, ignoring all inclemency. The frozen shelters were equally inclement. So he took care to rush for a place under a lamp. But his theory, in practice, turned out to be something else. The book became a wonderful soporific to suspend him between being asleep and awake without being either. Take a paragraph and roll it gently round in the mind until soft and pliable. The idea is now ready for the mind to mould as it drifts about in the grandiloquent delusion of magnificent cerebration, giving to the thinker a strange exhilaration which takes him even higher in pure delusion. It was a wonderful feeling. But John learned that there was one rule that must never be broken, *never halt an idea.* Never call it to attention and ask it to explain itself. This was fatal—for suddenly this wonderful idea would stand there tongue-tied with absolutely nothing to say: idiot. What had been wonderful resonance became flat, abject hollowness. Never stand these ideas to attention . . . just let them cavort pretentiously in your wandering mind and marvel at them.

There had been one attempt to build another shelter. They had dug into the wet clayey hill, timbering as they went. One day, as three prisoners were digging in there, about twenty feet in, some timbers broke and the roof collapsed. Two of them hugged the face according to the rule. One tried to run out. He was buried and crushed—pelvis, legs and chest. He died in hospital a couple of hours later. The other two were dug out and the shelter was abandoned. It was ironic that, down below, where conditions looked so risky and crazy, nothing had happened. Here, where the job had looked like child's play, there was a fatality.

Gradually the weather improved.

"Let's get some warm . . . we've had enough of this Pommy weather," Harry said.

"That's all right, chum, when we get your bleedin' Ossie weather you'll be right sorry."

"How come, cobber?"

"Fleas . . . millions of 'em . . . they'll all come out of the *tatami*, mate."

"Are they worse than the bugs?"

"Dunno, mate . . . haven't got bugs."

"Wanta bet?"

The fleas and bugs added a lot to the camp activity. Each man looked like a measles case. Bodies were covered with small

Each man looked like a measles case

red welts. The *tatami* gave the attackers perfect cover. When the men got to sleep, the fleas woke them up. It was not the bites that woke them—this they got used to. It was the constant crawling trails of ticklish irritation, as if somebody were deliberately trying to arouse them. For a week John kept a rough tally.

A single light was left on in the rooms all night, so that the guards could keep a constant check on them. John would wait until he could no longer stand the irritation. His blanket had once been white, now it was a yellowish brown. But it still gave enough contrast to the dark little fleas. In a blanket, a flea can crawl but he cannot jump. It was not hard to catch them and squash them between his nails. He thought he would keep a count. He would go down one side of his blanket, turn it over, and come down the other. A fair average was sixty fleas on each side. In not much more than an hour the population had built up again and asked for further Malthusian attention. This would happen four or five times a night. It meant that he was killing about five hundred fleas a night. He checked this result a number of times and got about the same answer. But he doubted that anybody outside the camp would ever believe him.

At the same time, in the other building the British were confronted with bugs. The Australians there assured the British that they were the finest pedigreed Siamese bugs you could get —they had bred them themselves, they said. This produced acrimonious comment. The British, in a determined attempt to get rid of the bugs, took all the *tatami* mats out of their rooms, and slept on the rough open-spaced boards underneath. Bugs only come out in the dark, so they would turn out their light then, without warning, snap it on—flailing about, slapping and squashing the running bugs with their rubber-soled boots. There were ten men in each room. In just under a week one room had tallied a kill (confirmed) of ten thousand bugs. They gave up counting but went on killing. But, to the end, the bugs and the fleas continued.

"Blessed are the meek."

"Blessed . . . the bastards . . . I know what *I'd* say!"

An Australian passing a room of flailing men, killing for all they were worth, said, "You'll find it easier to learn to live with them, you blokes . . . you're only farting against thunder."

Gardens had been made in the camp, more as a hobby for some of the officers who did not have to work, but who wanted to qualify for a larger rice ration. With food, the Japanese were very practical—the less work a man did, the less he needed to eat. The sick got only 420 grammes. Non-workers were classed with the sick. This was a point the officers sought continually to adjust. So the gardens were started, outside the camp on the rising hillside at the back. The prisoners could only work them by day. They planted sweet potatoes and tomatoes. On certain days the mine workers, in their time-off, worked as *benjo* party. The concrete camp *benjo* pits were ladled into buckets, several of which were carried on a pole between two men. One man had to go in front of the other. With uneven tracks and slopping buckets there was always strong competition to be the man in front, although the advantage was marginal. The prisoners found that they had to pick the tomatoes green, if they wanted them at all. The Japanese were free to roam at night while the prisoners were inside the camp. When they came to dig their sweet potatoes they found that the tops were intact, but most of the tubers were gone.

"Bandicooted!" they swore.

9

The war was creeping closer to Japan. The cigarette issue was cut from five to two. Then it vanished altogether. Rations became even more meagre. Men became more and more food-conscious. They could be seen staring hard at the last few grains of rice before they finally ate them. Their expressions were enigmatic. Like the look on the face of a miser counting his money; like someone malevolently contemplating something that was responsible for all his misery. Some had got hold of *saki* cups, like small coffee cups. They would get their rice issue and press it with their thumbs until it was all in one cup, just to prove to themselves how little they got. Some would not eat it in the dining-hall. They would take it to their rooms.

"Look at it! . . . *That's* a meal . . . you're expected to live on that!"

They might eat it finally an hour later. But some, getting more angry and depressed as they went on, sometimes threw it out. Squabbling petulance, self-righteousness, self-pity, cunning, deceit, thieving and selfishness became constant aggravations which brought violent reactions.

"God!" Harry said. "How pitiful can blokes get?"

"They can't help it, Harry," Boof said. "They've lost their grip."

"But they still make it miserable for the mob," Buck said. "As if we haven't got enough with the Nips!"

"You've got to come back at some of them," Alec said. "If they get away with it, they are really gone . . . and everybody with them."

On the way, single file down the mine, a group made a topic of food. All the food they could dream up. Food they would have when they could have what they liked. Food they would cook

THE SWORD AND THE BLOSSOM

themselves. One day they were preparing cauliflower to be
baked in a cheese sauce.

"I can smell it."

"Smell it . . . I'm eating it!"

"You would want one cauli on your own . . . be easy to
knock off that much. . . ."

"Yes, nothing else . . . just that . . . eat it straight out of the
dish with a spoon . . . woof the lot . . . then just lay back and
give a good belch every now and again. . . ."

"Boy! Roll on liberation . . . who wants to go to heaven. . . ."

A shaking voice, low at first, but rising to a kind of shriek,
said, "Can't you bastards shut up! What are you trying to do?
Torture us! Shut up, for Christ's sake! You just go on and on.
. . . SHUT UP!"

"Right-o boys, back on the rice," Buck said quietly.

As a result of the vegetable, meagre though it was, coming
from the *benjo*-fed gardens, worms made their appearance among
the men. They could hardly be ignored. John caught an objective glimpse of themselves one day as they were going below.

A long file of skinny men, no longer brown but dead white
like underground things. Irregularly cropped heads. Flapping
muddy black coats and trousers making them look whiter.
Each with an ungainly gait accommodated to his wasted frame
as he clawed with split-toed boots the slippery slope of the
descent. A line of men below the earth playing to no gallery,
intent on doing what they must do. There had been some
tangerines. The men had of course eaten the skins. Flatulent
foulness passed down the line of men in the narrow tunnel.
Habitual, rough and insulting protests were growled. With
equal force came the defence, "That's all right about *you* . . .
what would *you* do? . . . Bust?"

Men would begin coughing, strangling and hawking violently.
Gasping, they would put their fingers into their throats and pull
out a tangled knot of white worms and fling them away with a
kind of patient disgust.

So, they went below to dig coal.

They were being weighed each month. For the first few
months in Japan they had stayed about the same weight. But
now, each month, they watched a significant drop—sometimes
as much as a kilogramme, two and a fifth pounds. Now the

end of the war became much more than just speculation and patience. They began to realize that they each had just so much endurance left . . . and the scales seemed to be measuring it out.

Soya beans were added to the rice, but an equal weight of rice had already been deducted. Each afternoon there came a yell from the cookhouse, "Bean water!" Those in camp would rush down with rattling dixies to get into the queue. There was never enough for all of them, so men fought for positions—dangerous and pitiful fights. Their world had become small and mean.

10

One day John saw some women of the miners' terraces opposite the camp being put through Air Raid Drill by black-uniformed, silver-buttoned men. The flimsy wooden houses were perfect tinder. There were no hoses, no fire engines. Just buckets of sand and some water at a distance which had to be carried in buckets. The women were bundled in their coats and long pants caught at the ankles and had scarves tied over their hair. Wooden *geta* were on their feet. With unquestioning obedience they ran here and there with the buckets, chased by the hoarse shouts of the uniformed men. John had no doubt that these women would run about, just so, under real attack . . . but to what purpose? To finish as just so many bloody pulped bundles against a wall somewhere? This his own side would see to.

He thought of these women who always smiled at him with warm unspoken sympathy, who were always so gracious and polite, who could be equally gay and demure, who somehow emanated a humanity that had the warmth of mother's milk.

Their commonplaces. . . . He remembered seeing two girls in a muddy street outside the hospital. Ordinary village girls standing gracefully on high *geta*, conversing with pleasantly modulated voices and delicate hand movements. It could have been a carefully rehearsed court scene, except for the violet-like perfume of simplicity and sincerity that pervaded this. Then, the final courteous bow to each other. They parted, picking their way through the deep-rutted spring mud on their awkward wooden platforms with the grace of slowly wading cranes in smooth water.

And the two old women who had been working in the warm morning sun on their garden plots on the hillside. Their faces were fresh, wrinkled, and with a serene sweet expression on their mouths. They had a sober twinkle around their bright eyes which were calm pools in which swam so much of life—lived. They wore only the black trousers caught at the ankle above their sandals of rice straw. On their scarved heads each bore a bundle of sweet potato tops. Their brown naked shoulders

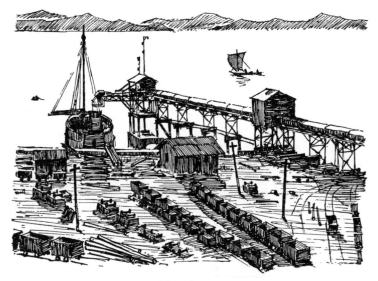

The mine yard

shone in the sun. Their naked spent breasts lay, not sad or old, but, autumnlike, quietly at peace. They too spoke with all the grace of the young girls . . . but added to this was the golden aura of life passing gently into the distance.

And the tiny women in the mine yard carrying large baskets of coal strapped on their backs with heavy crossed scarves biting into the quilted coats on their shoulders. Loads, the prisoners said, they would not like to have to carry—even when they were fit. Some of these women, as well, carried snug-tucked babies slung in front of them. Barbarous! some said. But they did not look barbarous. They were not hunched up or stagger-ing. They walked steadily, seemingly unconscious of the drag of the weight, with the simple strength of acceptance. The completeness of this acceptance and its obvious reward was shown by those who could walk so calmly and smile at the mite suckling them as they went. Madonna-and-child-looking, like the holiest of Christian paintings . . . yet 'heathen' with a hundredweight of coal dragging at her shoulders. Somehow it made John think of the nodding grasses his Voice had reminded him of.

And when the *B-ni-juu-ku's* came over with the stars on their wings that were not of Bethlehem, and rained down fire and high explosives, these women would run obediently with buckets until . . .

Well, the world would say, they had asked for it. *They*, John wondered. Were *these* women *they*? And do the bombs of either side ever fall on *they*?

But John was feeling soft. He was undermined. With these women he had also thought of his wife. He remembered what he had written when alone for twelve days in the Siamese jungle.

> *Gracious Lady, I to thee,*
> *In this mood of reverie,*
> *Could only faithful ever be—*
> *Always, deeply, I to thee.*
>
> *Gracious Lady, I would know*
> *If our love should ever go:*
> *Frozen grief and wretched woe*
> *Kill my heart—Ah! I should know.*
>
> *Gracious Lady, we will be*
> *Loving through eternity:*
> *Love through God, through thee, through me—*
> *Lovers' perfect trinity.*

Down below, the prisoners more and more heard the Japanese talk punctuated with *B-ni-juu-ku's*, as they gathered in knots to talk of the news. And there was awe in their voices.

Okada came to them one day. They had not seen him for some time and wondered if he had left the mine. They asked him where he had been. He had been to Tokyo. *"B-ni-juu-ku takusan."* Heavy raids had bombed and burnt much. He had been to see his people who were in trouble. Two brothers and their families were now all dead, except one little girl of five who was badly burned. Okada clawed his face until it was a hideous mask. Her face, he said. He had brought her back to his wife and their children. The little house he had built for his father was gone—but then his father no longer needed it.

II

They were working in a really wet heading. The water poured through the sandstone roof in cascades. The timberman told them that when they got through this section it would be all right. They had been provided with oilskins and sou'westers. The pneumatic pick was not enough here. They had to lay charges and blast their way through. When they retreated back along the drift to wait for the blow, they wondered.

"I hope they know what they are doing," Harry said.

"Of course they do," Buck said. "But I'm only saying it because I'm frightened to think anything else."

It went off. The ground shook all around them. Some timbers cracked. Smoke curled toward them like a groggy man staggering out of an accident.

"A couple more like that," Boof said, "and the whole bloody joint'll come in."

The timberman grinned.

"*O.K.-ca?*" Harry said, pointing to the roof.

"*O.K.-da.*"

"He's saying it like I said it . . . he only hopes," Buck said.

They went to work and were shovelling the heavy water-logged muck away when a violent shock shook them from above. Timbers broke and water seemed to spurt in from new places. Lumps of the roof fell in about them.

Harry looked scared, "Gawd strike me dead, what's going on *now?*"

The timberman said the explosion was not in the mine at all.

"*Nani?*" they said in disbelief.

No, he said, it was in the sea above them.

"Bloody mines!" John said, "The Yanks must've dropped them from the air—I've been noticing that they've been coming in low and there have been no explosions."

"Mined in a mine! Sounds funny . . . if you are not in the bloody mine!"

They never got used to these unpredictable explosions. The mine was so close to the seabed, and they felt as if they were in a submarine being depth-charged. They kept seeing walls of water rushing along the tunnels and drowning them—leaving them drowned and still like specimens in a bottle of alcohol, but with no one to look at them. They felt as many as eight explosions in a single shift.

Looking out from the top of Australians' building

Coming back to the camp one afternoon on a beautiful sunshiny day, they watched a small tug towing a string of five coal barges to Moji. These were constantly moving like so many little trains over the flat sea—sometimes they could see as many as four or five of them at once. Suddenly this tug and the first barge were hurled into the air, shattered, in one muddy explosion. Three of the remaining hulks drifted, rocking drunkenly near the debris. The fourth, planks shaken below the water, sank tiredly.

They wondered how the war would finish. Would they be alive for it? These were not mere idle speculations. The Americans were getting closer. Increased aircraft activity told them that. But they were still long-range bombers. *Mai Nichi* had printed the battle of Okinawa. They had said that their defeat was impossible. The splendid young men of the *Kami Kazes* would save them. The fate of the Americans must be humiliating defeat when they at last encountered the real might of Japan. The home islands would be defended with the death-before-dishonour *bushido* spirit of the Yamato race. This had conquered through the ages.

These noble Japanese sentiments had yet to be demonstrated. But the prisoners were right on the coast, and no move had been made to shift them inland. Surely they would become a menace to the defending Japanese when the attack came . . . unless . . .

"Unless," Buck said, "they simply do us over at the first sign . . . that'd be cheaper than sending us other places . . . what have they got to lose?"

"Buck, you're too bloody logical . . . it makes me shiver because you could be so right . . . one big bloody *hara kiri.*"

"We ought to organize."

"Like what? . . . Form a *tourabashi* brigade?"

"That might be all right among the locals . . . but you can bet they will send in a special Liquidating Squad to do us over."

"The bastards won't surrender . . . you can back *that* right in!"

A little later they came upon a small paragraph on the centre page of a copy of *Mai Nichi*. The general trend of the issue was on the *bushido* attitude, but this little paragraph said simply, "If Okinawa falls, then the home islands will become indefensible."

12

Smoking was not allowed in the rooms. Apart from the fire in the cookhouse, their only way to get a light was with a single magnifying glass or a kapok-and-flint lighter. If there was no sun the kapok lighter was used. But this made a noise, so a good lookout had to be kept. The Mamba was always on the track of the lighter, though he could not find out what it really was. He would sneak around trying to discover it, but the prisoners always had their 'cockatoo' who gave ample warning. The Mamba's vindictiveness grew with his frustration. One afternoon, when Boof and the others of the nightshift were sleeping, the Mamba heard the click, click, click of the lighter. He slipped silently into the building and crept along the corridors.

But the clicking had stopped and room after room yielded nothing. His temper was rising. Men were peacefully sleeping. Too peacefully, he thought. Men on nightshift, asleep in a room, did not have to get up and salute a passing guard. All others did.

The fleas had been active and Boof's bare chest showed a complete scatter of red bites. He rolled over and scratched his chest with one hand, relaxed, and began to snore just as the Mamba came to the door. Looking for an excuse, he saw in this an elaborate gesture by Boof to merely pretend that he was asleep to avoid saluting the Mamba. There was a running kick which took Boof right in the side.

"*Kurrah! Bageera! K'iotski nie! Kerei nie! Damme!*"

Boof rolled over just as another kick caught him on the side of the head and blackened an eye. He got ponderously to his feet, not realizing what was happening. The others were now awake. Boof stood, towering over the Mamba.

Harry said later, "I thought Boof was going to eat the little animal . . . but he just stood there."

The Mamba took this for insolence. He gave a couple of wild blows with his hands that hurt him as if he had been hitting a wall. He ordered Boof to the guardhouse. The Ape was there. They made him kneel on the gravel with his arms folded behind him. Some of the other guards joined in like children. They would jump up on his shoulders and make a great show of balancing, but swaying about in such a way to grind Boof's knees on the small stones. They would jump off with a high, hard spring. Boof was surprised when, after half an hour of this, they let him go with the usual *kurrah's* and *bageera's*.

He went to the bathroom and bathed his bleeding knees. Then he went to the sick bay to get some mercurochrome from the American U.S.N. Chief Pharmacist's Mate who lived permanently in the camp hospital. He was a dour man with a loose down-turned mouth, sad blue eyes and a joyless face. He did not know why men kept coming to him for stuff—he didn't have much. He really should save it for an emergency.

"Yes, mate," Boof said. "But just dab a bit on my knees . . . won't take much . . . take more if you have to take my leg off."

The other looked at him sourly, but dabbed it on with a long-suffering manner. This man had not seen what could happen to small sores and ulcers which had taken so many men's lives and legs in the jungle. But he got some idea later when another man came in after the kneeling treatment. This man was not so lucky as Boof. His legs had broken down. Poison swept through him and in less than a week he died in agony.

Boof went back to the room and told them he was all right. "Get your sleep in . . . don't worry about me."

"That's a decent shiner you've got there, old timer," Harry said. "If that bastard's about when it's over . . ."

"Forget him," Boof said. "Don't let it get you at this stage . . . it happens . . . let it go at that."

They slept on, between fleas and bladder calls until *tenko*, after which they had their evening meal before going down at 10 p.m.

At nine o'clock there was an air raid warning. All lights were put out but they were not sent to the shelters. In their rooms they lay on the *tatami* or sat about. In the dark they could feel the fleas crawling thickly over them. They took off their clothes and shook them hard. But, as they sat up, they could feel them crawling up their legs. They scratched and slapped and cursed monotonously. Quietly they slid back the windows and watched the starlit sky for intruders. They could hear distant explosions from behind the hill.

"Ube . . . I'm glad that joint's over there and bigger than Ohama."

It was well after eleven before the raid drew off. One of the American planes flew out over the Inland Sea, clear of the ack-ack, and switched on a powerful headlight, swooping low over the water.

"They must be confident."

More planes flew over and formed up, then they left.

"It won't be long now boys . . . I reckon they are right on top."

It was midnight before they got into the mine. The afternoon shift was just coming out. They had been kept inside the entrance until the all-clear. A lot of power had been cut from the mine. The story went around that a nearby power station had been hit. Over near Onada, they said. No *makkis* were working, no trucks were moving, and no pumps were working. They walked miles out into Ni Coda along a switchback main until they came to a long lane of water which had reached the roof at the far end.

"What do we do here?"

"I'll bite."

Heaped against the side of the main were pyramid stacks of logs. The rails were covered with water and the men stood knee-deep in the muddy stuff. Half a dozen Japanese stood in confused conference. At last they said, "*Yasume . . . yasume . . . sagio damme.*"

"This is the best raid to date . . . these are real results."

They climbed on the wet logs and arranged their sitting bones as best they could on the rough bark and uneven logs. They dug their heels in on the lower logs below the water so that, with their elbows on their knees, they could rest their heads in their hands and sleep. Some talked, but most were silent, shutting themselves each in his own dream-world, determined to enjoy this wind-fall—a night with nothing to do but doze. The luxury of sitting here on these wet logs, cap lamps out, water half-way up to their knees, counting their blessings, or, with dreaming fancies, slipping in and out of sleep with nothing to do.

There came a growl. Then a grumbling.

"Wouldn't it! The little bastards . . . there'll be little sleep tonight, mates."

The fleas in the men's boots were crawling up their legs to get above the water. Somehow they seemed more noticeable when they crawled with wet feet.

"They've got their bloody sea-boots on," John said.

Gunner Miles, a slow dry bush philosopher from north-west Tasmania, said with an unemotional drawling voice, "Wouldn't you know. . . . If it's not one Nip . . . it's another."

So the night was not quite so good as they had hoped. The water rose all night.

"She'll be flooded tomorrow . . . with a bit of luck."

And it was. They had to make their way back into the mine step by step with portable pumps, shovelling the sludge and silt into trucks as they went, foot by foot. It was more than a week before they were back at their jobs.

One day fighter aircraft came over, low. To their consternation the camp was cannon-shelled. It was over before they realized it. The shells had gone through the walls as if they were paper. Luckily no one was hit.

"They were carrier-borne aircraft," John said. "You know what that means!"

"What?"

"If they can fly off aircraft *this* close . . . what's happened to the Nip navy? They must have had it . . . things will really start now. . . . They might be here before the Nips knock us off yet."

"Yes . . . but I wish the enthusiastic bastards would lay off us!"

"Probably saw the minehead and had a bash for fun."

"Be just our rotten luck to be knocked off by one of our own side . . . instead of them," Buck said.

John had formed the habit of looking at the sky. Not because he was a weather prophet, though he tried to read the signs. But it was often the sky that set a mood. And with barbed wire and fences the sky was often all that there was left to look at. It had sharpened his interest in clouds. On this day it was clear and sunny. Looking south, there was a cluster of hazy Japanese-print islands nestling close to Kyushu—soft and blue. Low above them was a horizontal line of cumulus clouds like so many sheep grazing in a line. The weather showed no hint of thunder. None of the clouds had a hint of a thunderhead forming. Just placid woolly sheep. A low rumbling came from over in Kyushu. Probably ack-ack, John thought. He began to notice a change in the clouds. A thunderhead *was* forming, and it was climbing more rapidly than he had ever seen before. Up it went, growing convolution on convolution, swirling like a tall cauliflower. It was conventional enough, but something seemed strange. Had something happened to his sense of timing, for this seemed to be growing just too fast to make sense. Instead of it taking a quarter to half an hour, this 'anvil' grew and spread in what seemed to be a few minutes. He knew he was seeing it . . . yet . . . something strange . . . he wondered if there were any previous records of this sort of thing.

He found out later that there were indeed records. And in this cloud they would mention plutonium. It was August 1945 and, unbeknown to him, this cloud had given him a perfect bearing on Nagasaki. He had heard the timbermen talking about an 'earthquake' at a place he had never heard of. But it was in their prefecture of Fukuoka. Later, looking at the map, he saw that Ohama was almost exactly midway between Hiroshima and Nagasaki.

Later, a thought came to him. This pillar of cloud would be as significant as one in the Red Sea was to the Jews. This was the end of the Japanese this time. But what was it to those who had sent it? Those who were accelerating the swing of action and reaction, perhaps beyond man's control. Would *their* justification become also *everybody's* justification—so that morality became meaningless? The atrocities of one war were perhaps only the means of the next.

On *Yasume* day, Sunday, 14th, they had a Red Cross 'lob'. This was what the British called a Red Cross issue. The store in the camp was full of American cartons each containing a balanced parcel for one prisoner for one month. But over the twelve months that they had been here they received only three issues. And the Ape issued one parcel between each five men. This made division very difficult. Lots had to be drawn, and later there was bartering. There was always discontent and accusations of injustice no matter how the division had been made. In this issue cigarettes were the pot of gold for the smokers who had been three months without an issue.

This did not mean that the men did not smoke. The improvizations ranged from the purely makeshift to something smacking of alchemy. Buck was among the practical. He wanted to smoke and saw no virtue in giving it up. The lifelines coiled down in the corridor were made of coconut-fibre rope. Buck cut off just one cigarette's length. He teased it out and put it in his tobacco tin, polished bare of paint by use. He left it there for a day or so "so that when I go for it it won't seem so much like rope". At last he opened the tin and took out a pinch of fibre. He laid it in a torn piece of *Mai Nichi*. He rolled it into a cone and twisted and ends into a wick as the natives in Java had done. He lit it and drew hard on it.

"What's it like, Buck?" Harry asked. He had given up smoking.

"Paper . . . I'll tell you next draw. . . ."

He took it slowly and deeply and then gave a long dry *h-a-a-h* of exhalation.

"Well?"

"This is the answer to it . . . one draw and you don't *want* any more . . . it'll be two days before I can come at it again . . . this tin will last me the duration."

But the alchemists were different. Castor leaves, soya leaves. In fact any leaves they could lay their hands on. These would be dried and mixed in all sorts of proportions. Arguments and deep discussions surrounded it all. The pine logs of the mine yielded the most popular crops. The bark was stripped off the logs, rubbed into a ready mixture and smoked. But it was not just as simple as that. The logs were of differing lengths. Their lengths in *shakus* ranged from five to nine, that is, *go, roku, nana* or *shichi, hachi* and *ku*.

"What are you smoking?"

"*Nana shak*' "

"I'm on *rok' shak'* . . . try some . . . I reckon it's the best."

"One of the blokes . . . a Pom . . . mixed *go* and *hachi* . . . one of our mob smoked one . . . he said it was extra. . . . But I haven't seen many *rok' shak'* about lately . . . they're as scarce as rocking-horse manure."

"A Pom said he wouldn't smoke anything else."

"You can tell the difference, I reckon . . . but I don't reckon you should mix them."

But today the issue of parcels was one to four men. This was an omen, they said. But whatever optimism there was, it was always equally matched by pessimism. One room was having a £2-in-pool on the date the war would be over. It was now some months old. One man said the 15th—the next day. Did he want to change it now? They'd give him a chance. No, he'd bloodywell stick to it.

That night they were allowed a sing-song in the dining-hall. But, one of the guards told them, "Sing *sukoshi*—small, small— no more than twelve men at a time . . . or the villagers might think you are rejoicing".

PART 4

THE WAY OUT

Icicles and water
Old differences dissolved . . .
Drip down together.
                    (TEISHITSU)

Net mender

THE WAY OUT

I

"THERE's something doing!"
"Don't tell me . . . the war's over! We're going home tomorrow!"

"All right . . . be smart. But *something's* on. They just took a radio into the Nip's office. The *Shookoo's* told them all to be there at noon."

At noon there was silence in the camp. Apart from this, the Australians could see nothing different. But from the British side they could see into the office from the upper floor. They saw the *Shookoo* and the guards standing, caps off and heads bowed —as unmoving as the cold *hibachi* in the middle of the room. From the radio came a thin penetrating sing-song voice. They remained riveted.

The voice stopped. Still they stood unmoving. At last the *Shookoo* spoke a short subdued sentence. The guards put on their caps and straggled out in silence.

"Definitely something cooking!"

But at two o'clock they were at the gate being checked. At the minehead an unusual crowd of miners stood and sat about on the grass as if at a loss. Normally they would have already been below. Some were apart and silent. Others in groups were talking earnestly. There was a delay at the lamp room and the prisoners were watching the Japanese for a clue. John noticed one particular man sitting apart from the others. Possibly it was only by chance, but it looked as if the others were deliberately having nothing to do with him. He had red hair and a larger nose than the others, than Japanese normally have. It was as if this man had become to them now a symbol of invasion. As if fate had put him there as an evil omen.

The prisoners were hoping that whatever was in the wind might stop them having to go down the mine today. But they picked up their gaffers and went below.

Buck, Alec and John were taken to a heading in San Coda. The timberman poked his head about here and there and, after a thoughtful consideration, pointed out several timbers that needed replacing.

Was that all? Yes. What then? *Yasume*, I will return.

"I hope you're not as long as the other bloke who said that," Buck grinned.

"*Nani?*"

"*O.K.-da*," Buck said.

In less than an hour they had replaced the timbers.

"Well," Alec said. "Is this it? . . . What do you think?"

"After three and a half years . . . what do *you* think? . . . Ever since the Dutch in Java gave us that bull about the Indonesian legend which said that the invader would prevail only while the corn ripened . . . I don't think," John said.

"Well," Buck said, "it could be *anything*. What if it's the invasion they got told about? Where would that leave us? What about that silverpaper all over the joint last week?"

Coming off nightshift last week they had seen the whole countryside glittering like a Christmas tree with hundreds of thousand of strips of tinfoil. They knew that this was used to fox radar observations. But no bombs had been dropped then.

"Pretty," someone had said.

"Except we know it isn't Father Christmas . . . they must be giving this part of the coast a good louse-over . . . so it won't be Rudolph the red-bloody-nosed bloody reindeer, cobber . . . you can back *that* right in!"

"Be nice to know," Alec said now as he unclipped the top of his battery and settled back comfortably against a timber. "I hope the gaffer's not in a hurry to get back . . . whatever it is, this'll do me. . . . *Takusan yasume . . . sagio aware.*"

"Big rest . . . work finished . . . wonder how long before we are able to say that," John said.

"For the Battler," Buck said, "when he's dead."

All their lamps were out now. They did not sleep but dozed lazily, floating in the luxury of do-nothingness—the Nirvana they had all dreamed of. Occasionally an odd remark would come . . . but no reply was called for. It was as if they sat by a deep wide pool so perfectly still as to be not quite there. Into this pool they dropped these occasional remarks like stones— only to hear the resonant plop! plumbing the depths and rippling the silence with concentric rings. Like that old Japanese haiku: *Old pond . . . frog-jump-in-sound . . . silence.*

"Hey! You fellers in there! Where are you? Where's your bloody lamps?"

They clipped on their battery-tops and swung the lamps toward the entrance. There stood Eddie, his own lamp challenging theirs. Eddie was a Welsh sar'major from an ack-ack battery. He was also a miner. Now he was their shift sar'major who held a wandering commission for general liaison, to warn the men on safety and translate the shift boss's intentions to them.

"She's *O-O-OVER! It's bloody O-O-Over*, mates!"

"What is?" Buck said.

"The bloody *WAR*, man! The bloody *WAR!*"

"Got a light?" Buck asked, pulling out a Red Cross Camel.

"A *LIGHT!* The bloody *WAR's* over, man . . . I *TOLD* you . . . it's *O-O-OVER!*"

"Do you reckon? Dinkum?"

"It's ridge . . . pukka . . . real gen . . . Okada told me!"

"How'd he know? Tojo tell him?"

"You bastards won't believe anything . . . that's what the radio broadcast was about today. . . ."

"Could be a furphy . . . you know what newspapers are . . . what about *Mai Nichi?*"

"But it's *RIGHT*," the exasperated Eddie said. "What's wrong with you dopey bastards . . . you don't *want* to believe it. . . . *The Emperor spoke himself* . . . he told all the Japanese that he had surrendered because there was nothing else he could do."

"Oh, the old Imperial Benevolence himself . . . the first and only bit that's ever done us any good . . . what about that light?"

"You blokes are daft . . . I come to tell you the bloody war's over and you won't listen." He held the lighted cigarette out to Buck.

"Never mind, Eddie," Alec said. "Now it's *o-o-over* you can dig real Welsh coal again . . . and be shot of us."

"*Ger-cha!*"

"It's over," Buck said. "So we just sit here. Doesn't seem much different . . . when do we get out of this lousy hole?"

"Okada says all men come back at eight o'clock."

"Big deal! The war's over . . . so we get two hours off. . . . Big Nippon presento!"

Eddie left to tell the others.

They talked about the news, but it did not seem real somehow. As the shift started to straggle out past their heading, they joined them. They got to the dining-room just as the night shift was finishing its meal and bundling up the mine ration.

"Well . . . we are still going down!"

They fell in and marched to the gate. From the dining-hall they could hear the numbers being called.

"It's over all right," someone said sarcastically.

There was a thundering gallop down the hill ending with a burst of men into the dining-hall.

"The *Shookoo* said *KERIE NIE!* and *wakere-ed* us!"

"*Kerie nie* . . . no bloody salute . . . it's *got* to be over!"

Still the men were confused. Unconsciously they had conditioned themselves all these years against hopeless hopes and the habit could not be broken at will. Dreams were to dream— not to have come true. This they were unprepared for. Some talked all night. Some tried to sleep. Few did. After midnight a guard came around and said timidly, "*Speakoo sukoshi*, prease." They thought of food and cigarettes. Impatience mounted. It was over. But where was the real evidence? Roll on daylight. After the first short sleep men lay awake, waiting for the nevercoming dawn. They got up and wandered around aimlessly. *Tenko* was as usual, except that it went very quietly and the Japanese appeared to be in a hurry to get it over. They asked no questions. Breakfast brought the same rations. Still nothing, really.

But, at ten o'clock, the prisoners took over the Red Cross store. There they found, in beautiful tongue-and-grooved cases, some supplies. On the outside of the cases was the legend: FROM DETROIT BRANCH, RED CROSS SOCIETY OF U.S.A. YOKOHAMA EARTHQUAKE FUND, 1923. For twenty-two years they had remained unopened. At eleven o'clock there was an issue of a mug of Red Cross milk to each man. One parcel was issued between four men. The men set about enjoying these things in absurd ways. Some lit two cigarettes at once. Many made gluttons of themselves. They talked expansively of the future with deliberate fantasy. They compared their immediate past with the normal conditions they had known . . . and laughed at the comparisons.

"How'd it be to sit down at a party, and take off your G-string and start picking out the lice!"

This, until now, had been quite normal. Now they romanced about the shock effect this conduct would have in normal times. But some spoke of the 'awful' things to get sympathy. "What do you want? To bludge for the rest of your life . . . just because of this. . . . Remember, mate, you're no bloody hero . . . you're just another mug that got caught . . . you didn't volunteer."

The gate was open all day but, at first, few went out. Rumours spread. Leave in seven days. Where? How long before we get home? Which way will we go? But still it was not real. What *was* beginning to dawn on them was the fact that *tomorrow* they had a better chance of still being alive than they had had for the past three and a half years. They were beginning to realize how long they had lived with this uncertainty of life— that life had been purely a thing of chance between the capriciousness of the Japanese and their defencelessness against disease. This had been their norm. Now, with the first signs of freedom, its abnormality was dawning. The shock of their escape was beginning to act upon them. A deep, almost unbearable, exhilaration disturbed them. They talked wildly, said inflated things, made boasts, revelled foolishly in the new feeling. Some went to the village and marched possessively into houses. The people were quiet, but frightened. They expected the prisoners to assert their right of rape and pillage due to the conqueror at least for the first day. But the prisoners only took a couple of radios to contact the outside world. Suddenly all the fairy-tale dreams of the poignant years seemed within reach. But, like so many dreamed-of Utopias, they tarnish when many greedy hands seize them. They quickly smoked all the cigarettes in the Red Cross supplies and clamoured for more. Contentious argument sprang up. Officers and men pulled in opposite ways —each toward themselves. The officers saying that they were acting for the men's benefit and the men saying that they were only acting for their own. Gambling sprang up overnight. Men dug out old remnants of uniforms and wore them like peacocks.

One man in hospital was dying. Relief had come too late.

He was too weak to come back, although he hung on for days. He became a reminder of what they had been . . . and yet he suddenly seemed an anachronism to them now. Another went mad. A couple of months before he had been banned from the camp concerts because of his too-obscene songs. A month ago he had suddenly gone religious, haunting the hospital patients with a Bible and wild talk. He became violent and had to be restrained. In his quieter periods now he sat with his pay book and Bible, indiscriminately reading both and babbling nonsense about returning home and going to heaven, all pitifully mixed in his mind.

After five days the men grew restive from what they considered unwarranted restrictions. From one Red Cross issue the chocolate had been taken out. The men found this out and refused to draw one parcel. The officers said it was on doctor's orders. The men said "Balls!" The officers tried to maintain their authority but the men shouted raw opinions. At last the officers said that the chocolate was being withheld as a travelling ration in case they had to move.

"In this weather we'd need a bloody waterbottle to carry it in!"

"Might as well be under the Nips, still."

Rumours. We are moving. Tomorrow. Four a.m. Day after tomorrow. Old man says we will be here a long time. All British and Australians above 350 to go to Moji . . . the rest stay six weeks.

On the 21st the black-out restrictions were lifted. To the men, this was a definite sign. They had been thinking in terms of an armistice only. They were still cautious about believing. The books and 'valuables' that had been taken from them were returned. They got their packs out of the kit store. John got his watercolours back.

The madman, a non-smoker, suddenly took up obsessive smoking and became a walking chimney. "He's given up cutting his throat for a slower form of suicide," Harry said.

Tanaka said it could be from two to four weeks before they were taken out. Then they would go straight to Moji. The Americans were to go to Yokohama.

'Gundagai' sat dreaming in the sun. "If only we had more grub and plenty of fags . . . we could sit in the sun all day and

play two-up for cigarettes . . . playin' for this Nip coin's no
good . . . no bloody satisfaction."

At three o'clock in the afternoon, a black car pulled up outside the gate and a Japanese officer came into the camp. The
British and Australian C.O.s were called into the office. Later
the N.C.O.s were sent for and told the situation. From the next
day the camp was to be run by the prisoners. The guards would
still be outside, but only as protection. Medical supplies would
be handed over. Those who had died would be taken home as
ashes. Mail and papers were out of the question at the moment.
The country was devastated. A telegram from Tokyo took three
days. Food was not a question of money, but of devastation.
They would not be moved from this camp for three weeks or a
month. Then they would go straight to a ship because there was
no shore accommodation—again, devastation. It was not known
just how long they would remain, there had been no orders
from Manila. They were told to mark their roofs with large
white P.W. signs.

2

On the twenty-fourth a Union Jack and home-made
Australian and American flags were hoisted over the camp. The
British took over the guard duties. They took exceptional pride
in it. Leather boots which had been hoarded came out,
brightly polished. Gaiters and belts had the brasswork shining.
The skinny men inside the khaki strutted with a new importance.
After all this anonymity, they were determined to become *someone* again. They would show the shambling Japanese what a real
military bearing was.

"A bit late, poor bastards," Harry said, not without sympathy.

It was as if each man were looking for an identity lost somewhere along the way. The unreasonable complaints, the
undisciplined shouts against authority, were all part of this.
Their personal squabbling was like the conduct of children
trying to find themselves in a new group.

Four thousand kilos of potatoes, and two thousand eight
hundred of rice were on the way.

They heard a tale from the village that the women had been

told that if they had anything to do with the Australians they would give birth to kangaroos. The men laughed loudly. But Buck added a sobering thought. "Not so funny, you blokes . . . take a good gander at us . . . it wouldn't be kangaroos . . . it'd be bloody *bunyips!*"

There was a rumour that eighty cigarettes a man and some sugar was on its way. A bargeload of cucumbers and egg fruit came in. On the roofs, after the white P.W. they painted 400 to tell how many in the camp. They heard that the Americans had landed at Yokohama, and that seven thousand five hundred prisoners in the area had been fed from aircraft for the last three days. But they had still not had any contact with the outside world themselves.

For two days, heavy rain and gales swept over the country and the sea. Loose, low cloud made flying impossible. Then, one morning, a dozen fighters swept low along the coast and, on seeing their marks, made several passes and victory rolls over the camp. Now their excitement began to rise and impatience increased. At twelve-thirty, a four-engined aircraft, looking silver against the pale-blue sky, went over like a stately sailing-ship. Over Motoyama they watched dozens of coloured para-chutes tumble out in a cascade as the supplies were dropped. Only one plane came over Ohama and made a single drop which, because of the hill at the back, was not very accurate. Double-parachuted 44-gallon drums came down with great speed. Some chutes did not open. Two of these heavy drums crashed through the lamp-room roof at the mine. They ripped along the concrete floor, tearing out all the racks of the charging gear in a chaos of blue and white flashes and explosions. The girls ran screaming, badly frightened. But none was hurt.

One parachute landed just outside the gate, bringing down a large bale. The starving men ran out and ripped it open, impatient for what was inside.

"Boots . . . bloody boots!"

"If I had the strength I'd throw the bastards back!"

"That's not all I'd do with them."

"I've a bloody good mind to *eat* them!"

Parties went out to collect the rest of the scattered stuff. Much of it had burst and had to be brought back bundled in the canopies. There was dehydrated bullion, pea soup, tinned meat,

fruit juice, vitamin tablets, cigarettes and candy. They found
one man by a broken drum shovelling handfuls of vitamin
tablets into his mouth, and chewing them down as fast as he
could.

"You idiot! You'll poison yourself!"

"I don't care."

They had to take them off him by force.

The men were running about, not knowing which way to
turn first. So much, and *given* to them! CONTACT HAD BEEN MADE.
At last the outside world knew about them again. For the past
three and a half years it had never seemed to matter to anybody
whether they lived or died. Now, *they mattered!* People were concerned about them. There was a surge of emotion in them that
had no concise expression. It seemed that their bellies were
melting within them.

The wings of the dropping aircraft were marked, P.W.
SUPPLIES. One man, in the general rushing about, shouted,
"WHAT A GREAT DAY! THIS IS FUN . . . I WOULDN'T CHANGE WITH
ANYONE FOR QUIDS . . . IT'S *WORTH* BEING A P.O.W. FOR!"

A message came from International Red Cross Protective
Powers. *You are to be evacuated from a port near Osaka as soon as
possible. You are exhorted to be patient and co-operate to the last,
leaving Nippon in the face of its people with your dignity and honour
intact. Supplies and clothes will be dropped. Nominal rolls are to be
forwarded and an attempt will be made to broadcast survivors from
Tokyo. It is hoped to make the evacuation as comfortable as possible.
But we can only do so with your absolute co-operation, as other districts
will be evacuated through the same ports, and it is hoped to avoid bottle-
necks. Again we exhort patience.*

With the supplies came the stern warning: DO NOT OVER-EAT,
DO NOT OVER-MEDICATE.

As one of them, John had become used to the men. But he
watched a foraging party come into the camp loaded with this
new treasure in the coloured canopies of the parachutes. They
were thin with the skin tight over their cheekbones. Their eyes
were sunken and dark-ringed. They moved with the slouch that
came from discouragement and endurance. It seemed to John,
as they came in, that their sunken eyes were burning with an
excitement almost diabolically being repressed—as if they feared
being discovered with all this stuff, for their prisoner-reason

kept telling them this was impossible. This was the dream they had continually had, but from which they had previously always awakened before they could sample any of it. Gunner Miles said, "When things were tough and you had your guts knocked in . . . it was thoughts of days like today that kept you going."

Their first meal of the stuff made them think of all those who had not lived to eat it. The things of their captivity were already beginning to seem unreal.

3

It was still to be a fortnight before they finally left Ohama. Boof, Harry, Buck, Alec and John went rambling about the countryside during those days. John took his watercolours and looked for subjects. As he worked the others explored further, sat about and talked or skipped stones across the Inland Sea. They wandered over the little *yama* at the back of the camp, up a narrow path to its crest, from which they could see Ube with its twenty-two chimneys sticking up out of the flat country beyond. Among the pines and climbing vines on the ridge they came across a little cemetery. Small caskets and jars of ashes sat on little shelves in boxes that looked like doll's houses—as if some child's playthings lay forgotten in the undergrowth. To the prisoners they appeared child-like and toy-like with a great irrelevance to the pageant of death made in the west with ostentatious protocol. Here, it was as if children had left their well-loved dolls in the care of an understanding spirit. Not far away was a crude crematorium. A long, low cylindrical oven of iron, long enough to take one corpse on a curved iron tray that could be withdrawn and pushed in. The two iron doors were ajar. In the fireplace was some charred wood. On the tray were remnants of charred bones. In the trees about, black crows sat . . . a few flew about, cawing with dismal foreboding.

Also from the crest of the hill they could see the B29s roaring over Motoyama with parachutes tumbling from their bomb bays and bursting into coloured flowers with the supplies swinging like pendulums under them. Nothing further was dropped at Ohama. This hill made the seaward approach tricky at low altitude. At the western end of the little mountain, they came down a zig-zag path winding between the wooden houses that rose one over the other. The path was at once at the foot of one house and above the roof of the house below. John felt, all at once, that he was in Japan one hundred years too early for the war that had just finished. What had these people to do with it? he wondered, as they came down to the seawall of the little village of Neshi Ohama. They came back along the rocky shore to the camp.

"We'll have to go back there," John said. "Did you see those junks?"

Seawall of Neshi Ohama

"Don't worry," Boof said. "We'll take you back—you can have a whole day to draw them."

"I reckon he'd *eat* a bloody ship," Harry said to the others.

A party had gone to Motoyama with some commandeered handcarts and brought back a lot of supplies, and tales of Babylonian feasting that was going on there.

"They aren't eating rice at all . . . except as a chocolate pudding!"

That night they got a bigger ration. Rice, beans and potatoes —2000 grammes. There was also soup, a rice *d'œuvre* and a breakfast 'K' Ration. They all over-ate and spent the night in agony.

"Don't talk to me about crucifixion and childbirth . . . let them try this!" Buck said.

"Well, don't eat so much tomorrow."

"Are you kidding? Tomorrow I'll guts myself just the same ... after all this time without food ... I've got no willpower."

"That's stupid."

"I know ... but now I'm a *food addict* ... nothing can stop me ... I just like giving in to temptation."

"You'll suffer."

"Don't you think I don't know! But I'll tell you what—so will all the blokes making fancy resolutions ... as well as a guts-ache, they will feel guilty as well ... I'll know *I* did it."

"Well, *you're* buying it."

Motoyama mine and jetty

"Harry, when I sin, I do it on my own ... don't get shifty and say someone made me ... you do it—you fix it ... otherwise it's all front and not worth a pinch of nanny goat's ... doesn't fix a bloody thing."

Men began to put on weight rapidly—too rapidly. In fifteen days some put on twenty pounds. Stomachs were distended, limbs were swollen. Some were caricatures of humanity. Emaciated men with puffed-up pot-bellies thrust out turning their navels inside-out. Above this taut inflation were their slatted ribs, cheekbones and hollow temples. Their shoulder-blades stuck out like featherless wings. They walked with a stately gait as if they were unnaturally pregnant. They turned corners with a circumspect manoeuvre as if they had an invisible bass drum and were afraid the wind would snatch it away.

Some of the parcels brought from Motoyama had short messages scrawled on them by the exuberant Americans who had sent them. Eat up, there's plenty more where this came from. . . . Don't eat their wog food, you've been living on rice for 3½ years. . . . You eat the food, we'll — the women. . . . Smoke as much as you want to. . . . You've slept on boards for 3½ years, there's plenty of beds and women in Manila . . . You don't have to take any more from those bastards. . . . The men laughed and gloated over them. These prisoners who had sworn bloody revenge on the Japanese were now free to indulge it. The Ape and the rest of the guards had vanished. Somebody had seen Okada talking to the Tiger in the village.

"The Tiger! Wonder where he's sprung from?"

"I suppose he's just wandering about . . . must be a lot of blokes out of the army foot-loose now . . . the joint's in an uproar."

"Are you going to get the Tiger, Boof?" Doggie asked.

"I don't think so . . . reckon the Tiger's got all the trouble he wants just now . . . you know what surrender would do to *him* . . . probably won't have the front to go home."

"D'y'reckon?"

So the prisoners took their revenge.

The camp chores were now being done by the village people. Women carted *benjo*, and cleaned the camp. Each day they lined up, silent supplicants, hoping only for some rice.

The prisoners gave them what clothes they could spare. They gave the children what candy and chewing-gum they would take. There had been one gaffer whose wife had been sick. Only on the strictly limited food ration of this communal village, he had gone without himself so that she got more. He had lost weight and began to look quite ill himself. Now some of the prisoners made up a substantial food parcel and took it down to his house. The gratitude of the wife was more than they could stand. "She was a real little doll . . . the way she thanked us . . . it was bloody awful . . . nearly bawled like a kid . . . some other bastard can take the next lot down."

The gaffer had told them that the villagers could not understand this lack of revenge. Neither could they, really. They had

meant to take it. The American messages meant well, but they
could not know the people here.

They took John back to Neshi Ohama to draw the junks.
The day was overcast. Heavy storm clouds were lumbering up
from the west. Because of the weather threat, John made only
simple line-drawings. As he worked he burned the details into
his mind. The metre-wide keels as they rested on the low-tide
mud. The balanced, hoisted rudders. The gear and rigging.

John made only simple line drawings

The shape that spoke so clearly to him of how they would
behave in storm or calm. From the iron bell-tower he looked
down on them. From the mud he looked up at them. On board
he had the Japanese fishermen hoist, lower, and work the gear
for him. They showed him round and explained. From the
stone wharf Buck called, "Hey, Admiral! What time does the
fleet sail?"

Rain came and they took shelter in the noisy fish-market.
John made sketches of a Korean he had known down the mine.
They gave him some cigarettes. Then he drew a boy, shy almost
to the point of fear. When he had finished, John offered him
candy—but he bolted like a rabbit. Children crowded round
and they gave away all the candy they had brought with them.

After the rain lifted, they walked out beyond the village to a shrine in a small forest of giant cypress pines. John made drawings of the *torii* and stone lions. The *torii* was weathered and unpainted.

"Wonder what's the strength of these *torii's*?" Buck said.

"They started off only as bird roosts," John said.

"What!"

"That's right. Gifts of food used to be brought to the priests. Live fowls were hung up by the feet until sunset . . . at sunset they ate the food, but the birds were not killed. They let them go . . . to become the chanticleers of the temple to wake them in the morning. The *torii's* were put up as roosts. Until Bhuddism came they only had one bar."

"If they woke me at dawn," Buck said, "it would be a good way of getting themselves knocked off."

They walked back to the village and the rain started again. They took shelter in a shop-fronted house. The window framed a perfect profile of a three-masted junk, upright on the mud.

"Another bloody junk," Harry groaned as John began drawing it.

They had brought plenty of tinned rations with them in haversacks. They asked if they could heat some tins somewhere. Cooma San, a mine gaffer, fixed it up for them. They were taken to the back of the house where there was an earthen floor. Here firewood was piled and the fire pot was set. Two women, a mother and daughter, shyly showed them in. The frame of the house was of round unsawn poles. The floor proper was a raised platform covered with *tatami*. The portable paper-screen walls were now stacked at one end, making a spacious single room of the place.

They had much more food than they needed so they gave most of it to the mother, who became quite embarrassed and reluctant to take it. It was only when Boof made a great pantomime of lordly anger if she did not do as she was told, that she smiled and took it with a graciousness that they never tired of seeing. After they had eaten they took off their boots and sat on the *tatami* with the two women and talked. It was all so halted and repeated, but it was amazing how much real exchange there was.

Harry began by telling mamma that her daughter was very

lovely—*airoshi*. The old lady, who could easily have been the girl's grandmother, was puzzled but, after much perseverance, they made her understand. She smiled. But the girl was only fifteen!

Boof said, "O.K. draw her John—she's better looking than that Korean you did this morning."

John asked the girl to sit for him. She was shy, but she consented. She wore a dark-blue sailor blouse with a square

collar and a V-front. Her face was broad, smooth and un-awakened. She sat as still as Buddha with her eyes fixed. The others kept the talk going. The girl had a bit of school English, which helped them. They found that she had a brother who had gone to the war. They had had no word of him. Papa? Long ago in China. She had never seen him. One other brother was dead in New Guinea. They said they were sorry. The mother looked at them, the fine old face made sweet with the character of acceptance, gave a smile that did not move her kindly mouth— it came from deep within her eyes. It was a look she might have given a son.

"She's beautiful," Harry said. He insisted until she understood. Now her mouth smiled and her head ducked a little with embarrassment as she blushed.

"Draw her," Harry said. "She's the real beauty of this house."

She was so shy that it took all of them, including the daughter, to coax her. And then not until she had combed her hair and patted it into place. After which she took the small broken-toothed comb and stuck it in the back of her hair. The others thought the sketch was good and the old woman was pleased. But John would have to be content to take back within himself

She came to the shrine and stood before it, praying

all that he had failed to put on paper. He was so conscious then of all the beauty that is in humanity, despite the hate and stupidity with which it is enmeshed. This was the drive behind his drawing—he wanted to take some of this good back with him. He worked hard. When he was not getting subjects he chafed. Often, at 3 a.m., he was still sitting up writing the day's impressions.

He had been drawing a small shrine down towards Moto-yama. In the vegetable patch on the hillside near by, a woman worked all the morning with a baby on her back. About noon, before she went away, she came to the shrine and stood before it, praying. John could hear her voice. The simple peasant woman reciting some Oriental litany, he thought, to her ancestors in an effort to touch the hem of the garments of her gods. It mingled with the baby-talk on her back. John wrote that night, "I was deeply impressed—these are impressionable times. As always I was touched by the great simplicity of her acts of faith. Her country—this divine land under the hand of the illustrious Hirohito, Son of Heaven, dispenser of Imperial Benevolence and divine will—this, her country, was fallen. She would know a Westerner, a General, alien and vulgarly mortal, to whom the Son of Heaven was only the son-of-a-gun, and who was making an unpardonable travesty of Nipponese divinity. This is the second day of the full-scale occupation of Japan. What was the quality of her faith? Had she come to pray for the Son of Heaven? Would not that, in itself, be *lèse-majesté*? Or had she come in simple bewilderment to ask the help of her ancestors? Perhaps she understood nothing of the politico-religious mysteries of her country at all. She may have lost a son or husband. Perhaps the future held only the spectre of famine and pestilence so familiar to her kind. Perhaps she had come to pray only from habit, unmindful of what was happening to her country. Yet I felt that *she* was more fundamental than all the momentous chaos of victory and defeat around me. As simply as her womb had yearned for motherhood and begotten a child, so she came with a simple soul before the spirits of her ancestors—as childlike as the infant on her back. It was so simple. Yet so profound that I could only feel an un-nameable significance in it. I only know that I was touched by the common humanity of it all that these garbled sentences do little to describe."

That same night he wrote, "I have killed a hundred bugs. I could easily have killed five hundred (and the same number of fleas), but we are tolerant these days. Even if the vermin don't surrender like the Japanese, we kill only those that over-annoy us . . . and this is not all that bite us by any means. This, some day, I might find hard to believe. So I write it now as a normal incident to remind me later. When I remember later, it may perhaps make life seem a little sweeter then."

There had been no solution to the bugs and fleas all this time. But now they found it. The large room-sized mosquito nets of silk had not been used because they were too airless to sleep under. Now they strung them upside-down as you would a canvas swimming-pool. They then climbed over the walls and slept inside. The vermin could not intrude through the bottom and for some reason of their own, refused to climb over the walls.

4

The air drops were becoming dangerous. So many 'chutes did not open. Each was designed to carry 300 pounds at 150 miles per hour. With eighteen or more coming down together, some opening and some not, there was danger. These had crashed through the roofs, luckily into empty rooms. At the first sign of a drop, the bell rang the alarm and everybody streamed into the open where they could watch and dodge. The sick just had to take their chance. A story came from Ube that more had been killed in the air drops there than in the previous bombings. Two were hurt at Ohama, but there were some miraculous escapes. At Motoyama a man had a leg broken and a Japanese was killed. The noise of the breakaway drums ripping through the trees and undergrowth on the hillsides was frightening with its unexpected force. It was loud even a quarter of a mile away. They said that the Americans allowed for a fifty per cent loss.

Foraging parties went out to collect the stuff. Some of the villagers voluntarily brought in the scattered supplies with great honesty. They were allowed to keep all the damaged stuff and were given more besides. One day Harry and Boof were out. By the edge of a paddy they saw a little boy who had salvaged some candy from a scattered drop. A man was standing over him, taking it away.

"It's the bloody Mamba," Harry said.

With a flying boot, he lifted the Mamba into the paddy, where he fell flat in the swampy mud. "Get up, you bastard! *Kurrah!*"

The Mamba looked frightened and came out cautiously. Harry lifted his hand but did not strike. The Mamba cringed. "You dirty yellow-bellied no-good bastard. *Kurrah!*" He made the Mamba give the candy back to the boy. He made him wade about for more and give it to the child. He made him apologize, but the little boy ran away, frightened.

"Now, you . . . YOU . . . *KURRAH!*"

They made him pick up the yellow canopy and fill it with

supplies. "Just his colour," Boof said. "It matches the streak down his back." They made him hoist a killing load. Their threats were so menacing that he thought he was carrying it under the threat of death if he failed. Desperately he staggered with it, sometimes falling, but jumping up again fearfully straining the load up on his shoulders. Mercilessly they drove him back to the camp and turned him over to the English guard. "Teach the bastard a lesson." Men whom he had bashed visited him in the small cell. Some beat him, but most simply insulted and frightened him. A few days later, some black-uniformed police visited the camp. They turned the Mamba over to these, saying that the man had been caught stealing American supplies. That night the villagers said that the Mamba had been shot.

The food was bringing more suffering to the men who could not stop eating. John wrote, "It is horrible to see a man with a stomach so swollen that it seems it will burst. The distension is exaggerated above his emaciated thighs and legs. Wind and the horrible pains of indigestion leave no laws of etiquette which remain sensible under these conditions."

Over the wireless came impassioned pleas for men to remain where they were. "Wait until we come for you." The incidence of venereal disease was given; the number of deaths from home-made alcohol and substitutes—and the cases of blindness. Men were being killed in air crashes, hitching rides. This gave them an indication of the state of ferment among the prisoners generally. There were the stories other P.O.W.s were telling in the first flush of release. To the Ohama men they sounded distorted and exaggerated. John wrote, "It is a pity. The reality, which is bad enough, will be lost to the public confronted with the fantastic versions. It will get no real understanding, nor will it have an ear for the truth when it finally hears it."

Torrential rains set in.

A newspaper dropped from Manila carried some strange items. Aircraft without propellers, called jets. The bombs that had destroyed whole cities, Hiroshima and Nagasaki, atom bombs—chain reaction. Great fear was felt about this chain reaction: one atom set off the one next to it and so on . . . how did they stop the whole world from blowing up once it had started? They wondered. They felt like so many Rip Van

Winkles waking. But one item they would not swallow: a new pen they said would write for two years without a refill—a ballpoint, they called it. This was a lot of rubbish.

5

One day Buck, Alec and John walked across the neck of the island to a headland on the other side, on which stood a shrine. It was a beautiful morning after a brutal storm that had left its

A junk with limp sails dripped its reflection into
an horizonless sea

signature scrawled roughly along the shore. Stone lanterns were overturned, and the broken hulls of several small craft lay a hundred yards inland. A stone *torii* was askew. But now the mirrorlike sea was gentle again, hardly breathing. A junk with limp sails dripped its reflection into an horizonless sea, as if suspended in the sky. John wrote, "While I was working, I felt very deeply, as I have felt before, that to express adequately one must love the things and *feel* their oneness." Buck was walking further up the beach. John put him in the picture. Alec came over and sat by John.

"Well," Alec said, "it's over. Now you will have to come out from under your willow tree ... or from off your lotus leaf ... or down from your mountain crag ... or from wherever you philosophize ... now we are going back ... to what? ... I wonder ..."

"Things will be strange."

"No doubt about that."

"I meant that the things we did before will now seem different ... different from what they will be to people who have never been without them ... I hope I never lose this fresh taste of freedom."

"What have you made of it, John?"

"When you put it into words it sounds silly ... do you know, it just struck me, that's just about what old Lao Tzu said about six hundred B.C. ...."

"What?"

"*But the Way, when declared, seems so thin and flavourless. It is nothing to look at and nothing to hear ... but used, it will prove inexhaustible.* ... That's about what he said."

"But what do *you* say?"

"The first rule of life is *To accept it.* The greatest possible achievement in life can never be more than simply *To be.* (Animals do this better than man.) The greatest wisdom to be got is to learn *How to be.*"

"But what about religions?"

"Perhaps they are the *As-if* tales we must tell ourselves to assure and comfort us. Somehow it seems that man *must* have an *Answer.*"

"What do you mean by *As-if* tales?"

"The way you look at things. You see, your view of life is made up of what you choose (or are forced) to notice and what you ignore. You must do this because you can't take it *all* in. This is true from worm to man. The worm's world probably works better because the worm sticks to necessity—man's brains lead him to wishes and the obligation to do much that is useless essentially. To me, to try to define Purpose is *not* to have faith."

It was not so strange that John should have such a pat answer for Alec. They had discussed this sort of thing before.

But for John, this had been part of a continual search he had made as a prisoner, partly to help him live outside his circumstances. He had learned that simply by *sitting still* these thoughts would come to him. In a way it had started with a cup of strong black coffee which had been given to him in Java by an Indian he had befriended. It had kept him awake and brought him the question, "*I, Myself—what am I?*" He seemed to fall into a transcendental state then.

The next day he had written about it in his diary: "I had drunk it at sundown. At 10 p.m. I was still not able to sleep. I was still listening to the sounds of men changing as they went to sleep. I still did not sleep. Outside, the sweet, shrill chirping of the Java bush at midnight suggested an absolute purity of air. The toc-ta lizards were lazily calling. Then, clear, ringing silence. The imperceptible radar of a million distant pinpoints of starlight. The deep, black distance of the sky was eternity itself. The slow-turning stars passed their zenith and set beyond, immeasurably beyond, that death-still frieze of frozen ink-black palm fronds. This was the slow, endless turn of the universal loom weaving us all into the perfect incomprehensible fabric of being. My body remained unobtrusive: I had become a voyaging mind which sailed out and around those stars, deep into the nebulae of the unknowable. Never had my mind been so clear and so sure, with such a completely absorbed ego. No confusion. Only crystal clarity . . . I am that coincidence through which thought flows; that fantasy of being, the meeting-place of ideas in the conscious; the point in the path of the abstract transmuted to the sensual in me—sensing and being sensed; the imperfect reflector of those ideas. All things pass me in time; or I them; or we each other. All is movement in space. The difference of speed and velocity is the difference of things by co-incidence. . . ." And so on.

John had worked out various ways to beat mental despair and stagnation. With a month's supply of cigarettes he had traded for a small pocket-dictionary. He sewed a canvas cover on it and carried it about with him. In the Red Cross parcels were packets of spearmint chewing-gum. The inner green wrapper just fitted between the pages of the dictionary. These were not easy to get for although they were only one and a half inches by three and three-quarters, they were also in demand for toilet paper. But he managed to get twenty-six pieces—one for each letter of the alphabet. In small letters he put down the words he was not sure of. He went over and over them until he had most of the words in that small book in his mind. Some words became almost *things* to him. He had spoken to Alec about *scintillating* and *coruscating*. Where they touched his reality, they fascinated him. Down below in the mine, he would sometimes slip away and study them.

"Where have you been?" the others would ask. "Up with your old friends the rats?"

And he had. He had found the hint of what faith was in the invisible ends of those exquisitely fine white filaments of fungus slowly striving in Stygian silence beneath the sea. Those thread-like fingers acted as a catalyst to his thoughts.

"Let's face it," he thought deliberately. "What if *none* of the prisoners ever gets home? What if this war, or another one, destroys civilization? Or lays the whole face of the earth flat and dead? Then, what?" John had felt a calm as the answer came. *These filaments would continue to grow—to bridge again the infinite with the finite.*

Here he waded in and sat on a pile of wet slimy logs and wrote by the light of his cap-lamp. Around him the big, thick-furred rats picked their way about with great fastidiousness, avoiding the water with neat, but not athletic, jumps from one obstacle to the next.

He paused and looked up for an inspiration or a wandering Japanese. There, in a semicircle about him, shone the bright golden eyes of a dozen rats sitting still and intent, looking right into the beam of his lamp.

"Brother Rats," he said quite distinctly, "I think you already know what I am trying to say."

And now, as Alec had said, back to the world of victory. . . . But where, John wondered, does the one end and the other begin?

6

Rainstorms continued to sweep the countryside.

Some men from Ohama met some English who had come to Japan in the same convoy with them. Their ship had been driven ashore in the typhoon. After five days they had been taken off by a Japanese destroyer and put aboard a ship at Taiwan. The whale factory-ship that was with them was lost. And they had reached Japan before the Australians.

Some came back from a trip to Ube, where, they said, they found a camp of English who were too morose to talk to them. They had not been outside their camp. They did not fly a flag. Scraps of news blew about like so much torn paper. A couple of junks blew up just offshore at Ohama as a result of mines. The teeth of war were not yet drawn. A group went to Moji and came back with their pieces of the jig-saw of release.

In July 1944 a P.O.W. ship approaching Japan was torpedoed with 700 Australians and 100 Dutch, outside Nagasaki. Six hundred drowned. The Japanese took to the boats. The prisoners had to jump for it. Some of John's *Perth* shipmates were among them. An electrical artificer was finally able to launch a jammed lifeboat the Japanese had abandoned on board. He got it into the water and picked up some of the prisoners. Escort vessels picked up the Japanese from the boats and the prisoners took them over. But they were left there. Japan was in sight to the eastwards. China was invisible to the westward. All boats began pulling to the west. Most were never heard of again. One seaman petty-officer John had grown up in the Navy with, was last seen steering towards China with the tiller between his knees and leading the rowers singing, *Cheer up my lads —— 'em all*. This story came from the artificer whose boat was overtaken four days later by a Japanese destroyer. One ship of fifteen hundred Americans was reported in the news as having only one-third survived. They were bombed and harrassed by submarines all the way up. One American said that they had left Manila eight days after the invasion had begun. Conditions were so bad, he said, that he had seen men cut each other's throats for water. Four hundred only of them survived. British and Australian troops had been taken out of Nagasaki and replaced by Dutch. Eight days later the atom bomb was dropped there. Moji, they said, was attacked with incendiaries and laid waste by fire. Prisoners with the Japanese had fought fires and salvaged stores in a six-hour raid. People were now living there under sheets of old iron or any sort of shelter they could contrive. People had become scavengers to live. One of the camps there did not get any air drop, while a nearby camp of only one hundred and twenty were hoarding any amount. They would neither give nor sell any to their starving countrymen. The adamant British C.O. said that his position of plenty was purely an act of providence. The other camp must have sinned in some way, he maintained, and he was only acting in accordance with Divine Will in withholding it.

"He sounds like one of the Imperial Benevolence mob," Buck said. "But a B29's a bloody big angel."

After six days of rain and storm, the air drop started again. By 9.30 a.m. over two hundred parachutes had fallen. The bell went. The men streamed out into the open. The hospital was narrowly missed. Two went through the camp cookhouse roof. The village hospital, the lamp-room and the mine office and a house near by were all hit when parachutes did not open, or the packs broke away from the harness. Forty-three 'chutes came down in one drop—forty-one opened. The whole village was recruited and volunteered to recover them. Infants, mothers with babies slung over their backs, or on the breast, children, old men with thin straggling beards and pinched faces, ex-mine workers, all trooped into the camp draped over with red, white, blue, green and yellow canopies. They were all lined up later and freely *presento-ed*.

Surrounded by all this food, cigarettes and candy men began to break out in cantankerous complaint. A couple of weeks ago they had been starving. They had fought dangerously over bean water and whale blubber crackling. They had smoked coir rope and all sorts of bark and leaves. They had not tasted sugar for more than a year and none to speak of for three and a half years. Now they threatened mutiny—to 'jack-up'—because they had been given a carton of Camels. They had had those last time, now they wanted Chesterfields or some other brand. They complained because it was chicken soup again, wasn't there anything else! Why did they have to have *this* sort of candy! They were getting back to normal.

Their hair was beginning to grow again, some could part it now. It looked strange to them. "Blokes are looking like sheilas!"

There was much unreasonable pettiness and much unreasonable reaction to it. There was officer-and-man friction. It was all indulged in, yet, somehow, understood between them as if it were a part of some play they had to act out. But there were some meannesses that were not overlooked.

A girl came to the camp gate one night in the grip of the moon. She had come of her own accord, offering. Two of the guards played with her with a salacious peeping-Tom obscenity. Hands violated until she trembled and wept—but they did nothing for her. Instead they laughed at her and told her to clear off.

"All these bints are just bitches . . . that'll teach her a lesson . . . serve her right."

"Yeah . . . did you *see* her!"

A voice in the dark said, "I bloodywell did."

"Who's that?"

"I'm the bastard that's going to even-up on you pair of motherless bludgers—boots and all."

Without another word the voice was among them. With cold, unfeeling ruthlessness he was using every trick in his gutter-fighting repertoire. He punched, chopped, elbowed, kneed, butted and kicked in deadly sequence. He left them groaning and holding themselves in agony. He knew exactly what he had done.

When Buck came into the room his nose was skinned and his knuckles were bleeding. He wrapped a handkerchief around them.

"What happened, Buck?"

"Not looking where I was going."

"Too much *saki*, old son."

"When you hear some of our blokes talk about the Japs . . ."

"Yes?"

"Oh, nothing . . . but we've got some prize bastards in our mob, too."

"Strike me! You haven't just found that out, have you?"

That night there was a bottle of beer a man, and some biscuits, issued at supper. This was an extra meal they now put on at 9 p.m. Not all the men drank the beer, but others, who had now got the taste, finished it for them. Some of these had managed also to get some whisky on this night.

"Let's go down the village and stir some of these bastards up."

"Wait on. I know where there's another bottle of 'skey."

They went down the road and prowled round the houses. From one window a small light shone. They threw clods of earth on to the roof. A small man was silhouetted for a moment at the door as he came out to see what was happening. He stood in the garden looking about.

"Let's go over him!"

They ran drunkenly towards him. As he looked around they were on him in a heap. They stood up again. But, as the Japanese began to rise, they kicked him down again. Each time he tried they punched and kicked him. They swore at him ferociously. "Now it's *our* turn, you slit-eyed bastard." They did not wait for him to try to rise any more. They kicked and beat him until they were swaying and stumbling from exhaustion.

"That'll teach him," they said as they lurched away.

The beaten man writhed, gave a gasping screech, and lay still. In the sudden quietness a child's voice sounded in the house. A woman in kimono ran out in bare feet. She hesitated in the dark a moment, then, as if by instinct, ran directly to the fallen man. She saw him and, for an instant, both hands clutched below her breasts. She dropped to her knees with a sob and pulled the man's shoulders on to her knees, pillowing his head against her *obi*. Her face drew into a grimace. Koko San was dead.

7

Ohama was like an island, though it was joined to the mainland by a flat stretch that looked as if it had been recently reclaimed from the sea. One rainy morning John and the others went for a walk right around it. Passing a house, they saw a little boy standing outside watching a pair of fowls with incredibly long tails sitting on top of a fence. As usual, they offered him a few bars of candy. He took them, a little puzzled. They assured him it was all right. He thanked them ceremoniously with great politeness. Then he immediately turned toward his house. The front door was open and the walls stood on one side. On the farther wall they could see the *kami dana*, the family shrine, on a shelf. The boy went straight to the shrine, bowed, laid the candy on the shrine, bowed twice more and came away, leaving the present there.

"And these kids are starving . . . wouldn't have seen lollies in years . . . and yet he does this, , , ,"

"It's nice to see," Boof said.

"We call them heathens . . . *us!*" Buck said.

They went on and at the other side of the island they came to a large shrine in what looked like a flat parkland of giant firs which made living walls and roof for a vast green shadowy cave in which the temple stood. The rain-blackened trunks were like pillars in a cathedral. Big moss-grown stone lanterns of the moon and sun, and *shishi*, the stone lions, grew out of the ground, giving an aged look that somehow the inorganic expresses best. The stone lions looked as eternal as stalactite columns in a forgotten cave. The fine timber of the temple was without blemish or paint in the Shinto tradition which also aims 'to keep the old new'. They say that each twenty years or so the temples are practically rebuilt by constant replacement. This means that there are no really old wooden buildings in Japan— yet the spirit of antiquity seems imperishable. The tradition is the living thing. Many people were going and coming up and down the steps of this temple.

"Must be a holiday." Boof said.

"What would they want a holiday for?" Harry said. "After what's happened to them . . . what have they got to celebrate?"

"Maybe they are just wandering around wondering what will happen next."

They came out under the dark, dripping *torii*.

"The roosters have packed it in for the day," Buck said.

They walked along between the paddy fields. The kaledi leaves were luscious with their blue-green against the gamboge of the new rice. Fig trees threw up their gnarled livid limbs and held out broad handlike emerald flakes scattered shoulder-high across the distant siennas, madders and indigos of the rain-misted hills. It was new, young and growing. There was no hint of the past six years of destructive war. They came to Neshi Ohama. It was grey and dripping with silver shining roofs and streets and quays.

They turned toward Onada. The rain had stopped when they came to a school of about a thousand children, ranging from fifteen down to the tots. The children were now spread out in the grounds and formed up by classes for physical training. On a raised platform in the centre stood the headmaster giving directions. In front of each class was a teacher, repeating the exercises. All the pupils were bare-topped. The women teachers wore blouses and trousers buttoned at the ankle. All, except the headmaster, were bare-footed. All the exercises were free-standing ones requiring suppleness and co-ordination.

With silver shining roofs and streets and quays

"Look at that!" Harry said admiringly." ... Those kids are only knee-high to a duck ... *and they don't miss a beat!*"

"And they don't even know how good they are," Alec said.

They were back in camp by lunch-time. After a good meal they relaxed in their room.

8

Boof lay back on the *tatami*, his hands behind his head and his big chest expanded upwards. Across the ripple of his ribs were scars of the past three and a half years. Though part-grown, through his hair others could be seen. Boof was not thinking of the scars. He'd see Doris and the baby again. Baby? Not now ...

They had been talking about it.

"Just think, Boof . . . coming home from work every night! When you boil it all down . . . that's all we fought for . . . this whole bloody war!" Harry had said.

"Yes . . . we were unlucky . . . but we're lucky now . . . as you said, Harry, coming home from work every night . . . that's it."

"What about the Tiger? He's about, you know; somebody saw him the other day with Okada."

"He'll eat his heart out . . . what's the point now? . . . he's all Jap . . . I couldn't do any more to him than this. . . ."

When Boof had joined the army he had thought perhaps of a personal show-down with the enemy. He had been cheated in Syria . . . and in Java. The test with cold steel had been denied him. But, like a deliberate jibe, he repeatedly had to stand almost naked and be taunted by the enemy's cold steel. At first he had thought murderously of revenge. But before it devoured him, he overcame it. He endured silently because his common sense told him to. Now the way was clear for revenge, he no longer wanted it. Coming home from work every night, that was it. An end had come to killing, he thought.

Later in the afternoon they went for a walk by the village and along the shore. On the way back, Alec suggested that they go for a swim off the rocks below the seawall.

"Freshen us up before we get back."

"I'll be in it."

"You blokes go," Boof said. "I'll just mooch about up here . . . feel too lazy to go for a swim."

"Right-o, mate, see you back in camp."

Boof walked along the road by the side of the hill. He could see across the Inland Sea to Moji. The mountains of Kyushu were purple and blue. On the sea, flat like a floor, junks with slack sails lay, inviting the warm fitful breeze to bring them back to harbour. The wind was playing with them, breathing dark strips on the water all around them without ever quite touching them. Sailors call these dark patches 'cat's paws'—the wind that plays cat-and-mouse with ships. Stunted pines grew down by the sea above the rocks where the others were now swimming. These trees aroused something in Boof by the way they had withstood the weather. They suggested the quality of the

Australian gums growing gnarled and rugged in baked, drought-stricken paddocks. He almost caught the whiff of wet gum leaves ... of the smoke when they burned ... the sound of bell birds hanging their notes all about in the air—notes that stayed just where they were put ... the screech of cockatoos tearing strips out of the air ... it was as real as if he were walking there now. The country schoolhouse of his childhood ...

Boof walked along the road by the side of the hill

the sprawling country town ... the bush school ... he smiled ... long time now. .... These things were swamping out the past three and a half years of captivity ... these were now *real* things. For so long they had been unattainable dream-stuff it was painful to think about too much. But this was freedom, and Boof was savouring it to his fill. This was why he just wanted to mooch about on his own this afternoon.

By the road, he came to the small Ohama school. It had been closed since V.J. Day. He had seen the kids playing about and thought that kids were just about the same everywhere. He'd have a look in at their schoolroom. The door was unlocked. He pushed it open slowly, with some deference. He had taken a couple of steps into the dimmer light of the room before he realized somebody was there. He stopped while his eyes became adjusted from the glare outside.

There were four men in a rough semicircle, each kneeling back on his heels, Japanese fashion. Two were in some sort of black uniform, one was in a drab kimono, while the fourth was in a faded and patched Army uniform. Boof noticed the red patches at the collar and then recognized the Tiger. Okada was in the kimono.

Boof was about to go out, feeling sheepish.

The Tiger had been contemplating tragedy. They had listened to the Emperor's speech of capitulation. They felt awe at the sound of a voice they had never been permitted to hear before. *According to the dictates of time and fate . . . we have resolved to pave the way for a grand peace for all generations to come by enduring the unendurable and suffering what is insufferable.*

They were still stunned by it, unable to think the unthinkable. The great Yamato race was on its knees. They felt an incomprehensible mixture of grief, frustration of noble instinct, shame and impotence. They were trying to resolve it. Where lay their course of honour? How could they alleviate their country's dishonour? Swords lay naked before them like sacred symbols. Just as the Tiger's grief had reached a high pitch of nobility, there stood Boof—a Barbarian. With emotion he jumped to his feet, sword in hand. The others followed.

"*Kurrah!*"

The word exploded in Boof's head as he caught the gleam of the naked sword in the Tiger's hand. He became simple instinctive reaction perfected by his training. With one sweep, Boof's left arm backhanded across the neck of the nearest Japanese, Okada, and pulled him down to his knees. The big man's right hand came over and grabbed the man's sword arm from behind. The arm came up with a terrible jerk. The shoulder and elbow went with a double crack. The scream was cut short as Boof's knee came up sharply with a sinewy crunch into the man's neck. He had the sword before it dropped and shoved his victim violently towards the Tiger who was making a vicious swing at him. The Tiger was thrown off balance but his descending sword split the skull of the helpless man Boof had flung at him.

The Tiger recovered quickly and made another tremendous

two-handed swing at Boof, giving a peculiar grunting squeal of effort. Boof hardly thought what he was doing. He stepped *just* clear of the whistling blade and, with effortless and deceptive speed, he drove a short two-handed blow at the base of the Tiger's neck. All his unconscious power was in that short movement. It severed the spine and half-decapitated the Tiger. Without a pause he turned on the others and caught them irresolute. They went down as if they had nothing to defend themselves with. All Boof's past training, instinct for survival, uncanny natural ability, suddenly released from an iron-willed repression had become a single reaction. It was over.

He was left shaking and sick. He felt for the wall and slid into a sitting position. He thought bitterly, "Bloody *kurrah*."

At last he found a tap and washed himself and the sword, which he had not let go. With an inconsequential methodical detachment he sheathed it in a scabbard, closed the door and with deliberate steps, as if he were forcing himself, he made his way back to camp. He did not know why he took the sword with him. Not as a souvenir, or to brag about. He only ever told the story once, to Harry and the others. Back home he sometimes had found himself handling it . . . compulsively . . . the Tiger . . . he swung it . . . the Tiger, how had he . . . *why?* . . . he swung like the Tiger, as if he were trying to understand this last act of his old enemy . . . *Kurrah! Bageera!* . . . poor bastard. . . . And then, when Harry took it away, saying nothing . . . because he could not explain it to himself.

"Boof, don't blame yourself," they had said when he had told them.

"It was one of those things . . . war's war, as you bloodywell know . . . it's fate."

"It's that Arch Bastard who never shows his face . . . *he's* the Joker," Buck said with deep sudden feeling.

They felt it was pointless to talk about it more.

The next day a rumour went around.

"Hey, did you hear what the Tiger and some of the other Nips did?"

"No . . . what?"

"They Harry Careyed down at the school."

"Well I'm buggered!"

The Japanese made no fuss about it. It was one of those it-cannot-be-helped things.

"It was not fate . . . it was not anything but a sentence passed on both of them by Institution," John wrote in his diary that night. "Institution—the man-made fabric that could make a shroud for us all. The Jews have gone to the gas chambers and been boiled down for soap or fertilizer. Old men, women, children—non-combatants—have been slaughtered in Hamburg, Coventry, Warsaw, Rotterdam, Nankin . . . and now here in Nagasaki and Hiroshima. . . In each case some INSTITUTION has decided that this was RIGHT. Rabelais said it: *Till he has filled, by clamour and disputes, the sky with noise, the earth with trampling feet. Then faithless men will have authority, as great as have the champions of truth; for all shall follow the will and beliefs of the ignorant and stupid multitude, the dullest of whom shall be held as judge. O, hideous and most destructive flood. . . .*"

Two days later came the order to move.

9

At roll-call on the thirteenth, fifteen men were missing. They were to be ready to move at noon. Some came back with only minutes to spare. Just before four o'clock the trucks came for them.

The villagers had gathered. In their shabby and worn clothes which they wore with the unselfconsciousness of a skin, they waited—incongruous only to an outsider. Kimono, trousers, blouses, shirts, diapers (on men as well as children) and rags. Men on their way to the public bathhouse on *geta*, wearing only a G-string and carrying their little buckets and a towel. Blouses were buttoned or open wide. Some of the women who had been working in the gardens were half-naked. There were naked children. As eloquently as Shakespeare's Ages of Man, bare breasts told of the passage of man through this floating world: incipient, proud, suckling, barren, and completely senile. Frank or partly concealed—all innocently devoid of prudery or shame. Boys and girls, fat and lean, crooked and straight, with clear skins or sores, with boils or runny noses. John wrote, "These people have been kind and tolerant. They have lived on as little rice as we have, and now have hope of little better. They understand deprivation, hunger and catastrophe. They get little from life except what is born of their own appreciation of that little, and a constant thankfulness that it is no worse. They can laugh and have compassion. Without any sign of envy, they waved us *Sayonara* as we left for better prospects than they could imagine. They wished us well. I shall always remember these people of Ohama as they were then, having a humanity that rises above the false values of class, creed and race. I will remember them as the friendly enemy."

The people waved and called until the prisoners were around the corner of the road out of sight.

At Onada, they left their gear in a cinema, a fusty place with dusty black-curtained cubicles under and behind the stage. It was a strange place, redolent of the unimagined. Some lay down with their packs and waited. Boof and the others went for a walk around the paddy fields and small hamlets scattered through them. At seven p.m. they moved up to the station, but it was almost an hour after midnight before the train came through. At about ten p.m. the *Shookoo* from Ohama came on to the platform and wished them well in halting precise English. He shook hands with them and addressed many of them by their camp numbers—the only names he had ever known them by. His simple directness touched many of them and they genuinely wished him well.

"Poor old codger, I don't think he'll last . . . I reckon he's got T.B."

The train came in at last. The old *Shookoo* stood alone watching the train out of sight. At Manila, on a questionnaire about ill-treatment put to the prisoners, this harmless school-teacher was denounced by some as a war criminal.

They were sixty-nine to a carriage and all had seats, but they sat up all night. In the morning they awoke to see the livid surf breaking almost under the wheels of the running train. It steamed on around the rugged coast over the very edge of the sea. The swift smooth rhythm of the surf was all that was palpable at first in the darkness. Now and again they saw the weak golden glow of a cottage lamp placing but not revealing where the fishermen lived. It was a rocky pine-girt coast rich with breathlessly hanging crags and improbable islets which looked like sheer artistic invention. Each feature showed the individuality of its struggle against the continual assault of gale-lashed seas driven before the immense wind blowing right from the bleak Asiatic Steppes. This very discipline had also given a mass-conformity as if to say, 'We will conform to endless panels of Japanese art that will truthfully speak for us'. John tried to soak it up without one intellectualization—just to *feel* it. The sweep of the rain-swept sky over the moving grey-green ocean. The muted watery indigo of the distance melting around some sudden sharp dark brushstroke mountain coming through like the foundation of creation itself. The warm touches of bare earth, the clean precise pattern of terraced paddy cherished to the last square yard. Sawgum, kaledi, sweet potato. Clumps of small stunted pines preserved among the neat cultivation like ancestors. The swift swollen rivers, brown torrents as turbulent as stampeding horses in a narrow canyon, from which farmers fished fast-swimming driftwood for their fires. The bridges. The thatched houses on rock-bound mounds in paddy fields. The snug-harboured clustered huts of the fishermen in sheltered coves looking out over the restlessness of the surf boiling about the rocky promontories, and islands. The hiss of the swilling sea about the sterns of their updrawn boats made fast to the very stakes in their gardens somehow made to grow food in spite of salt. Sheltered harbours, sea-swept coasts, islands with *torii* and shrines . . . the *reality* without which art is but a performing eunuch . . . John's mind was following this thought when he was brought back to earth by a simple bird-scaring device. A man came out of his doorway on the edge of a field. From the house ran lines on which were strung tins and hollow bamboo pieces. On seeing the thieving birds the man indignantly pulled at the lines starting the rattling racket. The birds flew off without a backward glance. How his two children would love to see that, he thought. Then, with a thrill, John realized that, at last he *was* on his way to see them again. He had to start thinking of other things to bridle his impatience.

They carried their own K-rations. At four p.m. they drew into a large station with three double-sided platforms. As the train stopped, they heard a click and then the hum of loudspeakers which began in a metallic tone. A woman's voice with a touch of American accent said, "This is Tottori T-O-T-T-O-R-I. We welcome you here. The train will stay in the station about fifteen minutes. The boys will clean out the inside of the train. We have prepared hot water for you, so will you please have your cups ready at the windows. We are sorry it is raining, but this part of the island is noted for its rain—*it is always raining in Tottori*." Then it was repeated over.

There were small crowds of Japanese on the platforms waiting for their trains. The lady announcer had been sorry it was raining, but the prisoners were not. The water was pouring off the curved canopies of the platforms and splashing down. As prisoners they had learned to size up an opportunity quickly, and to abandon convention for the practical. So they left their clothes in the train and lined up naked under the streaming water, lathering up and telling each other how good it was after the soot and cinders. They rubbed themselves hard with their towels and got back into the train.

The tinny voice began again, "The train is about to depart. Will you please board the train. We are sorry we have not been able to completely gratify you. You are going to your home people. Tottori hopes you *bon voyage*. We think you will reach your destination tonight." Then she sang in a strained voice some sentimental song about a boy going home to his mother. She finished with a final *Good-by-e-e-e!* The prisoners shouted and cheered. *Encore encore!* She sang them another chorus, amid cheers.

They went on through heavy rain. The sky was low and clouds chased each other over sharp, saw-toothed, thickly wooded hills. Peasants stood in the rain and watched the passing train. They wore rice-straw hats thatched on them like a roof. They also wore straw capes and skirts yellow-gleaming and dripping. Some said they looked like walking stooks, others that they looked like Maoris.

They continued to skirt the coast, diving continually in and out of tunnels through spurs of mountains that ran like knuckles into the sea. Between the spurs they crossed small bays, some with clustered islets within them. On one of these islets John saw the wreck of a three-masted junk with the bare poles still standing but broken like the bowsprit, and like a show of mourning. Bare and weathered, this hull could have been the remains of some Elizabethan adventurer long-forgotten. It was like a half-told tale that haunted him.

The passage through the tunnels almost asphyxiated them with sulphurous fumes. The men cursed the Japanese loudly for it. They were on top now, and this elated them. They had to let the world know, even if the world were not listening. It was pure rhetorical invective for the hell of it. They had been reading how Lord Louis Mountbatten had established a no-nonsense policy with the enemy. So now one of them yelled from the swirling blackness of smoke.

"Come on, you slit-eyed bastards! Pack it up! Or . . ."

There was a slight pause. Then in one united chorus:

"WE'LL TELL LORD LOUIS!"

John was impressed by how the mountainsides were covered by conical-topped cypress pines, of all about the same size. They overlaid each other with such uniformity that they looked like the scales of some fish—was this the uncovered back of the giant carp upon which these islands were said to rest? It would have been easy to believe in this wet, swimming world drenched with the greys of antiquity . . . a world before man and war, in which even cataclysm seemed to release new good.

10

They did not arrive until the next morning. John wrote, "So dawned one of the eventful days of our lives . . . as in the Wizard of Oz, our feet seemed to be set on the yellow brick road to a land of beautiful fantasy. And so it still seems. I feel like an uninvited guest who will be discovered. I fear that the clock will strike twelve and my ragged state will be revealed to these beautiful, clean, well-fed people who see nothing special in their state. The threat of beatings and humiliation, of bugs, fleas, lice, hunger and plague are gone. It is hard to believe."

Word was passed forward in the train that they would arrive in about an hour. It was a sunshiny day with strong opaque light-drenched mists in the east. They passed through Osaka to Wakayama along miles of devastation, meagre heaps of rubble, scattered rusty, torn sheets of metal, and a few vestiges of baked mud-and-bamboo walls. There were square miles of destruction with here and there a ruined concrete building caught like a saurian monster on its knees about to die in a drying swamp.

There was not a person in sight—nothing left to salvage, even for a thrifty Japanese. The Americans had assessed Wakayama as 45 per cent destroyed. On occupation, they found it to be 90 per cent.

From the train they boarded open electric trams which took them to the quay. Here they embarked in L.S.T.s and were taken across the bay and landed on a beach below a large building on a headland. It was a fine piece of traditional wooden architecture. On the beach they were told to throw away everything. Already there were growing piles. Cans of petrol lay about waiting to burn it all. But some adamantly kept valueless stuff merely because they had carried it with them through it all.

"Throw it away, you guys—we'll give you everything."

This was well-meant but, to many prisoners, it revealed the difference of values between those who had been free and those who had not. It was no good trying to explain it. They would have to be quiet about it and let these well-meaning exuberant people go on shouting their heartiness. With all the things that were being showered upon them, the consideration and exaggerated sympathy because of propaganda, some could not help a slight feeling of guilt, of false pretence. Some thought of that humane little Ohama group who would be getting nothing. And somehow they felt closer then to Ohama than to this unbelievable prodigality.

They went up to the processing station on the hill. Suddenly they got the impression that they should have bells around their necks and be crying, "Unclean, unclean!" As they took their clothes off these were snatched away. They were given soap and towels and put through steaming showers. They came naked out of the showers and stood in unlaced leather boots. They were sprayed thoroughly with D.D.T. powder and had four-figured numbers painted in purple on their chests. In a loose, wandering line they moved into a big hall with many tables. At each table was a doctor and his aides. As each prisoner came before a table he was regarded, he could not help feeling, like some doubtful specimen on a slide. There seemed to be a reluctance to get too near him. This of course was only their subjective feeling.

Buck said, "Get on them, will ya! Each bloke specializes in a different hole."

Everybody was so well groomed, so sleek, so close shaven, so impeccably pressed, hair so exact that they seemed artificial to the prisoners. As they stood with unlaced boots, a towel around their middles (which was whipped off at a moment's notice), a number painted on their chests, half-grown, unparted hair and unshaven—they were sure that in fact they belonged to Ohama, not here. But they weren't going back—they would brazen it out.

The men went from doctor to doctor each with his own particular probing interest. Each added comments to an impressively growing file carried with them as they went. They went to a U.S.N. quartermaster who gave them a pair of socks, a pair of navy jeans, a singlet, a shirt and a belt. And they were given a circular which described the ship they were being sent to.

U.S. NAVY HOSPITAL SHIP *Consolation*

GENERAL INFORMATION FOR PATIENTS EN ROUTE
FROM WAKAYAMA, JAPAN TO OKINAWA

It is now well known that the United States Army will occupy and control the Japanese Islands. Occupation, by the U.S. Eighth Army, of the Tokio area is now well under way. The landings being supported by the Third U.S. Fleet. Control of the southern part of Japan will be the task of the Sixth U.S. Army. A considerable period of time is required to put an army in readiness for such a task, and it was not found possible to land the Sixth Army before the latter part of September. The Fifth U.S. Fleet will accomplish this landing. About a fortnight ago word was received that approximately 3000 Allied prisoners of war could be brought to Wakayama for evacuation. The Commander of the Fifth Fleet offered to effect this evacuation prior to the arrival of the Sixth Army. This offer was accepted by the Supreme Allied Command, and consequently a task force was formed to accomplish this mission. This force included the U.S. Navy Hospital ships *Consolation* and *Sanctuary*. Approach to Wakayama was made difficult by the presence of mines, many of which had been laid by the American Air Force. In a remarkably short period minesweepers of the Fifth Fleet cleared a channel thru the mine fields, allowing the task force to pass safely into the harbour of Wakayama. The rest of the story you know.

You may be interested to learn something about the ship on

which you are being carried back to Okinawa. The U.S.S. *Consolation* is one of six new hospital ships of the United States Navy, all of which have been commissioned in the last six months. These ships are all of the same basic design and are similarly equipped and staffed. Each of these new hospital ships has a displacement of approximately 18,000 tons, and has an overall length of 520 feet and a beam of 71 feet, six inches. The speed is $17\frac{1}{2}$ knots and the cruising radius 12,000 miles. The medical equipment of the ships of this class compares favourably with that of modern shore based hospitals. The ships are the first in the navy to have complete air conditioning of the medical and living spaces.

Each ship carries in addition to the line officers and crew the following complement: 19 Medical Officers, 3 Dental Officers, 30 Nurses, 5 Hospital Corps Officers, 2 American Red Cross Workers and 254 Hospital corpsmen.

> L. R. NEWHOUSER,
> Captain, (MC), USN,
> Senior Medical Officer.

They were taken out to the ship by L.S.T. where they were welcomed with gravity and sympathy.

"I reckon they must think we are pregnant, or something," Buck said.

"They probably think we are psycho and they're going easy in case we scream or something," Harry said.

In the ship there was space for six hundred and fifty bed patients. There were radio headphones to each bed. Each prisoner had a classification tag tied to him. It was solemnly inspected and he was directed with great deference. But the men said, "No matter what the vets say—there's nothing wrong with us that a good feed and a soft bed won't cure." But when they found themselves tucked into the hospital beds, in new pyjamas and between clean sheets, to be waited on hand and foot and to be able to watch the immaculate American nurses moving about the wards, they changed their tune.

"Boy! Am I going to lap this up! Now I'm real crook—I think I'll stay here for ever."

"Those lovely sheilas . . . it's been so long that I had to ask one of the Yanks what they were."

"Malaria never gave me a temperature like this!"

They lay back listening to the wireless as if it had just been invented. They drank fruit juice and drooled over the nurses.

Boof and the others were in the last boatload and found that all the beds had been filled. They were taken down and billeted in the main surgery on stretchers in the reception hall. For pyjamas they wore the green operating overalls of the surgeons.

The prisoners were the first patients the ship had ever had, and it was made a test of the ship's organization and routines. They were fussed over because of the stories of their ill-treatment that by now had been so widely circulated. But there was genuine humanity in it. This sudden contact with the nurses had an unnerving effect on many of them. More than one man, going along one of the narrow passageways, on seeing a nurse approaching the other way had turned back as if he had suddenly realized that he was going the wrong way. Somehow they could not face these women like that.

"I felt so scaley and un-human, I couldn't let her pass me close like that . . . they are so *clean*—we must look like animals to them."

John wrote, "We seem to be out of place among all this kindness and consideration, this work of new ships and great deeds. I spoke with a Quartermaster's Striker this afternoon. He showed me all over the bridge, wheelhouse, chartroom, etc. All the new gear up there! War has made us old-fashioned already. When I came below to go to bed, I found a Red Cross bag had been dumped on my stretcher. I thought it was merely a wash bag, but it was much more. Soap, washer, razor blades, talc, slippers, sweets, a novel, a pencil, paper and envelopes. It's these touches of thoughtfulness that do you in. I would prefer a little rougher handling—it is easier on the sentiments."

Sailing was delayed the next day by a typhoon report. On that day they got to know Sarah Stevens, the senior surgical sister. Blue-eyed with red hair and glasses, she had the five of them sitting in her office, talking until after midnight. With great understanding she kept them talking to get them used to mixing again with ordinary people (though in those emotional times, who *was* normal?). She was able to ask about some things in their captivity without the morbid curiosity that became so common. She helped them to tell. She was the first plank in their bridge from Ohama back to their own world. She spoke without that bigoted hatred so many non-prisoners used in relation to the Japanese which allowed no exceptions. They could tell her about the people of Ohama and she was touched. True, some prisoners aided and abetted all the virulence they could. Sarah Stevens was a strict practising Roman Catholic but she had a wide and generous sympathy with those outside her religion. It was plain that hatred and intolerance saddened her painfully. When they told her about the people of Ohama she nodded and her eyes shone.

"What a bonza woman," Boof said later.

That night the ship rolled heavily at anchor. News came that U.S.S. *Sanctuary* was right in the typhoon's path and getting it very rough. In the harbour three small ships were blown ashore, others were damaged and there were many casualties in the ships generally. Sailing was again delayed while a critical casualty was taken aboard. They saw him brought down to the operating theatre. Two doctors, Miss Stevens, two surgical sisters and two corpsmen went to work at once, unaffectedly but with a drama that Hollywood could never match. They watched through the glass-topped doors of the main theatre. It went on for just six hours. The man had been hit on the back of the skull by a run-away 44-gallon drum of oil in one of the smaller ships being thrown about by the wind and sea. The skull had been crushed inward, and they were looking for the fragments of bone. They worked without pause. Nurses passed instruments and mopped sweating heads bent in concentration over the patient. The corpsmen were wringing out towels in ice-water to keep the patient's temperature down. At one point a corpsman came out and rang for another 2000 c.c. of penicillin. They had never heard of it. He told them it was a new wonder drug. At last it was over and the patient was taken away. Before they left the ship he was out of danger.

John read an article in *Pocket Book* about the nervous numbness in P.O.W.s which leads to indifference and lack of emotional response. In his diary that night he wrote, "As far as our blokes are concerned, they are as curious as cats, as excited as children, and ready for anything. They are saying that this is a bit different from the old *Byōke Maru*."

Their first night at sea, with all lights burning, gave John an uncanny, uncomfortable feeling of distrust. It was six and a half years since he had been at sea in an undarkened ship and he could not readily throw off the uneasiness which took hold of him.

II

Two days later, at 11.30 a.m., they anchored in Okinawa. John wrote, "The harbour is full of ships—probably more ships than I have ever seen at once before. It is strange to think that this island, so unremarked before the war, is at the moment one of the busiest ports in the world. There are ships of all kinds. War- and weather-battered destroyers with side plates pushed in concave between their ribs like hungry greyhounds. Cruisers and battleships dark grey and grimed with salt and rust like sweat-streaked workers. The peace-time pomp and ceremony of ships 'showing the flag' has long been forgotten, their drabness now is an adornment of purpose only. And now, too, that purpose seems to have been achieved. There is no more need for guns to blaze in anger to perpetrate expedient murder—no more St George-and-the-dragon stuff for them. There seems to be a silent sadness about these ships no longer needed, whose jubilant crews can hardly wait to get them home to pay them off. There are also hundreds of merchantmen which have, for so long, worn the same grey as the warships. They have shared a war that has probably given the two services a closer kinship than at any other time in history. The war is over and all these ships will be dispersed back to the sharp class distinctions of peace. People too, I suppose, will separate again into classes and factions, forgetting the unity they once had. What irony is it in human affairs that takes the greatest folly of man to unite him?

"In this armada which must number thousands of ships, there is a fervour of excitement and activity like an ant-heap on a hot day. Boats plying through the water made choppy and turbulent, not by the wind, but by the traffic alone. Hurrying boats churning creaming wakes and bow-waves with diminutive importance. Coloured strings of flags going up and coming down over the heads of shouting hoisting signalmen, calling as if their words commanded the whole earth. Aircraft roaring low over the ships, mast-high, or through low clouds, looking as if they were only up there to work off the incontinent energy that the sudden end of the war has left unspent. We, the prisoners, are like country bumpkins, looking everywhere at once like kids at a carnival. We feel an elation that swells in our chests, that brings out silly exclamations of bragging pride, and of delighted contrast with our late lot. I cannot now but think of, among all this powerful well-found shipping, the old *Byōke Maru* alone in the typhoon. There are strangely sad things in life we cannot explain, and yet they have a form of beauty.

"But all this activity does not stop at sundown. Instead, it seems to become more frantic in an effort to relegate the stars to faint unimportance. Flashing lights from ships make a continuous visual babel with everybody talking at once. The ships that are boxed-in behind so many others all anchored with bare swinging room, send up flashing shouts with searchlight projectors on to the bellies of the low-flying clouds. The beams play hide-and-seek, hit-and-miss among them like the flickering of a lightning storm. All the red masthead air beacons look like storm warnings. The navigation-lights of the continually flying aircraft, like flies over a picnic, remind me of the fireflies in the jungle. I suppose I am a bit over-emotional now—but this is a great sight."

They were two days in Okinawa. They had made many friends in *Consolation*. Doctors, nurses, corpsmen and crew—all so ready to talk to them, to tell them of the outside world they were going back to. It had been good for them. There had been two picture-shows a night. The ship's band of crewmen put on jazz sessions and they heard songs that had become popular while they had been out of circulation. The prisoners had been given a farewell concert. Miss Stevens, and Miss Nelson, chief nurse, had, out of their own pockets, bought cigarettes and candy for fifty-four of the men that came within their care. The prisoners had no money of their own. "We have no adequate way of saying thanks," they told these Sisters.

At 3 p.m. came the high pipe over the broadcast system. "Attention all medical officers! Stand by to disembark all Class Four patients."

Each man was tagged and given a medical history sheet. John looked at his and found the deflating remark, '*His past history shows no significance*'. They went down the gangway into the waiting L.S.T. An orderly at the bottom of the gangway ripped off the lower portion of their tags as a tally. Lining the guard-rails on several decks were doctors, nurses and crew—all shouting names, good-lucks and good-byes. As the L.S.T. shoved off a formation of thirty-four Liberators, some fighters and some B29s flew over them. They threaded their way among the mass of ships as if through a labyrinthine maze until they came alongside the gangway of *Haskell*, an assault landing ship. On deck huge landing craft lay in chocks beneath the mass of heavy-lift gear that put them in the water. The ship had been in four landings and twice had debarked the whole two thousand troops in nine minutes.

They boarded and went below to the large living spaces filled with two-tiered bunks. Soon they were piped to 'chow' in the large cafeteria. There John met some of his own shipmates he had not seen since their ship had been sunk in Java in 1942. They had been in the same camp as some American officers who had been in the ship which was said to be three months from Manila to Nagasaki. "Only four hundred out of two thousand arrived. They said there were thirty murders in one night, and that men drank each other's blood. They had received almost no water—that's what they told us, anyway." They had come out through Nagasaki. They said the shipyard gantries were blown over like so much grass. They had come to Okinawa by air.

That night they got under way and awoke at sea the next day. Sunday church services were held for Protestant, Catholic, Jew and Mormon—in Dutch and English because there were also Dutch prisoners aboard. Before each service the shrill pipe came over, *Now hear this! Stop all skylarking and gaming on the upper deck. The smoking lamp is out for divine service.*

On Tuesday they passed in by Corregidor to Manila.

"There she is again," Harry said. "I'm a bit happier to see the old morgue again, this time."

12

The following morning they were taken to a recovery camp outside Manila in Army trucks. They were allowed to send a telegram and were told that they might receive a mail the next day. The sudden meeting again with many Australians they had not known whether alive or dead for so long unsettled them. Impatience to get home was mounting intolerably.

They went to a kit store and were given more clothes. They were given another medical inspection, worm pills, and they were weighed, measured, vaccinated and inoculated for cholera and typhus.

"This is to stop *us* giving it to *them*," Buck said.

They were given a pay book each with a credit of £6 5s. od. in it, and £1 in canteen coupons. British aircraft carriers were being made ready for them, but bad weather had already delayed them four days.

They went to open-air pictures at night and sat it out in the rain, huddled under gas-capes, refusing to miss a minute of it. They saw *The Battle of Britain, Battle of the Western Desert, The Eastern Blitz,* and *Stalingrad.* They felt humbled.

13

They joined H.M.S. *Speaker,* an escort carrier. The whole hangar was now a sea of stretcher beds. The sailors had willingly also given up their bunks and slung their hammocks in out-of-the-way places to give the prisoners as much comfort as possible. Great warmth developed between the naval ratings and the prisoners during the voyage south. They were under way and the next stop was Australia. It was hard for many of them to make themselves believe this. Silently they remembered the *Byōke Maru,* the coal mine, the railway they had built through the jungle in Siam, the dead men—dead skeletons, really, for that is all they were when they died, and how they so often remembered them. They remembered back to the sudden Japanese victories when all that it-can't-happen-here began to happen. When they got back, how could they ever describe what those it-can't-happen-here things were actually like? Most of them would have to live with it lonely and excommunicate within them. It would be there. But now it was being submerged as anticipation and realization of their returning became keener.

There were pictures on the flight deck at night, except when the weather was too bad. Meals came and went. Men paced the

flight deck endlessly from dawn, sometimes before *reveille*, until
pipe-down. Talking, talking—walking, walking impatiently. It
was almost as if they had all decided to walk to Australia. They
would walk for miles and miles and, after a meal and a doze,
restlessly they would be walking again. They steamed down the
north coast of New Guinea. New Britain was passed on their
port hand. They rounded the eastern tip of Papua and headed
south, across the Coral Sea—walking all the way.

They were walking up and down the flight deck with the
fresh southeast trade-wind blowing on to their port bow. The
bright morning sun sparkled on a lively aquamarine sea. Even
Boof was getting impatient. His control had seemed superhuman
to the others. But at last he said, "As the time gets shorter—*it
bloodywell gets longer!*"

They berthed in Sydney at 10 a.m. on the 14th of October
1945. It was just a few days more than two months since John
had seen that cloud over Nagasaki. Another gate was shutting
behind him.

Many of the men did not know their home addresses; whether
they still had wives or not; nor exactly what awaited them. They
would head for their home towns, not knowing for sure whether
anybody knew they were still alive.

In all the excitement and sorting out, the five men said good-
bye, sensibly not promising anything for the future. It was
sufficient for them to know that they would not forget each
other. The Army, Navy, and Air Force all came to claim their
own. They separated with a last handshake and not much else.

The Navy put John on a south-bound Melbourne train that
night. He travelled first class because he was now a Chief Petty
Officer. He was in a compartment with five naval officers. One,
a Commander he had known most of his seventeen years in the
service, filled him in on what had been going on in the Navy and
of the men he knew. John told him something of what had
happened to his ship at the last when she had been sunk, and
something of his captivity.

When the train arrived at Spencer Street a special car had
been sent to pick him up. He was the only naval survivor on
this train. He was taken straight to H.M.A.S. *Lonsdale*, the
Melbourne depot. Within ten minutes, the Commander was
shaking him warmly by the hand.

"Bloody glad you're back . . . good to see you! Just step into my office, will you—I'll be with you in a few minutes."

John pushed the door open and walked in.

There, he saw a clean and shining boy and girl standing, with his wife's arms about their shoulders. Sitting close by, quiet and silvery, were his mother and father.

FALLING LEAF

The sadness of it. . . .
Under the hero's helmet ,
tarnished now . . . a cricket.
　　　　　　(BASHO)

FALLING LEAF

Two years had passed.

It was dinner time on the wharf and Boof was watching the card game. The men were scattered about the cargo shed in groups—talking, arguing, reading papers, sleeping on bales of wool, or playing cards. Each game had its ring of watchers.

During the morning Boof had told Harry, "I'm going up to the Repat on Friday—they are going to give me a good going-over, they said. The local doctor was looking at the scars on my skull . . . he thinks I ought to go."

"Best thing, Boof, you don't want to let these things go on—after all, you copped some pretty good bashings up there . . . you never know."

"I had another black-out last night . . . lucky it was after I got the car into the garage . . . I just stayed there until I came good again . . . I didn't tell Doris."

And now Boof was watching Harry about to be 'shot' by the other players. A grin was spreading over his face and his eyes crinkled with anticipation. The whole ring of onlookers was waiting too. The card fell. SHOT HIM, the shout went up in good-natured derision.

But Boof's huge chesty laugh came in spasms like the roar of storm-driven surf.

They all chuckled, "Listen to Boof!"

"It's worth getting shot for," Harry said, "just to hear the old fella laugh."

At one o'clock the foreman blew his whistle which shrilled through the galvanized iron shed like an angry cricket. The port siren filled the air with a sinister air-raid scream. But, even this did not drown Boof's laugh.

"Come on, Boof, me son. No time to laugh . . . there's work . . . *takusan sagio*, mate!"

Boof reached up to get his hook hanging on the band of a bale of wool. As he caught hold of it, his laugh stopped. The hook tore the bale as Boof slid down to the floor.

"Steady on, Tanglefoot, or they'll think you've been up to the rubberty in the lunch hour."

943

Boof said nothing.

"Black-out," Harry thought. He looked up and saw John just coming out of the shipping office.

"Hey, John! Ring for the First Aid . . . it's Boof . . . tell them to hurry, for Christ's sake!"

Harry propped Boof up.

The fire-alarm clang of the First Aid unit sounded as it drew up in the shed.

"Over here, mate!" Harry called.

The First Aid man examined Boof for a few minutes, then he looked up.

"He's gone."

> *Leaf alone, fluttering*
> *Alas, leaf alone, fluttering . . .*
> *Floating down the wind.*
> (ANON)

PUBLISHER'S NOTE

The conclusion of the story of HMAS *Perth* was told by Ray Parkin in his Foreword to *The Bells of Sunda Strait* by David Burchell, published by Rigby Limited in 1971. Ray's Foreword and two drawings from that book are included here.

EPILOGUE

At just after midnight, twenty-nine years ago, 1 March 1942, with about one third of our ship's company I lay in the water coated with oil fuel watching our ship sinking. Exposed and helpless in the glare of searchlights from surrounding Japanese warships, she had come to the end of as violent an hour's action as was ever fought at sea. Not many minutes before I had been on board, steering her through this last battle—a vessel complex, expensive, and extremely efficient in speed and action. I had lived in her for two years and nine months, which was her whole life as an Australian warship. She had been hit by torpedoes and shell-fire had shattered her boats. The captain, just after he had given the order, "Abandon ship—*every man for himself*," had been killed on the bridge by a salvo of shells. We watched the ship go out of the searchlights' glare into the unknown blackness below, taking almost two-thirds of our shipmates with her.

Yet twenty-five years later a man left her alive.

This man was Dave Burchell. He was not a member of the ship's company but he brought back what we thought, on that night in 1942, had been blotted out for ever. This was a unique act carried out by a man of true sentiment: simply, directly, unselfishly, and at his own expense. Some few have thought that such an act might have been a desecration. In fact, nothing could be further from the truth. Most *Perth* survivors now know that Dave Burchell's sentiment, humour, and character, would have made him a most welcome shipmate in those hectic war years when men were held together by a single purpose. He has been made an honorary member of ex-*Perth* associations

947

throughout Australia. Almost all the relics he raised are now in the National Memorial at Canberra: as a visible reminder of the ship, her dead and her deeds. The general public may have forgotten her, new generations may never have heard of her, but she has an undeniable place in Australian tradition.

Dave Burchell does not argue "to be or not to be;" he *is* and *does*. He lost a leg when young but that did not stop him joining the R.A.A.F. as an aircraftsman in wartime. He is now a diver, a no-nonsense expert to whom other divers are willing to listen. He is powerful and fit, but he is self-effacing. From his modest accounts you are apt to miss the full significance of what he has done. When the Japanese proposed to raise the *Perth* for scrap, there was a public outcry in Australia. To Dave Burchell it meant that she was in a diveable depth of water, and it would not be long before people without sentiment or conscience would be able to reach her. This book tells what happened when he decided to act. At first his prime objective was to bring back the ship's bell. In this he failed. I feel, however, that he has brought back something far more precious.

I remember how the ship, in her second-last battle, made a vivid impression on men of another navy who saw her at work. During the action of the Java Sea, H.M.S. *Exeter* was hit in the boiler room and stopped. She came under the concentrated fire of the Japanese fleet. Without hesitation Captain Waller at once took *Perth* in at high speed to lay a protective screen between her and the enemy. At the end of each leg in front of *Exeter*, *Perth* made 180-degree turns at high speed under full helm—black smoke pouring away from her two funnels, and white smoke from the smokefloats on the quarterdeck filling the gap along the surface of the sea with a dense fog. (I can still feel the ship heeling away under my feet as I put the wheel over.) Thus she made an unforgettable picture for some men. Lieutenant Hamlin, of U.S.S.

Houston, wrote later of what he saw as he looked out from *Houston*'s Number 1 eight-inch turret, ". . . there was *Perth,* a beautiful white bone in her teeth . . . three battle flags streaming . . . smoke pouring . . . firing all the time . . . rapid salvoes . . . shells falling all around her . . . *It was one of the finest sights I have ever seen.*"

Now Dave Burchell has brought back a different picture—one, because of the fatal suddenness of that night, we never expected to get. When men die at a distance from home in an unimagined place, with their bodies unrecovered and their graves unmarked, a terrible lack of finality gnaws with doubt and futile hope at the hearts of those left behind. Many will travel across the world just to see a wooden cross or a mound of earth to try to get that final acceptance. Now the bereaved of *Perth* have been given some vision of finality.

Altogether he made thirty dives, arduously piecing it all together. It is as if the ship, at last, is able to speak. He was the first man near her since the lucky ones had left her to save their lives and the rest had come with her to this faintly translucent Eden. Here, at last, was one who could take back news of those entombed when four of the eighty-seven torpedoes fired at her had hit. Now it was quiet and there was time to tell—and time to listen. She lay on her side like a mammoth resting. She looms like a towering block of buildings. In heavy weather she had often seemed tiny in a vast turbulent ocean; but in dry dock she had dwarfed the men who walked the wet barnacle-littered floor beneath her. And so she dwarfed this diver. He patiently explored, extending his endurance underwater and carefully reducing the time between dives so that he was able to make two a day. It was a calculated risk and he was never free of the possibility of an attack of the "bends."

There could not have been a better first visitor to the shrine of these dead men—never could they have been safer from desecration or vandalism. As well as fine feeling, Dave Burchell also brought uncommon skill.

The equipment had to be serviced, the compressor run, the bottles recharged, and a hundred other things done that the non-expert has no idea of. Above all it took guts and perseverance to hang on and overcome the serious set-backs he unexpectedly met.

We know now that our shipmates' grave is not a sordid one. The relics were brought to the surface and photographed wet, just as they were. And they were unexpectedly beautiful, as if encrusted with gems. Coloured transparencies will attest the accuracy of this statement. Turquoise, topaz, emerald, pearl, onyx, opal and ruby were never more vivid than these sea-wet encrustations. They cloaked the profane relics with that kind of glory John Bunyan's Pilgrim might have expected in his heaven. The whole ship must look like this—555 feet of her— and each funnel having as much area as a brig's main mast with all sail set. The whole is splashed with living colour; covered with the innocent, unprejudiced rainbow growth of animal and vegetable in harmony affirming indefeasible life-to-come. A mute sermon on the continuance of life, notwithstanding the most devastating havoc Man can wreak. The men who died so suddenly are now in a vast coffin decorated with a touching beauty which has the quality of impartial eternal justice: the significance of which, sadly, seems to escape Man as he seeks dominance and wins his successive pyrrhic victories.

Groper and other fish have established particular territories of their own now about the wreck. Where once Captain H. M. L. Waller, D.S.O., R.A.N., commanded and was killed, a large good-natured but sagacious groper now is the steadfast caretaker of the Compass Platform, the erstwhile nerve-centre of the ship in action. As I read of this in this book it seemed to me an absolutely just and appropriate succession of command after our superb down-to-earth last Captain.

Nancy Waller, the Captain's widow who has become a special sort of mother to all *Perth* survivors, gave it the

EPILOGUE

nicest possible benediction when I told her about it. With
blue eyes shining and a face lit from within, she said
movingly, "Oh, I am glad . . . Hec would be tickled pink
to know that."

Ray Parkin,
Ivanhoe, Vic.
March 1971

1. Y 6" Turret (Trained to Port)
2. X 6" Turret (Trained to Starboard)
3. S.1. Twin 4" A.A. Mounting
4. After Control 36" Searchlight
5. Crow's Nest—Masthead Lookout
6. 4" High-Angle Director Tower
7. 6" Main Armament Director control tower
8. Starboard Bridge Signal Projector (Recovered)
9. Port & Starboard Bridge Rangefinders (with Plow Seats for Trainer & Rangetaker—one recovered)
10. Midship Wheelhouse Scuttle
11. 2 Quadruple .5" Machine-guns
12. Captain's Day Cabin
13. S.2. Twin 4" A.A. Mounting
14. Starboard Quadruple 21" Torpedo Tubes

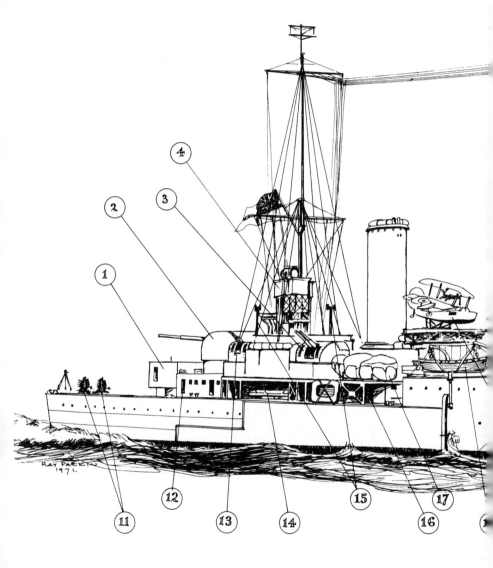

RAY PARKIN
1971.

15. "Charlie Nobles"—Officers Galley Funnels
16. Space Under Boat Skids where Fire Engine is stowed
17. 35 ft Motor Pinnace
18. 32 ft cutter rigged as Starboard sea boat
19. Amphibious Aircraft on Catapult (both blown over the side in final action) Note : Crane on Port side

20. Flag Deck Starboard Signal Projector
21. Starboard 36" Searchlight
22. Starboard Bridge Lookout Positions
23. Paravane on trolley
24. B 6" Turret trained to Port
25. A 6" Turret trained to Starboard
26. Starboard Bower Anchor
27. Paravane Shoe
28. Port Bower Anchor

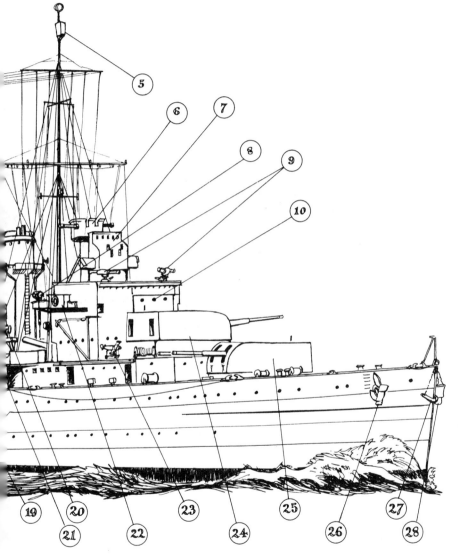

OUTLINE OF H.M.A.S. *PERTH*
Showing Starboard side and relevant features

H.M.A.S. *PERTH*

As she now lies sunk in Sunda Strait

DAVID BURCHELL
(Drawn to scale)

1-5. Diver's Buoy Ropes
6. Starboard Anchor in place
7. Wheel House below Compass Platform
   (Voicepipe, Saveall & Repeat Gyro recovered)
8. Starboard Bridge Signal Projector (Recovered)
9. Flag Deck
10. Catapult Structure (Catapult and Aircraft gone)
11. S.1. Twin 4″ Mounting
12. S.2. Twin 4″ Mounting (Shell cases recovered)
13. After Control (Secondary 6″)

14. Davits of Starboard cutter
15. Starboard 36″ Searchlight and Platform
16. Fire Engine (Embarked Tandjong Priok) in here
17. Quadruple 21″ Torpedo Tubes
18. Captain's Day Cabin
19. Starboard Outer & Inner Propellers
20. Port and Starboard Anchor and centre line
    Capstans
21. Breakwater
22. A 6″ Turret

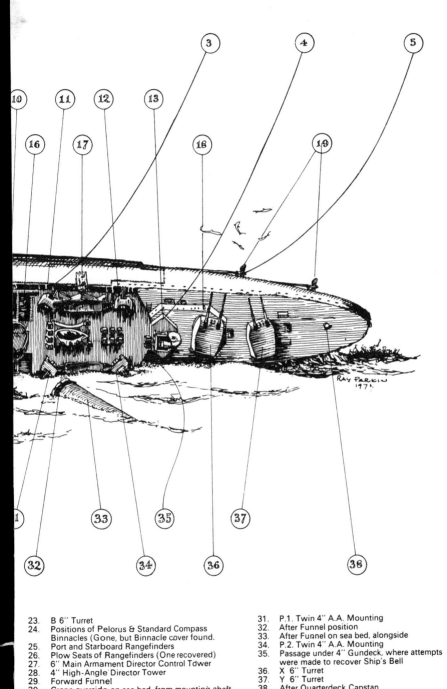

RAY PARKIN
1971.

23.	B 6″ Turret	31.	P.1. Twin 4″ A.A. Mounting
24.	Positions of Pelorus & Standard Compass Binnacles (Gone, but Binnacle cover found.	32.	After Funnel position
		33.	After Funnel on sea bed, alongside
25.	Port and Starboard Rangefinders	34.	P.2. Twin 4″ A.A. Mounting
26.	Plow Seats of Rangefinders (One recovered)	35.	Passage under 4″ Gundeck, where attempts
27.	6″ Main Armament Director Control Tower		were made to recover Ship's Bell
28.	4″ High-Angle Director Tower	36.	X 6″ Turret
29.	Forward Funnel	37.	Y 6″ Turret
30.	Crane overside on sea bed, from mounting abaft	38.	After Quarterdeck Capstan
	forward funnel	39.	Coral "tree" growth